THE GOOD MOUNTAIN BIKING GUIDE

ENGLAND & WALES

WITHDRAWN

Active Maps Limited

Published in Great Britain by Pioneer

© Pioneer Partners 2011

ISBN-13: 978 0 95680 290 3

Book produced by Active Maps Ltd.
Richard Ross: Book Design, Cartography
Ruth Jevons: Research & Compilation
Anne Ross: Book Administration
Active Maps Ltd
Ruskin Chambers, Drury Lane, Knutsford, WA16 6HA.
Tel: 01565 750049

Maps:
Contain Ordnance Survey data © Crown copyright & database right 2011.

Photographs:
Please see our Acknowledgements on page 18.
Copyright as stated on the photographs.

Printed and bound in the UK by St Ives Web Ltd (Peterborough).

Warnings

Mountain biking can be dangerous and carries a risk of personal injury or death. It should only be undertaken by those with a full understanding of the risks and the training and/or experience to be able to judge them.

Every effort has been made to ensure that the information shown in this book is accurate. The authors, publishers and copyright owners can take no responsibility for damage of any nature from the use of this book (including personal injury or death, damage to property or equipment).

The representation on the maps of roads, tracks and paths are no evidence of the existence of a Public Right of Way. Rights of Way change over time and trails may be on concessionary/permissive paths which are not pubic rights of way. Therefore whilst every care and effort has been made to show only trails where it is possible to ride we can not guarantee this.

General Advice

Pubs and cafés have varying opening times and food serving times, they may also close for business. Therefore it is recommended that you check with the relevant establishment(s) prior to your departure.

Trains are subject to change and it advisable to check with National Rail Enquiries on your intended route.

Route distances and drive times are approximate.

Front Cover Photo

Photographer: Seb Rogers
(www.sebrogers.co.uk)

Taken at The Batch, Long
Mynd (p266).

© Seb Rogers

Contents Overview

Contents by Regions
Mountain Biking Bases

5

MIDLANDS & EASTERN 220

6

7

WALES 526

Snowdonia, The Clwyds & North Wales 528

Introduction

The Good Mountain Biking Guide is very different to many of the excellent mountain biking books available. The Guide has been specifically designed for planning mountain biking adventures and leading you towards any other resources that may be necessary for your rides. In The Good Mountain Biking Guide we aim to give a practical overview of all the great mountain biking that is available in England and Wales and help you to always find somewhere great to ride, wherever you are. The Good Mountain Biking Guide is not designed to be taken out on the trail and used for navigational purposes and we make no apology for its size and weight!

As keen mountain bike riders ourselves we know how frustrating it is to be unsure what riding is available when you are visiting a new area. The Guide will save time, allowing you to go straight to the best locations. Never again arrive in a new area with only a vague idea of what might be possible - and waste valuable, hard earned, riding time trying to find a trail. No more frustrating excursions to a new area only to find the local maps or guides are unavailable and you can't find your way around the trails. Pack your bikes and gear with confidence. A family holiday or a weekend away can provide a great opportunity to find new areas to ride – use the book to get ahead with your plans. The Good Mountain Biking Guide allows you to go prepared – and get the most out of the time you have on your bike.

We hope that you will always have The Guide available to consult and that you will get many hours of pleasure from exploring new routes. It is all too easy to settle into the habit of riding well-trusted trails - although somehow they always seem to ride differently depending on how fit you feel, who you are with and what particular challenges the weather chooses to throw at you! Going out and finding somewhere new requires a bit more effort but can be an exhilarating and rewarding experience. Often you will meet new groups of riders who will be delighted to describe the best bits of their trails and you will find that your portfolio of favourite trails extends dramatically.

The Good Mountain Biking Guide is based on maps for specific areas across the whole of England and Wales that offer mountain biking. The maps provide a quick overview of the relevant area – you can immediately get a feel for its size, the density of the trail network, and the steepness of the terrain by the contours and the spot heights we have marked along the trails. Car parks are also shown, the main ones being grid referenced in the text along with Sat Nav friendly post codes (where available), and drive times from major nearby cities - allowing you to plan your whole trip as well as the ride itself. Perhaps most importantly, as mountain biking can certainly burn the calories, we have given details of suggested refuelling stops – cafés and pubs on, or close to the trails.

Whilst we do not suggest you use our maps for navigational purposes we would encourage you to study them carefully for route planning. They are purpose drawn to emphasise the features that are important to mountain bikers and are designed to be able to identify an interesting route that might justify further exploration with the relevant guidebook. In the text we have identified guide books that contain detailed instructions for any routes they feature in the area and we have highlighted the relevant map that you might use alongside the guide books. Where free routes are available on the internet we have shown where they can be found: since some web addresses are long and complicated, we have redirected via a simplified web link.

The photographs are of real riders out on the relevant trails and we are delighted by the support that we have been offered by mountain bikers in creating this book. We use photographs that illustrate the trails and scenery rather than focusing just on the rider and hope that the photographs give a reasonable representation of what to expect in the area.

The Good Mountain Biking Guide should appeal to every kind of mountain biker. Those that enjoy the jumps and berms of purpose built trails will find details of 100 Trail Centres and other similar facilities. The cross-country rider will find a huge variety of terrain in the 400 natural areas that we have covered. The determined downhiller or freerider might also be surprised to find some of the natural areas can replicate or exceed the thrills of the man made mountain biking centres. From the dedicated "all day/all terrain/all weather" mountain biker to the occasional rider who wants to escape from traffic to those who are teaching their children - there are trails for all in the book.

When selecting which areas to feature, we have tried to focus on the best mountain biking available in England and Wales but we have also tried to make sure that every area is represented. Where an area is relatively flat and comparatively unexciting we have still identified the best riding available in that area. This can lead to a situation where terrain similar to this, but in the middle of an area rich in mountain biking trails, may not be featured in the book.

The Good Mountain Biking Guide does not cover Scotland and this is not because we think the mountain biking there is unattractive. The reverse is true.

Scotland contains some of the biggest, highest, longest and wildest trails in the UK -and some of the best Trail Centres. When compared to England & Wales, Scotland has a more enlightened access policy for mountain bikers with riding possible on most footpaths. The abundance of trails explains why it is not covered in this edition - to include it would simply have made The Guide unwieldy.

It would take an extremely dedicated rider to explore all the great riding that England and Wales has to offer and there is over 17,000km of riding over 700 route suggestions covered in this guide. We would be surprised if any of our readers managed to ride every trail we feature or even one trail in every area, but we know some mountain bikers will love the idea of that sort of challenge! We'd like to hear your experiences good and bad of the areas featured and hope to update the Good Mountain Biking Guide in the future with more and more great riding. We hope to gather more photos and also to hear of any changes or omissions in the facilities that we have described. Thank you for buying our book and Happy Riding!

Stephen Ross
Pioneer Partners

March 2011

How To Use
The Good Mountain Biking Guide

Good Mountain Biking Bases

In selecting the chosen areas we have identified locations for which there are recognised maps, guidebooks, individual route guides or information on the web. We have not sought to identify 'secret' locations in this book. We have not treated every trail equally but have instead tried to make sure that we have included somewhere to ride that is reasonably close to you, wherever you are in the country. In some places, the best off road riding available may be a railway path or an easy forest route. We have included this if it has been referenced in a mountain bike guide book for that area.

Each area is focused on a "base" that will generally be a hamlet, village, or small town. Ideally, a good mountain biking base will have a car park, a café, a pub and best of all, a bike shop. Our view is that an ideal base is big enough to have these facilities but small enough that you are not cycling miles along busy roads at the start of your ride. Most bases are easily identified and have a network of good mountain biking trails around them. The book also includes 100 purpose built mountain biking sites, Trail Centres and other similar facilities. Some of these are Forestry Commission sites with full amenities: parking, café and bike shop with purpose-built waymarked trails. Others are less formal rider-built trails in woods and old quarries. We have not mapped the trails in these areas or shown a layout of the routes. Generally this information may be available when you get to the Trail Centre via maps, information boards and, most importantly, waymarks showing the course of the routes. Some of the venues charge to ride and some are restricted to organised events; we have attempted to state this where possible but venues change their policies; so always check in advance of going. In the past, we have had trouble finding some purpose built facilities ourselves so have aimed to show you both how to get to them and what you might find when you get there.

The book is divided into the five main regions of England and Wales: North, Midlands & Eastern, South East, South West and Wales. It is then further divided into 21 smaller regions, which cover recognisable mountain biking areas. Our regions do not necessarily follow standard areas, as trails do not always fit easily within county or National Park boundaries. The map on page 24 shows how we have divided the areas. The 'atlas style' maps from page 25 show the divisions in more detail along with the locations of the mountain bike bases.

Finding a base from which to ride

The book is structured so that you can find a base in a number of ways:

- If you know the base you want to visit, or the general area, then you can look in the appropriate region and sub-region. A list of all the bases is set out in the beginning of each chapter with natural areas listed first and purpose built facilities at the end.

- If you are visiting a specific village or hamlet then you could refer to the index (p609), which contains over 3000 names. The index lists any significant habitation identified on the maps and directs you to the relevant page number. The index includes place names within each map area so you can use the index to search for more than just base names.

- You can use the overview maps (p25) to identify the base that you would like to visit and then locate its page number from the list of bases at the beginning of the book (p5), refer to the index at the back (p609) or see the lists at the front of each sub region chapter (eg Lake District p38).

- Alternatively, simply flick through the book using the photographs to identify interesting places that you would like to visit!

We have tried to achieve a lot in this book in order to provide a resource that is genuinely useful to every mountain biker, irrespective of skill level or preferred riding type. We have included all the areas that we think are attractive but we may have missed some locations and others will develop and open up. We will aim to keep this book up-to-date and would appreciate your help with any feedback.

Using our maps

All of our maps are drawn specifically to make mountain biking route planning as simple as possible we have therefore tried to exclude features which are unnecessary in this respect and the maps do not therefore present a complete picture of the area.

We have shown roads, trails, habitations and other significant features in each area but then focused only on those that are important in planning your route.

The **trails** are shown on the map as ▬▬▬▬ , and we have tried to identify something about the trail surface itself. If there is a black "pecked" edge to the trail marked on map ▬▬▬▬ , then it is more likely the ground will be on a firm surface such as a farm track (even possibly tarmac – but this is generally in or close to urban areas). All the maps vary in **scale** but in order to make it easy to compare distances, each map shows **one kilometre grid squares** and includes a simple scale bar.

The number and closeness of **contours** is clearly a guide to steepness and they also give an indication of the type of riding terrain. Generally, closer contours indicating steeper gradients will also mean more technical trails. Contour lines are backed up with **spot heights in metres** (eg **140**) **along the trails**. These simplify calculating the steepness of climbs and descents and will give you a good gauge of how hard you are going to have to work. In planning equipment it is worth remembering that higher terrain is likely to be more open and therefore more exposed when the weather is cold wet and windy. On the other hand, in fine weather open land will mean fewer gates, less stopping for opening and closing and often more attractive views. Forests are naturally sheltered and provide good riding in all weathers but will naturally include more roots as obstacles.

Circular routes can obviously be ridden in both directions but many seem to ride better one way or the other. Many routes contain mixtures of off road trails and small lanes to access them (sometimes busier roads near major conurbations). When presented with a choice, most mountain bikers would prefer to use tarmac to climb and then enjoy an off road decent rather than the other way around.

One other factor that you may wish to consider when planning routes is giving yourself options along the way. This is very important if you are riding with a group of mixed ability and fitness or if the weather is poor or changeable. The best route planning will give you options to lengthen or shorten your route once you have a feel for how the ride is working out. Similarly it is worth noting the facilities and opportunities to take shelter and plan in a stop for a hot drink or a meal. **Cafés** ☕ and **pubs** 🍺 along the trails are marked but some, particularly in remote places, may have unusual opening hours (or be closed for a large part of the year). It is always worth checking in advance and we have therefore included phone numbers.

We have also included a selection of **Car Parks** 🅿 and other parking areas such as **Laybys or Roadside Parking** P where you can start a ride. In the text for each area we have included grid references and Sat Nav postcodes where applicable.

The Good Mountain Biking Guide maps are designed to make this route planning as easy as possible by removing extraneous features. **The Route Ideas** we have included are similarly brief and, as per the maps, are not designed for navigation on the ground. The descriptions in our text are written specifically so that you can follow a trail around on the page - with a finger rather than a bike! This is important to recognise since reference is often made to features on the map that may be invisible on the ground. For detailed instructions you will need one of the guide books we have recommended for that particular base. If you are confident in planning your own routes then you can use our maps to develop some ideas. We would then recommend you either transcribe your chosen route onto a paper map (such as OS Explorer 1:25,000 series), or input into one of the excellent computer mapping programs to then print-out or for loading the detailed route onto a GPS enabled device. If doing the latter we would still recommend taking a detailed map to deal with the situation where your batteries run out or the equipment loses its signal or malfunctions.

Despite advances in technology we are still great fans of paper based maps as a the fastest way of giving an overview of an area and the small details necessary for good navigation. We have referenced the appropriate OS Explorer 1:25,000 or Harvey's map or any purpose produced mountain biking maps for each area. The references are a guide only and it is advisable to check the map covers all of the area, for which you are interested in, before setting off on your ride. For big days out in the National Parks we find it hard to beat Harvey's 1:40,000 maps produced for BMC (British Mountaineering Council). These cover The Lake District, Yorkshire Dales, Peak District, Snowdonia and Dartmoor have a number of advantages for mountain bikers. The scale is large enough to show enough detail but small enough to make sure that a lot of ground is covered on one map and they are produced on a virtually indestructible material, which is a huge advantage when they end up wet at the bottom of a rucksack. Finally the bridleways are reasonably well marked and contours shaded in a way that makes navigation relatively easy.

Although you are unlikely to use it, we would recommend taking a compass on all trips. Navigating on tracks and roads is generally pretty easy but there are instances where bridleways cross open land and the trails can be indistinct on the ground. This can be a real problem when visibility is poor. A compass or GPS enabled device can really help.

Different Types of Riding

There is a huge variety of riding throughout England and Wales. Rides can be as short or as long, as easy or as tough, as natural or as man made as you want, though if you are looking for remote moorland challenges you clearly won't find them in Kent!

In the far west of England, Exmoor and Dartmoor can both offer some full on high moorland crossings; Wales is more mountainous than flat and the 'cross' formed by the five National Parks of the Peaks, the Lakes, the Dales, the North York Moors and Northumberland encompass some of the most dramatic scenery and trails in the North of England.

Lake District

Although the scenery might be less dramatic, Southern England also has some great mountain biking: Dorset and Wiltshire have a greater density of bridleways and byways than any other county in Britain; the Ridgeway and the South Downs Way are the two best long distance trails open to mountain bikes in the country and both make a good weekend challenge; Surrey and Kent offer many shorter trails along the North Downs; the Chilterns have some of the best natural woodland singletrack in the country and even amongst the honey coloured villages of the Cotswolds you will find some hidden gems.

If you are after Trail Centres, then what started in Wales and Scotland is now slowly being adopted by England, whether in the vast forests of Kielder, Grizedale, Dalby and Hamsterley or Lee Quarry in the north, Cannock Chase and Sherwood Pines in the Midlands, Haldon Forest in Devon, Aston Hill in the Chilterns or Bedgebury in Kent. There are even black grade trails in East Anglia, in Thetford. Wales still leads the field here and there are myriad trails from Cwmcarn and Afan

Lee Quarry © Blackshaw Outdoor

Forest in the south, to Nant yr Arian in Mid Wales, to Coed y Brenin and The Marin Trail in the north.

Riding In Different Regions

There is not much in common between the Chilterns and the Cheviots or the North Downs and the North York Moors except that, if you know where to look, you will find routes to suit every type of rider from woodland singletrack to big open views, your reward for a lung-bursting climb to the top of a hill. Broadly speaking, the further north and west you go, the higher the hills, the harder the rocks and the more likely that you will be able to ride the trails all year round.

Draw a line from Exeter to Hull and you have a rough geological divide of the country: to the south and east of this line the rocks are younger and softer offering some fantastic hard-packed trails from spring to autumn but it can get very sticky in the winter.

There are stunning chalk rides along the Ridgeway, the North and South Downs, and from the Isle of Wight and Dorset up through Wiltshire to the Chilterns.

The Cotswolds are like a wedge of cake on its side; tough rides on the steep bit (the escarpment) dropping hundreds of feet down to the Severn Vale and easier trails on the gently sloping side as it runs east down to the Thames and Oxford.

The Quantocks and Mendips are two compact mountain bike playgrounds to the south of Bristol, the Quantocks have an amazing variety of trails packed into a small area.

Into the Midlands the trails are harder to find until you get up into the Peak District, one of the most popular mountain biking areas in the country as it lies so close to the major conurbations of Manchester, Sheffield and the big cities of the Midlands.

Crossing over the geological line to the north and west there is huge variety on offer: all the National Parks in England and Wales to the west of this line have masses of trails, from Dartmoor in the far southwest to Northumberland in the northeast, from the Brecon Beacons in South Wales to Snowdonia in the north. These trails climb higher, descend further, explore more remote areas and should be treated with respect: if something goes wrong (a bad fall or a crisped wheel) when you are out on exposed moorland and a storm is coming in as the light is fading, you are in trouble. A little bit of common sense goes a long way - these are fantastic areas to ride and explore but treat with care.

Trail Centres or Natural Trails?

Coed y Brenin © Singletrack Safari

Snowdonia © Andrew Hill

Largely a development of the past 15 years, starting in Wales and Scotland and spreading to England more recently, Trail Centres have seen an explosion in numbers of visitors as more and more people choose to go somewhere where there is a consistency of quality, a variety of clearly graded trails, no need for maps or route finding and often facilities such as a café, bike wash and bike hire. People will travel hours to try out new trails, offering ever-greater challenges, as bikes themselves evolve to handle bigger jumps and more technical trails.

On the other hand, bridleways will always meet the demand to ride from your own doorstep, or to go somewhere that is only a half hour drive away compared to the several hours it can take to get to a good Trail Centre. Many people don't like crowds and prefer open spaces to enclosed tracks through woodland and actually like the challenge of reading a map or following a route. There can be a real sense of exploration and a sense of the unknown, which is somewhat unlikely in the confines of a planted forest. On the downside, natural trails can become impossibly wet or muddy in the winter; if you are riding 'blind' you may come up against ploughed fields, bridleways trashed by horses or overgrown with brambles and nettles or byways churned up by scramble bikers and 4x4 enthusiasts.

So, take your pick - there's much to be said for both types of riding and it's best to keep an open mind about what you are prepared to try out.

Riding In All Seasons

© Sheldon Attwood

© Mike Gill

Many mountain bikers enjoy their riding most on long summer days during a warm, dry spell when the trails are bone dry and fast. Nevertheless, with the right gear, there is no reason why you can't go out 365 days a year, even in snow. However, hypothermia on the top of a bleak moor in midwinter is serious stuff so preparation and common sense are essential. The key to temperature control is layering and zips. Several thin layers are better than one thick one and when it's cold pay special attention to your extremities: feet, hands and head. Think about where you will stow any gear you decide to take off and remember getting wet in a strong wind is a far quicker way to hypothermia than riding in sub zero temperatures but staying dry.

Between these two extremes there is scope to go out and enjoy yourself in most weather conditions - wet and muddy means slower riding and more time cleaning up but many people don't feel they have been properly off road unless there is some mud to show for it.

Safety While You Ride

Things go wrong. In a group, on a fine day, this is rarely a problem - you can help each other out. On your own, in bad weather, a bad fall or a bike failure can have serious consequences. Mobile phones cannot be relied on to get you out of every difficulty. Take a basic tool kit to tighten loose nuts and bolts or to fix a broken chain, a pump and a spare tube to mend punctures. Take a map so you know where you are, something waterproof so that you stay dry and water so that you don't dehydrate. A whistle takes up very little space but makes a lot of noise. Let people know where you are going, even if it is just the start point, so that if you don't come back when you said you would then people will know where to start looking for you.

Help us make the next edition of The Good Mountain Biking Guide even better...

This is the first edition of the book and we hope that it will become essential to every mountain biker who wants to get the best out of his or her bike. We would be delighted to feel, in part, responsible for people discovering new areas and riding in a greater variety of terrain. We have spent thousands of hours collecting and sifting relevant information, drawing maps, sorting photographs and presenting the information in a simple and clear fashion. Even as the book goes to print we know that some things will change by the time it reaches the shelves. New trails will be added as access arrangements improve, Trail Centres will be built and sadly some may also end up closing. Pubs, cafés and bike shops will also come into existence or stop trading.

We would like your help on keeping **The Good Mountain Biking Guide** as up to date as possible. There are some areas where you can specifically help:

- If you have a photograph that illustrates an area that where we don't currently have a photograph then please send it to us (or if you think you can improve on a photograph we have used in the book). We will provide a free copy of the next edition to the photographer and credit both photographer and rider if appropriate (please see www.goodmtb.co.uk for more details)

- If we have made any errors of fact in the text or the maps then we would like to correct them next time around.

- If you have better or alternative route ideas for particular bases then please send us details and, most importantly, if you are aware of new trails or areas that we have simply missed then let us know. We would also like to hear from you if you think any of our existing choice of bases do not provide attractive riding but do please recognise that this is fairly subjective and some riders may get enjoyment from a trail which others consider mundane.

Please send any suggestions to: editor@goodmtb.co.uk

Acknowledgements

One of the highlights of producing this guide has been meeting and talking to so many wonderful people. We are truly grateful for all the help, support and advice we have been given and without which it is likely this book would still be just a great idea.

Our thanks go to the contributors, in particular to **Nick Cotton** who is responsible for the majority of the descriptive text relating to mountain biking regions and sub regions. It is clear from the text that Nick has an unbridled passion for mountain biking and the scenery, history and geology are far more important to him having than having the latest bit of bike kit. Nick's knowledge is genuinely encyclopaedic, amassed through writing 40 mountain bike guides over the past 20 years, there can be few mountain bikers who have ridden as many trails in England and Wales. There are a couple of areas that Nick does not yet know and we are grateful to **Jon Barton** (*Vertebrate Publishing, www.v-publishing.co.uk*) and **Stephen Hall** (*Blackshaw Outdoor, www. blackshawoutdoor.co.uk*) for riding in to help on the The Peak District and South Pennines respectively. Jon is an author and publisher of the excellent Vertebrate range of Mountain Biking, Climbing & Outdoor Books. Stephen is author of Mountain Bike Guide South Pennines West Yorkshire & Lancashire and provides a range of MTB courses and guiding in the South Pennine moors and valleys. Thanks for his relentless enthusiasm and advice in providing detailed information about the riding in South Lancashire and numerous photos to illustrate the book.

When we set out to illustrate The Good Mountain Biking Guide with photos of real riders out on the trails we were not entirely sure what to expect. We were very lucky that our first contact was with **Simon Barnes** (MTB enthusiast, photographer and the webmaster for the Bog Trotters Mountain Bike Club *www.bogtrotters.org*). Simon's photography is fantastic and he also has the benefit of leading a photogenic group of riders in the Bog Trotters who have had an unparalleled determination to ride in all weathers in all parts of Northern England. **Sheldon Attwood** (*www.sheldonattwood.com*), professional photographer based in Worcestershire, a selection of his excellent photos can be found throughout this book. **Gavin Duthie** (*www.gavinduthie.com*), professional photographer based in Northumberland. **Duncan Snow** (*www.mbkphotos.co.uk*), professional photographer based in Wiltshire. **Iain McConnell** (*www.turniptowers.co.uk*), part-time freelance photographer based in the Welsh borders. **Seb Rogers** (*www.sebrogers.co.uk*), professional photographer. Seb provided the cover shot and we have yet to meet one mountain biker who would not wish to be flying down that trail on the Long Mynd. **Tony Harker** (*Muddy Bums, www.muddybums.org.uk*), author of North York Moors Mountain Biking and the man behind Muddy Bums Mountain Biking, a website providing information about riding the North York Moors. **Neil Gander**, author of Beyond Hamsterley for providing us with some great photos of Northumberland & County Durham. **Graham Cooke** (*glphotos.co.uk*), professional photographer based on the Isle of Man. **Matt Cope** (*mcope.photoshelter.com*), professional photographer based in South Wales. **Dave Kneen** (*www.ManxPhotosOnline.com*), professional photographer based on the Isle of Man. **Graeme Warren**, professional photographer based in Berkshire. Thanks also to **Andy Heading** (*Race Kit, www.racekit.co.uk*) for looking through his huge library of shots when he was preparing for one of the toughest trail races on earth and launching a new business at the same time. **Jacqueline Easton** (*Dirt Divas, www.dirtdivas.co.uk*), MTB coach and founder of Dirt Divas, providing day courses for women mountain bikers of all abilities in Swinley Forest. **Danielle Sheridan** (*Singletrack School, www.astoundingadventures.co.uk*), providing MTB skills coaching and guided rides in the Surrey Hills. **Anna Heywood** (*Drover Holidays, www.droverholidays.co.uk*), providers of Guided and Self-Guided MTB Holidays in Mid Wales, the Welsh Borders, Brecon Beacons & Black Mountains. **Steve Phipps** (*Chasing Trails, www.chasingtrails.com*), providing MTB skills coaching and guided rides on the North York Moors. **Lee Cave** (*Dragon Adventure, www.dragonadventure.co.uk*), providing guided MTB rides in the Brecon Beacons National Park. **Huw Dullea** (*Treads & Trails, www.treadsandtrails.co.uk*), based in the Brecon Beacons National Park, providing MTB instruction and guided rides. **Keith Lee** (*Bikes & Hikes, www.bikesandhikes.co.uk*), providing MTB courses and guided rides including MTB hire, in the Brecon Beacons National Park. **Sean Case** (*South Downs Mountain Biking, www.southdownsmountainbiking.co.uk*), offering skills workshops and guided rides for all abilities in the South Downs. **Darren Allgood** (*Macc Mountain Biking, www.maccmtbiking.co.uk*), offering guided rides for all abilities in Macclesfield Forest and the Peak

18

District. **Graham Pollard** (*Moors Mountain Biking, www.moorsmountainbiking.co.uk*), MTB guide and instructor based in the North York Moors also offering a unique experience to people with a disability in the form of Tandem Mountain Biking. **Pete Corson** (*Trailbrakes, www.trailbrakes.co.uk*), providing MTB holidays, tours and coast to coast rides across the UK. **Singletrack Safari** (*Singletrack Safari, www.singletracksafari. com*), offering a range of "roadtrip-style" holidays throughout Europe and the UK. Based from a central location (sometimes moving to a second base midweek) they will transport you in limousine-style vehicles, to ride the finest trails available in your chosen destination. **Phil Harrison** (*Trailbreak, www.trailbreak.co.uk*), offering specialist mountain bike holidays, fun events and challenges in the UK, French Alps and Peru for novices to experienced mountain bikers including full challenge rides along the whole SDW. **Richard Kelly** (*All Biked Up, www.allbikedup.com*), founder of All Biked Up, providing MTB skills training and coached rides in the Surrey Hills as well as author of the Technique pages for IMBikemag, for his help and advice about riding the Surrey Hills and some great photos of the area. **Roger Knight** (*The Bike Barn, www.cornwallcycletrails. com*), providing MTB hire, tuition, sales and repairs on the Cornish CTC trail. **Jim Holgate** (*MTB Instruction, www.mtbinstruction.co.uk*), offering training and skills courses for all levels of rider at Woburn Sands in Buckinghamshire. **Colin Down** (*www.flattyresmtbroutes.com*), author of Flattyres MTB Routes as well as MTB guide and instructor providing routes, rides and training in North Wales and the North West. **David Heath** (*www.cycletrails.co*), author of Dave's MTB Mania, an online MTB guide to the East Midlands, Derbyshire & Nottinghamshire. **Michael Paradowski** (*www.kent-trails.co.uk*), offering online route suggestions and the opportunity to join a group of dedicated mountain bikers riding some of the best trails in Kent. **Aaron Swan** (*www.mountainbikewriter.blogspot.com*), author of Mountain Bike Writer, an online blog inspiring people to ride with accounts of his MTB rides. **Mark Reynolds** (*VC Godalming & Haslemere, www.vcgh.co.uk*), Trustee of The Hurtwood for his help and advice on riding the Surrey Hills. **Andy Stewart** (*Bath University Mountain Bike Club, www.bathunimtb.com*). **Mike Gill** (*Brighton MTB.org, brightonmtb.org*), **Anita Hartley** (*Reservoir Chicks, www.reservoirchicks.co.uk*). **Mark James, Scott Hogan,** (*Reservoir Goats, www.reservoirgoats.co.uk*)**. Dominic Bowles** (*CAM MTB, www.cammtb.co.uk*). **Chris Green, Peter Joyner** (*Old Blokes on Bikes, www. oldblokesonbikes.co.uk*). **Steve Gordon, Rob Koppenhol, Phil Jessiman** (*Dorset Rough Riders, www. dorsetroughriders.co.uk*). **Phil Reynolds** (*Swansea University MTB, www.swan.ac.uk/AU/mtb*). **Steve Lloyd, Chris Robinson, Dave Bradbury, Claire Hayter, Jeremy Stevens, Dan Trent, Mark Hatton** (*The Muddy Bums, www.muddybums.org*). **Mat Clark, Gary Ewing** (*Hamsterley Trailblazers, www.hamsterley-trailblazers.co.uk*). **Vic Cheetham, Alistair Websdell** (*The Tribe, www.thetribembc.co.uk*). **David Pettitt** (*Crowborough MBC, www.daysofspeed.com*), **Richard Foster** (*Sussex Muddyarse MTB, sussexmuddyarse.wordpress.com*), **Chris 'Stan' Hargrave** (*Bad Brains MTB, www.orgsites.com/ak/badbrainsmbc*),**, Tom Stickland , Job Hutchings** (*MB Swindon, www.mbswindon.co.uk*). **Dave Robinson, Phil Miles, Steve Wallis** (*SPAM, www.spambiking.co.uk*), *SPAM)*. **Andrew Hill** for taking the trouble to call in on us and providing a great selection of photos. **Anthony Beggs** (*www.bikedowns.co.uk Author of Bike Downs, an online Cyclists Guide to the South Downs Way*), **Dave Cassidy, Seb Herrod, Annie Coxey, Enrique Salcedo Sora, Liam Grose, Margaret Wilson, Jason Curtis, Desmond Green, Sam Townsend, James Elkington, Tom Ivory, Alan Leather, Julie Young , Alex Leigh, Geoff Rawson, Martin Samman, Pete Austin, Jonathan Russell, Angus Muir, Graham McCrindle, Mark Foster, Simon Clayson, Jonathan Neale, Andrew Querelle, Polly Summerhayes, Cat Williams, Nick Matthews, Neil Tydeman. Simon Gribbon** (*Go Leicestershire, www.goleicestershire.com*). **Claire Critchison** (*Isle of Wight Cycling Festival, www.sunseaandcycling.com*). **Mary** (*Discover Rutland, www.discover-rutland.co.uk*), **Helen Critchlow** (*Peak District & Derbyshire Tourist Board, www.visitpeakdistrict.com*). **Lizzie Carr** (*Experience Nottinghamshire, www.visitnottingham.com*). **Alan Leather** (*The National Forest Company, www.nationalfor-est.org*). **Nigel Turner** (*Forestry Commission, www.forestry.gov.uk*). **Martin Charlesworth** (*The Forest of Bowland, www.forestofbowlandimages.com*). **KT Davies** (*Moors Valley Country Park Ranger, www. moors-valley.co.uk*). **Terence Crump. Huw Mellior-Smith.** To **Gerard Downes** for a helping hand when we needed it most. Thanks to all at St Ives Web Ltd, in particular **Mark Harvey** who has been very helpful throughout and **Jason Ayres** for his technical expertise. To our families who have been a huge support. Thanks and love to **Anne** (who has been invaluable in keeping Active Maps in order, and helped on the book in many ways), **Douglas** & **Stewart**. We are grateful to **Amy, Magnus** and **Oscar** for their willingness to explore new trails, even before they knew they might feature in the book and to **Sarah** for encouragement and advice. Thanks to **John, Nick, Chris** & **Matt** for their patience & enthusiasm. Lastly, **Tim Clifford, Emma, Francis, Gill, Hannah, Janice, Linda, Lucy, Mark, Matthew, Sarah, Werner** for their practical support and for making a very happy workplace, and to **Peter Ross** for his enthusiasm.

If we have neglected to mention anyone we sincerely apologise, please let us know so we can add you to the next edition.

Further Reading
Recommended Books, Guides and Maps

Below is a list of the books, guides and maps that we have referred to throughout The Good Mountain Biking Guide. These are shown by region and publisher for ease of reference. As space is precious in the information sections of the book we have generally used abbreviated titles; these are shown below along with the full title.

BOOKS & GUIDES

Full Title and Author by Publisher	Abbreviation used in The Good Mountain Biking Guide

NORTH

Vertebrate Publishing

Lake District Mountain Biking - Essential Trails Chris Gore & Richard Staton 2010	Lake District MTB (C.Gore & R.Staton)
Yorkshire Dales Mountain Biking: The North Dales Nick Cotton 2006	Yorkshire Dales MTB - N Dales (N.Cotton)
Yorkshire Dales Mountain Biking: The South Dales Nick Cotton 2006	Yorkshire Dales MTB - S Dales (N.Cotton)
North York Moors Mountain Biking: Moorland Trails Tony Harker 2008	N York Moors MTB (T.Harker)

The Ernest Press

Mountain Bike Guide: South Pennines of West Yorkshire & Lancashire Stephen Hall 2010	MTB Guide S Pennines of W Yorks & Lancs (S.Hall)
Mountain Bike Guide: County Durham Derek Purdy 1997	MTB Guide County Durham (D.Purdy)
Mountain Bike Guide: Mid Yorkshire Rye Dale & the Wolds Dennis Liversidge 1998	MTB Guide Mid Yorkshire (D.Liversidge)
Mountain Bike Guide: North York Moors Steve Willis 2010	MTB Guide N York Moors (S.Willis)
Mountain Bike Guide: West Yorkshire Nick Dutton-Taylor 1993	MTB Guide W Yorkshire (N.Dutton-Taylor)

Cicerone Press

Mountain Biking in the Lake District Ian Boydon 2011	MTB Lake District (I.Boydon)
The Lancashire Cycleway : A Comprehensive Guide John Sparks 2007	The Lancashire Cycleway (J.Sparks)

IPC Media Ltd

MBR Ride Guide 2010	MBR Ride Guide 2010

Excellent Books

Mountain Biking Eden Valley & North Cumbria Richard Peace 2000	MTB Eden Valley & N Cumbria (R.Peace)

Mountain Biking West & South Yorkshire
Richard Peace 1996

MTB W & S Yorkshire (R.Peace)

Trailblazer Publishing

Mountain Biking on the Yorkshire Wolds
J Brian Beadle 1994

MTB Yorkshire Wolds (J.Beadle)

Hillside Publications

Wharfedale Biking Guide
Paul Hannon 2002

Wharfedale Biking Guide (P.Hannon)

Neil Gander

Beyond Hamsterley - Where To Ride Your Mountain
Bike In And Around County Durham
Neil Gander 2005

Beyond Hamsterley (N.Gander)

MIDLANDS & EASTERN

Vertebrate Publishing

Peak District Mountain Biking: Dark Peak Trails
Jon Barton 2010

Peak District MTB - Dark Peak (J.Barton)

Wales Mountain Biking - Beicio Mynydd Cymru
Tom Hutton 2009

Wales MTB (T.Hutton)

White Peak Mountain Biking: The Pure Trails
Jon Barton 2006

White Peak MTB (J.Barton)

The Ernest Press

Mountain Bike Guide South Pennines of West
Yorkshire & Lancashire
Stephen Hall 2010

MTB Guide S Pennines of W Yorks & Lancs (S.Hall)

Mountain Bike Guide Derbyshire & The Peak District
Tom Windsor 2009

MTB Guide Derbyshire & Peak District (T.Windsor)

Mountain Bike Guide East Midlands
Dave Taylor 1998

MTB Guide E Midlands (D.Taylor)

Mountain Bike Guide Mid-Wales & The Marches
Jon Dixon   1998

MTB Guide Mid Wales & The Marches (J.Dixon)

Mountain Bike Guide North Midlands To Manchester
Cheshire & Staffs
Henry Tindell 2005

MTB Guide N Midlands (H.Tindell)

Mountain Bike Guide Quality Routes in The Peak
District & Derbyshire
Mike Pearce 2004

MTB Guide Peak District & Derbyshire (M.Pearce)

Mountain Bike Guide West Midlands
Dave Taylor 2000

MTB Guide W Midlands (D.Taylor)

Context Publications

Mountain Bike Guide Nottinghamshire
Stewart Thompson 2006

MTB Guide Nottinghamshire (S.Thompson)

Rough Ride Guide Ltd

Mountain Bike Rides to the South East
Max Darkins 2005

MTB Rides to the SE (M.Darkins)

Excellent Books

Mountain Biking West & South Yorkshire
Richard Peace 1996

MTB W & S Yorkshire (R.Peace)

IPC Media Ltd

MBR Ride Guide 2010

MBR Ride Guide 2010

SOUTH EAST

Vertebrate Publishing

South East Mountain Biking: North & South Downs
Nick Cotton 2007

South East MTB - N & S Downs (N.Cotton)

South East Mountain Biking: Ridgeway & Chilterns
Nick Cotton 2008

South East MTB - Ridgeway & Chilterns (N.Cotton)

Cicerone Press

Mountain Biking on the South Downs
Peter Edwards 2011

MTB on S Downs (P.Edwards)

The Ernest Press

Mountain Bike Guide: Kent
Gary Tompsett 1995

MTB Guide Kent (G.Tompsett)

Rough Ride Guide Ltd

Mountain Bike Rides to the South East
Max Darkins 2005

MTB Rides to the SE (M.Darkins)

Mountain Bike Rides to the South West
Max Darkins 2006

MTB Rides to the SW (M.Darkins)

IPC Media Ltd

MBR Ride Guide 2010

MBR Ride Guide 2010

SOUTH WEST

Vertebrate Publishing

Cotswolds Mountain Biking: 20 Classic Rides
Tom Fenton 2010

Cotswolds MTB (T.Fenton)

South West Mountain Biking: Quantocks Exmoor
Dartmoor
Nick Cotton 2005, new edition out 2011

South West MTB (N.Cotton)

Rough Ride Guide Ltd

Mountain Bike Rides to the South West
Max Darkins 2006

MTB Rides to the SW (M.Darkins)

The Ernest Press

Mountain Bike Guide Dorset
Colin Dennis 2007

MTB Guide Dorset (C.Dennis)

Mountain Bike Guide - Wiltshire
Ian White 2000

MTB Guide Wiltshire (I.White)

IPC Media Ltd

MBR Ride Guide 2010

MBR Ride Guide 2010

Vertebrate Publishing

Wales Mountain Biking - Beicio Mynydd Cymru   Wales MTB (T.Hutton)
Tom Hutton 2009

Bikefax Ltd

The Best Mountain Bike Trails in North East   MTB Trails NE Wales (S.Savege & T.Griffiths)
Wales: Including the Clwydian Range, the Berwyn
Mountains, Mynydd Hiraethog, and Coed Llandegla
Sue Savege & Tony Griffiths 2005

The Best Mountain Bike Trails in Snowdonia /Y   MTB Trails Snowdonia (Savege, Barbier, Davis)
Ilwybrav Beic Mynydd Gorav Yn Eryri: Including
Coed Y Brenin, the Gwydyr Forest and Snowdon
Sue Savege, Paul Barbier & Dafydd Davis 2005

IPC Media Ltd

MBR Ride Guide 2010   MBR Ride Guide 2010

The Ernest Press

Mountain Bike Guide - Mid-Wales & The Marches   MTB Guide Mid Wales & The Marches (J.Dixon)
Jon Dixon 1998

Mountain Bike Guide - North Wales   MTB Guide North Wales (P.Bursnall)
Peter Bursnall 1996 , new edition out 2011

Cordee

The Mountain Bike Guide to Gower, South Wales   MTB Guide Valleys S Wales (N.Cotton)
Valleys and Lower Wye: 21 All Terrain Routes
Nick Cotton 1999

23

MAPS

Ordnance Survey

Explorer Map Series: Nationwide coverage.
Scale 1:25,000

Harvey

British Mountain Map Series: Dark Peak, Dartmoor,
Lake District, Snowdonia, Yorkshire Dales. Scale
1:40,000 Harvey Superwalker Series: Brecon
Beacons, Cheviot Hills, Forest of Bowland, Howgill
Fells, Lakeland, Malvern Hills. Scale 1:25,000 Cycle
Maps: Dales North, Dales East, Dales South, Dales
West Cycle Map 1:40,000

Goldeneye

Routes marked on a number of individual maps
printed on a large folded sheet for areas such as The
Lake District, Cotswolds, Exmoor, North Devon, The
Quantocks, Dartmoor.

Wild Boar Mountain Bike Maps

Series for around the Peak District. Dedicated
mountain bike maps, surface descriptions, technical grading of trails, A4 size, sealed waterproof
cover: Around Hayfield, Hayfield/Edale /Castleton,
Ladybower/Castleton/Hope, Macclesfield Forest &
Wildboarclough Bollington to Lyme Park, Goyt Valley,
Around Gradbach, Mellor Magic, Mellor Mania.

Mountain Bike Maps

Series of 12 A4 size maps for around the Lake
District.

Trailmaps

Series of 5 A4 size maps for around the Surrey Hills.

Further info: www.bikemaps.co.uk

Regions used in this Guide

p72 Page numbers

Isle of Man
p214

p72
Northumberland National Park & The Cheviots

North Pennines & Central Northumberland
p82

Lake District
p38

NORTH

Yorkshire Dales & Forest of Bowland
p100

North York Moors & The Wolds
p152

South Lancashire, West Yorkshire & Cheshire
p184

p222
Peak District

East Midlands
p290

Snowdonia, Clwyds and North Wales
p528

MIDLANDS & EASTERN

p556 Mid Wales

Shropshire Hills, Malverns & West Midlands
p264

Norfolk, Suffolk & Cambridgeshire
p316

WALES

The Chilterns & North Home Counties
p322

Brecon Beacons & South Wales
p580

The Cotswolds & The Mendips
p416

SOUTH EAST

The Ridgeway & Hampshire Downs
p340

North Downs & Surrey Hills
p352

p480 Exmoor & The Quantocks

Salisbury Plain & Dorset
p446

South Downs, South Hampshire and Isle of Wight
p378

SOUTH WEST

Dartmoor & Cornwall
p504

Mountain Bike Base Locations

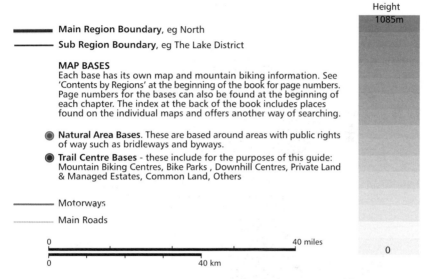

Height
1085m

——— **Main Region Boundary**, eg North

——— **Sub Region Boundary**, eg The Lake District

MAP BASES
Each base has its own map and mountain biking information. See 'Contents by Regions' at the beginning of the book for page numbers. Page numbers for the bases can also be found at the beginning of each chapter. The index at the back of the book includes places found on the individual maps and offers another way of searching.

● **Natural Area Bases**. These are based around areas with public rights of way such as bridleways and byways.

● **Trail Centre Bases** - these include for the purposes of this guide: Mountain Biking Centres, Bike Parks , Downhill Centres, Private Land & Managed Estates, Common Land, Others

——— Motorways

········· Main Roads

```
0                                          40 miles
|━━━━━━━━━━━━━━━━━━━━━━━━━━━━━━━━━━━━━━━━━|
0                          40 km
```

0

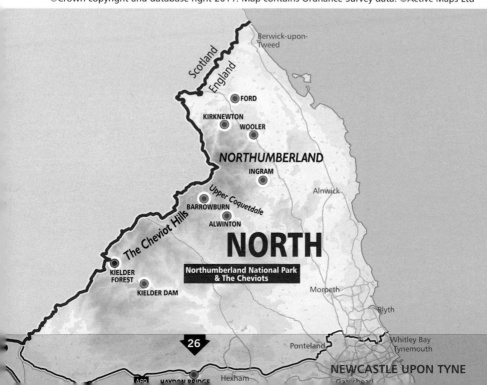

Berwick-upon-Tweed

Scotland

England

● FORD

KIRKNEWTON ● WOOLER

NORTHUMBERLAND

INGRAM

Alnwick

Upper Coquetdale

The Cheviot Hills

BARROWBURN

ALWINTON

NORTH

Northumberland National Park & The Cheviots

● KIELDER FOREST

● KIELDER DAM

Morpeth

Blyth

26

Ponteland

Whitley Bay
Tynemouth

NEWCASTLE UPON TYNE

Gateshead

HAYDON BRIDGE   Hexham

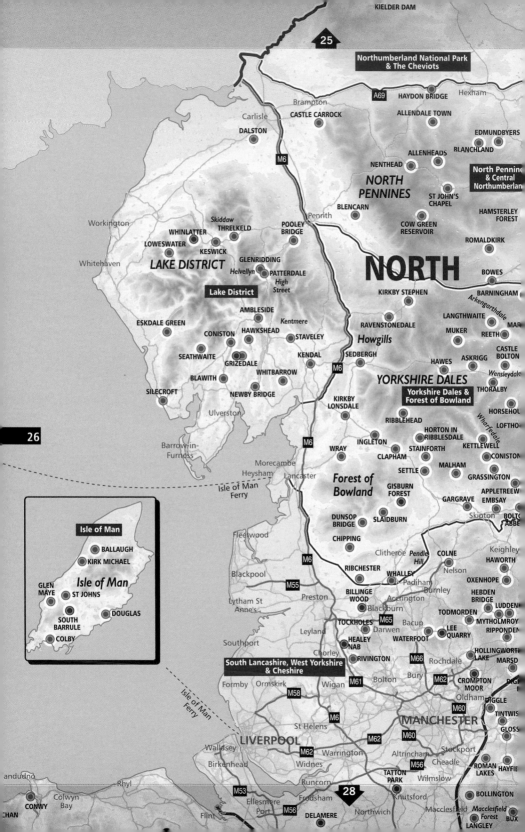

KIELDER DAM

Northumberland National Park
& The Cheviots

Brampton
A69 HAYDON BRIDGE   Hexham
Carlisle   CASTLE CARROCK   ALLENDALE TOWN
DALSTON   EDMUNDBYERS
                          ALLENHEADS   BLANCHLAND
                    NENTHEAD
                    NORTH   St JOHN'S   North Pennine
                    PENNINES   CHAPEL   & Central
                                              Northumberlan
Workington   Skiddaw THRELKELD BLENCARN   HAMSTERLEY
       WHINLATTER   FOREST
       LOWESWATER   POOLEY   COW GREEN
                    BRIDGE   RESERVOIR   ROMALDKIRK
       KESWICK   Penrith
Whitehaven GLENRIDDING   BOWES
       LAKE DISTRICT   NORTH
              Helvellyn PATTERDALE   BARNINGHAM
       Lake District High   KIRKBY STEPHEN   Arkengarthdale
                       Street   LANGTHWAITE
              AMBLESIDE   MUKER   REETH   MAR
ESKDALE GREEN   Kentmere   RAVENSTONEDALE
       CONISTON HAWKSHEAD STAVELEY   HAWES   ASKRIGG CASTLE
       SEATHWAITE   Howgills   BOLTON
              GRIZEDALE KENDAL SEDBERGH   Wensleydale
       BLAWITH WHITBARROW   YORKSHIRE DALES THORALBY
       SILECROFT NEWBY BRIDGE   HORSEHOL
       Ulverston   KIRKBY   Yorkshire Dales & LOFTHO
                          LONSDALE   Forest of Bowland
       Barrow-in-   RIBBLEHEAD   Wharfedale
       Furness   HORTON IN   KETTLEWELL
              Morecambe   INGLETON   RIBBLESDALE CONISTON
              Heysham   WRAY CLAPHAM STAINFORTH
       Lancaster   MALHAM GRASSINGTON
                          Forest of   SETTLE
                          Bowland   APPLETREEW
                          GISBURN   GARGRAVE EMBSAY
                          FOREST   Skipton BOLT
       Fleetwood   DUNSOP   SLAIDBURN   ABBE
                   BRIDGE
                   CHIPPING   Clitheroe Pendle   COLNE
       Blackpool   RIBCHESTER Hill   HAWORTH
                                          Nelson OXENHOPE
                          WHALLEY   HEBDEN
       Lytham St   Preston BILLINGE Padiham Burnley BRIDGE LUDDEN
       Anne's   WOOD   Accrington TODMORDEN MYTHOLMROY
                          Blackburn   RIPPONDEN
              Southport TOCKHOLES Bacup
                         Darwen WATERFOOT LEE
                    HEALEY   QUARRY
                    NAB   HOLLINGWORT
              Leyland RIVINGTON   LAKE MARSD
                    Chorley   Rochdale
                                          CROMPTON DIG
              Formby Ormskirk   Bury MOOR DIGGLE
                    Wigan   M61 Bolton Oldham TINTWIS
                                          M60   GLOSS
              St Helens   MANCHESTER HAYFIE
       LIVERPOOL   Altrincham Stockport ROMAN
       Wallasey   Cheadle   LAKES HAYFIE
       Birkenhead   Wilmslow BOLLINGTON BUX
andudno Colwyn Rhyl   Knutsford Macclesfield Macclesfield
CHAN CONWY Bay   Runcorn   Forest LANGLEY
              Flint Ellesmere Frodsham Northwich
                    Port DELAMERE

26
28

M6
M55
M58
M62
M65
M66
M60
M56
M53

Isle of Man
Ferry

Isle of Man
Ferry

Isle of Man

BALLAUGH
KIRK MICHAEL
GLEN
MAYE   Isle of Man
       St JOHNS
SOUTH
BARRULE   DOUGLAS
COLBY

South Lancashire, West Yorkshire
& Cheshire

North Pennine
& Central
Northumberlan

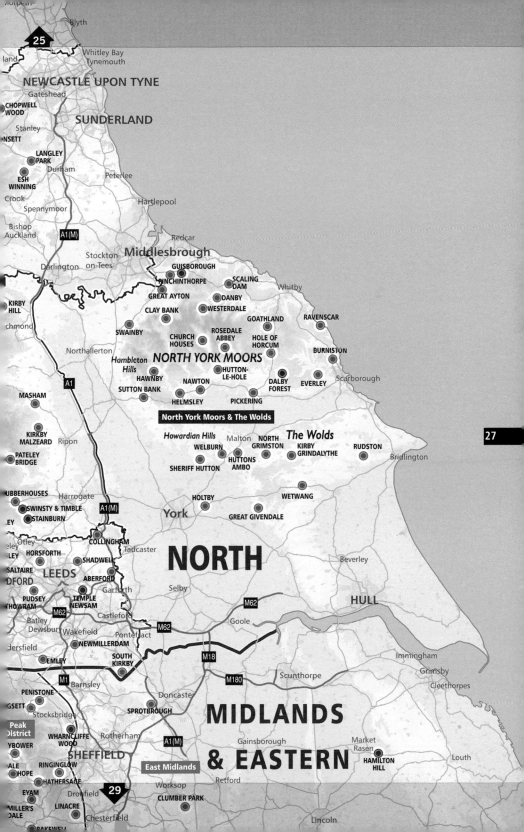

Blyth

Whitley Bay
Tynemouth

land

NEWCASTLE UPON TYNE

Gateseahd

**CHOPWELL
WOOD**

SUNDERLAND

Stanley

NSETT

Peterlee

**LANGLEY
PARK**

Durham

**ESH
WINNING**

Crook

Spennymoor

Hartlepool

Bishop
Auckland

A1(M)

Redcar

Stockton
on-Tees

Darlington

Middlesbrough

**KIRBY
HILL**

GUISBOROUGH

PINCHINTHORPE

GREAT AYTON

**SCALING
DAM**

Whitby

DANBY

chmond

CLAY BANK

WESTERDALE

GOATHLAND

RAVENSCAR

SWAINBY

Northallerton

**CHURCH
HOUSES**

**ROSEDALE
ABBEY**

**HOLE OF
HORCUM**

BURNISTON

A1

Hambleton
Hills

NORTH YORK MOORS

**HUTTON-
LE-HOLE**

Scarborough

HAWNBY

NAWTON

**DALBY
FOREST**

EVERLEY

MASHAM

SUTTON BANK

HELMSLEY

PICKERING

North York Moors & The Wolds

**KIRKBY
MALZEARD**

Ripon

Howardian Hills

Malton

The Wolds

27

**PATELEY
BRIDGE**

WELBURN

**NORTH
GRIMSTON**

**KIRBY
GRINDALYTHE**

RUDSTON

Bridlington

SHERIFF HUTTON

**HUTTONS
AMBO**

UBBERHOUSES

Harrogate

WETWANG

SWINSTY & TIMBLE

A1(M)

HOLTBY

EY

STAINBURN

York

GREAT GIVENDALE

Otley

Beverley

LEY

HORSFORTH

COLLINGHAM

Tadcaster

NORTH

SALTAIRE

SHADWELL

DFORD

LEEDS

ABERFORD

Selby

HULL

PUDSEY

**TEMPLE
NEWSAM**

Garforth

HOWRAM

Batley

M62

Castleford

Dewsbury

Wakefield

Pontefract

M62

Goole

dersfield

NEWMILLERDAM

M62

EMLEY

**SOUTH
KIRKBY**

Immingham

M1

Barnsley

M18

Scunthorpe

Grimsby

PENISTONE

Cleethorpes

GSETT

Stocksbridge

Doncaster

M180

SPROTBROUGH

MIDLANDS

Peak
District

**WHARNCLIFFE
WOOD**

Rotherham

A1(M)

Gainsborough

Market
Rasen

Louth

YBOWER

SHEFFIELD

& EASTERN

ALE

RINGINGLOW

East Midlands

**HAMILTON
HILL**

HOPE

HATHERSAGE

Worksop

Retford

EYAM

Dronfield

29

CLUMBER PARK

Lincoln

LINACRE

MILLER'S

Chesterfield

DALE

Holyhead

Llan

Anglesey

LLANFAIRFECHA

Bangor

LLANBERIS

CAPI
CURI

Snowdon

DOLWYDDE

BEDDGELERT
FOREST

NANT GWRTHEYRN

S N O W

Porthmadog

COED LLYN Y
GARNEDD

COEI
BRE

TAL-Y-BONT

Dolge

BARMOUTH

*Cad
Idr*

ABERGYNOLWYN

MACHYNLLET

Aberystwyth

NANT
ARIA

Cardigan

Fishguard

Preseli Hills

BRECHFA

St Davids

ROSEBUSH

Brecon Beacons & South Wales

PEMBROKESHIRE

Carmarthen

Haverordwest

Ammanford

Milford
Haven

Pembroke

Tenby

Llanelli

M4

N

Gower

Swansea

RHOSSILI

Ta

Louth

Skegness

Boston

Cromer

King's
Lynn

Wisbech

Downham
Market

Swaffham

Dereham

Norwich

Great Yarmouth

March

**Norfolk, Suffolk &
Cambridgeshire**

Lowestoft

Ely

THETFORD
FOREST

Thetford

**MIDLANDS
& EASTERN**

St Ives

Mildenhall

Newmarket

Bury
St Edmunds

Stowmarket

Cambridge

FULBOURN

Haverhill

RENDLESHAM
FOREST

ROYSTON

Saffron
Walden

Sudbury

35

Ipswich

M11

**The Chilterns &
North Home Counties**

Felixstowe

TTON
STONE

Bishop's
Stortford

Braintree

Colchester

Harwich

Ware

Hertford

Clacton-on-Sea

ETTY
REEN

Harlow

Chelmsford

Maldon

Cheshunt

Epping

EPPING
FOREST

HAINAULT
FOREST PARK

Brentwood

Basildon

field

Romford

Southend-on-Sea

O N

M25

South Benfleet

Woolwich

Tilbury

Haverordwest

Milford
Haven

Pembroke   Tenby

Ammanford

Llanelli

M4

Swansea

RHOSSILI   Gower

LYNTO

Ilfracombe

BARNSTAPLE

Bideford

SOUTH WEST
EXTREME

Bude

ABBEYFORD
WOODS

OKEHAMPTON

DREWSTEIGNTON

Dartmoor & Cornwall

Launceston

LYDFORD

DARTMOO

POSTBRIDGE

TAVISTOCK
WOODS

Tavistock

PRINCETOWN

Bodmin

Newquay

Liskeard

MADDACLEAVE
WOODS
(GAWTON)

SOUT
BREN

Saltash

PLYMOUTH

Ivybridge

St Austell

PORTREATH

THE TRACK   Truro

Redruth

POLDICE
VALLEY

Camborne

St Ives

Falmouth

Penzance   Helston

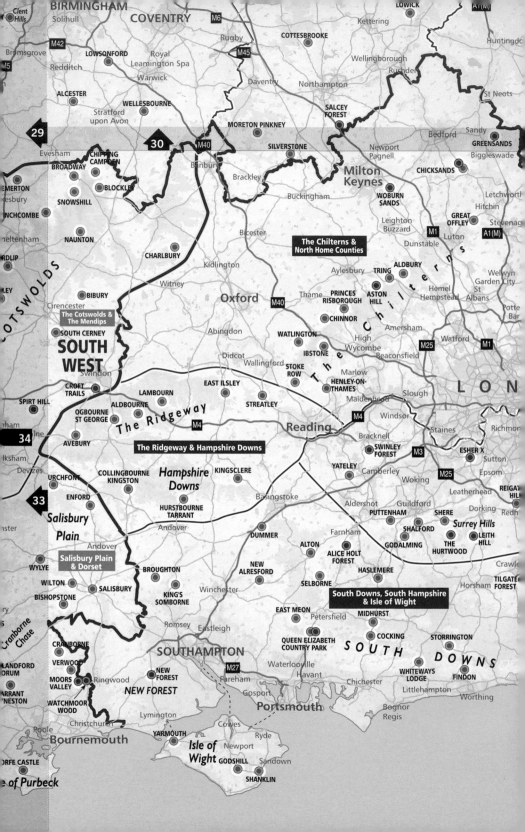

SOUTH EAST

31

Ely

Mildenhall

St Ives

Newmarket

Bury
St Edmunds

Stowmarket

Cambridge

FULBOURN

Haverhill

Ipswich

RENDLESHAM
FOREST

ROYSTON

Saffron
Walden

M11

Sudbury

Felixstowe

Harwich

WATTON
AT STONE

Bishop's
Stortford

Braintree

Colchester

Clacton-on-Sea

Ware

ertford

LETTY
GREEN

Harlow

Maldon

Cheshunt

Epping

Chelmsford

M25

EPPING
FOREST

HAINAULT
FOREST PARK

Brentwood

Enfield

Romford

Basildon

Southend-on-Sea

Southend-on-Sea

D O N

M25

South Benfleet

Margate

Woolwich

Tilbury

Dartford

Gravesend

Rochester

Herne Bay

Whitstable

Ramsgate

North Downs &
Surrey Hills

M20

Gillingham

Chatham

Sittingbourne

Faversham

BLEAN

NORTH DOWNS

TROTTISCLIFFE

NORTH DOWNS

Canterbury

FOWLMEAD
COUNTRY PARK

GODSTONE

Sevenoaks

AYLESFORD

M2

SHALMSFORD
STREET

Deal

Oxted

IGHTHAM

Maidstone

CHILHAM

IDE HILL

M20

CHARING

M23

Tonbridge

Royal

LYMINGE

Dover

East
Grinstead

VICEROY'S
WOODS

Tunbridge
Wells

BEWL
WATER

BEDGEBURY

Ashford

Folkestone

DEERS LEAP
PARK

Crowborough

HAMSTREET

HYTHE

aywards
Heath

High Weald

Uckfield

NETHERFIELD

Romney
Marsh

TCHLING
EACON

LEWES

Hailsham

Hastings

righton

Bexhill

Sussex
Downs

ALFRISTON

Eastbourne

Newhaven

FRISTON
FOREST

NORTH

The Lake District, Yorkshire Dales, North York Moors and Northumberland National Parks offer hundreds of miles of tough and exhilarating mountain biking. In the far north, rides in County Durham and Northumberland focus on the trail centres at Hamsterley and Kielder, the sandstone tracks around Allendale and the remote expanses of the Cheviot Hills. The Lake District has England's most distinctive mountain skyline, forming a backdrop to the rides that explore this stunning scenery. There are trail centres at Grizedale and Whinlatter. The best cross-country ride areas lie outside the central fells as the latter are filled with thousands of ramblers. The Yorkshire Dales have fewer visitors and fewer 'honeypots' so you can enjoy long unbroken stretches of superb stone-based tracks crossing the limestone scenery. The geology of the North York Moors and its drier climate offer a distinctive contrast, with a large trail centre in Dalby Forest. Another area covered here is the South Pennines between Manchester and Leeds, with its moorland riding on both fine single and double track, beautiful woodland and rocky trails. Many loops involve sections of the well maintained Pennine Bridleway. There are also the cutting edge routes at Lee Quarry Mountain Bike Centre which now has links to surrounding bridleways. Finally, the Isle of Man, a ferry trip from the mainland, offers an ideal weekend break with rides dominated by massive views across to Scotland, Ireland, Wales and England.

Howgill Fells. © Simon Barnes. www.bogtrotters.org

The Lake District

The Lake District National Park is surprisingly compact: a circle with a 20-mile radius drawn around *Ambleside* covers almost the entire area. Yet within this compact area there is an astonishing wealth of mountain biking tracks to discover: from the purpose-built Forestry Commission singletrack trails centres at *Grizedale* and *Whinlatter* to the big open spaces in the circuit of Skiddaw, north of *Keswick*, taking in *Threlkeld* and Bassenthwaite; from the ever more popular trails in Kentmere, north of *Staveley,* to the network of bridleways from *Eskdale Green* exploring Eskdale and Miterdale in the west; from the long established challenges of the wide stone tracks of Walna Scar near *Coniston* and Garburn

Grizedale p54. © Simon Barnes. www.bogtrotters.org

38

Pass in South Lakeland, to the grassy slopes of Askham Fell and the north end of the old Roman Road of High Street near *Ullswater*, accessed from *Pooley Bridge*, *Glenridding* or *Patterdale*. The central fells around *Ambleside* and the Langdales can be very busy with walkers: if you ride here it is well

Caw Moss, Coniston p56. © Simon Barnes. www.bogtrotters.org

worth choosing your time wisely ie midweek, outside holiday periods, and preferably early morning or early evening. This is one of the reasons that explains the popularity of **Staveley** as a cycling base: you don't have to contend with the traffic of the Central Lakes, various length trails start right from the doorstep exploring Kentmere and there are links to Longsleddale and Troutbeck, or High Street and Haweswater.

The further west you go in the Lake District, the quieter it becomes. There are easy and hard trails starting from picturesque **Loweswater**. **Eskdale Green** gives access to the bridleways around the base of Muncaster Fell, north to Miterdale or east to Eskdale at the start of the infamous Hardknott Pass.

In the southeast of the National Park, **Seathwaite** in the stunning Duddon Valley and **Blawith** at the south end of Coniston Water both give access to bridleways that are little visited by ramblers, exploring the Dunnerdale Fells, Woodland Fell and Subberthwaite Common.

In the very heart of the National Park, the three bases of **Coniston**, **Hawkshead** and **Ambleside** are linked by bridleways and narrow lanes, past scenically located Loughrigg and Elterwater, via the old quarries at Tilberthwaite and over the delights of Claife Heights.

Grizedale Forest is well known for the North Face Trail but there is plenty more in the area lying between Coniston Water and Windermere. Finally, **Whinlatter Forest**, to the west of **Keswick**, boasts the Altura Trail climbing to 500m with panoramic views over the northern Lakes.

Rider: Dave Yip. Longsleddale, Staveley p62

Keswick (north)

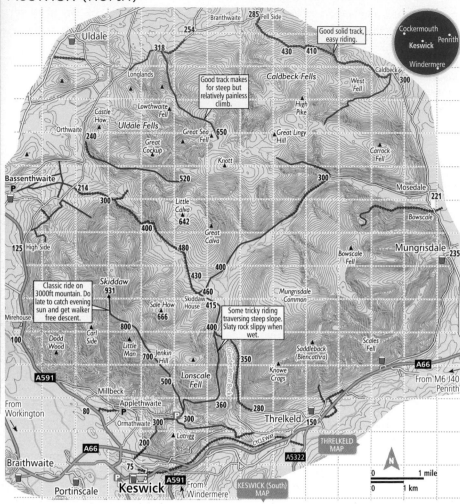

Map labels (reading across the map):

Branthwaite • 285 Fell Side • Cockermouth • Penrith • **Keswick** • Windermere • Caldbeck • 300

Uldale • 254 • 318 • Longlands • Good solid track, easy riding. • 430 • 410 • West Fell • Caldbeck Fells • Good track makes for steep but relatively painless climb. • High Pike • Great Lingy Hill • Castle How • Lowthwaite Fell • 240 • Uldale Fells • Orthwaite • Great Cockup • Great Sea Fell • 650 • Knott • Carrock Fell

Bassenthwaite • P • 214 • 300 • 520 • 300 • Mosedale • 221

High Side • 125 • Little Calva • 642 • Great Calva • 480 • 400 • 430 • Bowscale • Bowscale Fell • Mungrisdale • 235

Skiddaw • 931 • Classic ride on 3000ft mountain. Do late to catch evening sun and get walker free descent. • Sale How • 666 • Skiddaw House • 460 • 415 • Mungrisdale Common • 400 • Some tricky riding traversing steep slope. Slaty rock slippy when wet. • Scales Fell

Mirehouse • 100 • Dodd Wood • Carl Side • 800 • Little Man • 700 • Jenkin Hill • 400 • 350 • Saddleback (Blencathra) • A66 • From M6 J40 Penrith

A591 • 500 • Lonscale Fell • Knowe Crags • A66 • From Workington • Millbeck • Applethwaite • P • 80 • Ormathwaite • 300 • 300 • 360 • 280 • Threlkeld • 150

A66 • 200 • Latrigg • CYCLEWAY • THRELKELD MAP • 75 • P • A591 • Keswick • From Windermere • KESWICK (South) MAP • A5322

Braithwaite • Portinscale • Keswick

0 — 1 mile / 0 — 1 km • N

Situation: At the foot of the Skiddaw fells, in the north of the Lake District National Park, 15 miles west of M6 Jct 40 and Penrith.

About the Base: Keswick, a market town with plenty of pubs, cafés and accommodation. Further info: www.keswick.org. **Parking**: Car park behind Latrigg or parking roadside opposite Applethwaite Country House Hotel. Long stay car park in Keswick town centre. *Grid Ref: Latrigg NY280253. Applethwaite NY265256. Keswick NY265233.* **Post Code:** *Applethwaite CA12 4PL. Keswick CA12 5EX.*

Drive Times: Carlisle 50mins, Newcastle 2hr, Manchester 2hr10, Leeds 2hr30, Birmingham 3hr20.

Refreshments: Lots of choice in Keswick. The Old Sawmill Café at Mirehouse, Sun Inn 017687 79632 in Bassenthwaite, Snooty Fox 016973 71479 at Uldale, The Mill Inn 017687 79632 at Mungrisdale, pubs on A66 and at Threlkeld.

Books: Lake District MTB (C.Gore & R.Staton). MBR Ride Guide 2010.

Maps: Skiddaw Mountain Bike Map (Mountain Bike Maps). Lake District Mountain Bike Routes (Goldeneye). OS Explorer OL4 & OL5, Lakeland North (Harvey).

Routes on Web: www.goodmtb.co.uk/a41a & /a41b

Bike Shops: Keswick Bikes 017687 75202 and Whinlatter Bikes 017687 73940 for parts & hire. Keswick Leisure Pool 017687 72760 for hire.

© Simon Barnes. www.bogtrotters.org

Route Ideas

❶ From Keswick, head east along the cycleway to Threlkeld then up and around the Glenderaterra Beck valley and back to Keswick. Distance 18km.

❷ An out and back to the top of Skiddaw. Distance 17km.

❸ From Keswick head up the Glenderaterra Beck valley then follow the trail towards Bassenthwaite. Before reaching the village turn left onto the lane, follow to main road and back to Keswick. Distance 31km.

❹ This starts as option 3 but at Skiddaw House head to Mosedale, then Caldbeck, Fell Side and Longlands. Continue along the road then take the trail that leads back to Skiddaw House and then onto the finish. Distance 45km.

Crossing the Caldew. © Simon Barnes. www.bogtrotters.org

Keswick (south)

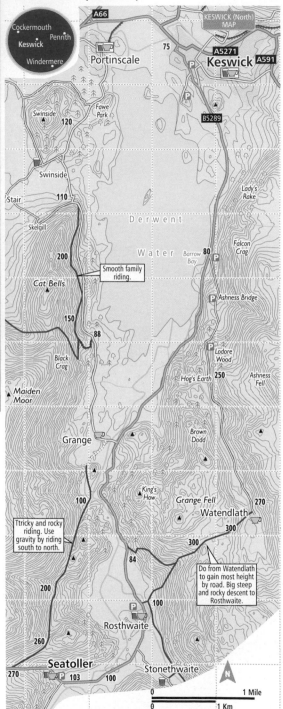

Smooth family riding.

Ttricky and rocky riding. Use gravity by riding south to north.

Do from Watendlath to gain most height by road. Big steep and rocky descent to Rosthwaite.

Situation: At the foot of the Skiddaw fells, in the north of the Lake District National Park, 15 miles west of M6 Jct 40 and Penrith. Keswick is on the shores of Derwentwater.

About the Base: Keswick, a market town with plenty of pubs, cafés and accommodation. Further info: www.keswick.org. **Parking:** Long stay car park in Keswick town centre and by the lake. Car parks at Seatoller, Rosthwaite, Lodore Wood, Ashness Bridge and Barrow Bay. *Grid Ref: Keswick NY265233, Lakeside NY265229, Seatoller NY245137, Rosthwaite NY257148, Lodore Wood NY268189, Ashness Bridge NY269196, Barrow Bay NY269203.*
Post Code: Keswick CA12 5EX, Lakeside CA12 5DJ, Seatoller CA12 5XN, Rosthwaite CA12 5XB.

Drive Times: Carlisle 50mins, Newcastle 2hr, Manchester 2hr10, Leeds 2hr30, Birmingham 3hr20.

Refreshments: Lots of choice in Keswick. The Farmer 017687 73442 and Portinscale Tea Rooms 017687 75307 in Portinscale. The Swineside Inn 017687 78253 at Swineside, Grange Café 017687 77077 at Grange, Honisters Yew Tree 017687 77634 in Seatoller, Langstrath Inn 08721 077077 in Stonethwaite, Flock Inn 017687 77675 and Royal Oak Hotel 017687 77214 in Rosthwaite and Caffle House Tea Rooms 017687 77219 at Watendlath.

Books: Lake District MTB (C.Gore & R.Staton).

Maps: Borrowdale Mountain Bike Map (Mountain Bike Maps). OS Explorer OL4, Lakeland Central (Harvey), Lake District British Mountain Map (Harvey).

Routes on Web: www.goodmtb.co.uk/a42

Bike Shops: Keswick Bikes 017687 75202 and Whinlatter Bikes 017687 73940 for parts and hire. Keswick Leisure Pool 017687 72760 also hire bikes.

Route Ideas

❶ Head S from Keswick, along the east side of Derwent Water, then on the road leading to Watendlath, trails to Rosthwaite, past Seatoller then to Grange and back to Keswick on the west of Derwent Water. Distance 29km.

❷ Start at Rosthwaite car park and loop around the southern area (Seatoller, Grange, Watendlath). Distance, 12km.

Nr Watendleth. © Simon Barnes

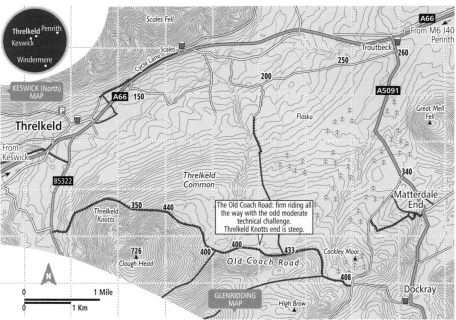

Situation: At the southern foot of Blencathra in the north of the Lake District National Park. 4 miles east of Keswick and Derwentwater, 14 miles west of Penrith.

About the Base: Threlkeld, a village with two pubs & accommodation. Further info: www.threlkeld.org.uk.

Parking: Car park on the north side of the village past the school. *Grid Ref: NY318256. Post Code: CA12 4SB.*

Drive Times: Carlisle 45mins, Newcastle 1hr50, Manchester 2hr, Leeds 2hr30, Birmingham 3hr40.

Refreshments: At Threlkeld, The Salutation Inn 017687 79614 or The Horse & Farrier 017687 79688. The White Horse Inn at Scales 017687 79883, The Troutbeck Inn 017687 83635 at Troutbeck and The Royal at Dockray 017684 82356.

Books: MTB Lake District (I.Boydon).

Maps: The Old Coach Road Mountain Bike Map (Mountain Bike Maps). Lake District Mountain Bike Routes (Goldeneye), OS Explorer OL4 & OL5, Lakeland North (Harvey), Lakeland Central (Harvey), Lake District British Mountain Map (Harvey).

Bike Shops: Keswick Bikes 017687 75202 and Whinlatter Bikes 017687 73940 for parts & hire. Keswick Leisure Pool 017687 72760 also hire bikes.

Route Idea

From Threlkeld, NE to Scales then on to Troutbeck via road to the south of A66. Head towards Matterdale End then on to the Old Coach Road (off road trail) all the way to join the B5322, stay on this back to start or use minor roads to the W. Distance 26km

43

The Old Coach Road. © Simon Barnes. www.bogtrotters.org

Glenridding

Penrith
Keswick
Glenridding
Ambleside

THRELKELD MAP

From A66
Troutbeck

A5091

500

400

600

High Brow

Dockray

290

P

Matterdale Common

700

Deepdale

800

Great Dodd
800

From M6 J40 Penrith

A592

Watson's Dodd

750

Hart Side

800

Stybarrow Dodd

830

Green Side

Glencoyne

Generally considered the easiest way up or down.

P
148
Glencoyne Bridge

Ullswater

Sticks Pass

750

550

Sheffield Pike

Glenridding Dodd

500

Raise
870

Stang

300

Glenridding Beck

Glenridding

800   700

400

200

P

815

600   500

148

White Side

863

Keppel Cove

Glenridding Common

Birkhouse Moor

The paths in the whole of this area are very popular with walkers: chose your time carefully

PATTERDALE MAP

Grisedale Bridge

150

44

Technical descent with drops on both sides.

800

Brown Cove

Catstye Cam

200

Patterdale

P

Swirral Edge

Lower Man

900

Red Tarn

Patterdale Common

Grisedale

A592

Helvellyn

950

Striding Edge

Highest point legally accessible by bike in England. Well worth it for the fit and technically proficient.

900

Nethermost Cove

Birks

From Ambleside Windermere

Nethermost Pike

880

250

Ridge top track largely ridable.

Grisedale Forest

300

The Cape

850

Dollywaggon Pike

400

N

800

700   500

0   1 Mile

550

0   1 Km

Grisedale Tarn

Situation: At the southern end of Ullswater below Helvellyn, near the foot of the Kirkstone Pass in the heart of the Lake District National Park. 14 miles south west of Penrith.

About the Base: Glenridding, a village with pubs, cafés and accommodation. **Parking:** Car Parks next to the information centre by the lake in Glenridding and opposite the pub in the roadside at Glencoyne Bridge or south of Dockray. **Grid Ref:** *Glenridding NY387169. Patterdale NY395160. Glencoyne Bridge NY386188. Dockray NY396211.* **Post Code:** *Glenridding CA11 OPB. Patterdale CA11 ONN.*

Drive Times: Carlisle 45mins, Newcastle 1hr50, Manchester 2hr, Leeds 2hr20, Birmingham 3hr.

Refreshments: Choice of pubs in Glenridding, Fellbites Café 017684 82664 and Greystones Coffee House 017684 82392. The White Lion Inn 017684 82214 or The Patterdale Hotel 017684 82231 in Patterdale and The Royal at Dockray 017684 82356.

Dropping off Great Dodd. © Simon Barnes. www.bogtrotters.org

Books: Lake District MTB (C.Gore & R.Staton).

Maps: OS Explorer OL5, Lakeland Central (Harvey), Lake District British Mountain Map (Harvey).

Bike Shops: Hire at St Patrick's Boat Landing 017684 82393 in Glenridding.

Route Ideas

This is a high mountaneous area, plan accordingly.

❶ From Glenridding, head north to Dockray then soon climbing on trails passing Great Dodd, Stybarrow Dodd and Raise. Take the bridleway after Raise back to Glenridding. Distance 23km.

❷ An out and back from Glenridding along Glenridding Beck, Glenridding Common to White Side. Distance 12km.

❸ Whilst the above options are far from easy it is possible to make the riding harder still by using the descent from Sticks Pass and also the bridleways passing Helvellyn, Dolywaggon Pike and along Grisedale. For an easy option head along Grisedale until the going becomes tough then about turn.

Lower Man. © Simon Barnes. www.bogtrotters.org

Patterdale

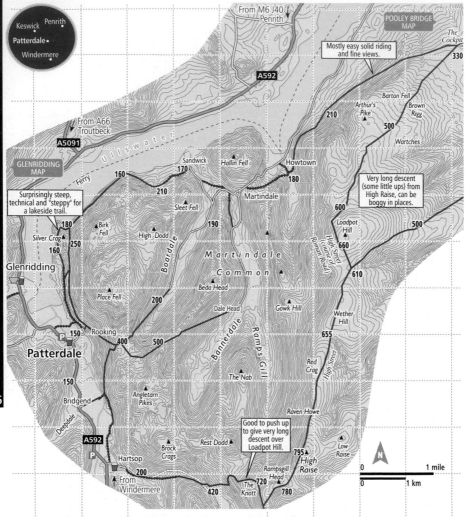

Keswick • Penrith •
Patterdale •
Windermere •

From M6 J40 / Penrith

POOLEY BRIDGE MAP

The Cockpit

Mostly easy solid riding and fine views.

330

A592

Barton Fell

Arthur's Pike

Brown Rigg

210

500

Wartches

From A66 Troubeck

A5091

Ullswater

Sandwick

Hallin Fell

Howtown

GLENRIDDING MAP

Ferry

160

170

180

Very long descent (some little ups) from High Raise, can be boggy in places.

Surprisingly steep, technical and "steppy" for a lakeside trail.

210

Martindale

600

500

Sleet Fell

190

Loadpot Hill

180

Birk Fell

High Dodd

660

Silver Crag

250

High Street (course of Roman Road)

160

Martindale Common

610

Glenridding

Beda Head

Place Fell

200

Dale Head

Gowk Hill

Wether Hill

150

Rooking

655

400

500

Bannerdale

Rampsgill

Patterdale

150

The Nab

Red Crag

High Street

Bridgend

Angletarn Pikes

Raven Howe

Good to push up to give very long descent over Loadpot Hill.

Deepdale

A592

Brock Crags

Rest Dodd

795

Low Raise

Hartsop

200

Rampsgill Head

High Raise

720

From Windermere

420

The Knott

780

N

0   1 mile
0   1 km

Situation: At the southern end of Ullswater, the head of the Kirkstone Pass and the foot of Helvellyn in the Lake District National Park. 14 miles SW of Penrith.

About the Base: Patterdale, a small village with pub, café and hotel. Further info: www.patterdale.org.

Parking: Car parks opposite the pub in the centre of the village or at Hartsop. *Grid Ref: Patterdale NY395160, Hartsop NY402134. Post Code: Patterdale CA11 0NN.*

Drive Times: Carlisle 45mins, Manchester 1hr50, Newcastle 1hr50, Leeds 2hr20, Birmingham 3hr.

Refreshments: The White Lion Inn 017684 82214 and The Patterdale Hotel 017684 82231 in Patterdale. The Brotherswater Inn 017684 82239 at Hartsop.

Books: Lake District MTB (C.Gore & R.Staton). MTB Lake District (I.Boydon).

Maps: Ullswater Mountain Bike Map (Mountain Bike Maps). OS Explorer OL5, Lakeland (Harvey), Lake District British Mountain Map (Harvey).

Routes on Web: www.goodmtb.co.uk/44a ; www.goodmtb.co.uk/44b

Bike Shops: Hire at St Patrick's Boat Landing 017684 82393 in Glenridding.

Route Ideas

❶ A loop that heads from Patterdale into Boardale to Sandwick, then along Ullswater and back to Patterdale. Distance 13km.

❷ From Patterdale, head S to Hartsop (or start from car park on the A592 near Hartsop) then up towards Rampsgill Head and along High Street to The Cockpit, onto Howtown and back to the finish via Boardale or along Ullswater. Distance 30km.

❸ For less extreme biking, follow the trail along Ullswater and turn around at any point, or loop around Silver Crag. It is also possible to use the Ullswater Steamer (ferry) to Howtown and then ride back to Patterdale.

46

Pooley Bridge

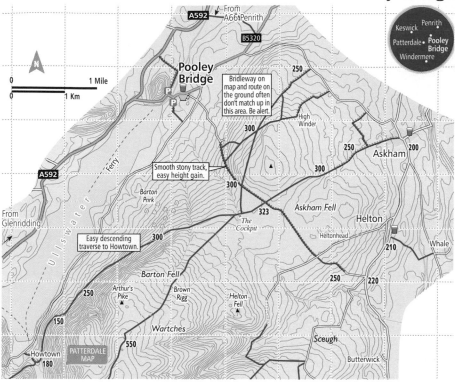

Situation: On the banks of the River Eamont, at the head of Ullswater on the north east edge of the Lake District National Park. 6 miles south west of Penrith.

About the Base: Pooley Bridge, a village with pubs and a café. **Parking:** Car parks in Pooley Bridge, north and south of the bridge. *Grid Ref: North NY469244, South NY470243. Post Code: CA10 2NE.*

Drive Times: Carlisle 40mins, Newcastle 1hr40, Manchester 2hr, Leeds 2hr20, Birmingham 3hr.

Refreshments: At Pooley Bridge, The Sun Inn 017684 86913, Pooley Bridge Inn 017684 86215, Crown Hotel 017684 86955 and Granny Dowbekins Tea Rooms 017684 86453. The Punch Bowl Hotel 01931 712443 at Askham and The Beckfoot House Hotel 01931 713241 at Helton.

Maps: Ullswater (Mountain Bike Maps). Lake District MTB Routes (Goldeneye).

Bike Shops: Arragons Cycle Centre 01768 890344 in Penrith, 6 miles away for parts & repairs.

Route Idea

SE from Pooley Bridge then trails passing High Winder, road to Askham and Helton then SW via Heltonhead to pick up trail heading NW. Take the bridleway to The Cockpit (stone circle) then onto Howtown and road back to start. Distance 22km.

Overlooking Ullswater. Rider: Magnus Ross © Stephen Ross

Loweswater / Buttermere

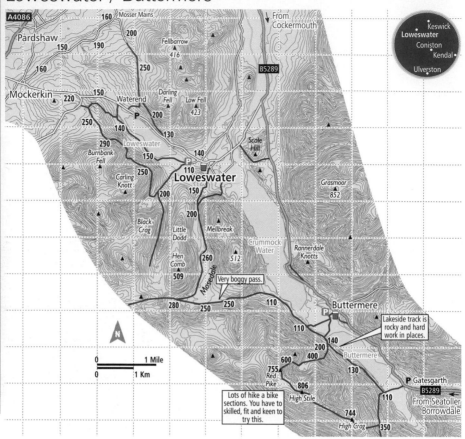

Situation: In the north west of the Lake District National Park, north of the Loweswater fells. Loweswater village is at the foot of Loweswater, 8 miles south east of Cockermouth. Buttermere village, between Crummock Water and Buttermere is 3 miles to the south east.

About the Base: Loweswater or Buttermere, both small villages with pubs and accommodation. **Parking:** Car park close to the lake outside Loweswater village or lakeside at Waterend. Car park in Buttermere village and roadside at Gatesgarth. *Grid Ref: Loweswater NY135210, Waterend NY121222, Buttermere NY173168, Gatesgarth NY195150. Post Code: Buttermere CA13 9UZ.*

Drive Times: Carlisle 1hr, Newcastle 2hr10, Manchester 2hr30, Leeds 2hr50, Birmingham 3hr40.

Refreshments: The Kirkstile Inn 01900 852191 at Loweswater. The Fish Hotel 017687 71253 and The Bridge Hotel 017687 70252 in Buttermere.

Maps: Lake District Mountain Bike Routes (Goldeneye). OS Explorer OL4, Lakeland West (Harvey).

Routes on Web: www.goodmtb.co.uk/a43

Bike Shops: Cyclewise 017687 78711 at Whinlatter Forest Park, 9 miles away, for repairs & hire.

Route Ideas

❶ From car park at Loweswater to Mosser Mains, Mockerkin, Waterend and back along S of the lake. Distance 14km.

❷ From Loweswater to trail across Scale Hill and road to Gatesgarth. Trails NW along Buttermere lake, through Mosedale and back to Loweswater. Distance 19km.

© Simon Barnes. www.bogtrotters.org

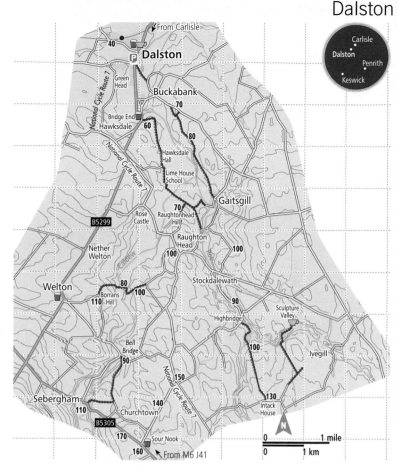

Situation: On the banks of the River Caldew, north of the Cumbrian mountains and east of the Solway Firth. 4 miles south of Carlisle.

About the Base: Dalston, a large village with two pubs and a café. Further info: www.dalston.org.uk.
Parking: In the square by the church at the centre of the village. *Grid Ref: NY369501. Post Code: CA5 7PJ.*

Drive Times: Newcastle 1hr30, Glasgow 1hr50, Manchester 2hr10, Leeds 2hr30, Birmingham 3hr20.

Trains: Dalston Railway Station is on the Cumbrian Coast line.

Refreshments: At Dalston, The Bluebell Inn 01228 712061, The Robin Hood 01228 675649 and Country Kitchen Café 07706 874541. The Bridge End Inn 01228 710161 in Bridge End, The Royal Oak Inn 07506 714852 in Welton and High Head Sculpture Valley Tea Rooms 01697 473552 in Ivegill.

Books: MTB Eden Valley & N Cumbria (R.Peace).

Maps: OS Explorer OL4 & 315.

Routes on Web: www.goodmtb.co.uk/a38

Bike Shops: Scotby Cycles 01228 546931, 4 miles away in Carlisle, for bikes, parts & repairs.

Route Ideas

❶ SE to Intack House via Buckabank, Gaitskill, Stockdalewath, Highbridge. W to Churchtown. Return to Dalson via Bell Bridge, Borrans Hill, Raughton Head and Hawksdale Hall.
Distance 27km.

❷ Short loop from Dalston to Gaitskill and onto Raughton Head. Return via Hawksdale Hall.
Distance 13km.

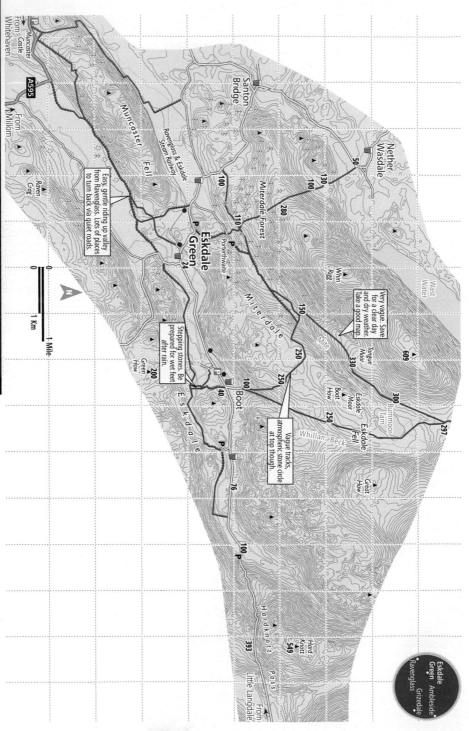

Easy, gentle riding up valley from Ravenglass. Lots of places to turn back via quiet roads.

Very vague. Save for a clear day and dry weather. Take a good map.

Stepping stones. Be prepared for wet feet after rain.

Vague tracks, atmospheric stone circle at top though.

From Castle Whitehaven

From Millom

A595

Muncaster

Raven Crag

Muncaster Fell

Ravenglass & Eskdale Steam Railway

Santon Bridge

Nether Wasdale

Miterdale Forest

Porterthwaite

Eskdale Green

Whin Rigg

West Water

Mite

Tongue Moor

Miterdale

Green How

Boot

Eskdale

Boot How

Eskdale Moor

Burnmoor Tarn

Eskdale Fell

Whillan Beck

Great How

Hardknott Pass

Hard Knott

From Little Langdale

0
1 Km
1 Mile

N

50
100
130
100
280
110
24
150
200
40
100
250
250
330
300
297
76
100
393
609
549

Eskdale Green • Ambleside
Ravenglass • Grizedale

Situation: In the Eskdale Valley, at the foot of Muncaster Fell in the west of the Lake District National Park. 10 miles west of Coniston.

About the Base: Eskdale Green, a village with a pub and accommodation.
Further info:www.eskdaleweb.co.uk. **Parking:** in Eskdale Green near the village store or layby north of the village at Porterthwaite. Car Parks at Dalegarth Station near Boot and opposite Muncaster Castle. Layby at the start of Hardnott Pass. *Grid Ref: Eskdale Green NY140001, Porterthwaite NY146010. Dalegarth Station NY172007, Muncaster Castle SD097966, Hardnott Pass NY210011. Post Code: Eskdale Green CA19 1TX, Dalegarth Station CA19 1TG, Muncaster Castle CA18 1RD.*

Drive Times: Carlisle 1hr30, Manchester 2hr20, Leeds 2hr50, Newcastle 2hr50, Birmingham 3hr30.

Trains: Eskdale Green is on the Ravenglass and Eskdale Steam Railway Line. Bikes must be pre booked, 01229 717171, giving you the possibility of a train out, cycle back ride.

Refreshments: At Eskdale Green, The Bower House Inn 019467 23244 and King George IV 019467 23470. The Brook House Inn 019467 23288 or Woolpack Inn 019467 23230 at Boot, The Bridge Inn 019467 26221 at Santon Bridge and The Screes Inn 019467 26262 at Nether Wasdale.

Books: Lake District MTB (C.Gore & R.Staton).

Maps: Lake District Mountain Bike Routes (Goldeneye). OS Explorer OL6, Lakeland South West (Harvey), Lakeland West (Harvey).

Routes on Web: www.goodmtb.co.uk/a39

Bike Shops: Budgie Bike Hire 019467 23226 at Dalegarth Station for MTB hire.

Route Ideas

❶ For a low level ride use the trails and roads keeping in the Eskdale valley. There are two loops (NE and SW of Eskdale Green) which can be ridden separately or combined. Distance 24km.

❷ For a higher level ride then head up and around Burnmoor Tarn, down to Boot then west on road before turning onto trails that lead back to Eskdale Green. Distance 25km

Above Burnmoor Tarn. © Simon Barnes. www.bogtrotters.org

Seathwaite

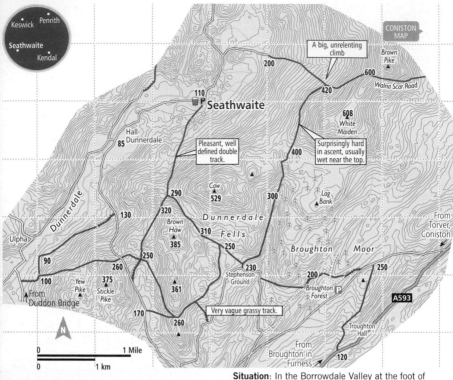

Dunnerdale Fell. © Simon Barnes. www.bogtrotters.org

Situation: In the Borrowdale Valley at the foot of Seathwaite Fell, in the south of the Lake District National park. 7 miles north of Broughton in Furness.

About the Base: Seathwaite, a hamlet with easy access to the trails. **Parking:** Layby north of Seathwaite or car park at Broughton Forest. **Grid Ref:** *Seathwaite NY236123, Broughton Forest SD252926,*

Drive Times: Carlisle 1hr40, Manchester 2hr20, Leeds 2hr40, Newcastle 2hr40, Birmingham 3hr20.

Refreshments: The Newfield Inn 01229 716208 at Seathwaite.

Books: Lake District MTB (C.Gore & R.Staton). MTB Lake District (I.Boydon).

Maps: OS Explorer OL6, Lakeland South West (Harvey).

Routes on Web: www.goodmtb.co.uk/a45

Route Ideas

❶ From Seathwaite head north then east to climb steeply. Follow trails south to Stephenson Ground then more trails to join a road near Hare Hall. Skirt Stickle Pike and Yew Pike and then on a trail running NE along Dunnerdale to road and follow back to Seathwaite. Distance 18km.

❷ Also possible to start at car park on A593 at Broughton Moor. Head up to Stephenson Ground and loop as described in Option 1 then the reverse of your start back to the car park.

❸ Start as above but at Stephenson Ground head on trailes straight to Seathwaite, then SW along Dunnerdale to trails to the north of Yew Pike. Follow road south towards Hare Hall then trails back to Stephenson Ground and then the reverse of your start back to the car park. Distance 22km.

Blawith

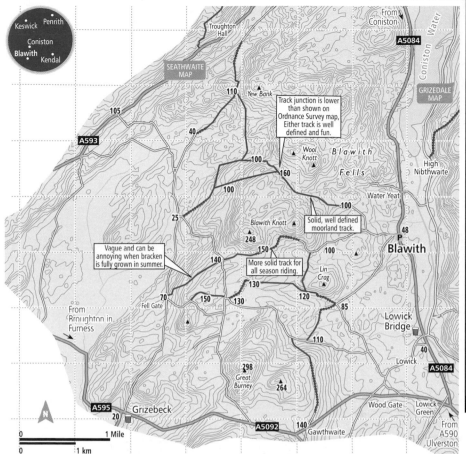

Keswick · Penrith
Coniston
Blawith · Kendal

Troughton Hall
From Coniston
A5084
Coniston Water
SEATHWAITE MAP
GRIZEDALE MAP
110 · Yew Bank
105
A593
40
100
160
Wool Knott
Blawith Fells
High Nibthwaite
100
100
Water Yeat
25
Blawith Knott
248
Solid, well defined moorland track.
48
P
Blawith
Track junction is lower than shown on Ordnance Survey map, Either track is well defined and fun.
Vague and can be annoying when bracken is fully grown in summer.
140
150
More solid track for all season riding.
100
Lin Crag
130
70 · Fell Gate
150
130
120
85
Lowick Bridge
From Broughton in Furness
110
40
Lowick
298 · Great Burney
264
A5084
N
A595
20
Grizebeck
Wood Gate
Lowick Green
From A590 Ulverston
0   1 Mile
0   1 km
A5092
140
Gawthwaite

Situation: West of the River Crake, a mile south of Coniston Water on the southern edge pf the Lake District National Park. 6 miles south of Coniston.

About the Base: Blawith, a hamlet with easy access to the trails. **Parking**: In front of the church in Blawith. *Grid Ref: SD288883. Post Code: LA12 8EQ.*

Drive Times: Carlisle 1hr20, Manchester 1hr50, Leeds 2hr20, Newcastle 2hr30, Birmingham 3hr.

Refreshments: The Red Lion 01229 885366 at Lowick Bridge. The Greyhound Inn 01229 889224 at Grizebeck or cafés in Coniston.

Books: Lake District MTB (C.Gore & R.Staton).

Maps: Coniston (Mountain Bike Maps), OS Explorer OL6 & OL7, Lakeland South West (Harvey).

Routes on Web: www. goodmtb.co.uk/a36

Bike Shops: Gill Cycles 01229 58116 in Ulverston, 7 miles away.

Route Idea

Head NW out of Blawith and skirt around the north of Blawith Knott to join road, follow to Fell gate then head E on road and trails back to Blawith. Distance 12km.

The Low. © Simon Barnes. www.bogtrotters.org

Grizedale

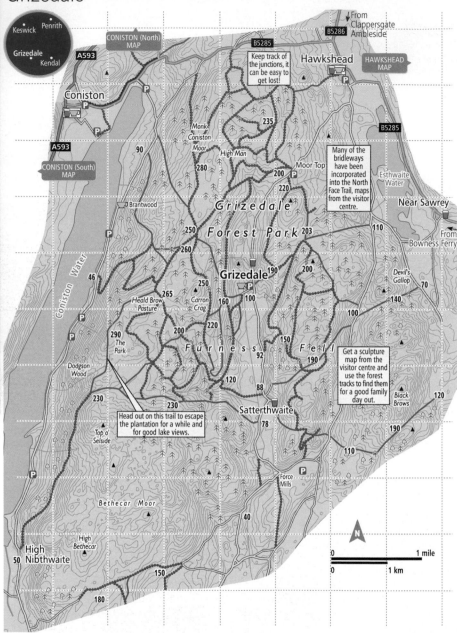

Keswick • Penrith
• Grizedale • Kendal
A593

CONISTON (North) MAP

↓From Clappersgate Ambleside
B5286
Hawkshead
HAWKSHEAD MAP

Keep track of the junctions, it can be easy to get lost!

B5285

235

Monk Coniston Moor
High Man
90
280
200
220
Moor Top

Many of the bridleways have been incorporated into the North Face Trail, maps from the visitor centre.

Esthwaite Water

Near Sawrey

Brantwood

G r i z e d a l e
F o r e s t   P a r k 203
250
260
110

From Bowness Ferry

Coniston Water

46
Grizedale 190
200
Devil's Gallop
70

265
250
160 100
Carron Crag
Heald Brow Pasture
140
100

200
220
290
The Park
Dodgson Wood

F ü r n e s s   F e l l
92
150
190
100

Get a sculpture map from the visitor centre and use the forest tracks to find them for a good family day out.

Black Brows
120

230
230
120
88
Satterthwaite
78
190

Head out on this trail to escape the plantation for a while and for good lake views.

Top o' Selside
110

Force Mills

Bethecar Moor
40

High Bethecar
50 Nibthwaite
High
150

180

N

0   1 mile
0   1 km

Situation: Between Coniston Water and Lake Windermere in the south of the Lake District National Park. 10 miles north west of Newby Bridge.

About the Base: Grizedale Forest, a rural location with a visitor centre, café and shop.
Further Info: www.forestry.gov.uk/grizedalehome.
Parking: Car park at Grizedale Forest visitor centre.
*Grid Ref: SD337944. **Post Code**: LA22 0QJ.*

Drive Times: Carlisle 1hr20, Manchester 2hr, Leeds 2hr30, Newcastle 2hr30, Birmingham 3hr.

Refreshments: Café in the Forest 01229 860010 at Grizedale Visitor Centre. Jumping Jenny Café 01539 441715 at Brantwood & The Eagles Head 01229 860237 in Satterthwaite.

Books: Lake District MTB (C.Gore & R.Staton). MTB Lake District (I.Boydon). MBR Ride Guide 2010.

Maps: Grizedale (Mountain Bike Maps). OS Explorer OL7, Lakeland South East (Harvey).

Bike Shops: Grizedale Mountain Bikes 01229 860369 for hire, bikes & parts.

Route Ideas

There are plenty of trails in this area; so many possibilties to make up rides to suit any desired distance.

❶ From the Moor Top Car Park head SW then loop round to Satterthwaite, then trails NE and back to Moor Top. Distance about 15km.

❷ From either Moor Top or the main Visitor Centre Car Park extend the main concentration of trails by heading to High Nibthwaite then around to Force Mills and various options back to the start.
Distance around 25 to 30km.

❸ See the Grizedale Trail Centre entry p70.

Above Satterthwaite. © Simon Barnes. www.bogtrotters.org

Coniston (south)

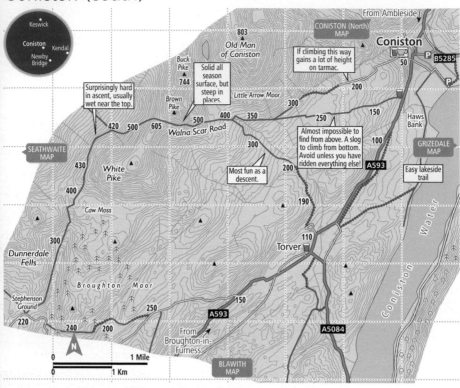

Keswick
Coniston Kendal
Newby
Bridge

803
Old Man
of Coniston

From Ambleside

CONISTON (North)
MAP

Coniston

P B5285

P

Buck
Pike
744

Solid all
season
surface, but
steep in
places.

If climbing this way
gains a lot of height
on tarmac.

200

50

Surprisingly hard
in ascent, usually
wet near the top.

Brown
Pike

Little Arrow Moor

300

150

Haws
Bank

420 500 605

500 400 350

250

100

Walna Scar Road

Almost impossible to
find from above. A slog
to climb from bottom.
Avoid unless you have
ridden everything else!

A593

GRIZEDALE
MAP

SEATHWAITE
MAP

430

White
Pike

300

200

Easy lakeside
trail

400

Most fun as a
descent.

190

Caw Moss

110

Torver

300

Dunnerdale
Fells

Broughton Moor

Stephenson
Ground

250

150

220

240 200

A593

From
Broughton-in-
Furness

A5084

Coniston Water

N

0   1 Mile
0   1 Km

BLAWITH
MAP

Situation: At the head of Coniston Water and the foot of Coniston Old Man in the south of the Lake District National park. 11 miles west of Windermere.

About the Base: Coniston, a village with pubs, cafés and accommodation.Further Info: www.conistonweb.co.uk.
Parking: Car park next to the lake in Coniston. *Grid Ref: SD308971. Post Code: LA21 8AN.*

Drive Times: Carlisle 1hr10, Manchester 2hr, Leeds 2hr20, Newcastle 2hr20, Birmingham 3hr.

Refreshments: Choice of pubs in Coniston, The Bluebird Café 015394 41649 and Meadowdore Café 015394 41638. The Church House Inn 015394 41282 at Torver and The Ship Inn 015394 41224 at Haws Bank.

Books: Lake District MTB (C.Gore & R.Staton). MTB Lake District (I.Boydon).

Maps: Coniston (Mountain Bike Maps). Lake District MTB Routes (Goldeneye), OS Explorer OL6 & OL7, Lakeland South West (Harvey).

Routes on Web: www. goodmtb.co.uk/a37

Bike Shops: In Ambleside, Bike Treks 015394 31245 for bikes, parts & guided rides or Ghyllside Cycles 01539 433592 also does hire. Highpoint 07970 138591 in Elterwater for hire.

Route Idea

Anticlockwise loop, south along Coniston Water to Torver, on to Stephenson Ground then north around White Pike Down Walna Scar Road and back to Coniston. Distance 28km. Also good clockwise.

Walna Scar Road. © Simon Barnes. www.bogtrotters.org

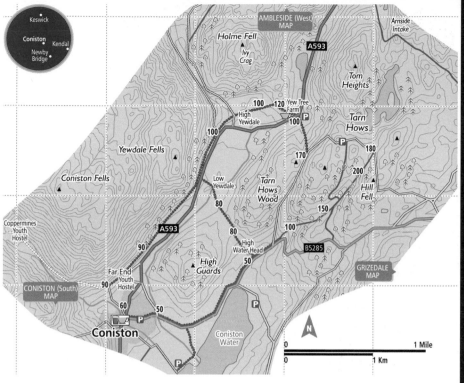

Situation: At the foot of Coniston Fells and the head of Coniston Water in the south of the Lake District National Park. 11 miles west of Windermere.

About the Base: Coniston, a village with pubs, cafés and accommodation. Further Info: www.conistonweb.co.uk.
Parking: Car parks next to the lake in Coniston, at Tom Heights & Tarn Hows. *Grid Ref: Coniston SD308971, Tarn Hows SD326995, Tom Heights SD321998. Post Code: Coniston LA21 8AN.*

Drive Times: Carlisle 1hr10, Manchester 2hr, Leeds 2hr20, Newcastle 2hr20, Birmingham 3hr.

Refreshments: Choice of pubs at Coniston, The Bluebird Café 015394 41649 and Meadowdore Café 015394 41638. Yew Tree Farm Tea Rooms 015394 41433 only open to groups booking ahead. Ice Cream Van at Tarn Hows car park April-September.

Bike Shops: In Ambleside, Bike Treks 015394 31245 for parts & guided rides or Ghyllside Cycles 01539 433592 also does hire. Highpoint 07970 138591 in Elterwater for hire.

Maps: OS Explorer OL7, Lake District British Mountain Map (Harvey). Off-road cycling around Coniston (www. nationaltrust.org.uk).

Route Idea

From Coniston, N on road then trail running close to the A593. On to Tarn Hows. S on trails through the woods. Cycle path running alongside the B5285 back to Coniston. Distance 9km.

Extend the Area: The route above would suit those wanting a relatively easy hour or two. There are adjoining maps to the N, S, & E, however these areas are for more serious mountain biking and therefore not ideal to combine with this area.

Hawkshead

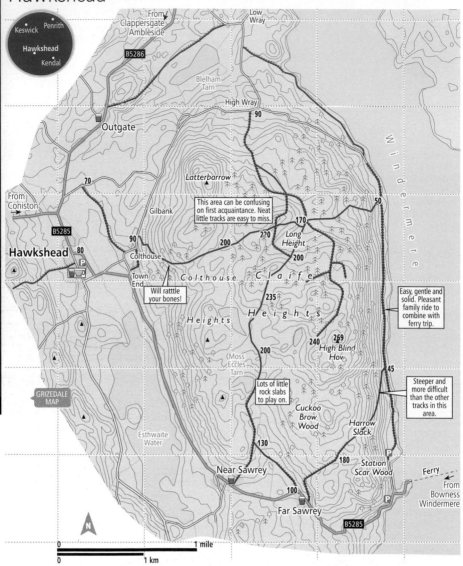

Keswick • Penrith
Hawkshead • Kendal

From Clappersgate Ambleside

Low Wray

B5286

Blelham Tarn

High Wray
90

Outgate

W i n d e r m e r e

Latterbarrow

70

From Coniston →

Gilbank

This area can be confusing on first acquaintance. Neat little tracks are easy to miss.

50

170

B5285

90

200

220

Long Height

Hawkshead

80

200

Colthouse

Town End

Colthouse

Claife

Will ratttle your bones!

235

Heights

Heights

Easy, gentle and solid. Pleasant family ride to combine with ferry trip.

269
High Blind How

240

200

45

GRIZEDALE MAP

Lots of little rock slabs to play on.

Cuckoo Brow Wood

Harrow Slack

Steeper and more difficult than the other tracks in this area.

Esthwaite Water

130

180

Station Scar Wood

Near Sawrey

Ferry

100

From Bowness Windermere

Far Sawrey

B5285

N

0   1 mile

0   1 km

Situation: In the Vale of Esthwaite at the heart of the Lake District National Park. North of Esthwaite Water and west of Lake Windermere, 17 miles north west of Kendal.

About the Base: Hawkshead, a village with pubs, cafés and accommodation.
Further Info: www.hawkshead-village.co.uk.
Parking: Car park in the centre of the village. Also at Far Sawrey or Station Scar Wood by Lake Windermere.
Grid Ref: Hawkshead SD353980, Far Sawrey SD387954, Station Scar Wood SD387960.
Post Code: Hawkshead LA22 ONT.

Drive Times: Carlisle 1hr10, Manchester 1hr50, Newcastle 2hr20, Leeds 2hr20, Birmingham 3hr.

Trains: Windermere Railway Station is on the Windermere-Kendal line, going on to join the main West Coast line at Oxenholme Lake District.

Refreshments: Several pubs & cafés in Hawkshead. The Tower Bank Arms 015394 36334 at Near Sawrey, The Sawrey Hotel 015394 43425 at Far Sawrey & The Outgate Inn 015394 36413 at Outgate.

Bike Shops: Bike Treks 015394 31245 in Ambleside, 5 miles away, for parts & guided rides or Ghyllside Cycles 01539 433592 in Ambleside also does hire. Grizedale Mountain Bikes 01229 860369, 3 miles away in Grizedale Forest, for hire & parts.

Books: Lake District MTB (C.Gore & R.Staton). MTB Lake District (I.Boydon).

Maps: Claife Heights Mountain Bike Map (Mountain Bike Maps). OS Explorer OL7, Lakeland South East (Harvey).

Routes on Web: www.goodmtb.co.uk/a40

Route Ideas

❶ Head south from Hawkshead on the road to the west of Esthwaite Water to Near Sawrey then onto Far Sawrey. Onto trails along Windermere to High Wray then south on trails back to Near Sawrey and back to Hawkshead as you started out.
Distance 14km.

❷ Start at the car park near the Windermere Ferry to miss the road section from Hawkshead.
Distance 15km.

❸ From Hawkshead follow road to High Wray via Colthouse then trails south to Far Sawrey. North along Windermere almost to Low Wray then onto Outgate and road back to start.
Distance 21km.

© Simon Barnes

Colthouse. © Simon Barnes. www.bogtrotters.org

Ambleside (west)

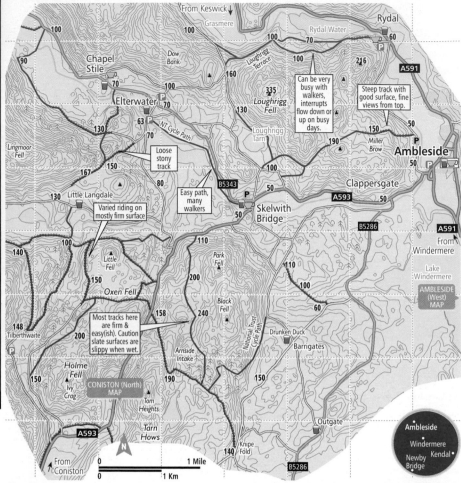

From Keswick
Grasmere
Rydal
Rydal Water
100
100
70
60
P
Chapel
Stile
Dow
Bank
100
216
A591
70
160
100
Can be very
busy with
walkers,
interrupts
flow down or
up on busy
days.
Steep track with
good surface, fine
views from top.
Elterwater
70
335
Loughrigg
Fell
130
Loughrigg
Terrace
150
50
NT Cycle Path
63
P
70
Loughrigg
Tarn
190
Miller
Brow
P
Lingmoor
Fell
130
150
Loose
stony
track
Ambleside
50
P
167
Little Langdale
80
Varied riding on
mostly firm surface
Easy path,
many
walkers
B5343
P
50
Clappersgate
130
50
50
A593
50
Skelwith
Bridge
B5286
A591
100
110
Park
Fell
110
From
Windermere
140
Little
Fell
200
100
Lake
Windermere
150
Oxen Fell
158
240
60
AMBLESIDE
(West)
MAP
148
Tilberthwaite
P
200
Most tracks here
are firm &
easy(ish). Caution
slate surfaces are
slippy when wet.
Black
Fell
National Trust Cycle Path
Drunken Duck
Barrigates
Holme
Fell
Ivy
Crag
CONISTON (North)
MAP
150
Arnside
Intake
190
150
Tom
Heights
Outgate
Ambleside
A593
Tarn
Hows
Knipe
Fold
Windermere
Kendal
Newby
Bridge
From
Coniston
140
B5286
N
0   1 Mile
0   1 Km

Situation: At the head of Lake Windermere and the foot of Loughrigg Fell, in the heart of the Lake District National Park.

About the Base: Ambleside, a small town with plenty of pubs, cafés & accommodation. Further Info: www.amblesideonline.co.uk. **Parking**: Car parks in Ambleside, best for the ride is next to the river. Also roadside west of the village or at Rydal, Elterwater & Tibberthwaite. *Grid Ref: Ambleside Car Park NY372040, Ambleside Roadside NY371044, Rydal NY365059, Elterwater NY328047, Tibberthwaite NY315016. Post Code: Ambleside LA22 0HQ, Rydal LA22 9LR, Elterwater LA22 9HW.*

Drive Times: Carlisle 1hr, Manchester 1hr40, Leeds 2hr10, Newcastle 2hr10, Birmingham 2hr50.

Trains: Windermere Railway Station is on the Windermere-Kendal line, going on to join the main West Coast line at Oxenholme Lake District.

Refreshments: Plenty of choice in Ambleside. Glen Rothay Hotel 015394 34500 & Cote How Organic Tea Rooms 015394 32765 at Rydal, Britannia Inn 015394 37210 at Elterwater, Wainwright Inn 015394 38088 & Brambles Café 015394 37500 at Chapel Stile, Three Shires Inn at Little Langdale 015394 37215, Skelwith Bridge Hotel 015394 32115 & Chesters Café 015394 32553 at Skelwith Bridge. The Drunken Duck 015394 36347 at Barngates, Outgate Inn 015394 36413 at Outgate.

Books: Lake District MTB (C.Gore & R.Staton). MTB Lake District (I.Boydon). **Maps**: Ambleside & Loughrigg (Mountain Bike Maps), OS Explorer OL7, Lake District British Mountain Map (Harvey).

Routes on Web: www.goodmtb.co.uk/a35

Bike Shops: In Ambleside, Bike Treks 015394 31245 for bikes, parts & guided rides or Ghyllside Cycles 01539 433592 also does hire. Highpoint 07970 138591 in Elterwater for hire.

Route Ideas

❶ A loop around Loughrigg via Miller Brow, Loughrigg Tarn, Loughrigg Terrace and Rydal Water. Distance 13km.

❷ From Ambleside, W to Elterwater via Rydal Water, Loughrigg Terrace then road. On to Little Langdale then skirt Little Fell and onto Arnside Intake, head N on trails to west of Black Fell to Skelwith Bridge. Back to the start via trail over Miller Brow. Dist 28km.

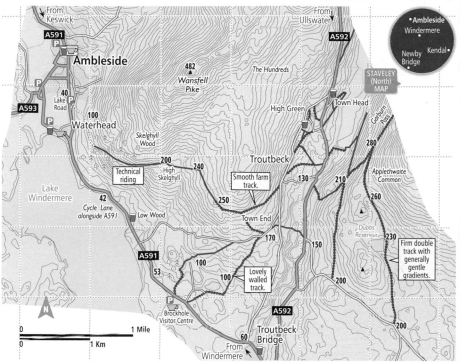

Ambleside · Windermere · Newby Bridge · Kendal

From Keswick · From Ullswater

A591 · A592 · A593

Ambleside · 482 Wansfell Pike · The Hundreds · STAVELEY (North) MAP

40 Lake Road · Waterhead · 100 · High Green · Town Head · Garburn Pass

Skelghyll Wood · 280

Lake Windermere · 200 · High Skelghyll · 240 · Troutbeck · 130 · 210 · Applethwaite Common

Technical riding · 42 Cycle Lane alongside A591 · Low Wood · 250 · Smooth farm track. · 260

Town End · 170 · 150 · Dubbs Reservoir · 230 · Firm double track with generally gentle gradients.

A591 · 53 · 100 · 100 · Lovely walled track. · 200

N · Brockhole Visitor Centre · A592 · 200

0 — 1 Mile · 0 — 1 Km · Troutbeck Bridge · 60 · From Windermere

61

Situation: At the head of Lake Windermere and the foot of Wansfell Pike, in the heart of the Lake District National Park. 4 miles north west of Windermere.

About the Base: Ambleside, a small town with plenty of pubs, cafés and accommodation. Further Info: www.amblesideonline.co.uk. **Parking**: Several car parks in Ambleside, best for the ride is Lake Road. Car park at Brockhole Visitor Centre on the A591. *Grid Ref: Ambleside Lake Road NY377037, Ambleside Roadside NY371044, Brockhole NY389011. Post Code: Lake Road LA22 0DR, Brockhole LA23 1LJ.*

Drive Times: Carlisle 1hr, Manchester 1hr40, Leeds 2hr10, Newcastle 2hr10, Birmingham 2hr50.

Trains: Windermere Railway Station is on the Windermere-Kendal line, going on to join the main West Coast line at Oxenholme Lake District.

Refreshments: Plenty of choice in Ambleside or at Waterhead by the lake. Café at Brockhole Visitor Centre 015394 46601, The Mortal Man 015394 33193 and The Queens Head 015394 32174 at Troutbeck.

Books: Lake District MTB (C.Gore & R.Staton).
Maps: OS Explorer OL7, Lake District British Mountain Map (Harvey). Ambleside to Toutbeck (Mountain Bike Maps)

Routes on Web:
www.goodmtb.co.uk/a34

Bike Shops: In Ambleside, Bike Treks 015394 31245 for bikes, parts & guided rides or Ghyllside Cycles 01539 433592 also does hire. Country Lanes Cycle Hire 015394 44544, 4 miles away in Windermere.

Route Ideas

❶ An anti-clockwise route heading south on the cycle lane running alongside the A591, up to Town End and Troutbeck, then back to Ambleside via High Skelghyll. Distance 12km.

❷ An extension within the area can be made by bearing east at Town End and incorporating the off-roads to the east of the A591. About 8km extra. For a longer ride combine with the Staveley Map to the east, or the Ambleside West Map.

Paul Stewart & Nick Matthews. Ambleside (west) p60, Loughrigg Terrace.

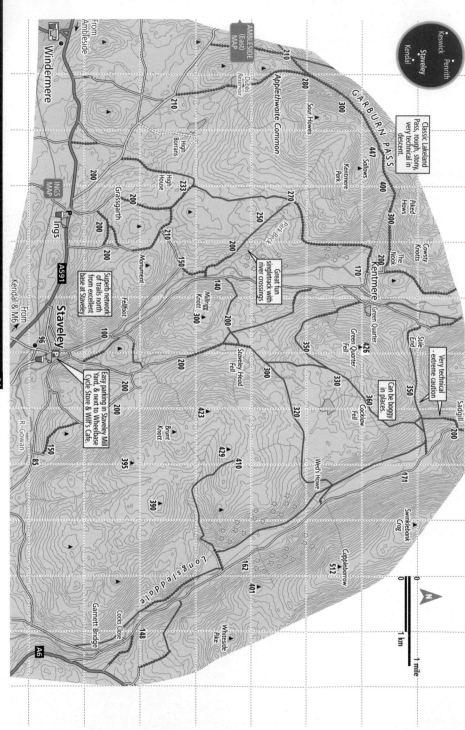

Classic Lakeland Pass, rough, stony, very technical in descent.

Superb network of trails north from excellent base at Staveley

Great fun singletrack with river crossings

Easy parking in Staveley Mill Yard, & next to Wheelbase Cycle Store & Wilf's Cafe.

Can be boggy in places.

Very technical - extreme caution

Situation: At the confluence of the River Kent and the River Gowan, at the mouth of the Kentmere valley in the south east corner of the Lake District National Park. 4 miles north west of Kendal.

About the Base: Staveley, a village with a pub, café, good parking and easy access to the trails. **Parking:** In the village at Staveley Mill Wood Yard (where Wheelbase Cycle Store & Wilf's Café are also located). *Grid Ref: Staveley SD471982, Ings SD446986. Post Code: Staveley LA8 9LR, Ings LA8 9PY.*

Drive Times: Carlisle 1hr10, Manchester 1hr40, Leeds 2hr, Newcastle 2hr20, Birmingham 2hr40.

Trains: Staveley Railway Station is on the Windermere-Kendal line, going on to join the main West Coast line at Oxenholme Lake District.

Refreshments: At Staveley, Wilfs Café (next to Wheelbase) 01539 822329 which caters especially for mountain bikers, The Eagle & Child 01539 821320. The Watermill Inn 01539 821309 and Café Zest 01539 821128 in Ings. Maggs Howe Café 01539 821443 at Green Quarter.

Books: Lake District MTB (C.Gore & R.Staton). MTB Lake District (I.Boydon).

Maps: Kentmere & Troutbeck Mountain Bike Map (Mountain Bike Maps).Lake District Mountain Bike Routes (Goldeneye). OS Explorer OL7, Lakeland South East (Harvey), Lakeland East (Harvey).

Routes on Web: www.goodmtb.co.uk/a46a & /a46b & /a46c

Bike Shops: Wheelbase 01539 821 443 in Staveley ("UK's largest Cycle Store").

Route Ideas

With so many good trails that intermingle with each other it is easy to vary the following or to make up your own routes alltogether. The area includes The Garburn Pass - a challenge to ride up it and down it.

❶ Three Rivers Ride. From Staveley, road NW past Fellfoot. Continue on the road as it bends & climbs to the SW. Trails N to Park Beck. SE along Park Beck then roads back to Staveley. Distance 13km.

❷ From Staveley, road N but cross first bridge & follow road to its end. Trails over Staveley Head Fell & Cocklaw Fell. W to stile End then Kentmere. Trails S to Park Beck. SE along Park Beck then roads back to Staveley. Distance 19km.

❸ As Route Idea 2 to Kentmere, then trails over the Garburn Pass. On to & past Dubbs Reservoir. Road SE then trails N past High House & on to Park Beck. SE along Park Beck then roads back to Staveley. Distance 29km.

Nick Cotton. Kentmere, Staveley (north) p62

Staveley (south)

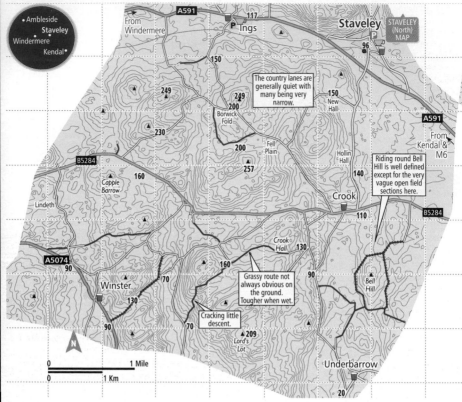

Situation: At the mouth of the Kentmere valley, on the banks of the River Kent in the south east corner of the Lake District National Park. 4 miles north west of Kendal.

About the Base: Staveley, a village with a pub and a café. **Parking**: In the village at Staveley Mill Wood Yard. Also roadside near the pub at Ings. *Grid Ref: Staveley SD471982, Ings SD446986. **Post Code**: Staveley LA8 9LR, Ings LA8 9PY.*

Drive Times: Carlisle 1hr10, Manchester 1hr40, Leeds 2hr, Newcastle 2hr20, Birmingham 2hr40.

Trains: Staveley Railway Station is on the Windermere-Kendal line, going on to join the main West Coast line at Oxenholme Lake District.

Refreshments: At Staveley, The Eagle & Child 01539 821320 & Wilfs 01539 822329 which caters especially for mountain bikers. The Watermill Inn 01539 821309 & Café Zest 01539 821128 at Ings. The Sun Inn 015398 21351 at Crook & The Brown Horse 015394 43443 at Winster. The Punch Bowl 015395 68234 at Underbarrow.

Books: Lake District MTB (C.Gore & R.Staton).

Maps: OS Explorer OL7, Lakeland South East (Harvey).

Bike Shops: Wheelbase 01539 821 443 in Staveley ("UK's largest Cycle Store").

Route Idea

For a more adventurous area head to the Stavaley North map. However for those wanting a low lying area with quiet lanes interspersed with some off-roads then this area should be ideal. From Staveley head south and start a loop past New Hall, Borwick Fold, Lindeth and Winster. Next head for Crook Hall and then either head back to Staveley or include a loop around Bell Hill. Distance 20-25km.

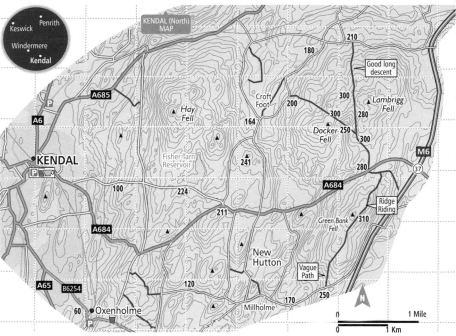

Situation: Just beyond the south eastern edge of the Lake District National Park, on the banks of the River Kent. 8 miles north west of junction 36 on M6.

About the Base: Kendal, a market town with plenty of pubs, cafés and accommodation. Further Info: www.kendalonline.co.uk. **Parking:** Car park next to Halfords on the north east side of the town centre. Pay & Display car park at Oxenholme Railway Station. *Grid Ref: Kendal SD522941, Oxenholme SD531900. Post Code: Kendal LA9 6NF, Oxenholme LA9 7RB.*

Drive Times: Carlisle 1hr, Manchester 1hr30, Leeds 2hr, Newcastle 2hr, Birmingham 2hr40.

Trains: Kendal Railway Station is on the Windermere-Kendal line, going on to join the main West Coast line at Oxenholme Lake District.

Refreshments: Choice of pubs & cafés in Kendal. The Station Inn 015397 24094 & Trekkers Café 015397 33680 at Oxenholme.

Maps: Kendal to Lambrigg Fell Mountain Bike Map (Mountain Bike Maps). OS Explorer OL7.

Bike Shops: Several bike shops in Kendal including Halfords 01539 735001. Askews Cycles 015397 28057 also does hire.

Route Idea

Out of Kendal on the A684 then minor roads keeping south of New Hutton to join trail near M6, follow N past Lambrigg Fell to join road then head back via road towards Fisher Tarn Reservoir and back to Kendal. Distance 24km.

Lambrigg Fell. Rider: Marc Coxey. © Annie Coxey

Kendal (north)

Situation: On the banks of the River Kent just beyond the south eastern edge of the Lake District National Park. 8 miles north west of junction 36 on M6.

About the Base: Kendal, a market town with plenty of pubs, cafés and accommodation. Further Info: www.kendalonline.co.uk. **Parking**: Car park next to Halfords on the north east side of the town centre. **Grid Ref**: SD522941. **Post Code**: LA9 6NF.

Drive Times: Carlisle 1hr, Manchester 1hr30, Leeds 2hr, Newcastle 2hr, Birmingham 2hr40.

Keswick • Penrith
• Windermere
• Kendal

A6
290
250
Borrowdale
Bretherdale Common
230
Combs Hollow
250
Roundthwaite Common
Fairly easy riding along the valley floor
Belt Howe
190
Old High
Whinfell Common
350
Fun, grassy descent
Whinfell Beacon
400
Mast
Mast
300
170
Tough tarmac climb
Selside
150
Watchgate
160
170
Deepslack
180
Garth Row
Grayrigg
Patton Bridge
180
Meal Bank
150
150
Mint
70
A685
A6
Hay Fell
200
50
NF
P
KENDAL (East) MAP
190
KENDAL
From M6 J37
A684
165
A65
60
P
Oxenholme

N

0 ——————— 1 Mile
0 ——————— 1 Km

Maps: Kendal to Whinfell & Borrowdale Mountain Bike Map (Mountain Bike Maps). OS Explorer OL7.

Bike Shops: Several bike shops in Kendal including Halfords 01539 735001. Askews Cycles 015397 28057 also does hire.

Route Idea

Out of Kendal on A685 and NE on roads past Patton Bridge and then across Whinfell Common passing near the two communication masts and follow into Borrowdale. Head NW along the valley to A6. South on trails and roads to Garth Row then back to Kendal. Distance 32km.

Belt Howe. © Simon Barnes. www.bogtrotters.org

Trains: Kendal Railway Station is on the Windermere-Kendal line, going on to join the main West Coast line at Oxenholme Lake District.

Refreshments: Choice of pubs & cafés in Kendal.

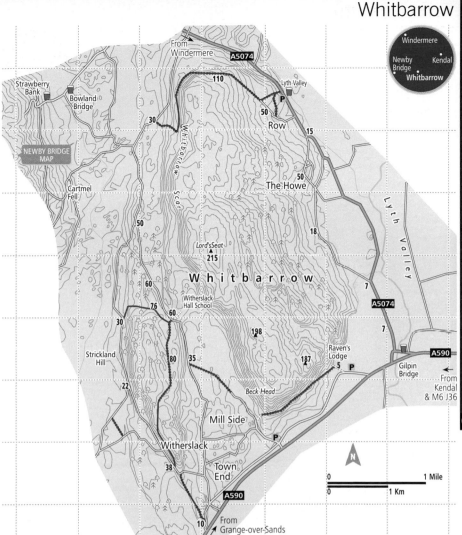

Situation: In the south east corner of the Lake District National Park. A National Nature Reserve, 5 miles south west of Kendal.

About the Base: Raven's Lodge, a rural location on the south edge of Whitbarrow with easy access to the trails.
Further Info: www.english-lakes.com/whitbarrow_scar.
Parking: On road parking near Raven's Lodge. Also, small layby near Mill Side on A590 or layby opposite the Lyth Valley pub on the A5074. *Grid Ref: Ravens Lodge SD463851, Mill Side SD452840, Lyth Valley SD452895.*

Drive Times: Carlisle 1hr20, Manchester 1hr30, Leeds 2hr, Newcastle 2hr20, Birmingham 2hr40.

Trains: Kendal Railway Station is on the Windermere-Kendal line, going on to join the main West Coast line at Oxenholme Lake District.

Refreshments: The Lyth Valley Hotel 01539 568233 near Row or The Gilpin Bridge Inn 01539 552206 at Gilpin Bridge.

Books: Lake District MTB (C.Gore & R.Staton).

Maps: OS Explorer OL7, Lakeland South East (Harvey).

Bike Shops: Halfords 01539 735001 in Kendal.

Route Idea

A route with a high percentage of tarmac but the off-road sections make for an enjoyable ride. Head anti-clockwise around Whitbarrow. Include the loop from Whitherslack Hall that goes off-road to Witherslack, road to Strickland Hall and off-road back to Witherslack Hall. Distance 22km.

Extend the area: Newby Bridge Map to the W.

Newby Bridge

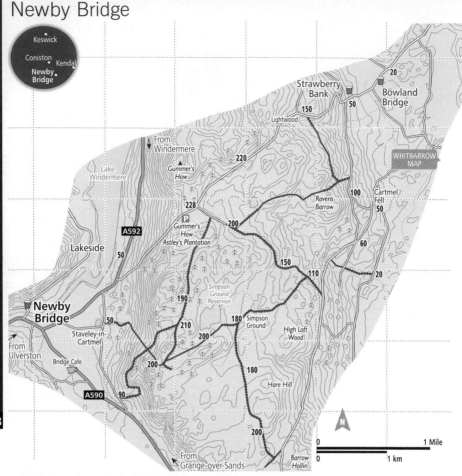

Ravens Barrow. © Simon Barnes

Situation: On the banks of the River Leven, at the southern end of Lake Windermere in the south of the Lake District National Park. 6 miles north west of Grange-over-Sands and 8 miles south of Windermere.

About the Base: Newby Bridge, a small village with several hotels and easy access to the trails.

Parking: Gummers' How Car Park at Astley's Plantation. *Grid Ref: SD391877.*

Drive Times: Carlisle 1hr20, Manchester 1hr40, Leeds 2hr, Newcastle 2hr20, Birmingham 2hr50.

Trains: Windermere Railway Station is on the Windermere-Kendal line, going on to join the main West Coast line at Oxenholme Lake District. Grange over Sands is on the Carlisle-Barrow-Preston line.

Refreshments: The Bridge Café 01539 530667 on A590 at Newby Bridge. The Masons Arms 015395 68486 at Strawberry Bank & The Hare & Hounds 015395 68333 at Bowland Bridge.

Books: Lake District MTB (C.Gore & R.Staton). **Maps**: OS Explorer OL7, Lakeland South East (Harvey).

Bike Shops: Country Lanes Bike Hire 015394 44544 at Lakeside.

Route Idea

Head to Strawberry Bank then Cartmell Fell and then use off-roads past Ravens Barrow and then a loop around Simpson Ground Reservoir. Dist 20km.

Extend the area: Whitbarrow Map to the E.

Silecroft

Map Labels

From Whitehaven

A595

200

200

100

300

70

Little Fell

Easy access track to warm up or down on.

Whitbeck

Townend Hall Farm

30

P

Unavoidable section on main road isn't busy but some people drive far too fast - take care.

A595

Irish Sea

N

Silecroft

200

300

400

450

500

580

▲600
Black Combe

500

400

300

200

100

40

Whicham

25

A5093

From Millom

Spectacular summit views - save this for a clear day. Legal route misses summit by 150m.

150

From Broughton in Furness

A595

Guidebooks recommend counter clockwise circuit but the climb feels long whichever way you do it!

Keswick
Coniston
Kendal
Silecroft

0   1 Mile
0   1 km

Situation: On the coast at the foot of Black Combe, where the Irish Sea meets the south west corner of the Lake District National Park. 8 miles south west of Broughton in Furness.

About the Base: Silecroft, a small village with a pub. **Parking:** Layby on A595 at Townend Hall, just north of Silecroft. *Grid Ref: SD120836.*

Drive Times: Carlisle 1hr40, Manchester 2hr10, Leeds 2hr40, Newcastle 2hr50, Birmingham 3hr20.

Trains: Silecroft Railway Station is on the Carlisle-Barrow-Preston line.

Refreshments: The Miners Arms 01229 772325 in Silecroft.

Books: Lake District MTB (C.Gore & R.Staton). MBR Ride Guide 2010.

Maps: OS Explorer OL6.

Route Idea

An anticklockwise loop to the hights of Black Combe (a climb of about 540m) then down passing Little Fell and onto Whitbeck and back.
Distance 15km.

Black Combe. © Simon Barnes. www.bogtrotters.org

Grizedale Forest Park

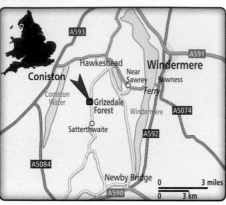

In the heart of the Lake District National Park, a challenging waymarked trail including 9 sections of all weather singletrack with fast descents and fantastic views. Several waymarked family trails.

Facilities:
Café In the Forest at Grizedale Visitor Centre. Grizedale Mountain Bikes 01229 860 369 for MTB hire and parts.

Parking:
Grid Ref: SD33594. Post Code: LA22 0QJ

Web: www.greatmb/b1

❶ **The North Face Trail, Red, XC, 16km.**
❷ **Family trails.**

Whinlatter Forest Park

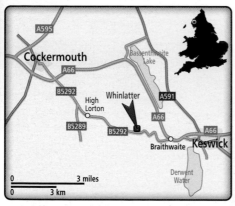

Two purpose built, waymarked, forest trails in the north of the Lake District National Park.

Choose the new blue trail with flowing singletrack, gentle berms and rolling jumps or the challenging red trail, rising to an altitude of 500 metres, with spectacular views, fast singletrack, exhilarating descents and some optional black grade features.

Facilities:
Siskins Café at Whinlatter Forest Park Visitor Centre. Cyclewise Whinlatter 017687 78711 for MTB hire, parts & repairs.

Parking:
Grid Ref: NY211244. Post Code: CA12 5TW

Web: www.greatmb/b2

The Trails
❶ **Altura Trail, Red, XC, 19km.**
❷ **Quercus Trail, Blue, XC, 7.5km.**

Whinlatter. Rider: Claire Hayter © Dan Trent

70

South of Keswick. © Simon Barnes. www.bogtrotters.org

Northumberland National Park & The Cheviots

In the far north of Northumberland the best riding areas are around the brooding, heather-clad Cheviot Hills. **Kirknewton**, **Wooler** and **Ingram** lie on the eastern edge of the National Park boundary giving access to the bridleways that climb deep into the heart of the Cheviots. **Barrowburn** lies northwest of **Alwinton**, set right in the heart of the National Park high up the valley of the River Coquet, on what must be one of the longest dead-end roads in the country. These tiny settlements are at the centre of a whole series of potential loops to the four points of the compass and up to the Scottish Border. This is big remote country where the mist can come down suddenly; so be prepared for a rapid change in the weather, even at the height of summer.

Hartside. Riders: The Muddy Bums. © Gavin Duthie

Located on the England/Scotland border in the west of the region, **Kielder Forest** Trail Centre is the main focus in this northern-most part of England. If you like your riding natural then several of the trails leading east from **Kielder Dam** exit the forest to explore the valley of the River North Tyne, flowing east from Kielder Water towards the North Sea.

© Gavin Duthie

Ford

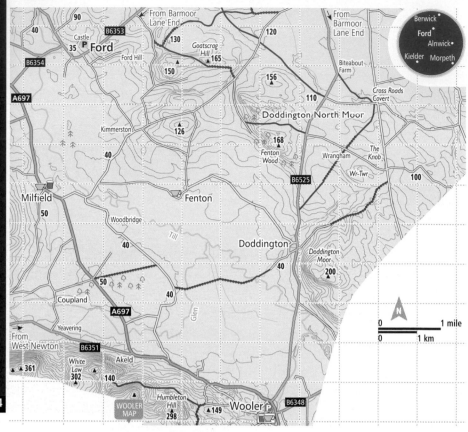

Ford Moss. Riders: The Muddy Bums. © Gavin Duthie

Situation: Overlooking the Till valley in the heart of the English Borders, 12 miles south west of Berwick-Upon-Tweed.

About the Base: Ford, a small village with a village shop. Further Info: www.ford-and-etal.co.uk.
Parking: Parking area in the village near to the castle. *Grid Ref: NT945375. Post Code: TD15 2PX.*

Drive Times: Newcastle 1hr20, Edinburgh 1hr30, Leeds 3hr20, Manchester 3hr50, Birmingham 4hr50.

Refreshments: No refreshments in Ford. The Red Lion Inn 01668 216224 and Milfield Country Café 01668 283333 in Milfield. Café at the Fenton Centre in Fenton 01668 216216 as well as pubs & cafés in Wooler.

Maps: OS Explorer 339 & 340.

Bike Shops: Haugh Head Garage 01668 281316, one mile south of Wooler on the A697, for hire, parts & repairs.

Route Idea

From Ford, NE on the B6353 then lanes and trails SE past Goatscrag Hill. Road NE then trail and road to Cross Roads Covert. Road S past The Knob then trails and roads to Doddington. Trail SW across the Rivers Till and Glen then roads back to Ford via Woodbridge then Kimmerston. Distance 26km. Extend the area: Wooler map to the S.

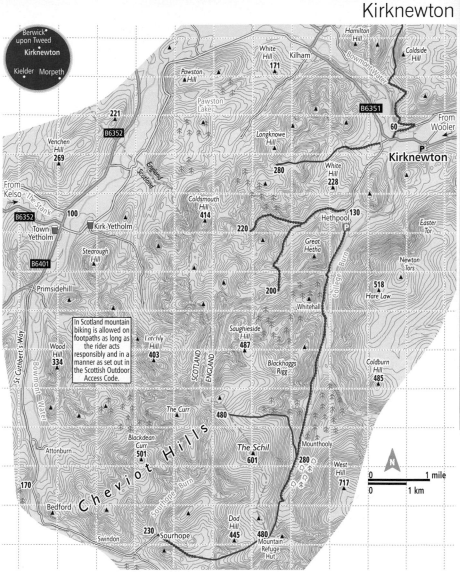

Situation: In the valley of Glendale, 20 miles south west of Berwick-Upon-Tweed, on the northern edge of the Cheviot Hills & Northumberland National Park.

About the Base: Kirknewton, a small village with easy access to the trails. **Parking:** Roadside in Kirknewton. Car park south of the village at Hethpool. **Grid Ref:** *Kirknewton NT913303, Hethpool NT894283.* **Post Code:** *Kirknewton NE71 6XF, Hethpool NE71 6TW.* **Drive Times**: Newcastle 1hr20, Edinburgh 1hr30, Leeds 3hr, Manchester 3hr50,Birmingham 4hr40.

Refreshments: The Border Hotel 01573 420237 in Kirk Yetholm & The Plough Hotel 01573 420215 in Town Yetholm. Town Yetholm also has a village shop.

Maps: OS Explorer OL16 & 339. Cheviot Hills Map (Harvey).

Route Idea

From Kirknewton, W on the B6351 then road S to Hethpool (or use car park there). Trails along College Burn valley before climbing steeply to the mountain refuge hut. Descend to Sourhope then roads to Town Yetholm, Kirk Yetholm, Kilham and back to Kirknewton. Distance 43km.

Berwick upon Tweed
Wooler
Kielder • Morpeth

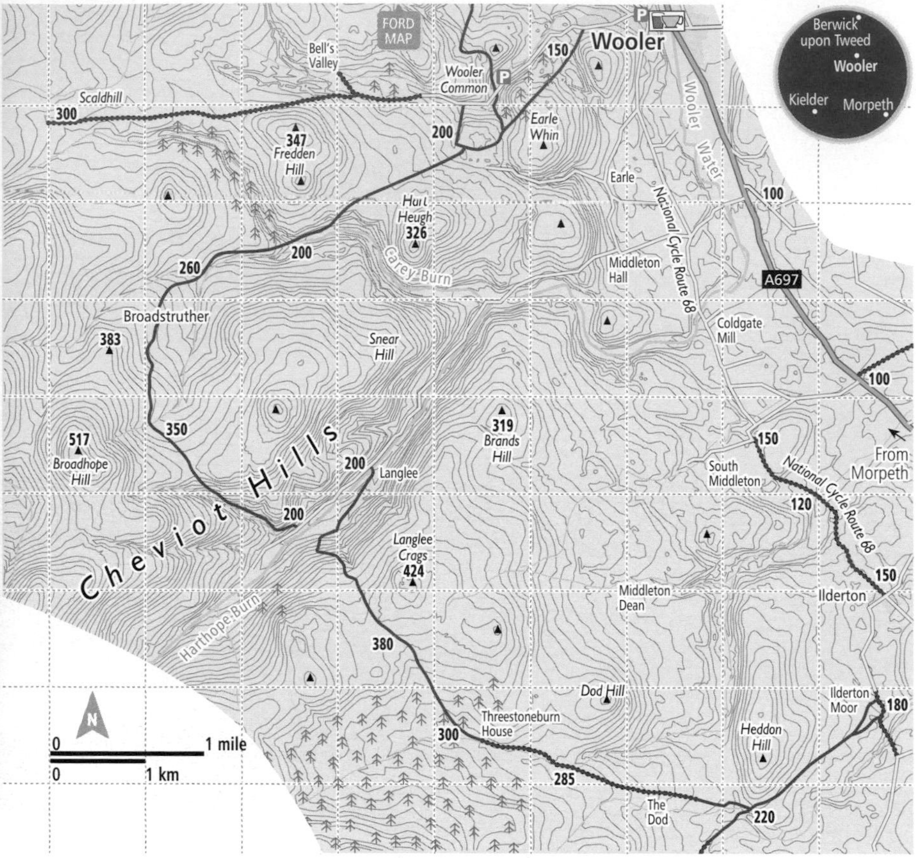

Situation: In the Cheviot Hills, at the north east edge of the Northumberland National Park. 17 miles south of Berwick-Upon-Tweed.

About the Base: Wooler, a small market town with pubs, cafés and accommodation.
Further Info: www.wooler.org.uk. **Parking:** Car park in the centre of Wooler. Also at Wooler Common, south west of the town. *Grid Ref: Wooler NT992279, Wooler Common NT977274. **Post Code:** Wooler NE71 6LH.*

Drive Times: Newcastle 1hr, Edinburgh 1hr40, Leeds 2hr50, Manchester 3hr30, Birmingham 4hr30.

Refreshments: At Wooler, The Tankerville Arms 01668 281581, The Black Bull Hotel 01668 281309 and The Anchor Inn 01668 281412. Market Place Café 01668 282282 and Breeze Café 01668 283333.

Books: MTB Guide Northumberland (D.Purdy).

Maps: Ordnance Survey OL16. Cheviot Hills Map (Harvey).

Bike Shops: Haugh Head Garage 01668 281316, one mile south of Wooler on the A697, for hire parts & repairs.

Route Idea

Head SW towards Broadstruther then using a mixture of trails and roads continue SE past Langlee, Threestoneburn House, Heddon Hill to Ilderton Moor. N to Ilderton then National Cycle Route 68 to Coldgate Mill and back to Wooler. Distance 27km. Extend the area: Ford map to the N.

Riders: The Muddy Bums. ©Gavin Duthie

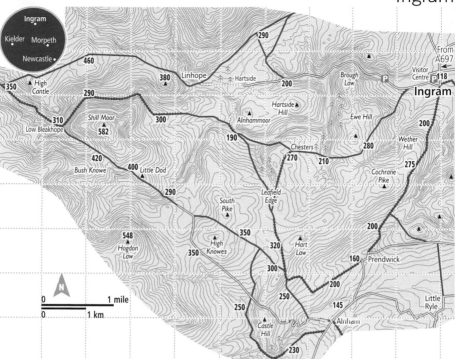

Map labels: Ingram, Kielder, Morpeth, Newcastle, 290, From A697, 460, 380, Linhope, Hartside, 200, Brough Law, Visitor Centre, 118, Ingram, 350, High Cantle, 290, 310, Low Bleakhope, Shill Moor, 582, 300, Alnhammoor, Hartside Hill, Ewe Hill, 200, 420, Bush Knowe, 400, Little Dod, 190, Chesters, 270, 210, 280, Wether Hill, 275, Cochrane Pike, 290, Leafield Edge, South Pike, 200, 548, Hogdon Law, 350, High Knowes, 350, 320, Hart Law, 160, Prendwick, 300, 200, 250, 145, Little Ryle, 250, Castle Hill, Alnham, 230

0 — 1 mile
0 — 1 km

Situation: In the Breamish Valley on the eastern edge of the Northumberland National Park. 14 miles west of Alnwick.

About the Base: Ingram, a small village with a Visitor Centre. **Parking**: Car park at the Visitor Centre in Ingram. Also half a mile outside the village heading west. *Grid Ref: Ingram Visitor Centre NU017162, Ingram West NU007163.* **Post Code**: *Ingram Visitor Centre NE66 4LT.*

Drive Times: Newcastle 1hr, Edinburgh 1hr50, Leeds 2hr50, Manchester 3hr30, Birmingham 4hr30.

Refreshments: National Park Visitor Centre 01665 578890.

Books: MTB Guide Northumberland (D.Purdy).

Maps: OS Explorer OL16. Cheviot Hills Map (Harvey).

Routes on Web: www.goodmtb.co.uk/a2

Route Ideas

❶ Head W to Hartside then S to pick up trail at Alnhammoor, on to Chesters then S to Alnham. Road and trails back to Ingram. Distance 19km.

❷ As above to Alnhammoor but then follow trail to Low Bleakhope. Pass Little Dod then on to Alnham and back to Ingram via Prendwick. Distance 26km.

Riders: The Muddy Bums. © Gavin Duthie

Barrowburn

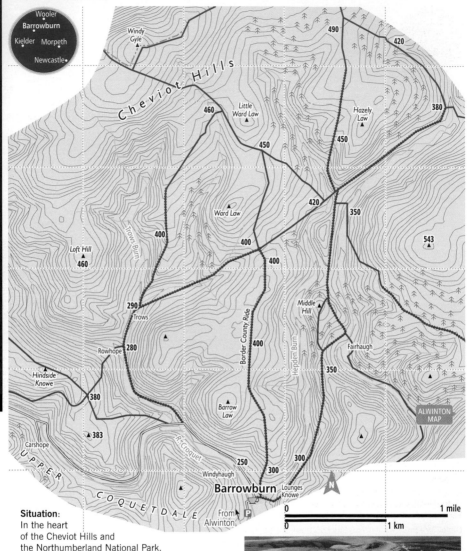

Situation:
In the heart
of the Cheviot Hills and
the Northumberland National Park.
25 miles west of Alnwick.

About the Base: Barrowburn, a hamlet with easy
access to the trails.
Further Info: www.barrowburn.com. **Parking:** Car park
south of the village. *Grid Ref: NT866103.*

Drive Times: Newcastle 1hr20, Edinburgh 2hr30,
Leeds 3hr, Manchester 3hr50, Birmingham 4hr50.

Refreshments: Barrowburn Farm Tea Rooms 01669
621176.

Books: MTB Guide Northumberland (D.Purdy).
Maps: OS Explorer OL16. Cheviot Hills (Harvey).

Route Idea

Head N on the Border Country Ride trail. At path junction (SE of Ward Law) head NE, cross Hepden Burn
then head S past Middle Hill and on to Barrowburn.
Distance 8km.

Extend the area: Alwinton Map to the E.

Windy Gyle. © Gavin Duthie

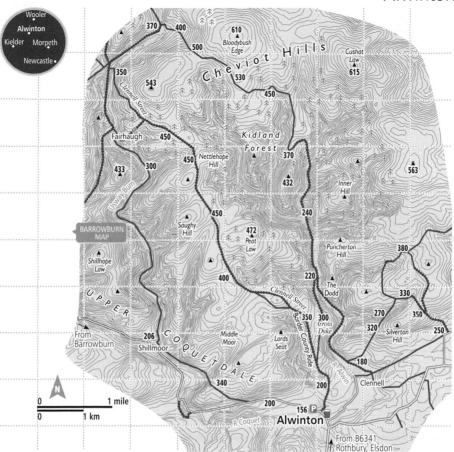

Situation: In Upper Coquetdale, on the eastern edge of the Northumberland National Park. 18 miles west of Alnwick.

About the Base: Alwinton, a small village with a pub and accommodation.
Further Info: www.coquetdale.net/alwinton.

Parking: Car park just past the pub in the village. *Grid Ref: NT919063. Post Code: NT65 7BQ.*

Drive Times: Newcastle 1hr, Edinburgh 2hr10, Leeds 2hr50, Manchester 3hr30, Birmingham 4hr30.

Refreshments: The Rose & Thistle Inn 01669 650226 in Alwinton.

Books: MTB Guide Northumberland (D.Purdy).

Maps: OS Explorer OL16. Cheviot Hills Map (Harvey).

Routes on Web: www.goodmtb.co.uk/a1

Route Ideas

❶ For a short route head to Clennell then take the NE trail following the River Alwin. When W of The Dodd pick up the trail that heads back to Alwinton. Distance 8km.

❷ For a longer route head on road to Shillmoor then trails along Usway Burn to Fairhaugh, link to Clennell Street (a Roman road) & follow back to Alwinton. Distance 20km.

Extend the area: Barrowburn Map to the W.

Kielder Dam

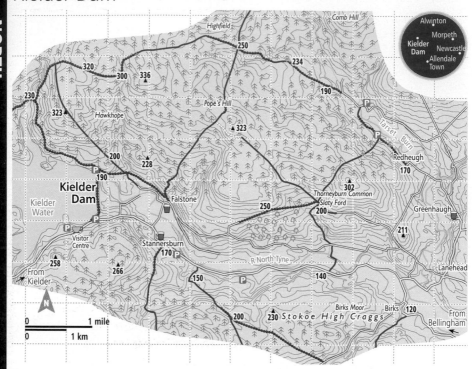

Situation: At the eastern end of Kielder Water, on the western edge of the Northumberland National Park. 38 miles north east of Carlisle.

About the Base: Kielder Dam, a rural location with a visitor centre. Further Info: www.visitkielder.com.
Parking: Several car parks close to the dam and the visitor centre. Also a car park at Stannersburn.
Grid Ref: Visitor Centre NY699868, Stannersburn NY728860. **Post Code:** *Visitor Centre NE48 1BX.*

Drive Times: Newcastle 1hr20, Carlisle 1hr30, Edinburgh 2hr, Leeds 3hr, Manchester 3hr10, Birmingham 4hr20.

Refreshments: Café at Tower Knowe Visitor Centre 0845 1550236. The Pheasant Inn 01434 240382 in Stannesburn, The Blackcock Inn 01434 240200 and Falstone Old School Café 01434 240459 in Falstone.

Maps: OS Explorer OL42.

Routes on Web: www.goodmtb.co.uk/a3

Bike Shops: Purple Mountain Bike Centre 01434 250532 in Kielder for hire, repairs & tuition.

Route Idea

From Kileder Dam, head E to Falstone then road & trails to Slaty Ford & continue NE to road. Then its mostly trails towards Highfield then on to Kielder Reservoir and back to the start. Distance 24km.

Also see Kielder Forest Trail Centre (opposite).

Kielder Forest (Trail Centre)

In the breathtaking borders around the North Tyne Valley, England's largest forest. Waymarked cross country trails for more experienced riders include fast sections of singletrack and Deadwater Summit, with views across South Scotland, Northumberland and the Lake District.

New Blue Osprey Trail, built in conjunction with the Kielder Trail Reavers, offers swooping singletrack and great views.

Easier family trail means that there is something for everyone.

Parking:
Grid Ref: NY629934. Post Code: NE48 1EQ

Web:
www.goodmtb.co.uk/b3a & /b3b

Facilities:
Kielder Castle Visitor Centre. Café at Tower Knowe Visitor Centre in Falstone. Purple Mountain Bike Centre 01434 250532 for MTB hire and repairs on site.

Trails

❶ Borderline, Green, XC, 11km.

❷ Osprey, Blue, XC, 20km.

❸ Lonesome Pine, Red, XC, 17km.

❹ Bloody Bush Trail, Red, XC, 33km.

❺ Deadwater Trail, Red, XC, 14.7km.

❺ Up & Over, Black, XC, 2.3km.

❻ Castlewood Training Loop.

Rider: The Muddy Bums. © Gavin Duthie

North Pennines & Central Northumberland

Hexhamshire Common. © Neil Gander

Cross-country rides can be found to the south of the Tyne Valley in the land rising towards the high Pennines, especially on the heather clad moorland of Hexhamshire Common above **Allendale Town,** or northeast from **Allenheads**. These are both located in East Allendale; to the west, the old mining town of **Nenthead** is a good base for the bridleways to be found in West Allendale. Further east, **Blanchland** is your starting point for the trails climbing north over Blanchland Moor into Slaley Forest or east via Edmundbyers Common to the village of **Edmundbyers**, set high above Derwent Reservoir. An 'expedition' style crossing of the high Pennines is possible starting from **Blencarn** in the Eden Valley to the west of the fells. This long, tough and often bleak moorland crossing should only be undertaken in excellent conditions by fit and experienced riders as it climbs to over 700m and passes through some very remote territory.

Other trails to the south west of Newcastle and west of Durham make use of the extensive network of old mining railways converted to recreational use, many of which form part of the National Cycle Network, including the Sea to Sea (C2C), the most popular long distance cycle route in the country. As some of the railway trails climb right up into the Pennines they present a reasonable challenge. Bases to use these railway paths include **Consett**, **Castleside**, **Langley Park** and **Esh Winning**. In the far south of the region the high peat moorland of Cotherstone Moor, lying between **Bowes** and **Middleton in Teesdale** is criss-crossed with bridleways.

The main trail centre is the large 2000 acre site at **Hamsterley Forest**, on the edge of Teesdale and Weardale, with challenges ranging from a skills loop to a highly acclaimed downhill track for expert riders. Chopwell Woods is a 360-hectare mixed woodland set right on the fringe of Gateshead offering short cross country trails.

Riders: The Muddy Bums. © Gavin Duthie

Castle Carrock

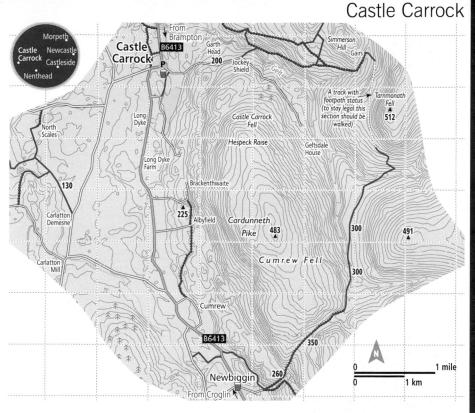

Situation: On the edge of the North Pennines overlooking the Eden Valley. 10 miles east of Carlisle and 18 miles north of Penrith.

About the Base: Castle Carrock, a small village with a pub and a hotel. **Parking:** Roadside in the centre of the village. *Grid Ref: NY542554. Post Code: CA8 9LU.*

Drive Times: Carlisle 25mins, Newcastle 1hr10, Manchester 2hr20, Leeds 2hr40, Birmingham 3hr30.

Trains: Brampton Railway Station, 4 miles away, is on the Newcastle-Carlisle line.

Refreshments: At Castle Carrock, The Weary Hotel 01228 670230 and the Duke of Cumberland Inn 01228 670341. The Bluebell Inn 01768 896615 at Newbiggin.

Books: MTB Eden Valley & N Cumbria (R.Peace).

Maps: OS Explorer 315.

Bike Shops: Halfords 01228 514041 in Carlisle.

Route Idea

From Castle Carrock, head E on road to Jockey Shield then trail to cross River Gelt. Trails then continue E to Gairs before heading S to Newbiggin. Head back to Castle Carrock via Cumrew, Albyfield and Long Dyke Farm.
Distance 20km.
A section of trail should be walked to stay legal, see map.

© Neil Gander

Haydon Bridge

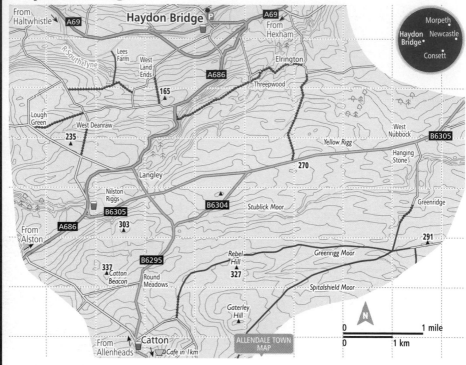

Situation: On the River South Tyne in the foothills of the North Pennines. 7 miles west of Hexham.

About the Base: Haydon Bridge, a village with a pub and accommodation.
Further Info: www.haydon-bridge.co.uk.

Parking: Car Park at Haydon Bridge railway station in the centre of the village.
Grid Ref: *NY842645.* **Post Code:** *NE47 6HD.*

Drive Times: Newcastle 40mins, Carlisle 45mins, Leeds 2hr20, Manchester 2hr40, Birmingham 3hr50.

Trains: Haydon Bridge Railway Station is on the Newcastle-Carlisle line.

Refreshments: The Railway Hotel 01434 684338 in Haydon Bridge. The Carts Bog Inn 01434 684338 in Langley and The Crown 01434 683447 in Catton. Allendale Bakery Café 01434 618879, half a mile south of Catton, caters especially for cyclists.

Books: Beyond Hamsterley (N.Gander).

Maps: OS Explorer OL43.

Bike Shops: The Bike Shop 01434 601032 in Hexham.

Route Idea

From Haydon Bridge, follow road SW to West Lane Ends then trails and roads past West Deanraw to Langley. Continue on B6295, just before Catton take the trail over Rebel Hill and Greenrigg Moor, N to join the B6305 then follow to join the trails to Elrington, Threepwood to the A686. Link back to West Lane Ends and return to the start.
Distance 30km.

Riders: The Muddy Bums. © Gavin Duthie

Allendale Town

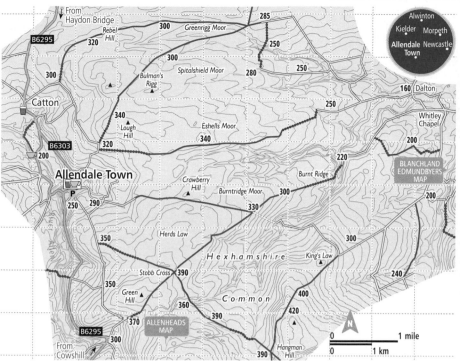

Situation: In the East Allen Valley, within the North Pennines Area of Outstanding Natural Beauty. 10 miles southwest of Hexham.

About the Base: Allendale, a large village with pubs, cafés and accommodation. **Parking**: Roadside in the centre of the village. *Grid Ref: NY837556.* **Post Code:** *NE47 9BU.*

Drive Times: Newcastle 50mins, Carlisle 1hr, Leeds 2hr30, Manchester 2hr40, Birmingham 3hr40.

Trains: Haydon Bridge Railway Station, 7 miles away, is on the Newcastle-Carlisle line.

Refreshments: At Allendale, The Allendale Inn 01434 683246, The Kings Head 01434 683681 and The Golden Lion 01434 683225. Allendale Tea Rooms 01434 683575 and Pebbles Café 01434 683975. The Crown Inn 01434 683447 at Catton. Allendale Bakery Café 01434 618879, between Allendale and Catton, caters especially for cyclists.

Books: MTB Guide Northumberland (D.Purdy). Beyond Hamsterley (N.Gander). **Maps**: OS Explorer OL43.

Bike Shops: The Bike Shop 01434 601032 in Hexham for bikes parts & repairs.

Route Ideas

❶ From Allendale Town, head SE to Stobb Cross then NE and circle Herd's Law taking trial S of Cranberry Hill then back to the start. Distance 11km.

❷ Extend the above route by continuing from Stobb Cross to Hangman Hill , then past King's Law and NW on road and trails back to Allendale Town.
Distance 17km.

❸ The above can also be easily extended – at King's Law continue to Whitley Chapel then follow road and trails to Eshells Moor and back to the start.
Distance 25km.

❹ Explore the north of the area by following road and trails to Rebel Hill and Greenrigg Moor, then use road and trails to Burnt Ridge and Cranberry Hill then back to the start. Distance 21km.

Riders: The Muddy Bums. © Gavin Duthie

Nenthead

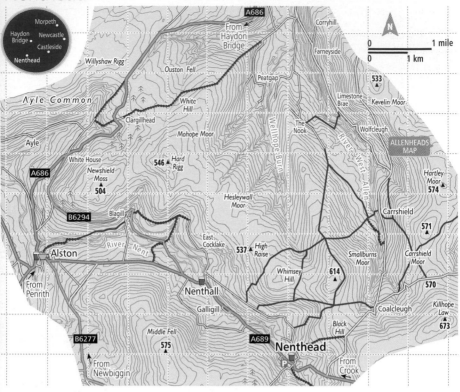

Situation: In the North Pennines at the head of the River Nent. 20 miles south west of Hexham and 24 miles north east of Penrith.

About the Base: Nenthead, a small village with a pub and accommodation. Further Info: www.nenthead.com.
Parking: Car park in the centre of the village. *Grid Ref: NY779438. Post Code: CA9 3QA.*

Drive Times: Carlisle 55mins, Newcastle 1hr10, Leeds 2hr20, Manchester 2hr20, Birmingham 3hr30.

Refreshments: The Miners Arms 01434 381427 in Nenthead, The Coach House Inn 08721 077077 in Nenthall or pubs & cafés in Alston.

Books: Beyond Hamsterley (N.Gander).

Maps: OS Explorer OL31.

Bike Shops: North Pennine Cycles 01434 381324 in Nenthead offer a parts, repair & rescue service.

Route Idea

From Nenthead, follow roads and trails W past East Cocklake Farm, to Blagill then Clargillhead then trails over White Hill. Just before reaching River West Allen head S on lanes to The Nook then trails E over the river to Limestone Brae. Stay on road to Black Hill then a final trail section back to Nenthead.
Distance 32km.

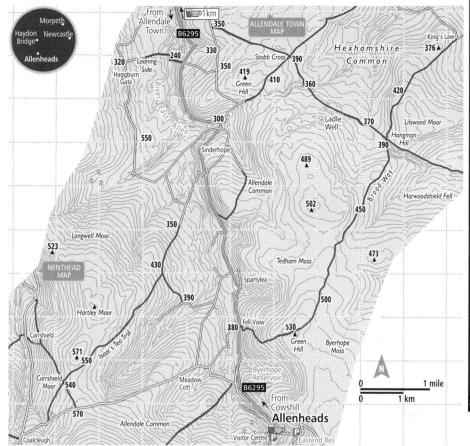

Situation: High in the North Pennines, north of Weardale. 18 miles south of Hexham and 30 miles north west of Penrith.

About the Base: Allenheads, a small village with a pub and a visitor centre. **Parking:** Car parks next to the visitor centre and on the eastern edge of the village next to Eastend Reservoir. *Grid Ref: Allenheads Visitor Centre NY859452, Eastend Reservoir NY864452. Post Code: Allenheads Visitor Centre NE47 9HN.*

Drive Times: Newcastle 1hr, Carlisle 1hr10, Leeds 2hr20, Manchester 2hr40, Birmingham 3hr40.

Refreshments: The Allenheads Inn 01434 685200 and The Hemmel Café 01434 685568 in Allenheads.

Books: Beyond Hamsterley (N.Gander).

Maps: OS Explorer OL31 & OL43.

Bike Shops: North Pennine Cycles 01434 381324, 7 miles away in Nenthead, offer a parts, repair & rescue service.

Route Idea

Head N out of Allenheads before taking the road past Meadow Cottage. Follow the trail to Carrshield Moor then NE on Isaac's Tea Trail. Use roads to pass Haggburn Gate then head E & cross B6295. Continue to Stobb Cross, arriving via the SE trail then on to Hangman Hill. Link to Broad Way & follow to Fell View & back to Allenheads. Distance 34km.

Hexhamshire Common. © Neil Gander

Blanchland / Edmundbuyers

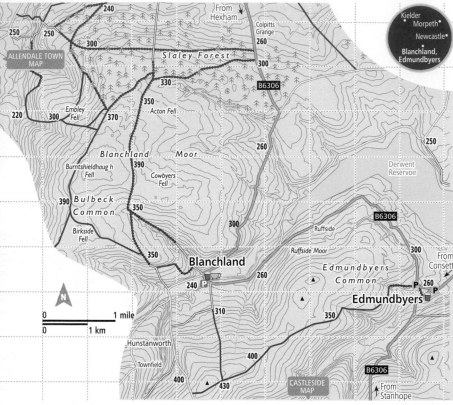

Kielder
Morpeth•
Newcastle•
**Blanchland,
Edmundbyers**

Situation: At the upper end of the Derwent Valley, near to Derwent Reservoir, on the Northumberland/Durham Border. 10 miles south of Hexham and west of Consett.

About the Base: Blanchland or Edmundbuyers, both small villages with pubs and accommodation. Blanchland also has tearooms. **Parking**: Car park at the north edge of Blanchland village. Also small area roadside in Edmundbuyers. *Grid Ref: Blanchland NY964504, Edmundbuyers NZ013501. Post Code: Blanchland DH8 9SS, Edmundbuyers DH8 9NP.*

Drive Times: Newcastle 45mins, Carlisle 1hr10, Leeds 2hr10, Manchester 2hr50, Birmingham 3hr50.

Refreshments: At Blanchland, The Lord Crewe Arms 01434 675251 and The White Monk Tea Rooms 01434 675044. The Punch Bowl Inn at Edmundbuyers 01207 255545.

Books: MTB Guide Northumberland (D.Purdy). Beyond Hamsterley (N.Gander). MBR Ride Guide 2010.

Maps: OS Explorer 307.

Bike Shops: The Bike Shop 01434 601032 in Hexham, Geared 4 01207 501188 and Bits 4 Bikes 01207 501188 in Consett.

Route Idea

From Blanchland, head S on road to pick up the NE trail to Edmondbyers, next follow road back to Blanchland then head to Slaley Forest via Blanchland Moor then trail back via Bulbeck Common. Distance 29km.

The ride can be shortened into either a southern loop of 16km or northern loop of 13km.

Edmundbuyers Common. Muddy Bums Mountain Biking. © Tony Harker

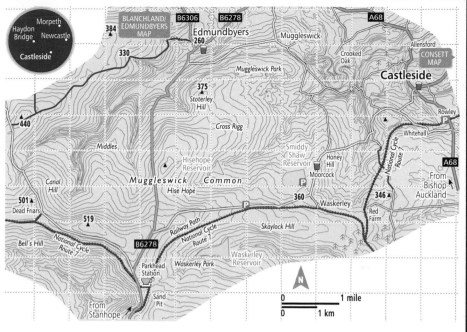

Situation: On the north east edge of the Pennines, 3 miles south west of Consett and 15 miles west of Durham.

About the Base: Castleside, a small village with two pubs.

Parking: Roadside in the centre of Castleside. Old station car park at Rowley just south of the village.

*Grid Ref: Castleside NZO77487, Rowley NZO86477, **Post Code:** Castleside DH8 9EB,*

Drive Times: Newcastle 40mins, Carlisle 1hr10, Leeds 2hr, Manchester 2hr40, Birmingham 3hr40.

Refreshments: At Castleside, The Horse and Groom Inn 01207 590419 and The Smelters Arms 01207 509265. The Punch Bowl Inn 01207 255545 at Edmundbuyers, Parkhead Station Tea Rooms 01388 526434 and The Moorcock 01207 508233 at Waskerley.

Bike Shops: Geared 4 01207 501188 & Bits 4 Bikes 01207 501188 in Consett.

Books: Beyond Hamsterley (N.Gander).

Maps: OS Explorer 307.

Route Idea

From Rowley car park, follow National Cycle Route 7 W for a short distance to pick up roads NW to Muggleswick then Edmundbyers, continue SW on trail to join minor road heading S and pick up Cycle Route 7, follow back to the start. Distance 36km.

Consett

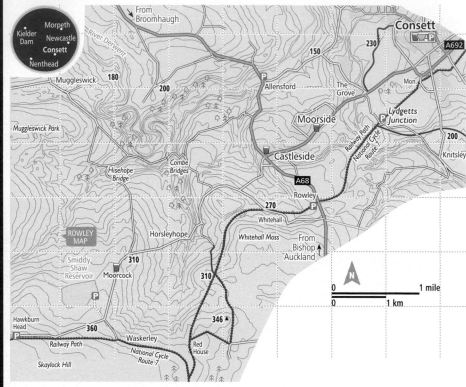

Situation: High on the north east edge of the Pennines, on the banks of the River Derwent. 14 miles north west of Durham.

About the Base: Consett, a small town with several pubs and cafes.

Parking: Several car parks in Consett. Also at Lydgetts Junction, Rowley and Allensford.

Grid Ref: Consett NZ104516, Lydgetts Junction NZ098494, Rowley NZ086477, Allensford NZ077502.
Post Code: Consett DH8 5UJ.

Drive Times: Newcastle 40mins, Leeds 2hr, Edinburgh 2hr40, Manchester 2hr50, Birmingham 3hr40.

Refreshments: Several pubs & cafés in Consett. The Castleside Inn 01207 581443 and The Stanefordham Inn 01207 504594 at Moorside, The Smelters Arms 01207 509265 and the Horse & Groom 01207 590419 in Castleside or The Moor Cock 01207 508233 at Waskerley.

Books: MTB Guide County Durham (D.Purdy).

Maps: OS Explorer 307.

Bike Shops: Geared 4 01207 501188 and Bits 4 Bikes 01207 501188 in Consett.

Route Idea

Off-roads are easy going railway paths. From Lydgetts Junction, National Cycle Route 7 to Whitehall, then to Waskerley then Hawkburn Head, road to Hisehope Bridge, Comb Bridges, Whitehall and Route 7 back to the start.
Distance 23km.

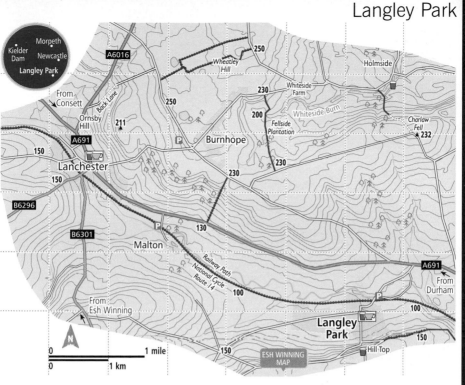

Situation: In the foothills of the North Pennines, 5 miles north west of Durham, on the banks of the River Browney.

About the Base: Langley Park, a village with pubs and a cafe. Further Info: www.langleypark.eu.

Parking: Car park to the north of the village before you cross the river approaching from the A691.
Grid Ref: NZ217453. Post Code: DH7 9TR.

Drive Times: Newcastle 35mins, Carlisle 1hr30, Leeds 1hr50, Manchester 2hr40, Birmingham 3hr30.

Trains: Durham Station, 5 miles away, is on the Leeds-Newcastle-Edinburgh line.

Refreshments: At Langley Park, The New Board Inn 0191 373 6914, The Rams Head 0191 373 7767 and Café Planet-Lan 01362 854126. Also several pubs & cafés in Lanchester.

Books: MTB Guide County Durham (D.Purdy).

Maps: OS Explorer 307 & 308.

Bike Shops: Specialist Cycles 0191 378 3753, 6 miles away in Meadowfield, for hire & repairs. Halfords 0191 383 0822 in Durham

Route Idea

Follow National Cycle Route 14 to Lanchester then on to Ornsby Hill, follow Back Lane, trails and roads to Wheatley Hill, Whiteside Farm, Fellside Plantation and back to Langley Park.
Distance 19km.

Esh Winning

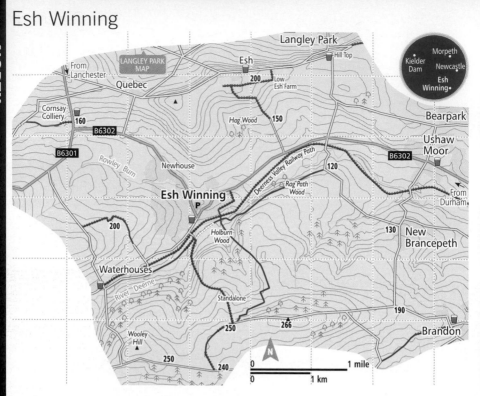

Situation: Lying in the Deerness Valley, a former mining village, 5 miles west of Durham.

About the Base: Esh Winning, a village with a pub.

Parking: In the centre of the village opposite the pub. *Grid Ref: NZ191416. Post Code: DH7 9HT.*

Drive Times: Newcastle 40mins, Carlisle 1hr30, Leeds 1hr50, Manchester 2hr40, Birmingham 3hr30.

Trains: Durham Station, 5 miles away, is on the Leeds-Newcastle-Edinburgh line.

Refreshments: The Staggs Head 0191 373 4139 in Esh Winning. The Black Horse Inn 0191 373 4576 at Waterhouses, The Royal Oak Inn 0191 373 4224 at Cornsay Colliery, The Cross Keys 0191 373 1279 in Esh, The New Board Inn 0191 373 6914 at Hill Top, The Flass Inn 0191 373 2467 at Ushaw Moor and The Bay Horse 0191 378 0498 in Brandon.

Books: MTB Guide County Durham (D.Purdy).

Maps: OS Explorer 307 & 308.

Bike Shops: Specialist Cycles 0191 378 3753, 6 miles away in Meadowfield, for hire & repairs. Halfords 0191 383 0822 in Durham.

Route Idea

Easy going railway paths. From Esh Winning, railway path SW to Waterhouses then head back towards Esh Winning on the trail close to the River Deerness. Continue to Standalone farm, Holburn Wood, Rag Path Wood then back on the railway path. Distance 12km.

Blencarn

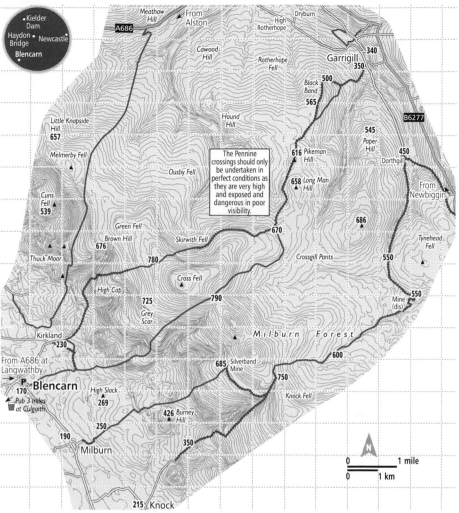

The Pennine crossings should only be undertaken in perfect conditions as they are very high and exposed and dangerous in poor visibility.

0 ————— 1 mile
0 ————— 1 km

Situation: On the eastern edge of the Eden Valley in the foothills of the north west Pennines. 10 miles east of Penrith.

About the Base: Blencarn, a small village with easy access to the trails. **Parking:** Roadside in the centre of the village *Grid Ref: NY636313. Post Code: CA10 1TZ.*

Drive Times: Carlisle 45mins, Newcastle 1hr30, Leeds 2hr10, Manchester 2hr10, Birmingham 3hr10.

Trains: Langwathby Station, 5 miles away, is on the Newcastle-Carlisle line.

Refreshments: Nothing in the map area but try The Black Swan Inn, 01768 88223 in Culgaith, 3 miles south west of Blencarn.

Maps: OS Explorer OL31.

Routes on Web: www.goodmtb.co.uk/a4

Bike Shops: Halfords 01768 8929606 in Penrith.

Route Idea

Road NE to Kirkland then trails to Garrigill via Skirwith Fell then Pikeman Hill. Return on road towards Dorthgill then trails S then SE to road junction near Knock, and finally roads to Milburn & Blencarn. Distance 44km.

© Neil Gander

St John's Chapel

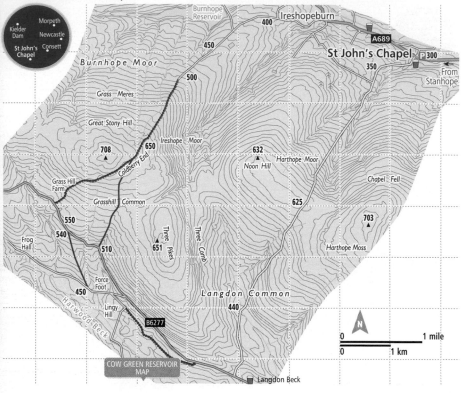

Situation: In the North Pennine hills, on the south side of the River Wear in Weardale. 24 miles west of Bishop Auckland.

About the Base: St John's Chapel, a village with two pubs.

Parking: In the market place in the centre of the village, or car park next to the Tourist Information Point as you enter the village from the east. *Grid Ref: St Johns Chapel NY884379, Information Point NY886378.*
Post Code: St Johns Chapel DL13 1QF,

Drive Times: Newcastle 1hr, Carlisle 1hr10, Leeds 2hr10, Manchester 2hr40, Birmingham 3hr40.

Refreshments: The Bluebell Inn 01388 537256 and The Golden Lion 01388 537231 at St Johns Chapel. The Weardale Inn 01388 537764 at Ireshopeburn and The Langdon Beck Hotel 01833 622267 at Langdon Beck.

Books: MTB Guide County Durham (D.Purdy).

Maps: OS Explorer OL31.

Route Idea

From St John's Chapel, road over Harthope Moor to Langdon Common then on to Grass Hill Farm via road or a mixture of trails & lanes just S of the B6277. Trails to Coldberry End which link to roads back to the start. Distance 22km.

Cow Green Reservoir

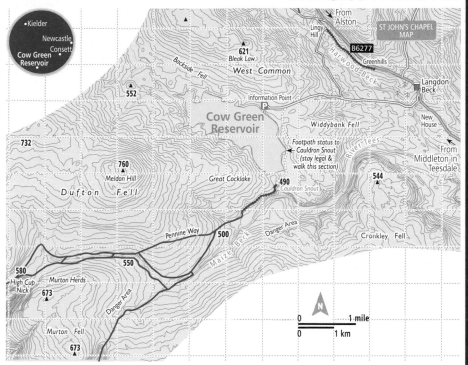

Situation: In Upper Teesdale, on the border of Cumbria and County Durham in the North Pennines. 30 miles west of Bishop Auckland and 35 miles east of Penrith.

About the Base: Cow Green Reservoir, a rural location with an information point. **Parking:** Car park next to the tourist information point as you approach the reservoir from the B6277. *Grid Ref: NY810309.*

Drive Times: Carlisle 1hr20, Newcastle 1hr20, Leeds 2hr, Manchester 2hr40, Birmingham 3hr40.

Refreshments: The Langdon Beck Hotel 01833 622267 in Langdon Beck.

Books: Beyond Hamsterley (N.Gander).

Maps: OS Explorer OL19.

Route Idea

An out & back from Cow Green Reervoir to High Cup Nick. At end of the reservoir , walk footpath to join the Pennine Way keeping N of Maize Beck to start, then crossing to the S for last few kilometres to High Cup Nick, reverse route back to start. Distance 22km.

Rider: The Muddy Bums. © Gavin Duthie

Romaldkirk / Middleton in Teesdale

Route Idea

From Romaldkirk, trails S then road and trails W to Blackton Reservoir. Road and trails NW to Holwick. Roads and railway path SE back to Romaldkirk. Distance 40km. Shortcut options: eastbound road after Blackton Reservoir, road running alongside Grassholme Reservoir.

This area is also fairly close to Hamsterley Forest Trail Centre (p99).

Situation: In Upper Teesdale in the Pennine Hills of west County Durham, six miles north of Barnard Castle.

About the Base: Romaldkirk, a small village with two pubs or Middleton-in-Teesdale, a small market town with pubs, cafes and accommodation. Further Info: www.hectorparr.freeuk.com/RomaldkirkV/index. htm. **Parking:** Roadside parking around the village green in Romaldkirk or in front of the Tourist Information Centre in Middleton-in-Teesdale. Car parks at Hury Reservoir & Grassholme Reservoir Visitor Centre. **Grid Ref:** Romaldkirk NY995220, Middleton-in-Teesdale NY947254, Hury Reservoir NY964197, Grassholme Visitor Centre NY946224. **Post Code:** Romaldkirk DL12 9ED, Middleton-in-Teesdale DL12 0QG.

Drive Times: Newcastle 1hr10, Carlisle 1hr20, Leeds 1hr30, Manchester 2hr20, Birmingham 3hr20.

Refreshments: At Romaldkirk, The Kirk Inn 01833 650260 & The Rose & Crown 01833 650213. Blacksmiths Arms 01833 640605 in Mickleton, Strathmore Arms 01833 640362 in Holwick & Fox & Hounds 01833 650241 in Cotherstone. Cafes & pubs in Middleton.

Books: Beyond Hamsterley (N.Gander).

Maps: OS Explorer OL31.

0 1 mile
0 1 km

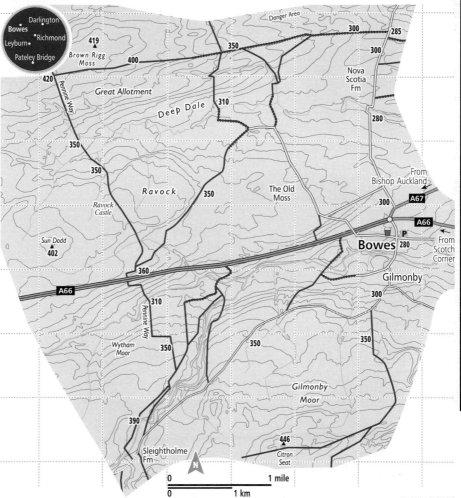

Situation: In the Pennine Hills on the edge of Deepdale in west County Durham. Just beyond the northern boundary of the Yorkshire Dales National Park, 4 miles west of Barnard Castle.

About the Base: Bowes, a village with a pub/B&B. Further Info: www.bowes.org.uk. **Parking**: Parking behind the village hall (by permission, which may be withdrawn). **Grid Ref: NY996135. Post Code: DL12 9HU.**

Drive Times: Newcastle 1hr10, Carlisle 1hr10, Leeds 1hr30, Manchester 2hr10, Birmingham 3hr10.

Refreshments: The Ancient Unicorn Inn 01833 628321 in Bowes.

Books: MTB Guide County Durham (D.Purdy).

Maps: OS Explorer OL31.

Routes on Web: www.goodmtb.co.uk/a5

Route Ideas

The area is exposed and the paths get boggy; so best during a dry spell.

❶ From Bowes, head N on the road towards Novia Scotia Farm. Trail W to Brown Rigg Moss, then Pennine Way S to Sleightholme Farm and road back to start.
Distance 23km.

❷ NW out of Bowes via The Old Moss, then SW on trails skirting Ravock. Pass the A66, on to Sleightholme Farm and road back to finish.
Distance 14km.

Chopwell Wood

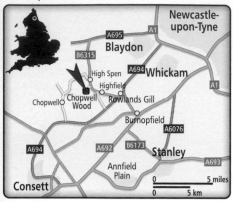

A 360 hectare mixed woodland on the fringes of Gateshead with short waymarked cross country trails offering fast technical singletrack and lots of freeride features. Two easier trails with scenic views follow the extensive forest road network.

Facilities:
None on site. Plenty of refreshments in nearby Gateshead.

Parking:
Grid Ref: NZ137580. Post Code: NE39 1LT

Web: www.goodmtb.co.uk/b4

The Trails

❶ Powerline, Red, XC, 3.5km.

❷ High Voltage, Black, XC, 0.3km.

❸ Outside Line, Blue, XC, 5.8km.

❹ Festival Trail, Green, XC, 2.5km.

Rider: Mat Clark. © Gary Ewing

Hamsterley Forest
and Descend Bike Park

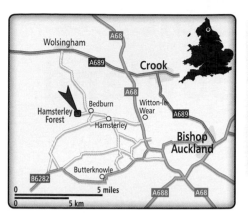

Two thousand hectares of mixed woodland on the edge of the North Pennines Area of Outstanding Natural Beauty. Waymarked trails to suit all abilities, including a new flowing singletrack, Skills Loop and Trail Quest, are built and maintained by the Hamsterley Trailblazers in conjunction with the Forestry Commission.

Descend Bike Park has tough downhills, a duel track, dirtjumps and a 4X. Run by local riders, you must pay to ride. Plenty of unofficial trails to explore.

Parking:
Grid Ref: NZ091312. Post Code: DL13 3QH

Web: www.goodmtb.co.uk/b5a /b5b & /b5c

Facilities:
Tea room at Hamsterley Forest Visitor Centre. Wood 'n' Wheels 0333 8008 222 MTB hire and repairs on site. Descend Hamsterley 07795 514251 organise an uplift Service at Descend Bike Park.

The Trails
❶ Blue, XC, 14.4km.
❷ Red, XC, 22.5km.
❸ Black, XC, 11.2km.
❹ The Loop, Freeride.
❺ Descend Bike Park, DH, 4X, Freeride.

Rider: Craig Cummings. © Gary Ewing

Yorkshire Dales & Forest of Bowland

Stretching from the M6 in the west almost as far as the A1 in the east, the Yorkshire Dales National Park sits squarely over the dramatic Central Pennines, rising to 736m on Whernside, the highest of the famous Three Peaks (the others being Ingleborough and Pen y Ghent). This is unmistakeable scenery with ever changing views of U-shaped valleys, field barns and drystone walls snaking their way up the hillsides. There is more consistently good riding, with longer, unbroken stretches of top quality stone bridleways than anywhere else in the country. As visitors are fewer and less concentrated around honeypots than is the case in the Lake District, there is far less potential for walker / biker conflict.

Challenging rides on the superb network of stone-based bridleways are spread throughout the National Park. In the far northwest are the distinctive smooth, rounded hills of the Howgills. Accessed from *Sedbergh* or *Ravenstonedale*, the only way to the top is via some very steep grassy climbs but once you have reached the ridge there is some superb open riding on well-drained tracks and fast smooth descents

Twistleton Scar. © Simon Barnes www.bogtrotters.org

Near Grinton. Amy & Magnus Ross © Stephen Ross

to make you whoop with joy. The area east of **Ingleton**, towards, **Settle**, **Horton in Ribblesdale** and **Ribblehead** is known as Three Peaks country and there is a maze of top grade tracks linking them altogether, including the unforgettable tunnels west of **Clapham**. Other highlights include the descent down Artengill above Dentdale, southwest of **Hawes** and the much improved track over Gorbeck connecting **Settle** to **Malham**.

South and west of **Hawes**, Bainbridge and **Askrigg** there are some long sections of wonderful stone-based tracks, whether Lady Ann Clifford's Highway parallel with Mallerstang, the old Roman Road over Common Allotments or the tracks over Stake Moss linking Wensleydale to Wharfedale. Jumping again from one dale to the next, the trails from **Kettlewell** linking Wharfedale to Littondale are some of the toughest in the

whole area, with brutal climbs rewarded by long and testing descents. **Conistone** offers an out and back route to a height of 540m on generally good surfaces.

To the east of **Malham**, Mastiles Lane is a wide stone-based track that acts as a spine for several rides exploring the limestone scenery to the north and south. In the southeast the trails merge seamlessly with those in Nidderdale, best explored from **Pateley Bridge**, **Lofthouse** or **Appletreewick**. To the north, the rides in Swaledale and Arkengarthdale based at **Muker**, **Reeth** and **Langthwaite** have a very different feel with stone ruins along the course of the routes giving a clue to the area's old mining history. Further northwest, beyond the boundaries of the National Park, there are many easy tracks to explore over the limestone outcrops of Great Asby Scar between Orton and **Kirkby Stephen**. To the south and west of the National Park lies the Forest of Bowland, with a superb 'roof of the world' ridge ride from **Wray** climbing to a highpoint of over 400m on Salter Fell and dropping down to **Slaidburn**. Other good Forest of Bowland bases are located at **Dunsop Bridge**, **Chipping** and **Whalley**. The latter is at the mid point on the Lancashire Cycleway, an ideal base from which to explore the Ribble Valley and ride around Pendle Hill.

Included here, although just outside the National Park are the Trail Centres at **Gisburn Forest** and **Stainburn**.

South of Sedbergh. Oscar Ross. © Amy Ross

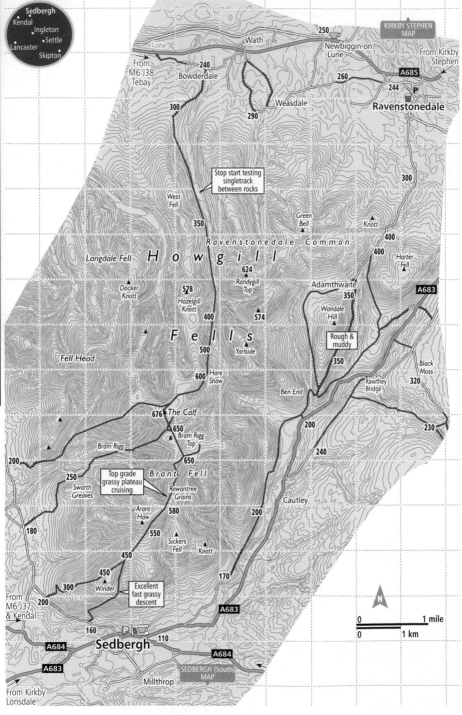

Sedbergh
Kendal
Ingleton
Lancaster
Settle
Skipton

KIRKBY STEPHEN MAP

Lune
Wath
Newbiggin-on-Lune
250
From Kirkby Stephen
From M6 J38 Tebay
240
Bowderdale
260
A685
244 P
290
Weasdale
300
Ravenstonedale

Stop start testing singletrack between rocks

West Fell
350
Green Bell
Knott
300
Ravenstonedale Common
400
400
Langdale Fell
H o w g i l l
Harter Fell
624
Docker Knott
578
Randygill Top
Adamthwaite
350
A683
Hazelgill Knott
400
574
Wandale Hill
F e l l s
500
Yarlside
Rough & muddy
350
Fell Head
600
Hare Shaw
Black Moss
320
Ben End
Rawthey Bridge
676 The Calf
650
Bram Rigg Top
200
230
Bram Rigg
650
240
200
Top grade grassy plateau cruising
B r a n t F e l l
250
Swarth Greaves
Rowantree Grains
Cautley
180
Arant Haw
580
200
200
550
Sickers Fell
Knott
450
170
450
Winder
Excellent fast grassy descent
300
200
From M6 J37 & Kendal
160
P
A683
Sedbergh
110
A684
A684
A684
A683
SEDBERGH (South) MAP
Millthrop
From Kirkby Lonsdale

N

0 _____ 1 mile
0 _____ 1 km

Situation: Sedbergh is south of Howgill Fells on the western edge of the Yorkshire Dales National Park, 7 miles east of Kendal. Ravenstonedale, on the north side of the fells, is 11 miles to the north west of Sedbergh.

About the Base: Sedbergh, a market town with plenty of refreshments and accommodation or Ravenstonedale, a vtillage with a pub. Further Info: www.sedbergh.org.uk. **Parking:** Car park off Main Street in the centre of Sedburgh or roadside in the centre of Ravenstonedale village. *Grid Ref: Sedburgh SD658921, Ravenstonedale NY722041. Post Code: Sedburgh LA10 5AS, Ravenstonedale CA17 4NH.*

Drive Times: Carlisle 1hr, Manchester 1hr30, Leeds 1hr50, Newcastle 1hr50, Birmingham 2hr40.

Refreshments: Sedbergh has a choice of pubs & cafés. The Black Swan 015396 23204 in Ravenstonedale or café at Lune Spring Garden Centre 01539 623318 in Newbiggin-on-Lune.

Books: Yorkshire Dales MTB – N Dales (N.Cotton).

Maps: OS Explorer O19. Dales West Cycle Map (Harvey).

Routes on Web: www.goodmtb.co.uk/a49

Bike Shops: Stonetrail Mountain Bike Hire 015396 623444 in Ravenstonedale. Sedbergh Bike Hire 07920 864586.

Route Ideas

❶ A loop connecting Sedbergh with Ravenstonedale. It can be ridden any direction; the following describes clockwise. There are three variations to the top of The Calf. The shortest option via Arant Haw will give a total ride length of about 40km. From The Calf head to Bowderdale, Ravenstonedale, Adamthwaite & back to Sedbergh.

❷ Road NW from Sedbergh, then trail NE past Swarth Greaves, around Bram Rigg Top then descent to Sedbergh via Arant Haw. Distance 16km.

❸ From Sedbergh, NE on trails along the valley. Loop around Rawthey Bridge then back to Sedbergh via the main road or the trails again in the valley. Distance 23km.

© Simon Barnes www.bogtrotters.org

Sedbergh (south)

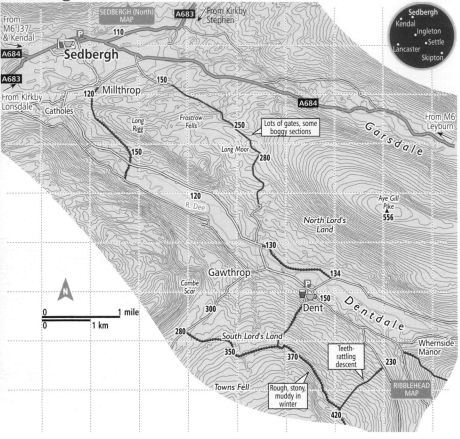

From M6 J37 & Kendal

SEDBERGH (North) MAP

A683

From Kirkby Stephen

110

P

A684

Sedbergh

A683

From Kirkby Lonsdale

120

Millthrop

Catholes

150

Long Rigg

150

Frostrow Fells

250

Lots of gates, some boggy sections

A684

From M6 Leyburn

Garsdale

Long Moor

280

120

R. Dee

North Lord's Land

Aye Gill Pike

556

130

Gawthrop

134

Combe Scar

300

280

P

150

Dent

Dentdale

South Lord's Land

350

370

230

Teeth-rattling descent

Whernside Manor

Towns Fell

Rough, stony, muddy in winter

RIBBLEHEAD MAP

420

N

0 _____ 1 mile
0 _____ 1 km

Sedbergh
Kendal
Ingleton
Settle
Lancaster
Skipton

Situation: At the foot of the Howgill Fells on the banks of the River Rowthey, at the western edge of the Yorkshire Dales National Park. 7 miles east of Kendal.

About the Base: Sedbergh, a small market town with plenty of refreshments and accommodation. Further Info: www.sedbergh.org.uk. **Parking**: Car parks off Main Street in the centre of Sedbergh & next to the information point in Dent. *Grid Ref: Sedburgh SD658921, Dent SD704870. Post Code: Sedburgh LA10 5AS, Dent LA10 5QJ.*

Drive Times: Carlisle 1hr, Manchester 1hr30, Leeds 1hr50, Newcastle 1hr50, Birmingham 2hr40.

Refreshments: Sedbergh has a choice of pubs & cafés. Meadowside Café 015396 25329, Stone Close Café 015396 25231, The Sun Inn 015396 25208 & The George & Dragon 015396 25256 at Dent.

Books: Yorkshire Dales MTB – N Dales (N.Cotton).

Maps: OS Explorer OL2 & O19. Dales West Cycle Map (Harvey).

Bike Shops: Sedbergh Bike Hire 07920 864586.

Route Idea

From Sedbergh, S to Millthrop then trail & road to Gawthorp. Trail across South Lord's Land & either descent to Dent or continue to the next trail junction before descending. On to Long Moor & back to Sedbergh. Distance 26km.

South Lords Land. Oscar Ross. ©Amy Ross

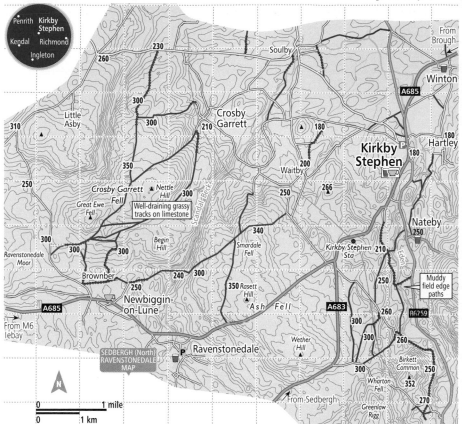

Situation: In the Upper Eden valley on the banks of the River Eden, just outside the northern boundary of the Yorkshire Dales National Park. 24 miles north east of Kendal.

About the Base: Kirkby Stephen, a small market town with pubs, cafés and accommodation. Further Info: www.kirkby-stephen.com. Further Info: www. ravenstonedale.org. **Parking**: Car park in Kirkby Stephen town centre on the road to Soulby or roadside parking in the centre of Ravenstonedale. *Grid Ref: Kirkby Stephen NY773088, Ravenstonedale NY722041.* **Post Code**: *Kirkby Stephen CA17 4HA, Ravenstonedale CA17 4NQ.*

Drive Times: Carlisle 1hr, Newcastle 1hr30, Manchester 1hr50, Leeds 1hr50, Birmingham 2hr50.

Trains: Kirkby Stephen Railway Station (about 1 mile south of the town) is on the Settle-Carlisle line.

Refreshments: Plenty of pubs & cafés in Kirkby Stephen. The Black Swan 015396 23204 in Ravenstonedale & a café at Lune Spring Garden Centre 01539 623318 in Newbiggin-on-Lune.

Books: Yorkshire Dales MTB – N Dales (N.Cotton).

Maps: OS Explorer OL19.

Routes on Web: www.goodmtb.co.uk/a57

Bike Shops: Kirby Stephen Cycle Centre 017683 71658.

Route Idea

From Kirkby Stephen, W to Waitby then road & trail towards Newbiggin-on-Lune. Trails N skirting the E side of Nettle Hill to Crosby Garrett & then back to Kirkby Stephen. Distance 20km. To extend this route, when at Crosby Garrett continue NE to Soulby, then Winton, S to Hartley & back to the finish.

©Nick Cotton

105

Muker

Kirkby Stephen • Muker • Richmond • Pateley Bridge • Settle

Tan Hill 526

Much better as gravity-assisted descent

450 540

Stonesdale Moor 450

566

440 Black Moor

400

West Stonesdale

East Stonesdale

Swale 400

B6270

Wain Wath Force

Park Bridge 320 350

From Kirkby Stephen

Keld Side Keld

Thorns 320

400

Kisdon 499

Angram

Hooker Mill Scar 490

450

Thwaite 350

300 Ivelet Moor

Black Hill

REETH/LANGTHWAITE MAP

Ann Gill Head

250

pub & cafe in Gunnerside 1.2km

Ramps Holme

290 Ivelet

Muker

P 250

Beautiful easy track along valley floor

B6270 247

From A6108 Richmond

0 1 mile
0 1 km

N

Situation: In Upper Swaledale, close to the River Swale in the north of the Yorkshire Dales National Park.

About the Base: Muker, a small village with a cafe, pub and accommodation.
Further Info: www.mukervillage.co.uk. **Parking**: Car park in the centre of Muker next to the bridge.
Grid Ref: SD910978.
Post Code: DL11 6QG.

Drive Times: Carlisle 1hr20, Newcastle 1hr30, Leeds 1hr50, Manchester 2hr10, Birmingham 3hr10.

Refreshments: At Muker, The Farmers Arms 01748 886297 & Village Tea Shop 01748 88640. Tan Hill Inn 01833 628246 at Tan Hill in the north of the map.

Books: Yorkshire Dales MTB – N Dales (N.Cotton).

Maps: OS Explorer OL30. Yorkshire Dales British Mountain Map (Harvey).

Routes on Web: www.goodmtb.co.uk/a59

© Nick Cotton

Route Ideas

❶ From Muker, roads E to Ivelet. Road then trails NW to Keld. Back to Muker via the trail over Kisdon. Distance 16km.

❷ Start as above to Ivelet then road & trails NW to West Stonesdale. Road N to Tan Hill. Trails S to Keld & back to Muker via the trail over Kisdon. Distance 30km.

Barningham

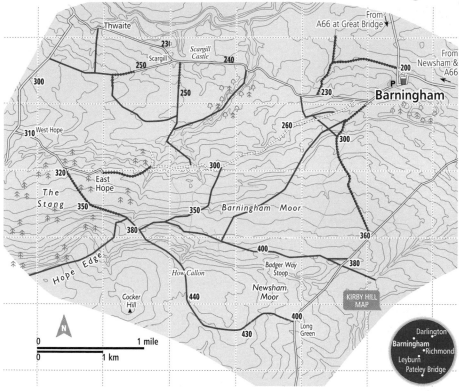

Thwaite

From A66 at Great Bridge

From Newsham & A66

Scargill
Scargill Castle

Barningham

West Hope

East Hope

The Stang

Barningham Moor

Hope Edge

How Callon

Badger Way Stoop

Newsham Moor

Cocker Hill

KIRBY HILL MAP

Long Green

0 ——— 1 mile
0 ——— 1 km

N

Darlington
Barningham • Richmond
Leyburn
Pateley Bridge

Situation: In the Pennine Hills of west County Durham, just beyond the north western boundary of the Yorkshire Dales National Park. South of the A66 between Barnard Castle and Scotch Corner.

About the Base: Barningham, a very small village with a pub.
Further Info: www.communigate.co.uk/ne/barn/index.phtml
Parking: Roadside in the centre of the village, opposite the village green.
Grid Ref: NZ084102. Post Code: DL11 7DR.

The Stang. © Tony Harker

Drive Times: Newcastle 1hr, Carlisle 1hr20, Leeds 1hr20, Manchester 2hr10, Birmingham 3hr.

Refreshments: Take your own.

Books: Beyond Hamsterley (N.Gander).

Maps: OS Explorer OL30.

Route Idea

From Barningham, a clockwise loop skirting around Barningham & Newsham Moors, on to The Stang & then via East Hope, tracks & lanes back to Barningham.
Distance 17km.

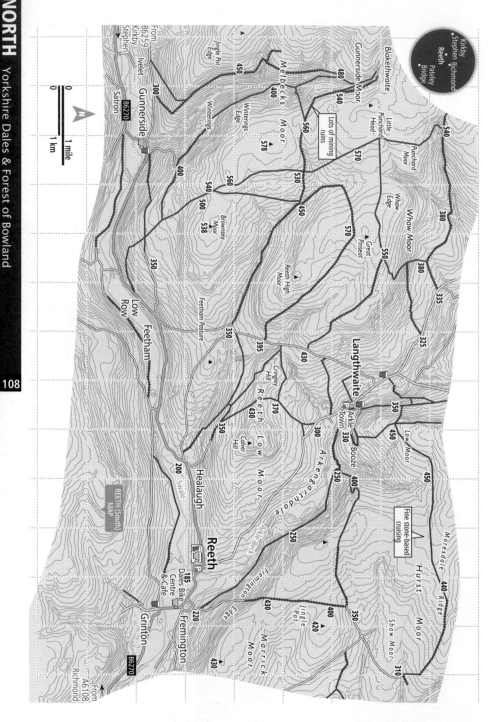

Kirkby
• Stephen
Reeth
Richmond
•
• Pateley
Bridge

N
0 ——— 1 mile
0 ——— 1 km

From
B6259
Kirkby
Stephen
Ivelet
Satron
B6270
Gunnerside

Jingle Pot Edge
300
450
Winterings
400
480
540
Melbecks Moor
Gunnerside Moor
Blakethwaite
Little Punchard Head
Lots of mining ruins
Punchard Moor
560
570
Whaw Edge
530
578
Winterings Edge
560
540
500
538
Brownsey Moor
450
570
Great Pinseat
550
Whaw Moor
380
380
335
325
530
380

400
350
Low Row
Feetham
Reeth High Moor
Feetham Pasture
350
395
430
Cringley Hill
Reeth Low Moor
370
430
Calver Hill
350
300
330
250
Langthwaite
Arkle Town
350
Booze
450
Low Moor
450
400
Molesdale Ridge
Hurst Moor
440

REETH (South) MAP

200
Healaugh
Swale
Arkengarthdale
Arkle Beck
250
430
Jingle Pot
420
400
350
Shaw Moor
310

Reeth
185
Dales Bike Centre & Cafe
220
Fremington
Fremington Edge
Marrick Moor
430

Grinton
B6270
From
A6108
Richmond

Fine stone-based cruising

Situation: On the north west edge of the Yorkshire Dales National Park, at the confluence of Swaledale and Arkengarthdale. 10 miles west of Richmond.

About the Base: Reeth, a village with pubs, cafés and accommodation or Langthwaite, a small village with a pub and easy access to the trails. Further Info: www.reeth.org. **Parking:** In Reeth at the village green, adjacent to the B6270. Car park just before Langthwaite village as you approach from Reeth.
Grid Ref: *Reeth SE038992, Langthwaite NZ005022.*
Post Code: *Reeth DL11 6SY, Langthwaite DL11 6RD.*

Drive Times: Newcastle 1hr20, Leeds 1hr30, Carlisle 1hr30, Manchester 2hr20, Birmingham 3hr10.

Refreshments: Full range of refreshments & accommodation in Reeth. The Red Lion 01748 884 218 in Langthwaite or The Charles Bathhurst Inn 01748 884 567 just to the north. The Dales Bike Centre & Café in Fremington & The Bridge Inn in Grinton.
On the big 40km route, Overton House Café 01748 884332 or The Bridge Inn 01748 886 126, both at Gunnerside.

Books: Yorkshire Dales MTB – N Dales (N.Cotton).

Maps: OS Explorer OL30. Yorkshire Dales British Mountain Map (Harvey).

Routes on Web: www.goodmtb.co.uk/a60a & /a60b

Bike Shops: The Dales Bike Centre 01748 884 908 in Fremington.

Route Ideas

❶ From Langthwaite, Road NW, trails W to Whaw Moor then SE to road. Link to trail skirting Cringley Hill. N back to the start.
Distance, 12km.

❷ A clockwise loop around Hurst Moor.
Distance 17km.

❸ From Reeth, road NW towards Langthwaite, SW on trail to skirt Cringley Hill, road N then bridleway back down to road S of Langthwaite, return to Reeth on trail on N side of Arkle Beck.
Distance 16km.

❹ From Reeth, E to Fremington then N across Fremington Edge past Jingle Pot. trails W towards Langthwaite then W across Cringley Hill. Trails over Reeth High Moor & on to Melbecks Moor. SE past Winterings Edge to Gunnerside. Trails & roads S of River Swale to Grinton & back to Reeth.
Distance 40km.

Extend the area: Reeth South Map.

Gunnerside Gill. Riders: Muddy Bums Mountain Biking. ©Tony Harker

Reeth (south)

Darlington
Richmond
Reeth
Settle   Pateley
Bridge

REETH (North)
MAP

Reeth

MARSKE
MAP

Healaugh

Fremington

Dales Bike
Centre
& Cafe

B6270

180
190

180

Swale

190

Swaledale

190
200

B6270

Grinton

190

From B6259
Kirkby Stephen

Low
Whita

250

250

220

Loads of options on
heather-clad hillside

Harker Mires

High Harker
Hill

400

300

From
A6108
Richmond

370

450

Long Scar

Harkerside   Moor

290
400

330

Cogden
Moor

360

450

450

Kendell
Bottom

Gibbon
Hill

Grinton
Moor

380

400

High
Carl
555

500

Good climb or
descent past
mining ruins

Greet's
Hill   500

Greet's
Moss

450

Whitaside
Moor.

550   Apedale
Head   500

450

460

N

East   Bolton
Moor

Apedale

400

380

410

0   1 mile
0   1 km

CASTLE BOLTON
MAP

Situation: At the confluence of Swaledale and Arken-garthdale on the north west edge of the Yorkshire Dales National Park, 10 miles west of Richmond.

About the Base: Reeth, a village with pubs, cafés and accommodation. Further Info: www.reeth.org. **Parking:** At the village green, adjacent to the B6270. *Grid Ref: SE038992. Post Code: DL11 6SY.*

Drive Times: Newcastle 1hr20, Leeds 1hr30, Carlisle 1hr30, Manchester 2hr20, Birmingham 3hr10.

Refreshments: Plenty of refreshments in Reeth, The Dales Bike Centre & Café 01748 884908 in Fremington & The Bridge Inn 01748 884224 at Grinton.

Books: Yorkshire Dales MTB – N Dales (N.Cotton).

Maps: OS Explorer OL30. Yorkshire Dales British Mountain Map (Harvey).

Routes on Web: www.goodmtb.co.uk/a61

Bike Shops: The Dales Bike Centre 01748 884 908 in Fremington.

Route Ideas

❶ From Reeth SE to Grinton. Road S past Grinton Moor. Trail W along Apedale. Just past Apedale Head either pick the bridleway that skirts Kendell Bottom & follow back to Grinton, or drop down to the road, a bit of zigzagging to the trails close to the River Swale & follow back to Grinton then Reeth. Distance 24km.

❷ From Reeth, SE to Grinton, W along the river Swale then climb towards Whitaside Moor. Trails NE past Kendel Bottom & back to Grinton then Reeth. Distances around 20km.

Extend the area: Reeth North Map.

Near Grinton. Rider: Magnus Ross © Stephen Ross

Kirby Hill

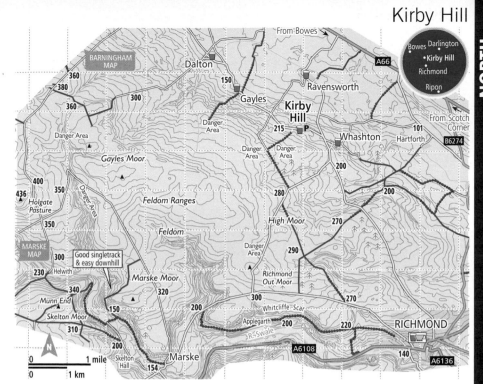

Situation: In the valley of Holmedale on the north east edge of the Yorkshire Dales National Park. 5 miles north of Richmond.

About the Base: Kirby Hill, a small village with a pub.
Parking: Roadside in the centre of the village. *Grid Ref: NZ139065. Post Code: DL11 7JH.*

Drive Times: Newcastle 1hr, Leeds 1hr20, Carlisle 1hr30, Manchester 2hr10, Birmingham 3hr.

Refreshments: At Kirby Hill, The Shoulder of Mutton Inn 01748 822772. The Hack & Spade 01748 823721 in Whashton, The Travellers Rest 01833 621225 in Dalton & The Foxhall Inn 01325 718262 in Gayles. The Bay Horse Inn in Ravensworth 01325 718328. Also several pubs & cafés at Richmond.

Books: Beyond Hamsterley (N.Gander).

Maps: OS Explorer 304.

Bike Shops: Arthur Caygill Cycles 01748 825469 in Richmond.

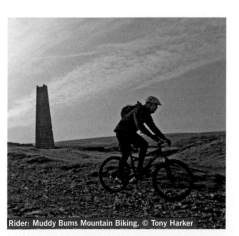

Rider: Muddy Bums Mountain Biking. © Tony Harker

Route Ideas

❶ From Kirby Hill, NW to Dalton. SW around Gayles Moor to Holgate Pasture. Trails S across Skelton Moor & on to Marske. Road to Richmond Out Moor then trails to Whaston. Road back to start.
Distance 30km.

❷ The following route uses a trail through Applegarth to Richmond that is now MTB friendly, with gates replacing stiles. As route above but after Marske pick up trail S of Whitcliffe Scar to detour via Applegarth into Richmond. Road to Richmond Out Moor then as above. Adds 7km to the ride.

❸ From Kirby Hill head S to pick up road across High Moor then head SE towards Marske before taking trail S of Whitcliffe Scar to Richmond. Follow road to Richmond Out Moor then trails to Whaston. Road back to the start. Distance 23km.

Extend the area: Marske Map to SW. Barningham Map to NW

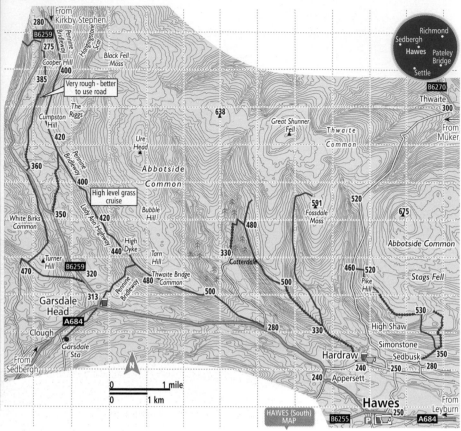

From Kirkby Stephen
280
B6259
275
Hartbrigstone Scar
Pennine Bridleway
Cooper Hill
400
385
Black Fell Moss
Very rough - better to use road
The Riggs
Cumpston Hill
420
Ure Head
638
Great Shunner Fell
Thwaite Common
360
400
Abbotside Common
White Birks Common
350
420
Lady Ann Highway
Bubble Hill
High level grass cruise
480
591 Fossdale Moss
520
675
Abbotside Common
High Dyke
440
Tarn Hill
330
Cotterdale
Turner Hill
470
B6259
320
Thwaite Bridge Common
480
500
500
460 520 Pike Hill
Stags Fell
Garsdale Head
313
Pennine Bridleway
280
330
530
High Shaw
Simonstone
Sedbusk
350
Clough
A684
Garsdale Sta
Hardraw
240 250 280
From Sedbergh
0   1 mile
0   1 km
N
240 Appersett

Richmond
Sedbergh
Hawes Pateley Bridge
Settle

B6270
Thwaite
300
From Muker

HAWES (South) MAP

Hawes
250
B6255
A684
From Leyburn

Situation: On the banks of the River Ure, in Upper Wensleydale and the heart of the Yorkshire Dales National Park. 16 miles from both Leyland and Sedbergh, on the A684.

About the Base: Hawes, a small market town with pubs, cafés and accommodation.
Further Info: www.wensleydale.org/hawes.
Parking: Car park on Gayle Lane, close to Wensleydale Creamery. *Grid Ref: SD870896. Post Code: DL8 3RL.*

Drive Times: Carlisle 1hr20, Leeds 1hr40, Newcastle 1hr40, Manchester 1hr50, Birmingham 3hr.

Trains: Garsdale Head Railway Station, 6 miles away, is on the Settle-Carlisle line.

Refreshments: Plenty of choice of cafés & pubs in Hawes. Cart House Tea Room 01969 667691 & The Green Dragon Inn 01969 667392 in Hardraw. The Moorcock Inn 01969 667488 at Garsdale Head.

Books: Yorkshire Dales MTB – N Dales (N.Cotton).

Maps: OS Explorer OL30. Yorkshire Dales British Mountain Map (Harvey).

Route Ideas

❶ From Hawes, N to Hardraw then trails to Cotterdale. Road back to Hawes. Distance 14km. Make longer by combining with trails to the NE of Sedbusk.

❷ From Hawes, NW on the A684. Trail NE across Thwaite Bridge Common follow to the B6259. Return by road. Distance 34km.

© Nick Cotton

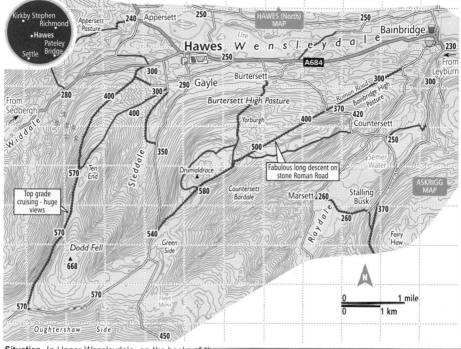

Map labels: Kirkby Stephen, Richmond, Appersett Pasture, Appersett, 240, 250, HAWES (North) MAP, 250, Bainbridge, Hawes, Pateley Bridge, Settle, Ure, 230, Hawes Wensleydale, From Leyburn, 250, A684, 300, Burtersett, 300, 300, Gayle, 290, Burtersett High Pasture, Roman Road, Bainbridge High Pasture, 300, From Sedbergh, 280, 400, 400, Yorburgh, 370, 420, 400, Countersett, Widdale, 350, 500, 250, Sleddale, Ten End, 570, Drumaldrace, Fabulous long descent on stone Roman Road, Semer Water, ASKRIGG MAP, Top grade cruising - huge views, 580, Countersett Bardale, Marsett 260, Stalling Busk, 570, 540, Green Side, Raydale, 260, 370, Dodd Fell, 668, Fairy Haw, 570, 570, Fleet Moss, 570, Oughtershaw Side, 450

N 0 — 1 mile / 0 — 1 km

Situation: In Upper Wensleydale, on the banks of the River Ure in the heart of the Yorkshire Dales National Park. 16 miles from both Leyland and Sedbergh, on the A684.

About the Base: Hawes, a small market town with pubs, cafés and accommodation. Further Info: www.wensleydale.org/hawes. **Parking:** Car park on Gayle Lane, close to Wensleydale Creamery.
Grid Ref: SD870896. Post Code: DL8 3RL.

Drive Times: Carlisle 1hr20, Leeds 1hr40, Newcastle 1hr40, Manchester 1hr50, Birmingham 3hr.

Trains: Garsdale Head Railway Station, 6 miles away, is on the Settle-Carlisle line.

Refreshments: Plenty of choice of cafés & pubs in Hawes. The Rose & Crown 01969 650225 & Cornmill Tea Room 01969 650212 in Bainbridge.

Books: Yorkshire Dales MTB – N Dales (N.Cotton).
Maps: OS Explorer OL30. Yorkshire Dales British Mountain Map (Harvey).

Routes on Web: www.goodmtb.co.uk/a55

Route Ideas

❶ From Hawes, roads to Bainbridge. Roman road SW past Drumaldrace then SW on roads to skirt Dodd Fell. N on trails back to Hawes. Distance 30km.

❷ From Hawes, SW on trails towards Dodd Fell. Road NE & then trail past Drumaldrace then N to Burtersett & main road to Hawes. Distance 21km.

❸ From Hawes take the road S that follows Sleddale around the back of Dodd Fell then N on trails back to Hawes. Distance 18km.

Extend the Area: Hawes North Map. Askrigg Map to the E.

© Simon Barnes www.bogtrotters.org

Askrigg

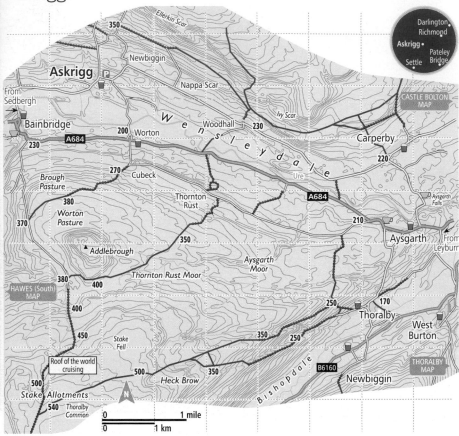

Situation: In the centre of Wensleydale, close to the River Ure in the Yorkshire Dales National Park. A mile from the A684 Leyburn to Sedbergh road.

About the Base: Askrigg, a small village with two pubs. Further Info: www.wensleydale.org/villages/askrigg.html.

Parking: Small car park in the centre of the village. *Grid Ref: SD950911.*
Post Code: DL8 3HJ.

Drive Times: Newcastle 1hr30, Carlisle 1hr30, Leeds 1hr40, Manchester 2hr, Birmingham 3hr10.

Refreshments: The Crown Inn 01969 650298 & Kings Arms 01969 650817 in Askrigg. The Wheatsheaf 01969 663216 in Carperby, The George Inn 01969 663256 in Thoralby & Victoria Arms 01969 650314 in Worton. George & Dragon 01969 663358 in Aysgarth, Mill Race Tea Shop 01969 663446 & Coppice Coffee Shop 01969 663763 at Aysgarth Falls. Pubs & café in Bainbridge.

Books: Yorkshire Dales MTB – N Dales (N.Cotton).

Maps: OS Explorer OL30. Yorkshire Dales British Mountain Map (Harvey).

Routes on Web: www.goodmtb.co.uk/a50

Route Ideas

❶ From Askrigg, S to Worton then climb to Stake Allotments via Worton Pasture. E to Thoralby & on to Aysgarth & Carperby. Trails W back towards Askrigg. Distance 28km.

❷ From Askrigg, roads N, then use the trails to Carperby. W along the lane to Woodhall, continue S to Thornton Rust then up & around Addlebrough before dropping to Worton & back to Askrigg. Distance 23km.

Extend the area: Castle Bolton Map to the E. Thoralby Map to the SE. Hawes South Map to the W.

Thornton Rust Moor. © Tony Harker

Castle Bolton

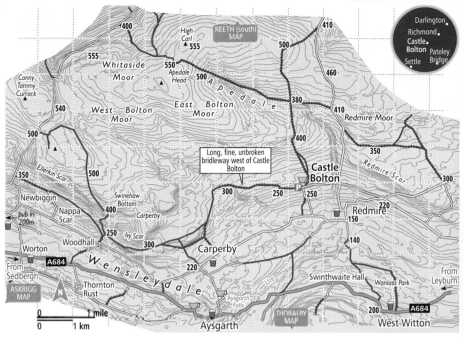

Long, fine, unbroken bridleway west of Castle Bolton

Situation: In Wensleydale, on the north east edge of the Yorkshire Dales National Park. 5 miles west of Leyburn.

About the Base: Castle Bolton, a village ideally placed on the corner of the main mountain bike loop.
Further Info: www.boltoncastle.co.uk.
Parking: Car park next to Bolton Castle. *Grid Ref: SE033918.*
Post Code: DL8 4ET.

Drive Times: Newcastle 1hr20, Leeds 1hr30, Carlisle 1hr40, Manchester 2hr, Birmingham 3hr 10.

Refreshments: Tea room in the castle 01969 62398 (no need to pay for admission). The Bolton Arms 01969 624336 in Redmire, The Wheatsheaf 01969 663216 in Carperby & Fox & Hounds in West Witton 01969 623650. The George & Dragon 01969 663358 in Aysgarth, Mill Race Tea Shop 01969 663446 & Coppice Coffee Shop 01969 663763 at Aysgarth Falls.

Books: Yorkshire Dales MTB – N Dales (N.Cotton).

Maps: OS Explorer OL30. Dales North Cycle Map (Harvey).

Routes on Web: www.goodmtb.co.uk/a52

Route Ideas

❶ A clockwise loop from Castle Bolton, W on trails to north of Newbiggin. Road N past Whitaside Moor. E along Apedale & back to the start.
Distance 24km.

❷ Trails W to Carperby then road E to Redmire. Roads & trails anti-clockwise around Redmire Scar. W along Apedale then S to the finish (or stay on the road N for a couple of km before turning left on to trail & follow back to Castle Bolton).
Distance 22-26km.

Extend the area: Reeth (south) Map to the N, Askrigg Map to the SW or Thoralby map to the S.

Rider: Muddy Bums Mountain Biking. © Tony Harker

Thoralby

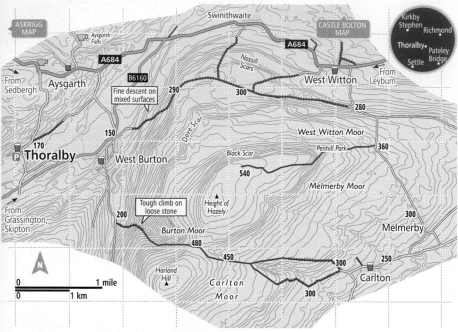

Situation: At the entrance to Bishopdale in the heart of the Yorkshire Dales National Park, just south of Askrigg. 8 miles west of Leyburn.

About the Base: Thoralby, a small village with a pub. Further Info: www.wensleydale.org/villages/thoralby.html.
Parking: Car park in the centre of the village. *Grid Ref: SE000867. **Post Code: DL8 3SU.***

Drive Times: Leeds 1hr30, Newcastle 1hr30, Carlisle 1hr40, Manchester 1hr50, Birmingham 3hr10.

Refreshments: The George Inn 01969 663256 in Thoralby. The Fox & Hounds 01969 663111 in West Burton, Foresters Arms in Carlton & Fox & Hounds 01969 623650 in West Witton.

Books: Yorkshire Dales MTB – N Dales (N.Cotton).

Maps: OS Explorer OL30. Dales North Cycle Map (Harvey).

Route Idea

From Thoralby, E to West Burton then an anticlockwise loop passing Carlton & Melmerby, skirting West Witton Moor before heading back to West Burton & Thoralby. Distance 22km.

Looking towards Settle Scar (Settle p127). Magnus Ross © Stephen Ross

Fremington Edge (Reeth p108). Rider: Angie Rawson. © Geoff Rawson

Marske

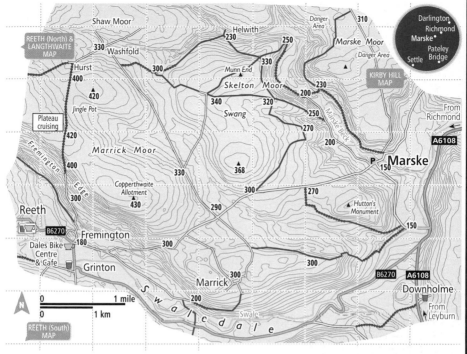

Situation: On Marske Beck in Swaledale, on the north east edge of the Yorkshire Dales National Park. 5 miles west of Richmond.

About the Base: Marske, a small village with easy access to the trails. **Parking:** Small laybynext to the bridge in Marske.
Grid Ref: NZ103004. Post Code: DL11 7NB.

Drive Times: Newcastle 1hr, Leeds 1hr20, Carlisle 1hr30, Manchester 2hr10, Birmingham 3hr.

Refreshments: No refreshments for the short routes around Markse. On the longer route, Dales Bike Centre & Café 01748 884908 in Fremington or The Bridge Inn 01748 884224 at Grinton.

Books: Yorkshire Dales MTB – N Dales (N.Cotton).

Maps: OS Explorer OL2. Dales North Cycle Map (Harvey).

Bike Shops: The Dales Bike Centre 01748 884 908 in Fremington.

Route Ideas

❶ From Marske, trails N along Marske Beck, up to & around Skelton Moor then return to Marske on the W side of Marske Beck. Distance 8km.

❷ From Marske, road S then trail W towards Marrick. On to Fremington then N to Hurst & Washfold. Choice of trails back to Marske. Distance about 18km.

Above Marske Beck. © Tony Harker

Kirkby Lonsdale

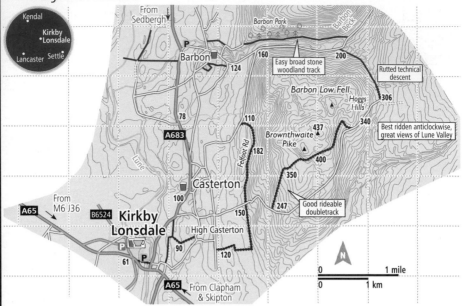

Barbon Park

From Sedbergh

Barbon Beck

Kendal
Kirkby Lonsdale
Lancaster Settle

Barbon 124

160 200

Easy broad stone woodland track

Rutted technical descent

Barbon Low Fell

Hoggs Hills 306

78

110

340

437 Brownthwaite Pike

Best ridden anticlockwise, great views of Lune Valley

A683

182

400

Fellfoot Rd

Lune

350

Casterton

100

247

Good rideable doubletrack

From M6 J36

A65

B6524

Kirkby Lonsdale

150

High Casterton

90

120

61 P.

A65 From Clapham & Skipton

0   1 mile
0   1 km

Situation: Just outside the western edge of the Yorkshire Dales, 5 miles from M6 Jct 36 and 12 miles south east of Kendal.

About the Base: Kirkby Lonsdale, a small town with pubs, cafés and accommodation.
Further Info: www.kirkbylonsdale.co.uk.

Parking: Long stay car park in Kirby Lonsdale or roadside at Devils Bridge south east of the town. Hodge Bridge layby near the turn off from the A683 into Barbon. *Grid Ref: Kirby Lonsdale SD609785, Devil's Bridge SD617782, Barbon SD623826.*

Drive Times: Carlisle 1hr10, Leeds 1hr40, Manchester 1hr30, Newcastle 2hr, Birmingham 2hr30.

Refreshments: At Barbon, The Barbon Inn 01524 276 233. Several pubs & cafés in Kirkby Lonsdale.

Books: Yorkshire Dales MTB - S Dales (N.Cotton).
Maps: OS Explorer OL2.
Dales West Cycle Map (Harvey).

Route Idea

From Kirkby Lonsdale, roads E to pick up the trail towards & past Brownthwaite Pike. Roads and trails north of Barbon Beck to Barbon. Road W along south of Barbon Beck then road S. Trails to High Casterton. Roads back to Kirkby Lonsdale. Distance 20km

Fells East of Casterton. © Simon Barnes www.bogtrotters.org

Ingleton

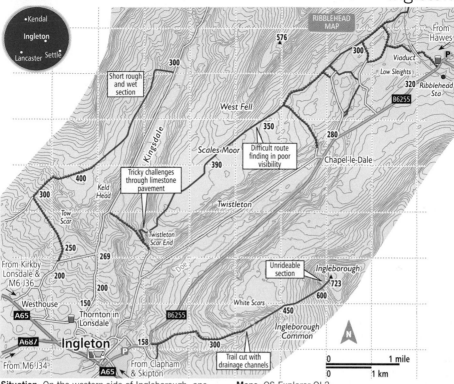

Situation: On the western side of Ingleborough, one of the famous 'Three Peaks', and the south west edge of the Yorkshire Dales National Park. 11 miles north west of Settle.

About the Base: Ingleton, a village with pubs and cafés. Further Info: www.ingleton.co.uk. **Parking:** Car park in the centre of Ingleton. *Grid Ref: SD696730. Post Code: LA6 3HG.*

Drive Times: Carlisle 1hr20, Leeds 1hr30, Manchester 1hr30,Carlisle 1hr40, Newcastle 2hr, Birmingham 2hr40.

Refreshments: At Ingleton, The Craven Heifer Inn 01524 242515, The Wheatsheaf 01524 2412785 & The Café at Inglesport 01524 241146. Marton Arms 01524 241281 in Thornton in Lonsdale & The Station Inn at Ribblehead 01524 241274.

Books: Yorkshire Dales MTB - S Dales (N.Cotton).

Maps: OS Explorer OL2.
Dales West Cycle Map (Harvey).

Bike Shops: Ingleton Mountain Bike Hire 01524 241422. Inglesport 01524 241146 in Ingleton has some bike repair stock.

Route Ideas

❶ From Ingleton, N to Twistleton Scar End then road along Kingsdale. Trails S past Tow Scar. Roads back to Ingleton. Distance 16km.

❷ From Ingleton, N to Ribblehead by roads & trails. Return to Ingleton by a long trail passing Scales Moor & Twistleton End Scar. Distance 22km. The above two routes can be combined. Distance 33km.

❸ An out & back up Ingleborough, involving quite a bit of pushing. Distance 10km.

Extend the area: Ribblehead Map to the N.

Twistleton Scar End. © Simon Barnes www.bogtrotters.org

Clapham

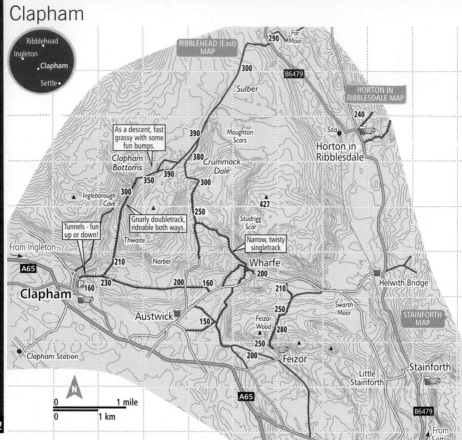

Situation: By Clapham Beck, on the south west edge of the Yorkshire Dales. 6 miles north west of Settle.

About the Base: Clapham, a village with a pub, cafés and group accommodation.
Further Info: www.claphamyorkshire.co.uk. **Parking**: Car park in the centre of the village close to the New Inn.
Grid Ref: SD745692. Post Code: LA2 8EA.

Drive Times: Leeds 1hr25, Manchester 1hr20, Carlisle 1hr20, Newcastle 2hr10, Birmingham 2hr40.

Trains: Clapham Railway Station, south of the village, on the Leeds-Morecambe line. Horton-in-Ribblesdale Station is on the Settle-Carlisle line.

Refreshments: At Clapham, The New Inn 01524 251203, Brook House Café 01524 251280 & Croft Café. Clapham Bunk at The Old Manor House 01524 251144 serves food. The Game Cock Inn 01524 251226 in Austwick, Elaine's Tearoom 01729 824114 in Feizor & The Craven Heifer 01729 850824 in Stainforth. Pubs & cafés in Horton-in-Ribblesdale.

Books: Yorkshire Dales MTB - S Dales (N.Cotton).

Maps: OS Explorer OL2. Yorkshire Dales British Mountain Map (Harvey).

Routes on Web: www.goodmtb.co.uk/a53

Bike Shops: In Settle, 3 Peaks Cycles 01729 824232. Off the Rails 01729 824419 (next to Settle station) for hire & guided rides.

Route Idea

From Clapham, E on trails to Austwick & on to Feizor & Wharfe. Climb NW to Crummack Dale. Trails SW to Clapham. Distance 18km. If arriving at Clapham Station this will add about 4km. From Horton-in-Ribblesdale Station, NW on the B6479 then trails over Sulber to join the main loop (described above). Return to the station as per outward start. Distance 31km.

Extend the area: Ribblehead East Map to the N.
Horton-in-Ribblesdale Map to the NE.

Above Wharfe. Rider: Magnus Ross

Ribblehead (north)

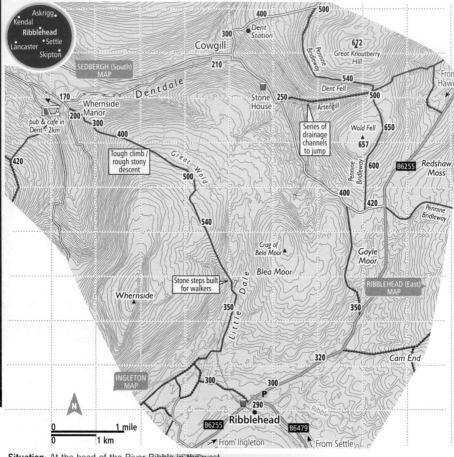

Situation: At the head of the River Ribble in the west Yorkshire Dales, 12 miles north of Settle.

About the Base: Ribblehead, a rural location with a pub and a railway station. **Parking:** Layby north of the junction of B6255 & B6479. *Grid Ref: SD766793.*

Drive Times: Leeds 1hr30, Manchester 1hr30, Carlisle 1hr30, Newcastle 2hr, Birmingham 2hr40.

Trains: Ribblehead Station, Settle-Carlisle line.

Refreshments: The Station Inn at Ribblehead. The Sportsmans Inn 015396 25282 south of Cowgill. Pub & café in Dent (outside map area: see top left of map).

Books: Yorkshire Dales MTB - S Dales (N.Cotton).
Maps: OS Explorer OL2. Yorkshire Dales British Mountain Map (Harvey).

Bike Shops: In Settle, 3 Peaks Cycles 01729 824232. Off the Rails 01729 824419 (next to Settle station) for hire & guided rides.

Route Idea

From Ribblehead, N to Dentdale via Little Dale & Great Wold. Roads past Cowgill & Dent Station. Trails S past Great Knoutberry Hill then W along Artengill to Stone House. Road & trail past Gayle Moor back to Ribblehead. Distance 32km.
Extend the area: Ribblehead East Map

Rider: The Tribe MBC. © Vic Cheetham

Ribblehead (east)

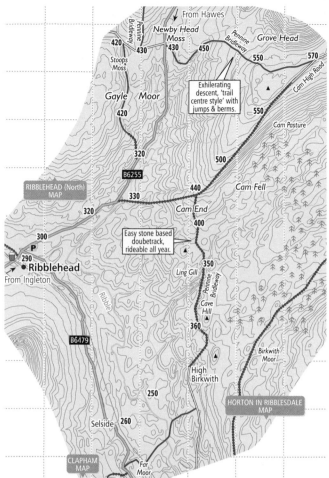

Map labels:
From Hawes
Pennine Bridleway
Newby Head Moss
Grove Head
420
430
430
450
550
570
Stoops Moss
Cam High Road
Gayle Moor
Exhilerating descent, 'trail centre style' with jumps & berms.
420
550
Cam Pasture
320
500
B6255
440
Cam Fell
RIBBLEHEAD (North) MAP
330
320
Cam End
400
300
P
290
Ribblehead
From Ingleton
350
Easy stone based doubetrack, rideable all year.
Ling Gill
Pennine Bridleway
Ribble
Cave Hill
360
B6479
Birkwith Moor
High Birkwith
250
HORTON IN RIBBLESDALE MAP
Selside 260
CLAPHAM MAP
Far Moor
From Settle

Situation: In the west of the Yorkshire Dales National Park, an area of moorland at the head of the River Ribble. 12 miles north of Settle.

About the Base: Ribblehead, a rural location with a pub and a railway station.

Parking: Layby north of the junction of B6255 & B6479. *Grid Ref: SD766793.*

Drive Times: Leeds 1hr30, Manchester 1hr30, Carlisle 1hr30, Newcastle 2hr, Birmingham 2hr40.

Trains: Ribblehead Railway Station is on the Settle-Carlisle line.

Refreshments: The Station Inn at Ribblehead.

Maps: OS Explorer OL2. Yorkshire Dales British Mountain Map (Harvey).

Bike Shops: In Settle, 3 Peaks Cycles 01729 824232, Off the Rails 01729 824419 (next to Settle station) for hire & guided rides.

Route Idea

From Ribblehead, S on the B6479 to Selside. Pennine Bridleway N to Newby Head Moss. Road W then trails S across Gayle Moor. SW on the B6255 back to Ribblehead. Distance 25km.

Cam High Road. Rider: Magnus Ross

Horton in Ribblesdale

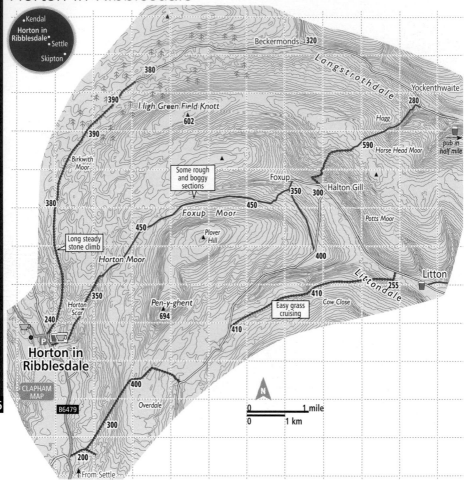

Kendal
Horton in Ribblesdale
Settle
Skipton

Beckermonds 320

Langstrothdale

Yockenthwaite 280

380

390

Hagg

High Green Field Knott
602

590
Horse Head Moor

pub in half mile

390

Birkwith Moor

Foxup

350 300 Halton Gill

380

450

Foxup Moor

Potts Moor

450

Plover Hill

400

Horton Moor

Littondale

Litton
255

350

Pen-y-ghent
694

410

Cow Close

Easy grass cruising

Horton Scar

240

410

Horton in Ribblesdale

P

CLAPHAM MAP

400

Overdale

N

B6479

0   1 mile
0   1 km

300

200
From Settle

Situation: On the banks of the River Ribble in Ribblesdale, west of Pen-y-Ghent. In the south west of the Yorkshire Dales National Park, 10 miles north of Settle.

About the Base: Horton-in-Ribblesdale, a village with two pubs and cafés. **Parking**: Car park next to the tourist information point as you enter the village from the south. *Grid Ref: SD807726.*
Post Code: BD24 0HF.

Drive Times: Leeds 1hr30, Manchester 1hr30, Carlisle 1hr30, Newcastle 2hr, Birmingham 2hr40.

Trains: Horton-in-Ribblesdale Railway Station is on the Settle-Carlisle line.

Refreshments: The Crown Inn 01729 860209, The Golden Lion 01729 860206 & the Pen-y-Ghent Café 01729 860333 in the village & Blindbeck Tea Room 01729 860396 just to the north. The Queens Arms 01756 770208 in Litton.

Books: Yorkshire Dales MTB - S Dales (N.Cotton).
Maps: OS Explorer OL2 & OL30. Yorkshire Dales British Mountain Map (Harvey).

Routes on Web: www.goodmtb.co.uk/a56

Bike Shops: In Settle, 3 Peaks Cycles 01729 824232. Off the Rails 01729 824419 (next to Settle station) for hire & guided rides.

Route Ideas

❶ N over Birkwith Moor to Beckermonds & Yockenthwaite then return via Foxup & Horton Moor. Distance 30km.

❷ S on the B6479 to pick up the trails & lanes NE to Foxup. Back via Foxup Moor. Distance 24km.

Views of Pen-y-Ghent. John Ingham

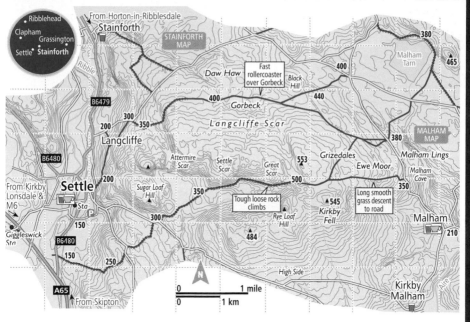

Situation: On the banks of the River Ribble in Ribblesdale, on the south west edge of the Yorkshire Dales National Park. 16 miles north west of Skipton.

About the Base: Settle, a small market town with plenty of pubs, cafés and accommodation. Further Info: www.settle.co.uk. **Parking**: Greenfoot car park east of the town centre & several other car parks in the centre of Settle. *Grid Ref: SD820633. Post Code: BD24 9RB.*

Drive Times: Leeds 1hr15, Manchester 1hr15, Carlisle 1hr30, Newcastle 2hr10, Birmingham 2hr40.

Trains: Settle Railway Station is on the Settle-Carlisle line. Giggleswick Station, a mile from Settle, is on the Leeds-Lancaster-Morecambe line.

Refreshments: A choice of pubs & cafés in Settle or The Craven Heifer 01729 850824 in Stainforth. The Victoria Inn at Kirkby Malham 01729 830499 or pubs & cafés in Malham.

Books: Yorkshire Dales MTB - S Dales (N.Cotton).

Maps: OS Explorer OL2. Yorkshire Dales British Mountain Map (Harvey).

Routes on Web: www.goodmtb.co.uk/a62a & /a62b

Bike Shops: 3 Peaks Cycles 01729 824232. Off the Rails (next to Settle station) for hire & guided rides 01729 824419.

Route Idea

From Settle, trails E towards Ewe Moor. W along trails to the north of Langcliffe Scar & back to Settle. Distance 22km.

The above can be extended by about 6km - when at Ewe Moor head N to Malham Tarn. W along trails to the north of Langliffe Scar && back to Settle.

Extend the area: Malham Map to the E. Stainforth Map to the N.

Great Scar. © Simon Barnes www.bogtrotters.org

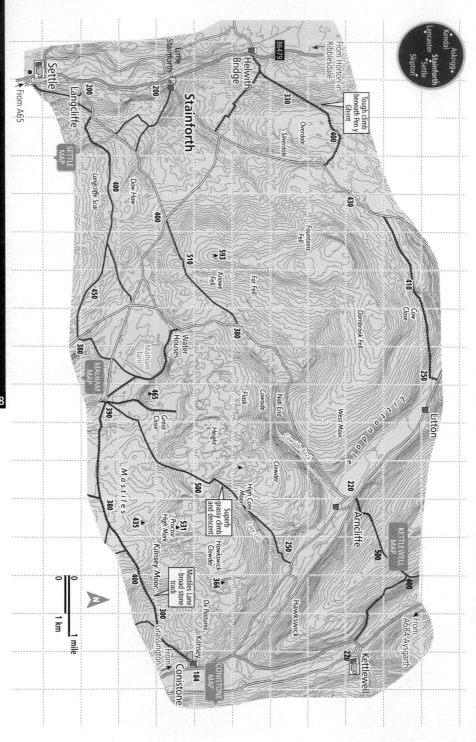

Settle

From A65

Langcliffe

Little Stainforth

Helwith Bridge

B6479

From Horton-in-Ribblesdale

Tough climb beneath Pen y Ghent

Stainforth

200

200

330

400

430

Langcliffe Scar

Daw How

400

400

510

450

380

593

Knowe Fell

Far Fell

Fountains Fell

380

Darnbrook Fell

410

Cow Close

250

Litton

Water Houses

Malham Tarm

465

390

Great Close

Height

Flask

Cowside

Nab End

West Moor

Cowside Beck

220

Arncliffe

250

Mastiles

500

435

531

Proctor High Mark

High Cote Moor

Clowder

Clowder

Superb grassy climb and descent

Cote Gill

Hawkswick Clowder

500

Kettlewell MAP

From A684 Aysgarth

400

Kilnsey Moor

380

400

300

Mastiles Lane - broad stone track

366

Hawkswick

Ox Pastures

Kilnsey

184

Conistone

From Grassington

CONISTONE MAP

220

Kettlewell

SETTLE MAP

MALHAM MAP

N

0   1 km
0   1 mile

Askrigg
Kendal • Lancaster • Stainforth • Settle
Skipton

Situation: In Ribblesdale, just north of Settle on the south west edge of the Yorkshire Dales National Park.

About the Base: Stainforth, a small village with a pub. Further Info:
www.yorkshiredales-stay.co.uk/tourist/Stainforth.html.

Parking: Car park as you enter the village from the B6499. *Grid Ref: SD820672. Post Code: BD24 9QB.*

Drive Times: Leeds 1hr20, Manchester 1hr15, Newcastle 2hr10, Birmingham 2hr40, Carlisle 2hr50.

Trains: Settle Railway Station is on the Settle-Carlisle line. Giggleswick Station, a mile south of Settle, is on the Leeds-Lancaster-Morecambe line.

Refreshments: The Craven Heifer 01729 850824 in Stainforth. Queens Arms Inn 01756 770208 in Litton, Falcon Inn 01756 770205 in Arncliffe & The Tennants Arms 01756 752301 in Kilnsey. Pubs & cafés in Kettlewell.

Books: Yorkshire Dales MTB - S Dales (N.Cotton).

Maps: OS Explorer OL2 & OL30. Yorkshire Dales British Mountain Map (Harvey).

Routes on Web: www.goodmtb.co.uk/a63

Bike Shops: 3 Peaks Cycles 01729 824232. Off the Rails (next to Settle station) for hire & guided rides 01729 824419.

Route Idea

From Stainforth, road & trails NE to Litton. On to Arncliffe & Hawkswick. SW across High Cote Moor then roads & trails W past Langcliffe Scar back to Stainforth.
Distance 45km.

The above loop can be extended by a few km at Hawkswick by carrying on to Kilnsey. Trail over Kilnsey Moor then back as above.

Extend the area: Malham Map to the SW. Settle Map to SW. Kettlewell Map to the N.

High Cote Moor. © Simon Barnes www.bogtrotters.org

© Simon Barnes www.bogtrotters.org

Malham

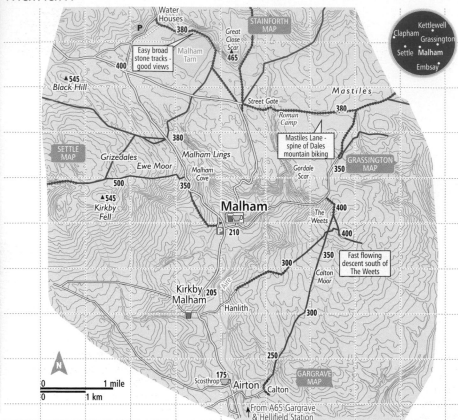

On the map: Water Houses, P, 380, Great Close Scar 465, STAINFORTH MAP, Kettlewell, Clapham, Grassington, Settle, Malham, Embsay, Easy broad stone tracks - good views, Malham Tarn, 400, 545 Black Hill, Mastiles, Street Gate, 380, 380, Roman Camp, Mastiles Lane - spine of Dales mountain biking, SETTLE MAP, Grizedales, Ewe Moor, Malham Lings, Malham Cove, Gordale Scar, 350, GRASSINGTON MAP, 500, 350, 545 Kirkby Fell, Malham, 210, P, The Weets, 400, 400, 300, 350, Calton Moor, Fast flowing descent south of The Weets, Kirkby Malham 205, Hanlith, 300, Ave, 300, 250, 175 Scosthrop, Airton, Calton, From A65 Gargrave & Hellifield Station, N, 0 1 mile, 0 1 km, 130

Situation: In the south west corner of the Yorkshire Dales National Park. 7 miles east of Settle.

About the Base: Malham, a small village with pubs, cafés and accommodation. Further Info: www.malhamdale.com. **Parking:** Car park next to the National Park Information Centre as you enter the village from the south. Also layby at Malham Tarn. **Grid Ref:** *Malham: SD900627, Malham Tarn: SD883672.* **Post Code:** *Malham: BD23 4DG, Malham Tarn: BD24 9PT.*

Drive Times: Leeds 1hr10, Manchester 1hr20, Carlisle 1hr50, Newcastle 2hr, Birmingham 2hr40.

Trains: Settle Railway Station is on the Settle-Carlisle line. Giggleswick Station, a mile from Settle, is on the Leeds-Lancaster-Morecambe line.

Refreshments: At Malham, The Buck Inn 01729 830317, The Lister Arms 01729 830330, The Old Barn Café 01729 830486, Beck Hall Café 01729 830332 & YHA café 01729 830321.The Town End Tea Room 01729 83090 in Airton & Victoria Inn 01729 830499 in Kirkby Malham.

Books: Yorkshire Dales MTB - S Dales (N.Cotton). **Maps**: OS Explorer OL2. Yorkshire Dales British Mountain Map (Harvey).

Bike Shops: In Settle, 3 Peaks Cycles 01729 824232. Off the Rails 01729 824419 (next to Settle station) for hire & guided rides.

Route Ideas

❶ From Malham, E on road. Trail S over Calton Moor to Airton. N on roads back to Malham. Distance 12km.

❷ From Malham, roads NW toWaterhouses. Trails E around Malham Tarn to Street Gate. E towards Mastiles. S to Airton. Roads back to Malham. Distance 24km. This route can be shortened by heading SW to Kirkby Malham on the trail just S of The Weets.

The Grizedales. © Simon Barnes www.bogtrotters.org

Kettlewell

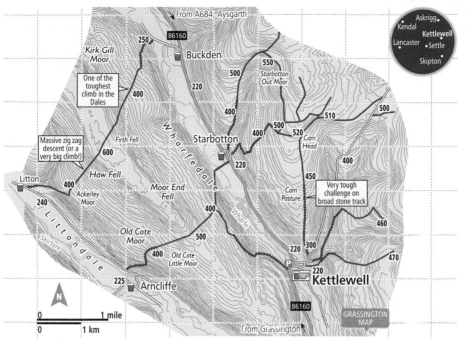

Situation: In Upper Wharfedale on the banks of the River Wharfe. North east of Settle and 15 miles north of Skipton in the heart of the Yorkshire Dales National Park.

About the Base: Kettlewell, a village with two pubs and a cafe. Further Info: www.kettlewell.info.
Parking: Car park as you cross the river on the B6160 before you enter the village. *Grid Ref: SD968722. Post Code: BD23 5QZ.*

Drive Times: Leeds 1hr10, Manchester 1hr30, Newcastle 1hr40, Carlisle 1hr50, Birmingham 2hr50.

Refreshments: At Kettlewell, The Racehorses Hotel 01756 760223, The Kings Head 01756 760242 & The Bluebell Inn 01756 760230; The Cottage Tea Room 01756 760405 & Zarinas Café 01756 761188. The Queens Arms Inn 01756 770208 in Litton, Fox & Hounds 01756 760269 in Starbotton, Falcon Inn 01756 770205 in Arncliffe & The Buck Inn 01756 760220 in Buckden.

Books: Yorkshire Dales MTB - S Dales (N.Cotton).

Maps: OS Explorer OL30. Yorkshire Dales British Mountain Map (Harvey).

Bike Shops: Outdoor Human 01756 751865, 7 miles away in Grassington.

Route Ideas

❶ From Kettlewell, N to Cam Head (300m of ascent). For a quick return head to Starbotton & road back to Kettlewell. Distance 9km.

❷ For a longer ride & one that adds about 650m of climbing to the total head N at Starbotton & pick up the trail W of Buckden to Littondale. At Arncliffe head over Old Cote Moor & link to the trail back to Kettlewell.

Extend the area: Grassington Map to the S.

© Simon Barnes www.bogtrotters.org

Conistone

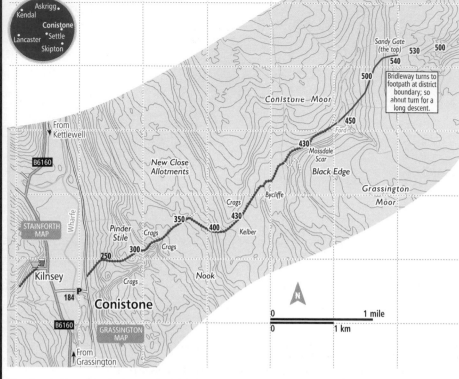

Askrigg
Kendal
Lancaster
Conistone
Settle
Skipton

From Kettlewell

B6160

New Close Allotments

STAINFORTH MAP

Wharfe

Pinder Stile
Crags
350
400
430
Kelber
Crags
Bycliffe

Conistone Moor

Mossdale Scar
430
450
Ford
500
Sandy Gate (the top) 530 500
540

Bridleway turns to footpath at district boundary; so about turn for a long descent.

Black Edge

Grassington Moor

Crags
300
250
Crags
Nook
Kilnsey
184 P
Conistone
B6160
GRASSINGTON MAP
From Grassington

N

0   1 mile
0   1 km

Situation: In Upper Wharfedale on the banks of the River Wharfe, in the Yorkshire Dales National Park. 11 miles north of Skipton.

About the Base: Conistone, a very small village with access straight onto the fells. No refreshments but cross the river to the pub in Kilnsey. Further Info: www.kilnseyandconistone.co.uk. **Parking:** Roadside parking on the wide section of road between the village & bridge. *Grid Ref: SD979674. Post Code: BD23 5HS.*

Drive Times: Leeds 1hr10, Manchester 1hr30, Newcastle 1hr50, Carlisle 2hr, Birmingham 2hr50.

Refreshments: The Tennants Arms 01756 752301 in Kilnsey & café at Kilnsey Park 01756 752150.

Books: Wharfedale Biking Guide (P.Hannon).

Maps: OS Explorer OL2. Yorkshire Dales British Mountain Map (Harvey).

Bike Shops: Outdoor Human 01756 751865, 3 miles away in Grassington.

Route Idea

An out & back ride. Climb from Conistone to Sandy Gate at the top of Conistone Moor. About face & descend back to Conistone. Distance 13km.

The ford on Conistone Moor. © Simon Barnes www.bogtrotters.org

Map labels:
- Askrigg
- Appletreewick
- Settle
- Skipton
- Leeds
- Grimwith Res
- From Pateley Bridge
- 390
- B6265
- Greenhow
- B6265
- 322
- Stump Cross
- 318 P
- Craven Moor
- Caverns
- Black Hill
- High Crag
- Redlish
- 350
- 300
- From Grassington
- Langerton Hill
- 278
- Appletreewick Pasture
- 300
- Trollers Gill
- 300
- Washburn
- Braithwaite Moor
- Burnsall
- Hartlington 230
- 144
- 145
- Kail Hill
- 300
- 400
- Fine climb / descent on broad stone track
- 430
- Pock Stones
- Skyreholme
- Great Pock Stones Moor
- 300
- Appletreewick 170
- 486 Simon's Seat
- 240
- 345
- 284
- Whit Moor
- Howgill
- Wharfe
- B6160
- 449 Carncliff Top
- Barden Fell
- N
- Bramley Head
- BOLTON ABBEY/EMBSAY MAP
- Barden Bridge
- From Bolton Abbey
- 0   1 mile
- 0   1 km

Situation: In Wharfedale on the banks of the River Wharfe, in the south east corner of the Yorkshire Dales National Park. 9 miles north of Skipton.

About the Base: Appletreewick, a small village with two pubs and a Mountain Bike Livery.
Parking: Limited parking in the centre of the village. Small layby opposite the Craven Cruck Barn. Seasonal parking in a field near the village centre. *Grid Ref: SE050601.*
Post Code: BD23 6DD.

Drive Times: Leeds 1hr, Manchester 1hr30, Newcastle 2hr, Carlisle 2hr10, Birmingham 2hr50.

Refreshments: At Appletreewick, The Craven Arms 01756 720 27 & The New Inn 01756 720252 (home to The Bike Livery). The Stump Cross Caverns Café 01756 752780 & The Miners Arms 01423 711227 in Greenhow.

Books: Wharfedale Biking Guide (P.Hannon).

Maps: OS Explorer OL2. Dales South and Dales East Cycle Maps (Harvey).

Bike Shops: The Bike Livery 01756 720 319 for guided rides, bike storage & tools for repairs.

133

Route Ideas

❶ From Appletreewick, head NE via Skyreholme to the B6265, W on to trails towards Hartington & back to start. Distance 15km.

❷ As above to the B6265, then clockwise loop via Stump Cross, Greenhow, Pock Stones Moor & back to start.
Distance 25km.

Grassington / Gargrave

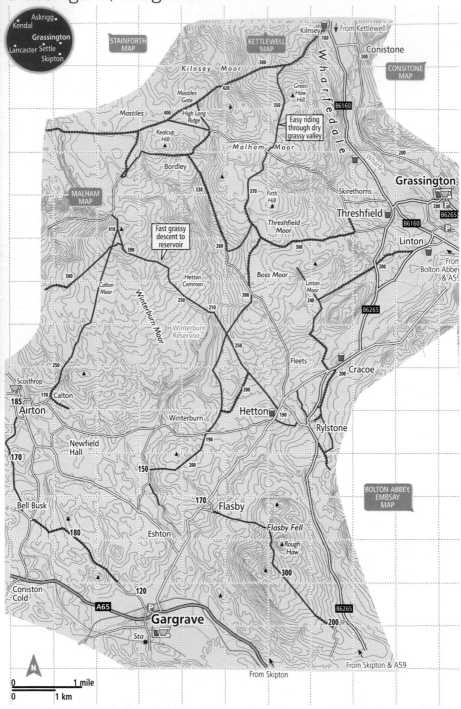

Askrigg
Kendal
Grassington
Lancaster Settle
Skipton

STAINFORTH MAP

KETTLEWELL MAP

Kilnsey   From Kettlewell
180
Conistone
200

Kilnsey Moor
300

CONSITONE MAP

Mastiles Gate
420
Green Haw Hill
350
B6160

Mastiles   400   High Long Ridge

Kealcup Hill

Malham Moor
200

Easy riding through dry grassy valley

Wharfe   200

Bordley

Grassington
200   P
B6265
Skirethorns

MALHAM MAP
330   370   Firth Hill
Threshfield
B6160   P

Fast grassy descent to reservoir
410   260
Threshfield Moor
Linton

390   300   Boss Moor
200
From Bolton Abbey & A59

300
Calton Moor   *Hetton Common*   250   210
Linton Moor   240
B6265

Winterburn Moor
Winterburn Reservoir
250

Fleets
Cracoe
200

250   Scosthrop
170   Calton
185
Airton
200

Winterburn   **Hetton**   190
Rylstone

Newfield Hall   190
150   200

Bell Busk
180   Eshton   170   **Flasby**
Flasby Fell
Rough Haw
300

Coniston Cold   120
A65   P
Gargrave
200   B6265
Sta

BOLTON ABBEY, EMBSAY MAP

From Skipton & A59
From Skipton

0 ___ 1 mile
0 ___ 1 km

N

Situation: In the south of the Yorkshire Dales National Park. Grassington is on the banks of the River Wharfe in Upper Wharfedale, north of Skipton. Gargrave is on the River Aire, 4 miles north west of Skipton.

About the Base: Grassington, a small town with cafés, pubs and accommodation or Gargrave, a large village with pubs and cafés.
Further Info: www.grassington.uk.com & www.gargrave.org.uk.

Parking: Car parks in Grassington at the National Park Information Centre or just south of the river. Car Park in Gargrave on North Street. *Grid Ref: Grassington SE002637, Gargrave SD932543.* **Post Code:** *Grassington BD23 5DG, Gargrave BD23 3RL.*

Drive Times: Leeds 1hr, Manchester 1hr30, Carlisle 2hr, Newcastle 2hr. Birmingham 2hr40.

Trains: Gargrave Railway Station is on the Leeds-Morecambe line.

Refreshments: Many cafés & pubs in Grassington & Gargrave. The Town End Farm Shop & Café in Airton, Angel Inn 01756 730263 in Hetton, Devonshire Arms 01756 730237 in Cracoe, Fountaine Inn 01756 752210 in Linton, Old Hall Inn 01756 752441 in Threshfield & The Tennants Arms 01756 752301 in Kilnsey.

Books: Yorkshire Dales MTB - S Dales (N.Cotton). Wharfedale Biking Guide (P.Hannon).

Maps: OS Explorer OL2. Yorkshire Dales British Mountain Map (Harvey).

Routes on Web: www.goodmtb.co.uk/a54

Bike Shops: Outdoor Human 01756 751865 in Grassington. In Skipton, Dave Ferguson Cycles 01756 795367.

Route Ideas

❶ From Grassington, W to Threshfield Moor. N across Malham Moor & past Green Haw Hill. Trails SW to Mastilles Gate. Trails across Bordley to road. S to Winterburn Reservoir & on to Hetton. Road & trails N to Grassington. Distance 32km. There are a good selection of trails & roads to shorten as required.

❷ From Gargrave, NW to Airton. N past Calton Moor, on to Mastilles, Malham Moor & S to Winterburn Reservoir. SE to Hetton. Roads back to Gargrave. Distance 30km (numerous trails & roads to shorten as required).

Extend the Area: Malham Map to the W. Kettlewell Map to the N. Bolton Abbey/Embsay Map to the SE.

Threshfield Moor. © Simon Barnes www.bogtrotters.org

Bolton Abbey / Embsay

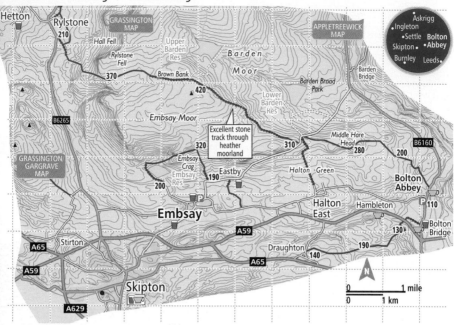

Situation: On the southern edge of the Yorkshire Dales National Park, Embsay is 2 miles north west of Skipton. Bolton Abbey, a further 4 miles away, is on the banks of the River Wharfe.

About the Base: Bolton Abbey, a country estate with tea rooms or Embsay, a small village with a pub. Further Info: www.boltonabbey.com. **Parking:** Car park south of Bolton Abbey on the B6160. Car park in the centre of Embsay village. *Grid Ref: Bolton Abbey SE070539, Embsay SE009538.*
Post Code: Bolton Abbey BD23 6EY, Embsay BD23 6RE.

Drive Times: Leeds 45mins, Manchester 1hr20, Carlisle 2hr, Newcastle 2hr, Birmingham 2hr40.

Trains: Skipton Railway Station is on the Airedale line.

Refreshments: At Embsay, The Elmtree Inn 01756 790717 & Cavendish Arms 01756 793980. The Mason Arms 01756 792754 in Eastby, Hambleton Tea Rooms 01756 711256 & Devonshire Arms Hotel at Bolton Bridge. Abbey Tea Rooms 0175671 0797

at Bolton Abbey, the Angel Inn in Hetton 01756 730263 or pubs & cafés in Skipton.

Books: Yorkshire Dales MTB - S Dales (N.Cotton).

Maps: OS Explorer OL2. Yorkshire Dales British Mountain Map (Harvey).

Routes on Web: www.goodmtb.co.uk/a51a & /a51b

Bike Shops: Dave Ferguson Cycles 01756 795367 in Skipton.

Route Idea

Two loops forming a figure of 8;can be done as two individual rides (9km & 21km). From Bolton Abbey, W to Halton East then N over Halton Green. Trail past Brown Bank to Rylstone & road S towards Skipton. Turn left to Embsay before reaching Skipton. Road past Eastby before a final trail over Middle Hare Head & back to Bolton Abbey. Distance 30km.

Middle Hare Head. © Simon Barnes www.bogtrotters.org

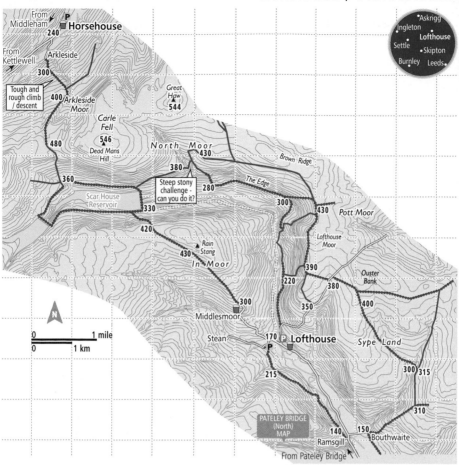

Situation: In the east of the Yorkshire Dales, Horsehouse is within the Yorkshire Dales National Park. Lofthouse, on the banks of the River Nid, is in the Nidderdale Area of Oustanding Natural Beauty, 7 miles north of Pateley Bridge.

About the Base: Horsehouse or Lofthouse, both small villages with a pub. Further Info: www.nidderdale. co.uk. **Parking**: Car park in the centre of Lofthouse & a layby just to the west. In Horsehouse, small area of roadside parking to the north of the village. *Grid Ref: Lofthouse SE101734, Horsehouse SE047813. Post Code: Lofthouse, HG3 5RZ, Horsehouse DL8 4TT.*

Drive Times: Horsehouse: Leeds 1hr30, Newcastle 1hr40, Manchester 1hr50,Carlisle 2hr, Birmingham 3hr15.
Lofthouse: Leeds 1hr, Manchester 1hr50, Newcastle 2hr, Carlisle 2hr20, Birmingham 3hr.

Refreshments: At Horsehouse, The Thwaite Arms 01969 640206. The Crown Hotel 01423 755204 in Middlesmoor or The Crown Hotel 01423 755206 in Lofthouse.

Books: Yorkshire Dales MTB - S Dales (N.Cotton).
Maps: OS Explorer OL30. Dales East Cycle Map (Harvey).

Routes on Web: www.goodmtb.co.uk/a58

Route Ideas

❶ From Lofthouse, head to Scar House Reservoir via In Moor. The loop then continues via North Moor, Pott Moor, Sype Land & Ramsgill. Distance 24km.

❷ From Horsehouse, a tough out & back to Scar House Reservoir. Distance 17km.

Woo Gill. © Simon Barnes www.bogtrotters.org

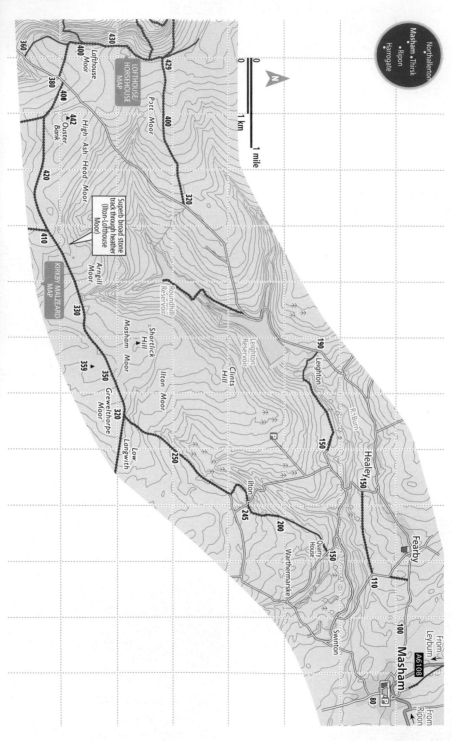

Lofthouse Moor

LOFTHOUSE HORSEHOUSE MAP

High Ash Head Moor

442 ▲ Ouster Bank

Pott Moor

430

429

400

400

360

380

400

420

410

Superb broad stone track through heather (Ilton-Lofthouse Moor)

320

Arngill Moor

KIRKBY MALZEARD MAP

330

Masham Moor

Shortlick Hill

359 ▲

350

Grewelthorpe Moor

320

Low Langwith

250

Roundhill Reservoir

Leighton Reservoir

Ilton Moor

Clints Hill

Leighton

190

150

Healey 150

R. Burn

P

Ilton

245

200

Warthermarske

Quarry House

150

110

Fearby

Swinton

100

Masham

A6108

80

From Leyburn

From Ripon

Northallerton

Masham ● Thirsk

● Ripon

Harrogate

0   1 km

0   1 mile

Situation: In Wensleydale, east of the Yorkshire Dales National Park, on the western banks of the River Ure. 10 miles north west of Ripon.

About the Base: Masham, a small market town with several pubs, cafés and accommodation. Further Info: www.visitmasham.com. **Parking:** In the market place at the centre of Masham.
Grid Ref: SE225807. Post Code: HG4 4DZ.

Drive Times: Leeds 1hr, Newcastle 1hr 20, Carlisle 1hr50, Manchester 1hr50, Birmingham 2hr40.

Refreshments: At the town centre, The White Bear 01765 689319, The Bay Horse Inn 01765 689236 & The Bruce Arms 01765 689372. The Black Swan 01765 689372 & The Kings Head Inn 01765 689 448 in Fearby. Several cafés in the centre of Masham.

Books: Yorkshire Dales MTB - S Dales (N.Cotton).

Maps: Dales East Cycle Map (Harvey).

Bike Shops: Blaze A Trail Cycles 01677 427831, 6 miles away in Bedale.

Route Ideas

❶ From Masham, E on road, before Fearby head S on trail then mixture of road & trails to arrive at Leighton. Road SW to W of Ouster Bank, trails to Ilton & Quarry House. Road to Swinton & back to Masham. Distance 31km.

❷ Road towards Fearby then on to Healey by trails & road. Road to Leighton. Trail E then road to Ilton. Trail to Quarry House & road back to Masham. Distance 17km.

Extend the area: Lofthouse/Horsehouse Map to the W. Kirkby Malzeard Map to the S.

Around Masham © Tony Harker

Blubberhouses

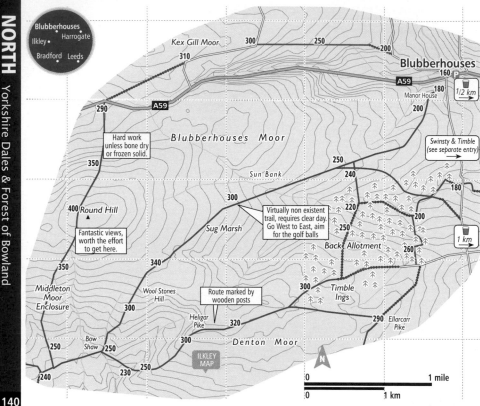

Blubberhouses
Ilkley • Harrogate
Bradford Leeds

Kex Gill Moor 300 250 200
310

Blubberhouses 160 P
A59 180
Manor House 1/2 km
290 A59 200

Hard work unless bone dry or frozen solid.

Blubberhouses Moor

Swinsty & Timble (see separate entry)
250 180
350 Sun Bank 240

400 Round Hill
Fantastic views, worth the effort to get here.

300
Sug Marsh

Virtually non existent trail, requires clear day. Go West to East, aim for the golf balls

220
250 200

Back Allotment 260

1 km

350 340
Middleton Moor Enclosure
Wool Stones Hill
300

Route marked by wooden posts

300 Timble Ings

250 Bow Shaw 250
Heligar Pike 320
290 Ellarcarr Pike

300 Denton Moor

N

240 230 250

ILKLEY MAP

0 1 mile
0 1 km

Situation: In the Washburn Valley, at the south eastern edge of the Yorkshire Dales National Park in North Yorkshire. 10 miles west fo Harrogate.

About the Base: Blubberhouses, a small village with easy access to the trails. **Parking**: Car park in the centre of Blubberhouses. *Grid Ref: Blubberhouses SE168553. Post Code: Blubberhouses LS21 2NY.*

Drive Times: Leeds 40mins, Manchester 1hr30, Newcastle 1hr50, Carlisle 2hr10, Birmingham 2hr40.

Refreshments: No refreshments in Blubberhouses. Try the Hopper Lane Hotel 01943 880232 or the The Timble Inn 01943 880530 east of the map.

Books: MTB Guide S Pennines of W Yorks & Lancs (S.Hall).

Maps: OS Explorer 297. Dales East Cycle Map (Harvey).

Bike Shops: Chevin Cycles 01943 462773, 7 miles away in Otley & JD Cycles 01943 816101, 8 miles away in Ilkley.

Route Idea

From Blubberhouses, W to Kex Gill Moor then on to Round Hill, Middleton Moor Enclosure & Bow Shaw. NE across Sug Marsh & back to Blubberhouses. Distance 15km.

Extend the area: Ilkley Map to the S. The Swinsty & Timble Trails to the E.

Blubberhouses Moor. Rider:Andy Hind. © Blackshaw Outdoor

Kirkby Malzeard

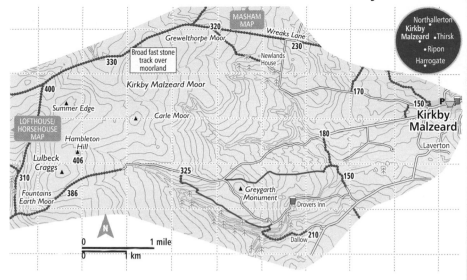

Situation: In the Nidderdale Area of Outstanding Natural Beauty, east of the Yorkshire Dales National Park. 6 miles north west of Ripon.

About the Base: Kirkby Malzeard, a village with a pub and tea rooms. **Parking:** Roadside in the centre of the village. **Grid Ref:** *SE234743.* **Post Code:** *HG4 3RP.*

Drive Times: Leeds 1hr, Newcastle 1hr30, Manchester 1hr50, Carlisle 2hr, Birmingham 2hr40.

Refreshments: At Kirkby Malzeard, Henry Jenkins Inn 01765 658557 & Roselea Tea Rooms 01765 658693. The Drovers Inn 01765 658510 in Dallowgill.

Books: Yorkshire Dales MTB - S Dales (N.Cotton).

Maps: OS Explorer 298. Dales East Cycle Map (Harvey).

Bike Shops: Monglu 01765 601106 in Ripon.

Route Idea

W out of Kirkby Malzeard on road to Wreaks Lane. Trail W over Grewelthorpe Moor, S to Fountains Earth Moor then E to road. Road past Drovers Inn then trails N to join road back to start. Distance 30km.

Extend the area: Masham Map to the N. LoftHouse/Horsehouse Map to the W.

© Nick Cotton

Pateley Bridge (north)

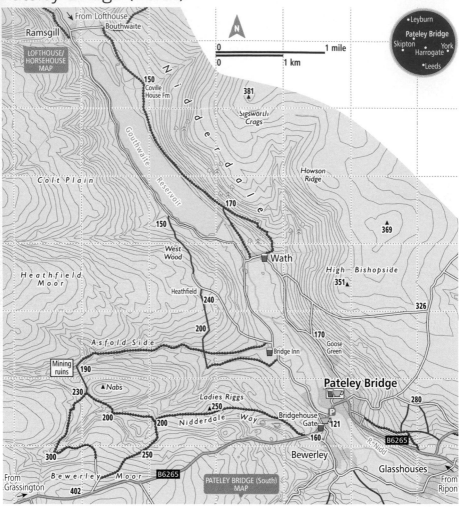

From Lofthouse
Bouthwaite
Ramsgill

LOFTHOUSE/
HORSEHOUSE
MAP

N

0 ──────── 1 mile
0 ──────── 1 km

• Leyburn
Pateley Bridge
Skipton ● ● York
Harrogate ●
● Leeds

150
Coville
House Fm

381 ▲

Sigsworth
Crags

Nidderdale

Gouthwaite Reservoir

Howson
Ridge

Colt Plain

170

369 ▲

150

West
Wood

■ Wath

High Bishopside
351 ▲

Heathfield
Moor

Heathfield

240

326

200

170

Goose
Green

■ Bridge Inn

Asfold Side

Mining
ruins 190

▲ Nabs

230

200 200

Ladies Riggs
▲ 250

Nidderdale Way

Pateley Bridge

280

Bridgehouse
Gate 121

P

300

250

B6265

160

Bewerley

B6265 R. Nidd

Glasshouses

From
Grassington

402

Bewerley Moor

PATELEY BRIDGE (South)
MAP

From
Ripon

Situation: In Nidderdale, on the banks of the River Nidd and south east of the Yorkshire Dales National Park. 14 miles north west of Harrogate.

About the Base: Pateley Bridge, a small market town with several pubs and cafés. **Parking**: Car park across the river, west of the town centre.
Grid Ref: SE152650. Post Code: HG3 5HW.

Drive Times: Leeds 50mins, Manchester 1hr40, Newcastle 1hr40, Carlisle 2hr15, Birmingham 2hr50.

Refreshments: At the town centre, The Crown Inn 01423 712455, Wildings Tea Room 01423 711152 & The Apothecary's House 01423 711767 cafe. In Bridgehouse Gate, The Royal Oak 01423 711571 & The Lemon Meringue Tea Rooms 01423 711013. The Bridge Inn 01423 711484 & The Sportsmans Arms 01423 711306 in Wath.

Maps: OS Explorer 298. Dales East Cycle Map (Harvey).

Routes on Web: www.goodmtb.co.uk/a48

Bike Shops: Stif Activities 01423 780738, 3 miles away in Summerbridge.

Route Idea

Head N to Wath then anticlockwise around reservoir. Before reaching Bridge Inn head W to Ashfold Side then along Nidderdale Way & back to start. Distance 21km.

Extend the area: Lofthouse/Horsehoue Map to N or Pateley Bridge South Map to S.

© Nick Cotton

Pateley Bridge (south)

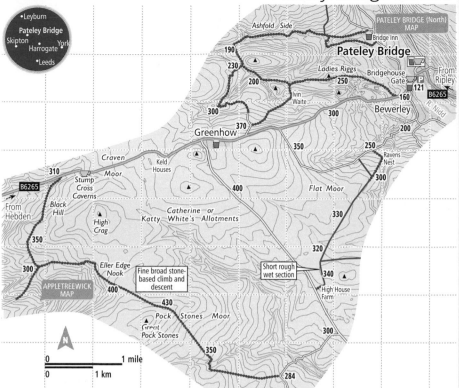

Situation: South east of the Yorkshire Dales National Park, on the banks of the River Nidd in Nidderdale. 14 miles north west of Harrogate.

About the Base: Pateley Bridge, a small market town with several pubs and cafés. **Parking:** Car park across the river, west of the town centre. *Grid Ref: SE152650. Post Code: HG3 5HW.*

Drive Times: Leeds 50mins, Manchester 1hr40, Newcastle 1hr40, Carlisle 2hr15, Birmingham 2hr50.

Refreshments: At the town centre, The Crown Inn 01423 712455, Wildings Tea room 01423 711152 & The Apothecary's House 01423 711767 cafe. In Bridgehouse Gate, The Royal Oak 01423 711571 & The Lemon Meringue Tea Rooms 01423 711013. Stump Cross Caverns Tea Rooms 01756 752780 & The Miners Arms 01423 711227 in Greenhow.

Books: Yorkshire Dales MTB - S Dales (N.Cotton).

Maps: OS Explorer 298. Dales East Cycle Map (Harvey).

Bike Shops: Stif Activities 01423 780738, 3 miles away in Summerbridge.

Route Ideas

❶ From Pateley Bridge, road N past Bridge Inn, trail to Ashold Side, on to Ivin Waite Farm then to B6265. Pass Stump Cross Caverns then trails around Black Hill & Pock Stones Moor. Road to High House Farm then trail across Flat Moor & road to finish. Distance 28km.

❷ As above but at Greenhow take road straight to High House Farm. Distance 18km.

Extend the area: Pateley Bridge North Map to N or Appletreewick Map to SW.

© Nick Cotton

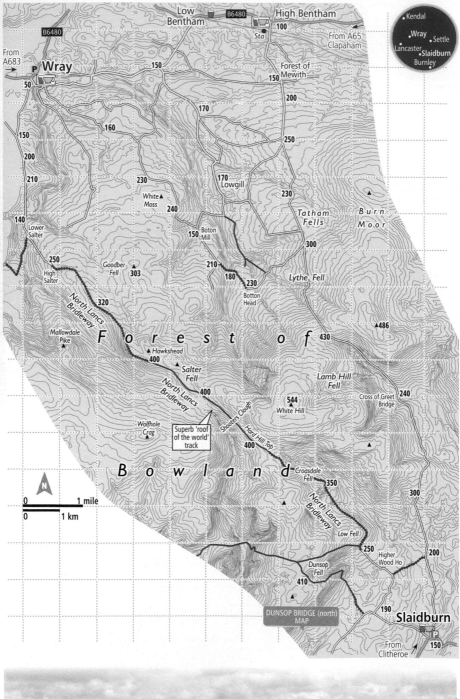

Low Bentham

High Bentham

B6480

B6480

Sta

100

From A65 Clapaham

Forest of Mewith

Wray

P

From A683

50

150

150

150

200

210

140

Lower Salter

250

High Salter

320

Mallowdale Pike

North Lancs Bridleway

160

170

150

White Moss

Goodber Fell

303

Boton Mill

150

210

180

230

Botton Head

F o r e s t   o f

Hawkshead

400

Salter Fell

North Lancs Bridleway

400

Wolfhole Crag

Superb 'roof of the world' track

Shooters Clough

230

170

Lowgill

250

230

Tatham Fells

B u r n   M o o r

300

Lythe Fell

430

▲486

Lamb Hill Fell

Cross of Greet Bridge

240

544

White Hill

Hard Hill Top

400

B o w l a n d

Croasdale Fell

350

North Lancs Bridleway

Low Fell

250

Higher Wood Ho

200

300

Dunsop Fell

410

DUNSOP BRIDGE (north) MAP

190

Slaidburn

P

150

From Clitheroe

N

0   1 mile

0   1 km

Kendal

Wray

Settle

Lancaster

Slaidburn

Burnley

Situation: In he Forest of Bowland, west of Lancaster in Lancashire. Wray is in the north, Slaidburn the south east, 9 miles north of Clitheroe.

About the Base: Wray or Slaidburn, both small villages with pubs and a café. **Parking:** Car park at Slaidburn, east of the bridge over the River Hodder. Roadside parking in the centre of the village at Wray. *Grid Ref: Slaidburn SD713523, Wray SD598672. Post Code: Slaidburn, BB7 3ES, Wray LA2 8QN.*

Drive Times: Carlisle 1hr20, Manchester 1hr20, Leeds 1hr40, Newcastle 2hr20, Birmingham 2hr20.

Trains: Bentham Railway Station, 5 miles east of Wray at High Bentham, is on the Leeds-Morecambe line.

Refreshments: At Wray, The George & Dragon 015242 21403, The Inn at Wray 015242 21722 & Bridge House Farm café 01524 222496. In Slaidburn, Riverbank Tearooms 01200 446398 & Hark to Bounty Pub 01200 446246. If arriving by train at High Bentham, The Nose Bag Coffee Shop 01524 263150 or Horse & Farrier 015242 61381.

Books: The Lancashire Bridleway (J.Sparks).

Maps: OS Explorer OL41. Forest of Bowland Map (Harvey).

Routes on Web: www.goodmtb.co.uk/a64 & /a64b

Bike Shops: Pedal Power 01200 422066 in Clitheroe for hire, parts & repairs.

Route Idea

From Slaidburn, NW on the North Lancs Bridleway & roads to Wray. Pick your choice of roads to return to Slaidburn. Distance 50km.

Alternatively ride anticlockwise to do the road section first.

If arriving by train at High Bentham Station this will add about 7km to the route.

North Lancs Bridleway, near High Salter looking south east © www.forestofbowlandimages.com / Graham Cooper

Dunsop Bridge (north)

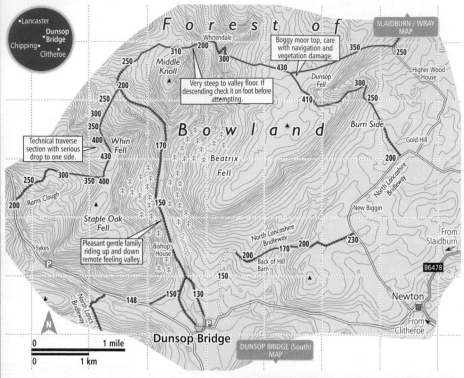

- Lancaster
- Dunsop Bridge
- Chipping
- Clitheroe

SLAIDBURN / WRAY MAP

F o r e s t o f

Whitendale

Boggy moor top, care with navigation and vegetation damage.

Middle Knoll

310
200
250
300
350
250

Higher Wood House

430

Dunsop Fell

300

Very steep to valley floor. If descending check it on foot before attempting.

200

410

250

B o w l a n d

300

350

Burn Side

Gold Hill

Technical traverse section with serious drop to one side.

400

Whin Fell

170

200

430

Beatrix Fell

North Lancashire Bridleway

250
300
350
400

New Biggin

200

Rams Clough

150

200

Staple Oak Fell

North Lancashire Bridleway

230

From Slaidburn

Sykes

Pleasant gentle family riding up and down remote feeling valley.

Bishop's House

North Lancashire Bridleway

170
200

B6478

200

Back of Hill Barn

P

150

148

150

130

P

Newton

From Clitheroe

N

0   1 mile

0   1 km

Dunsop Bridge

DUNSOP BRIDGE (South) MAP

Situation: At the confluence of the River Dunsop and the River Hodder, in the Forest of Bowland in Lancashire. 9 miles north west of Clitheroe.

About the Base: Dunsop Bridge, a small village with a café and easy access to the trails. **Parking:** Car parks east of the river at Dunsop Bridge & next to the information point at Sykes. *Grid Ref: Dunsop Bridge SD660501, Sykes SD632511,*

Post Code: Dunsop Bridge BB7 3AZ.

Drive Times: Manchester 1hr10, Leeds 1hr30, Sheffield 2hr, Birmingham 2hr20, Newcastle 2hr40.

Refreshments: At Dunsop Bridge, Puddleducks Café & Post Office 01200 422066. The Parkers Arms 01200 446236 at Newton.

Books: MTB Guide S Pennines of W Yorks & Lancs (S.Hall). **Maps**: OS Explorer OL41. Forest of Bowland Map (Harvey).

Bike Shops: Pedal Power 01200 422066 in Clitheroe for hire, parts & repairs.

Route Ideas

❶ From Dunsop Bridge, road NW to Rams Clough. Trails NE over Whinfell. S along the River Dunsop back to Dunsop Bridge. Distance 12km.

❷ As above to Whinfell then trails past Middle Knoll, Whitendale & Dunsop Fell. Road past New Biggin & North Lancashire Bridleway back to Dunsop Bridge. Distance 20km.

Extend the area: Dunsop Bridge South Map.

This area is close to Gisburn Trail Centre (p150).

© Blackshaw Outdoor

Dunsop Bridge (south) / Chipping

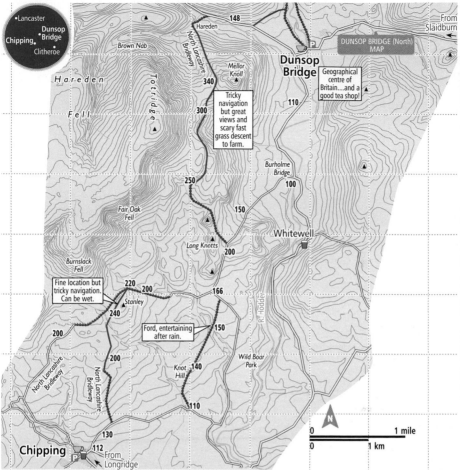

Map labels:
- •Lancaster
- Dunsop Bridge
- Chipping•
- •Clitheroe
- Hareden
- Brown Nab
- 148
- From Slaidburn
- DUNSOP BRIDGE (North) MAP
- P
- Mellor Knoll
- Dunsop Bridge
- Geographical centre of Britain....and a good tea shop!
- Hareden Fell
- Totridge
- 340
- 300
- Tricky navigation but great views and scary fast grass descent to farm.
- 110
- Fair Oak Fell
- 250
- Burnslack Fell
- Burholme Bridge
- 100
- 150
- Whitewell
- Long Knotts
- 200
- Fine location but tricky navigation. Can be wet.
- 220
- 200
- Stanley
- 240
- 166
- R. Hodder
- Ford, entertaining after rain.
- 150
- 200
- 200
- Knot Hill
- 140
- Wild Boar Park
- North Lancashire Bridleway
- 110
- 130
- Chipping
- 112
- From Longridge
- 0   1 mile
- 0   1 km
- N
- 147

Situation: In the Forest of Bowland, Dunsop Bridge stands at the confluence of the River Dunsop and the River Hodder. Chipping, 6 miles to the south west is on the edge of the Trough of Bowland in the Ribble Valley. Both 9 miles north west of Clitheroe.

About the Base: Dunsop Bridge, a small village with a café and easy access to the trails or Chipping, a village with pubs and a café. Further Info: www.chippingvillage.co.uk. **Parking:** Car parks at Dunsop Bridge, east of the river, & in the centre of Chipping village. **Grid Ref:** *Dunsop Bridge SD660501, Chipping SD621432.* **Post Code:** *Dunsop Bridge BB7 3AZ, Chipping PR3 2QL.*

Drive Times: Manchester 1hr10, Leeds 1hr30, Sheffield 2hr, Birmingham 2hr20, Newcastle 2hr40.

Refreshments: At Dunsop Bridge, Puddleducks Café & Post Office 01200 422066. The Inn at Whitewell 01200 448222. The Sun Inn 01995 61206, Tillotsons Arms 01995 61568 & Cobbled Corner Café 01995 61551 in Chipping.

Books: MTB Guide S Pennines of W Yorks & Lancs (S.Hall). **Maps**: OS Explorer OL41. Forest of Bowland Map (Harvey).

Routes on Web: www.goodmtb.co.uk/a47

Bike Shops: Pedal Power 01200 422066 in Clitheroe for hire, parts & repairs.

Route Ideas

❶ Road S from Dunsop Bridge towards Burholme Bridge then Long Knotts. Trail N then road back to start. Distance 10km.

❷ Start as above but continue past Long Knotts to take trail S past Knot Hill. W on road then either N on trail past Stanley or into Chipping & loop to Stanley from the SW. On to Long Knotts & trail N past Mellor Knoll & road back. Distance 22km.

❸ The above route can be started from Chipping. For a short route from Chipping head to Stanley then back to start via trail past Knott Hill. Distance 10km.

© Blackshaw Outdoor

Ribchester

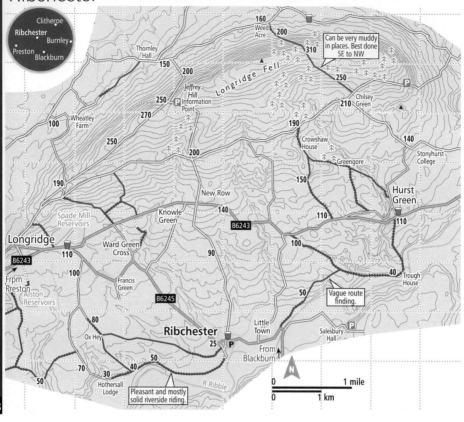

Clitheroe
Ribchester • Burnley •
Preston • Blackburn

Thornley Hall
Longridge Fell
160 Weed Acre 200
310
Can be very muddy in places. Best done SE to NW
150 200 250
Jeffrey Hill Information Point 250 270
210 Chilsey Green
Wheatley Farm 100
190
250 200
Crowshaw House 140
Stonyhurst College
Greengore
150
New Row
Spade Mill Reservoirs
Knowle Green 140
B6243 110
Hurst Green 110
Longridge
Ward Green Cross 110
90
100
B6243
Frpm Preston 100
Francis Green
B6245
40 Trough House
50 Vague route finding.
Ox Hey 80
Ribchester 25 P
Little Town
Salesbury Hall P
From Blackburn
70 30 40 50
Hothersall Lodge
Pleasant and mostly solid riverside riding.
R Ribble
50

0 ——— 1 mile
0 ——— 1 km

Situation: On the banks of the River Ribble at the foot of Longridge Fell in Lancashire. 7 miles north of Blackburn and 9 miles south west of Clitheroe.

About the Base: Ribchester, a village with pubs, tea rooms and accommodation. **Parking:** In the centre of the village. Also car parks at Salesbury Hall, Chilsey Green & next to the information point at Jeffrey Hill. *Grid Ref: Ribchester SD649353, Salesbury Hall SD676356, Chilsey Green SD680407, Jeffrey Hill SD639401. Post Code: Ribchester PR3 3YP.*

Drive Times: Manchester 1hr, Leeds 1hr20, Sheffield 1hr50, Birmingham 2hr, Newcastle 2hr50.

Trains: Ramsgreave & Wilpshire Railway Station, 4 miles away, is on the Manchester-Blackburn-Carlisle line.

Refreshments: At Ribchester, The White Bull 01254 878303, The Black Bull 01254 878291 & The Ribchester Arms 01254 820888 as well as The Carmen Rose Tea Rooms 01254 878431. The Punch Bowl 01254 826678 & The Bayley Arms 01254 826478 in Hurst Green & The Corporation Arms 01772 782644 outside Longridge.

Maps: OS Explorer 287.

Routes on Web: www.goodmtb.co.uk/a71

Bike Shops: Ewood Bikes 01254 55515 & Halfords 01254 681774 in Blackburn. Pedal Power 01200 422066 in Clitheroe for hire, parts & repairs.

Route Idea

E from Ribchester to Little Town. Minor road N to B6243, SE on trail to Trough House then N to Hurst Green. Trail NW past Greengore & Crowshaw House. Road NE to Chisley Green then trail to Weed Acre. Road towards Longridge then trail past Spade Mill Reservoirs. Back to Ribchester via Hothersall Lodge. Distance 29km.

Hurst Green. © Simon Barnes www.bogtrotters.org

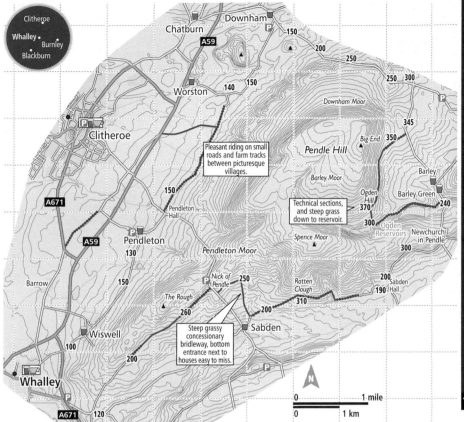

Clitheroe
Whalley • Burnley
Blackburn

Chatburn

Downham

Worston

Clitheroe

Pleasant riding on small roads and farm tracks between picturesque villages.

Downham Moor

Pendle Hill

Big End

Barley Moor

Barley

Pendleton Hall

Technical sections, and steep grass down to reservoir.

Ogden Hill

Barley Green

Pendleton

Pendleton Moor

Spence Moor

Ogden Reservoirs

Newchurch in Pendle

Barrow

Nick of Pendle

The Rough

Ratten Clough

Sabden Hall

Wiswell

Steep grassy concessionary bridleway, bottom entrance next to houses easy to miss.

Sabden

Whalley

0 .... 1 mile
0   1 km

Situation: At the foot of Whalley Nab on the banks of the River Calder and at the heart of the Ribble Valley in Lancashire. 4 miles south of Clitheroe and 7 miles north east of Blackburn.

About the Base: Whalley, a large village with pubs and a café. **Parking:** Car park east of Whalley village centre near to the golf course. Also at Clitheroe, Pendleton, Nick of Pendle & Downham next to the information centre. *Grid Ref: Whalley SD741360, Clitheroe SD742419, Nick of Pendle SD772384, Pendleton SD755395, Downham SD784441.*
Post Code: Whalley BB7 9UE, Clitheroe BB7 2JW, Pendleton BB7 1PX, Downham BB7 4BN.

Drive Times: Manchester 50mins, Leeds 1hr10, Sheffield 1hr40, Birmingham 2hr10, Newcastle 2hr40.

Trains: Whalley Railway Station is on the Manchester-Blackburn-Clitheroe line.

Refreshments: At Whalley, several pubs & Marmalade Café 01254 822462. The Freemasons Arms 01254 822218 at Wiswell, The Swan with Two Necks 01200 423 112 at Pendleton, pubs & cafés in Clitheroe. The Calf's Head 01200 441218 at Worston, The Brown Cow 01200 440 878 at Chatburn, The Assheton Arms 01200 441 227 in Downham, The Pendle Inn 01282 614808 & The Barley Mow 01282 614293 at Barley, The White Hart Inn & The Pendle Witch 01282 778277 at Sabden.

Books: MTB Guide S Pennines of W Yorks & Lancs (S.Hall).

Maps: OS Explorer OL41 & 287. Forest of Bowland Map (Harvey).

Routes on Web: www.goodmtb.co.uk/a75

Bike Shops: Pedal Power 01200 422066 in Clitheroe for hire, parts & repairs.

Route Idea

From Whalley, NE past Wiswell, Pendleton, Pendleton Hall & on to Downham. Roads E then S to join trails past Ogden Hill & the reservoirs. S to Sabden Hall then back to Whalley via Ratten Clough, Nick of Pendle & the trail along The Rough. Dist 31km.

Above Barley © Blackshaw Outdoor

Gisburn Forest

Within the Forest of Bowland Area of Outstanding Natural Beauty in Lancashire, two exciting new waymarked trails designed as part of the Adrenaline Gateway project. A short trail suitable for novices with simple singletrack and fun, sweeping descents or challenging new singletrack including tricky boardwalk, downhill features and optional technical sections.

©Blackshaw Outdoor

Facilities:
None on site. Refreshments at The Dog & Partridge in nearby Tosside.

Parking:
Grid Ref: SD745550.

Web: www.goodmtb.co.uk/b9a & /b9b

The Trails

❶ **Bottoms Beck, Blue, XC, 9.5km.**

❷ **The "8", Red (optional)**

❸ **Black lines and features), XC, 18km.**

Stainburn

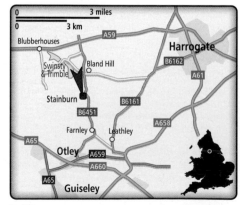

Forestry Commission land in North Yorkshire, developed in conjunction with Singletraction and constantly evolving. Three purpose built waymarked trails and a small pump track offer short, technically challenging routes including the "toughest Black Trail in the UK?" The Norwood Edge Trails are natural trails within the forest that have been discovered and cleared by SingletrAction. Almost entirely singletrack, natural features make them technical and far from easy.

Parking:
Grid Ref: SE210508.

Web: www.goodmtb.co.uk/b10

Facilities: None on site.

The Trails

❶ **Warren Boulder Trail, Black, XC, 4km.**

❷ **Our lil' ole Red Loop, Red, XC, 2km.**

❸ **The Descent Line, Red, XC, 1.5km.**

❹ **Norwood Edge Trails, Gold, XC.**

❺ **Pump Track.**

Swinsty & Timble Trails

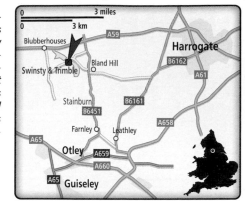

In the Washburn Valley, west of Harrogate in North Yorkshire. Waymarked trails linking the public bridleways to Swinsty Moor Plantation with those across Blubberhouses Moor. With something for everyone, trails offer varied surfaces with short sections of road, hard stoned forest tracks and grassed areas which can be soft and muddy. Two alternative unsurfaced trails offer rooty technical sections for more experienced riders.

Parking:
Grid Ref: SE187538

Web: www.goodmtb.co.uk/b11

Facilities:
None on site. Timble Inn for refreshments at nearby Timble.

The Trails

XC, 9km plus optional extensions.

A Summer's Evening in The Dales. Simon Thompson, Steve Wroe, Neil Fleetwood, Mark Willacy. © Nick Matthews

North York Moors & The Wolds

Lying to the east of the Pennines and in the rain shadow of the prevailing westerly winds, the North York Moors tend to enjoy a much drier climate than the National Parks further west. Many of the trails are fast draining and offer excellent year-round riding. Rising to just 454m on Urra Moor, this is clearly moorland rather than mountain scenery. Never fear! The North York Moors are the location of two of the finest ridge rides in the country: northwest of **Hutton-le-Hole** and west of **Church Houses**, the track over Rudland Rigg runs for over 17km with magnificent views over the heather-clad moorland and down into the forested valleys below. The second ridge ride, the Cleveland Way, can be started from the **Sutton Bank** Visitor Centre and runs along the top of the escarpment with mighty views west out over the Vale of York, eventually dropping down to **Swainby**. Other bases in the northern half of the park including **Danby**, **Westerdale** and **Goathland** lie either side of the valleys cut through by the River Esk and its tributaries. Further south, **Rosedale Abbey** lies tucked down in the valley at the foot of Spaunton Moor. By contrast, **Hole of Horcum** is a viewpoint high up on the A169, the main road connecting **Pickering** to Whitby with trails running east and west from here.

© www.chasingtrails.com

Hidden away in Upper Ryedale, **Hawnby** would make a fine base for exploring tracks to the north, south and west up through the thickly wooded valleys onto the open heather of Hawnby Moor and Arden Great Moor. In the southeastern corner of the National Park, just inland from the coast at Scarborough, the Broxa Forest north of **Everley** is criss-crossed with wide forest roads. Though it may be hard to believe, there is a 'tough' railway path running along the stunning coast between Whitby and Scarborough, passing through **Burniston** and **Ravenscar**.

In the south of the area, the gently rolling countryside of the Yorkshire Wolds offers much easier riding, rarely rising above 200m. Good bases are dotted around the area, from **Sheriff Hutton** in the west to **Rudston** in the east, from **Great Givendale** to the south to the more centrally located bases at **Welburn**, **Huttons Ambo**, **North Grimston** and **Kirkby Grindalythe**.

If you are looking for purpose-built single-track then the Trail Centre at **Dalby Forest** has it in bucket loads to suit riders of all abilities and includes the nearby Pace Bike Park. The trails at **Guisborough Forest** are a convenient alternative, close to the conurbations of Tyneside.

Swainby

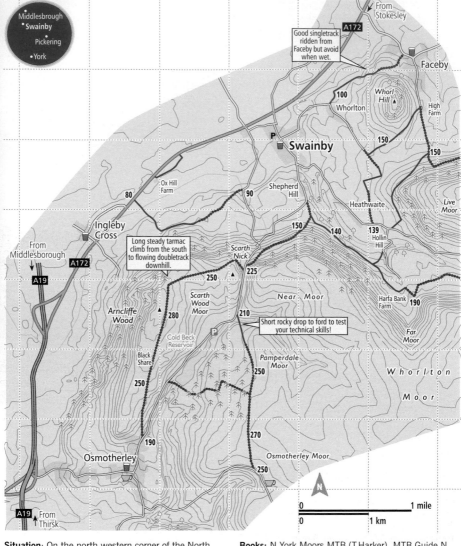

- Middlesbrough
- **Swainby**
- Pickering
- York

From Stokesley

A172

Good singletrack ridden from Faceby but avoid when wet.

Faceby

100
Whorl Hill
Whorlton
High Farm

150

150

Swainby

Ox Hill Farm

80

90

Shepherd Hill

Heathwaite

Live Moor

Ingleby Cross

From Middlesborough

A172

A19

Long steady tarmac climb from the south to flowing doubletrack downhill.

150

140

139 Hollin Hill

250

225

Scarth Nick

Near Moor

Harfa Bank Farm

190

Scarth Wood Moor

Arncliffe Wood

280

210

Short rocky drop to ford to test your technical skills!

Far Moor

Cold Beck Reservoir

Black Share

250

250

Pamperdale Moor

250

W h o r l t o n

M o o r

270

320

Osmotherley Moor

190

Osmotherley

250

N

A19 From Thirsk

| 0 | | 1 mile |
| 0 | | 1 km |

Situation: On the north western corner of the North York Moors National Park. 10 miles north east of Northallerton.

About the Base: Swainby, a village with 3 pubs.
Parking: Roadside in the village or car park at head of Cod Beck Reservoir. *Grid Ref: Swainby NZ477020, Cod Beck Reservoir SE468992. Post Code: Swainby DL6 3EG.*

Drive Times: Middlesbrough 20 mats, Leeds 1hr10, Newcastle 1hr10, Manchester 2hr, Birmingham 2hr50.

Refreshments: At Swainby,The Black Horse 01642 700436, The Blacksmiths Arms 01642 700303 & The Miners Arms 01642 700457. The Sutton Arms 01642 700382 at Faceby & The Bluebell Inn 01609 882272 at Ingleby Cross. Pubs & cafés at Osmotherley. Chequers Tea Room 01609 883710 at Osmotherley Moor.

Books: N York Moors MTB (T.Harker). MTB Guide N York Moors (S.Willis). **Maps**: OS Explorer OL26.

Bike Shops: Westbrook Cycles 01642 710232, 5 miles away at Stokesley.

Route Ideas

❶ Route consisting of two loops: Road S from Swainby past Shepherd Hill then Scarth Nick. Trail across Pamperdale Moor then W through wood to the reservoir. Road S then trail N to Scarth Nick. Trails E to Hollin Hill then N to High Farm & Faceby. Trail to Whorlton & road back to start.
Distance 19km.

❷ North loop only. Distance 10km.

❸ South loop only. Distance 12km.

Clay Bank

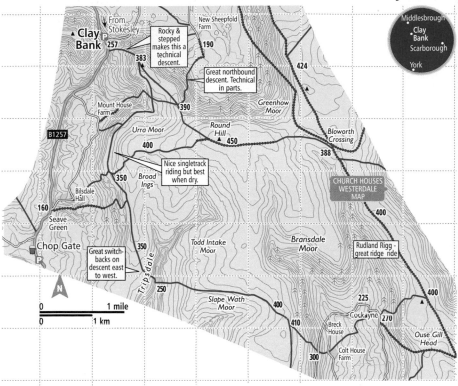

Situation: Between the Cleveland Hills and the High Moors, Clay Bank is at the north west corner of the North York Moors National Park, 12 miles north of Helmsley.

About the Base: Clay Bank, a rural location with a car park and easy access to the trails. **Parking:** Car parks at Clay Bank & at Chop Gate next to the information point. *Grid Ref: Clay Bank NZ573035, Chop Gate SE558993.*

Drive Times: Middlesbrough 30mins, Leeds 1hr20, Newcastle 1hr20, Manchester 2hr10, Birmingham 3hr.

Trains: Battersby Railway Station, 3 miles away, is on the Middlesbrough-Whitby 'Esk Valley' Line.

Refreshments: The Buck Inn at Chop Gate 01642 778334.

Books: MTB Guide N York Moors (S.Willis).

Maps: OS Explorer OL26.

Routes on Web: www.goodmtb.co.uk/a11

Bike Shops: Westbrook Cycles 01642 710232, 5 miles away in Stokesley, for bikes. Parts & repairs.

Route Idea

A clockwise loop from Clay Bank, to Round Hill, Bloworth Crossing then on to Cockayne, Slape Wath Moor, Urra Moor & back to start.
Distance 28km.

Extend the Area: Churchouses/Westerdale Map to the E.

©Tony Harker

Great Ayton / Pinchinthorpe

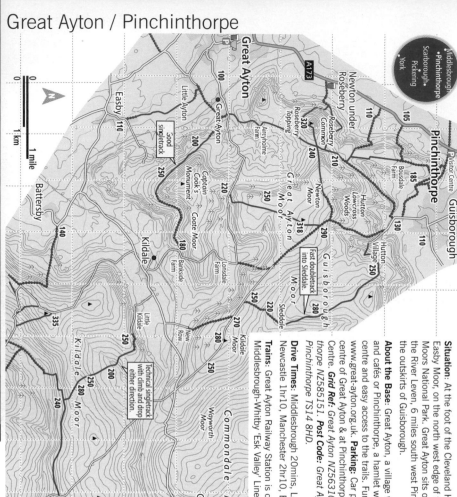

Situation: At the foot of the Cleveland Hills beneath Easby Moor, on the north west edge of the North York Moors National Park, Great Ayton sits on the banks of the River Leven, 6 miles south west Pinchinthorpe on the outskirts of Guisborough.

About the Base: Great Ayton, a village with two pubs and cafés or Pinchinthorpe, a hamlet with a visitor centre and easy access to the trails. Further Info: www.great-ayton.org.uk. **Parking:** Car parks in the centre of Great Ayton & at Pinchinthorpe Visitor Centre. **Grid Ref:** Great Ayton NZ563106, Pinchinthorpe NZ585151. **Post Code:** Great Ayton TS9 6PN, Pinchinthorpe TS14 8HD.

Drive Times: Middlesbrough 20mins, Leeds 1hr20, Newcastle 1hr10, Manchester 2hr10, B'ham 3hr.

Trains: Great Ayton Railway Station is on the Middlesbrough-Whitby 'Esk Valley' Line.

Refreshments: The Royal Oak Hotel 01642 722361 & The Buck Hotel 01642 722242, No 5 Coffee Shop 01642 722646 & Coffee Bean 01642 725236 at Great Ayton. At Castleton, The Eskdale Inn 01287 660333, The Downe Arms 01287 660135, The Cleveland Inn 01287 660223 & Castleton Tea Rooms 01287 660135. The Cleveland Inn 01287 660214 at Commondale & The Kings Head at Newton under Roseberry 08714 329005.

Books: N York Moors MTB (T.Harker), MTB Guide N York Moors (S.Willis). **Maps:** OS Explorer OL26.

Routes on Web: www.goodmtb.co.uk/a15

Bike Shops: Bike Traks 01642 724444 at Gt Ayton.

Route Ideas

❶ From Pinchinthorpe SE on trail & road to Hutton Village. Trail across Gisborough Moor then road NW to trails past Newton Moor & N back to start. Dist 15km.

❷ From Great Ayton SE on trails to Bankside Farm. Road to Kildale & Little Kildale. Onto Castleton via Kildale Moor. Road then trails to Commondale. W to Kildale Moor, Newton Moor & Rosebury Common. S past Aireyholme Farm & back to start. Distance 39km.

❸ As above but at Kildale head past New Row to miss out Castleton & Commondale. Distance 13km. Extend the area: Danby to the E.

Also see Guisborough Trail Centre (p183).

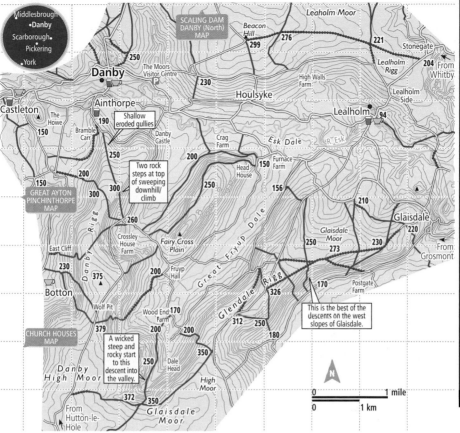

Situation: On the banks of the River Esk in the Esk Valley at the heart of the North York Moors National Park. 15 miles west of Whitby.

About the Base: Danby, a village with a pub and a visitor centre. **Parking**: Car park at The Moors Visitor Centre, east of the village. *Grid Ref: NZ716083. Post Code: YO21 2NB.*

Drive Times: Middlesbrough 40mins, Newcastle 1hr30, Leeds 1hr40, Manchester 2hr30, Birmingham 3hr20.

Trains: Danby & Leaholm Railway Stations are on the Middlesbrough-Whitby 'Esk Valley' Line.

Refreshments: At Danby, The Duke of Wellington 01287 660362 & Café at The Moors Visitor Centre 01287 660362. The Board Inn 01947 897279, Beck View Tea Room 01947 897318 & Shepherds Hall Tea Room 01947 897361 at Leaholm. The Fox & Hounds 01287 660218 at Ainthorpe & Botton Village Café 01287 660871 at Botton. Also pubs & cafés at Castleton.

Books: N York Moors MTB (T.Harker). MTB Guide N York Moors (S.Willis).

Maps: OS Explorer OL26 & 27.

Route Ideas

❶ From Visitor Centre to Danby, through Ainthorpe & S on to trails towards Crossley House Farm. Road S to Danby High Moor. Trails across Glaisdale Moor. To Glaisdale via Glaisdale Rigg. N to Lealholm Rigg. Trail W to Beacon Hill & road back to start. Distance 27km.

❷ From Visitor Centre towards Danby Castle then W towards Bramble Carr. S on trail towards Crossley House Farm then trails to West Cliff & Wolf Pit. S on road to Danby High Moor. Trail NE then S to Wood End Farm. Road back to Danby. Distance 19km.

Extend the area: Scaling Dam/Danby North Map to the N. Great Ayton/Pinchinthorpe Map to the W. Church Houses Map to the SW.

Glaisdale Moor. Rider: Christine Finlay. © www.trailbrakes.co.uk

Danby (north) / Scaling Dam

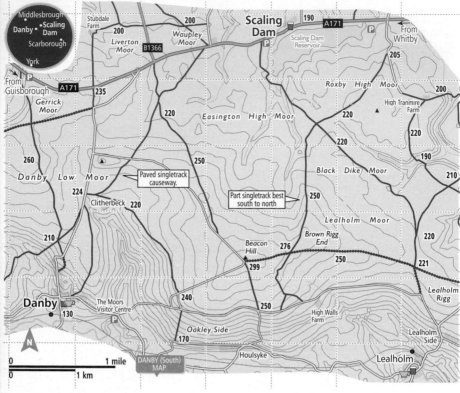

Situation: In the heart of the North York Moors National Park in the Esk Valley, 15 miles west of Whitby. Scaling Dam, to the north east, is the largest lake in the national park.

About the Base: Danby, a village with a pub and a visitor centre or Scaling Dam, a rural location with a pub and easy access to the trails. **Parking:** Car park at the The Moors Visitor Centre, east of Danby. Also at Scaling Dam Reservoir & roadside at Gerrick Moor. *Grid Ref: Danby NZ716083, Scaling Dam NZ740125, Gerrick Moor NZ704120. Post Code: Danby YO21 2NB, Scaling Dam TS13 4TP.*

Drive Times: Middlesbrough 40mats, Newcastle 1hr30, Leeds 1hr40, Manchester 2hr30, Birmingham 3hr20.

Trains: Danby & Leaholm Railway Stations are on the Middlesbrough-Whitby 'Esk Valley' Line.

Refreshments: At Danby, The Duke of Wellington 01287 660362 & Café at The Moors Visitor Centre

01287 660362. The Board Inn 01947 897279, Beck View Tea Room 01947 897318 & Shepherds Hall Tea Room 01947 897361 at Leaholm or The Grapes Inn 01287 640461 at Scaling Dam.

Books: N York Moors MTB (T.Harker). MTB Guide N York Moors (S.Willis).

Maps: OS Explorer OL27.

Routes on Web: www.goodmtb.co.uk/a12

Route Ideas

❶ From car park on E of Scaling Dam head S to cross Roxby High Moor to Brown Rigg End & S to join road. W on road then NW trail to Clitherbeck. Trail NE to A171 at Waupley Moor. Road back to finish. Distance 17km.

❷ As start above but head to High Tranmire Farm then S towards Lealholm Rigg. Trail W to Brown Rigg End then S to road W of High Walls Farm. W on road then on trail NW to Clitherbeck. Trail NE then road to Beacon Hill, on to Brown Rigg End, NE to Roxby High Moor & back to start. Distance 20km.

❸ From car park on W of Scaling Dam W on A170. Trails around Waupley Moor to Stubdale Farm then S to cross A170. Trails W across Gerrick Moor & S across Danby Low Moor to road N of Danby. NE on road then trail SE passing Clitherbeck. Follow road to Beacon Hill then E to Brown Rigg End, N across Black Dike Moor & NW back to start. Distance 19km.

Extend the area: Danby South Map to the S.

Riders: Muddy Bums Mountain Biking. © Tony Harker

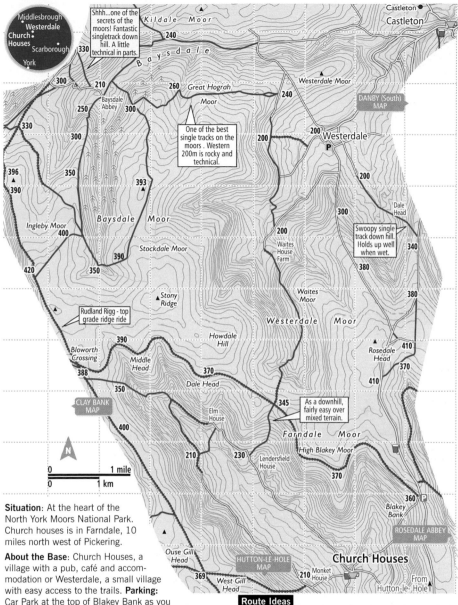

Shhh...one of the secrets of the moors! Fantastic singletrack down hill. A little technical in parts.

One of the best single tracks on the moors. Western 200m is rocky and technical.

Swoopy single track down hill. Holds up well when wet.

Rudland Rigg - top grade ridge ride

As a downhill, fairly easy over mixed terrain.

DANBY (South) MAP

CLAY BANK MAP

HUTTON-LE-HOLE MAP

ROSEDALE ABBEY MAP

Situation: At the heart of the North York Moors National Park. Church houses is in Farndale, 10 miles north west of Pickering.

About the Base: Church Houses, a village with a pub, café and accommodation or Westerdale, a small village with easy access to the trails. **Parking:** Car Park at the top of Blakey Bank as you head north east out of Church Houses. Roadside parking in Westerdale. *Grid Ref: Blakey Bank SE683989, Westerdale NZ665058.*

Drive Times: Middlesbrough 50mins, Leeds 1hr40, Newcastle 1hr40, Manchester 2hr30, B'ham 3hr20.

Refreshments: The Feversham Arms 01751 433206 & the Daffy Caffy Café 01751 430363 at Church Houses The Lion Inn 01751 417320 on Blakey Ridge.

Books: N York Moors MTB (T.Harker).

Maps: OS Explorer OL26.

Route Ideas

❶ From car park at top of Blakey Bank head N on road. Trails & road to Dale Head then on to Westerdale. Road NW then trail along Baysdale & S to Bloworth Crossing. E to Middle Head, Dale Head, High Blakey Moor & back to start. Distance 34km.

❷ NW from car park across Farndale Moor then N across Westerdale Moor. W over Great Hograh Moor & S over Baysdale Moor to Bloworth Crossing. E to Middle Head, Dale Head, High Blakey Moor & back to start. Distance 30km.

Extend the area: Danby South Map to the NE, Hutton-Le-Hole Map to the S. Clay Bank Map to the the W. Rosedale Abbey Map to the SE

Rosedale Abbey (north)

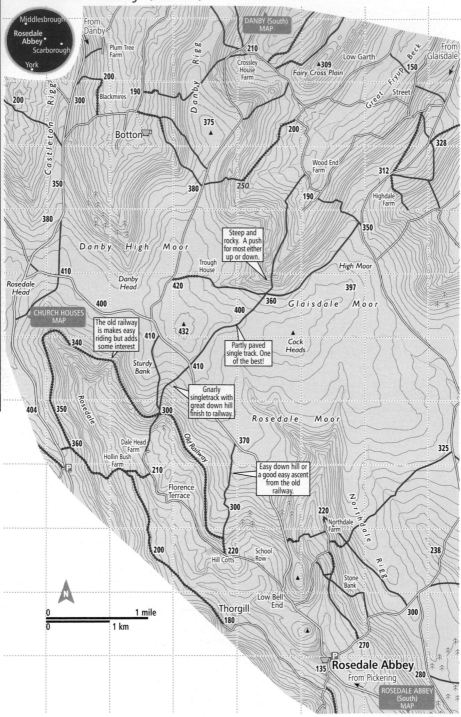

Middlesbrough
Rosedale Abbey
Scarborough
York

From Danby

Plum Tree Farm

DANBY (South) MAP

From Glaisdale

210

Crossley House Farm

Low Garth

▲309 Fairy Cross Plain

150

200

190

Blackmires

375 ▲

Botton

380

250

200

Great Fryup Beck

Street

328

Wood End Farm

190

312

Highdale Farm

Castleton Rigg

350

380

200

300

Danby Rigg

High Moor

350

Danby High Moor

Trough House

Steep and rocky. A push for most either up or down.

360

Glaisdale Moor

397

High Moor

Rosedale Head

410

Danby Head

420

400

CHURCH HOUSES MAP

400

The old railway is makes easy riding but adds some interest

410

432 ▲

Cock Heads ▲

Partly paved single track. One of the best!

Sturdy Bank

340

410

404

350

Rosedale

300

Gnarly singletrack with great down hill finish to railway.

Rosedale Moor

360

Dale Head Farm

Old Railway

325

Hollin Bush Farm

P

210

370

Easy down hill or a good easy ascent from the old railway.

Florence Terrace

220

Northdale Farm

Northdale Rigg

300

238

200

300

220
Hill Cotts

School Row

Stone Bank

N

Thorgill

Low Bell End

270

300

0   1 mile

180

280

0   1 km

135 Rosedale Abbey

From Pickering

ROSEDALE ABBEY (South) MAP

Situation: In a valley at the centre of Rosedale, at the heart of the North York Moors National Park. 10 miles north west of Pickering.

About the Base: Rosedale Abbey, a village with cafés and a shop. **Parking:** Roadside in the centre of the village or car park as you leave the village heading east. Car park at Blakey Bank in the west of the map. *Grid Ref: Rosedale Abbey SE724959, Blakey Bank SE683989.* **Post Code:** *Rosedale Abbey, YO18 8RA.*

Drive Times: Middlesbrough 1hr, Leeds 1hr30, Newcastle 1hr40, Manchester 2hr20, Birmingham 3hr20.

Refreshments: Graze on the Green Café 01751 417468 or Abbey Tea Room & Store 01751 417475 at Rosedale Abbey. Botton Village Café 01287 660871 at Botton. The Lion Inn 01751 417475 on Blakey Ridge.

Books: N York Moors MTB (T.Harker). MBR Ride Guide 2010 **Maps**: OS Explorer OL26 & 27.

Routes on Web: www.goodmtb.co.uk/a27

Route Ideas

❶ N from Rosedale Abbey to Hill Cottages. N on trail to Rosedale Moor. NW on road. S to Dale Head Farm via Sturdy Bank then on to Hollin Bush Farm. Loop clockwise around Rosedale & back to Hill Cottages. Road to the finish.
Distance 20km.

❷ N from Rosedale Abbey to Hill Cottages. N on trail to Rosedale Moor then NW on road. Trail NE towards Glaisdale Moor then on to Wood End Farm. Road N then S across Danby High Moor. W towards Rosedale Head then SW trail to cut road corner. Clockwise on trail around Rosedale then either drop down to Dale Head Farm or follow trail to Hill Cottages & road back. Distance 35km.

Extend the area: Church Houses Map to W, Rosedale Abbey South Map to the S. Danby South Map to the N.

Above Botton. Riders: Muddy Bums Mountain Biking. ©Tony Harker

Rosedale Abbey (south)

Situation: Heart of the North York Moors National Park in Rosedale, 10 miles NW of Pickering.

About the Base: Rosedale Abbey, a village with cafés and a shop. **Parking**: Roadside in the centre of the village or car park as you leave the village heading east. Car park in Hutton le Hole next to the information point. **Grid Ref**: Rosedale Abbey SE724959, Hutton-le-Hole SE705901. **Post Code**: Rosedale Abbey YO18 8RA, Hutton Le Hole YO62 6UB.

Drive Times: Middlesbrough 1hr, Leeds 1hr30, Newcastle 1hr40, Manchester 2hr20, B'ham 3hr20.

Refreshments: Graze on the Green Café 01751 417468 or Abbey Tea Room & Store 01751 417475 at Rosedale Abbey. The Blacksmiths Inn 01751 417331 at Hartoft, The New Inn 01751 417330 at Cropton, The Blacksmiths Arms 01751 417247 at Lastingham, The Crown Inn 01751 417343, Barn Tea Rooms 01751 417311 & Forge Tea Shop 01751 417444 at Hutton-le-Hole.

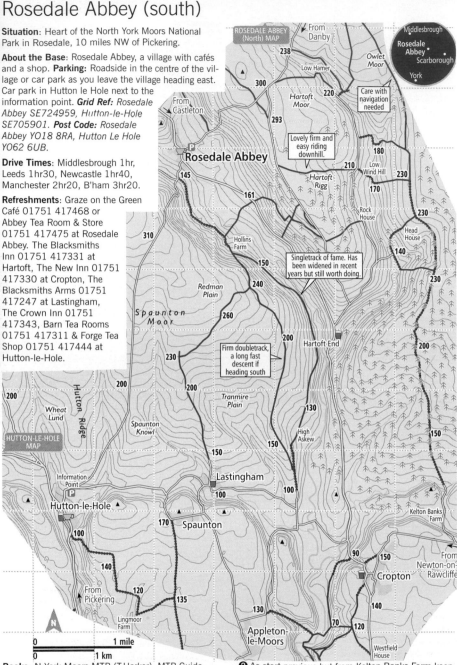

Books: N York Moors MTB (T.Harker). MTB Guide N York Moors (S.Willis).MTB Guide Mid Yorkshire (D.Liversidge). **Maps**: OS Explorer OL26 & 27.

Routes on Web: www.goodmtb.co.uk/a28

Route Ideas

❶ From Rosedale Abbey, SE to Hollins Farm and High Askew then road to Cropton. On to Kelton Banks Farm then trails N. Pass Low Wind Hill then S to Rock House followed by trails W to join road back to start. Dist 23km.

❷ As start previous but from Kelton Banks Farm keep heading N passing Owlet Moor to meet road (See Rosedale Abbey North Map) & follow SW back to start. Distance 26km.

❸ Head SE to Hollins Farm, High Askew then road W to Lastingham. Trail N across Spaunton Moor, on to Hollins Farm & back to start. Distance 15km.

Extend the area: Hutton-le-Hole Map to the W. Rosedale Abbey North Map to the N.

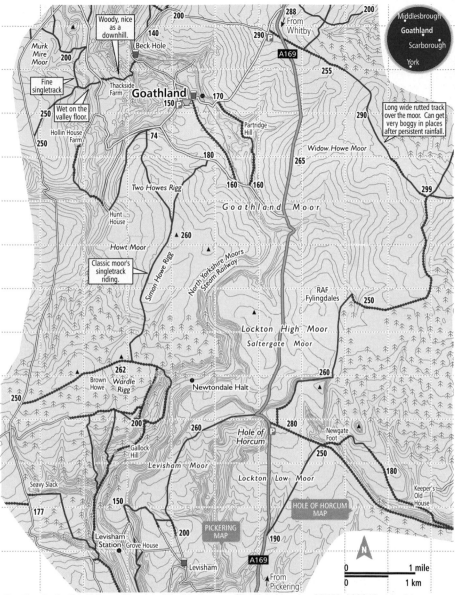

Map labels:

Middlesbrough
Goathland
Scarborough
York

From Whitby
A169

200
288
290
200
255
290

Woody, nice as a downhill.
200
140
Beck Hole
Murk Mire Moor
200

Fine singletrack
Thackside Farm
Goathland
150
170
Wet on the valley floor.
250
Hollin House Farm
250
74
180
Partridge Hill

Two Howes Rigg
160   160
265

Widow Howe Moor
299

Goathland Moor

Long wide rutted track over the moor. Can get very boggy in places after persistent rainfall.

Hunt House
▲ 260
Howt Moor
▲
Classic moor's singletrack riding.
Simon Howe Rigg
North Yorkshire Moors Steam Railway
RAF Fylingdales
250

Lockton High Moor
Saltergate Moor
▲

262
Brown Howe   Wardle Rigg
Newtondale Halt
260
▲
250
200
260
280
Gallock Hill
Hole of Horcum
Newgate Foot
250
180
Levisham Moor
Lockton Low Moor
Keeper's Old House
Seavy Slack
150
HOLE OF HORCUM MAP
177
Levisham Station   Grove House
200
PICKERING MAP
190
Levisham
A169
From Pickering

N

0   1 mile
0   1 km

Situation: In the Esk Valley at the east of the North York Moors National Park.

About the Base: Goathland, a village with pubs, a tea room and accommodation. **Parking:** Car parks in the village & at Hole of Horcum. *Grid Ref: Goathland NZ833013, Hole of Horcum SE853936.*

Drive Times: Middlesbrough 1hr10, Leeds 1hr40, Newcastle 1hr50, Manchester 2hr30.

Trains: Goathland Station is on the North York Moors Steam Railway Line.

Refreshments: At Goathland, The Inn on the Moor 01947 896296, The Goathland Hotel 01947 896203 & Goathland Tea Rooms 01947 896446. The Birch Hall Inn 01947 896245 at Beck Hole & The Horseshoe Inn 01751 460240 at Levisham.

Books: N York Moors MTB (T.Harker). MTB Guide N York Moors (S.Willis). **Maps:** OS Explorer OL27.

Routes on Web: www.goodmtb.co.uk/a14

Bike Shops: Dr Cranks Bike Shack 01947 606661 & Trailways Cycle Hire 01947 820207 in Whitby.

Route Idea

From Goathland, head NE to cross the A169 then trails to S Hole of Horcum. Cross Levisham Moor & on to Levisham Station. N to Gallock Hill, Wardle Rigg & along Simon Howe Rigg. NW across Two Howes Rigg & back to start. Distance 37km.

Extend the area: Hole of Horcum Map to the E.

Hole of Horcum

Middlesbrough
Hole of Horcum•
Scarborough
York

Worm Sike Rigg
245
250
A long forest track downhill if heading SE
From Whitby
Saltergate Moor
A169
Nab Farm
Allerston High Moor
LANGDALE FOREST
205
High Langdale End
GOATHLAND MAP
250
244
280
Hole of Horcum
P
From Pickering
250
Blakey Topping
Newgate Foot
Dalby Snout
139
Thompson's Rigg
Crossscliff Wood
150
North Side
Birch Hall Cott
EVERLEY MAP
N
0   1 mile
0   1 km
Deepdale Farm
100
233
DALBY FOREST
Moorcock
Langdale End

Situation: On the edge of Langdale and Dalby Forests, at the south east corner of the North York Moors National Park. 7 miles north of Pickering.

About the Base: Hole of Horcum, a rural location with easy access to the trails.
Further Info: www.holeofhorcum.co.uk. **Parking**: Hole of Horcum car park. *Grid Ref: SE853936.*

Drive Times: Middlesbrough 1hr, Leeds 1hr30, Newcastle 1hr50, Manchester 2hr20, Birmingham 3hr10.

Trains: Levisham Railway Station, 4 miles away, is on the North York Moors Steam Railway Line.

Refreshments: The Moorcock Inn 01723 882268 at Langdale End.

Books: N York Moors MTB (T.Harker). MTB Guide N York Moors (S.Willis). **Maps**: OS Explorer OL27.

Routes on Web: www.goodmtb.co.uk/a19

Bike Shops: Purple Mountain Bike Centre 01751 460011 in Dalby Forest, 4 miles away, for hire. Big Bear Bikes 01751 474220 & The Cycle Centre 01751 472581 in Pickering.

© Tony Harker

Route Idea

From Hole of Horcum, a clockwise loop via Allerston High Moor, Langdale Forest, North Side & Thompson's Rigg.
Distance 27km.

Extend the area: Goathland Map to the W. Evereley Map to the E.

This base is also very close to Dalby Forest Trail Centre (p183).

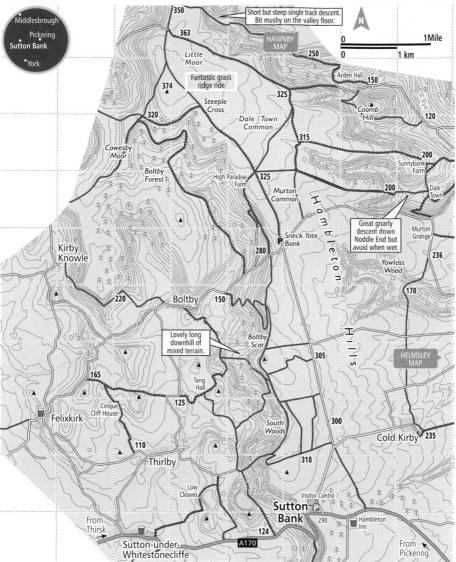

Short but steep single track descent. Bit mushy on the valley floor.

HAWNBY MAP

Fantastic grass ridge ride.

Great gnarly descent down Noddle End but avoid when wet.

Lovely long downhill of mixed terrain.

HELMSLEY MAP

Situation: High on the edge of the Hambleton Hills and the south western edge of the North York Moors National Park. 6 miles east of Thirsk.

About the Base: Sutton Bank, a rural location with a visitor centre. **Parking:** Car park at the Sutton Bank National Park Visitor Centre or roadside at Sneck Yate Bank. **Grid Ref**: *Sutton Bank SE515830, Sneck Yate Bank SE510877*. **Post Code: YO7 2EH.**

Drive Times: Middlesbrough 40min, Leeds 1hr, Newcastle 1hr30, Manchester 1hr50, B'ham 2hr40.

Trains: Thirsk Station, York-Newcastle line.

Refreshments: Café at Sutton Bank Visitor Centre 01845 597426. Hambleton Inn 01845 597202 east of Sutton Bank, The Whitestonecliffe Inn 01845 597271 at Sutton-under-Whitestonecliffe.

Books: N York Moors MTB (T.Harker). MTB Guide N York Moors (S.Willis). **Maps:** OS Explorer OL26.

Routes on Web: www.goodmtb.co.uk/a31
Bike Shops: Millgate Cycles 01845 527666 Thirsk.

Route Ideas

❶ From Sutton Bank, road N then trails E & N to pass South Woods & Boltby Scar to road. At Sneck Yate Bank N on trail to Little Moor then SE to Dale Town Common & S past Murton Common to road. Road to Murton Grange then trails to Cold Kirby & road back to start. Distance 27km.

❷ As above to road after passing Boltby Scar. SW on road then NW on trails through Boltby Forest, up to & around Little Moor. At Murton Common W then S to Sneck Yate Bank Road back to start. Distance 25km.

Extend the area: Hawnby Map to the NW. Helmsley Map to the E.

Hawnby

Middlesbrough
Hawnby
• Pickering
•York

Super singl track with rock steps. Short steep drop into Arns Gill.

400

350

Head House

390

Sandy tracks become hard going after rain.

Snilesworth Moor

300

Long double track fast downhill.

Cow Ridge

Bilsdale West Moor

From Stokesley

P Square Corner

280

250

360

350

Wetherhouse Moor

300

200

Low Thwaites

Fangdale Beck 150

Technical rocky section

Dale Head

200

320

200

Black Hambleton

Short but nice singletrack. Gets boggy in parts after heavy rain. Best east to west towards Dale Head.

220

530

Helm House Wood

Helm House

Great Views

Whitestones

300

B1257

Arden Great Moor

Hawnby Moor

250

130

Kepwick Moor

350

350
300

290

220

Low Ewe Cote

200

Dak House

From Cowesby

Thorodale

Crow Nest

170

170 250

Little Moor

350

150

170 P

BannisClue Wood

370

Coomb Hill

Hawnby

Rievaulx Moor

200

R. Rye

250

Dale Town Common

SUTTON BANK MAP

330

315

Broadway Foot

250

250

High Paradise Farm

150
Dale Town

B1257

N

245

From Helmsley

0 ————— 1 mile
0 1 km

303

150

Situation: In Upper Ryedale, at the heart of the North York Moors National Park, 7 miles north west of Helmsley and 10 miles north east of Thirsk.

About the Base: Hawnby, a village with a pub, tea rooms and accommodation. **Parking**: Car park next to the pub in the village or at Square Corner car park. *Grid Ref: Hawnby SE543898, Square Corner SE479959. Post Code: Hawnby YO62 5QS.*

Drive Times: Middlesbrough 40mins, Leeds 1hr10, Newcastle 1hr30, Manchester 2hr, Birmingham 2hr50.

Refreshments: The Inn at Hawnby 01439 798202 & The Hawnby Stores & Tea Room 01439 798223 at Hawnby.

Books: N York Moors MTB (T.Harker). MTB Guide N York Moors (S.Willis).

Maps: OS Explorer OL26.

Routes on Web: www.goodmtb.co.uk/a17

Route Ideas

❶ Road N out of Hawnby. Trail over Hawnby Moor & Bilsdale West Moor. SW across Snilesworth Moor then W via Dale Head. Trails S to Little Moor & around Coomb Hill & back to start. Distance 31km.

❷ From Hawnby, road & trails SE to Broadway Foot & on to B1257. Minor road & trails past Helm House to Fangdale Beck. Trail SW skirting Helm House Wood to road. N then SW on trail towards Coomb Hill. W on road then anti-clockwise loop around Thorodale. Trails S of Coomb Hill then road back to start. Distance 30km.

❸ For a shorter variation of above miss out the loop Thorodale. Distance 18km.

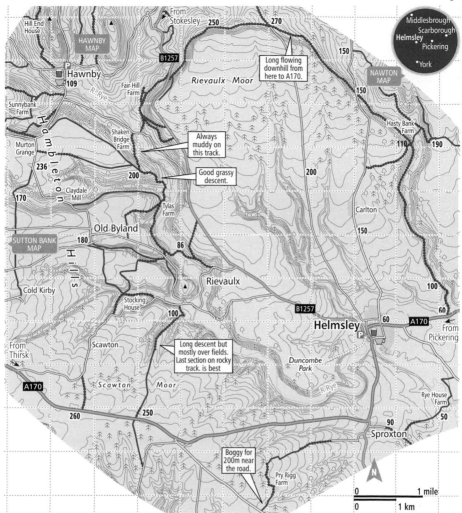

Hill End House

HAWNBY MAP

B1257

Hawnby 109

Fair Hill Farm

Sunnybank Farm

R. Rye

Murton Grange

236

Shaken Bridge Farm

200

Claydale Mill

170

Tylas Farm

Old Byland

180

86

SUTTON BANK MAP

Cold Kirby

Stocking House

100

From Thirsk

A170

Scawton

Scawton Moor

260

250

From Stokesley 250

270

150

Long flowing downhill from here to A170.

Rievaulx Moor

Always muddy on this track.

Good grassy descent.

NAWTON MAP

150

Hasty Bank Farm

110 190

200

Carlton

150

Rievaulx

100

B1257

60

Helmsley

60

A170

From Pickering

Duncombe Park

R. Rye

Rye House Farm

90

50

Sproxton

Long descent but mostly over fields. Last section on rocky track. is best

Boggy for 200m near the road.

Pry Rigg Farm

Middlesbrough
Scarborough
Helmsley • Pickering
• York

N

0 _____ 1 mile
0 _____ 1 km

Situation: On the banks of the River Rye in Ryedale, on the southern edge of the North York Moors National Park. 14 miles east of Thirsk.

About the Base: Helmsley, a market town with several pubs and cafes. **Parking**: Car parks west of Helmsley town centre & next to the pub in Hawnby. **Grid Ref**: *Helmsley SE609836, Hawnby SE543898.* **Post Code**: *Helmsley YO62 5AH, Hawnby YO62 5QS.*

Drive Times: Middlesbrough 50mins, Leeds 1hr10, Newcastle 1hr40, Manchester 2hr, B'ham 2hr50.

Refreshments: At Helmsley, The Royal Oak 01439 770450 The Black Swan Hotel 01439 770466 & The Feathers Hotel 01439 771101 as well as several cafes. The Inn at Hawnby 01439 798202 & The Hawnby Stores & Tea Room 01439 798223 at Hawnby.

Books: N York Moors MTB (T.Harker). MTB Guide N York Moors (S.Willis).MTB Guide Mid Yorkshire (D.Liversidge).

Maps: OS Explorer OL26.

Routes on Web: www.goodmtb.co.uk/a18

Route Ideas

❶ From Helmsley, S on road & trails to Sproxton, on to Pry Rigg Farm. Road NW to A170. W on A170 then N on trail over Scawton Moor. Road then trail N past Tylas Farm to Shaken Bridge Farm. Head NE on trails to cross B1257.Trails around Rievaulx Moor to reach A170 & back to start. Distance 38km.

❷ For a shorter variation to above head NW on B1257, minor roads to Rievaulx. Trails to Old Byland. Trails to Tylas Farm then as directions above 'from Tylas Farm'. Distance 18km.

Extend the area: Nawton to the E. Hawnby to the NW. Sutton Bank to the E.

Nawton

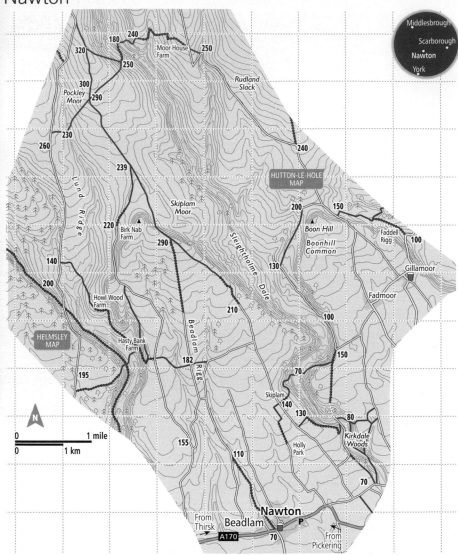

Situation: In Ryedale, on the south west edge of the North York Moors National Park. 3 miles east of Helmsley and 10 miles west of Pickering.

About the Base: Nawton, a small village with two pubs. **Parking:** Roadside, just east of the village on the A170. *Grid Ref: SE660848.*

Drive Times: Middlesbrough 1hr, Leeds 1hr20, Newcastle 1hr40, Manchester 2hr, Birmingham 3hr.

Refreshments: The Rose & Crown 01439 770247 & White Horse Inn 01439 770627 at Nawton. The Royal Oak Inn 01751 431414 at Gillamoor.

Books: MTB Guide Mid Yorkshire (D.Liversidge).
Maps: OS Explorer OL26.

Routes on Web: www.goodmtb.co.uk/a23

Route Idea

Trail N from Nawton then on towards Hasty Bank Farm & Howl Wood Farm. Along Lund Ridge then trails NE to Moor House Farm. Road SE then trail W of Boon Hill. Continue to Skiplam & through Kirkdale Woods. Road back to start.
Distance 34km

Extend the area: Helmsley Map to the W. Hutton-le-Hole Map to the NE.

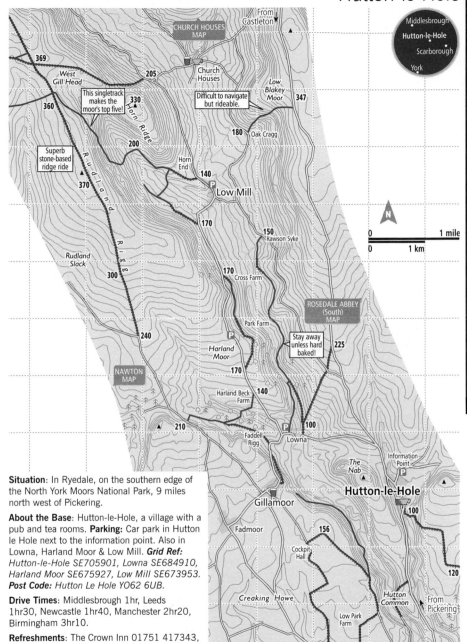

Situation: In Ryedale, on the southern edge of the North York Moors National Park, 9 miles north west of Pickering.

About the Base: Hutton-le-Hole, a village with a pub and tea rooms. **Parking:** Car park in Hutton le Hole next to the information point. Also in Lowna, Harland Moor & Low Mill. *Grid Ref: Hutton-le-Hole SE705901, Lowna SE684910, Harland Moor SE675927, Low Mill SE673953. Post Code: Hutton Le Hole YO62 6UB.*

Drive Times: Middlesbrough 1hr, Leeds 1hr30, Newcastle 1hr40, Manchester 2hr20, Birmingham 3hr10.

Refreshments: The Crown Inn 01751 417343, The Barn Tea Rooms 01751 417311 & Forge Tea Shop 01751 417444 at Hutton-le-Hole. The Royal Oak Inn 01751 431414 at Gillamoor, The Feversham Arms 01751 433206 & the Daffy Caffy Café 01751 430363 at Church Houses.

Books: N York Moors MTB (T.Harker). MTB Guide N York Moors (S.Willis).
Maps: OS Explorer OL26.

Routes on Web: www.goodmtb.co.uk/a21

Route Idea

From Hutton-le-Hole, road s then trail across Hutton Common. NW to Gillamoor via Cockpit Hall. N on roads & trails to pass Faddell Rigg. NW along Rudland Rigg. SE trail to Low Mill. Road back to start via Rawson Syke. Distance 27km.

Extend the area: Church Houses Map to N. Rosedale Abbey Map to the E. Nawton Map to the W.

Pickering

Middlesbrough
Scarborough
Pickering
York

Cawthorn Moor
200
From Whitby
GOATHLAND MAP
100

Thornsby House
Stony Moor
150

170

200

Levisham Station

Newton-on-Rawcliffe

Cawthorn Banks

East Moor

150

Cawthorne
160

150

High Nova Farm
150

Haugh Rigg

126

150

High Blansby

130

Blansby Park

Broats Farm

100

100

Blansby Park Farm
100

Wrelton

Aislaby

From Thirsk

40

Middleton

Park Gate

Newbridge

North York Moors Steam Railway

About the Base: Pickering, a market town with several pubs, cafés and accommodation. Further Info: www.pickering.uk.net.
Parking: Eastgate car park in the town centre on the A170. Several other car parks in the centre of Pickering. *Grid Ref*: SE802835. *Post Code*: YO18 7DY.

A170

A169

Pickering

30
From Malton

From Scarborough

Situation: At the foot of the North York Moors National Park, overlooking the Vale of Pickering to the south, 18 miles east of Scarborough.

Drive Times: Middlesbrough 1hr10, Leeds 1hr20, Newcastle 2hr, Manchester 2hr10, Birmingham 3hr.

Trains: Pickering & Levisham Railway Stations are on the North York Moors Steam Railway line to Whitby.

0 ____ 1 mile
0 ____ 1 km

Refreshments: Plenty of pubs & cafés at Pickering. Middleton Arms 01751 475444 at Middleton, Blacksmiths Arms 01751 472182 at Aislaby, Mucky Duck 01751 472505 at Newton Rawcliffe.

Books: MTB Guide Mid Yorkshire (D.Liversidge).
Maps: OS Explorer OL27.

Routes on Web: www.goodmtb.co.uk/a25

Bike Shops: Big Bear Bikes 01751 474220 & The Cycle Centre 01751 472581 in Pickering. Big Bear Active 01751 475111 offer instruction, guided rides & accommodation in Pickering.

Route Ideas

❶ Pickering to Aislaby then N on road followed by trails. Past Cawthorn Banks to Cawthorn Moor then E to road. Trail to Newton-on-Rawcliffe. Back to Pickering via Blansby Park Farm & Newbridge. 27km.

❷ N from Pickering to Newbridge. N on trail to W of river (now see Goathland Map). Pass Gallock Hill then up & around N of Wardle Rigg & SW to road. S to join road to Cawthorn Moor (now back on this map), on to Cawthorn Banks & East Moor. Trails S to A170 on E side of Aislaby & back to start. 32km.

Extend the area: Goathland Map to the N.

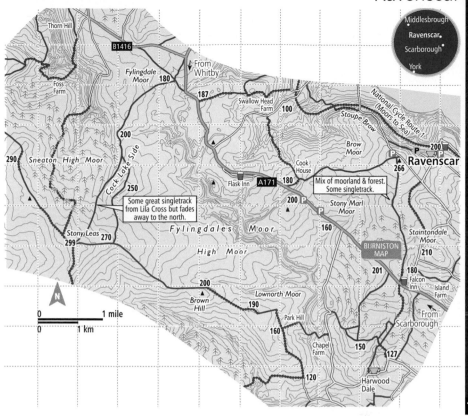

Situation: On the north east coast, 12 miles north of Scarborough, at the edge of the North York Moors National Park.

About the Base: Ravenscar, a village with a hotel and tea rooms. **Parking**: Roadside in the centre of the village or car park before you enter the village from the west, next to the radio mast. Also at Stony Marl Moor. *Grid Ref: Ravenscar NZ980015, Car Park NZ969012, Stony Marl NZ945002.*
Post Code: Ravenscar YO13 0NE.

Drive Times: Middlesbrough 1hr20, Leeds 2hr, Newcastle 2hr, Manchester 2hr50, Birmingham 3hr40.

Refreshments: The Raven Hall Hotel 01723 870353 & Ravenscar Tea Rooms 01723 870444 at Ravenscar. Wykeham Tea Rooms 01723 865212 & The Grainary 01723 870717 at Harwood Dale. The Falcon Inn 01723 870717 on the A171.

Books: N York Moors MTB (T.Harker). MTB Guide N York Moors (S.Willis). **Maps**: OS Explorer OL27.

Routes on Web:
www.goodmtb.co.uk/a26

Route Idea

Out of Ravenscar & S on to trail to Falcon Inn then on to Harwood Dale. Approach Lownorth Moor from the S then head past Brown Hill to Stony Leas. N across Sneaton High Moor & on to the B1416. S on the A171. E on trails to join railway path (Moors to Sea Route) back to Ravenscar.
Distance 37km.

Extend the Area: Burniston Map to the SE.

© Tony Harker

Burniston

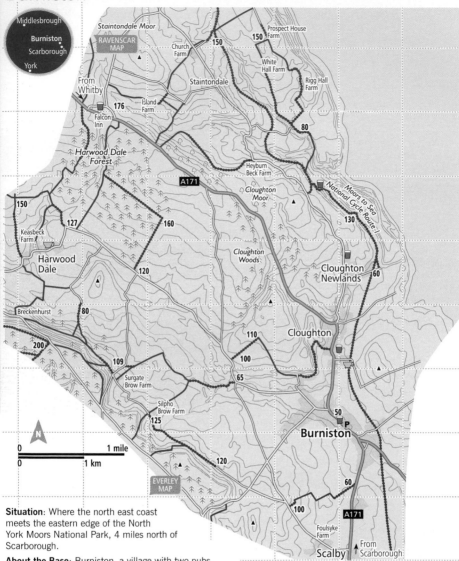

Situation: Where the north east coast meets the eastern edge of the North York Moors National Park, 4 miles north of Scarborough.

About the Base: Burniston, a village with two pubs.
Parking: Roadside in the centre of the village or car park at Reasty Hill Top in the west of the map.
Grid Ref: Burniston TA013929, Reasty Hill Top SE964943. Post Code: Burniston YO13 0HU.

Drive Times: Middlesbrough 1hr20, Leeds 1hr50, Newcastle 2hrs, Manchester 2hr40, B'ham 3hr30.

Trains: Scarborough Station has services to York.

Refreshments: At Burniston, The Three Jolly Sailors 01723 871259 & The Oakwheel 01723 870230. The Blacksmiths Arms 01723 870244, The Red Lion 01723 870702 & The Station Tea Room 01723 870896 at Cloughton. The Brytherstones 01723 870744 & The Hayburn Wyke Hotel 01723 870202 at Cloughton Newlands. The Falcon Inn 01723 870717, Wykeham Tea Rooms 01723 865212 & The Grainary 01723 870026 at Harwood Dale.

Maps: OS Explorer OL27.

Routes on Web: www.goodmtb.co.uk/a10

Bike Shops: Richardsons Cycles 01723 352682, Bike It UK 01723 507332 & Halfords 01723 500488 in Scarborough.

Route Idea

From Burniston, on to the 'Moors to Sea' trail N then to Rigg Hall & Prospect House Farms. SW to Church Farm & Island Farm then on to Harwood Dale via the eastern trail through Harwood Dale Forest. S towards Breckenhurst then SE passing Silpho Brow Farm. Road & trails to join A171 & back to start. Distance 25km.

Extend the area: Everley Map to the SW. Ravenscar Map to the NW.

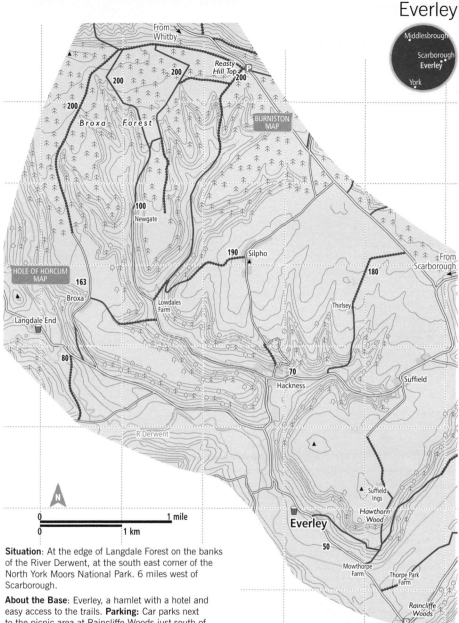

Middlesbrough
Scarborough
Everley
York

Situation: At the edge of Langdale Forest on the banks of the River Derwent, at the south east corner of the North York Moors National Park. 6 miles west of Scarborough.

About the Base: Everley, a hamlet with a hotel and easy access to the trails. **Parking:** Car parks next to the picnic area at Raincliffe Woods just south of Everley. Also car park at Reasty Hill Top in the north of the map. *Grid Ref: Raincliffe Woods SE984875, Reasty Hill Top SE964943.*

Drive Times: Middlesbrough 1hr20, Leeds 1hr40, Newcastle 2hr10, Manchester 2hr30, Birmingham 3hr20.

Trains: Scarborough Railway Station has services to York.

Refreshments: The Everley Country Hotel 01723 882202 serves refreshments. The Moorcock Inn 01723 882268 at Langdale End.

Maps: OS Explorer OL27.

Routes on Web: www.goodmtb.co.uk/a13

Bike Shops: Richardsons Cycles 01723 352682, Bike It UK 01723 507332 & Halfords 01723 500488 in Scarborough.

Route Idea

From car park at Raincliffe Woods, road to Everley & on to Broxa. Trail through Broxa Forest to Reasty Hill Top. Trails to Newgate. Onto Hackness & Suffield then S to Hawthorn Wood, Everley & back to car park. Distance 24km.

Extend the area: Burniston Map to the N. Hole of Horcum Map to the W.

Sheriff Hutton

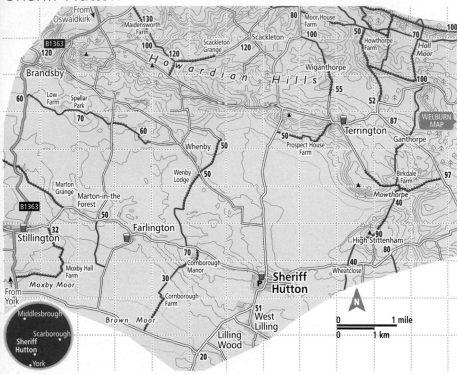

Situation: South of the Howardian Hills in Ryedale, 10 miles north east of York.

About the Base: Sheriff Hutton, a village with two pubs. Further Info: www.sheriffhutton.co.uk.

Parking: Roadside in the centre Sheriff Hutton. *Grid Ref: SE650663. Post Code: YO60 6QX.*

Drive Times: Leeds 1hr, Middlesbrough 1hr, Manchester 1hr50, Newcastle 1hr50, Birmingham 2hr40.

Refreshments: At Sheriff Hutton, The Highwayman Inn 01347 878328 & The Castle Inn 01347 878335. The Blacksmiths Arms 01347 810581 at Farlington, White Dog Inn 01347 810372 at Stillington & Bay Horse Inn 01653 648416 at Terrington.

Books: MTB Guide Mid Yorkshire (D.Liversidge).

Maps: OS Explorer 300.

Routes on Web: www.goodmtb.co.uk/a30

Bike Shops: Cycle Scene 01904 653286, 8 miles away on B1363 & Halfords 01904 611844 in York.

Route Idea

SW from Sheriff Huton past Lilling Wood to Brown Moor. Trail to Cornborough Manor then to Brandsby via Whenby & Spellar Park. NE on B1363 then trails to Scackleton. Continue to Moor House Farm then on to Hall Moor. Trails S past Ganthorpe & High Stittenham to Wheatclose, then road back to start.
Distance 42km.

Extend the area: Welburn Map to the E.

Welburn

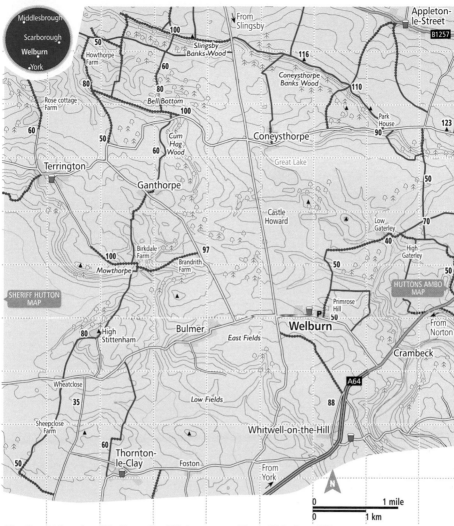

Situation: At the edge of the Howardian Hills in Ryedale.Close to Castle Howard and 14 miles north east of York.

About the Base: Welburn, a village with a pub and accommodation. **Parking**: Roadside in the centre of Welburn. *Grid Ref: SE720680. Post Code: YO60 7EE.*

Drive Times: Leeds 1hr, Middlesbrough 1hr10, Manchester 1hr50, Newcastle 2hr, Birmingham 2hr40.

Trains: Malton Railway Station, 5 miles away, is on the York-Scarborough line.

Refreshments: At Welburn, The Crown & Cushion 01653 618304. The Stone Trough Inn 01653 618713 at Kirkham, The White Swan Inn 01653 618286 at Thornton le Clay, The Bay Horse Inn 01653 648416 at Terrington & The Cresswell Arms at Appleton-le Street 01653 693647. Arboretum Café 01653 648767 at Castle Howard.

Books: MTB Guide Mid Yorkshire (D.Liversidge).

Maps: OS Explorer 300.

Routes on Web: www.goodmtb.co.uk/a32

Route Ideas

❶ FromWelburn, N on trail to High Gaterley & on to Park House. Continue to Ganthorpe via Slingsby Banks Wood, Howthorpe Farm, Bell Bottom & Cum Hag Wood. Road to Terrington then on to Mowthorpe, Brandrith Farm & back to Welburn. Distance 27km. Also suitable in reverse direction.

❷ From Welburn, head on road past Bulmer then S on trail to Thornton-le-Clay. Road & trails W past Sheepclose Farm. N to Ganthorpe, Cum Hag Wood & Slingsby Banks Wood. Trails to Park House, Low Gaterley annd Back to Welburn. Distance 29km.

Extend the area: Huttons Ambo Map to the E. Sheriff Hutton Map to the W.

Huttons Ambo

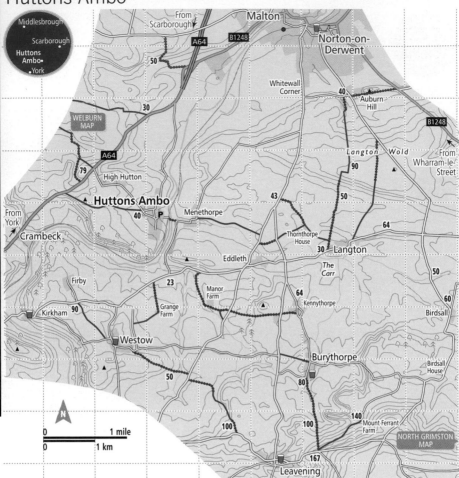

Situation: On the north west bank of the River Derwent at the edge of the Howardian Hills, 17 miles north east of York.

About the Base: Huttons Ambo, a small village with easy access to the trails.
Further Info: www.huttonsambo.com.

Parking: Roadside in the centre of the village. *Grid Ref: SE761677*. *Post Code: YO60 7HG.*

Drive Times: Leeds 1hr, Middlesbrough 1hr20, Manchester 1hr50, Newcastle 2hr, Birmingham 2hr50.

Trains: Malton Railway Station, 3 miles away, is on the York-Scarborough line.

Refreshments: The Stone Trough Inn 01653 618713 at Kirkham, The Blacksmiths Arms 01653 619606 at Westow, The Jolly Farmer 01653 658276 at Leavening & The Bay Horse Inn at Burythorpe. Several pubs & cafés at Malton.

Books: MTB Guide Mid Yorkshire (D.Liversidge). **Maps**: OS Explorer 300.

Routes on Web: www.goodmtb.co.uk/a22

Route Idea

From Huttons Ambo, E to Menethorpe & on to Thrornthorpe House. N on trails across Langton Wold. Road & trails S back across Langton Wold to Langton. Continue to Leavening using road & trails via Kennythorpe & Burythorpe. NW to Westow. Back to start via Grange Farm. Distance 23km.

Extend the area: Welburn Map to the NW, North Grimston Map to the E.

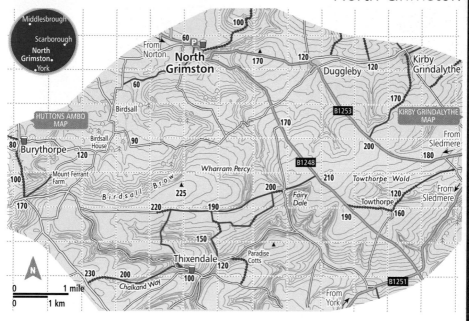

Situation: In Ryedale and the Yorkshire Wolds, 4 miles south east of Malton.

About the Base: North Grimston, a small village with a pub.
Parking: At the pub in the centre of the village. *Grid Ref:* SE842676. **Post Code:** YO17 8AX.

Drive Times: Leeds 1hr10, Middlesbrough 1hr20, Manchester 2hr, Newcastle 2hr10, Birmingham 2hr50.

Trains: Malton Railway Station, 4 miles away, is on the York-Scarborough line.

Refreshments: The Middleton Arms 01944 768255 at North Grimston. The Cross Keys 01377 288272 at Thixendale & The Bay Horse Inn 01653 658302 at Burythorpe.

Books: MTB Guide Mid Yorkshire (D.Liversidge).

Maps: OS Explorer 300.

Routes on Web: www.goodmtb.co.uk/a24

Route Ideas

❶ From North Grimston, roads E to Kirby Grindalythe then SW trail to B1253. Continue on trail past Towthorpe, then along trail N of Fairy Dale to then drop down to Thixendale. Head W on Chalkland Way then roads to just N of Birdsall to take trail back to start. Distance 40km.

❷ Shorten above but head straight to Fairy Dale from North Grimston. Distance 27km

Extend the area: North Grimston to the W, Kirby Grindalythe to the E.

Kirby Grindalythe

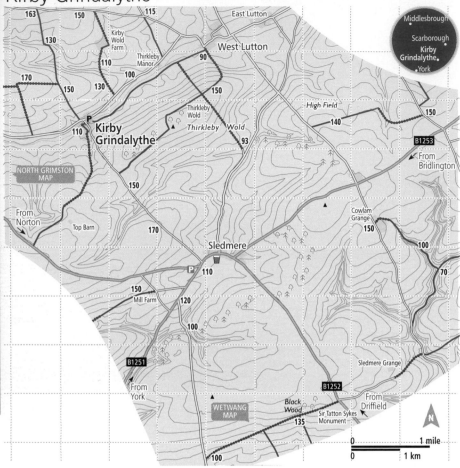

Situation: Midway between Scarborough and York in the Ryedale area of the Yorkshire Wolds. 9 miles south east of Malton.

About the Base: Kirby Grindalythe, a small village with easy access to the trails. **Parking**: Roadside in the centre of Kirby Grindalythe or car park opposite the church in Sledmere. **Grid Ref**: *Kirby Grindalythe SE905675, Sledmere SE927645*. **Post Code**: *Kirby Grindalythe YO17 8DE.*

Drive Times: Leeds 1hr20, Middlesbrough 1hr30, Manchester 2hr10, Newcastle 2hr20, Birmingham 2hr50.

Refreshments: The Triton Inn 01377 236078 at Sledmere.

Books: MTB Yorkshire Wolds (J.Beadle).

Maps: OS Explorer 300.

Route Ideas

❶ From Kirby Grindalythe , NE on trail to West Lutton then S across Thirkleby Wold to road. NE then SE to Cowlam Manor to take trail & roads past Sir Tatton Sykes Monument & Black Wood. Roads back to start. Distance 29km.

❷ Start as above but just before return to Kirby Grindalythe take trail NE to West Lutton then use road or trail back. Distance 34km.

Extend the Area: North Grimston Map to the W, Wetwang Map to the S.

Rider: Angie Rawson. © Geoff Rawson

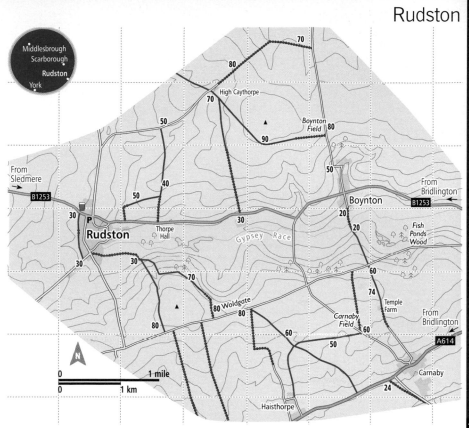

Situation: In the Gypsey Race Valley on the eastern side of the Yorkshire Wolds. 6 miles west of Bridlington.

About the Base: Rudston, a village with a pub and easy access to the trails.

Parking: Roadside in the centre Rudston. *Grid Ref: TA095678. Post Code: YO25 4UB.*

Drive Times: Leeds 1hr30, Middlesbrough 1hr50, Manchester 2hr20, Newcastle 2hr40, Birmingham 3hr.

Trains: Bridlington Railway Station is on the Scarborough-Hull line.

Refreshments: The Bosville Arms 01262 420259 at Rudston.

Maps: OS Explorer 295.

Routes on Web: www.goodmtb.co.uk/a29

Bike Shops: Hilderthorpe Cycles 01262 677555 in Bridlington.

Route Idea

From Rudston, Trails SE to Woldgate then to Carnaby Field. N to Boynton & Boynton Field. W to High Caythorne & back to Rudston with mixture of road & trails. Distance 17km.

Holtby

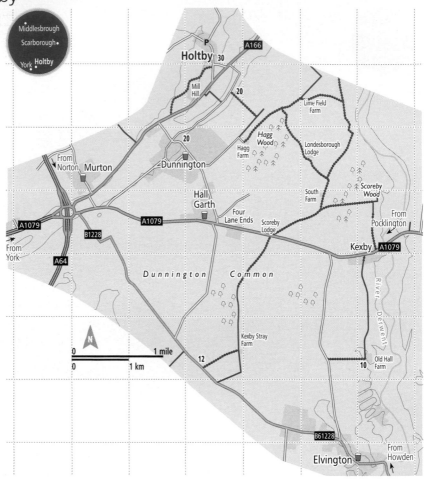

Situation: West of the Yorkshire Wolds in the Derwent Valley, 5 miles east of York.

About the Base: Holtby, a small village with easy access to the trails. **Parking:** Roadside in the centre of the village. *Grid Ref: SE674541. Post Code: YO19 5UD.*

Drive Times: Leeds 45mins, Midd lesbrough 1hr20, Manchester 1hr40, Newcastle 2hr, Birmingham 2hr30.

Trains: York Railway Station is on the main east coast line.

Refreshments: The Bay Horse Inn 01904 489684 at Murton, The Cross Keys 01904 488847 & The Greyhound 01904 488018 at Dunnington, The Windmill 01904 481898 at Hall Garth, The Grey Horse 01904 608335 & the Naafi Café 01904 608595 at Yorkshire Air Museum, both at Elvington.

Books: MTB Guide Mid Yorkshire (D.Liversidge). **Maps**: OS Explorer 290.

Routes on Web: www.goodmtb.co.uk/a20

Bike Shops: Evans Cycles 01904 629473 & Halfords 01904 611844, 4 miles away in York.

Route Idea

From Holtby, head S to Scoreby Lodge via Hagg Wood & Londesborough Lodge. S on trails across Dunnington Common. B61228 to Elvington. On to Kexby via Old Hall Farm then N to Scoreby Wood. Back to Holtby via South Farm & Lime Field Farm. Distance 22km.

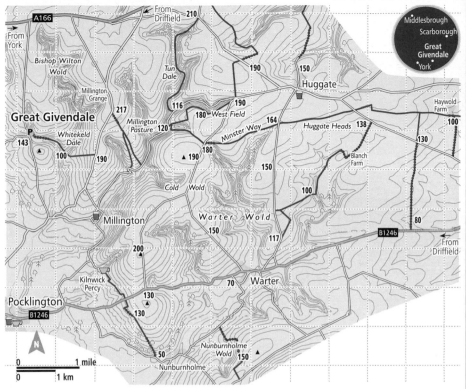

Situation: In the East Riding of Yorkshire at the edge of the Yorkshire Wolds, 17 miles east of York.

About the Base: Great Givendale, a hamlet with easy access to the trails.
Parking: Roadside opposite the church, just east of the village. *Grid Ref: SE813538. Post Code: YO42 1TT.*

Drive Times: Leeds 1hr, Middlesbrough 1hr30, Manchester 1hr50, Newcastle 2hr20, Birmingham 2hr30.

Refreshments: The Gate Inn 01759 302045 at Millington, World Peace Café 01759 304832 at Kilnwick Percy & The Wolds Inn 01377 288217 at Huggate. Pubs & cafés at Pocklington.

Maps: OS Explorer 294.

Routes on Web: www.goodmtb.co.uk/a16

Bike Shops: Wheelies Cycle Care 01759 388716, 6 miles away on the A1079, for hire, parts & repairs.

Route Idea

From Great Givendale, E on trail across Whitekeld Dale. N on minor roads to trail N through Tun Dale. Road & trail S again to West Field. Minster Way E across Huggate Heads. Onto Blanch Farm, Warter, Nunburnholme then NW to Kilnwick Percy, Millington & back to the start. Distance 38km.

Wetwang

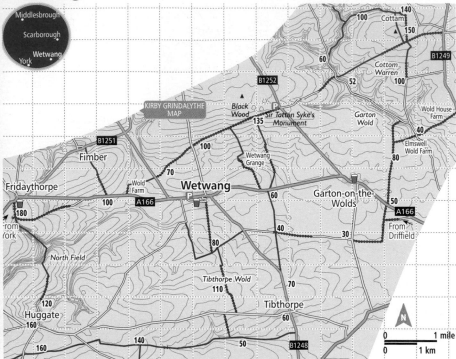

Situation: In the heart of the Yorkshire Wolds and the East Riding of Yorkshire, 6 miles west of Driffield.

About the Base: Wetwang, a village with two pubs.

Parking: In front of The Black Swan pub at the centre of Wetwang. Car park next to the Sir Tatton Sykes monument, north east of the village. *Grid Ref: Wetwang SE933591, Monument SE957618. Post Code: Wetwang YO25 9YB.*

Drive Times: Leeds 1hr10, Middlesbrough 1hr40, Manchester 2hr, Newcastle 2hr20, Birmingham 2hr40.

Trains: Driffield Railway Station is on the Scarborough-Hull line.

Refreshments: At Wetwang, The Black Swan 01377 236237 & The Victoria Inn 01377 236677. St Quintins Arms 01262 490329 at Garton on the Wolds, The Farmers Arms 01377 288221 & The Rose & Crown 01377 252211 at Fridaythorpe.

Maps: OS Explorer 294 & 300.

Routes on Web: www.goodmtb.co.uk/a33

Bike Shops: Bells Cycles 01377 253070, 6 miles away in Driffield.

Route Ideas

❶ From Sir Tatton Syke's Monument, W on trails then main road to Fridaythorpe. S to Huggate then using mostly trails on to Tibthorpe. N on the B1248 then trails & minor roads to the A166 (E of Garton-on-the-Wolds). Straight across the A166 then up & around Cottam & back to start. Distance 45km.

❷ From Sir Tatton Syke's Monument, W on trails then S on road to Wetwang. S on the B1248 then E on minor roads & trails to the A166 (E of Garton-on-the-Wolds). Straight across the A166. Before reaching Cottam use the SW trail to head back to start. Distance 23km.

Guisborough Forest Trails

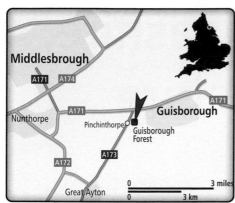

At the edge of the North York Moors, a challenge for riders of all abilities with plenty of unmarked singletrack and way-marked trails including long climbs and technical challenges. Built and maintained by Singletraction.

Facilities:
Guisborough Forest and Walkway Visitor Centre. Refreshments at nearby Guisborough.

Parking:
Grid Ref: NZ586152. Post Code: TS14 8HD

Web: www.goodmtb.co.uk/b7

The Trails

❶ Blue, XC, 7.2km.
❷ Black, XC, 12km.

Dalby Forest Trails
Pace Bike Park
DOA Downhill Trail

On the southern slopes of the North York Moors National Park. Waymarked cross country trails on forest roads and flowing singletrack with plenty of technical features for more experienced riders. Pace Bike Park, a disused quarry with a 4X course, plenty of Northshore and freeride features. DOA Downhill, a well planned, short trail with changes made regularly as part of Singletraction and Team DOA's on-going project.

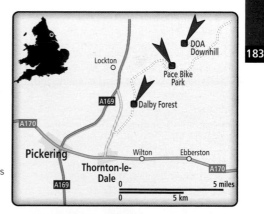

Facilities:
Purple Mountain Café in Dalby Courtyard and Treetops in Dalby Forest Visitor Centre. Purple Mountain Bike Centre 01751 460011 for hire, parts & repairs.

Parking:
Main Car Park - Grid Ref: SE856875. Post Code: YO18 7LT
Pace Bike Park - Grid Ref: SE882900
DOA Downhill - Grid Ref: SE895914

Web: www.goodmtb.co.uk/b6a /b6b & /b6c

The Trails

❶ Ellersway, Green, XC, 3.2km.
❷ Adderstone, Green, XC, 9.6km.
❸ Blue, XC, 12.9km.
❹ Red, XC, 37km.
❺ World Cup Cycle Trail, Black, XC, 6.4km.
❻ Pace Bike Park, Black, Freeride, 4X.
❼ DOA Downhill.

Rider: Dan Trent. © Claire Hayter

South Lancashire, West Yorkshire & Cheshire

The South Pennines lie between the Peak District and the Yorkshire Dales. To the west the hills reach almost as far as the M6 and to the east you can find excellent riding on the doorsteps of Leeds and Harrogate. The whole region is criss-crossed with old drovers routes and

Descending to Marsden. Rider: Paul Fox. © Blackshaw Outdoor

packhorse trails, most of which are now bridleways, many being stone-flagged for serious full suspension entertainment.

Calderdale has one of the densest network of bridleways in the country. This, combined with several canal towpaths, means tarmac is easily avoided and, as this is not a National Park, your descents are less likely to be interrupted by other users than in The

Lake District or The Peak District. Many of the descents drop more than 300m from panoramic gritstone moorland tops to the tree-covered valleys below. This obviously means that there are lots of climbs too: luckily the many towns in the valleys such as *Ilkley*, *Haworth*, *Hebden Bridge* and Holmfirth, mean that a café or pub is never far away.

To the north of the area there is some excellent open riding near *Ilkley* and Otley, north of *Horsforth* taking you over wild open moors. Further south the Aire Valley contains some excellent packhorse trails and plenty of singletrack. Several loops can be done from *Haworth* or *Oxenhope* and the nearby *Bingley* Circuit is a classic, especially now that more concessionary bridleways have been created as part of the Calder Aire Link route.

This leads us over to Calderdale where trails can get much rockier and steeper with technical climbs and descents to keep the best riders satisfied. The buses from *Hebden Bridge* have bike racks so if you organise things ahead you could do an uplift day courtesy of public transport. Classic routes in Calderdale, with bases at **Hebden Bridge**, **Todmorden**, **Mytholmroyd** and **Luddenden Foot** explore some breathtaking moors on both fine single and double track as well as through beautiful woodland on the hillsides. The 47-mile Mary Towneley Loop and the spectacular track across Rooley Moor, both part of the Pennine Bridleway, can be accessed from **Waterfoot**.

South again the bases of **Marsden** and **Digley Reservoir** have their own network of trails, with enough variety to keep any rider happy no matter what their energy or skill level. The descents of Willykay Clough (3km) or the Wessenden Valley (5km) into Marsden are excellent finales to any ride.

On the Lancashire side of the South Pennines, **Whalley** is a great base from which to explore Pendle Hill and the foothills of the Pennines, whilst from **Colne** you can ride out to the tranquil Wycoller Country

Park and join the Pennine Bridleway. **Rivington** offers a dense network of legal routes from waterside family rides to some killer climbs and descents off the Pike itself. There is also the opportunity to extend your ride around Winter Hill from **Tockholes** or take in the purpose-built downhill at **Healey Nab**. Good quality Trail Centres are becoming a major part of Lancashire riding with further trails set up at **Billinge Wood** in Blackburn, **Lee Quarry** near Bacup in Rossendale and several more in planning or under construction.

Gently undulating mountain biking can be found in bases north and south of Leeds such as at **Shadwell**, **South Kirkby**, **Emley** and **Newmillerdam**.

Descending from Shackleton Knoll. © Blackshaw Outdoor

Colne

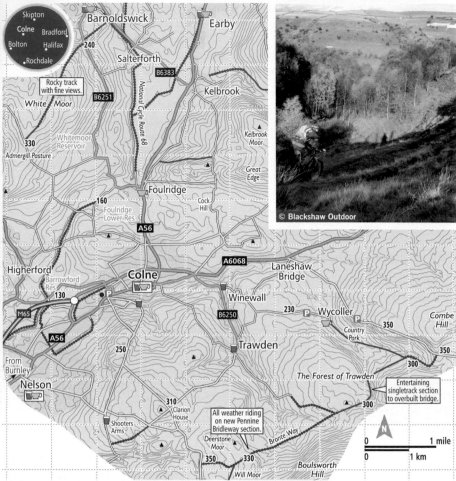

Skipton
Colne Bradford
Bolton Halifax
Rochdale

Barnoldswick

Earby

240

Salterforth

B6383

B6251

Rocky track with fine views.

White Moor

Kelbrook

National Cycle Route 68

330

Whitemoor Reservoir

Admergill Pasture

Kelbrook Moor

Great Edge

Foulridge

160

Cock Hill

Foulridge Lower Res

A56

A6068

Laneshaw Bridge

Higherford

Barrowford Res

130

Colne

M65

A56

250

From Burnley

Nelson

Winewall

B6250

230

Wycoller

P

P

350

Country Park

Combe Hill

350

Trawden

300

The Forest of Trawden

Entertaining singletrack section to overbuilt bridge.

310

Clarion House

Shooters Arms

All weather riding on new Pennine Bridleway section.

Deerstone Moor

350

330

Bronte Way

300

Boulsworth Hill

Will Moor

N

0   1 mile

0   1 km

© Blackshaw Outdoor

Situation: In the Aire Gap, close to the Yorkshire border, in the Pendle district of Lancashire. 8 miles north east of Burnley at the end of the M65.

About the Base: Colne, an ancient market town with plenty of pubs, cafés and accommodation.
Parking: Car Parks at Colne Leisure Centre and Wycoller Country Park. *Grid Ref: Colne Leisure Centre SD882398, Trawden Road Car Park SD926395. Post Code: Colne Leisure Centre BB8 9NF.*

Drive Times: Manchester 50mins, Leeds 1hr, Sheffield 1hr40, Birmingham 2hr10, Newcastle 2hr30.

Trains: Colne Railway Station is at the start of the Burnley line.

Refreshments: Choice of pubs & cafés in Colne and The Admiral Lord Rodney 01282 870083, south of the town next to the river. The Cottontree and Winewall 01282 863406 in Winewall, Tea Rooms at Wycoller Craft Centre 01282 868395 (phone ahead for large groups), The Trawden Arms 01282 863005 or The Sun Inn 01282 867985 at Trawden and the Shooters Arms 01282 614153. Café Cargo 01282 870284 in Foulridge and choice of pubs or Café on the Square 01282 812882 in Barnoldswick.

Books: MTB Guide S Pennines of W Yorks & Lancs (S.Hall). **Maps:** OS Explorer OL21.

Routes on Web: www.goodmtb.co.uk/a66

Bike Shops: Foxs Cycles 01282 863 017 in Colne. Halfords

Route Ideas

❶ S from Colne to Deerstone Moor then Bronte Way E followed by trail NW to Wycoller. Road to Laneshaw Bridge and on to Foulridge via Cock Hill. Road to Whitemoor Reservoir and Admergill Pasture. Trail across White Moor to Barnoldswick and Salterforth. National Cycle Route 68 to Foulridge. Road to the W of Foulridge Lower Reservoir, trails SW to Barrowford Reservoir and road back to start. Distance 39km.

❷ From Wycoller to Trawden to Clarion House. Road S then Bronte Way E. Trail descent back to Wycoller. Distance 14km.

Ilkley

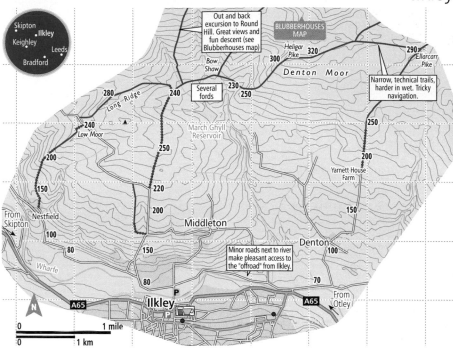

Situation: On the south bank of the River Wharfe in Wharfedale, just south of the Yorkshire Dales National Park. 6 miles north east of Keighley and 12 miles north of Bradford.

About the Base: Ilkley, a small town with pubs, cafés and accomodation. Further info: www.ilkley.org.
Parking: Car park in the centre of Ilkley.
Grid Ref: Ilkley LS29 9DX. Post Code: Ilkley SE115477.

Drive Times: Leeds 40mins, Manchester 1hr20, Sheffield 1hr30, Newcastle 2hrs, Birmingham 2hr40.

Trains: Ilkley Railway Station has services to Leeds & Bradford.

Refreshments: A choice of refreshments in Ilkley.

Books: MTB Guide S Pennines of W Yorks & Lancs (S.Hall). **Maps**: OS Explorer 297. Dales East Cycle Map (Harvey).

Bike Shops: JD Cycles 01943 816101 in Ilkley.

Route Idea

From Ilkley, road E to Denton then trails N past Yarnett House Farm. Trails W across Denton Moor, across Long Ridge and down to Nestfield. Road back to Ilkley. Distance 20km.

Extend the area: Blubberhouses Map to the N.

© Blackshaw Outdoor

Rivington

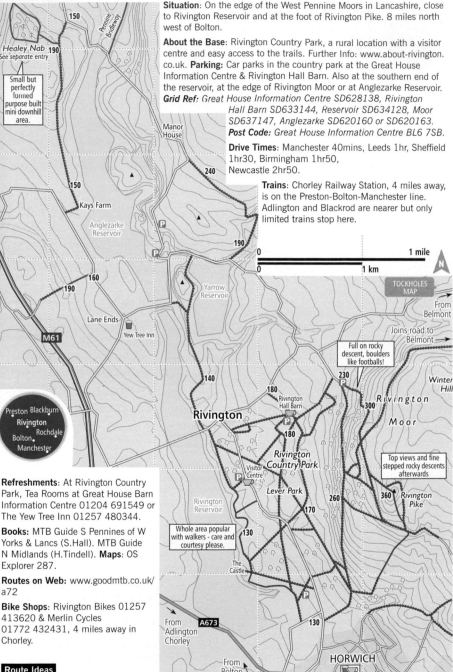

Situation: On the edge of the West Pennine Moors in Lancashire, close to Rivington Reservoir and at the foot of Rivington Pike. 8 miles north west of Bolton.

About the Base: Rivington Country Park, a rural location with a visitor centre and easy access to the trails. Further Info: www.about-rivington. co.uk. **Parking**: Car parks in the country park at the Great House Information Centre & Rivington Hall Barn. Also at the southern end of the reservoir, at the edge of Rivington Moor or at Anglezarke Reservoir. *Grid Ref: Great House Information Centre SD628138, Rivington Hall Barn SD633144, Reservoir SD634128, Moor SD637147, Anglezarke SD620160 or SD620163.* **Post Code**: *Great House Information Centre BL6 7SB.*

Drive Times: Manchester 40mins, Leeds 1hr, Sheffield 1hr30, Birmingham 1hr50, Newcastle 2hr50.

Trains: Chorley Railway Station, 4 miles away, is on the Preston-Bolton-Manchester line. Adlington and Blackrod are nearer but only limited trains stop here.

Refreshments: At Rivington Country Park, Tea Rooms at Great House Barn Information Centre 01204 691549 or The Yew Tree Inn 01257 480344.

Books: MTB Guide S Pennines of W Yorks & Lancs (S.Hall). MTB Guide N Midlands (H.Tindell). **Maps**: OS Explorer 287.

Routes on Web: www.goodmtb.co.uk/a72

Bike Shops: Rivington Bikes 01257 413620 & Merlin Cycles 01772 432431, 4 miles away in Chorley.

Route Ideas

❶ From the Visitor Centre S on trails to The Castle. SE to road then N on trail across slopes of Rivington Pike to car park . Road NW to Yarrow Reservoir. Trail followed by road past Manor House to Healey Nab & S to Kays Farm. Trail and road to cross over M61 twice. Trail from Yarrow Reservoir to Rivington and back to start. Distance 21km.

❷ Explore trails around Rivington Pike.

Extend the area: Tockholes Map to the E. Also see Healey Nab (p210), located at NW of this map.

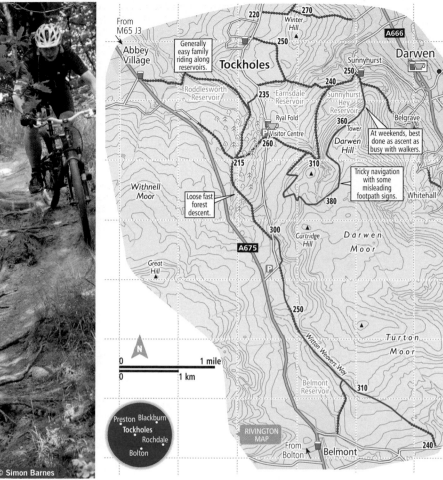

© Simon Barnes

Situation: On the West Pennine Moors in Lancashire at the foot of Winter Hill. 5 miles south west of Blackburn.

About the Base: Tockholes, a small village with pubs, a café and a visitor centre.
Further Info: www.tockholes.org.uk.
Parking: Car park at Tockholes Visitor Centre in Ryal Fold. Also at Tockholes Plantation. *Grid Ref: Visitor Centre SD665214, Tockholes Plantation SD663202.*
Post Code: Visitor Centre BB3 OPA.

Drive Times: Manchester 45mins, Leeds 1hr10, Sheffield 1hr40, Birmingham 2 hr, Newcastle 2hr50.

Trains: Cherry Tree Railway Station, 3 miles away, is on the Preston-Blackburn-Halifax line. Darwen Railway Station, 4 miles away is on the Blackburn-Bolton-Manchester line.

Refreshments: At Tockholes, The Rock Inn 01254 702733 and The Victoria Hotel 01254 701622. The Royal Arms 01254 705373 and Vaughns Café 01254 708568 at Ryal Fold. The Hare & Hounds 01254 830334 at Abbey Village, The Sunnyhurst Inn 01254 873035 in Sunnyhurst and The Black Dog 01204 811218 in Belmont.

Books: MTB Guide S Pennines of W Yorks & Lancs (S.Hall). **Maps:** OS Explorer 287.

Routes on Web: www.goodmtb.co.uk/a74

Bike Shops: Ewood Bikes 01254 55515, 3 miles away on A666 into Blackburn.

Route Ideas

❶ From Ryal Fold SW through wood and NW to Abbey Village. Turn E on trails to the N of Roddlewsworth, Earnsdale and Sunnyhurst Reservoirs. S past Darwen Hill and back to Ryal Fold. Distance 14km.

❷ An out and back from Ryal Fold to Belmont on Witton Weavers Way. Distance 14km.

Extend the area: Rivington Map to the W provides possibility of connecting to Belmont.

Waterfoot

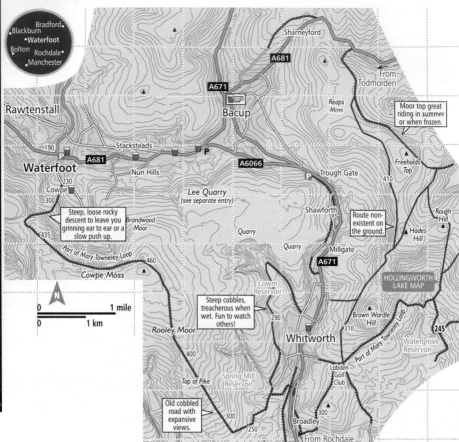

Map labels:
Bradford, Blackburn, •Waterfoot, Bolton, Rochdale, Manchester

Sharneyford

A681

From Todmorden

A671

Reaps Moss

Moor top great riding in summer or when frozen.

Rawtenstall

Bacup

Stacksteads

A681

Waterfoot

Nun Hills

A6066

Trough Gate

410

Freeholds Top

P

190

Cowpe

230

300

Lee Quarry (see separate entry)

Shawforth

Route non-existent on the ground.

Rough Hill

Steep, loose rocky descent to leave you grinning ear to ear or a slow push up.

Brandwood Moor

Quarry

Quarry

Hades Hill

435

Part of Mary Towneley Loop

460

Quarry

Millgate

A671

HOLLINGWORTH LAKE MAP

Cowpe Moss

Cowm Reservoir

0   1 mile
0   1 km

Steep cobbles, treacherous when wet. Fun to watch others!

290

Brown Wardle Hill

310

245

Rooley Moor

400

Whitworth

Part of Mary Towneley Loop

Watergrove Reservoir

Lobden Golf Club

Top of Pike

Spring Mill Reservoir

Old cobbled road with expansive views.

300

250

300

Broadley

From Rochdale

Situation: In the Rossendale Valley, 8 miles south of Burnley.

About the Base: Waterfoot, a small mill town with a pub and a tea shop. **Parking:** Car Park in the centre of Waterfoot. Roadside at the entrance to Lee Quarry or car park at Trough Gate.*Grid Ref: Waterfoot SD834217, Lee Quarry SD863219, Trough Gate SD885214. Post Code: Waterfoot BB4 7AL, Lee Quarry OL13 0BB, Trough Gate OL13 9SN.*

Drive Times: Manchester 40mins, Leeds 1hr, Sheffield 1hr20, B'ham 2hr, Newcastle 2hr40.

Trains: Burnley Railway Station is on the Halifax-Preston-Blackpool line.

Refreshments: At Waterfoot, the Duke of Buccleugh 01706 250059 and The Tea Shop 01706 225294. The Rose n Bowl 01706 879555 and Snack Attack 01706 870666 at Stacksteads, The Red Lion 01706 861441 in Whitworth, The Buck Inn 01706 213612 at Cowpe and a choice of pubs & cafés in Bacup.

Books: MTB Guide S Pennines of W Yorks & Lancs (S.Hall). **Maps**: OS Explorer OL21.

Routes on Web: www.goodmtb.co.uk/a76

Bike Shops: Ride On 01706 831101, a mile away in Rossendale.

Route Idea

From Waterfoot S along Mary Towneley Loop to Whitworth. Continue on Mary Towneley Loop but leave it at Lobden Golf Club to go N past west side of Brown Wardle Hill. Before Hades Hill head N to Reaps Moss and to A681. To Bacup on trails & roads. Roads back to start. Distance 30km.

Extend the area: Hollingworth Lake Map to E or look to tackle the whole Mary Towneley Loop, a tough 76km.

Also see Lee Quarry (p211).

Rooley Moor Road. © Simon Barnes www.bogtrotters.org

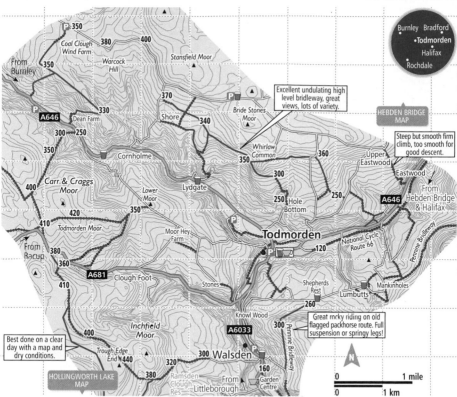

Burnley Bradford
•Todmorden
Halifax
Rochdale

Excellent undulating high level bridleway, great views, lots of variety.

HEBDEN BRIDGE MAP

Steep but smooth firm climb, too smooth for good descent.

Great rocky riding on old flagged packhorse route. Full suspension or springy legs!

Best done on a clear day with a map and dry conditions.

HOLLINGWORTH LAKE MAP

Situation: In the Upper Calder Valley, at the junction of three steep sided valleys in the heart of the Pennine hills. 4 miles south west of Hebden Bridge.

About the Base: Todmorden, a small market town with a choice of pubs and cafes.
Further Info: www.visittodmorden.co.uk.

Parking: Car parks in the centre of Todmorden and next to Ewood Hall west of the town. Also at Bride Stones Moor, Coal Clough Wind Farm and south on the A646. Small car park near the station in Walsden. *Grid Ref: Todmorden SD937243, Ewood Hall SD927248, Bride Stones Moor SD928272, Coal Clough Wind Farm SD898285, A646 SD888271, Walsden SD932221. Post Code: Todmorden OL14 5DN, Ewood Hall OL14 7DF, Walsden OL14 6SF.*

Drive Times: Leeds 50mins, Manchester 50mins, Sheffield 1hr30, B'ham 2hr10, Newcastle 2hr40.

Trains: Todmorden and Walsden Railway Stations are on the Manchester-Leeds line.

Refreshments: At Todmorden, plenty of pubs, Cherries Tearoom 01706 817828 and Costermonger Café 01706 812600. The Shepherd's Rest Inn 01706 813437 and The Top Brink Inn 01706 812696 at Lumbetts. Pubs & Café at Gordon Riggs Garden Centre 01706 813374 in Walsden. The Staff of Life Inn 01706 819033 and the White Hart Hotel 01706 812198 at Lydgate, The Glen View Inn 01706 812 796 at Cornholme and The Sportsmans Arms 01706 813 449 at Bride Stones Moor.

Books: MTB Guide S Pennines of W Yorks & Lancs (S.Hall). **Maps**: OS Explorer OL21.

Bike Shops: Blazing Saddles 01422 844435 in Hebden Bridge. Hebden Bridge Cycle Hire 07790 648 842 for MTB Hire.

© Blackshaw Outdoor

Route Ideas

❶ From Todmorden, N to Hole Bottom then NW on trails past Whirlaw Common and on to road north of Shore. Continue to the Wind Farm then trails S past Dean Farm to the A646. S across Carr & Craggs Moor. E across Todmorden Moor to Lower Moor. Road & trails SE past Moor Hey Farm to Stones and on to the A6033. Roads and cycle paths back to the start. Distance 22km.

❷ As above to cross Carr Craggs Moor. Then S on trails past Trough Edge End to Walsden. Road link to the Pennine Bridleway. N to the Shepherds Rest Inn. Road W then link to trails N back to Todmorden. Distance 26km.

Extend the area: Hebden Bridge Map to the N. Hollingworth Lake Map to the S.

Hebden Bridge

Map labels:

- Shackleton Moor
- 290
- Flask
- Calder-Aire Link
- 300
- 290
- New Laithe Moor
- Pack Horse
- 275
- Calder-Aire Link
- "Take no prisoners" descents to pretty Lumb Falls. Push back out.
- Colne · Keighley · Bradford
- Hebden Bridge · Halifax
- Rochdale
- From Keighley
- Gorple Lower Reservoir
- 350
- All weather stony track
- 380
- Heptonstall Moor
- Hardcastle Crags
- Awesome rocky, rooty switchback descent. A6033
- 230
- Pecket Well
- 350
- Easy picturesque hardpack trail.
- Shackleton
- 280
- 270
- Hoar Side Moor
- 350
- 400
- Highgate Farm
- 300
- Colden
- 145
- Midgehole
- 430
- 340
- Slack
- Old Town
- Chiserley
- Jack Bridge
- 270
- Heptonstall
- Hebden Bridge
- 260
- 380
- 350
- 340
- Steep enough to make for a challenging climb.
- 210
- Blackshaw Head
- 300
- Calderside
- 110
- Staups Moor
- Very steep, bottom half on tarmac
- 250
- Charlestown
- 115
- A646
- From Halifax
- N
- 0 — 1 mile
- 0 — 1 km
- A646
- Eastwood
- Edge End Moor
- Kershaw Farm
- 330
- Mytholmroyd
- RIPPONDEN/ MYTHOLMROYD MAP
- From Todmorden
- Canal towpath
- Erringden Moor
- 300

Situation: In the Pennine Hills, where the River Calder meets the River Hebden in the Upper Calder Valley. 8 miles west of Halifax.

About the Base: Hebden Bridge, a market town with plenty of pubs, cafés and accommodation. Further Info: www.hebdenbridge.co.uk. **Parking**: Market Place car park or any of the long stay car parks in the town centre. National Trust car park at Midgehole, north of the town. *Grid Ref: Hebden Bridge SD992274, Midgehole SD988292, Calder Aire Link SD947323. Post Code: Hebden Bridge HX7 7DD.*

Drive Times: Leeds 40mins, Manchester 1hr, Sheffield 1hr20, Birmingham 2hr10, Newcastle 2hr30.

Trains: Hebden Bridge Railway Station is on the Leeds-Bradford-Manchester line.

Refreshments: Plenty of choice in Hebden Bridge. The Hare & Hounds Inn 01422 842671 at Chiserley, Robin Hood Inn 01422 842595 at Packet Well and The Blue Pig at Midgehole. The Pack Horse Inn 01422 842803, Highgate Farm shop 01422 842 897 at Colden, New Delight Inn 01422 846178 at Jack Bridge and The Cross Inn 01422 847563 at Heptonstall.

Books: MTB Guide S Pennines of W Yorks & Lancs (S.Hall). **Maps**: OS Explorer OL21.

Routes on Web: www.goodmtb.co.uk/a69

Bike Shops: Blazing Saddles 01422 844435 in Hebden Bridge. Hebden Bridge Cycle Hire 07790 648 842 for MTB Hire.

Route Ideas

❶ From Hebden Bridge, main road (A6033) then minor road N to Midgehole. Trails NW past Shackleton and New Laithe Moor. On to Gorple Lower Reservoir. Pennine Bridleway now all way to and across A646 and up to Kershaw Farm. Trails NE to station and back to start. Distance 23km.

❷ Extend the above route by heading to Midgeghole via Chiserley, Pecket Well, trails SW then continue as above. Distance 27km.

❸ Shortcuts back to Hebden Bridge at Highgate Farm, Jack Bridge or along the canal beside the A646 to avoid the last climb.

Extend the area: Ripponden/Mytholmroyd Map to the SE.

Descent from Pecket Well © Blackshaw Outdoor

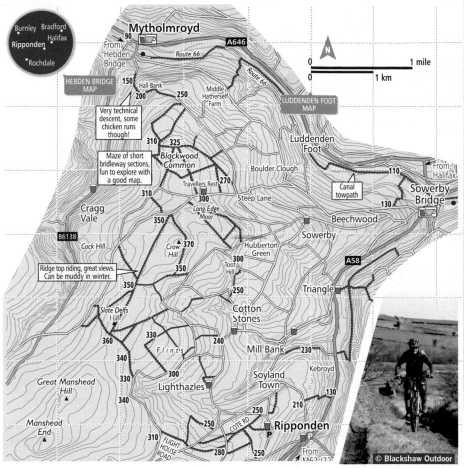

Burnley Bradford
Halifax
Ripponden
Rochdale

Mytholmroyd

From Hebden Bridge

A646

Route 66

0 —— 1 mile
0 —— 1 km

HEBDEN BRIDGE MAP

150 Hall Bank

200

250

Middle Hatherself Farm

Route 66

LUDDENDEN FOOT MAP

Very technical descent, some chicken runs though!

310 325

Maze of short bridleway sections, fun to explore with a good map.

Blackwood Common

310

300

270 Travellers Rest

Long Edge Moor

Steep Lane

Luddenden Foot

Boulder Clough

110 From Halifax

Canal towpath

130

Sowerby Bridge

Cragg Vale

350

Beechwood

B6138

Cock Hill

Crow Hill 370

350

350

Hubberton Green

300

Toot Hill

250

Sowerby

A58

Triangle

Ridge top riding, great views. Can be muddy in winter.

Slate Delfs Hill

Cotton Stones

360

330

240

340

Flints

Mill Bank 230

Kebroyd

Great Manshead Hill

330

300

Soyland Town

130

Lighthazles

340

210

Manshead End

310 FLIGHT HOUSE ROAD

250 COTE RD

280 250

Ripponden
P   P

From M62

© Blackshaw Outdoor

Situation: In Calderdale, West Yorkshire. Ripponden, is on the banks of the River Ryburn, 6 miles south west of Halifax. Mytholmroyd, on the River Calder, is 6 miles away between Halifax and Hebden Bridge.

About the Base: Ripponden, a village with a couple of pubs or Mytholmroyd, a small town with pubs, cafés and a railway station. **Parking:** Car park in Ripponden (short stay except Sundays) or roadside on A58 nearby. Also opposite The Beehive Inn outside the village. **Grid Ref:** Ripponden SE039198, A58 SE037196, Beehive Inn SE033199. **Post Code:** Ripponden HX6 4AT, A58 HX6 4DS, Beehive pub HX6 4LU

Drive Times: Leeds 40mins, Manchester 40mins, Sheffield 1hr10, B'ham 2hr, Newcastle 2hr20.

Trains: Mytholmroyd Railway Station is on the Halifax-Preston & Leeds-Preston lines.

Refreshments: At Ripponden, The Old Bridge Inn 01422 822595 and The Golden Lion 01422 822887 or The Beehive 01422 824670 outside the village. The Queens Hotel 01422 820563 at Lighthazles and Robin Hood Inn 01422 885899 at Crag Vale. Choice of pubs and Riverside Café 01422 in Mytholmroyd. The Travellers Rest 01422 832124 at Longedge

Moor, The Rush Cart 01422 831956 at Sowerby. Pubs & cafés in Sowerby Bridge. The Triangle Inn 01422 831512, The Alma Inn 01422 823334 at Cotton Stones or The Mill Bank Inn.

Books: MTB Guide S Pennines of W Yorks & Lancs (S.Hall). MTB W & S Yorkshire (R.Peace). **Maps:** OS Explorer OL21.

Bike Shops: Blazing Saddles 01422 844435 in Hebden Bridge.

Route Ideas

❶ NW from Ripponden then along Cote Road, Flight House Road and NW to Slate Delfs Hill. NE to road then S past Crow Hill. Road & trails to Lighthazles and back to Ripponden. Distance 12km.

❷ Start as above then NE past Slate Delf Hill to road, across Blackwood Common and down to Mytholmroyd. E on cycle route 66. Up to Middle Hatherself Farm then back across Blackwood Common to Travellers rest. Trail to E side of Crow Hill then on to Lighthazles and back to Ripponden. Distance 21km.

Luddenden Foot

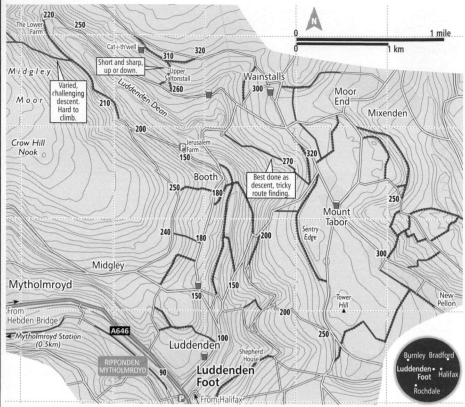

The Lower Farm 220 250

Midgley Moor

Cat-i-th'well 310 320

Short and sharp, up or down.

Upper Saltonstall 260

Wainstalls 300

Moor End

Mixenden

Varied, challenging descent. Hard to climb. 210

Luddenden Dean 200

Crow Hill Nook

Jerusalem Farm 150

Booth 270 320

250 180

Best done as descent, tricky route finding.

250

Mount Tabor

Sentry Edge

240 180 200 300

Midgley

Mytholmroyd 150 150

From Hebden Bridge

Mytholmroyd Station (0.5km)

A646

RIPPONDEN/MYTHOLMROYD 90

200 Tower Hill New Pellon

250

Luddenden 100

Shepherd House

Luddenden Foot

From Halifax

Burnley Bradford
Luddenden • Foot • Halifax
• Rochdale

Situation: Lying along the Upper Calder Valley in Calderdale, West Yorkshire. 4 miles south east of Hebden Bridge and 5 miles west of Halifax.

About the Base: Luddenden Foot, a village with a pub and easy access to the trail. **Parking**: Car park on Station Road, next to the canal at Luddenden Foot. Also parking at Jerusalem Farm in Booth. *Grid Ref: Luddenden Foot SE035251, Booth SE037278. Post Code: Luddenden Foot HX2 6AD.*

Drive Times: Leeds 40mins, Manchester 50mins, Sheffield 1hr10, Birmingham 2hr10, Newcastle 2hr20.

Trains: Mytholmroyd Railway Station is on the Halifax-Preston & Leeds-Preston lines.

Refreshments: At Luddenden Foot, The Kershaw House Inn 01422 882222. The Lord Nelson Inn

01422 882176 in Luddenden, The Crossroads Inn 01422 241511 and The Delvers 01422 244863 at Wainstalls and The Cat-I-Th'well 01422 244841.

Books: MTB Guide S Pennines of W Yorks & Lancs (S.Hall). MTB W & S Yorkshire (R.Peace). **Maps**: OS Explorer OL21.

Bike Shops: Blazing Saddles 01422 844435 in Hebden Bridge.

Route Idea

From the car park next to the canal, N on road to Luddenden then trails and tracks to Booth. NW to The Lower Farm then E to Wainstalls via Upper Saltonstall. S on roads and trails past Sentry Edge. On to Shepherd House and back to start. Distance 15km.

© Blackshaw Outdoor

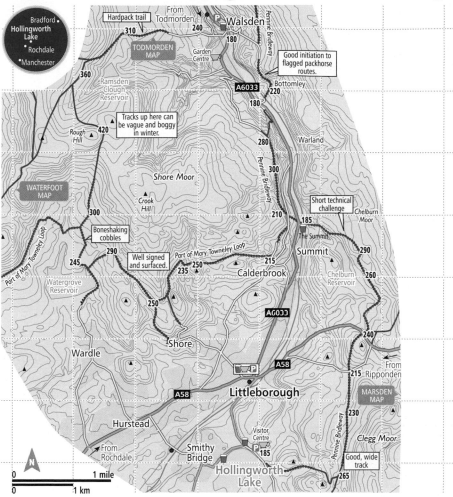

Situation: In the Roch valley between the Rossendale Fells and the South Pennines. 3 miles north east of Rochdale.

About the Base: Littleborough, a town with a choice of pubs and accommodation or Hollingworth Lake, south of the town, with pubs, a visitor centre and a café. Further Info: www.littleboroughlocal.co.uk. **Parking:** Car park in Littleborough town centre or at Hollingworth Lake, next to the visitor centre. Small car park near the station in Walsden. *Grid Ref: Littleborough SD936162, Hollingworth Lake SD940152, Walsden SD932221. Post Code: Littleborough OL15 8AQ, Hollingworth Lake OL15 0AQ, Walsden OL14 6SF.*

Drive Times: Manchester 40mins, Leeds 45mins, Sheffield 1hr20, Birmingham 2hr, Newcastle 2hr30.

Trains: Littleborough and Walsden Railway Stations are on the Halifax-Rochdale-Manchester line.

Refreshments: Choice of pubs in Littleborough. At Hollingworth Lake, Café in Visitor Centre 01706 373421, The Wine Press 01706 378168 and The Beach 01706 378163. The Summit Inn 01706

378011. In Walsden, Café at Gordon Rigg's Garden Centre 01706 813374, The Boarder Rose Inn 01706 812142, Hollins Inn 01706 815843 and The Cross Keys 01706 810210.

Maps: OS Explorer OL21.

Routes on Web: www.goodmtb.co.uk/a70

Bike Shops: Plenty in Rochdale. Chris Paulson Cycles 01706 633426, as you enter the town from Littleborough.

Route Ideas

❶ From Hollingworth Lake E to Pennine Bridleway. N to Bottomley and then leaving Pennine Bridleway down to Walsden. Road and trails past Rough Hill and down to Watergrove Reservoir. E on Mary Towneley Loop to The Summit pub. Retrace your tyre treads back to the start. Distance 31km.

❷ Shorten by starting at Walsden and riding the loop only and so avoiding Hollingworth Lake to The Summit section. Distance 16km.

Marsden

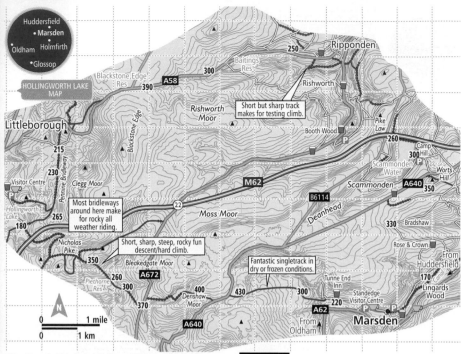

Huddersfield
• Marsden
Oldham   Holmfirth
• Glossop

HOLLINGWORTH LAKE MAP

Blackstone Edge Res
A58   390
300
Baitings Res
250
Ripponden

Littleborough
Rishworth Moor
Short but sharp track makes for testing climb.
Rishworth
Booth Wood   P
Pike Law
260
Camp Hill   300
Scammonden Water   P
Worts Hill
350

215
230
Visitor Centre   P
Hollingworth Lake   265
180
Clegg Moor
Most bridleways around here make for rocky all weather riding.
22
Moss Moor
M62
B6114
Deanhead
Scammonden   A640
330   Bradshaw

Nicholas Pike
350
Short, sharp, steep, rocky fun descent/hard climb.
Bleakedgate Moor
A672
Fantastic singletrack in dry or frozen conditions.
Rose & Crown
From Huddersfield

Piethorne Res
260   300
370
400 Denshaw Moor
430
300
Tunne End Inn
220
Standedge Visitor Centre   P
170
Lingards Wood

A640
From Oldham
A62   P   P
Marsden

0   1 mile
0   1 km
N

Situation: In the Colne Valley, at the foot of the Pennine Moors and the northern edge of the Peak District National Park in West Yorkshire. 7 miles south west of Huddersfield and north east of Saddleworth.

About the Base: Marsden, a large village with pubs and cafes. Further Info: www.bellastown.demon.co.uk.

Parking: Car park in the centre of Marsden and at Standedge Visitor Centre. Also at Scammonden Water, Booth Wood Reservoir and Hollingworth Lake Visitor Centre. *Grid Ref: Marsden SE049118, Standedge Visitor Centre SE040120, Booth Wood Reservoir SE035167, Hollingworth Lake SD940152. Post Code: Marsden HD7 6AB, Standedge Visitor Centre HD7 6NQ, Hollingworth Lake OL15 0AQ.*

Drive Times: Manchester 40mins, Leeds 45mins, Sheffield 1hr10, Birmingham 2hr10, Newcastle 2hr30.

Trains: Marsden Railway Station is on the Manchester-Huddersfield-Leeds line.

Refreshments: Pubs & Cafés in Marsden, The Tunnel End Inn 01484 844636 and Café 01782 785 703 at Standedge Visitor Centre west of the village. The Rose & Crown 01484 844410 in Cop Hill End. Nont Sarahs 01484 842 848 at Scammonden. The Turnpike Inn 01422 822789 and The Old Bore 01422 822 291 at Boothwood. The Malt House 01422 822382 in Rishworth and The Butchers Arms 01422 823100 at Ripponden.

Books: MTB Guide S Pennines of W Yorks & Lancs (S.Hall). **Maps**: OS Explorer OL21.

Bike Shops: Colne Valley Cycles 01484 843498, 3 miles away on A62 to Huddersfield. The Cyclery 01457 879955 in Saddleworth. Several bike shops in Huddersfield.

Route Idea

From Marsden, canal towpath then N to Worts Hill. Trails and minor roads N towards Ripponden then W to join the A58 near Baitings Reservoir. W on the A58. Pennine Bridleway S. Cross under the M62 then trails past Piethorne Reservoir to the A672. E on trails plus small road sections back to Marsden. Distance 40km.

Extend the area: Hollingworth Lake Map to the E.

Pennine Bridleway. Rider: Paul Fox. © Blackshaw Outdoor

Northowram

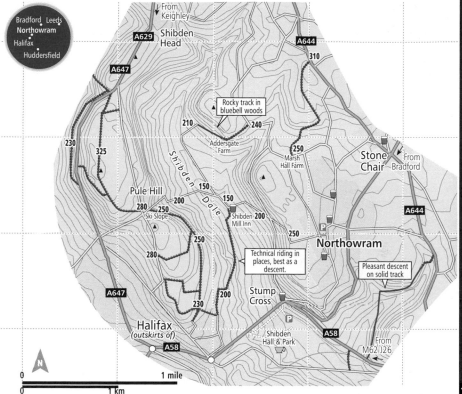

Situation: On the north side of the Shibden Valley in Calderdale, West Yorkshire. 3 miles north east of Halifax.

About the Base: Northowram, a village with pubs and easy access to the trails. **Parking:** Car park in the centre of the village. Also at Shibden Park. *Grid Ref: Northowram SE110270, Shibden Park SE107261. Post Code: Northowram HX3 7EE, Shibden Park HX3 6XJ.*

Drive Times: Leeds 30mins, Manchester 1hr, Sheffield 1hr, Newcastle 2hr10, Birmingham 2hr10.

Trains: Halifax Railway Station is on the Leeds-Bradford-Preston line.

Refreshments: At Northowram, The Yew Tree Inn 01422 202316, Windmill Tavern 01422 202464 and Shoulder of Mutton 01422 206229. The Duke of York 01422 203925 at Stone Chair, The Stump Cross Inn 01422 321066 and Shibden Mill Inn 01422 365840. Also, Café at Shibden Hall and Park 01422 352246.

Books: MTB W & S Yorkshire (R.Peace).
Maps: OS Explorer 288.

Bike Shops: Cycle Gear 01422 344602 in Halifax.

Route Idea

From Northowram, N on minor roads to A644. NW on A644. S on trails to Marsh Hall Farm. Roads and trails to Pule Hill via Addersgate Farm. Trail N then road back to Pule Hill. SE on trails past Ski Slope then N to Shibden Mill Inn and road back to start. Distance 14km.

Oxenhope

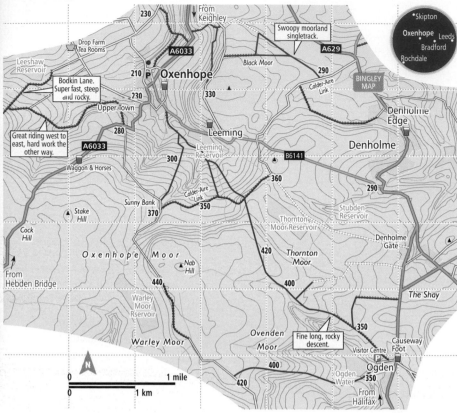

Situation: At the foot of Oxenhope Moor in West Yorkshire. Close to Haworth, at the heart of 'Bronte Country'. 5 miles south west of Keighley.

About the Base: Oxenhope, a village with a pub and easy access to the trails. **Parking:** In the centre of the village or car park at Ogden Water close to the visitor centre. *Grid Ref: Oxenhope SE031353, Ogden Water SE066309. Post Code: Oxenhope BD22 9SF, Ogden Water HX2 8XZ.*

Drive Times: Leeds 40mins, Manchester 1hr, Sheffield 1hr20, Newcastle 2hr30, Birmingham 2hr30.

Trains: Oxenhope Railway Station is at the end of the Keighley & Worth Valley Railway line to Keighley. Keighley Railway Station is on the Hull-Leeds-Carlisle line.

Refreshments: At Oxenhope, The Bay Horse Inn 01535 642209 or the Buffet Car at Oxenhope Station. The Dog & Gun 01535 643159 at Leeming Reservoir, The Causeway Foot Inn 01422 240273 and The Moorlands Inn 01422 248943 in Ogden, The Waggon & Horses 01535 643302 on Oxenhope Moor or The Drop Farm Tea Rooms 01535 645297 at Leeshaw Reservoir as you return to Oxenhope.

Books: MTB Guide S Pennines of W Yorks & Lancs (S.Hall). MTB W & S Yorkshire (R.Peace). MTB Guide W Yorkshire (N.Dutton-Taylor). **Maps:** OS Explorer OL21.

Bike Shops: Aire Valley Cycles 01535 610839, in Keighley.

Route Ideas

❶ N from Oxenhope then W over to and across Black Moor. Road SW to cross the B6141. Trails across Thornton Moor to Ogden Water. Across Ovenden Moor. NW past Warley Moor and Oxenhope Moor to Sunny Bank. NW to A6033. Calder-Aire Link trail W then trail NE past Leeshaw Reservoir and back to start. Distance 23km.

❷ Shorten above when at Sunny Bank by taking N trail back to Oxenhope. Distance 18km.

Extend the area: Bingley Map to the N.

Haworth

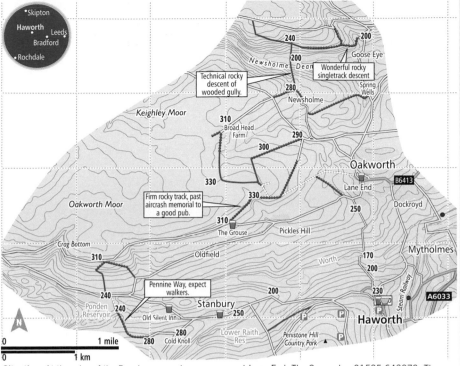

Skipton
Haworth • Leeds
Bradford
Rochdale

240
200
Goose Eye
200
Newsholme Dean
Wonderful rocky singletrack descent
Technical rocky descent of wooded gully.
280
Spring Wells
Newsholme
Keighley Moor
310
Broad Head Farm
290
300
Oakworth
330
Lane End
B6413
330
Firm rocky track, past aircrash memorial to a good pub.
250
Dockroyd
Oakworth Moor
310
The Grouse
Pickles Hill
Crag Bottom
310
Oldfield
Worth
170
200
Mytholmes
240
Pennine Way, expect walkers.
200
230
A6033
250
Stanbury
Haworth
Ponden Reservoir
240
Old Silent Inn
P
P
280
Cold Knoll
Lower Raith Res
Penistone Hill Country Park
P
0   1 mile
0   1 km

Situation: At the edge of the Pennine moors in West Yorkshire. 3 miles south west of Keighley and 10 miles west of Bradford.

About the Base: Haworth, a village with a choice of pubs and cafes.
Further Info:www.haworth-village.org.uk.
Parking: Car parks in the centre of Howarth and just outside the village at Penistone Hill Country Park. *Grid Ref: Howarth SE029372, Penistone Hill SE025369 or SE020369. Post Code: Howarth BD22 8DS.*

Drive Times: Leeds 50mins, Manchester 1hr10, Sheffield 1hr20, Newcastle 2hr30, Birmingham 2hr30.

Trains: Keighley Railway Station is on the Leeds-Carlisle line.

Refreshments: At Haworth, The Fleece Inn 01535 642172, Haworth Old Hall 01535 642709, 10 The Coffee House 01535 644694, Cobbles & Clay Café 01535 644218. The Golden Fleece 01535 642574 at Lane End. The Grouse Inn 01535 643073. The Old Silent Inn 01535 647437 and The Wuthering Heights 01535 643332 at Stanbury.

Books: MTB Guide S Pennines of W Yorks & Lancs (S.Hall). **Maps:** OS Explorer OL21.

Bike Shops: Aire Valley Cycles 01535 610839, in Keighley.

Route Idea

A figure of 8. From Haworth road N to Lane End. Trails NW to Broad Head Farm. On to Goose Eye via trails along Newsholme Dean. S to Spring Wells then trail W. Road and trails to The Grouse pub. Road W then trails S past Ponden Reservoir to Cold Knoll. Back to Haworth by roads and small trail section east of Lowe Raith Reservoir. Distance 11km.

© Blackshaw Outdoor

Bingley

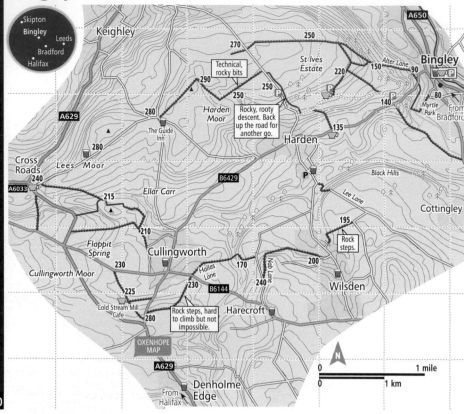

© Blackshaw Outdoor

Situation: On the banks of the River Aire in the West Riding of Yorkshire. 5 miles north west of Bradford.

About the Base: Bingley, a market town with pubs, cafés and accommodation. Further Info: www.bingley. org.uk. **Parking**: Long stay car park in the centre of Bingley. Also car park at the edge of St Ives Estate and roadside parking in Harden. *Grid Ref: Bingley SE108390, St Ives SE082391, Harden SE087378. Post Code: Bingley BD16 2NG, Harden BD16 1JQ.*

Drive Times: Leeds 40mins, Manchester 1hr10, Sheffield 1hr10, Newcastle 2hr20, Birmingham 2hr20.

Trains: Bingley Station, Bradford-Carlisle line.

Refreshments: Plenty of choice in Bingley. The Malt Shovel 01535 272357 in Harden, The Villager 01535 275700, The New Inn 01535 272551 and Brewers Arms 01535 272430 in Wilsden, The Station Hotel 01535 272430 at Harecroft, The Fleece 01535 272439 and Coldspring Mill Café 01535 275647 in Cullingworth, The Kitchen Café 01535 647755 at Cross Roads, The Three Acres 01535 644895 at Lees Moor and The Guide Inn at Harden Moor. Readers at St Ives on the St Ives Estate 01274 515887.

Books: MTB Guide S Pennines of W Yorks & Lancs (S.Hall). **Maps:** OS Explorer OL21 & 288.

Routes on Web: www.goodmtb.co.uk/a65

Bike Shops: Keith Lambert Cyclesports 01274 560605 in Bingley. All Terrain Cycles 01274 588488, 2 miles away in Saltaire.

Route Idea

From Bingley past Myrtle Park, to and up Alter Lane. Follow to road. Cross Harden Moor to The Guide Inn. Road towards Lees Moor then trails SE to west of Cullingworth. Trails past Cold Stream Café. Trails NE on to Hallas Lane, Nab Lane and to Lee Lane. NW to Harden. E on B6429 then trail N into St Ives Estate. Pass café then trails to Alter Lane. Retrace the start to arrive back at Bingley. Distance 22km.

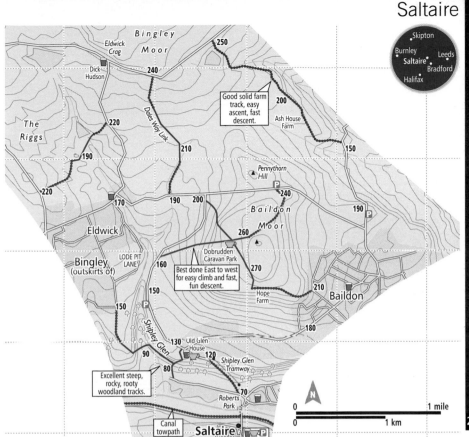

Map labels:

Bingley Moor · Eldwick Crag · Dick Hudson · 250 · 240 · 200 · Good solid farm track, easy ascent, fast descent. · Ash House Farm · 150 · Dales Way Link · 220 · 210 · The Riggs · 190 · 220 · 170 · 190 · 200 · Pennythorn Hill · 240 · Baildon Moor · 190 · Eldwick · 260 · LODE PIT LANE · Bingley (outskirts of) · 160 · Dobrudden Caravan Park · Best done East to west for easy climb and fast, fun descent. · 270 · 150 · 150 · Hope Farm · 210 · Baildon · 130 · Old Glen House · 180 · Shipley Glen · 90 · 120 · Shipley Glen Tramway · 80 · Excellent steep, rocky, rooty woodland tracks. · 70 · Roberts Park · N · Canal towpath · Saltaire

Skipton · Burnley · Saltaire · Leeds · Bradford · Halifax

0 ——— 1 mile
0 ——— 1 km

Situation: By the River Aire and the Leeds-Liverpool Canal below Baildon Moor, a mile west of Shipley in West Yorkshire.

About the Base: Saltaire, a model village with pubs and tea rooms. Further Info: www.saltairevillage.info.

Parking: Car park next to the Salt Mills in Saltaire. Also on Glen Road in Shipley Glen, at Baildon Moor or north of Baildon village. *Grid Ref: Saltaire SE140379, Shipley Glen SE129395, Baildon Moor SE142407, Baildon SE153404.* **Post Code:** *Saltaire BD17 7EZ.*

Drive Times: Leeds 30mins, Manchester 1hr10, Sheffield 1hr10, Newcastle 2hr10, Birmingham 2hr30.

Trains: Saltaire Railway Station is on the Bradford-Carlisle line.

Refreshments: At Saltaire, The Boathouse Inn 01274 585690 and Victoria Tea Rooms 01274 823092. The Cricketers Arms 01274 592578 across the river at Lower Baildon. The Old Glen House Inn 01274 589325 and Old Glenhouse Tea Rooms 01274 595364 at Shipley Glen, The Acorn 01274 567653 at Eldwick, Dick Hudsons 01274 552121 at Bingley Moor and Café at Dobrudden Caravan Park 01274 404278.

Books: MTB Guide S Pennines of W Yorks & Lancs (S.Hall). MTB Guide W Yorkshire (N.Dutton-Taylor).

Maps: OS Explorer 288.

Bike Shops: All Terrain Cycles 01274 588488 in Saltaire.

Route Idea

From Saltaire N across canal, walk through Roberts Park then head to the Dales Way Link by trails and road W of Shipley Glen and via Lode Pit Lane. N on Dales Way Link towards Bingley Moor. E on road. S past Ash House Farm then roads towards Pennythorn Hill. W across Baildon Moor and down to road. S to Old Glen House. S on trail then E on road back to Roberts Park. Reverse outward start back to finish. Distance 16km.

Horsforth

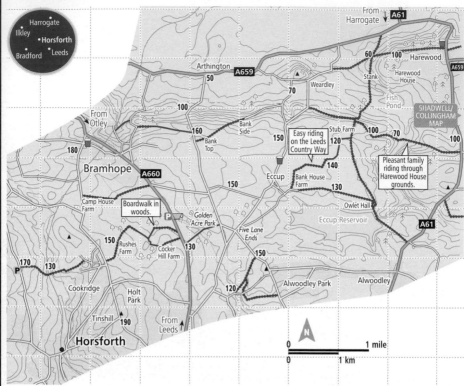

Harrogate
Ilkley
•Horsforth
Bradford •Leeds

From Harrogate — A61
From Otley
Arthington — A659
50
60 100 Harewood — A659
Stank
Harewood House
Weardley
70
100
Bank Side
Bank Top
160
150
Stub Farm
Easy riding on the Leeds Country Way
120 100 70
100
Fish Pond
SHADWELL/ COLLINGHAM MAP
180
Bramhope — A660
150
Eccup
Bank House Farm
140
130
Pleasant family riding through Harewood House grounds.
Camp House Farm
Boardwalk in woods.
Golden Acre Park
Owlet Hall
Eccup Reservoir
A61
150 Rushes Farm
Cocker Hill Farm
130
Five Lane Ends
150
170 130
Cookridge
Holt Park
120
Alwoodley Park
Alwoodley
Tinshill 190
From Leeds
Horsforth

N

0 ——— 1 mile
0 ——— 1 km

Situation: In West Yorkshire, 7 miles north west of Leeds city centre. 7 miles north east of Bradford.

About the Base: Horsforth, a town with pubs, cafés and accommodation.

Parking: Roadside north of Horsforth or car park at Golden Acre Park. *Grid Ref: Horsforth SE235407, Golden Acre Park SE266417. Post Code: Golden Acre Park LS16 9JY.*

Drive Times: Leeds 15mins, Manchester 1hr, Sheffield 1hr, Newcastle 2hr, Birmingham 2hr20.

Trains: Horsforth Railway Station is on the Leeds-Harrogate line.

Refreshments: Café at Golden Acre Park 01132 613064, The New Inn 01132 886335 at Eccup and Harewood Arms Hotel 01132 886566 at Harewood. Fox & Hounds 01132 842448 in Bramhope.

Books: MTB W & S Yorkshire (R.Peace).

Maps: OS Explorer 297.

Bike Shops: Crosstrax 01132 554747 in Rodley, 2 miles away.

Route Idea

From the car park north of Horsforth (on the very west of the map) head E towards Owlet Hall (near Eccup Reservoir) via Rushes Farm, Five Lane Ends, & Eccup. N on trails past Stank then W to Weardley. Continue to Bank Top then S on road. Retrace the start of the route when near Five Lane Ends. Distance 22km.

Riders: Elle & Jess Booth. © Blackshaw Outdoor

Lumb Falls, Hebden Bridge p192. Rider: Stephen Hall. © Blackshaw Outdoor

Calder Aire Link near Shackleton (Hebden Bridge p192). Riders: Molly Heltz & Helen Hodgkinson. © Blackshaw Outdoor

Pudsey

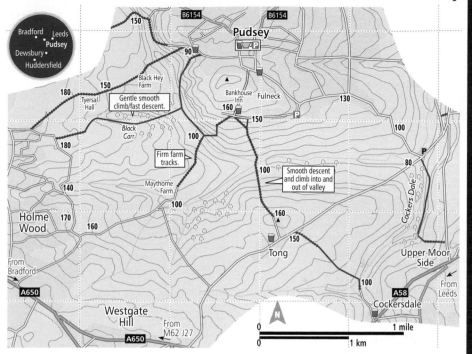

Situation: In West Yorkshire, 5 miles west of Leeds city centre and 5 miles east of Bradford.

About the Base: Pudsey, a market town with plenty of pubs, cafés and accommodation.
Parking: Car parks in the town centre as well as south east of Pudsey at Fulneck or layby on Tong Lane. *Grid Ref: Pudsey SE223333, Fulneck SE224319, Tong Lane SE238316.*
Post Code: Pudsey LS28 7BG, Fulneck LS28 9LH.

Drive Times: Leeds 15mins, Sheffield 1hr, Manchester 1hr, Newcastle 2hr, Birmingham 2hr10.

Trains: Pudsey Railway Station is on the Leeds-Bradford line.

Refreshments: Plenty of pubs & cafés in Pudsey. The Bankhouse Inn 01132 564662 at Fulneck, The Greyhound Inn 01132 852427 at Tong. The Gas House Tavern at Cockersdale.

Books: MTB Guide W Yorkshire (N.Dutton-Taylor). **Maps:** OS Explorer 288.

Bike Shops: Plenty in Leeds and Bradford.

Route Idea

From Pudsey, roads SE to Cockers Dale then trail to Upper Moor Side and road to Cockersdale. NW to Tong then N to Bankhouse Inn. SW to Maythorne Farm. Roads then trail past Tyersall Hall and back to Pudsey. Distance 16km.

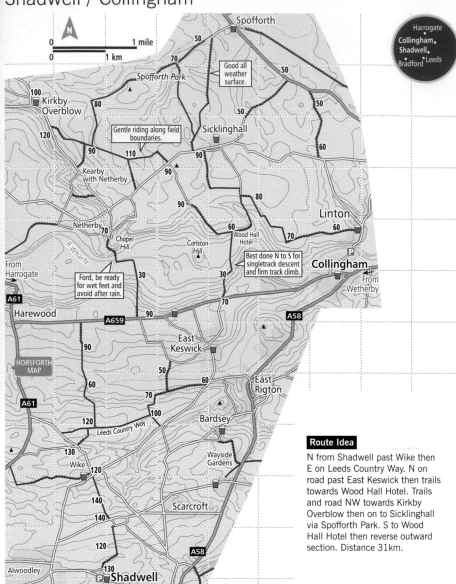

Harrogate
Collingham
Shadwell
Bradford Leeds

Spofforth

0 ——— 1 mile
0 ——— 1 km

50

70

50

Good all weather surface.

Spofforth Park

100 Kirkby Overblow

80

50

50

Gentle riding along field boundaries.

120

Sicklinghall

90

110

60

90

Kearby with Netherby

90

80

Linton

90

Netherby

70

60

60

R Wharfe

Chapel Hill

Carlston Hill

Wood Hall Hotel

70

60

Collingham

From Harrogate

Ford, be ready for wet feet and avoid after rain.

30

30

Best done N to S for singletrack descent and firm track climb.

From Wetherby

70

A61

Harewood

A659

90

A58

East Keswick

90

50

60

East Rigton

A61

60

70

120

100

Bardsey

Leeds Country Way

130

Wayside Gardens

Wike

120

140

Scarcroft

140

120

A58

Alwoodley

130 Shadwell

HORSFORTH MAP

Route Idea

N from Shadwell past Wike then E on Leeds Country Way. N on road past East Keswick then trails towards Wood Hall Hotel. Trails and road NW towards Kirkby Overblow then on to Sicklinghall via Spofforth Park. S to Wood Hall Hotel then reverse outward section. Distance 31km.

Situation: Between Leeds and Wetherby in West Yorkshire. Collingham is on the River Wharfe, 2 miles south east of Wetherby. Shadwell is 6 miles north east of Leeds city centre.

About the Base: Shadwell or Collingham, both small villages with pubs. **Parking:** Car parks in Shadwell and on the north side of Collingham on the road to Linton. *Grid Ref: Shadwell SE339401, Collingham SE388463. Post Code: Shadwell LS17 8HF.*

Drive Times: Leeds 20mins, Sheffield 1hr, Manchester 1hr10, Newcastle 1hr50, Birmingham 2hr10.

Trains: Crossgates Railway Station, 4 miles away, is on the Leeds-York & the Leeds-Hull line.

Refreshments: The Red Lion 01132 737463 in Shadwell. The Wike Ridge Inn 01132 886160 at Wike, The Scotts Arms 01937 582100 in Sicklinghall. The Windmill Inn 01937 582209 at Linton, The Half Moon 01937 572641 or The Old Star 01937 579310 in Collingham as well as pubs in East Keswick and The Bingley Arms 01937 572462 at Bardsey.

Books: MTB Guide W Yorkshire (N.Dutton-Taylor).
Maps: OS Explorer 289.

Bike Shops: Plenty in Leeds.

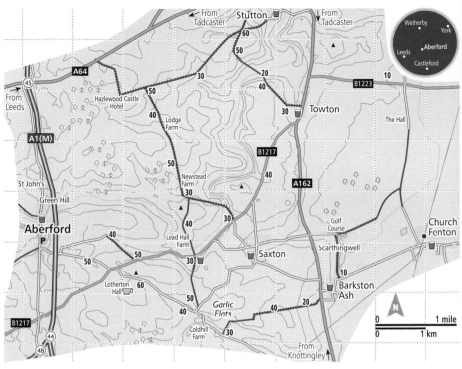

Situation: Just east of Leeds and only 15 miles south west of York in the heart of Yorkshire, close to the A1M.

About the Base: Aberford, a large village with three pubs and a village shop.
Further Info: www.aberford.net.
Parking: In the centre of the village. *Grid Ref: SE433372.*
Post Code: LS25 3BR.

Drive Times: Leeds 20mins, Manchester 1hr10, Nottingham 1hr30, Newcastle 1hr40, Birmingham 2hr10.

Trains: Garforth Railway Station, 3 miles away, is on the Leeds-York & Leeds-Hull lines.

Refreshments: At Aberford, The Arabian Horse 0113 281 3312, The Royal Oak 0113 281 1035 and The Swan Hotel 0113 281 3205 . Stables Café 0113 281 3259 at Lotherton Hall outside the village. Pubs at Saxton, The Boot and Shoe 01937 557374 in Barkston Ash, The White Horse 01937 557143 at Church Fenton and The Hare & Hounds 01937 883164 at Stutton.

Books: MTB Guide Mid Yorkshire (D.Liversidge).

Maps: OS Explorer 289 & 290.

Bike Shops: Fine Fettle Cycles 0113 3935688 in Barwick-in-Elmet, 2 miles away. Halfords 0113 2648311 in Leeds.

Route Idea

From Aberford, SE past Lotherton Hall then trails N past Lodge Farm and NE towards Stutton. SE to Towton. E on the B1223 then S on minor roads and trails to Barkston Ash. Trails past Garlic Flats then roads back to start.
Distance 27km

© Blackshaw Outdoor

Newmillerdam

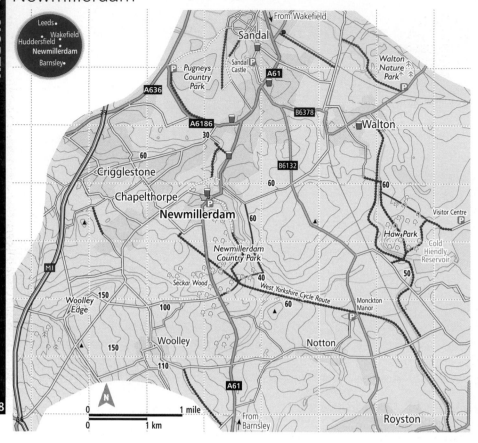

Situation: Adjacent to Newmillerdam Country Park in West Yorkshire. 4 miles south of Wakefield.

About the Base: Newmillerdam, a small village with a pub and a café. **Parking:** Car parks at Newmillerdam Country Park, Sandal Castle, Pugney Country Park, Walton Nature Park and Haw Park Visitor Centre next to the reservoir. **Grid Ref:** Newmillerdam SE330157, Sandal Castle SE338181, Pugney Country Park SE324179, Walton Nature Park SE363176, Haw Park SE374153. **Post Code:** Newmillerdam WF2 7SY, Sandal Castle WF2 7NF, Haw Park WF4 2EE.

Drive Times: Leeds 30mins, Sheffield 40mins, Manchester 1hr10, Birmingham 2hr, Newcastle 2hr.

Trains: Sandal and Agbrigg Railway Station, 2 miles away, is on the Wakefield-Sheffield line. Calder Grove, 3 miles away, is on the Wakefield-Manchester line.

Refreshments: At Newmillerdam, The Fox & Hounds 01924 255474 and Beulay Café 01924 251569. The Castle 01924 256981 at Sandal and The New Inn 01924 251569 in Walton.

Books: MTB W & S Yorkshire (R.Peace). **Maps**: OS Explorer 278.

Bike Shops: Halfords or GTP Cycles 01924 367070 in Wakefield.

Route Ideas

❶ N from Newmillerdam to Pugneys Country Park, Sandal and on to Walton via the Nature Park. Trails to Haw Park. Back to Newmillerdam through the Country Park via West Yorkshire Cycle Route, railway path. Distance 18km.

❷ Extend the above by a few km of road by leaving the railway path S of Newmillerdam Country Park and looping up to Woolley Edge and back via Woolley.

Emley

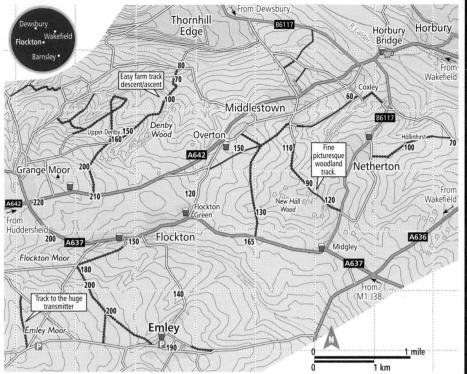

Situation: At the foot of Emley Moor in West Yorkshire, 8 miles south west of Wakefield and south east of Huddersfield.

About the Base: Emley, a village with pubs and easy access to the trails.

Parking: Car park in the centre of the village or car park at Emley Moor, west of Emley. *Grid Ref: Emley SE243130, Emley Moor SE223130. Post Code: Emley HD8 9RJ.*

Drive Times: Leeds 30mins, Sheffield 40mins, Manchester 1hr, Birmingham 2hr, Newcastle 2hr.

Refreshments: At Emley, The White Horse 01924 840937 and The Green Dragon 01924 848275. The Sun 01924 848605 and George & Dragon 01924 840975 in Flockton, The Reindeeer Inn 01924 848374 at Overton and The Kaye Arms 01924 840228 at Grange Moor. The Star Inn 01924 274496 at Netherton or The Black Bull 01924 830260 in Midgley.

Books: MTB W & S Yorkshire (R.Peace).

Maps: OS Explorer 288 & 289.

Bike Shops: Try Cycling 01484 607830, 3 miles away in Kirkburton.

Route Idea

From Emley N on road to Flockton, Flockton Green and Overton then trails NE to Coxley. Road NW to Thornhill Edge then trails SE past Denby Wood to A642. Back to Emley via roads then trail SE from Flockton Moor. Distance 19km.

South Kirkby

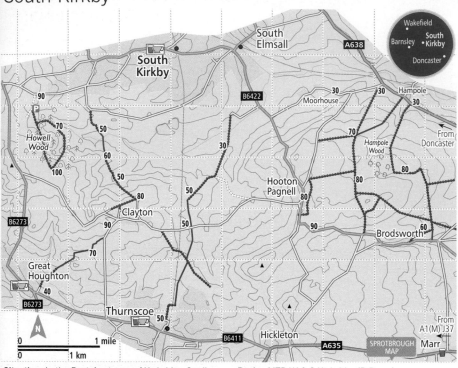

Situation: In the Pontefract area of Yorkshire, 9 miles north east of Barnsley.

About the Base: South Kirkby, a small town with pubs and a café. **Parking**: Car park at Howell woods, as you leave the village heading west. *Grid Ref: SE432098.*

Drive Times: Leeds 40mins, Nottingham 1hr10, Manchester 1hr20, Birmingham 1hr50.

Trains: Moorthorpe Station, in the town, is on the York-Sheffield line. South Elmsall Station, to the east, is on the Leeds-Wakefield-Doncaster line.

Refreshments: At South Kirkby, The Travellers Inn 01977 642284, The Forresters 01977 651468 and Janet's Café 01977 641000.

Books: MTB W & S Yorkshire (R.Peace).
Maps: OS Explorer 278 & 279.

Bike Shops: Don's Cycles 01977 642593 in South Elmsall.

Route Idea

From Howell Woods, a circuit of the woods then towards South Kirkby to take trails S to Clayton. Trails NE to the B6422 then road through Moorhouse to Hampole. Trails S to Brodsworth. Roads W to Hooton Pagnell and Clayton then reverse start of route back to Howell Woods. Distance 30km.

Extend the area: Sprotbrough Map to the S.

Healey Nab Trails

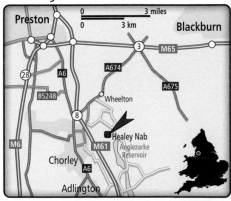

At the edge of the West Pennine Moors. Designed by Rowan Sorrel. Two challenging woodland trails combining swooping descents, interesting climbs, natural and technical features with adrenaline pumping downhill.

Facilities: Wood 'n' Wheels 0333 8008 222 for parts and repairs on site.

Parking: SD620163.

Web: www.goodmtb.co.uk/b14a /b14b

The Trails

❶ Red, XC.

❷ Black, Downhill.

Lee Quarry Mountain Bike Centre
and Cragg Quarry

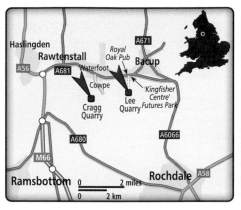

At Lee Quarry there is over 8km of technical riding designed by Dafydd Davis as part of the Adrenaline Gateway project in South Lancashire. A mix of flowing berms, rewarding climbs and scenic views, a dedicated skills area including 'rocky drop offs', 'skinny logs', a 'pump track' and an extensive trials area.

A second phase of trail design and build, led by Rowan Sorrell, includes links to the Pennine Bridleway and Cragg Quarry. Extend your riding here to find flowing singletrack, banked berms and pumps as well as some bigger jumps to test your skills.

Facilities:
None on site. Refreshments at nearby Waterfoot and Buck Inn at Cowpe.

Parking:
Lee Quarry
Grid Ref: SD865212, Post Code: OL13 0BB.
Cragg Quarry
Grid Ref: SD831203

Web: www.goodmtb.co.uk/b15a & /b15b

Lee Quarry Trails
❶ Black, XC, 3km.
❷ Red, XC, 5km.
❸ Skills Area.

Cragg Quarry Trails
❶ 4.5km loop.

© Simon Barnes. www.bogtrotters.org

Crompton Moor

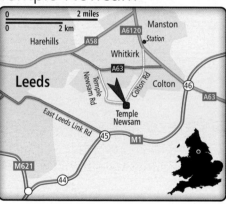

On the outskirts of Oldham in the South Pennines, two purpose built trails funded by the National Lottery. A new family orientated green trail and a pump track designed and built in cooperation with North West Riders.

Parking:
Grid Ref: SD951100. Post Code: OL2 8NA

The Trails
❶ Green, 1km, XC.
❷ Pump Track.

Temple Newsam

Set within 1500 acres of parkland on the outskirts of Leeds, The Trax Bike Track is a 250 metre downhill mountain bike track designed as a partnership between Leeds City Council and Leeds Mountain Bike Club. Built by volunteers, it offers plenty of berms, jumps and bends for all abilities. A circular bridleway runs around the perimeter of the estate but cycling is not allowed within the park.

Facilities:
Tearooms in the Stable Courtyard within the estate, plenty of refreshments nearby.

Parking:
Grid Ref: SE354324. Post Code: LS15 0AD

Web: www.goodmtb.co.uk/b17

The Trails
❶ XC, 11km.
❷ DH Track.

Billinge Wood Trails

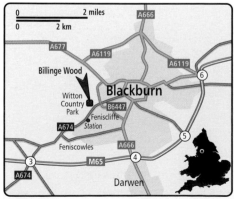

Within Witton Country Park, just west of Blackburn in Pennine Lancashire. Designed by Phil Saxena and built in conjunction with the local council and Blackburn & District Mountain Bikers, two all weather waymarked cross country trails. Technical and challenging, making the best of natural features, in a figure of eight loop with the majority graded red and a few sections of black for more expert riders.

Facilities:
Pavillion Café or Old Stables Tearoom at Witton Country Park Visitor Centre.

Parking:
Grid Ref: SD658272. Post Code: BB2 2TP

Web: www.goodmtb.co.uk/b12

The Trails
❶ Tricky Sixty, Red, XC, 600m.
❷ Trail of Two Trees, Red, XC, 600m.

Delamere Forest

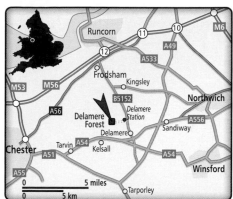

On the Cheshire Plain, Forestry Commission land with waymarked family trails and plenty of unmarked singletrack on smooth sandy forest trails. Dedicated Skills Area with dirt jumps, northshore and a 4X course.

Facilities:
Café and bike wash at Linmere Information Centre. Tracs Cycle Hire 07949 088477 for MTB hire, parts, repairs and coaching on site. Delamere Railway Station nearby.

Parking:
Grid Ref: SJ548704. Post Code: CW8 2JD

Web: www.goodmtb.co.uk/b13a & /b13b

The Trails

Hunger Hill, Family, XC, 6.4km.

Whitemoor Trail, Family, XC, 11.2km.

Skills Area

Delamere, © Mark Foster

Tatton Park Estate

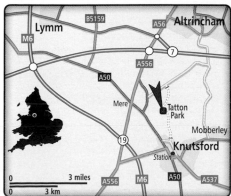

A managed estate in the heart of Cheshire. The area is fairly flat but with some looking and exploring short 30m singletrack climbs and descents can be found, just don't expect an adrenaline rush! There is also a small and casual skills area at the north end of Tatton Mere.

As most of the paths are on grass it is best saved for dry conditions.

Facilities:
Café & cyclehire on the estate. Cyclelife Hire Shop 01625 374458.

Parking:
Grid Ref: SJ741816. Post Code: WA16 6QN

Web: www.goodmtb.co.uk/b16

The Trails

No specific waymarked trails.

Isle of Man

Measuring approximately 30 miles long by 10 miles wide the Isle of Man is located in the Irish Sea mid-way between the Cumbrian Coast and Northern Ireland. It is only a few hours by ferry from Liverpool or Heysham (near Morecambe), making it a perfect weekend's destination if you are looking for something a little unusual.

Many of the rides climb to over 400m and as this is a small island, almost every climb is rewarded with sea views stretching across to England, Wales, Scotland and Ireland.

Rides can be started from **Douglas**, the ferry terminal. Other bases are located near to the coast, in the south of the island at **Colby**, to the west at **Glen Maye** and in the north at **Kirk Michael** and **Ballaugh**. The newly established **South Barrule** Mountain Bike

Trails combine singletrack and technical sections to suit both intermediate and more skilled riders.

The Isle of Man has achieved some high regard in mountain bike circles for its annual End to End race, a gruelling 46 miles (75km) that attracts a field of over 1500 riders to do battle with the challenging terrain of the island and the 1500m of climbing involved. In common with most of the shorter circular rides that are possible from various bases around the island, the End to End is a thrilling mixture of fast fire roads, sweeping moorland paths, country lanes and forest singletrack with stunning views. There is also the added bonus that some trail sections are only open for this event.

Towards Slieu Whallian. © Dave Kneen

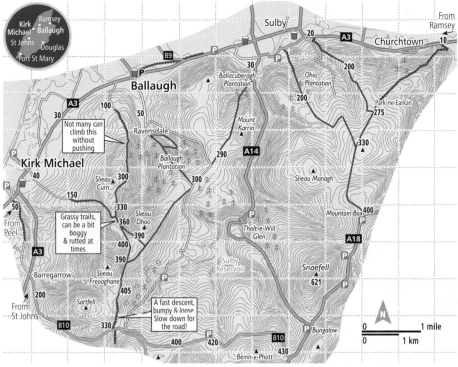

Ramsey
Kirk
Michael • Ballaugh
St Johns
Port St Mary • Douglas

Sulby

From
Ramsey

Churchtown

Ballaugh

Ballacuberagh
Plantation

Ohio
Plantation

Park-ne-Earkan
275

Not many can
climb this
without
pushing

Ravensdale

Mount
Karrin

Ballaugh
Plantation

Slieau Managh

Kirk Michael

Slieau
Curn

Slieau
Dhoo

Grassy trails,
can be a bit
boggy
& rutted at
times

Mountain Box

Tholt-e-Will
Glen

From
Peel

From
St Johns

Barregarrow

Slieau
Freoaghane

Sartfell

A fast descent,
bumpy & loose
Slow down for
the road!

Sulby
Reservoir

Snaefell
621

Bungalow

Beinn-y-Phott

0   1 mile
0   1 km

Situation: Three miles apart on the north west coast of the Isle of Man. Kirk Michael, 6 miles north of Peel and Ballaugh, 6 miles west of Ramsey.

About the Base: Ballaugh or Kirk Michael, both small villages with pubs. Further Info: www.iomguide.com.

Parking: Roadside in the centre of Ballaugh or car park next to the beach in Kirk Michael. Also other car parks in the map area. *Grid Ref: Kirk Michael SC309905, Ballaugh SC347934.*

Refreshments: The Raven Hotel 01624 896128 in Ballaugh, The Mitre Hotel 01624 878244 in Kirk Michael, The Sulby Glen Hotel 01624 8972540 and Ginger Hall Hotel 01624 897231 in Sulby.

Maps: OS Isle of Man Outdoor Leisure Map. Isle of Man (Harvey).

Routes on Web: www.goodmtb.co.uk/a6

Bike Shops: Isle of Man Cycle Hire 07624 422843 in Sulby, serve the whole island and will deliver. Bikestyle 01624 673576 in Douglas.

Route Ideas

❶ From Kirk Michael SE past Slieau Curn then S to B10, W to Barregarrow and back to Kirk Michael. Distance 14km.

❷ From Ballaugh S to the E of Slieau Curn, around Slieau Dhoo and back to Ballaugh via Ballaugh Plantation. Distance 12km.

❸ Combination of the above two routes which link just S of Slieau Curn. Distance 26km.

❹ From Ballaugh S to the E of Slieau Curn and S to B10. E to Bungalow then NE to Mountain Box. Trails past Ohio Plantation, on to A3 and back to Ballaugh on trails N of A3. Distance 30km.

❺ From Ballaugh S to the E of Slieau Curn and around Slieau Dhoo. NE to Ballaugh Plantaion and on to Sulby. Trails SE to parc-ne-Earkan then NE to A3. A3 back to Ballaugh using trail for last 2km. Distance 30km.

© Dave Kneen

St John's / Glen Maye

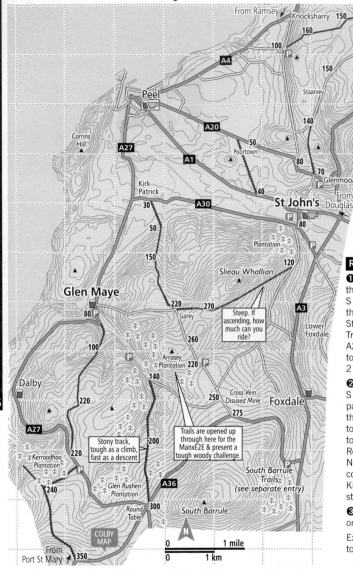

Route Ideas

❶ From St Johns, S on road through plantation. Trail on S side of Slieau Whallian then N to A30 and back to St Johns. N past Staarvey. Trail W to road then S to A20. W to Poortown, trail S to A1 and back to St Johns. 21km.

❷ From Glen Maye head S on trail to A27. Trail SW past Kerroodhoo Plantation then SE to A36 and NE to Round Table. Trail N towards Arrasey Plantation. Road E to Cross Vein then NW passing Garey to continue on trail to A30 and Kirk Patrick. Road back to start. 21km.

❸ See South Barrule trails on p219

Extend the area: Colby Map to the S.

Steep. If ascending, how much can you ride?

Trails are opened up through here for the ManxE2E & present a tough woody challenge.

Stony track, tough as a climb, fast as a descent

Situation: St Johns is in the central valley of the Isle of Man, 8 miles north west of Douglas.

About the Base: St Johns, a village with pubs and cafés or Glen Maye, a small village with a hotel. Further Info: www.iomguide.com. **Parking:** Car parks in the centre of St Johns and in Glen Maye next to the Waterfall Hotel. Other car parks in the area. *Grid Ref: St Johns SC276817, Glen Maye SC235797.*

Refreshments: At St Johns, The Glen Helen Inn 01624 801294, The Farmers Arms 01624 801372, The Tynwald Hill Inn 01624 801249 and The Hop Garden 01624 619527. The Waterfall Hotel 01624 840626 in Glen Maye and The Ballacallin Hotel 01624 841100 in Dalby. The Baltic Inn in Foxdale 01624 801305 or pubs and cafés in Peel.

Maps: OS Isle of Man Outdoor Leisure Map. Isle of Man (Harvey).

Routes on Web: www.goodmtb.co.uk/a9

Bike Shops: Isle of Man Cycle Hire 07624 422843 in Sulby, serve the whole island and will deliver. Bikestyle 01624 673576 in Douglas.

© Graham Cooke, GL Photos

Map Labels

Kerroodhoo Plantation
ST JOHN'S/ GLEN MAYE MAP
Glen Rushen Plantation
A36 From St Johns
Ramsey
St Johns
Colby Douglas
Port St Mary
200
240
A27
300
South Barrule
Wide track, as a climb its quite long but not too tough
Cronk Fedjag
Cronk ny Arrey Laa
Boyr ny Skeddan (Herring Road)
Cringle Plantation
B39
350
The Sloc
200
Enjoyable Singletrack
A27
B41
200
Lhiattee ny Beinnee
A36
80 Grenaby
260
110
250
B42
B40
Fast Descent
Cronk-e-dhooney
Ballakilpheric
150
Ballachrink
50
Surby
Ballabeg
Bradda East
100
Colby
A7
Ballafesson
25
Ballagawne
Pubs & Cafes in Port Erin & Port St Mary, 2km
Ballachurry
A7

N

0 ——————— 1 mile
0 ——————— 1 km

Situation

Situation: Close to the south coast of the Isle of Man between the towns of Port Erin and Castletown.

About the Base: Colby, a small village with a pub. Further Info: www.iomguide.com. **Parking**: Car park next to the Colby Glen pub in the village. *Grid Ref: SC233701*. Also several car parks in the map area

Trains: Colby Railway Station is on the Douglas-Port Erin Isle of Man Steam Railway line. Bikes can be carried at modest cost, subject to space being available. It is recommended that you check in advance 01624 663366.

Refreshments: The Colby Glen 01624 834853 in Colby. Pubs and cafés in Port Erin or Port St Mary.

Maps: OS Isle of Man Outdoor Leisure Map. Isle of Man (Harvey).

Routes on Web: www.goodmtb.co.uk/a7

Bike Shops: Isle of Man Cycle Hire 07624 422843 in Sulby, serve the whole island and will deliver. Bikestyle 01624 673576 in Douglas.

Route Idea

From Colby E to Ballabeg and on to Grenaby. NW to Herring Road then A27 to Kerroodhoo Plantation. S towards Cronk ny Arrey Laa, SW along The Sloc (trail here may be closed at various times through the year, but road runs parallel) and on to Surby. Roads back to start. Distance 23km.

Extend the area: St John's/Glen Maye Map to the N

The Sloc. © Dave Kneen

Douglas

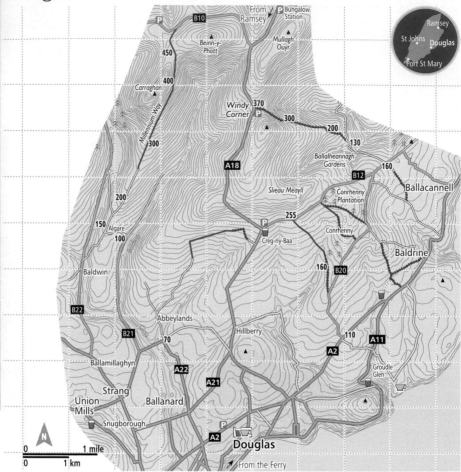

Situation: On the east coast of the Isle of Man, overlooking Douglas Bay, with hills to the north west and to the south east.

About the Base: Douglas, the largest town on the Isle of Man with several pubs, cafés and accommodation. Further Info: www.iomguide.com. **Parking:** At the TT Grandstand, just north of the town centre. Car parks at Creg ny Bar, Windy Corner, Bungalow Station or Beinn y Phott. *Grid Ref: Douglas SC383774, Creg ny Baa SC392819, Windy Corner SC391844, Bungalow Station SC395866, Beinn y Phott SC368864.*

Trains: Isle of Man Steam Railway runs from Douglas to Port Erin. Manx Electric Railway runs from Douglas to Ramsey. Bikes can be carried at modest cost on both, subject to space being available. It is recommended that you check in advance 01624 663366.

Refreshments: Many pubs & cafés in Douglas. Groudle Glen Hotel 01624 675740 or Sea Lion Rocks Café in Groudle Glen. The Liverpool Arms 01624 674787 in Baldrine, The Creg ny Baa Inn 01624 674787 or The Railway Inn 01624 853006 in Union Mills.

Maps: OS Isle of Man Outdoor Leisure Map. Isle of Man (Harvey).

Routes on Web: www.goodmtb.co.uk/a8

Bike Shops: Isle of Man Cycle Hire 07624 422843 in Sulby, serve the whole island and will deliver. Bikestyle 01624 673576 in Douglas.

Route Idea

From Douglas, head NW to B21 and on to the Millenium Way via Algare Farm. E on B10 then S on A18 to Windy Corner. SE to Ballaheannagh Gardens then along to Conrhenny Plantation. SE trail past Conrhenny to B20. Roads back to start. Distance 28km.

South Barrule

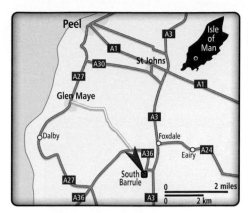

In the south of the Isle of Man, purpose built by Manx Mountain Bike Club in association with the Department of Agriculture, Fisheries and Forestry, two waymarked forest trails. Forest roads, singletrack, board walk and technical sections offer a challenge to both intermediate and more experienced riders.

Facilities:
None on site. Nearest refreshments, The Baltic Inn at Foxdale

Parking:
Grid Ref: SC275766.

Web: www.goodmtb.co.uk/b8

The Trails

❶ **Kipper Trail, Blue, XC, 1km.**
❷ **Viking Trail, Red, XC, 5km.**

MIDLANDS & EASTERN

From the high moorland of the Dark Peak rising to over 600m, to the pancake flat landscape of Cambridgeshire, this region has a wide variety of terrain although, truth to be told, less mountain biking than almost any other part of England and Wales. The best places are the very popular trails of the Peak District National Park, the Shropshire Hills along the Welsh Border (especially the area around the Long Mynd) and the trail centres at Cannock Chase north of Wolverhampton, Sherwood Pines Forest Park north east of Mansfield and Thetford Forest in the centre of East Anglia. This is not to say that there is nowhere to go mountain biking anywhere else: there are networks of bridleways across the Midlands and East Anglia, although the hills disappear the further east you go.

The Peak District

The Peak District National Park is big, busy and beautiful. There's very little forestry, it's ringed by huge cities with urban sprawl stretching up its river valleys and surrounding its foothills. The land is well used and has been for millennia. A great hunk of limestone sits hundreds of metres thick in the middle of it all, overlain with a crust of millstone grit, scoured by glacial water courses, landslips, endless streams and valleys with remnant high moorland and rock faces hinting at the naturalness of it all. And then Man arrived, with pack horses, mining, ploughs, forts, canals, railways and roads.

Ever the opportunist, the mountain biker in the Peak District can devise incredible varied and, in the most part, challenging rides. Fabulous swooping moorland singletrack, dropping down rock-strewn packhorse tracks, past medieval waymarks, cruising along canal towpaths, linking farm tracks and forcing tired limbs up steep quarry roads. This is the Peak.

We split the Peak north and south, the northern bit we refer to as the Dark Peak, and to the south, the White Peak. The Dark Peak is characterised by high moorland, bisected by some classic river valleys, the Goyt, Derwent, Edale, Woodhead and

South Head. © Simon Barnes www.bogtrotters.org

Snake to name a few. The riding here can be good all year round, with a bit of local knowledge. Many routes rely on well drained tracks, rides out of **Hope**, from **Ladybower** and around Stanage are superb, but beware they destroy bikes, the rock is millstone grit, excellent for grinding, whether it be flour or shiny groupsets it bothers not. In the summer the high moorland of the Dark Peak offers brilliant views, fast slick sandy trails, long do-able yet intimidating climbs and descents. All starting from bike-friendly cafés, and finishing to the aroma of coffee or local real ale. Base yourself in **Hope**, **Hathersage** or **Edale** in the heart of the area, in **Hayfield** or **Glossop** to the west, **Holme** or **Langsett** in the north.

By contrast the White Peak is all dales and greenery. Less frequented by mountain bikers, the riding is every bit as good, the trails are less rocky, more rooty, but can be very muddy in wet conditions. Where the scenery in the Dark Peak is harsh, here it is idyllic, to such an extent you sometimes feel you're intruding on forgotten farmsteads, undisturbed wildlife and the odd local. Start your ride from anywhere in the triangle formed by **Bakewell**, **Carsington Water** and **Waterhouses** and enjoy a circuit of the many fine trails dropping into and out of the small limestone dales, often linked by two of the most popular railway trails in the country, the High Peak and Tissington, passing near or through **Parsley Hay**, **Middleton Top**, **Hartington** and **Ashbourne**. Or explore the industrial heritage of quarries, railways and mill towns around Matlock and **Ashover.** However, for a real treat head to the east of the park and explore the trails and tracks around **Linacre Reservoirs**, simply superb on a dry sunny summer evening.

Why not enjoy the White and the Dark together? Indulge in that great journey that is the Pennine Bridleway. Starting its life in the south of the Peak, it takes in much of the mainstream mountain biking in the area, a great glimpse of the best trails, as it links towns and villages south to north, leaving the Peak on its way to the Yorkshire Dales. Finally the Peak is famous for its hidden nooks and crannies, some known and well documented, some less so. These include the tracks of Sheffield's Blacka Moor south of **Ringinglow** where you share the fast technical trails with red deer, the splendour around Macclesfield Forest near **Langley**, the picturesque Three Shire Heads above **Wincle,** the hardcore descents around **Longnor** and Goyt Valley west of **Buxton**. There is something for everyone.

For trail centre style riding there is **Wharncliffe Woods**, just north of Sheffield where you will find a cross country loop and some downhill.

223

Digley Reservoir

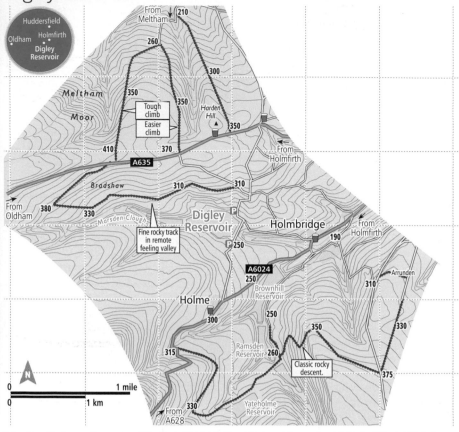

Huddersfield
Oldham • Holmfirth
Digley
Reservoir

From
Meltham 210

260

300

Meltham 350

Moor 350

Tough
climb

Easier
climb

Harden
Hill 350

410 370

A635

Bradshaw 310 310

From
Holmfirth

From
Oldham 380 330

Marsden Clough

Fine rocky track
in remote
feeling valley

Digley
Reservoir

Holmbridge 190

From
Holmfirth

250

A6024
250

Brownhill
Reservoir

Arrunden

310

Holme 250

300

Ramsden
Reservoir 260

350

Classic rocky
descent.

330

375

315

From
A628 330

Yateholme
Reservoir

0   1 mile
0   1 km

224

Situation: On the northern edge of the Peak District National Park and the north east flank of Black Hill, below Meltham Moor. 3 miles south west of Holmfirth.

About the Base: Digley Reservoir, a rural location with easy access to the trails. **Parking:** Car Parks on either side of the reservoir. *Grid Ref: North SE111071, South SE109067.*

Drive Times: Manchester 45mins, Leeds 50mins, Sheffield 1hr, Birmingham 2hr, Newcastle 2hr30.

Refreshments: The Fleece Inn 01484 683449 at Holme, The Bridge Tavern 01484 688122 at Holmbridge, The Ford Inn 01484 854741 and The Huntsman 01484 850205 at Harden Hill.

Books: MTB Guide S Pennines of W Yorks & Lancs (S.Hall). Peak District MTB - Dark Peak (J.Barton). MTB W & S Yorkshire (R.Peace). MTB Guide Peak District & Derbyshire (M.Pearce).

Maps: OS Explorer 288. Dark Peak British Mountain Map (Harvey).

Routes on Web: www.goodmtb.co.uk/a68

Bike Shops: Bikes for All 01484 688887 in Holmfirth. Halfords 01484 426677 in Huddersfield.

Route Ideas

❶ S from Digley Reservoir to Holme. A6024 SW. Trails past Yaeholme Reservoir. On to Holmridge via Arrunden. Road N to A635 then trail N past Harden Hill then back S across Meltham Moor. Trails around Bradshaw & back to start. Distance 24km.

❷ Short loop, N from Digley Reservoir to A635 then trail N past Harden Hill. S across Meltham Moor, trails around Bradshaw & back to start. Distance 12km.

Bad Brains MBC. ©Chris Hargrave

Penistone / Cawthorne

Map labels: Huddersfield, Barnsley, Penistone, Glossop, Sheffield, A636, 170, Denby Dale, Cannon Hall Country Park, Jowett House, 90, 110, Cawthorne, Lower Denby, A635, 110, 100, 90, From Huddersfield, 250, Upper Denby, 150, Low Mill, A629, 190, Ingbirchworth, Gunthwaite Hall, 150, 180, 100, 230, Gadding Moor, Silkstone, From Barnsley, 250, Cat Hill, 300, Scout Dike Reservoir, Hoylandswaine, A628, 120, Silkstone Common, Royd Moor Reservoir, Windmill Nursery, LANGSETT MAP, 330, 300, Thurlstone, 200, A629, 190, Millhouse Green, 230, B6462, R Don, Hazlehead Hall Farm, Penistone, 230, 230, Four Lane End, A628, 220, 180, Trans Pennine Trail, From Manchester, Thurlcliff Hill, Cubley, Oxspring, Roughbirchworth, 260, 250, 0 1 mile, 0 1 km

Situation: In the foothils of the Pennines, on the banks of the River Don, Penistone is 8 miles west of Barnsley. Cawthorne, 5 miles to the north east, is on the edge of Cannon Hall Country Park.

About the Base: Penistone, a small market town with plenty of pubs, cafés and accommodation or Cawthorne a small village with a pub and tea rooms nearby. Further Info: www.visitpenistone.co.uk.

Parking: Car parks in the centre of Penistone & at Cannon Hall Country Park. *Grid Ref: Penistone SE244032, Cannon Hall SE272079.Post Code: Penistone S36 6BY, Cannon Hall S75 4AR.*

Drive Times: Sheffield 30mins, Leeds 40mins, Manchester 50mins, Birmingham 1hr50, Newcastle 2hr20.

Trains: Penistone Railway Station is on the Sheffield-Huddersfield-Leeds line.

Refreshments: Pubs and cafés at Penistone. The Huntsman 01226 764892 at Thurlstone, The Rose and Crown 01226 763280 at Ingbirchworth, The Spencer Arms 01226 791398 or Tea Rooms at Cannon Hall Country Park 01226 790270 at Cawthorne. The Ring O'Bells 01226 790298 or Potting Shed Café 01226 792525 at Silkstone, The Station Inn 01226 790248 at Silkstone Common, Travellers Inn 01226 762518 at Four Lane Ends and Waggon & Horses 01226 763259 at Oxspring.

Books: MTB Guide Peak District & Derbyshire (M.Pearce).

Maps: OS Explorer OL1.

Bike Shops: Lex's Mountain Bike Heaven 01226 763763 in Penistone.

Route Idea

From Penistone, N to Scout Dike Reservoir then trails to Gunthwaite Hall. E to Gadding Moor. Road and trails to Cawthorne then E on A635 to pick up trail past Low Mill to Silkstone. On to Four Lane End, Oxspring and then back to start. Distance 28km.

Diggle

Situation: On the moorlands of the Pennine hills at the north western edge of the Peak District National Park. 7 miles north east of Oldham.

About the Base: Diggle, a village with two pubs. Further Info: www. digglevillage.org.uk. **Parking:** Car Parks in the centre of Diggle. Also at Uppermill, Castleshaw Reservoirs & parking on the Pennine Bridleway at Standedge Tunnels. *Grid Ref: Diggle SE006079, Uppermill SD995055, Castleshaw Reservoirs SD996092, Pennine Way SE017094. Post Code: Diggle OL3 5PU, Uppermill OL3 6HR, Castleshaw OL3 5LZ.*

Drive Times: Manchester 40mins, Leeds 50mins, Sheffield 1hr10, Birmingham 2hrs, Newcastle 2hr30.

Trains: Greenfield Station, on the Manchester-Huddersfield-Leeds line.

Refreshments: At Diggle, The Diggle Hotel 01457 872741 and The Hanging Gate 01457 871164. The Swan Inn 0871 261 1469 or The Woolpack 0871 261 1466 at Dobcross. Pubs and cafés at Uppermill. If arriving by train, The Railway Inn 01457 872307 at Greenfield.

Maps: OS Explorer OL1.

Routes on Web:
www.goodmtb.co.uk/a67

Bike Shops: The Cyclery 01457 879955 in Uppermill. Halfords 0161 627 5091 in Oldham.

Route Idea

From Diggle, E to Kiln Green then Pennine Bridleway S to Greenfield. Main road past the station then N onto Ladcastle Road. Section of Delph Donkey Trail W. Roads through Dobcross to trails along Harrop Edge. Continue to Castleshaw Reservoir to pick up the Pennine Bridleway all the way back to Diggle. Distance 17km.

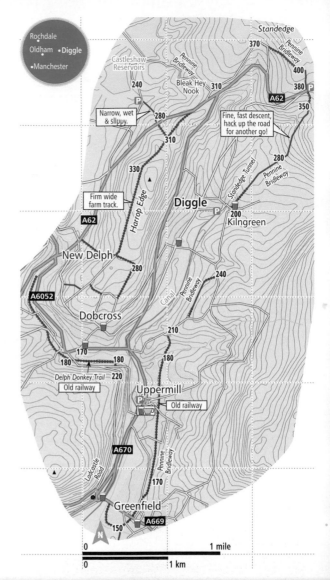

Pennine Bridleway near Standedge

Tintwistle

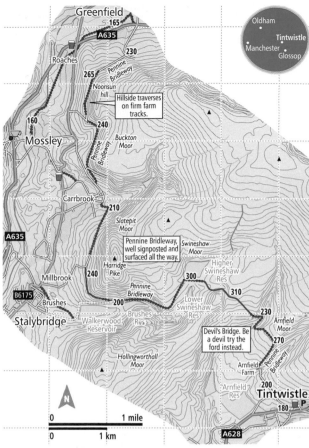

Situation: At the lower end of the Longdendale Valley, on the western boundary of the Peak District National Park. 3 miles north of Glossop.

About the Base: Tintwistle, a small village with a pub and easy access to the trails. **Parking:** Roadside parking in the centre of the village. *Grid Ref: Tintwistle SK026974. Post Code: Tintwistle SK13 1JZ.*

Drive Times: Manchester 40mins, Leeds 50mins, Sheffield 1hr10, Birmingham 2hrs, Newcastle 2hr30.

Trains: Mossley Station is on the Manchester-Huddersfield-Leeds line.

Refreshments: The Bulls Head 01457 853 365 at Tintwistle. The Buckton Castle 01457831911 and The Stamford Arms at Carrbrook. Cafés at Mossley and The Roaches Lock Inn 01457 837151 at Roaches.

Books: MTB Guide S Pennines of W Yorks & Lancs (S Hall).

Maps: OS Explorer OL1.

Routes on Web:
www.goodmtb.co.uk/a73

Bike Shops: High Peak Cycles 01457 861 535 in Glossop & The Cyclery 01457 879955 in Uppermill, a mile north of the map.

Route Idea

From Tintwistle, Pennine Bridleweay NE to Greenfield. Cycle paths S past the Roaches to Mossley. On to Carrbrook then return back on the Pennine Brdileway to Tintwistle. Distance 26km.

Arnfield Moor

Glossop

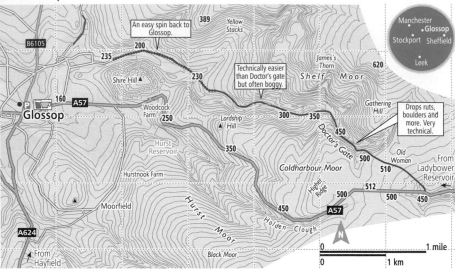

An easy spin back to Glossop.

Technically easier than Doctor's gate but often boggy.

Drops ruts, boulders and more. Very technical.

Manchester • Glossop
Stockport • Sheffield
Leek

Situation: At the foot of the moors, on the north western edge of the Peak District National Park, 13 miles east of Manchester.

About the Base: Glossop, a small market town with pubs, cafés and accommodation.
Further Info: www.glossop.com. **Parking:** Car park at Glossop Railway Station. *Grid Ref: Glossop SK035941.*
Post Code: Glossop SK13 8BS.

Drive Times: Manchester 30mins, Leeds 1hr, Birmingham 1hr50, Bristol 3hr10, London 3hr30.

Trains: Glossop Station has services to Manchester.

Refreshments: Plenty of pubs and cafés at Glossop after the ride.

Books: Peak District MTB - Dark Peak (J.Barton).

Maps: OS Explorer OL1.

Bike Shops: High Peak Cycles 01457 861 535 in Glossop.

Route Idea

From Glossop E along A57. Trails back via Doctor's Gate. Distance 16km.

© Simon Barnes www.bogtrotters.org

Roman Lakes

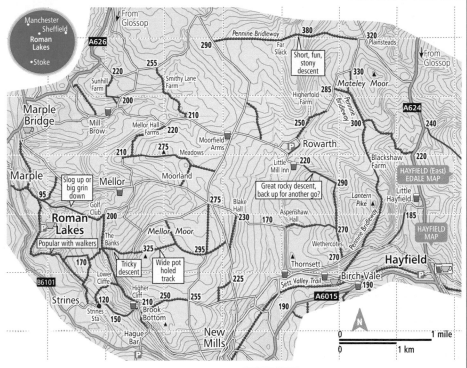

Situation: In the lower reaches of the Goyt Valley just west of the Peak District National Park. Between Mellor and Marple, 5 miles east of Stockport.

About the Base: Roman Lakes, a country park with a café and a visitor centre.
Further Info: www.romanlakes.co.uk. **Parking:** Car Park at Roman Lakes Country Park. Also Sett Valley car park in Hayfield and parking at Rowarth. *Grid Ref: Roman Lakes SJ969878, Hayfield SK036869, Rowarth SK012892. Post Code: Roman Lakes SK6 7HB, Hayfield SK22 2PB, Rowarth SK22 1EF.*

Drive Times: Manchester 30mins, Leeds 1hr, Birmingham 1hr50, Bristol 3hr, London 3hr40.

Trains: Marple Station, a mile from Roman Lakes, is on the Sheffield-Manchester & Buxton-Manchester lines.

Refreshments: Takeaway café at Roman Lakes Country Park 0161 427 2039. The Oddfellows Arms 0161 449 7826 and The Moorfield Arms 0161 427 1580 at Mellor. Little Mill Inn 01663 746305 at Rowarth, Special Touch café 01663 746 157 at Birch Vale. Several pubs or Rosies Tea Room 01663 745 597 at Hayfield. The Pack Horse Inn 01663 742365 at New Mills and The Hare & Hounds 0161 427 4042 or Christies Café 0161 44901332 at Marple Bridge.

Books: Peak District MTB - Dark Peak (.I Barton). MTB Guide Peak District & Derbyshire (M.Pearce).

Maps: Wild Boar Map Series: Mellor Magic & Mellor Mania. OS Explorer OL1.

Bike Shops: Sett Valley Cycles 01663 742 629, 3 miles away in New Mills. North West Mountain Biking Centre 0161 4283311 in Cheadle.

Route Ideas

❶ From Roman Lakes to Mellor via Golf Club. Road and trails NE to Mellor Hall Fams then Smithy Lane Farm. Pennine Bridleway E then S past Mateley Moor and Lantern Pike. Trail NW towards Rowarth then Moorfield Arms. Road S then trails and roads to Brook Bottom and Strines Station. Trails N back to the start. Distance 25km.

❷ S from Roman Lakes to Strines Station. On to Brook Bottom then Rowarth via Blake Hall and Aspenshaw Hall. NE towards Mateley Moor then S past Lantern Pike. Roads and trails past Wethercotes , Aspenshaw Hall and Blake Hall. Trails across Mellor Moor to The Banks. N to Golf Club then W down trail and back to start. Distance 23km.

Extend the area: Hayfield Map to the S, Hayfield/Edale Map to the E.

Tricky rock steps, east of the Little Mill Inn, Rowarth

Ladybower (north)

Manchester
Ladybower
Stockport Sheffield
• Leek
• Stoke

From
Chapeltown &
M1 J36 & 35a

A628

340

PENISTONE
MAP

270

250

Visitor
Centre Langsett

250

A616

Steep cobbled
track.

Barmings

Hingcliff
Hill

330

Langsett
Reservoir

Langsett Moors

300

Round
Hill

Harden Moor

250

275

350

400

Midhope

H a r d e n M o o r

Moors

A trail that can be brilliant in the
right conditions (dry) through to
a nightmare in the wrong
conditions (saturated ground).
The wettest sections have been
'improved' with flagstones.

450

Pike Lowe Stones

478

Howden Moors

500

510

Cut Gate

Upper Commons

Steep with
steps, check on
foot before
riding.

520

Margery
Hill

Mosley
Bank

N

545

Ronksley Moor

400

0   1 mile

507

Slippery
Stones

290

0   1 km

Ox Hey

Along east side
of reservoirs.
Nothing too
tricky but a
good one for
families who
want more than
easy flat trails.

Ridge Nether
Moor

285

Howden
Reservoir

300

Beaver's
Croft

U p p e r

260

Birchinlee Pasture

D e r w e n t

Derwent Reservoir

483

260

Fun, flowing
descent

V a l l e y

Rowlee Pasture

LADYBOWER (South)
MAP

A57 250 Rowlee
Farm

Lockerbrook
Farm

Fairholmes
Visitor Centre

210

Ladybower
Res

Rider: Andrew Hill. ©Dave Cassidy

Situation: In the Upper Derwent Valley, close to the north east edge of the Peak District National Park. 12 miles west of Sheffield.

About the Base: Ladybower Reservoir, a rural location with a visitor centre. **Parking:** Car parks at Fairholmes Visitor Centre (Ladybower) and Langsett Visitor Centre. *Grid Ref: Fairholmes Visitor Centre SK173893, Langsett Visitor Centre SE210004.* **Post Code:** *Fairholmes Visitor Centre S33 0AQ, Langsett Visitor Centre S36 4GY.*

Drive Times: Manchester 50mins, Leeds 1hr, Birmingham 1hr50, Bristol 3hr20, London 3hr20.

Trains: Bamford Railway Station, 2 miles south of Ladybower, is on the Sheffield-Manchester line.

Refreshments: At Ladybower, Refreshment Kiosk 01433 650953 at Fairholmes Visitor Centre. The Waggon and Horses 01226 763 147 and Bank View café 01226 762 337 at Langsett.

Books: Peak District MTB - Dark Peak (J.Barton). MBR Ride Guide 2010

Maps: OS Explorer OL1. Dark Peak British Mountain Map (Harvey).

Routes on Web: www.goodmtb.co.uk/a87

Bike Shops: 18 Bikes 01433 621111 in Hope. Trail Monkeys 01433 620 586 in Bradwell, for repairs, hire & guided rides. Derwent Cycle Hire at Fairholmes Visitor Centre 01433 651261.

Route Ideas

❶ From Fairholmes Visitor Centre, N along W of reservoirs to Slippery Stones. N along Cut Gate. Fork NE on Midhope Moors and descend almost to Langsett Reservoir then W towards Hingcliff Hill followed by S back along Cut Gate. Back to the start via the E side of Howden and Derwent Reservoirs. Distance 30km.

❷ Extend the above by continuing to and around Langsett Reservoir.
Distance 35km.

Extend the area: Ladybower South Map.

Rider: Andrew Hill. ©Dave Cassidy

Near Coldwell Clough, Hayfield p236 © Simon Barnes www.bogtrotters.org

Langsett

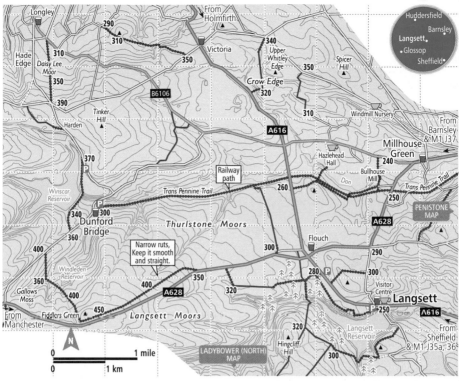

Situation: On the north east edge of the Peak District National Park, at the edge of Langsett Reservoir, below Langsett & Thurlstone Moors. 11 miles south west of Barnsley.

About the Base: Langsett, a small village with a pub, café and visitor centre. **Parking:** Car park next to the visitor centre in Langsett. Also at Flouch or Dunford Bridge. *Grid Ref: Langsett SE210004, Flouch SE200012, Dunford Bridge SE157023. Post Code: Langsett S36 4GY.*

Drive Times: Sheffield 30mins, Leeds 40mins, Manchester 40mins, Birmingham 1hr50, Newcastle 2hr20.

Trains: Penistone Railway Station, 4 miles away, is on the Sheffield-Huddersfield-Leeds line.

Refreshments: At Langsett, The Wagon and Horses 01226 763147 and Bank View Café 01226 762337. The Dog and Partridge 01226 763173 at Flouch, The Stanhope Arms 01226 763104 at Dunford Bridge, The Bay Horse Inn at Longley, Pratty Flowers 01226 761692 at Crow Edge. at Millhouse Green, The Blacksmiths Arms 01226 762211 and Hazelhead Hall Farm Coffee Shop 01226 764800 or Café at Windmill Nursery 01226 765599 close to the Royd Moor viewing point.

Books: Peak District MTB - Dark Peak (J.Barton). MTB Guide Peak District & Derbyshire (M.Pearce).

Maps: OS Explorer OL1.

Bike Shops: Lex's Mountain Bike Heaven 01226 763763, 4 miles away in Penistone.

Route Ideas

❶ From Langsett, trails across S of Langsett Reservoir then W towards Fiddlers Green and on to Dunford Bridge. E on Trans Pennine Trail then S before reaching A616. Return to start along N of the reservoir. Distance 22km.

❷ Start as above but before Dunford Bridge head N past Winscar Reservoir. Cross Daisy Lee Moor then road and trails to Victoria. E on road then S past Crow Edge. A616 S to Trans Pennine Trail. W on the Trail to pick up S trails back to Langsett. Distance 31km.

Rider: Alan Leather. ©Alan Leather

Ladybower (south) / Hope

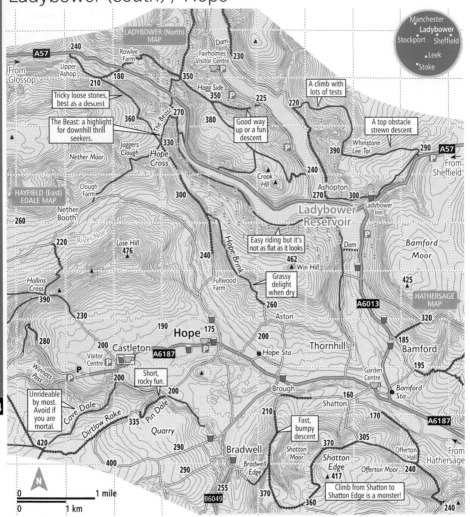

LADYBOWER (North) MAP

Manchester
Ladybower
Stockport   Sheffield
Leek
Stoke

A57

240

Rowlee Farm

Upper Ashop

From Glossop

210

180

350

Hogg Side

Fairholmes Visitor Centre

Dam

230

225

A climb with lots of tests

220

Tricky loose stones, best as a descent

360

The Beast

270

380

The Beast: a highlight for downhill thrill seekers.

330

Jaggers Clough

Hope Cross

Good way up or a fun descent

390

Whinstone Lee Tor

A top obstacle strewn descent

290

A57

From Sheffield

Nether Moor

300

Crook Hill

240

270

Ashopton

300

Ladybower Inn

Clough Farm

Nether Booth

260

220

River Noe

Lose Hill 476

240

Hope Brink

Easy riding but it's not as flat as it looks

Dam

Ladybower Reservoir

Bamford Moor

425

HATHERSAGE MAP

Hollins Cross

390

230

Fullwood Farm

462 Win Hill

Grassy delight when dry

260

Aston

A6013

320

280

190

Hope 175

200

Thornhill

Bamford

185

195

Castleton

A6187

Visitor Centre

Hope Sta

Garden Centre

Bamford Sta

Short, rocky fun.

Winnats Pass

200

200

200

Brough

160

Shatton

170

A6187

Unrideable by most. Avoid if you are mortal.

Cave Dale

Dirtlow Rake

Pin Dale

335

Quarry

210

Fast, bumpy descent

305

Offerton Hall

From Hathersage

420

290

Bradwell

Bradwell Edge

370

Shatton Moor

Shatton Edge

417

Offerton Moor

240

400

290

255

B6049

370

360

Climb from Shatton to Shatton Edge is a monster!

240

N

0   1 mile
0   1 km

© Seb Herrod

Books: Peak District MTB - Dark Peak (J.Barton). White Peak MTB (J.Barton). MTB Guide Derbyshire & Peak District (T.Windsor). MTB Guide Peak District & Derbyshire (M.Pearce). MBR Ride Guide 2010

Maps: Wild Boar Map Series: Ladybower/Castleton/ Hope. OS Explorer OL1. Dark Peak British Mountain Map (Harvey).

Routes on Web: www.goodmtb.co.uk/a88a & /a88b

Bike Shops: 18 Bikes 01433 621111 in Hope. Trail Monkeys 01433 620 586 in Bradwell, for repairs, hire & guided rides. Derwent Cycle Hire at Fairholmes Visitor Centre 01433 651261.

Route Ideas

❶ From Fairholmes Visitor Centre, road along E side Ladybower then trail to Whinstone Lee Tor and Ladybower Inn. Rd S then walk across Dam to ride trails NW along reservoir to bottom of the Beast and along to A57. NW on A57 then past Rowlee Farm. Trails E past Hagg Side to road and back to start. Distance 23km.

❷ Start as above to Ladybower Inn, then onto Thornhill, Shatton, up along Shatton Edge and down to Bradwell. Roads S of quarry to Dirtlow Rake then Pindale trails and road to Hope. To Hope Cross via Fullwood Farm. Down The Beast, cross A57 and follow trails N to join road (see Ladybower North Map) then S back to Fairholmes. Distance 38km.

Extend the Area: Ladybower North Map to the N, Hathersage Map to the E and Hayfield/Edale Map to the W.

Situation: Close to the north east edge of the Peak District National Park, Ladybower Reservoir is in the Upper Derwent Valley, 12 miles west of Sheffield. Hope lies on the River Noe in the Hope Valley, 3 miles south west of Ladybower, beyond Win Hill.

About the Base: At Ladybower Reservoir or at Hope or Castleton - villages with pubs, cafés and accommodation. **Parking:** Large car park at Fairholmes Visitor Centre (Ladybower), several smaller car parks on the approach road. Also on A57 east of the reservoir. Car park in the centre of Hope, next to the information centre. Car park in Castleton next to the TIC or west of Castleton at the foot of Winnats Pass. *Grid Ref: Fairholmes Visitor Centre SK173893, Hope SK171834, Castleton SK148829, Winnats Pass SK140828.*
Post Code: Fairholmes Visitor Centre S33 0AQ, Hope S33 6RS, Castleton S33 8WN.

Drive Times: Manchester 50mins, Leeds 1hr, Birmingham 1hr50, Bristol 3hr20, London 3hr20.

Trains: Hope Railway Station is on the Sheffield-Manchester line.

Refreshments: Refreshment kiosk 01433 650953 at Fairholmes Visitor Centre. The Woodbine Café 07778 113 882 at Hope plus pubs. Plenty of pubs and cafés at Castleton.

Also, The Ladybower Inn 01433 651241 and The Yorkshire Bridge 01433 651361 at south end of the reservoir . At Bamford a Coffee Shop at High Peak Garden Centre 01433 651484. The Travellers Rest 01433 620 363 at Brough, Shoulder of Mutton 01433 620427 or Ye Olde Bowling Green 01433 620 450 at Bradwell.

Top of 'The Beast'.

Hayfield / Edale

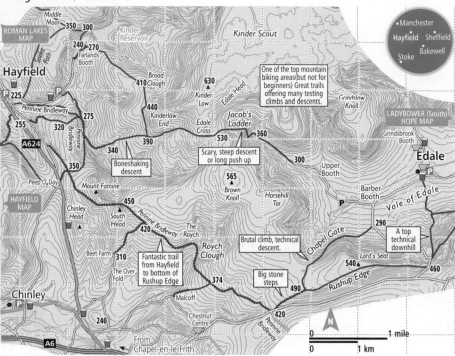

Middle Moor
ROMAN LAKES MAP
350 — 300
Kinder Reservoir
Kinder Scout
240 — 270
Farlands Booth
Snake Path
Hayfield
Broad Clough 410
630
Kinder Low
Edale Head
One of the top mountain biking areas(but not for beginners) Great trails offering many testing climbs and descents.
Grindslow Knoll
P 225
P
275
440
Kinderlow End
Edale Cross
Jacob's Ladder
LADYBOWER (South) HOPE MAP
Pennine Bridleway
255
320
390
530
360
Grindsbrook Booth
Edale
A624
340
Pennine Bridleway
Scary, steep descent or long push up
300
Upper Booth
P
350
Boneshaking descent
565
Brown Knoll
Horsehill Tor
Barber Booth
Vale of Edale
Peep O' Day
Mount Famine
HAYFIELD MAP
450
P
290
Chinley Head
South Head
Pennine Bridleway
The Roych
Brutal climb, technical descent.
Chapel Gate
A top technical downhill
420
Beet Farm 310
Roych Clough
Lord's Seat
540
460
The Over Fold
Fantastic trail from Hayfield to bottom of Rushup Edge
374
Big stone steps
490
Rushup Edge
Chinley
P
Malcoff
420
240
Chestnut Centre
Pennine Bridleway
N
0 .... 1 mile
0   1 km
A6
From Chapel-en-le-Frith

Situation: At the foot of Kinder Scout, Hayfield is in the Sett Valley on the western edge of the Peak District National Park. Edale is 6 miles to the east in the Edale Valley, 7 miles north east of Chapel-en-le-Frith.

About the Base: Hayfield, a village with pubs, cafés and accommodation or Edale, a village with two pubs and cafés. Further Info: www.edale-valley.co.uk.

Parking: Car park in Edale village next to station. Sett Valley car park in Hayfield or smaller car park on Kinder Road, east of the village. *Grid Ref: Edale SK124853, Barber Booth SK107846, Hayfield SK036869, Kinder Road SK048869. Post Code: Edale S33 7ZQ, Hayfield SK22 2PB.*

Drive Times: Manchester 50mins, Leeds 1hr20, Birmingham 1hr50, Bristol 3hr20, London 3hr20.

Trains: Edale Railway Station is on the Sheffield-Manchester line.

Refreshments: At Edale, Penny Pot Café 01433 670 293 and The Old Nags Head 01433 670291. The Rambler Inn 01433 670 268 and Coopers Café 01433 670 401 just north of the village. The Oddfellows Arms 01663 751257 and The Crown & Mitre 01663 751 114 at Chinley, The Lamb Inn 01663 750519 at Chinley Head or Café at The Chestnut Centre 01298 812 322. Several pubs or Rosies Tea Room 01663 745 597 at Hayfield as well as The Sportsman 01663 741 565 east of the village.

Books: MTB Guide Derbyshire & Peak District (T.Windsor). MBR Ride Guide 2010

Maps: Wild Boar Map Series: Hayfield/ Edale/Castleton. OS Explorer OL1. Dark Peak British Mountain Map (Harvey).

Routes on Web: www.goodmtb.co.uk/a83a & /a83b

Bike Shops: 18 Bikes 01433 621111, 5 miles away in Hope. Trail Monkeys 01433 620 586, 7 miles away in Bradwell, for repairs, hire & guided rides.

Route Ideas

❶ A classic loop that can be ridden anticlockwise or clockwise. From Hayfield SE on road then trails to Mount Famine, Roych Clough and bottom of Rushup Edge. Trails over Rushup Edge then trails N to Edale. W to Upper Booth, Jacob's Ladder then Edale Cross. W to Pennine Bridleway and back to Hayfield. Distance 26km.

❷ Extend the above; after Edale Cross continue to Kinderlow End, Broad Clough, then Kinder Reservoir. Up to Snake Path and follow down to Hayfield. Distance 29km.

Extend: Hayfield Map to the W, Roman Lakes Map to the NW, Ladybower/Hope Map to the E.

© Andrew Hill

Hathersage

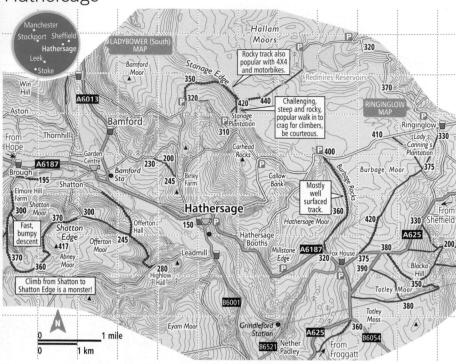

Situation: On the north bank of the River Derwent in the Hope Valley, close to the eastern edge of the Peak District National Park. 11 miles west of Sheffield.

About the Base: Hathersage, a village with pubs, cafés and accommodation. **Parking:** Car park in centre of Hathersage. Also parking at Stanage Edge, Stanage Plantation, Redmires Reservoir, Ringinglow, Burbage Rocks, Carhead Rocks, Fox House & Millstone Edge. **Grid Ref:** *Hathersage SK231813, Stanage Edge SK227843, Stanage Plantation SK238838, Redmires Reservoir SK255857, Ringinglow SK291837, Burbage Rocks SK259828, Carhead Rocks SK244828, Fox House SK266800, Millstone Edge SK251800.* **Post Code:** *Hathersage S32 1DU.*

Drive Times: Manchester 1hr, Leeds 1hr10, Birmingham 1hr40, Bristol 3hr10, London 3hr10.

Trains: Hathersage Railway Station is on the Sheffield-Manchester line.

Refreshments: At Hathersage, a choice of cafés including Outside Café 01433 651159, The Scotsman Pack Inn 01433 650 253 or The Little John Inn 01433 650 225. The Plough Inn 01433 650 319 at Leadmill, The Fox House Inn 01433 630374, The Norfolk Arms 0114 230 2197 at Ringinglow. At Bamford, The Anglers Rest 01433 659955, Ye Derwent 01433 651395 and Coffee shop at High Peak Garden Centre 01433 651484. The Travellers Rest 01433 620 363 at Brough.

Books: Peak District MTB - Dark Peak (J.Barton).

Maps: OS Explorer OL1. Dark Peak British Mountain Map (Harvey).

Routes on Web: www.goodmtb.co.uk/a85

Bike Shops: 18 Bikes 01433 621111, 4 miles away in Hope. Trail Monkeys 01433 620 586, 4 miles away in Bradwell, for repairs, hire & guided rides.

Route Idea

From Stanage Edge Car Park E along road to Lady Canning's Plantation. SE to A625 then trails around Blacka Hill and W across Totley Moor. NE on trails across Burbage Moor to Ringinglow. N to reservoirs and trails back to start. Distance 30km.

Extend the area: From Hathersage, head over Shatton Edge to combine with the Ladybower South Map.

Rider: Tim Ordway. © Blackshaw Outdoor

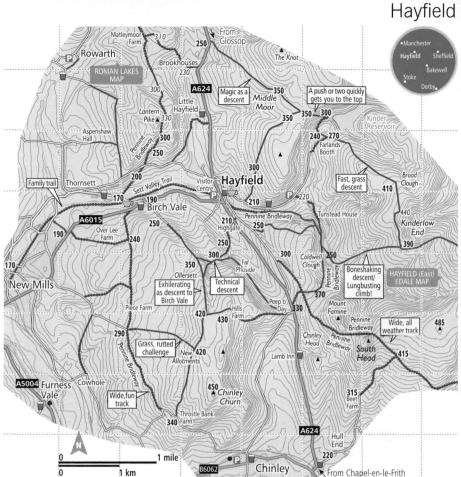

Situation: At the foot of Kinder Scout on the western side of the Peak District National Park. 3 miles east of New Mills and 5 miles south of Glossop.

About the Base: Hayfield, a village with pubs, cafés and accommodation.
Further Info: www.hayfieldvillage.co.uk.
Parking: Sett Valley car park in Hayfield or smaller car park on Kinder Road, east of the village. Also car park next to station in Chinley. **Grid Ref:** Hayfield SK036869, Kinder Road SK048869, Chinley SK039826.
Post Code: Hayfield SK22 2PB, Chinley SK23 6AY.

Drive Times: Manchester 35mins, Leeds 1hr10, Birmingham 2hr, Bristol 3hr10, London 3hr30.

Trains: Chinley Station, Manchester-Sheffield line.

Refreshments: Several pubs & Rosies Tea Room 01663 745 597 at Hayfield. Lantern Pike 01663 747590 at Little Hayfield, The Waltzing Weasel 01663 743402, The Sycamore Inn 01663 742715 and Special Touch café 01663 746 157 at Birch Vale. The Oddfellows Arms 01663 751257 at Chinley.

Books: Peak District MTB - Dark Peak (J.Barton). White Peak MTB (J.Barton). MTB Guide Derbyshire & Peak District (T.Windsor). MBR Ride Guide 2010.

Maps: Wild Boar Map: Around Hayfield. OS Explorer OL1. Dark Peak British Mountain Map (Harvey).

Routes on Web: www.goodmtb.co.uk/a86a & a86b

Bike Shops: Sett Valley Cycles 01663 742 629 in New Mills.

Route Ideas

❶ From Hayfield, W on Sett Valley Trail to Birch Vale. Trails S past Piece Farm then to Throstle Bank Farm. N to Peep o' Day via New Allotments and Hills Farm. Back to Hayfield via Coldwell Clough on the Pennine Bridleway. Distance 13km.

❷ From Hayfield SE on Pennine Bridleway to South Head. S to Beet Farm and then to Chinley, Throstle Bank Farm, New Allotments, Ollersett, Birch Vale, and Hayfield. Distance 17km.

❸ NE from Hayfield towards Kinder Reservoir. Over Middle Moor to A624. Trails past Lantern Pike via Brookhouses and Matleymoor Farm. At Birch Vale S past Piece Farm to Throstle Bank Farm. N to Ollersett then NE to Highgate and back to Hayfield. Dist 19km.

Extend the Area: for the classic Hayfield Edale loop which includes Jacobs Ladder see the Hayfield Edale Map. Also Roman Lakes Map to the N.

Bollington

Manchester
Stockport • Sheffield
Bollington • • Buxton
• Stoke

Small skills area.
Always check for walkers

Lyme Park

The Knott

Wood Lane End Farm

Wood Lanes 150

P

Booth Green

Family riding railway trail

Bridge 10

Middlewood Way

Towpath

Harrop Brow

Birchencliff

200

275

Grassy moorland fun, good views, tricky descents, tough climbs

350

Bakestonedale Moor

280

Styperson Park

Shrigley Hall (Hotel)

Macclesfield Canal

Clark Green

Pott Shrigley

Nab Head

Long Lane

Whitley Green

150

Poachers

240

300

Billinge Head Farm

B5091

Bollington

Tarmac track footpath status, Walk to stay legal

210

330

From Macclesfield

P

220

280

Stony fun

300

Kerridge

High Cliff

260

From Whaley Bridge

Enjoyable, undulating grassy trail

240

Rainow

Kerridge Ridge

310

200

Canal

250

From Macclesfield

B5470

N

0 _____ 1 mile

0 _____ 1 km

Situation: In the foothills of the Pennines on the western edge of the Peak District National Park in Cheshire. On the Middlewood Way, 3 miles north of Macclesfield.

About the Base: Bollington, a large village with plenty of pubs and cafés. Further info: www.happy-valley.org. uk. **Parking:** In Bollington, car parks on Adlington Road next to the Middlewood Way & Clough Bank on Grimshaw Lane. Also at Wood Lanes in the north of the map. *Grid Ref: Middlewood Way SJ930780, Clough Bank SJ928772, Wood Lanes SJ939825.*
Post Code: Middlewood Way SK10 5JT, Clough Bank SK10 5JA.

Drive Times: Manchester 40mins, Leeds 1hr20, Birmingham 1hr30, Bristol 2hr50, London 3hr35.

Trains: Macclesfield Railway Station is on the Manchester-Stoke on Trent-London line.

Refreshments: Plenty of pubs & cafés in the centre of Bollington. Best for the trails, The Poachers 01625 572 086, The Vale Inn 01625 575 147 and Waterside Café 01625 576 689. The Windmill 01625 574 222 at Whiteley Green, The Miners Arms 01625 872 731 at Wood Lane, Café at Lyme Park 01663 762 023, The Coffee Tavern 01625 576 370 at Harrop Brow, The Robin Hood 01625 574 060 or The Rising Sun 01625 424 235 at Rainow and The Bulls Head 01625 575 522 at Kerridge.

Maps: Wild Boar Map Series: Bollington to Lyme Park. OS Explorer OL24.

Bike Shops: Peak Cycle Sport 01625 426 333, Bikes 01625 611375 & Halfords 01625 430328 in Macclesfield. Royles 01625 543440 in Wilmslow. Cycle Store 01260 297837 in Congleton.

Route Ideas

❶ From Clough Bank Car Park to Kerridge. Road along W side of Kerridge Ridge then trail along E side of the ridge. Continue to The Poachers then road E to then N past Pott Shrigley to Harrop Brow. Trail E over Bakestonedale Moor, road to Pott Shrigley then S and E to Billinge Head Farm. Trails S then N over High Cliff and back to The Poachers. Roads back to the start. Distance 21km.

❷ An out and back extension at Harrop Brow to The Knott at Lyme Park, a small informal area to practice skills (though note that for most of Lyme Park mountain biking is not permitted).

Darren Allgood www.maccmtbiking.co.uk, Macclesfield Forest, Langley p243

Riders: Douglas and Anne Ross. Cumberland Brook, Wildboarclough p243

Langley (Macclesfield Forest)

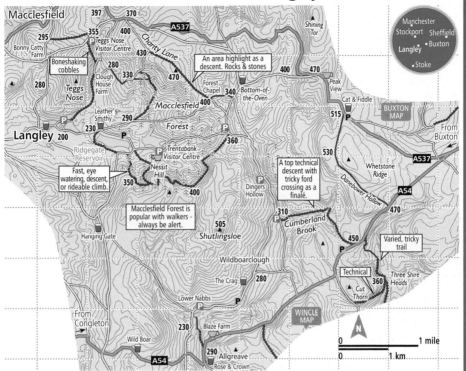

Situation: On the River Bollin and the western edge of the Peak District National Park in Cheshire. 3 miles south east of Macclesfield.

About the Base: Langley, a small village with a pub and easy access to the trails. **Parking:** Car park east of Langley village next to reservoir. Also roadside next to Ridgegate Reservoir. Car parks at Trentabank Visitor Centre, Macclesfield Forest, Teggs Nose Country Park, Dingers Hollow, Cumberland Brook & Lower Nabbs Farm in Wildboarclough. Also roadside at The Cat & Fiddle. **Grid Ref:** *Langley SJ945717, Ridgegate SJ957713, Trentabank Visitor Centre SJ961711, Macclesfield Forest SJ977714, Teggs Nose Country Park SJ950732, Dingers Hollow SJ984705, Cumberland Brook SJ987698, Lower Nabbs Farm SJ973679, Cat & Fiddle SK000718.* **Post Code:** *Langley SK11 0NB.*

Drive Times: Manchester 50mins, Leeds 1hr30, Birmingham 1hr30, Bristol 2hr50, London 3hr30.

Trains: Macclesfield Railway Station is on the Manchester-Stoke on Trent-London line.

Refreshments: The St Dunstan Inn 01260 252 615 at Langley. The Leather's Smithy 01260 252 313 at Ridgegate Reservoir, refreshments at Trentabank Visitor Centre, The Stanley Arms 01260 252 414 at Bottom-of-th-Oven, Cat & Fiddle or Peak View Tea Rooms 01298 22103 on A537, The Crag 01260 227 239 or Blaze Farm Café 01260 227 229 at Wildboarclough, The Rose & Crown 01260 227 232 at Allgreave, The Wild Boar 01260 227219 at Wincle and The Hanging Gate.

Books: White Peak MTB (J.Barton). MTB Guide Peak District & Derbyshire (M.Pearce). MBR Ride Guide 2010

Maps: Wild Boar Map Series: Macclesfield Forest & Wildboarclough. OS Explorer OL24. Dark Peak British Mountain Map (Harvey).

Bike Shops: Peak Cycle Sport 01625 426 333, Bikes 01625 611375 & Halfords 01625 430328 in Macclesfield. Royles 01625 543440 in Wilmslow Cycle Store 01260 297837 in Congleton.

Route Ideas

❶ From Trentabank Visitor Centre car park, head to the Leather's Smithy pub via trail at Ridgegate Reservoir. W on road then trail N through the forest. Trail (Charity Lane) SE to Forest Chapel. Road S then trails past Nessit Hill to start. Distance 10km.

❷ Start as above. After first section of trail in the N part of the forest head to Clough House Farm then to Langley. Roads N past Bonny Catty Farm. Trail then roads E to A537. Along Charity Lane to Forest Chapel, down to Bottom-of-the-Oven and up to Cat & Fiddle. Trail SE then A54 SW to link to trail alongside Cumberland Brook. Road N then trails though southern area of Macclesfield Forest & back to start. Distance 26km.

Extend the area: Buxton Map to the NE. Wincle Map to the S.

Wincle

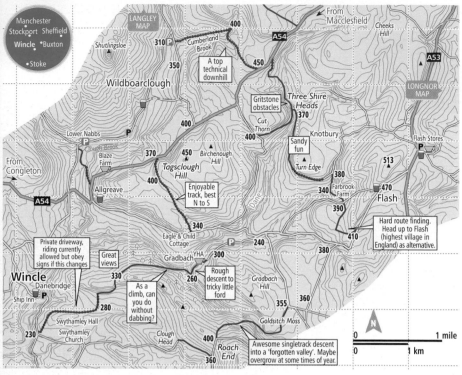

Manchester
Stockport Sheffield
Wincle •Buxton
•Stoke

LANGLEY MAP

Shutlingsloe

310 P Cumberland Brook

400

From Macclesfield

Cheeks Hill

A54

350 A top technical downhill

450

A53

Wildboarclough

Gritstone obstacles

Three Shire Heads
370

LONGNOR MAP

Cut Thorn

400

Knotbury

Sandy fun

Flash Stores
P

Lower Nabbs P

400

370 450 Birchenough Hill

Turn Edge

513

Blaze Farm

Tagsclough Hill

400 Enjoyable track, best N to S

380

470 Flash

Farbrook Farm

340

390

From Congleton

A54

Allgreave

340

Eagle & Child Cottage

Hard route finding. Head up to Flash (highest village in England) as alternative.

410

Rose & Crown

Great views

Gradbach YHA 300 240

380

Wincle 330

260 Rough descent to tricky little ford

Gradbach Hill

360

Danebridge

As a climb, can you do without dabbing?

355

Ship Inn P

280

Goldsitch Moss

230 Swythamley Hall
Swythamley Church

Clough Head

400 Roach End 360

Awesome singletrack descent into a 'forgotten valley'. Maybe overgrow at some times of year.

N

0   1 mile
0   1 km

244

Situation: On the River Dane and the Cheshire/ Staffordshire border in the west of the Peak District National Park. 6 miles south east of Macclesfield.

About the Base: Wincle, a small village with a pub and easy access to the trails. Further Info: www. wincle.org.uk. **Parking:** Roadside parking in Wincle near to The Ship Inn. Car parks at Gradbach, Cumberland Brook & Lower Nabbs Farm in Wildboarclough. **Grid Ref:** Wincle SJ962652, Gradbach SJ998662, Cumberland Brook SJ987698, Lower Nabbs Farm SJ973679. **Post Code:** Wincle SK11 0QE.

Drive Times: Manchester 1hr, Birmingham 1hr25, Leeds 1hr40, Bristol 2hr50, London 3hr30.

Refreshments: The Ship Inn 01260 227 217 at Wincle and Riverside Café at Gradbach 01260 227625. The New Inn 01298 22941 at Flash, The Travellers Rest 01298 23695 or Flash Stores & Coffee Shop 01298 22763 just north of Flash on A53. The Crag 01260 227 239 or Blaze Farm Café 01260 227 229 at Wildboarclough and The Rose & Crown 01260 227 232 at Allgreave.

Maps: Wild Boar Map Series: Around Gradbach. OS Explorer OL24.

Bike Shops: Peak Cycle Sport 01625 426 333, Bikes 01625 611375 & Halfords 01625 430328 in Macclesfield. Cycle Store 01260 297837 in Congleton.

Route Ideas

❶ From Wincle head S past Swythamley Church and to Clough Head and Roach End. N to Goldsitch Moss then to Flash. Trail N at Farbrook Farm then to Three Shire Heads. N to A54 then down Cumberland Brook. S on road to A54. W on A54, then SE on trail by Tagsclough Hill. Road to Gradbach then trail to Swythamley (the last part is on Swythamley Hall driveway where cycling is allowed by the landowners permission, please ride with extra respect). Road N back to the start. Distance 26km.

❷ From Wincle head S then along driveway (see note above) by Swythamley Hall. Continue to Gradbach. Road to Farbrook Farm. Trails N to Three Shire Heads then SW to Cut Thorn. Road S then trail N by Eagle & Child Cottage. A54 past Blaze Farm then trail N to cross Clough Brook. Roads S back to start. Distance 22km.

Extend the area: Langley Map to the N. Longnor Map to the E.

Buxton

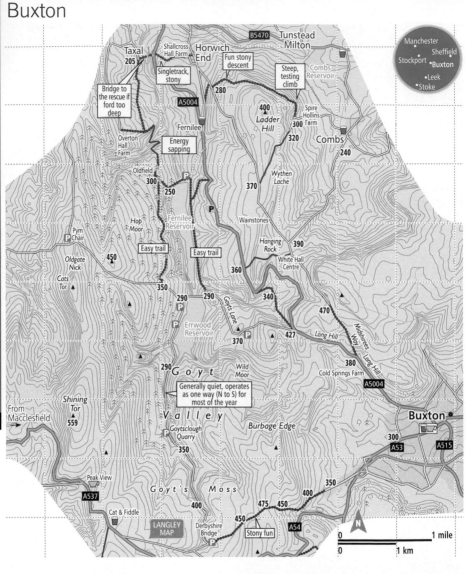

Taxal
205

Shallcross Hall Farm

Horwich End

B5470

Tunstead Milton

Manchester
Sheffield
Stockport • Buxton
• Leek
• Stoke

Singletrack, stony

Fun stony descent

Steep, testing climb

Combs Reservoir

280

Bridge to the rescue if ford too deep

A5004

400
Ladder Hill

Spire Hollins Farm

300

Fernilee

Energy sapping

Overton Hall Farm

320

Combs

240

Oldfield

300

P

250

Wythen Lache

370

Hop Moor

Fernilee Reservoir

P

Wainstones

Pym Chair

450

Easy trail

Easy trail

Hanging Rock

390

Oldgate Nick

White Hall Centre

Cats Tor

360

340

350

290

290

470

Goyts Lane

Midshires Way Long Hill

Errwood Reservoir

370

P

427

Long Hill

380

Cold Springs Farm

A5004

290

Goyt

Generally quiet, operates as one way (N to S) for most of the year

Wild Moor

Buxton

300

A53

A515

Shining Tor
559

Valley

Burbage Edge

From Macclesfield

Goytsclough Quarry

P

350

Peak View

Goyt's Moss

350

400

A537

Cat & Fiddle

400

475

450

450

LANGLEY MAP

Derbyshire Bridge

Stony fun

A54

N

0   1 mile
0   1 km

Situation: On the western edge of the Peak District National Park, centred on Goyt Valley. 12 miles east of Macclesfield.

About the Base: Buxton, a market town with pubs, cafés and accommodation.
Further Info: www.visitbuxton.co.uk.

Parking: Several car parks in Buxton. Car parks on west shore of Errwood Reservoir, on Goyts Lane as you approach from Buxton & south at Goytsclough Quarry or Derbyshire Bridge parking on A5004 east of Fernilee Reservoir. *Grid Ref: Buxton SK056735, Errwood SK013756, Goyts Lane SK024752, Goytsclough Quarry SK011733, Derbyshire Bridge SK018715, Fernilee SK018772. **Post Code:** Buxton SK17 6XW.*

Drive Times: Manchester 1hr, Leeds 1hr30, Birmingham 1hr30, Bristol 2hr50, London 3hr20.

Trains: Buxton Station has services to Stockport & Manchester.

Refreshments: Good choice of pubs and cafés at Buxton. The Beehive Inn 01298 812 758 at Combs, Hanging Gate 01298 812 776 at Tunstead Milton and Shady Oak 01663 733 658 at Fernilee. Cat & Fiddle or Peak View Tea Rooms 01298 22103 on A537.

Books: Peak District MTB - Dark Peak (J.Barton). MTB Guide Derbyshire & Peak District (T.Windsor).

Maps: Wild Boar Maps: Goyt Valley. OS Explorer OL24. Dark Peak British Mountain Map (Harvey).

Routes on Web: www.goodmtb.co.uk/a82

Bike Shops: Mark Anthony 01298 72114 in Buxton.

Route Ideas

❶ From Errwood Reservoir N along E side of Fernillee Reservoir. Then Fernilee, Horwich End and W to Taxal. S to Oldfield Farm and along W of Fernilee Reservoir back to start. Distance 11km.

❷ NW from Buxton on A5004 then Midshires Way. Pass White Hall Centre then trails past Wythen Lache and anticlockwise around N of Ladder Hill. To Taxall then S along W of Fernilee Reservoir. Road to Derbyshire Bridge then trail E back into Buxton. Distance 26km.

Extend the area: Langley Map to the SW.

© Simon Barnes www.bogtrotters.org

Longnor

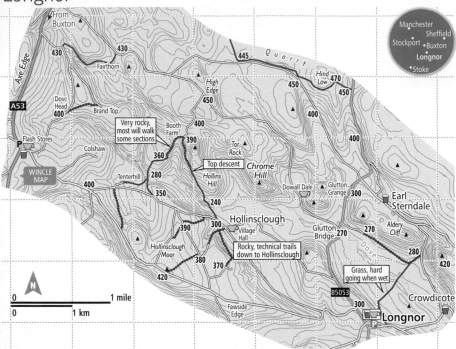

Manchester
Sheffield
Stockport • Buxton
Longnor
• Stoke

Situation: On a high ridge between the Manifold Valley and the River Dove in the Staffordshire Moorlands. In the south of the Peak District National Park, 6 miles south of Buxton.

About the Base: Longnor, a village with two pubs and a coffee shop.
Further Info: www.longnorvillage.co.uk.
Parking: Car Park in the centre of Longnor or layby just north of Flash on A53.
Grid Ref: Longnor SK088649, Flash SK030679.
Post Code: Longnor SK17 0NT, Flash SK17 0TF.

Drive Times: Manchester 1hr, Birmingham 1hr30, Leeds 1hr40, Bristol 2hr50, London 3hr10.

Trains: Buxton Railway Station has services to Stockport & Manchester.

Refreshments: At Longnor, The Cheshire Cheese Inn 01298 83218, The Horse Shoe Inn 01298 83262 and Longnor Craft and Coffee Shop 01298 83587. The Travellers Rest 01298 23695 or Flash Stores & Coffee Shop 01298 22763 just north of Flash on A53. Dowall Dale Tea Rooms 01298 23695, The Quiet Woman 01298 83211 at Earl Sterndale and Pack Horse Inn 01298 83618 at Crowdicote.

Books: White Peak MTB (J.Barton).

Maps: OS Explorer OL24.

Routes on Web: www.goodmtb.co.uk/a89

Bike Shops: Mark Anthony 01298 72114, Buxton.

Route Idea

From Longnor, NE then NW on trails to Glutton Bridge. N on B5053. Trail W skirting Hind Low and Quarry. Trail past Fairthorn and on to Brand Top and Dove Head. Continue on road to Tenterhill then trail NE to Booth Farm and S towards Hollinsclough. Anticlockwise loop to Hollinscough via Hollinsclough Moor and back on road to Longnor. Distance 25km.

Extend the area: Wincle Map to the W.

Darren Allgood. Skirting Hollins Hill, near Booth Farm

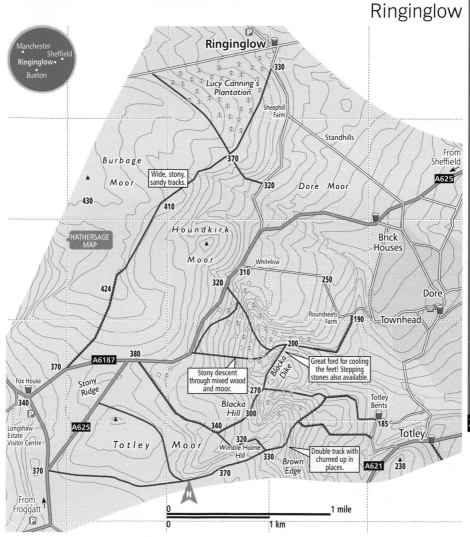

Ringinglow

Lucy Canning's Plantation

Sheephill Farm

Standhills

From Sheffield

A625

Burbage

Moor

Wide, stony, sandy tracks.

Dore Moor

Brick Houses

430

410

Houndkirk

Moor

Whitelow

Dore

424

320

310

250

Roundseats Farm

190

Townhead

HATHERSAGE MAP

Great ford for cooling the feet! Stepping stones also available.

200

A6187

380

Stony descent through mixed wood and moor.

Blacka Dike

Fox House

370

Stony Ridge

270

Totley Bents

185

Totley

340

Blacka Hill 300

Longshaw Estate Visitor Centre

A625

340

320

Totley Moor

Wimble Holme Hill

Double track with churned up in places.

370

370

330

Brown Edge

A621

230

From Froggatt

N

0   1 mile

0   1 km

Situation: At the foot of the moors on the eastern edge of the Peak District National Park. 5 miles south west of Sheffield city centre.

About the Base: Ringinglow, a village with a pub and easy access to the trails. **Parking:** Layby opposite the Norfolk Arms in the village. Car parks at Fox House & Totley Moor. *Grid Ref: Ringinglow SK291837, Fox House SK266800, Totley Moor SK266790. Post Code: Ringinglow S11 7TS.*

Drive Time s: Manchester 1hr, Leeds 1hr, Birmingham 1hr40, Bristol 3hr10, London 3hr10.

Trains: Dore Railway Station is on the Manchester-Sheffield line.

Refreshments: The Norfolk Arms 0114 230 2197 at Ringinglow. The Dore Moor Inn 0114 2621031, Hare & Hounds 0114 235 6623 and The Dore Café 0114 236 4397 at Dore, The Cricket Inn 0114 236 5256 at Totley Bents and The Fox House Inn 01433 630374.

Bike Shops: The Bike Tree 0114 236 5858 in Dore.

Books: Peak District MTB - Dark Peak (J.Barton). MTB Guide Derbyshire & Peak District (T.Windsor). MTB Guide Peak District & Derbyshire (M.Pearce). MBR Ride Guide 2010. **Maps:** OS Explorer OL1.

Route Idea

From Ringinglow, SW past Burbage and Houndkirk Moors and to Fox House Inn. Road S then trails E across Totley Moor. Around Wimbole Holme Hill then Blacka Hill, Blacka Dike, Roundseats Farm to Whitelow. Back to Ringinglow via trail alongside Lucy Canning Plantation. Distance 16km.

Burbage Moor. ©Aaron Swann, Diary of a Mountain Biker

Eyam

Map labels:

0 — 1 mile
0 — 1 km

Manchester · Sheffield
Stockport · Buxton · Eyam
Stoke

255 P
Eyam
250
B6521
280
Housley
225
A623
From Tideswell
P
Stoney Middleton 150
A625
Technical singletrack through bracken.
Wardlow
300
A623
150
270
P
330
Middleton Moor
High Fields
Calver Peak 280
Calver
Curbar
Baslow Edge
Black Harry Gate
Mostly hardpack quarry tracks (if you want National Park scenery go elsewhere).
Peak Pasture
290
Longstone Moor
High Rake
335
Deep Rake
Stony double track moortop riding
270
B6465
Bleaklow
200
B6001
From Chesterfield
360
Hassop Common
310
Bridleway between walls, a good descent.
250
Baslow 160
MILLER'S DALE MAP
Rowland
A623
P
230
140
Hassop
Monsal Head
Little Longstone
Great Longstone
From Bakewell
120
A619

MILLER'S DALE MAP

250

Situation: Above the River Derwent and below Eyam Moor, in the heart of the Peak District National Park in Derbyshire. 13 miles north west of Chesterfield.

About the Base: Eyam, a village with a pub, tea rooms and accommodation. **Parking:** Car park in Eyam. Layby on A623 west of Stony Middleton. Also car parks at Baslow Edge & in Baslow village. *Grid Ref: Eyam SK216767, Stony Middleton SK222757, Baslow Edge SK262747, Baslow SK257720. Post Code: Eyam S32 5QQ, Baslow DE45 1SS.*

Drive Times: Manchester 1hr, Leeds 1hr20, Birmingham 1hr40, London 3hr, Bristol 3hr10.

Trains: Grindleford Railway Station, 2 miles away, is on the Sheffield-Manchester line.

Refreshments: At Eyam, The Miners Arms 01433 630 853 and Eyam Tea Rooms 01433 631 274. The Moon Inn and Lovers Leap Café 01433 630 300 at Stoney Middleton, The Derwent Water Arms 01433 639 211 and Outside Café 01433 631111 at Calver. The Bridge Inn 01433 630 415 at Calver Bridge, The Rutland Arms 01246 582 276 and Café on the Green 07768 772 178 at Baslow.The Eyre Arms 01629 640 390 at Hassop, The White Lion 01629 640 252 at Great Longstone and The Packhorse Inn 01629 640 471 at Little Longstone. Monsal Head Hotel or Hobbs Café 01629 640 346 at Monsal Head. The Bulls Head 01298 871 431 or Three Stags Heads Inn 01298 872 268 at Wardlow.

Books: White Peak MTB (J.Barton). MTB Guide Derbyshire & Peak District (T.Windsor).

Maps: OS Explorer OL24. Dark Peak British Mountain Map (Harvey).

Routes on Web: www.goodmtb.co.uk/a84

Bike Shops: Trail Monkeys 01433 01433 620 586, 5 miles away in Bradwell, for repairs, hire & guided rides.

Route Ideas

❶ From Eyam, trail SE to Stoney Middleton, Road to Calver. S past Peak Pasture then W past Deep Rake, Bleakow and High Rake. N over High Fields and back to Eyam. Distance 12km.

❷ Extend the above; after Bleaklow descend S to Rowland and onto Great Longstone. NW trail to B6465. Road and trails to Black Harry Gate the N back to Eyam. Distance 19km.

Extend the area: Miller's Dale Map to the W.

Monsal © Greg Walker www.visitpeakdistrict.com

Miller's Dale

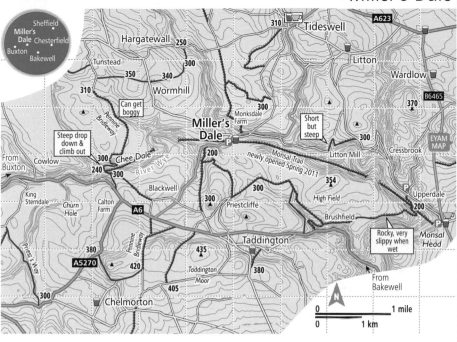

Situation: On the River Wye in the Derbyshire Dales and the heart of the Peak District National Park. 8 miles east of Buxton.

About the Base: Miller's Dale, a hamlet with a pub and easy access to the trails. **Parking:** Car park at Miller's Dale or parking at Upperdale & Monsal Head. *Grid Ref: Miller's Dale SK136733, Upperdale SK176721, Monsal Head SK184714. Post Code: Miller's Dale SK17 8SN.*

Drive Times: Manchester 1hr, Leeds 1hr30, Birmingham 1hr50, Bristol 3hr10, London 3hr10.

Refreshments: At Miller's Dale, The Anglers Rest 01298 871 323. Pubs and cafés at Tideswell, The Red Lion 01298 871 458 at Litton, Bulls Head 01298 871 431 and Three Stags Heads Inn 01298 872 268 at Wardlow, Monsal Head Hotel and Hobbs Café 01629 640 346 at Monsal Head, Queens Arms 01298 85245 at Taddington or Church Inn 01298 85319 at Chelmorton.

Books: White Peak MTB (J.Barton). MTB Guide Derbyshire & Peak District (T.Windsor).

Maps: OS Explorer OL24. Dark Peak British Mountain Map (Harvey).

Routes on Web: www.goodmtb.co.uk/a90

Bike Shops: Mark Anthony 01298 72114 in Buxton.

Route Ideas

❶ N past Monksdale Farm then road and trails past Wormhill. S across Chee Dale. W on A6 then S to Chelmorton via Priest's Way. Return N to Miller's Dale by roads and trails via Priestcliffe. Distance 24km.

❷ E from Miller's Dale to Litton Mill, Cressbrook, Upperdale. Trails W to Brushfield then Priestcliffe. Road to Blackwell then Pennine Bridleway N across Chee Dale. Trails past Wormhill then back to Miller's Dale via Monksdale Farm. Distance 23km.

Extend the area: Eyam Map to the E.

©Greg Walker www.visitpeakdistrict.com

Linacre (north)

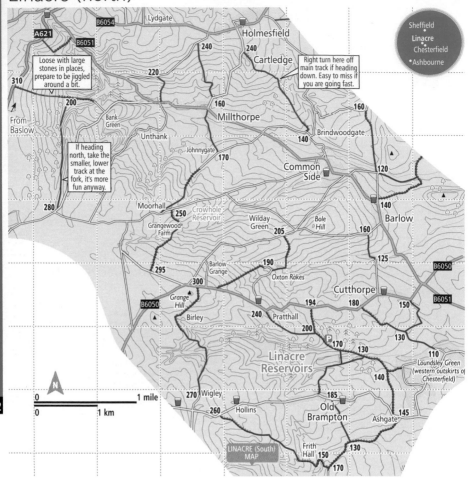

Sheffield
Linacre
Chesterfield
•Ashbourne

Loose with large stones in places, prepare to be jiggled around a bit.

Right turn here off main track if heading down. Easy to miss if you are going fast.

If heading north, take the smaller, lower track at the fork, it's more fun anyway.

Situation: On the eastern edge of the Peak District National Park, 4 miles north west of Chesterfield

About the Base: Linacre Reservoirs, a rural location with easy access to the trails. **Parking:** Parking at Linacre Reservoirs. *Grid Ref: Linacre SK337725.*

Drive Times: Leeds 1hr10, Manchester 1hr20, Birmingham 1hr30, London 2hr50, Bristol 3hr.

Trains: Chesterfield Railway Station is on the Sheffield-Nottingham & Sheffield-Derby lines.

Refreshments: No refreshments at the reservoir. The George & Dragon 01246 567826 at Old Brampton, The Royal Oak 01246 568 092 at Hollins, The Fox and Goose 0800 3894044 at Wigley, The Gate Inn 01246 276 923 at Pratthall. The Angel 0114 289 0336 at Holmeside, The Trout 0114 289 0893 or The Old Pump 0114 289 0296 at Barlow and Three Merry Lads 01246 277 593 at Cutthorpe.

Books: White Peak MTB (J.Barton). MTB Guide Derbyshire & Peak District (T.Windsor).
Maps: OS Explorer OL24 & 269.

Bike Shops: JE James Cycles 01246 453 453 & Halfords 01246 559897 in Chesterfield.

Route Ideas

❶ From car park at reservoir, SE to Ashgate then onto Frith Hall, Wigley and Birley. NE past Oxton Rakes and road past Bole Hill. S to Cutthorpe. W on B6050 then back to start. Distance 15km.

❷ From car park at reservoir, S to Old Brampton then to Wigley via Frith Hall. N to Holmesfield via Grange Hill, Grangewood Farm, Millthorpe and Holmesfield Common. S to Brindwoodgate, Barlow & Cutthorpe. W on B6050 then back to start. Distance 23km.

Extend the area: Linacre South Map

©www.visitpeakdistrict.com

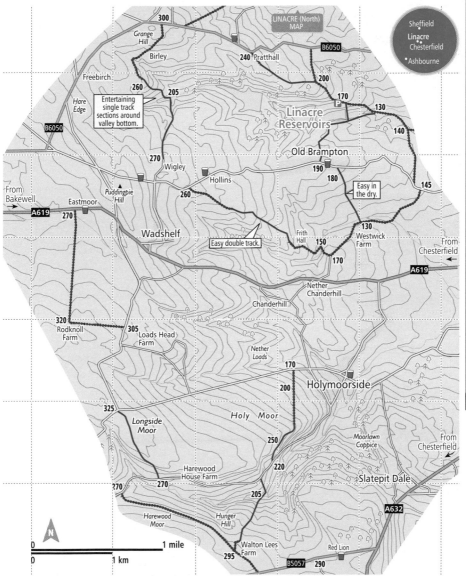

Sheffield
Linacre
Chesterfield
Ashbourne

LINACRE (North) MAP

300
Grange Hill
Birley
240 Pratthall
B6050
200
Freebirch
170
260
205
P
130
Hare Edge
Entertaining single track sections around valley bottom.
Linacre Reservoirs
140
B6050
270
Wigley
Old Brampton
190
Hollins
180
145
260
Easy in the dry.
Puddingpie Hill
Eastmoor
130
From Bakewell
A619
270
Wadshelf
Easy double track.
Frith Hall
150
Westwick Farm
From Chesterfield
170
A619
320
Rodknoll Farm
305
Loads Head Farm
Nether Chanderhill
Chanderhill
Nether Loads
170
325
Longside Moor
200
Holymoorside
Holy Moor
250
Moorlawn Coppice
From Chesterfield
220
Harewood House Farm
205
Slatepit Dale
270
270
A632
Harewood Moor
Hunger Hill
Walton Lees Farm
Red Lion
295
290
B5057

N
0 _____ 1 mile
0 _____ 1 km

Situation: In woodland on the eastern edge of the Peak District, 4 miles NW of Chesterfield

About the Base: Linacre Reservoirs, a rural location with easy access to the trails. **Parking:** Parking at Linacre Reservoirs. *Grid Ref: Linacre SK337725.*

Drive Times: Leeds 1hr10, Manchester 1hr20, Birmingham 1hr30, London 2hr50, Bristol 3hr.

Trains: Chesterfield Railway Station is on the Sheffield-Nottingham & Sheffield-Derby lines.

Refreshments: The Gate Inn 01246 276 923 at Pratthall, The George & Dragon 01246 567826 at Old Brampton, The Royal Oak 01246 568 092 at Hollins, The Fox and Goose 0800 3894044 at Wigley. The Highwayman 01246 566 330 at Eastmoor, The Bulls Head 01246 568 022 at Holymoorside.

Books: White Peak MTB (J.Barton). MTB Guide Peak District & Derbyshire (M.Pearce).
Maps: OS Explorer OL24 & 269.

Bike Shops: JE James Cycles 01246 453 453 & Halfords 01246 559897 in Chesterfield.

Route Idea

From car park at reservoirs, NW to Patthall, road W to Grange Hill then trails S to Wigley. Roads to Eastmoor. then S to Rodknoll Farm and on to Longside Moor, Harewood Moor, around Hunger Hill and NE across Holy Moor to Holymoorside. N to Nether Chanderhil, trails to Old Brampton and back to the start. Distance 21km.

Extend the area: Linacre North Map

Ashover

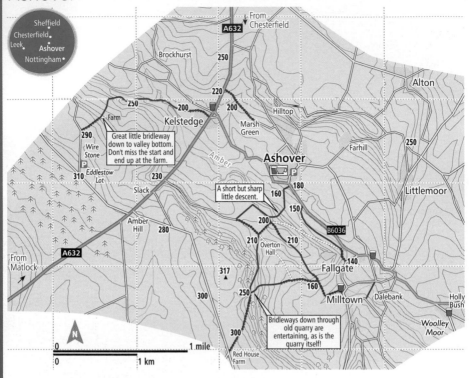

Situation: In the Amber Valley east of the Peak District National Park in Derbyshire. 4 miles north east of Matlock.

About the Base: Ashover, a village with two pubs. **Parking:** Parking in the centre of Ashover or car park next to picnic area at Wire Stone Quarry. *Grid Ref: Ashover SK348633, Wire Stone Quarry SK324632. Post Code: Ashover S45 0AE.*

Drive Times: Leeds 1hr20, Birmingham 1hr20, Manchester 1hr30, Bristol 2hr50, London 2hr50.

Trains: Matlock Railway Station has services to Derby-Leicester & Derby-Stoke on Trent.

Refreshments: At Ashover, The Old Poets Corner 01246 590 888 or The Black Swan 01246 591 648. The Miners Arms 01246 590 218 at Milltown and The Kelstedge Inn 01246 590 448 at Kelstedge. The Nettle Inn 01246 590 462 at Fallgate or The New Napoleon 01246 590 413 at Wooley Moor.

Books: White Peak MTB (J.Barton). MTB Guide Derbyshire & Peak District (T.Windsor).

Maps: OS Explorer 269.

Routes on Web: www.goodmtb.co.uk/a81

Bike Shops: Stanley Fearn Cycles 01629 582 089 in Matlock.

Route Idea

SE from Ashover on B6036 then trails to Fallgate. NW from Milltown to take trails around Overton Hall and then to Red House Farm. NW on road to Amber Hill and Eddlestow Lot then trails to Kelstedge. N on A632. Back to Ashover via Marsh Green. Distance 13km.

Bakewell

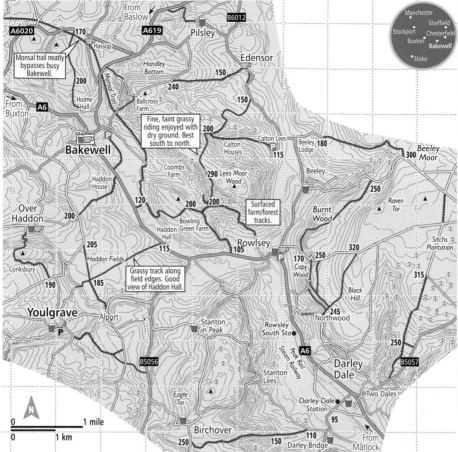

MIDLANDS & EASTERN

The Peak District

Situation: In the Derbyshire Dales and the heart of the Peak District National Park. Bakewell lies 8 miles north west of Matlock.

About the Base: Bakewell, a small market town with pubs, cafés and accommodation or Youlgrave, a village with a pub and tea rooms.
Further info: www.bakewellonline.co.uk.

Parking: Car park next to the river in Bakewell. Also at Calton Lees & Rowsley parking in the centre of Youlgrave. *Grid Ref: Bakewell SK220686, Calton Lees SK259683, Rowsley SK256657, Youlgrave SK210642. Post Code: Bakewell DE45 1BU, Rowsley DE4 2EE, Youlgrave DE45 1UR.*

Drive Times: Manchester 1hr10, Leeds 1hr30, Birmingham 1hr40, Bristol 3hr, London 3hr.

Trains: Peak Rail Steam Railway runs from Rowsley South to Matlock. Matlock Railway Station has services to Derby-Leicester & Derby-Stoke on Trent.

Refreshments: Plenty of pubs & cafés at Bakewell. Hassop Station Café 01629 815 668, The Devonshire Arms 01246 583 258 at Pilsley and Edensor Post Office Tea Rooms 01246 582 283. Cauldwells Mill Café 01629 733185 and The Grouse & Claret 01629 733 233 at Rowsley. The Church Inn 01629 732 291 at Darley Dale, Devonshire Arms 01629 733 259 at Beeley and Druid Inn 01629 650 302 at

Birchover. The Flying Childers Inn 01629 636 333 at Stanton in the Peak, Meadow Cottage Tea Garden 01629 636 523 or Farmyard Inn 01629 636 221 at Youlgrave. Lathkil Hotel 01629 812 501 or Courtyard Tea Room 01629 815 058 at Over Haddon.

Books: White Peak MTB (J.Barton). MTB Guide Derbyshire & Peak District (T.Windsor). MTB Guide Peak District & Derbyshire (M.Pearce).
Maps: OS Explorer OL24.

Bike Shops: Bike Active Cycle Hire 01629 814004 in Bakewell. Stanley Fearn Cycles 01629 582 089 in Matlock.

Route Ideas

❶ N from Bakewell via Holme Hall to join Monsal Trail, follow SE to end. Trails past Bowling Green Farm. N past Lees Moor Wood to Edensor. Trail W then road and trails back to Bakewell. Dist 17km.

❷ From Bakewell, SE on Monsal Trail and follow to end. Continue on trails to A6. S on A6 then trail SW across Haddon Fields to Youlgrave. SE on trails and road to Birchover. Trail E to Darley Bridge. NE to Two Dales. Trial and road to Sitchs Plantation. NW to Beeley Moor then W to Beeley Lodge. W past Calton Houses then S through Lees Moor Wood and back to Bakewell. Distance 31km.

Parsley Hay

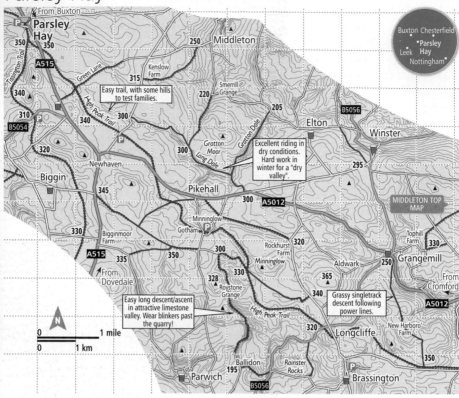

Situation: In the south of the Peak District National Park on both the Tissington & High Peak Trails. 8 miles south of Buxton.

About the Base: Parsley Hay, a rural location with a visitor centre, cycle hire and refreshments. **Parking:** Car parks at Parsley Hay Visitor Centre & Minninglow. Also along the Tissington & High Peak Trails. Parking in centre of Middleton village or car park north of Brassington. *Grid Ref: Parsley Hay SK146637, Minninglow SK194581. Post Code: Parsley Hay Visitor Centre SK17 0DG.*

Drive Times: Manchester 1hr10, Birmingham 1hr30, Leeds 1hr40, Bristol 3hrs, London 3hrs.

Refreshments: Refreshments at Parsley Hay Visitor Centre. The Jug & Glass 01298 84848 and The Waterloo Inn 01298 84284 at Biggin, The Miners Arms 01629 540 222 at Brassington or Sycamore Inn 01335 390 212 at Parwich. The Duke of York 01629 650 367 at Elton, The Bowling Green Inn 01629 650 219 at Winster or The Hollybush 01629 650300 at Grangemill.

Books: White Peak MTB (J.Barton). MTB Guide Derbyshire & Peak District (T.Windsor).

Maps: OS Explorer OL24.

Bike Shops: Cycle hire at Parsley Hay Visitor Centre 01298 84493.

Route Ideas

❶ SE from Parsley Hay on High Peak Trail then NE to Middleton via Green Lane and Kenslow Farm. S on roads and trails to Long Dale and A5012. On to Pikehall then W on trails and road to Biggin then Tissington Trail back to start. Distance 24km.

❷ From Minninglow Car Park head to Grangemill first on the High Peak Trail then N past New Harboro' Farm. Road W to Aldwark. Trail W from Rockhurst Farm then road back to start. Distance 17km.

Extend the area: Middleton Top Map to the E.

Hartington / Waterhouses

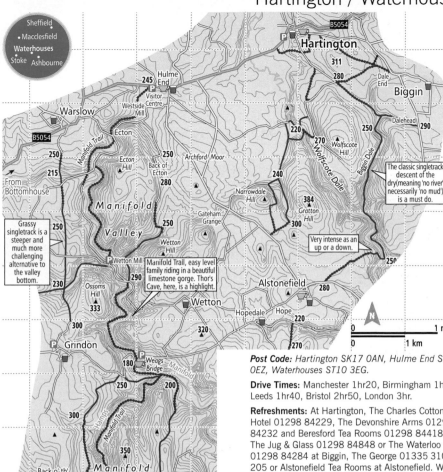

The classic singletrack descent of the dry (meaning 'no river' necessarily 'no mud') is a must do.

Very intense as an up or a down.

Grassy singletrack is a steeper and much more challenging alternative to the valley bottom.

Manifold Trail, easy level family riding in a beautiful limestone gorge. Thor's Cave, here, is a highlight.

Situation: In the south of the Peak District National Park, Hartington is 12 miles south east of Buxton. Waterhouses is at the southern end of the Manifold Trail, 8 miles north west of Ashbourne.

About the Base: Hartington, a village with a hotel, pub and tea rooms or Waterhouses, a village with 2 pubs and easy access to the Manifold Trail. Further Info: www.hartingtonvillage.co.uk. **Parking:** car park in Hartington village, also next to the visitor centre at Hulme End, on the Manifold Trail at Wetton Mill & Weags Bridge or next to the cycle hire centre at Waterhouses. *Grid Ref: Hartington SK127603, Hulme End SK103593, Wetton Mill SK094561, Weags Bridge SK099542, Waterhouses SK085501.*

Post Code: *Hartington SK17 0AN, Hulme End SK17 0EZ, Waterhouses ST10 3EG.*

Drive Times: Manchester 1hr20, Birmingham 1hr30, Leeds 1hr40, Bristol 2hr50, London 3hr.

Refreshments: At Hartington, The Charles Cotton Hotel 01298 84229, The Devonshire Arms 01298 84232 and Beresford Tea Rooms 01298 84418. The Jug & Glass 01298 84848 or The Waterloo Inn 01298 84284 at Biggin, The George 01335 310 205 or Alstonefield Tea Rooms at Alstonefield. Watts Russell Arms 01335 310 126 at Hopedale or Ye Olde Royal Oak 01335 310 287 at Wetton. Riverside Café 01538 308 434, The George Inn 01538 308 804 and Ye Olde Crown 01538 308 204 at Waterhouses. The Cavalier Inn 01538 304 285 at Grindon, Tea Rooms at Wetton Mill and The Greyhound 01298 84249 at Warslow. The Tea Junction 01298 687 368 or The Manifold Inn 01298 84537 at Hulme End.

Books: White Peak MTB (J.Barton). MTB Guide Derbyshire & Peak District (T.Windsor).

Maps: OS Explorer OL24.

Bike Hire: Manifold Valley 01538 308 609 & Brown End Farm 01538 308313 at Waterhouses.

Route Ideas

❶ From Hartington SE on trails to Dale End. Road to Dalehead then trail NW. Roads and trails S past Narrowdale Hill then Wetton. Road to Wetton Mill then Manifold Trail N to Hulme End. B5054 back to Hartington or SE to Wolfscote Dale then trails and road N to Hartington. Distance 25km.

❷ From Waterhouses N to Back o' th' Brook. Trail and road N to Grindon then Warslow. Roads to Ecton then Back of Ecton and trail S past Wetton Hill. Manifold Trail S back to Waterhouses. 29km.

Middleton Top

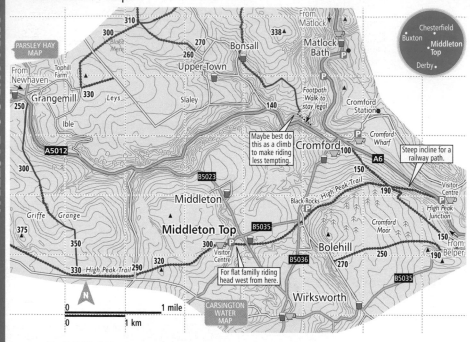

Situation: On the High Peak Trail, just beyond the south east edge of the Peak District National Park, 4 miles south west of Matlock.

About the Base: Middleton Top, a rural location with a visitor centre, café and easy access to the trails. Further Info: www.derbyshire-peakdistrict.co.uk/middletontop. **Parking:** Car parks at Middleton Top, Black Rocks, Cromford Wharf & High Peak Junction. Also in Matlock Bath or south of village on A6. *Grid Ref: Middleton Top SK275551, Black Rocks SK290556, Cromford Wharf SK300569, High Peak Junction SK314560, Matlock Bath SK297583, A6 SK293581. **Post Code:** Middleton Top DE4 4LS. Cromford Wharf DE4 3RP, Matlock Bath DE4 3NT.*

Drive Times: Birmingham 1hr20, Manchester 1hr20, Leeds 1hr30, Bristol 2hr50, London 2hr50.

Trains: Matlock Bath & Cromford Railway Stations are on the Matlock-Derby line.

Refreshments: At Middleton Top, refreshments at Visitor Centre 01629 823 204 or The Rising Sun Inn 01629 822 420. The Hollybush 01629 650300 at Grangemill, The Barley Mow 01629 825 685 at Upper Town or The Kings Head 01629 822 703 at Bonsall. Pubs and cafés at Cromford, Wheatcrofts Wharf Café 01629 823256 at Cromford Wharf and refreshments at High Peak Junction Visitor Centre. The Nelson Arms 01629 825 154 at Middleton or pubs and cafés at Matlock Bath and Wirksworth.

Books: White Peak MTB (J.Barton). MTB Guide Peak District & Derbyshire (M.Pearce).

Maps: OS Explorer OL24.

Bike Shops: Cycle Hire at Middleton Top Visitor Centre 01629 823 204. Stanley Fearn Cycles 01629 582 089 in Matlock.

Route Idea

From Middleton Top, W on High Peak Trail then N to Grangemill. Trail and roads to Bonsall via Blake Mere and along trail to Cromford. Trail SE to the B5035 then trail across Cromford Moor to Bolehill. Road N then High Peak Trail back to the start. Distance 21km.

Extend the area: Parsley Hay Map to the W. Carsington Water Map to the S.

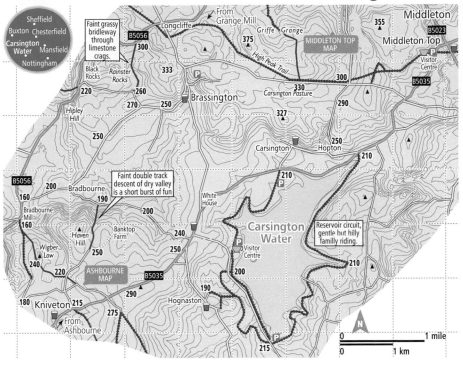

Sheffield
Buxton Chesterfield
Carsington Water Mansfield
Nottingham

From Grange Mill

Longcliffe

Faint grassy bridleway through limestone crags. B5056

300

Black Rocks Rainster Rocks

333

Griffe Grange

375

355

Middleton

B5023

Middleton Top

MIDDLETON TOP MAP

High Peak Trail

Visitor Centre

B5035

300

220 260 270 250

250

Brassington

330 Carsington Pasture

290

Hipley Hill

250

327

Carsington Hopton

250

210

B5056 200 Bradbourne

160 190

Faint double track descent of dry valley is a short burst of fun

White House

210

Bradbourne Mill 160

200

240

Carsington Water

Reservoir circuit, gentle but hilly familly riding.

Haven Hill

Banktop Farm

Wigber Low 250

240 250

220

ASHBOURNE MAP

B5035

290

250

Visitor Centre

200

210

180 Kniveton 215 275

190

Hognaston

From Ashbourne

215

N

0   1 mile
0   1 km

© www.cycletrails.co

Situation: Just beyond the south east edge of the Peak District National Park in Derbyshire, close to the High Peak Trail. 6 miles north east of Ashbourne and 8 miles south west of Matlock.

About the Base: Carsington Water, a rural location with a visitor centre and cycle hire. Further Info: www.carsingtonwater.com. **Parking:** Car park next to the visitor centre at Carsington Water, on the north of the lake at Carsington & south of the lake next to the picnic area. Also north of Brassington village & at Middleton Top Visitor Centre. **Grid Ref:** *Visitor Centre SK241515, North Carsington SK248528, South Carsington SK247498, Brassington SK233546, Middleton Top SK275551. Post Code: Visitor Centre DE6 1ST.*

Drive Times: Birmingham 1hr20, Manchester 1hr30, Leeds 1hr40, Bristol 2hr50, London 2hr50.

Refreshments: At Carsington Water, The Knockerdown Inn 01629 540 209 or The Galley Café 01629 540363 in the Visitor Centre. The Miners Arms 01629 540 207 at Carsington. At Middleton Top, refreshments at Visitor Centre 01629 823 204 or The Rising Sun Inn 01629 822 420. Ye Olde Gate Inn 01629 540 448 at Brassington, The Red Lion 01335 345 554 at Kniveton or The Red Lion Inn 01335 370 396 at Hognaston.

Books: MTB Guide Peak District & Derbyshire (M.Pearce).

Maps: OS Explorer OL24.

Bike Shops: Cycle Hire at Carsington Water Visitor Centre 01629 540478. Also at Middleton Top Visitor Centre 01629 823 204. Stanley Fearn Cycles 01629 582 089 in Matlock.

Route Ideas

❶ Circuit around the lake. Distance 13km.

❷ From Carsington Water Visitor Centre anti-clockwise around lake to Hopton. Road N then High Peak Trail to Longcliffe. S past Rainster Rocks. To Bradbourne then Bradbourne Mill. Trail over Wigber Low. Road and trail N past Haven Hill. Roads back to start. Distance 31km.

Extend the area: Middleton Top Map to the N. Ashbourne Map to the SE.

Ashbourne

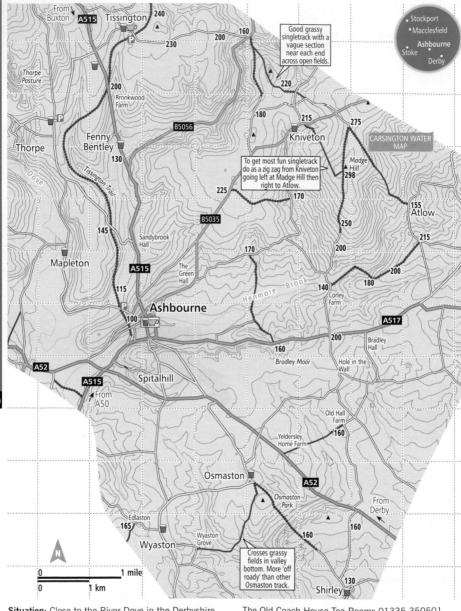

From Buxton
A515 Tissington
240
200 160
Good grassy singletrack with a vague section near each end across open fields.
230
220
Thorpe Pasture
200
Brookwood Farm
180
215
275
CARSINGTON WATER MAP
B5056
Kniveton
Madge Hill
298
To get most fun singletrack do as a zig zag from Kniveton going left at Madge Hill then right to Atlow.
Fenny Bentley
130
170
225
155
Atlow
Thorpe
Dove
Tissington Trail
250
215
B5035
145
Sandybrook Hall
170
200
Mapleton
A515
200
180
The Green Hall
115
140
Corley Farm
Henmore Brook
P
100
Ashbourne
A517
A52
200
Bradley Hall
A515
160
Spitalhill
Bradley Moor
Hole in the Wall
From A50
Old Hall Farm
160
Yeldersley Home Farm
Osmaston
A52
Edlaston
165
Osmaston Park
From Derby
Wyaston Grove
160
160
Wyaston
Crosses grassy fields in valley bottom. More 'off roady' than other Osmaston track.
130
Shirley

Stockport
Macclesfield
Ashbourne
Stoke
Derby

N
0   1 mile
0   1 km

Situation: Close to the River Dove in the Derbyshire Dales, at the southern tip of the Peak District National Park, 13 miles south west of Matlock.

About the Base: Ashbourne, a small market town with pubs, cafés and accommodation. Further Info: www.visitashbourne.co.uk. **Parking:** Car park at cycle hire centre in Ashbourne. Also on the Tissington Trail at Tissington. *Post Code: Ashbourne DE6 1FD, Tissington DE6 1RA.*

Drive Times: Birmingham 1hr10, Manchester 1hr25, Leeds 1hr40, Bristol 2hr40, London 2hr50.

Refreshments: Plenty of pubs & cafés at Ashbourne. At Tissington, The Bluebell Inn 01335 350317 and

The Old Coach House Tea Rooms 01335 350501 at Tissington Hall. The Red Lion 01335 345 554 at Kniveton, The Saracens Head 01335 360 330 at Shirley, The Shoulder of Mutton 01335 342 371 at Osmaston.

Books: MTB Guide Derbyshire & Peak District (T.Windsor). **Maps:** OS Explorer 259.

Bike Shops: Ashbourne Cycle Hire 01335 343156.

Route Idea

From Ashbourne, N to Tissington on Tissington Trail. Road and trails SE to Atlow. SW to Corley Farm, Hole in the Wall, then Shirley. NW to Osmaston then trail to Wyaston. Roads back to start. Distance 32km.

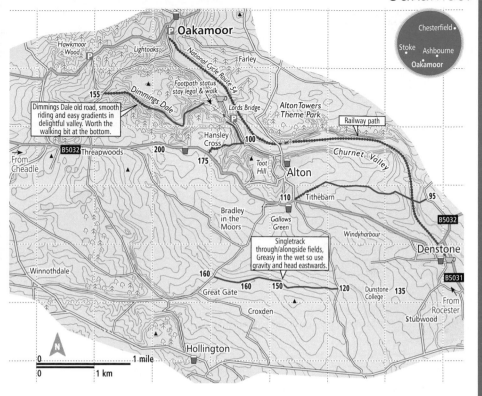

Situation: On the River Churnet in the Churnet Valley, just south of the Peak District National Park in Staffordshire. 12 miles east of Stoke on Trent.

About the Base: Oakamoor, a small village with a pub and easy access to the trails. **Parking:** Car Park next to the river in Oakamoor. Also at Hawkmoor Wood & Hawks Bridge. **Grid Ref:** Oakamoor SK052446, Hawkmoor Wood SK039441, Hawks Bridge SK062431. **Post Code:** Oakamoor ST10 3AG.

Drive Times: Birmingham 1hr10, Manchester 1hr30, Leeds 2hr, Bristol 2hr30, London 3hr.

Refreshments: The Cricketers Arms 01538 702 548 at Oakamoor. Ramblers Retreat 01538 702 730 in the Churnet Valley and The Bulls Head 01538 702 307 at Alton. Café at Denstone Hall Farm Shop and The Tavern 01889 590 847 at Denstone. The Blacksmiths Arms 01538 702 213 at Tithebarn and The Peakstones Inn 01538 755 776. The Yew Tree Inn 01335 360 723 at Hollington.

Books: MTB Guide N Midlands (H.Tindell).

Maps: OS Explorer 259.

Bike Shops: Brian Rourke Cycles 01782 835368 & Halfords 01782 744474 in Stoke on Trent.

Route Idea

From Oakamoor, road W towards Hawkmoor Wood. S through Dimmings Dale to Hansley Cross (walking footpath section to stay legal). Roads SW towards Great Gate then trail E. Roads to Denstone via Stubwood. National Cycle Route 54 back to Oakamoor. Distance 26km.

Wharncliffe Woods

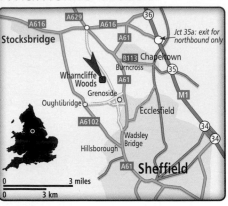

A steep and rocky wood situated on the Northern fringes of Sheffield. Developed and maintained by Wharncliffe Riders Collective in conjunction with the Forestry Commission, super technical rocky drops and fantastic technical single track. A new 16km XC route is under construction, very nearly all on new trail. Several highly technical downhill trails where local riders are planning to create a high quality, well managed venue for downhill riding.

Facilities:
None on site. Refreshments in nearby Grenoside.

Parking:
Grid Ref: SK324950. Post Code: S35 8RS

Web: www.goodmtb.co.uk/b98

The Trails

❶ Red, XC, 18km.

❷ DH

Rider: Anita Hartley Reservoir Chicks. ©Mark James

Above Jacob's Ladder p236, with view towards Higher Booth & Edale. Rider: Sam Townsend. © James Elkington

Shropshire Hills, Malverns & West Midlands

With the exception of Cannock Chase to the north of Wolverhampton and the Malvern Hills to the west of **Great Malvern**, all the best mountain biking in this region lies in Shropshire and most of this is located within 15 kilometres of the border with Wales. The central feature of this area is the Long Mynd, a whaleback of a hill rising to over 500m west of **Church Stretton** and criss-crossed with bridleways. It is one of the few places in the country where you should keep an eye out for gliders, as the ridge track crosses a landing strip! West from the Long Mynd to Stiperstones and Corndon Hill, east to Caer Caradoc Hill and The Lawley and north to Pulverbatch and **Snailbeach** there are a myriad of tracks to allow you to plan a weekend's riding. **Clun** offers a compact selection of trails utilising part of the Offa's Dyke Path.

A little further east from the Long Mynd there is a 20km ridge ride along Wenlock Edge, running northeast from near Craven Arms to **Much Wenlock**, at times following the course of the Marches Way or the Jack Mytton Way. On eastwards one of the highest points in Shropshire is Titterstone Clee Hill which rises to 533m and can be cirumnavigated from **Cleehill.**

The Malvern Hills offer some good riding in the south of the region, accessed from **Great Malvern** and **Alfrick.** The tops of the hills are criss-crossed with bridleways but you will need a good map. Further east into the borders of Staffordshire and Worcestershire, Kinver Edge (**Kinver**) has dramatic drops to test your downhill skills and the Clent Hills (**Clent**) offer a multitude of bridleways with some technical singletrack.

Eastridge Wood lies at the very northern end of the Long Mynd and is one of the several Forestry Commission holdings in Shropshire with waymarked trails. Others are at **Hopton Castle Woods** and **Bringewood**, both great downhill venues west of **Ludlow** or **Wapley Hill**, north east of **Kington**.

In addition to these smaller woodlands along the Welsh border, the two larger forestry holdings in the area, **Wyre Forest** to the west of Kidderminster and **Cannock Chase** to the north of Wolverhampton, both have waymarked trails.

Snailbeach

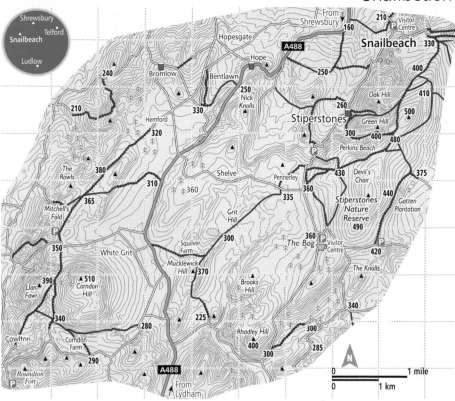

Situation: At the foot of the Stiperstones in Shropshire, close to the Welsh border. 12 miles south west of Shrewsbury.

About the Base: Snailbeach, a village with easy access to the trails. **Parking:** Car parks at Snailbeach, Stiperstones, The Bog Visitor Centre, The Knolls, Mitchells Fold & Roundton Fort. *Grid Ref: Snailbeach SJ373022, Stiperstones SO356997, The Bog Visitor Centre SO357978, The Knolls SO369976, Mitchells Fold SO302980, Roundton Fort SO292946. Post Code: Snailbeach SY5 0NZ, The Bog Visitor Centre SY5 0NG.*

Drive Times: Birmingham 1hr10, Manchester 2hr10, Bristol 2hr30, Leeds 2hr40, London 3hr20.

Refreshments: No refreshments at Snailbeach. The Stables Inn 01743 891 344 at Hopesgate or The Callow Inn 01743 891933 at Bromlow. The Miners Arms 01938 561352 at Priest Weston, Café at The Bog Visitor Centre 01743 792 484 and The Stiperstones Inn 01743 791 327 at Stiperstones.

Books: MTB Guide Mid Wales & The Marches (J.Dixon).

Maps: OS Explorer 216.

Routes on Web: www.goodmtb.co.uk/a94

Bike Shops: Shrewsbury Bicycles & Halfords 01743 270277 in Shrewsbury.

Route Idea

From Snailbeach, SW to Stiperstones. Trails S of Green Hill and down to Pennerley. Roads W to Shelve & Hemford. Trails S to Llan Fawr then E past Corndon Farm to road. Roads around Rhadley Hill to The Bog. Road E then trails past Gatten Plantation and N back to Snailbeach.
Distance 40km.

Church Stretton (west)

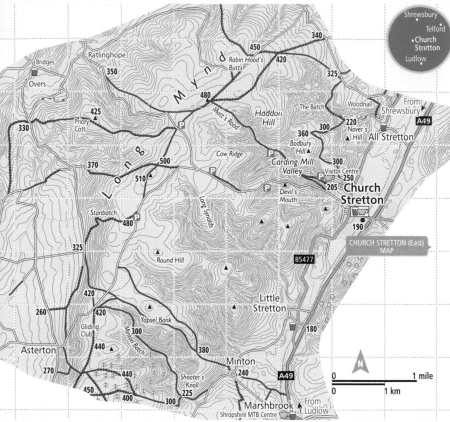

Map labels (Long Mynd area):
Shrewsbury, Telford, Church Stretton, Ludlow
Bridges, Ratlinghope, 350, Robin Hood's Butts, 450, 420, 340, 325
Overs, Mynd, 480, Matt's Road, Haddon Hill, The Batch, Woodnall, From Shrewsbury, A49
425, Priory Cott, Long, Cow Ridge, 360, Bodbury Hill, 300, 220, Nover's Hill, All Stretton, 250
330, 370, 500, Mo, Carding Mill Valley, Visitor Centre, 300
510, Devil's Mouth, 205, Church Stretton, 190
Stanbatch, 480, Long Synalds, CHURCH STRETTON (East) MAP
325, Round Hill, B5477
420, 260, 420, Yapsel Bank, Little Stretton
Gliding Club, 300, Minton Batch, 180
Asterton, 440, 380
270, 440, Minton, 240, A49
450, 300, Shooter's Knoll, 225, Marshbrook, From Ludlow
400, Shropshire MTB Centre
0   1 mile
0   1 km
N

Situation: East of Long Mynd in the heart of the Shropshire Hills. 15 miles south of Shrewsbury and 15 miles north of Ludlow.

About the Base: Church Stretton, a market town with pubs, cafés and accommodation.
Further Info: www.churchstretton.co.uk. **Parking:** Car park next to the National Trust visitor centre, west of Church Stretton. Also at Bodbury Hill, Devils Mouth, Cow Ridge, Wild Moor & Pole Cott on Long Mynd. *Grid Ref: Church Stretton SO448943, Bodbury Hill SO440948, Devils Mouth SO437942, Cow Ridge SO426944, Wild Moor SO420953, Pole Cott SO412937. Post Code: Church Stretton SY6 6JF.*

Drive Times: Birmingham 1hr10, Manchester 2hr, Bristol 2hr10, Leeds 2hr40, London 3hr10.

Trains: Church Stretton Station is on the Shrewsbury-Hereford & Shrewsbury-Carmarthen lines.

Refreshments: Plenty of pubs and cafés at Church Stretton. Chalet Pavillion Tea Rooms 01694 723068 at National Trust Carding Mill Valley. The Yew Tree Inn 01694 722 228 at All Stretton and The Green Dragon Inn 01694 722 925 at Little Stretton. The Station Pub 01694 781208 and Café 01694 781515 at Shropshire Hills MTB Centre at Marshbrook.

Books: MTB Guide W Midlands (D.Taylor). Wales MTB (T.Hutton). MTB Guide Mid Wales & The Marches (J.Dixon). MBR Ride Guide 2010

Maps: OS Explorer 217.

Bike Shops: Plush Hill Cycles 01694 720 133. Blazing Bikes 01694 781515 at Shropshire Hills MTB Centre in Marshbrook.

Route Idea

From the Visitor Centre, N past The Batch then W towards spine of Long Mynd. S along the Long Mynd then W past Priory Cottage. S on road. Trail E past Stanbatch. Road S then trail SE along Minton Batch. Roads back to start via Minton & Little Stretton. Distance 30km.

Carding Mill Valley. Rider: Amanda. © Sheldon Attwood

Church Stretton (east)

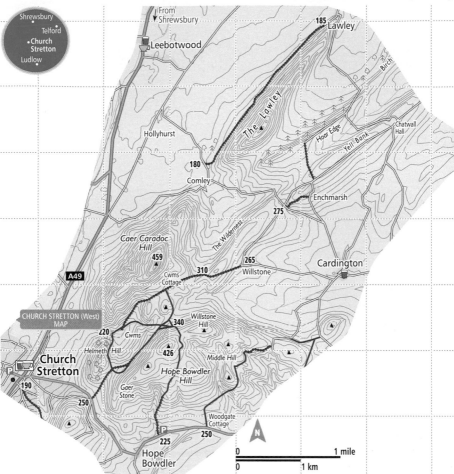

Situation: At the foot of the Caradoc Hills and east of Long Mynd in the heart of the Shropshire Hills. 15 miles south of Shrewsbury and 15 miles north of Ludlow.

About the Base: Church Stretton, a market town with pubs, cafés and accommodation. Further Info: www.churchstretton.co.uk. **Parking:** Car park in the centre of Church Stretton on Easthope Road parking on B4371 east of Hope Bowdler. *Grid Ref: Church Stretton SO454936, Hope Bowdler SO478927. Post Code: Church Stretton SY6 6BJ, Hope Bowdler SY6 7DB.*

Drive Times: Birmingham 1hr10, Manchester 2hr, Bristol 2hr10, Leeds 2hr40, London 3hr10.

Trains: Church Stretton Railway Station is on the Shrewsbury-Hereford & Shrewsbury-Carmarthen lines.

Refreshments: Plenty of pubs and cafés at Church Stretton. The Royal Oak 01694 771 266 at Cardington. The Pound Inn 01694 751 255 and The Copper Kettle Café 01694 751 238 at Leebotwood.

Books: MTB Guide W Midlands (D.Taylor).

Maps: OS Explorer 217.

Bike Shops: Plush Hill Cycles 01694 720 133. Blazing Bikes 01694 781515 at Shropshire Hills MTB Centre in Marshbrook.

Route Idea

From Church Stretton, road SE to Hope Bowdler & Woodgate Cottage. NE to Cardington, Enchmarsh & along Hoar Edge to Lawley. SW along The Lawley, Road to Willstone. Trails past Cwms Cottage & S over Hope Bowdler Hill. Road back to start. Distance 20km.

Much Wenlock

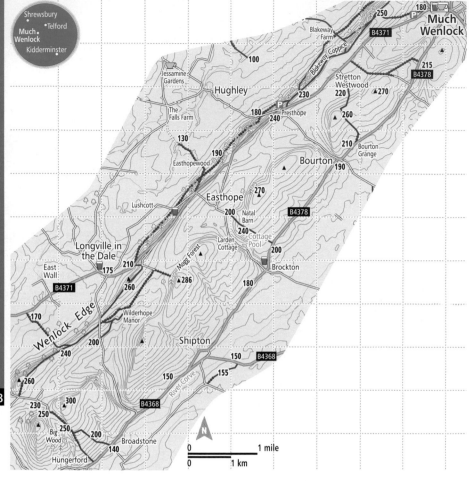

Situation: North east of Wenlock Edge in Central Shropshire. 8 miles north west of Bridgnorth and 12 miles south east of Shrewsbury.

About the Base: Much Wenlock, a small town with pubs, cafés and accommodation.
Further Info: www.muchwenlockguide.info. **Parking:** National Trust car park west of Much Wenlock on B4371. Car park at Blakeway Coppice. **Grid Ref:** *Much Wenlock SO613996, Blakeway Coppice SO581975.*
Post Code: Much Wenlock TF13 6AS.

Drive Times: Birmingham 1hr, Bristol 2hrs, Manchester 2hrs, Leeds 2hr40, London 3hrs.

Refreshments: Plenty of pubs and cafés at Much Wenlock. The Feathers Inn 01746 785 202 at Brockton, The Longville Arms at Longville in the Dale and The Wenlock Edge Inn at Easthopewood.

Books: MTB Guide W Midlands (D.Taylor).

Maps: OS Explorer 217.

Bike Shops: Pauls Pedals 01746 768 792 in Bridgnorth.

Route Idea

Trails SW through Blakeway Coppice to Presthope.
Road to Easthope & trail SE to Brockton. SW to
Broadstone then trails up to Wenlock Edge. Trails
NE along the Edge & back to Much Wenlock.
Distance 36km.

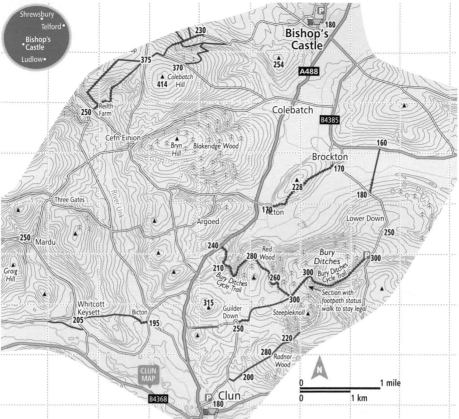

Situation: In Shropshire, just east of the Welsh border. 18 miles north west of Ludlow and south west of Shrewsbury.

About the Base: Bishops Castle, a small market town with pubs and cafés.
Further Info: www.bishopscastle.co.uk.

Parking: Car parks in Bishops Castle, at Bury Ditches & in Clun next to the community centre.
*Grid Ref: Bishops Castle SO322887, Bury Ditches SO333839, Clun SO302811. **Post Code:** Bishops Castle SY9 5AH, Clun SY7 8LE.*

Drive Times: Birmingham 1hr30, Bristol 2hr20, Manchester 2hr20, Leeds 2hr50, London 3hr30.

Trains: Broome Railway Station, 5 miles east of Clunton in the south of the map, is on the Shrewsbury-Carmarthen line.

Refreshments: At Bishops Castle, The Three Tuns 01588 638 797, The Six Bells 01588 630 144 and The Boars Head 01588 638521. Capricho 01588 638 181, Kirstys 01588 638 115 and The Poppy House Café 01588 638443. The White Horse 01588 640 305, The Sun Inn 01588 640559 and Clun Bridge Tea Rooms 01588 640 634 at Clun.

Books: MTB Guide W Midlands (D.Taylor).

Maps: OS Explorer 216 & 201.

Bike Shops: Plush Hill Cycles 01694 720 133, 12 miles away in Church Stretton.

Route Idea

From Bishops's Castle W on road & trails to Cefn Einion. S to A488 then along Bury Ditches Cycle Trail. The trail can be extended by detouring to Guilder Down, Radnor Wood and a walking section to link back to Bury Ditches. N to Brockton and back to Bishop's Castle. Distance 30km.

Clun

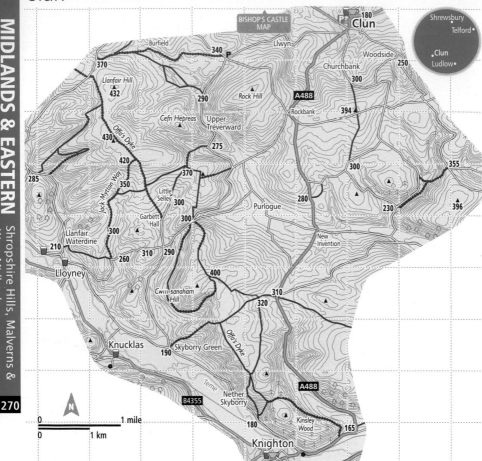

Situation: On the River Clun, east of Offa's Dyke, in the Shropshire Hills Area of Outstanding Natural Beauty. 8 miles north of Knighton in Wales and 17 miles north west of Ludlow.

About the Base: Clun, a small town with two pubs and tea rooms. **Parking:** Car park in Clun next to the Castle or roadside west of the town near Rock Hill. *Grid Ref: Clun SO299807, Rock Hill SO276800. Post Code: Clun SY7 8JQ.*

Drive Times: Birmingham 1hr40, Bristol 2hr20, Manchester 2hr30, Leeds 3hrs, London 3hr40.

Trains: Knighton Railway Station is on the Shrewsbury-Carmarthen line.

Refreshments: At Clun, The White Horse 01588 640 305, The Sun Inn 01588 640559 and Clun Bridge Tea Rooms 01588 640 634. The Waterdine 01547 528214 at Llanfair Waterdine or The Lloyney Inn 01547 528 498 at Lloyney. If arriving by train, The Castle Inn 01547 528 150 at Knucklas or pubs and cafés at Knighton.

Books: MTB Guide W Midlands (D.Taylor).

Maps: OS Explorer 201.

Bike Shops: Dale Street Sports 01588 673 388, 9 miles away in Craven Arms, for bikes, parts, repairs & hire.

Route Ideas

❶ W past Llwyn & Burfield. S along Offa's Dyke then descent along Jack Mytton Way to road. E to Garbett Hall & Little Selley. Trail up and over to road then onto Upper Treverward and back to Clun. Distance 19km.

❷ If arriving by train at Knighton, NW on road to Llanfair Waterdine, E to Garbett Hall, Little Selley & Upper Treverward. Trail W past Burfield then S on Offa's Dyke & Jack Mytton Way. Return as outward start. Distance 27km.

Kington

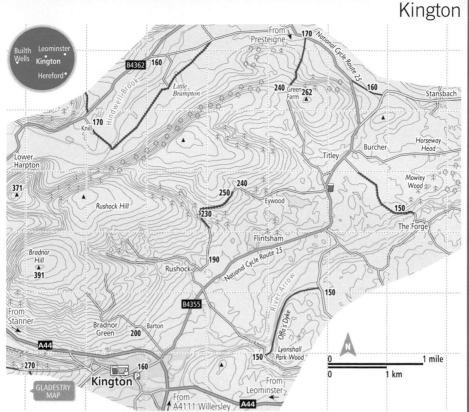

Situation: At the foot of Hergest Ridge on the River Arrow in Herefordshire. Close to the Welsh border, 11 miles north of Hay-on-Wye and 20 miles north west of Hereford.

About the Base: Kington, a market town with a choice of pubs and cafés. Further Info: www.kington.org.uk.
Parking: Car park in the centre of Kington. *Grid Ref: SO295565. Post Code: HR5 3BH.*

Drive Times: Bristol 1hr50, Birmingham 1hr50, Manchester 3hr, Leeds 3hr30, London 3hr40.

Refreshments: Choice of pubs and cafés at Kington. The Stagg Inn 01544 230 221 at Titley.

Maps: OS Explorer 201.

Routes on Web: www.goodmtb.co.uk/a93

Route Idea

NE on B4355. SE towards Lyonshall Park Wood. Trail and roads NE to Forge then on to Titley. N past Green Farm to rejoin B4355. Loop back to Green Farm via Little Brampton & Knill. Return to Kington via Eywood & Rushock.
Distance 31km.

Rider: Graham. © Sheldon Attwood

Ludlow

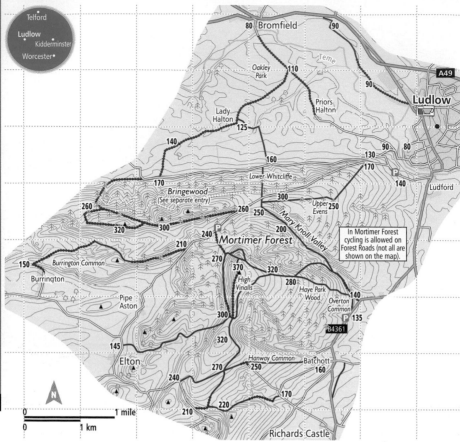

In Mortimer Forest cycling is allowed on Forest Roads (not all are shown on the map).

Situation: Beneath the Clee Hills, on the River Teme, in the Welsh Marches of Shropshire. 24 miles west of Kidderminster and north of Hereford.

About the Base: Ludlow, a market town with a choice of pubs, cafés and accommodation.
Further Info: www.ludlow.org.uk. **Parking:** Car park just south west of Ludlow town centre. *Grid Ref: SO506741.*
Post Code: SY8 2HB.

Drive Times: Birmingham 1hr30, Bristol 2hrs, Manchester 2hr30, Leeds 3hrs, London 3hrs.

Trains: Ludlow Railway Station is on the Shrewsbury-Hereford line.

Refreshments: Good choice of refreshments in Ludlow.

Books: MTB Guide W Midlands (D.Taylor).

Maps: OS Explorer 203.

Bike Shops: Pearce Cycles 01584 876 016 for parts & repairs.

Route Idea

Roads to Priors Halton then trails around to Bringewood. Trails around the forest then road link to trails W across Burrington Common. Road SE to Elton. Trail up to High Vinalls then down to Overton Common. NW along Mary Knoll Valley, E past Upper Evens & back to start.
Distance 31km.

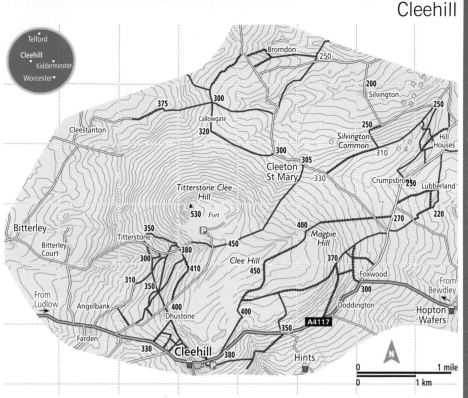

Situation: On the slope of Titterstone Clee Hill in the Clee Hills and Shropshire Hills Area of Outstanding Natural Beauty. 6 miles east of Ludlow.

About the Base: Cleehill, a village with three pubs and a cafe. **Parking:** Car parks in Cleehill & at Titterstone Clee Quarry. **Grid Ref:** *Cleehill SO594753, Quarry SO591776. **Post Code:** Cleehill SY8 3QE.*

Drive Times: Birmingham 1hr10, Bristol 1hr50, Manchester 2hr30, Leeds 3hrs, London 3hrs.

Trains: Ludlow Railway Station is on the Shrewsbury-Hereford line.

Refreshments: At Cleehill, The Kremlin 01584 890 950, The Royal Oak 01584 890 754 and The Golden Cross 01584 890 741. Craven Place Café 01584 891632 on A4117 just east of the village. The Colliers Arms 01584 890 445 at Hints or The Crown Inn 01299 270 372 at Hopton Wafers.

Books: MTB Guide Mid Wales & The Marches (J.Dixon).

Maps: OS Explorer 203 & 217.

Bike Shops: Pearce Cycles 01584 876 016, in Ludlow or Team Cycles 01584 819 196, 5 miles away in Tenbury Wells for parts & repairs.

Route Idea

From Cleehill NW to Dhustone. Road NE then small trail link to join roads W to Titterstone, Bitterley & Cleestanton. E to Cleeton St Mary. Trails NE past Silvington Common. S to Crumpsbrook. Trails up over Magpie Hill, Clee Hill and back down to the start.
Distance 27km.

Chelmarsh

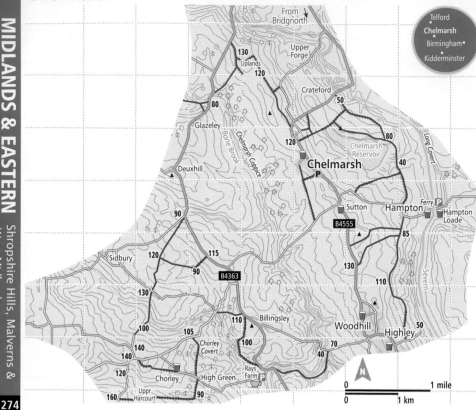

Situation: West of the River Severn above the Severn Valley in Shropshire. 4 miles south of Bridgnorth.

About the Base: Chelmarsh, a village with two pubs. **Parking:** In Chelmarsh next to the school. Car parks next to the river in Hampton Loade & at Rays Farm in Billingsley. **Grid Ref:** *Chelmarsh SO724871, Hampton Loade SO747865, Rays Farm SO713832.* **Post Code:** *Chelmarsh WV16 6BA, Hampton Loade WV15 6HD, Rays Farm WV16 6PF.*

Drive Times: Birmingham 1hr, Bristol 2hrs, Manchester 2hr10, Leeds 2hr40, London 3hrs.

Refreshments: At Chelmarsh, The Bulls Head 01746 861 469 and The Kings Arms 01746 861 455. The Unicorn 01746 861 515 and The River and Rail 01746 780 404 at Hampton Loade, The Malt Shovel 01746 862 894, The Bache Arms 01746 861 266 or Jays Café 01746 862 626 at Highley. Café at Rays Farm 01299 841255 and The Duck Inn 01746 718 267 at Chorley.

Books: MTB Guide W Midlands (D.Taylor).

Maps: OS Explorer 218.

Bike Shops: Pauls Pedals 01746 768 792 in Bridgnorth.

Route Idea

From Chelmarsh, trails past the reservoir to Hampton then S to Highley. Roads and trails W to Rays Farm, High Green, Upper Harcourt. Roads N. Trails after Glazeley to Uplands then S back to Chelmarsh. Distance 27km.

Kinver

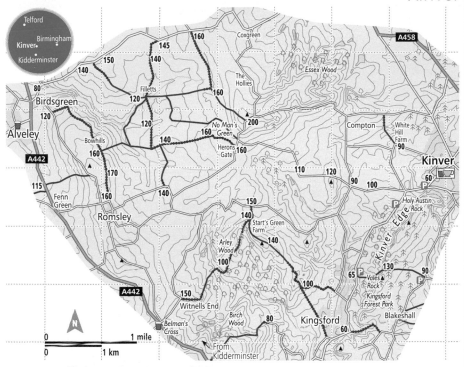

Rider: Stu Brettle. © Sheldon Attwood

Situation: At the foot of Kinver Edge and on the River Stour in the far south west of Staffordshire, close to Shropshire and Worcestershire. 5 miles west of Stourbridge and 7 miles north of Kidderminster.

About the Base: Kinver, a large village with pubs and a coffee shop. **Parking:** Car parks west of Kinver village, at Holy Austin Rock, east of Kinver Edge & at Kingsford. *Grid Ref: Kinver SO836836, Holy Austin Rock SO831834, Kinver Edge SO835821, Kingsford SO824821. **Post Code:** Kinver DY7 6DL, Kingsford DY11 5SB.*

Drive Times: Birmingham 45mins, Bristol 1hr40, Manchester 2hr, London 2hr40, Leeds 2hr40.

Trains: Stourbridge Junction & Kidderminster Railway Stations are on the Birmingham-Worcester line.

Refreshments: Choice of pubs or Maori Coffee Shop 01384 873 471 at Kinver. The Squirrel Inn 01746 780 235 or The Royal Oak 01746 781 163 at Alveley and The Bellmans Cross Inn 01299 861322 at Bellmans Cross.

Books: MTB Guide W Midlands (D.Taylor).

Maps: OS Explorer 218 & 219.

Bike Shops: Two Wheels 01384 394 653 in Stourbridge. Halfords 01562 861993 in Kidderminster.

Route Idea

From Kinver, road W to Herons Gate. Trails past the Filletts. Road to Birdsgreen. Trails S to Romsley. On to Belman's Cross, Witnells End, Kingsford & Blakeshall. Trail W past Vales Rock. Road back to start. Distance 26km.

Clent

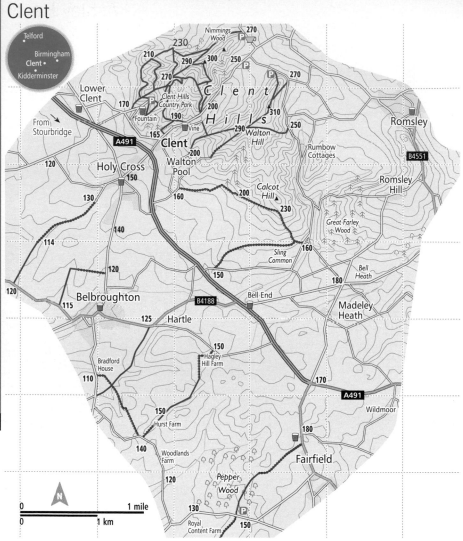

Situation: At the foot of the Clent Hills in north Worcestershire. 4 miles south of Stourbridge and 6 miles east of Kidderminster.

About the Base: Clent, a village with three pubs and easy access to the trails. **Parking:** Parking at Clent Hills Country Park. Also north east of the village in the Clent Hills, at National Trust Nimmings Wood & Pepper Wood in the south of the map. *Grid Ref: Clent Hills Country Park SO926798, Clent Hills SO943802 or SO939803, Nimmings Wood SO936801, Pepper Wood SO938744.*

Drive Times: Birmingham 30mins, Bristol 1hr30, Manchester 1hr50, London 2hr20, Leeds 2hr30.

Trains: Stourbridge Junction & Kidderminster Railway Stations are on the Birmingham-Worcester line.

Refreshments: At Clent, The Vine Inn 01562 882 491, The Fountain 01562 883 286 and The Hill Tavern 01562 885 024. Café at National Trust Nimmings Wood car park 01562 712822, The

French Hen 01562 883 040 at Lower Clent, Ye Olde Horseshoes at Belbroughton and The Swan 01527 837196 at Fairfield. The Bell 01562 731 928 at Bell End or The Sun 01562 710 417 at Romsley.

Maps: OS Explorer 219.

Routes on Web: www.goodmtb.co.uk/a91

Bike Shops: Two Wheels 01384 394 653 in Stourbridge. Midland Cycle Hire 01562 711 144, 2 miles away in Romsley, for hire & guided tours. Will deliver to Clent.

Route Idea

From the Nimmings Wood Car Park. Roads S then trails SW over Walton Hill to Walton Pool. Trail SE past Calcot Hill. Roads S to Fairfield. Trail through Pepper Wood. N to Belbroughton on road and trails. Road to Clent Hills Country Park. Trails over the hills and back to the start. Distance 19km

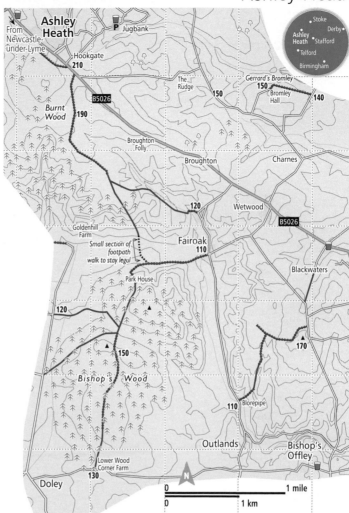

Situation: In Staffordshire, close to the Shropshire border, 5 miles north east of Market Drayton and 10 miles south west of Newcastle Under Lyme.

About the Base: Ashley Heath, a village with a pub and easy access to the trails. **Parking:** Roadside by the Robin Hood Pub at Jug Bank. *Grid Ref: SJ753356. Post Code: TF9 4NL.*

Drive Times: Birmingham 1hr, Manchester 1hr20, Leeds 1hr50, Bristol 2hr20, London 3hr.

Refreshments: The Robin Hood Inn 01630 672 237 at Ashley.

Books: MTB Guide W Midlands (D.Taylor).

Maps: OS Explorer 243.

Bike Shops: Brenin Bikes 01630 656614 in Market Drayton.

Route Idea

S past Burnt Wood and through Bishop's Wood. Roads E to Outlands then N to Blorepipe. Trails NE to road then onto Fairoak. Trails past Burnt Wood and back to start. Distance 19km.

Brocton

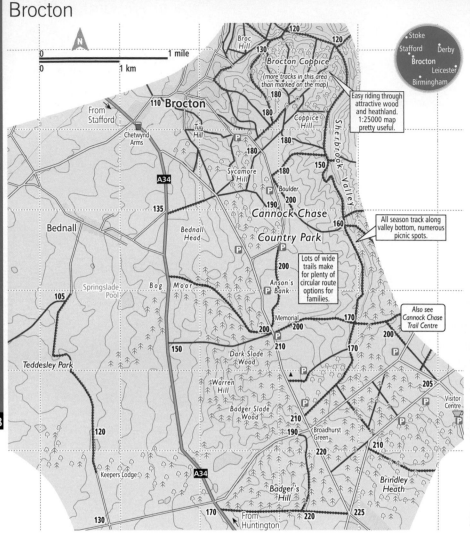

Situation: On the edge of Cannock Chase, an Area of Outstanding Natural Beauty. 4 miles south east of Stafford.

About the Base: Brocton, a village with a post office and easy access to the trails. **Parking:** Several car parks in Cannock Chase Country Park and at the visitor centre. **Grid Ref:** *Visitor Centre SJ999153.* **Post Code:** *Visitor Centre WS12 4PP.*

Drive Times: Birmingham 40mins, Manchester 1hr30, Leeds 2hr, Bristol 2hr, London 2hr40.

Trains: Milford Railway Station, a mile north of Brocton, is on the Rugby-Stafford-Crewe line.

Refreshments: The Chetwynd Arms 01785 661 089, west of Brocton on the A34. Café at Cannock Chase Country Park 01543 878690.

Books: MTB Guide W Midlands (D.Taylor).

Maps: OS Explorer 244.

Bike Shops: Mammoth Lifestyle & Fitness 01785 66455, a mile north of the village on the A513 at Milford. Halfords 01785 279810 in Stafford.

Route Idea

From car park SE of Brocton, W to Bednall, S through Teddesley Park then E to Badger's Hill. N along Sherbrook Valley, anticlockwise around Brocton Coppice and back to start.
Distance 19km.

For waymarked trails see Cannock Chase (p286).

Alfrick

Route Idea

From car park south of Alfrick, N to Alfrick, W to Round Hill. N past Ravenshill Wood & on to Knightwick. S past Brickhall Farm. Trails & roads S to Longley Green & Storridge. NE past Crumpton Hill. N past The Norrest & back to start. Distance 24km.

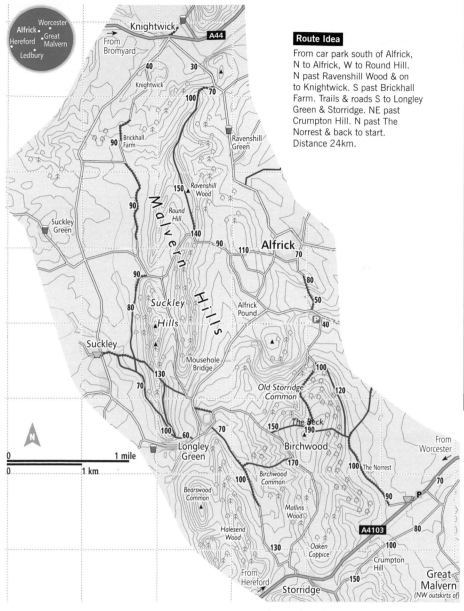

Situation: In the Malvern Hills, south of the River Teme in Worcestershire. 7 miles north of Great Malvern and west of Worcester.

About the Base: Alfrick, a village with easy access to the trails. **Parking:** Car park south of Alfrick next to Leigh Brook. Large layby on A4103 at Storridge. *Grid Ref: Alfrick SO751520, A4103.*

Drive Times: Birmingham 1hr, Bristol 1hr30, Manchester 2hr20, London 2hr50, Leeds 2hr50.

Trains: Malvern Link Railway Station, 6 miles away, is on the Worcester-Hereford line.

Refreshments: No refreshments at Alfrick. The Fox and Hounds 01886 821 228 at Ravenshill Green, The Talbot 01886 821235 at Knightwick, The Cross Keys 01886 884 494 or The Greenhouse Café 01886 884 665 at Suckley and The Nelson Inn 01886 884 530 at Longley Green.

Books: MTB Guide W Midlands (D.Taylor).

Maps: The Malverns Offroad Cycling Map West. OS Explorer 190 & 204.

Bike Shops: Back on Track Bikes 01684 565 777 & Halfords 01684 577835 in Great Malvern.

Great Malvern

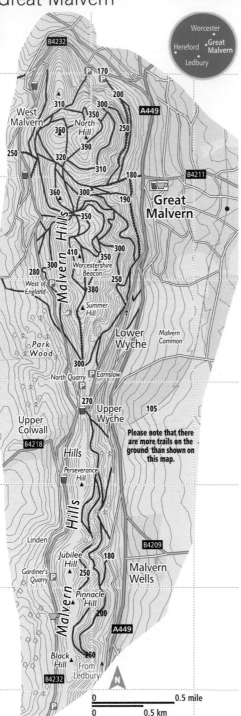

Situation: West of the River Severn on the eastern slopes of the Malvern Hills in Worcestershire. 8 miles south west of Worcester.

About the Base: Great Malvern, a market town with pubs, cafés and accommodation.

Parking: North Quarry Car Park on the outskirts of Great Malvern at North Hill. Car parks at West of England, Upper Wyche & Jubilee Hill. *Grid Ref: North Quarry SO770469, West of England SO765449, Upper Wyche SO770440, Jubilee Hill SO766420,*
Post Code: *North Quarry WR14 4LX, West of England WR14 4DG, Upper Wyche WR14 4EG, Jubilee Hilll WR13 6DN.*

Drive Times: Birmingham 1hr, Bristol 1hr20, Manchester 2hr20, London 2hr40, Leeds 2hr50.

Trains: Malvern Link & Great Malvern Railway Stations are on the Worcester-Hereford line.

Refreshments: Plenty of pubs and cafés at Great Malvern. The Lamb Inn 01684 577 847 and The Brewers Arms 01684 568 147 at West Malvern. The Wyche Inn 01684 575 396 at Upper Wyche, The Kettle Sings Café 01684 540 244 at Pinnacle Hill and The Chase Inn 01684 540 276 at Upper Colwall.

Books: MBR Ride Guide 2010

Maps: OS Explorer 190.
Malvern Hills Map (Harvey).

Routes on Web: www.goodmtb.co.uk/a92

Bike Shops: Back on Track Bikes 01684 565 777 & Halfords 01684 577835 in Great Malvern.

Route Idea

Very tightly packed bridleways make this area very hard to stay on your intended route if new to the area; so be prepared for a bit of exploring and maybe one or two unplanned extra climbs! There is a natural split in the hills at Upper Wyche and a popular ride would be to combine a loop on the N of Upper Wyche with one on the S. Distance about 16km.

© Sheldon Attwood

Around Clent p276. Rider: Mick Votchey. © Sheldon Attwood

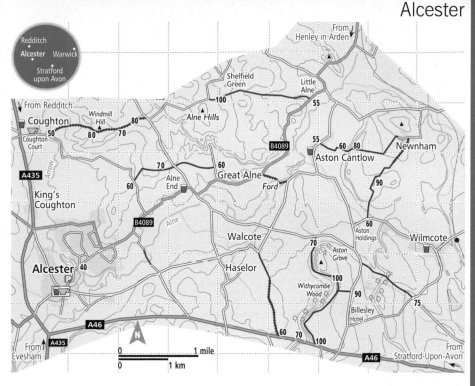

Alcester

Situation: At the confluence of the River Alne and the River Arrow in Warwickshire. 8 miles west of Stratford-upon-Avon.

About the Base: Alcester, a market town with a choice of pubs, cafés and accommodation.
Further Info: www.alcester.co.uk. **Parking:** Car parks in Alcester and at National Trust Coughton Court, north of Alcester. **Grid Ref:** *Alcester SP088577, Coughton Court SP085603.* **Post Code:** *Alcester B49 5DJ, Coughton Court B49 5JA.*

Drive Times: Birmingham 45mins, Bristol 1hr20, Manchester 2hr10, London 2hr10, Leeds 2hr30.

Refreshments: Good choice of pubs and cafés at Alcester. Tearooms at Coughton Court 01789 400777, The Throckmorton Arms 01789 766366 at Coughton, The Kings Head 01789 488 242 at Aston Cantlow and The Huff Cap 01789 488800 at Great Alne. If arriving by train, The Mary Arden Inn 01789 267 030 or The Masons arms 01789 297 416 at Wilmcote.

Books: MTB Guide W Midlands (D.Taylor).

Maps: OS Explorer 205 & 220.

Bike Shops: The Cycle Centre 01789 763 872 in Alcester. Halfords 01782 744474 in Stratford upon Avon.

Route Idea

From Alcester, NE on B4089 then N on minor road towards Coughton. Trail E over Windmill Hill. Road & trails to Little Alne. S to Aston Cantlow . E to Newnham then S to Aston Holdings. W to Great Alne across ford (if not too deep) otherwise detour around. Trails W from Great Alne and roads back to start.
Distance 26km.

Lowsonford

Situation: On the Stratford-on-Avon Canal in the Forest of Arden, Warwickshire. 4 miles north east of Henley-in-Arden and 10 miles north of Stratford-on-Avon.

About the Base: Lowsonford, a small village with a pub. **Parking:** Roadside in the centre of Lowsonford. *Grid Ref: SP188678. Post Code: B95 5FJ.*

Drive Times: Birmingham 35mins, Bristol 1hr40, Manchester 2hr10, London 2hr10, Leeds 2hr20.

Trains: Henley in Arden & Wootten Wawen Railway Stations are on the Birmingham-Stratford line.

Refreshments: At Lowsonford, The Fleur de Lys 01564 782 431. The Crabmill 0192684 3342 at Preston Bagot. The Bulls Head 01564 792 511

at Wootton Wawen or pubs and cafés at Henley-in-Arden.

Books: MTB Guide W Midlands (D.Taylor).

Maps: OS Explorer 220.

Bike Shops: The Cycle Studio 01789 205 057 & Halfords 01789 265510 in Stratford Upon Avon.

Route Idea

From Lowsonford, N to Bushwood Grange. S past Coppice Corner, Preston Fields & Preston Bagot. Road S then Monarch's Way SE to Cutler's Farm. N to Kington Grange, Barnmoor Green, Holywell, High Cross & back to finish. Distance 19km.

Wellesbourne

Situation: In the south west of Warwickshire, 6 miles east of Stratford Upon Avon and 7 miles south of Warwick.

About the Base: Wellesbourne, a large village with two pubs and a café. **Parking:** Roadside in the centre of Wellesbourne. Car park at National Trust Charlecote Park. *Grid Ref: Wellesbourne SP277551, Charlecote SP262564. Post Code: Wellesbourne CV35 9QR.*

Drive Times: Birmingham 40mins, London 1hr50, Bristol 1hr50, Manchester 2hr10, Leeds 2hr20.

Trains: Stratford Upon Avon Railway Station has services to Birmingham, Oxford & London.

Refreshments: At Wellesbourne, The Kings Head 01789 840 206, The Slags Head 01789 840 266 and The Coffee Stop 01789 470 800. Touchdown Café 01789 470 575 at Wellesbourne Mountfield Airfield. Refreshments at National Trust Charlecote Park 01789 470277. The Boars Head 01789 840 533 at Hampton Lucy, Cottage Tavern 01926 651

410 at Ashorne and The Black Horse 01926 651 231 at Moreton Morrell.

Books: MTB Guide W Midlands (D.Taylor).

Maps: OS Explorer 205.

Bike Shops: The Cycle Studio 01789 205 057 & Halfords 01789 265510 in Stratford Upon Avon.

Route Idea

From Wellesbourne, NW to Charlecote then road and trails N to Wasperton. On to Barford then E to Oakley Wood. Trails past the wood then S on road to Little Morrell. SE on trails & road to Westfields Farm then S to Combrook. W to Walton Hall House & back to Wellesbourne. Distance 29km.

Nantmawr Quarry

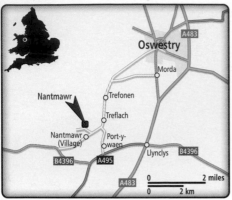

In the foothils of the Berwyn Mountains, on the Shropshire / Welsh border, a long, steep, fast competition standard downhill course. A XC trail over a variety of surfaces across the Moelydd hill, with alternative routes for beginners to professional, as well as a skills area with plenty of jumps, drop offs and technical features.

Facilities:
Refreshments at The "Engine House" bunk & club house. Pay to Ride.

Parking:
Grid Ref: SJ252249. Post Code: SY10 9HJ

Web: www.goodmtb.co.uk/b47

The Trails
❶ DH
❷ XC, 5.6k

Cannock Chase

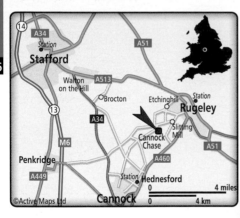

A small Area of Outstanding Natural Beauty in Staffordshire. Classic woodland riding maintained by Chase Trails. Purpose built XC and short, varied, downhill trails and three leisure trails.

Facilities:
Birches Valley Forest Centre. Birches Valley Café and Swinnerton Cycle Centre 01889 575170 for MTB hire, parts & repairs.

Parking:
Grid Ref: SK017170. Post Code: WS15 2UQ

Web: www.goodmtb.co.uk/b44a & /b44b

The Trails
❶ Follow The Dog, Red, XC, 11.3km.
❷ Monkey Trail, Red, XC, 11.3km extension to Follow the Dog.
❸ Birches Valley, XC, Green.
❹ Fairoak Pools, XC, Green.
❺ Sherbrook Valley, XC, Green.
❻ Stile Cop, DH.

Rider: Ed. © Sheldon Attwood

Eastridge Wood

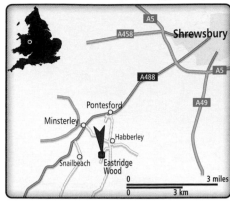

In the Shropshire Hills Area of Outstanding Natural Beauty. The Forestry Commission work with the Eastridge Trail Parnership to improve and maintain waymarked cross country trails on unsurfaced singletrack and two fast, technical downhill tracks.

Facilities:
None on site.
Parking:
Grid Ref: SJ391027.
Web: www.goodmtb.co.uk/b45

The Trails

❶ Blue Trail, XC, Blue, 2.4km.

❷ Yellow Trail, XC, Blue, 4.8lm.

❸ Brown Trail, XC, Red, 7km.

❹ 2x DH, Black.

Wyre Forest

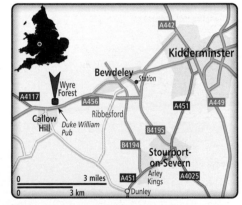

On the borders of Worcestershire and Shropshire, 6,000 acres of woodland with waymarked family trails through a varied landscape.

Facilities:
The Whitty Pear Café at Wyre Forest Discovery & Visitor Centre.
Parking:
Grid Ref: SO749740. *Post Code:* DY14 9XQ
Web: www.goodmtb.co.uk/b50

The Trails

❶ Blue, XC, 8km.

❷ Green, XC, 5.6km

Rider: Neil Smith MB Swindon. © Tom Stickland

Hopton Wood

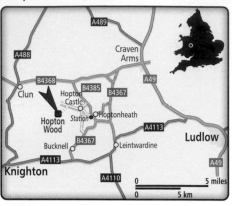

On the Shropshire/Welsh Border, coniferous woodland forming part of The Marches Forest in the South Shropshire Hills. Forest roads, tracks and singletrack or tough, rooty, technical downhills.

Facilities:
None on Site. Refreshments at nearby Craven Arms. Hopton Heath Railway Station , 2 miles away. Pearce Cycles 01584 879288 at Ludlow for parts, repairs, upliift service and organised events.

Parking:
Grid Ref: SO347777.

Web: www.goodmtb.co.uk/b46a

The Trails

XC. DH.

©Turnip Towers

Ribbesford DH

On the edge of Wyre Forest, a few miles west of Kidderminster. Three downhill tracks of varying difficulty. Maintained by local riders with the support of the Forestry Commission and designed to suit riders of all abilities, a fast paced single-track with flowing jumps; big berms, roots and drops or a smooth, black, free ride route with plenty of challenging features.

Facilities:
Refreshments in nearby Bewdley.

Parking:
Grid Ref: SO778729. Post Code: DY12 2TX

Web: www.goodmtb.co.uk/b48

The Trails
DH: Black, Red, Green.

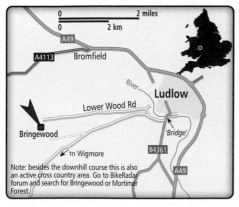

Bringewood. ©Turnip Towers

Bringewood

In the Shropshire Welsh Marches, Forestry Commission land with steep, fast down-hills for experienced riders. Peace Cycles run regular races and uplift days.

Facilities:
None on site. Train station and refreshments 2 miles away at Ludlow. Pearce Cycles 01584 879288 at Ludlow for parts, repairs, upliift service and organised events.

Parking:
Grid Ref: SO461740.

Web: www.goodmtb.co.uk/b99

Note: besides the downhill course this is also an active cross country area. Go to BikeRadar forum and search for Bringewood or Mortimer Forest.

The Trails
DH

East Midlands

The gently rolling countryside of Nottinghamshire and Leicestershire, rising to a highpoint of 278m to the southwest of Loughborough, offers some easy undulating riding through the Jurassic limestone and Triassic sandstone that gives the area its typical yellow stone villages.

Many bases in the south of the region offer access to the bridleway network through what the tourist boards like to call 'The Heart of England'. These might include **Cottesbrooke** and **Lowick** in Northamptonshire or a whole sheaf of options in Leicestershire, especially in the hilly area to the west of Rutland Water at **Tugby**, **Tilton on the Hill** and **Braunston,** north to the handsome town of **Melton Mowbray** and the villages of **Stathern** and **Hickling**, lying just south of the Vale of Belvoir.

In the very south of the area, the network of byways and bridleways around **Silverstone** and **Moreton Pinkney** offer a challenging ride

through very gently rolling countryside but avoid if the ground is soft.

This is a vast area and further north it touches on the old mining areas of Nottinghamshire and Derbyshire. Many old railways in the area around **Teversal**, to the east of Mansfield have been turned into a fine network of trails. As a complete contrast, the elegant surroundings of **Clumber Park** can be explored on a series of waymarked trails, most of these aimed at the easier end of the scale.

In the north of the area, **Sprotbrough** is beautifully set by the River Dearne, located on the course of the Trans Pennine Trail which crosses the country from the Irish Sea at Southport to the North Sea at Hornsea.

The main Trail Centre in the area is at **Sherwood Pines**, north east of Mansfield, whilst Salcey Forest and Rutland Water offer a choice of trails suitable for all the family.

©Daniel Bosworth / East Midlands Tourism

Sprotbrough

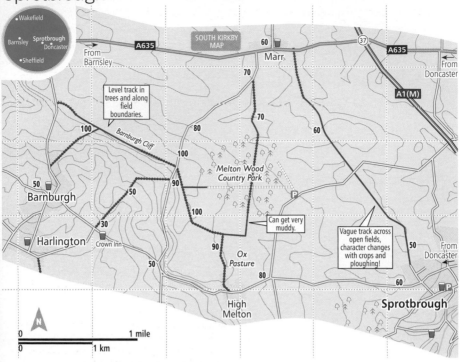

Wakefield
Barnsley • Sprotbrough • Doncaster
Sheffield

A635

From Barnsley

SOUTH KIRKBY MAP

Marr

60

37

A635

From Doncaster

70

A1(M)

Level track in trees and along field boundaries.

70

100

Barnburgh Cliff

80

70

60

100

Melton Wood Country Park

100

90

P

Barnburgh

50

50

50

100

Can get very muddy.

Vague track across open fields, character changes with crops and ploughing!

50

From Doncaster

30

Harlington   Crown Inn

90

Ox Pasture

80

60

P

50

Sprotbrough

N

High Melton

0 — 1 mile
0 — 1 km

Situation: On the banks of the River Don in South Yorkshire, north east of Sprotbrough Gorge. 4 miles west of Doncaster.

About the Base: Sprotbrough, a village with two pubs. **Parking:** At the far end of The Boat Inn car park (with permission from the landlord). **Grid Ref:** SE536013. **Post Code:** DN5 7NB.

Drive Times: Leeds 40mins, Nottingham 1hr, Manchester 1hr20, Birmingham 1hr40, Newcastle 2hr10.

Trains: Doncaster Railway Station is on the main London-Edinburgh East Coast line & Hull-Sheffield-Nottingham line.

Refreshments: At Sprotbrough, The Boat Inn 01302 858500 and The Ivanhoe 01302 853130. The Marr Lodge 01302 390355 at Marr, The Coach and Horses 01709 892306 and The Crown Inn 01709 893450 at Barnburgh. The Harlington Inn 01709 892300 at Harlington.

Books: MTB W & S Yorkshire (R.Peace).

Maps: OS Explorer 278.

Bike Shops: Several bike shops in Doncaster including Extreme Sports 01302 738388 for repairs and Halfords 01302 767030.

Route Idea

From Sprotbrough, NW on trails to Marr. SW on minor road, trail along Barnburgh Cliff then S into Barnburgh. Road towards Crown Inn. Trails to and around Melton Wood. Back to Marr and trails S to Sprotbrough. Distance 20km.

Extend the areas: South Kirkby Map to the N.

© Desmond Green

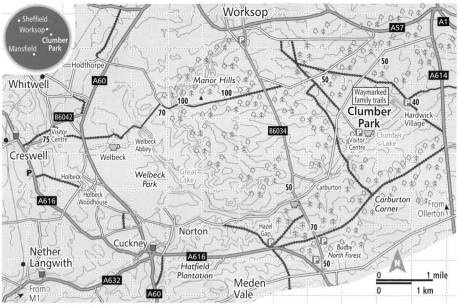

© Experience Nottinghamshire www.visitnotts.com

Situation: In The Dukeries, the northernmost part of Sherwood Forest, 5 miles south of Worksop.

About the Base: Clumber Park, a country park with a café and a visitor centre. Further Info: www.nationaltrust.org.uk/clumberpark. **Parking:** Car parks at Clumber Park visitor centre, Hardwick Village & south of Clumber Lake. Also south of Worksop at Manor Hills, Budby North Forest & Hazel Gap or roadside south of Cresswell on the A616.
Grid Ref: Visitor Centre SK625746, Hardwick Village SK638754, Clumber Lake SK622739, Manor Hills SK590771, Budby Foest SK611709 or SK613716, Hazel Gap SK599713, Cresswell SK532734. Post Code: Visitor Centre S80 3BD, Hardwick Village S80 3PB.

Drive Times: Leeds 1hr, Manchester 1hr40, Birmingham 1hr40, London 3hr, Bristol 3hr.

Trains: Worksop Railway Station is on the Sheffield-Grimsby & Nottingham-Grimsby lines. Cresswell Railway Station is on the Nottingham-Worksop line.

Refreshments: Café 01909 544917 at Clumber Park. The Lime House Café 01909 542704 at Welbeck, The Rose & Crown 01909 721547 at Cresswell and Old School Tea Room 01909 483517 at Carburton. The Greendale Oak Inn 01623 844441 at Cuckney or The Jug & Glass 01623 742283 at Nether Longwith.

Books: MTB Guide E Midlands (D.Taylor). MTB Guide Nottinghamshire (S.Thompson).

Maps: OS Explorer 270.

Bike Shops: Halfords 01909 530521 in Worksop.

Route Idea

From the Visitor Centre S to Carburton Corner then W to Norton. Roads & trail past Holbeck to A616. N to Creswell then E past Welbeck Abbey, into the Manor Hills then back into Clumber Park. Distance 26km.

Teversal

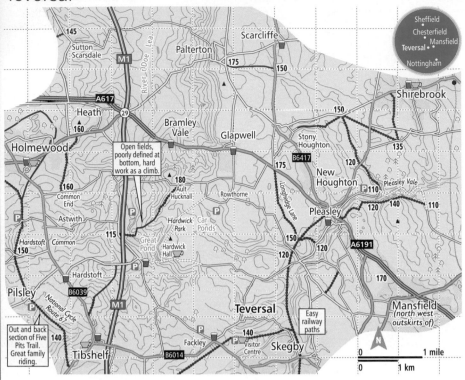

Open fields, poorly defined at bottom, hard work as a climb.

Out and back section of Five Pits Trail. Great family riding.

Easy railway paths

Situation: On the Teversal Trails and the Nottingham-shire/Derbyshire border. 4 miles west of Mansfield.

About the Base: Teversal, a small village with a pub and a visitor centre. **Parking:** Car Parks at Teversal Trails Visitor Centre, Hardwick Hall & Rowthorne. Also on 5 Pits Trail, west of Hardstoft & west of Astwith or next to the river east of Pleasley. *Grid Ref: Teversal SK478613, Hardwick Hall SK456633 or SK454640, Rowthorne SK475647, Hardstoft SK430624, Astwith SK427643, Pleasley SK508648. Post Code: Teversal NG17 3HJ*

Drive Times: Leeds 1hr, Birmingham 1hr15, Manchester 1hr30, Bristol 2hr40, London 2hr40.

Trains: Mansfield Railway station is on the Retford-Nottingham line.

Refreshments: At Teversal, The Carnavon Arms 01623 559 676 and Café in the Teversal Trails visitor centre 01623 442021. The White Hart 01773 873 099 or Tibshelf Café 01773 590 757 at Tibshelf, The Famous Shoulder 01246 850276 at Hardstoft, The Hardwick Inn 01246 850 245 or Café at Hardwick Hall 01246 850430. The Jolly Farmer 01246 855 608 or Silly Moos Café 01246 859 000 at Holmewood. The Hardwick Inn 01246 850 245 at Bramley Vale, The Young Vanish 01623 810 238 at Glapwell and The Nags Head 01623 810 235 at Pleasley. The Horse and Groom 01246 823 152 at Scarcliffe or pubs & cafés at Shirebrook.

Books: MTB Guide Nottinghamshire (S.Thompson). MTB Guide Derbyshire & Peak District (T.Windsor).

Maps: OS Explorer 269 & 270.

Bike Shops: On Yer Bike 01623 421 033 in Mansfield.

Route Ideas

❶ From the Visitor Centre, trails towards Pleasley then Longhedge Lane N to A617. On to Rowthorne, Ault Hucknall then SW on trails and road to Tibshelf. Trails N to Holmewood. Roads to Sutton Scarsdale and Palterton. Trail E then road to Stony Houghton. Trails to Pleasley Vale then track E followed by trail W to Pleasley. Trails back to start. Distance 40km.

❷ From the Visitor Centre, trails towards Pleasley then Longhedge Lane N to main road and onto Stony Houghton. Trails to Pleasley Vale then track E followed by trail W to Pleasley. Trails back to start. Distance 19km.

Also see Teversal Trails (p312).

© www.cycletrails.co

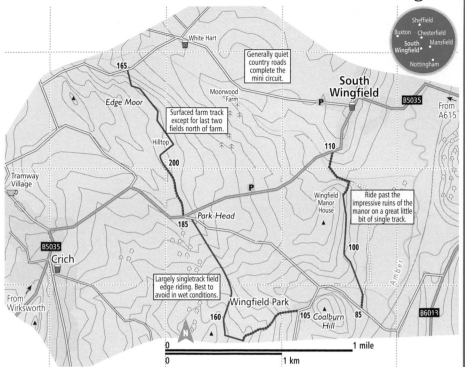

Situation: In the Amber Valley on the banks of the River Amber in north east Derbyshire. 3 miles west of Alfreton.

About the Base: South Wingfield, a village with a pub.

Parking: Roadside as you leave the village heading west. Also, layby south of the village at Park Head. **Grid Ref:** *South Wingfield SK373555, Park Head SK367548.* **Post Code:** *South Wingfield DE55 7LW.*

Drive Times: Birmingham 1hr10, Leeds 1hr10, Manchester 1hr40, Bristol 2hr40, London 2hr40.

Trains: Alfreton Railway Station is on the Sheffield-Nottingham line.

Refreshments: The Yew Tree Inn 01773 833 763 at South Wingfield. The White Hart Inn 01629 534 229, The Kings Arms 01773 853 544 or Tea Rooms at Tramway Village at Crich.

Books: MTB Guide Peak District & Derbyshire (M.Pearce).

Maps: OS Explorer 269.

Bike Shops: Cyclemania 01773 836 203 in Alfreton.

Route Idea

From South Wingfield, W to the White Hart Pub then SW across Edge Moor to Park Head. S around Wingfield Park to Coalburn Hill. Trail N past Wingfield Manor House and road back to start. Distance 9km.

Doveridge

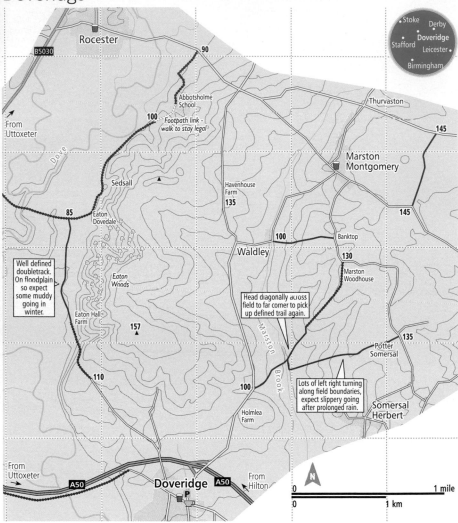

Rocester

B5030

From Uttoxeter

Abbotsholme School

100 Footpath link - walk to stay legal

Sedsall

85 Eaton Dovedale

Well defined doubletrack. On floodplain so expect some muddy going in winter.

Eaton Woods

Eaton Hall Farm

157

110

From Uttoxeter

A50 Doveridge A50 From Hilton

Thurvaston

145

Marston Montgomery

Havenhouse Farm
135

100 Banktop

Waldley

130

Marston Woodhouse

Head diagonally across field to far corner to pick up defined trail again.

Marston Brook

100

Lots of left right turning along field boundaries, expect slippery going after prolonged rain.

Holmlea Farm

145

135

Potter Somersal

Somersal Herbert

N

0 .... 1 mile
0 .... 1 km

Stoke Derby
Doveridge
Stafford Leicester
Birmingham

Situation: On the River Dove in Derbyshire. Close to the Staffordshire border, 3 miles east of Uttoxeter.

About the Base: Doveridge, a village with a pub and easy access to the trails.
Further Info: www.doveridge-village.org.

Parking: Roadside in the centre of the village close to the Cavendish Arms. *Grid Ref: Doveridge SK116343. Post Code: Doveridge DE6 5NJ.*

Drive Times: Birmingham 1hr, Manchester 1hr25, Leeds 1hr45, Bristol 2hr20, London 2hr40.

Trains: Uttoxeter Railway Station is on the Stoke on Trent-Derby line.

Refreshments: At Doveridge, The Cavendish Arms 01889 563 820 and Café at Doveridge Post Office & Stores 01889 562591. The Red Lion 01889 590 337 at Rocester and The Crown Inn 01889 591 430 at Marston Montgomery.

Books: MTB Guide Derbyshire & Peak District (T.Windsor).

Maps: OS Explorer 259.

Bike Shops: Uttoxeter Cycle Centre 01889 567 608.

Route Idea

NW from Doveridge past Eaton Hall Farm, Sedsall, Abbotsholme School. Roads S to Waldley, E to Banktop then S past Marston Woodhouse, Holmlea Farm and back to start. Distance 13km.

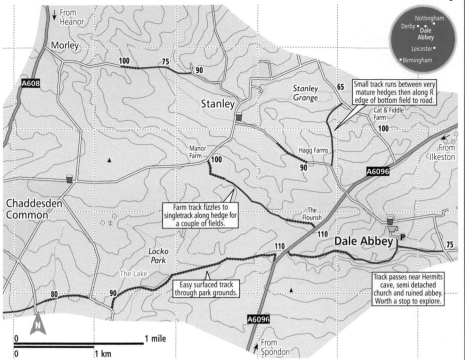

The map contains the following labels:

From Heanor
Morley
100 · 75 · 90
A608
Stanley
Stanley Grange · 65
Small track runs between very mature hedges then along R edge of bottom field to road.
Cat & Fiddle Farm · 100
From Ilkeston
Manor Farm · 100
Hagg Farms
90
A6096
Chaddesden Common
Farm track fizzles to singletrack along hedge for a couple of fields.
The Flourish
110
Dale Abbey · P · 75
Locko Park
The Lake
110
80 · 90
Easy surfaced track through park grounds.
Track passes near Hermits cave, semi detached church and ruined abbey. Worth a stop to explore.
A6096
From Spondon
1 mile
1 km

Locator map: Nottingham, Derby, Dale Abbey, Leicester, Birmingham

Situation: In Derbyshire in the East Midlands, close to the Nottinghamshire border. 7 miles north east of Derby and 10 miles west of Nottingham.

About the Base: Dale Abbey, a village with a pub and tea rooms. **Parking:** Roadside on the south of the village. *Grid Ref: Dale Abbey SK437386. Post Code: Dale Abbey DE7 4PN.*

Drive Times: Birmingham 1hr, Leeds 1hr25, Manchester 1hr50, Bristol 2hr30, London 2hr30.

Trains: Spondon Railway Station, 3 miles away, is on the Derby-Leicester-London line.

Refreshments: At Dale Abbey, The Carpenters Arms 0115 932 5277 and The Friars House Tea Rooms 01159 309152. The White Hart Inn 0115 932 5048 at Stanley and The Kings Corner 01332 678 410 at Chaddesden Common.

Books: MTB Guide Derbyshire & Peak District (T.Windsor).

Maps: OS Explorer 259 & 260.

Bike Shops: Urban Air 0115 932 8427 and Halfords 0115 944 7415, 4 miles away in Ilkeston.

Route Idea

From Dale Abbey, NW to A6096. SW to The Flourish then NW to Manor Farm. Continue to Hagg Farms then around Stanley Grange to Stanley. W to Morley then roads S to pick up trails through Locko Park & back to Dale Abbey. Distance 20km.

Ticknall

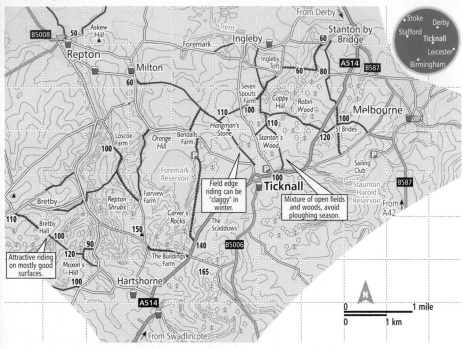

Situation: Just south of the River Trent in South Derbyshire, close to Foremark Reservoir. 8 miles east of Burton on Trent and 10 miles south of Derby.

About the Base: Ticknall, a small village with three pubs. Further Info: www.derbyshire-peakdistrict.co.uk/ticknal.

Parking: Car parks in Ticknall village & at Foremark Reservoir. *Grid Ref: Ticknall SK352240, Foremark Reservoir SK335240. Post Code: Ticknall DE73 7JX.*

Drive Times: Birmingham 45mins, Leeds 1hr 40, Manchester 1hr50, Bristol 2hr10, London 2hr30.

Refreshments: At Ticknall, The Wheel Inn 01332 864 488, The Staff of Life 01332 862 479 and Chequers Inn 01332 864 392. The Admiral Rodney Inn 01283 216 482 at Hartshorne, a choice of pubs or Brook Farm Tea Rooms 01283 704 438 at Repton, Swan Inn 01283 703 188 at Milton, The John Thompson at Ingleby. Choice of pubs and The Welcome Café 01332 862 582 at Melbourne.

Books: MTB Guide Derbyshire & Peak District (T.Windsor).

Maps: OS Explorer 245.

Routes on Web: www.goodmtb.co.uk/a79

Bike Shops: Lloyds Cycles, 5 miles away in Swadlincote. Halfords 01283 495160 in Burton on Trent.

Route Ideas

❶ From Ticknall, NW to Hangman's Stone, NE towards Ingleby Toft then onto St Brides. W through Robin Wood then back to Ticknall via Stanton's Wood.
Distance 15km.

❷ From Ticknall N past Stanton's Wood then to St Brides and around Robin Wood to Hangman's Stone and NW to Milton. S to Orange Hill, trail to Fairview Farm, across to Bretby. E to Moxon's Hill then The Buildings Farm. N to Bendalls Farm and back to Ticknall via Hangman's Stone.
Distance 32km.

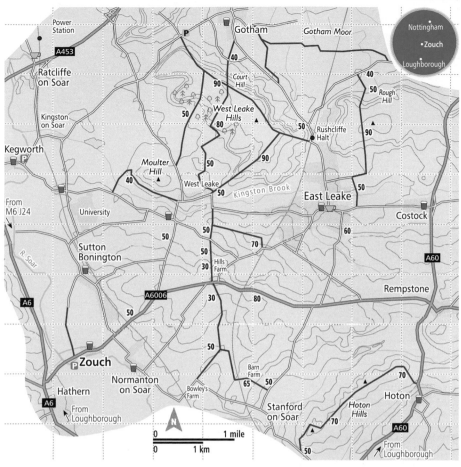

Situation: On the River Soar, just south of the West Leake Hills. 4 miles north west of Loughborough.

About the Base: Zouch, a village with a pub and easy access to the trails. **Parking:** Car park west of the village before you cross the river on the A6006. Also at Kegworth Lock. Roadside parking west of Gotham village. *Grid Ref: Zouch SK504233, Kegworth SK494272, Gotham SK527294. Post Code: Zouch LE12 5EQ, Kegworth DE74 2FS.*

Drive Times: Birmingham 50mins, Leeds 1hr30, Manchester 2hr, London 2hr20, Bristol 2hr20.

Trains: East Midlands Parkway Station (Ratcliffe-on-Soar) is on the Leicester, Nottingham, Derby Lines.

Refreshments: At Zouch, The Rose & Crown 01509 842240. The Kings Head 01509 672 331 and The Star Inn 01509 852233 at Sutton Bonnington, The Anchor Inn 01509 672722 and Station Hotel 01509 672252 at Kegworth, The Sun Inn 0115 983 1583 at Gotham, Three Horse Shoes 01509 856658 and Chefs Café 853488 at East Leake or The Plough Inn 01509 842228 at Normanton-on-Soar. Pubs at Costock and Hoton. If arriving by train, The Redhill Lock Tea Rooms 01509 670888 is at Ratcliffe-on-Soar.

Books: MTB Guide E Midlands (D.Taylor).

Maps: OS Explorer 246.

Routes on Web: www.goodmtb.co.uk/a80

Bike Shops: Pedal Power 01509 269663, Cycle Trax 01509 233532, The Bike Shed 01509 214927 & Halfords 01509 210301 in Loughborough.

Route Ideas

❶ Roads from Zouch to Normanton on Soar then on to Bowley's Farm. Trails N past Hills Farm and West Leake then over the West Leake Hills to Gotham. Across Gotham Moor then trail S to East Leake. Road then trail W to S of Moulter Hill, roads to Sutton Bonnington and trail back to Zouch.
Distance 32km.

❷ Start as above to West Leake Hills then NW at Court Hill followed by S to Moulter Hill. Trail at back of Moulter Hill, roads to Sutton Bonington and trail back to Zouch.
Distance 20km.

Netherseal

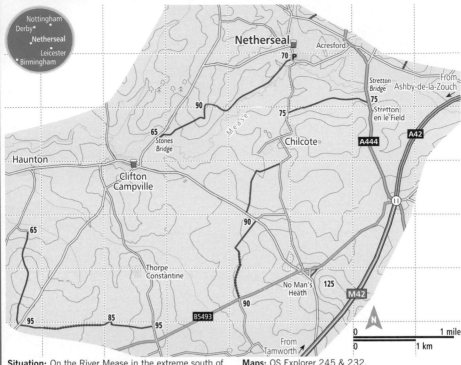

Situation: On the River Mease in the extreme south of Derbyshire close to the Leicestershire border. 8 miles south of Burton Upon Trent.

About the Base: Netherseal, a village with two pub. **Parking:** Roadside in the centre of the village. *Grid Ref: SK287128. Post Code: DE12 8DW.*

Drive Times: Birmingham 30mins, Leeds 1hr50, Manchester 2hr, Bristol 2hr, London 2hr20.

Refreshments: At Netherseal, The Holly Bush 01283 760 390 and The Seal Inn 01283 760 180. The Green Man 01827 373262 at Clifton Campville.

Books: MTB Guide Peak District & Derbyshire (M.Pearce).

Maps: OS Explorer 245 & 232.

Bike Shops: Lloyds Cycles 01283 214 727, 6 miles away in Swadlincote. Halfords 01283 495160 in Burton on Trent.

Route Idea

From Netherseal, E to Acresford then S across Stretton Bridge and trail W to Chilcote. S, mainly on trails, to B5493. Continue W then N to Haunton on road and trails. Road E to Clifton Campville then Stones Bridge. Trail back to start. Distance 16km.

© National Forest

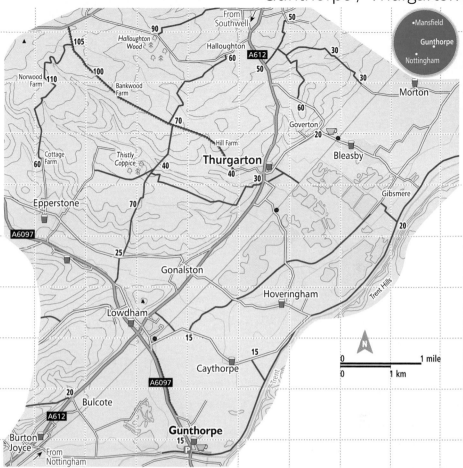

Situation: On the banks of the River Trent, Gunthorpe is 10 miles east of Nottingham. Thurgarton, 2 miles away to the north, is 11 miles south west of Newark.

About the Base: Gunthorpe, a village with pubs and tea rooms, or Thurgarton, a small village with a pub and a railway station.
Further Info: www.gunthorpe.org.uk.

Parking: Roadside in the village or car park beside the river at Gunthorpe Lock. *Grid Ref: Gunthorpe SK682437, Gunthorpe Lock SK686437. Post Code: Gunthorpe NG14 7RP.*

Drive Times: Birmingham 1hr20, Leeds 1hr30, Manchester 2hrs, London 2hr30, Bristol 2hr50.

Trains: Thurgarton Railway Station is on the Nottingham-Newark line.

Refreshments: At Gunthorpe, The Unicorn Hotel 0115 966 3612 and Anchor Inn 0115 966 3291. The Black Horse 0115 966 3520 at Caythorpe, The Reindeer Inn 0115 966 3629 at Hoveringham, The Waggon & Horses 01636 830283 or Manor Farm Tea Shoppe 01636 831316 at Bleasby, The Coach and Horses 01636 831311 or The Red Lion 01636 830351 at Thurgarton, The Cross Keys 0115 966 3033 at Epperstone, pubs at Lowdham or The Full Moon 01636 830251 at Morton.

Books: MTB Guide Nottinghamshire (S.Thompson).

Maps: OS Explorer 260.

Bike Shops: Halfords 0115 9400811, 5 miles away in Netherfield. Plenty in Nottingham & Newark.

Route Idea

From Gunthorpe, N to Lowdham. Trail N then road W to Epperstone, N past Cottage Farm and Norwood Farm then SE past Bankwood Farm to Thurgarton. Roads E to Bleasby and Gibsmere. Trail to Hoveringham then on to Gunthorpe.
Distance 29km.

Stathern

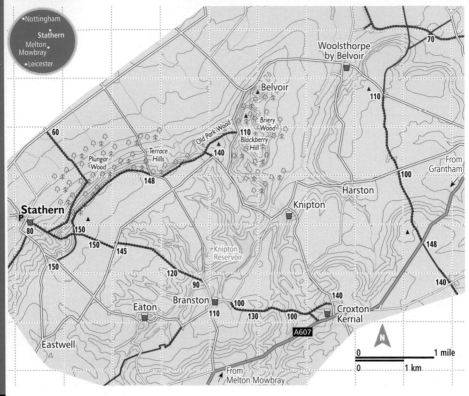

Situation: In the Vale of Belvoir in Leicestershire , 10 miles north of Melton Mowbray and 13 miles south west of Grantham.

About the Base: Stathern, a village with two pubs. Further Info: www.valeofbelvoir.co.uk.

Parking: Roadside in the centre of the village. *Grid Ref: SK772310. Post Code: LE14 4HS.*

Drive Times: Birmingham 1hr30, Leeds 1hr40, Manchester 2hr20, London 2hr30, Bristol 2hr50.

Trains: Bottesford Railway Station, 6 miles away, is on the Grantham-Nottingham line.

Refreshments: At Stathern, The Red Lion Inn 01949 860868 and The Plough 01949 860411. The Castle Inn 01476 870949 at Eaton, The Wheel Inn 01476 870376 at Branston, The Peacock Inn 014576 870324 at Croxton Kerrial, Chequers Inn 01476 870701 at Woolsthorpe or The Manners Arms 01476 879222 at Knipton.

Maps: OS Explorer 260 & 247.

Routes on Web: www.goodmtb.co.uk/a78

Bike Shops: Pedal Power 016674 566166 and Halfords 01664 566923 in Melton Mowbray.

Route Idea

Stathern to Belvoir via trails past Plungar Wood and Old Park Wood. Road through Woolsthorpe by Belvoir then trail S to and across A607. Back to Stathern mostly on trails via Croxton Kerrial and Branston. Distance 28km.

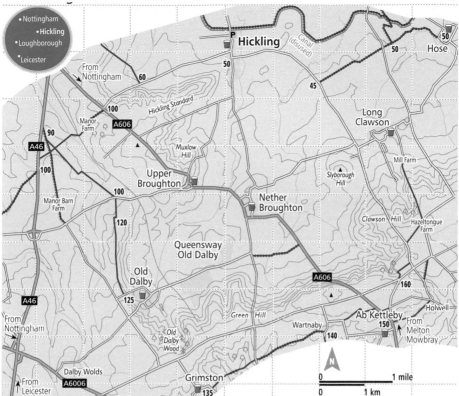

Situation: Close to the Vale of Belvoir, on the Grantham Canal and the border of Nottinghamshire and Leicestershire. 8 miles north west of Melton Mowbray.

About the Base: Hickling, a village with a pub.

Parking: Roadside next to the canal basin in the village. *Grid Ref: Hickling SK690294. Post Code: Hickling LE14 3AH.*

Drive Times: Birmingham 1hr10, Leeds 1hr40, Manchetser 2hr, London 2hr20, Bristol 2hr40.

Refreshments: At Hickling, The Plough Inn 01664 822223. The Rose & Crown 01949 860424 at Hose, The Sugar Loaf Inn 01664 822473 at Ab Kettleby, Stonepit Farm Tea Rooms 01664 822473 at Wartnaby, The Black Horse 01664 812358 at Grimston and Crown Inn 01664 823134 at Old Dalby. The Anchor Inn 01664 822461 at Nether Broughton or The Golden Fleece 01664 822262 at Upper Broughton.

Books: MTB Guide Nottinghamshire (S.Thompson).

Maps: OS Explorer 246.

Bike Shops: Pedal Power 016674 566166 and Halfords 01664 566923 in Melton Mowbray.

Route Idea

From Hickling, road W to A606, then trails past Manor Farm and Manor Barn Farm. Roads to Grimston then E to Wartnaby, Ab Kettleby and Holwell. N past Hazeltongue Farm to Mill Farm & Long Clawson. Road N to to disused canal, towpath back to Hickling.
Distance 28km.

Melton Mowbray

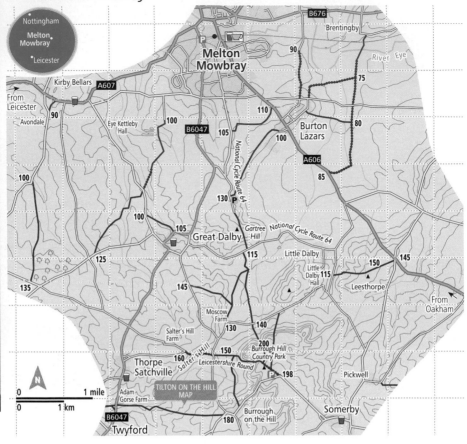

Situation: Lying along the course of the River Eye and the River Wreake in Leicestershire. 15 miles north east of Leicester and 18 miles south east of Nottingham.

About the Base: Melton Mowbray, a market town with plenty of pubs, cafés and accommodation. Further Info: www.melton.co.uk. **Parking:** Several car parks in Melton Mowbray. Best for ride is on B6047 to Great Dalby. Also roadside north east of Great Dalby or car park at Burrough Hill. **Grid Ref:** *Melton Mowbray SK749187, Great Dalby SK755157, Burrough Hill SK766114.* **Post Code:** *Melton Mowbray LE13 0AF.*

Drive Times: Birmingham 1hr10, Leeds 1hr50, Manchester 2hr20, London 2hr20, Bristol 2hr40.

Trains: Melton Mowbray Railway Station is on the Peterborough-Leicester-Birmingham & Peterborough-Nottingham/Derby lines.

Refreshments: Choice of pubs and cafés at Melton Mowbray. The Flying Childers 01664 813972 at Kirby Bellars, Royal Oak 01664 563147 at Great Dalby, The Fox Inn 01664 840257 at Thorpe Satchville and The Stag & Hounds 01664 452141 at Burrough-on-the-Hill.

Books: MTB Guide E Midlands (D.Taylor).

Maps: OS Explorer 246.

Routes on Web: www.goodmtb.co.uk/a77

Bike Shops: Pedal Power 016674 566166 and Halfords 01664 566923 in Melton Mowbray.

Route Idea

S from Melton Mowbray on Cycle Route 64 to Gartree Hill. Trails S to Burrough Hill Country Park. Road past Moscow Farm to take outward trail back to Gartree Hill and then Cycle Route 64 back to Melton Mowbray. Distance 17km.

Extend the area: Tilton on the Hill Map to the S.

©GoLeicestershire

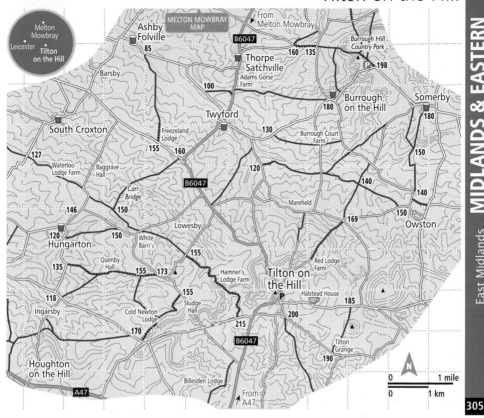

Situation: In East Leicestershire, 219m above sea level. 8 miles west of Oakham, 10 miles south of Melton Mowbray and 12 miles east of Leicester.

About the Base: Tilton-on-the-Hill, a village with a pub. **Parking:** Roadside in the centre of the village or car park at Burrough Hill. *Grid Ref: Tilton-on-the-Hill SK742056, Burrough Hill SK766114. Post Code: Tilton-on-the-Hill LE7 9LB.*

Drive Times: Birmingham 1hr20, Leeds 2hr, London 2hr20, Manchester 2hr30, Bristol 2hr40.

Trains: Oakham Railway Station is on the Peterborough-Leicester-Birmingham & Peterborough-Nottingham/Derby lines.

Refreshments: At Tilton-on-the-Hill, The Rose & Crown 0116 259 7234 and Halstead House Tea Rooms 0116 259 7239 east of the village. The Black Boy 0116 259 5410 at Hungarton, Carrington Arms 01664 841234 at Ashby Folville, The Fox Inn 01664 840257 at Thorpe Satchville, The Saddle 01664 841108 at Twyford and The Stag & Hounds 01664 452141 at Burrough-on-the-Hill.

Books: MTB Guide E Midlands (D.Taylor).

Maps: OS Explorer 233 & 246.

Bike Shops: Pedal Power 016674 566166 and Halfords 01664 566923 in Melton Mowbray.

Route Idea

From Tilton on the Hill, road W to Sludge Hall then trails and roads to Cold Newton Lodge then Ingarsby. N to Quenby Hall, White Barn's, over Carr Bridge & S on the B6047. E on road to Marefield then S back to start. Distance 24km.

Extend the area: Melton Mowbray Map to the N.

Braunston-in-Rutland

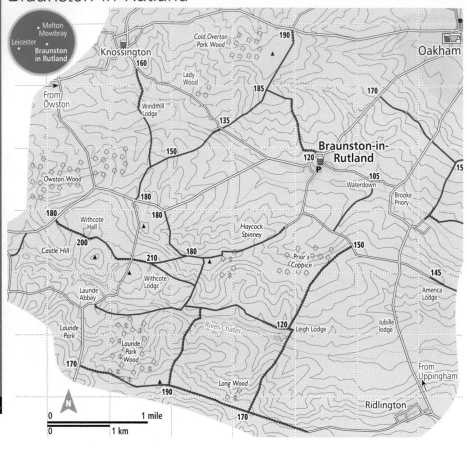

Situation: Close to Rutland Water in the East Midlands. 2 miles south west of Oakham.

About the Base: Braunston-in-Rutland, a village with a pub.
Parking: Roadside in the centre of the village. *Grid Ref: SK833066. Post Code: LE15 8QS.*

Drive Times: Birmingham 1hr30, Leeds 2hr, London 2hr20, Manchester 2hr40, Bristol 2hr50.

Trains: Oakham Railway Station is on the Peterborough-Leicester-Birmingham & Peterborough-Nottingham/Derby lines.

Refreshments: The Blue Ball Inn 01572 722135 and The Old Plough 01572 722714 in the village or The Fox & Hounds 01664 454676 at Knossington. A choice of pubs and cafés at Oakham.

Books: MTB Guide E Midlands (D.Taylor).

Maps: OS Explorer 234.

Bike Shops: Rutland Cycling, 6 miles away in Whitwell nea r Oakham, for parts & hire.

Route Idea

From Braunston-in-Rutland , road S then trails
past Haycock Spinney and onto Witchcote Hall.
Road and trails past Launde Park. Trail E then N
after Long Wood, past Prior's Coppice. NW trail to
Waterdown and then back to start.
Distance 19km.

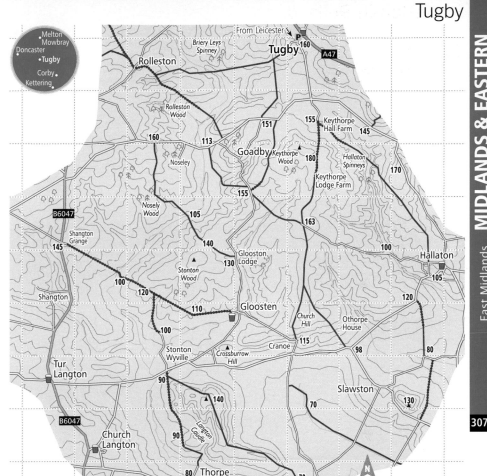

Situation: South west of Rutland Water in east Leicestershire. 12 miles east of Leicester and 10 miles north of Market Harborough

About the Base: Tugby, a village with a pub and easy access to the trails. Further Info: www.leicestershirevillages.com/tugby.

Parking: Roadside in the centre of Tugby. *Grid Ref: SK761009. Post Code: LE7 9WA.*

Drive Times: Birmingham 1hr20, Leeds 2hr10, London 2hr20, Bristol 2hr40, Manchester 2hr40.

Refreshments: At Tugby, The Fox & Hounds 0116 259 8282. The Fox Inn 01858 555 278 and The Bewicke Arms 01858 555 217 at Hallaton, The Old Red Lion 01858 565253 at Welham, The Bakers Arms 01858 545 201 at Thorpe Langton or The Old Barn Inn 01858 545 215 at Gloosten. The Bell Inn 01858 545 278 at East Langton, Langton Arms 01858 545 181 at Church Langton or The Crown Inn 01858 545 264 at Tur Langton.

Books: MTB Guide E Midlands (D.Taylor).

Maps: OS Explorer 233.

Bike Shops: George Halls Cycle Centre 01858 465 507 in Market Harborough.

Route Idea

From Tugby, SE to Hallaton via Keythorpe Hall Farm. S on roads & trails to Welham. W to Thorpe Langton. N to Stonton Wyville & NW to Shangton Grange. N to Rolleston. Trail E back to Tugby. Distance 30km.

Lowick

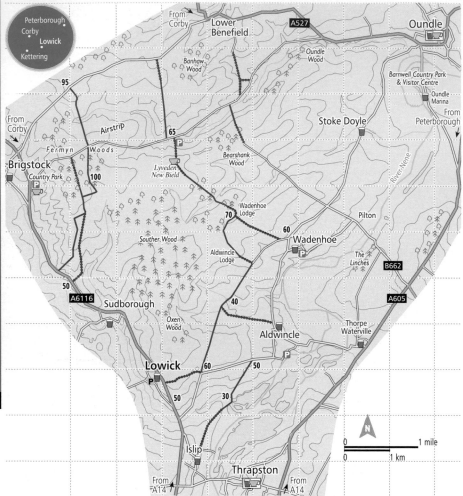

Situation: Just west of the River Nene, overlooking the Nene Valley in Northamptonshire. 8 miles east of Kettering.

About the Base: Lowick, a small village with a pub.
Parking: Roadside in the centre of Lowick. Car park near the marina at Aldwincle. Also at Wadenhoe, Lyvedon New Bield & Brigstock Country Park. *Grid Ref: Lowick SP977807, Aldwincle TL007813, Wadenhoe TL010833, Lyvedon New Bield SP981860, Brigstock SP953849. Post Code: Lowick NN14 3BH, Aldwincle NN14 3EE, Wadenhoe PE8 5ST.*

Drive Times: Birmingham 1hr10, London 2hrs, Leeds 2hr30, Bristol 2hr40, Manchester 2hr40.

Trains: Kettering Railway Station is on the Leicester-London line.

Refreshments: At Lowick, The Snooty Fox. The Vane Arms 01832 730 033 at Sudborough, Refreshments at Lyvedon New Bield 01832 205358, Café at Fermyn Woods Country Park 01536 373 625, The Kings Head 01832 720 024 at Wadenhoe or Hare & Hounds 01536 330 701 at Aldwincle. The Shuckburgh Arms 01832 272339 at Stoke Doyle,

Oundle Marina for refreshments, The Fox Inn 01832 720 274 at Thorpe Waterville, The Rose & Crown 01832 733 118 at Islip or pubs & cafés at Brigstock, Oundle and Thrapston.

Books: MTB Guide E Midlands (D.Taylor).

Maps: OS Explorer 224.

Bike Shops: C&D Cycles 01536 411 313 and Halfords 01536 310404 in Kettering.

Route Ideas

❶ From Lowick, N past Sudborough on A6116. Trails N through Fermyn Woods. Road E to Lower Benefield. S to Wadenhoe via Lyveden New Bield. Trails SW back to Lowick. Distance 24km.

❷ For a shorter route that avoids the main road, reverse the above to Lyveden New Build then E onto Pilton via Bearshank Wood. S to Wadenhoe & Aldwincle. Trail W to join outward start then S back to Lowick. Distance 21km.

Cottesbrooke

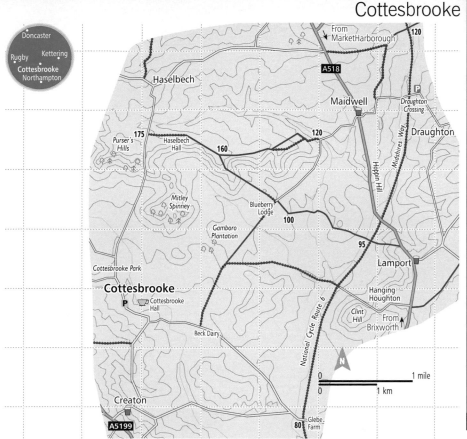

Situation: Close to the Brampton Valley Way in Northamptonshire, 9 miles north of Northampton and 10 miles south of Market Harborough.

About the Base: Cottesbrooke, a small village with easy access to the trails. **Parking:** Roadside in the centre of Cottesbrooke. Car park next to the picnic area east of Maidwell. *Grid Ref: Cottesbrooke SP709735, Maidwell SP756773. Post Code: Cottesbrooke NN6 8PQ.*

Drive Times: Birmingham 1hr, London 1hr50, Leeds 2hr10, Bristol 2hr20, Manchester 2hr30.

Refreshments: At Cottesbrooke, Café 01604 505808 at Cottesbrooke Hall. The Stags Head 01604 686 700 at Maidwell. The Kings Head 01604 847 351 at Creaton or The Lamport Swan 01604 686 555 at Lamport.

Books: MTB Guide E Midlands (D.Taylor).

Maps: OS Explorer 223.

Bike Shops: Pitsford Cycles 01604 881777, 5 miles away in Brixworth for hire, parts & repairs. Halfords 01604 684880 in Northampton.

Route Idea

From Cottesbrooke, head E to Beck Dairy. Trail N then E to take National Cycle Route 6 N to Loughton Crossing. Exit for Maidwell then W past Haselbech Hall and road S back to start. Distance 19km.

Moreton Pinkney

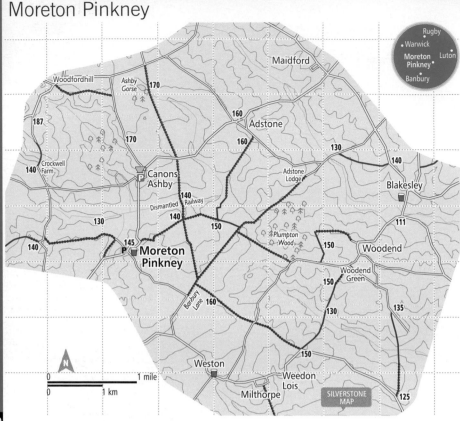

Situation: In Northamptonshire, in the south west of the county close to the Oxfordshire border. 9 miles south of Daventry and 10 miles north east of Banbury.

About the Base: Moreton Pinkney, a village with a pub. **Parking:** Roadside in the centre of Moreton Pinkney. Car park at National Trust Canons Ashby. *Grid Ref: SP575492. Post Code: NN11 3SH.*

Drive Times: Birmingham 1hr10, London 1hr50, Bristol 2hr10, Leeds 2hr30, Manchester 2hr40.

Refreshments: Englands Rose 0129576 0353 at Moreton Pinkney. Tea Rooms at National Trust Canons Ashby 01327 860044. The Bartholomew Arms 01327 860 292 at Blakesley or The Crown 01295 760 310 at Weston.

Books: MTB Guide E Midlands (D.Taylor).

Maps: OS Explorer 207.

Bike Shops: Town & Country Cycles 01295 710 518, 7 miles away in Middleton Cheney.

Route Idea

From Moreton Pinkney, W on trail then N to Woodfordhill. Trail E then then road to link to trail running S past Ashby Gorse. Cross over the Dismantled Railway (S of Canons Ashby) then to Adstone Lodge and trail link to Blakesley. S to Woodend Green. Trail S then before reaching Weedon Lois trails and road NW back to Moreton Pinkney. Distance 22km.

Extend the area: Silverstone Map to the S.

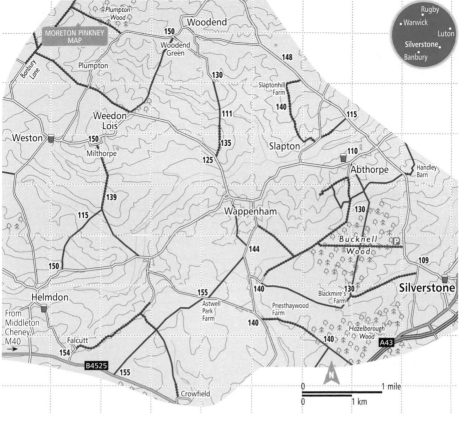

Situation: Close to Whittlewood Forest in Northamptonshire. 5 miles south west of Towcester.

About the Base: Silverstone, a village with a pub. **Parking:** Car park in Bucknell Wood north west of Silverstone. *Grid Ref: SP657447.*

Drive Times: Birmingham 1hr10, London 1hr40, Bristol 2hr10, Leeds 2hr30, Manchester 2hr40.

Refreshments: At Silverstone, The White Horse 01327 858 550. The Bell 01295 768155 at Helmdon, The Crown 01295 760 310 at Weston and The New Inn 01327 857 306 at Abthorpe.

Books: MTB Guide E Midlands (D.Taylor).

Maps: OS Explorer 207.

Bike Shops: Baines Racing 01327 858510 in Silverstone.

Route Idea

From Bucknell Wood car park, head W to Falcutt via Blackmire's Farm & Astwell Park Farm. N through Helmdon. N on trails to Weedon Lois. Trail W to Banbury Lane then up to Plumpton Wood and E along to Woodend Green. S to Wappenham. Back to the start through Bucknell Wood. Distance 30km.

Extend the area: Moreton Pinkney Map to the N.

Sherwood Pines

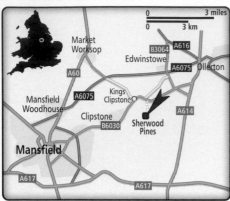

The largest single tract of forest open to the public in the East Midlands with something for everyone, from family cyclists to experienced riders. A network of waymarked trails for all abilities including an all weather family trail as well as cross country loops with tight, twisty, fast singletrack and slow technical sections. 72km of unmarked, technical singletrack to exploreas well as an ever developing bike park and dirt jumps for more experienced riders.

Facilities:
Café at Sherwood Pines Forest Park Visitor Centre. Sherwood Pines Cycles 01623 822 855 for MTB hire, parts & repairs .

Parking:
Grid Ref: SK610638. Post Code: NG21 9JL

Web: www.goodmtb.co.uk/b51

The Trails
❶ Singletrack, XC, 72km.
❷ Kitchener, Red, XC, 9.6km.
❸ Adventure, Blue, XC, 9.6km.
❹ Family, Green, XC, 4.8km.
❺ Dirt Jump Area.
❻ Skills Loop.

Teversal Trails

In Nottinghamshire, a choice of all weather, off road family trails following the tracks of the former colliery railways. Suitable for riders of all abilities.

Facilities:
Café at Teversal Trails Visitor Centre.

Parking:
Grid Ref: SK479613. Post Code: NG17 3HJ

Web: www.goodmtb.co.uk/b95

The Trails
❶ Teversal & Skegby Tracks, XC.
❷ Five Pits Trail, XC, 12km.
❸ Silverhill Trail, XC, 6.4km.

Recent improvements on the Teversal Track © www.cycletrails.co

©Daniel Bosworth / East Midlands Tourism

National Forest Cycle Centre

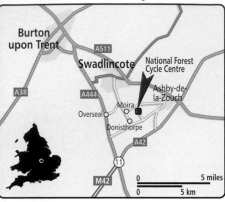

In the National Forest, a new purpose built facility located between Moira and Ashby-de-la-Zouch, developed by The National Forest Company in conjunction with the Forestry Commission.

Facilities:
Visitor Centre and café. Bike shop with bike hire and a repair workshop. Interpretative area with information on other routes exploring The National Forest.

Parking:
Grid Ref: SK329155. Post Code: DE12 6ED

Web: www.goodmtb.co.uk/b91

The Trails

12km of safe offroad trails with links into the wider Public Rights of Way. Aimed at family, young and novice riders.

Salcey Forest

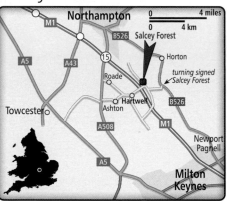

In Northamptonshire, a family cycle trail though medieval forest managed by the Forestry Commission.

Facilities:
Refreshments at Salcey Forest Café.

Parking:
Grid Ref: SP794513. Post Code: NN7 2HX

Web: www.goodmtb.co.uk/b94

The Trails

Green, XC, 8km.

Hamilton Hill Freeride Park

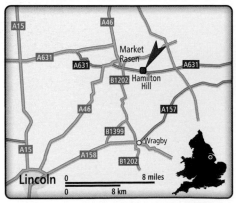

Situated within Willingham Woods, east of Market Rasen in Lincolnshire. A successful project undertaken by the Rasen Area Trailblazerz MTB Club and Forestry Commission to develop North Shore, Freeride, Cross Country and Downhill trails in this otherwise flat area.

Facilities:
Refreshments at Willingham Woods Kiosk on site.

Parking:
Grid Ref: TF139883

Web: www.goodmtb.co.uk/b92a & /b92b

The Trails

XC, DH & Freeride.

Rutland Water

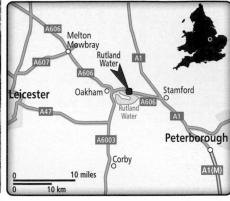

©Discover Rutland

In Rutland, a circular waterside cycling route around one of Europe's largest man made lakes. Off road, family friendly, way-marked trails with great views.

Facilities:
Four Foxes, Waters Edge and Harbour Cafés around the lake. Rutland Cycling at Normanton & Whitwell and Visitor Centres for MTB hire, parts & repairs.

Parking:
Grid Ref: SK923083. Post Code: LE15 8BL

Web: www.goodmtb.co.uk/b93a & /b93b

The Trails

XC, 27km.

©Discover Rutland

Norfolk, Suffolk & Cambridgeshire

Further east, into East Anglia, the land becomes very flat but there are still opportunities for mountain biking. These are mainly at *Thetford Forest*, right in the heart of East Anglia and *Rendlesham Forest* to the northeast of Ipswich. However, *Fulbourn* just east of Cambridge, is definitely worth a mention with its access to a long stone and chalk based section of Roman Road.

Fulbourn

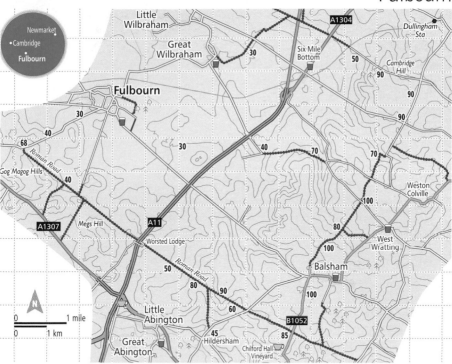

Situation: At the foot of the Gog Magog Hills. 5 miles south east of Cambridge.

About the Base: Fulbourn, a village with two pubs and easy access to the trails. **Parking:** Roadside in the centre of Fulbourn. *Grid Ref: CB21 5DH. Post Code: TL520562.*

Drive Times: London 1hr20, Birmingham 2hr, Leeds 2hr50, Bristol 3hr, Manchester 3hr30.

Trains: Cambridge Station has services to London, Peterborough, Kings Lynn, Norwich & Ipswich.

Refreshments: At Fulbourn, The White Hart 01223 880 264 and The Six Bells 01223 880 244. The Carpenters Arms 01223 882 093 at Great Wilbraham, The Chestnut Tree 01223 290 384 at West Wratting. The Black Bull 01223 893 844 and The Bell 01223 894 415 at Balsham. Café at Chilford Hall Vineyard 01223 895625. The Three Tuns 01223 891467 and The Comfort Café 01223 837 891 at Little Abingdon.

Books: MTB Rides to the SE (M.Darkins).

Maps: OS Explorer 209 & 210.

Bike Shops: Several bike shops in Cambridge. Billys 01223 568368 & Giant Cambridge 01223 415 349 are closest to Fulbourn. Halfords 01223 454280. Cambridge Station Cycles 01223 307 125 for hire.

Route Ideas

❶ From Fulbourn to Great Wilbraham. Trails and roads E past Cambridge Hill. SW to Balsham. Return to Fulbourn on the Roman Road. Distance 36km.

❷ Shorten the above by heading SE from Great Wilbraham to Balsham. Distance 31km.

Riders: Cam MTB. ©Dominic Bowles

Royston

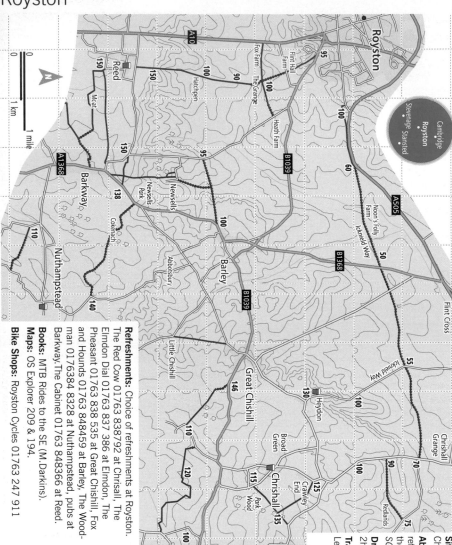

Situation: On the northern slopes of the Hertfordshire Chalk Downs. 13 miles south west of Cambridge.

About the Base: Royston, a town with a good choice of refreshments and accommodation. **Parking:** Car park in the centre of Royston. **Grid Ref:** TL358408. **Post Code:** SG8 7BS.

Drive Times: London 1hr20, Birmingham 2hr, Bristol 2hr50, Leeds 3hr, Manchester 3hr30.

Trains: Royston Railway Station is on the Cambridge-Letchworth-London line.

Route Ideas

❶ From Royston, head E (mostly on the Icknield Way) to meet road S of Chrishall Grange. S to Crawley End. Trails and roads to Elmdon and onto Green Wood, Bridge Green, Great Chishill. SW to Barkway via Abbotsbury & Cokenach. W to Reed then N on trails back to Royston. Distance 45km.

❷ Shorten the above, when heading out on the Icknield Way towards Chrishall Grange take the road to Heydon and onto Great Chishill, then see above. Distance 29km.

Refreshments: Choice of refreshments at Royston. The Red Cow 01763 838792 at Chrisall, The Elmdon Dial 01763 837 386 at Elmdon, The Pheasant 01763 838 535 at Great Chishill, Fox and Hounds 01763 848459 at Barley, The Woodman 0176384 8328 at Nuthampstead, pubs at Barkway. The Cabinet 01763 848366 at Reed.

Books: MTB Rides to the SE (M.Darkins).

Maps: OS Explorer 209 & 194.

Bike Shops: Royston Cycles 01763 247 911

Thetford Forest

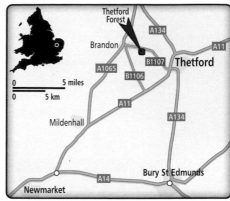

On the border of Norfolk and Suffolk in the heart of East Anglia. 65km of waymarked trails providing safe riding for families and access to more challenging terrain for experts. Wide, open trails, winding forest singletrack and a highly technical black route mean that there is something for everyone.

Facilities:
Café at High Lodge Forest Centre. Bike Art 01842 810090 for MTB hire, parts and reairs.

Parking:
Grid Ref: TL810851. Post Code: IP27 0AF

Web: www.goodmtb.co.uk/b96

The Trails

❶ Black, XC, 16km.

❷ Red, XC 17.7km

❸ Blue, XC, 12.8km

❹ Green, XC, 9.6km.

Rendlesham Forest

In Suffolk's coastal heathland belt, Forestry Commission managed, waymarked family trails on a variety of surfaces. Brand new challenging bike park with two routes including 'table tops', 'rhythm bumps', ramps and North Shore. Plenty of unmarked, relatively flat, fast singletrack in nearby Tunstall Forest to extend your ride.

Facilities:
Rendlesham Forest Visitor Centre. Refreshments in nearby Butley.

Parking:
Grid Ref: TM353484. Post Code: IP12 3NF

Web: www.goodmtb.co.uk/b97a & /b97b

The Trails

❶ Green, XC, 16km.

❷ Green, XC, 9.6km.

❸ Bike Park.

© Forestry Commission

SOUTH EAST

Mountain biking in the South East is dominated by four long ridges: the ancient track known as the Ridgeway runs east from near Marlborough in Wiltshire as far as the River Thames at Goring; from here the wooded Chiltern Hills escarpment continues northeast as far as Dunstable; the North Downs (part chalk and part sandstone) run all the way from Farnham in Surrey to Dover in Kent; finally, the great rounded whaleback chalk hills of the South Downs lie just inland from the South Coast offering some superb airy riding with fine views out into the English Channel.

Other Interesting areas to ride are the North Hampshire Downs, south west of Newbury, the highest chalk upland in Southern England and the New Forest which offers lots of easy riding on gravel tracks. As for Trail Centres, try Friston Forest (Eastbourne), Bedgebury Forest (south east of Tunbridge Wells), Queen Elizabeth Country Park (Petersfield), Swinley Forest (Bracknell) and Aston Hill (south east of Aylesbury).

321

The Chilterns & North Home Counties

Within this area, stretching from Oxfordshire to the Essex coast, the main focus for mountain biking is the Chilterns, a ridge of chalk hills running from the River Thames at Goring northeast to Dunstable. The hills are covered in beech woods and some of the best natural woodland singletrack in the country is to be found here beneath the green cathedral of mighty beech trees, often painted with white arrows indicating the course of the bridleways.

The Chiltern Hills are a continuation of the chalk uplands that carry the Ridgeway from Wiltshire to the Thames where the river has cut through the chalk escarpment at the Goring Gap. To the west of the Thames, the Ridgeway has bridleway or byway status along its entire length from the start at Overton Hill (near Avebury) to Goring. To the east of the Thames it is more confusing: there are three waymarked trails that follow the escarpment - the Ridgeway, Icknield Way and Swan's Way - and their status varies from footpath to bridleway to byway.

Look carefully at the maps and you will see that there is a plethora of bridleways to use to make your own customised rides, from a beauty that runs right alongside the Thames between Goring and Whitchurch to tough climbs up the escarpment from *Watlington* to Christmas Common or the dense network of woodland tracks radiating from *Stoke Row*, with its famous Maharajah's Well.

If you are looking for somewhere to stay for the weekend, *Henley* is an excellent base and there are even trails starting from close to the town centre heading west to Rotherfield Peppard and Bix. The whole of the Chilterns is full of hidden valleys, small villages with good pubs and a network of lanes that offer alternatives should the mud

Whiteleaf Hill. Riders: MTB Berkhamsted. © Steve Lloyd

get too much. As ever, this being Southern England, it is best to avoid the depths of winter as the tracks can get very sticky. This is definitely a case of building up intimate local knowledge, as some trails remain passable year round whereas others can have you axle deep in some very nasty energy sapping gloop.

Good centres are strung out along the base of the Chilterns escarpment, from **Watlington, Ibstone** and **Chinnor**, connected by a good long stretch of the Ridgeway, to **Princes Risborough**, **Tring** and **Aldbury**. Although the woodlands end here, the chalk ridge continues north east, offering rides to the north of Luton starting from **Great Offley**, using a fine section of the Icknield Way or south east of Stevenage at **Watton at Stone**.

If you are looking for trail centres, **Aston Hill, Chicksands** and **Hainault Forest Park** have waymarked trails. Alternatively, try the downhills at **Woburn Sands** or the expanse of woodland trails in **Epping Forest**.

323

Chicksands

Drive Times: Northampton 50mins, Cambridge 1hr, London 1hr20, Birmingham 1hr40, Bristol 2hr40.

Trains: Stations at Kempston Hardwick, Stewartby & Lidlington on the Bedford-London line.

Refreshments: Refreshments at Chicksands Bike Park weekends and bank holidays. The Red Lion Lodge 01234 381381 or The Greyhound 01234 381 239 at Haynes. The Red Lion 01234 740 246 at Wilstead, The Knife & Cleaver

01234 740387 at Houghton Conquest, Chequers 01525 404 853 at How End, The Royal Oak 01525 840 233 at Lidlington, Bell Inn 01234 768 310 at Marston Moretaine, Rose & Crown 01234 764 765 or Lakeside Cafe 01234 767037 at Stewartby Lake. Pubs at Cranfield or Rose & Crown 01234 851 103 at Wootton.

Bike Shops: Transition Cycles 01234 351154 in Bedford.

Books: MTB Rides to the SE (M.Darkins).

Maps: OS Explorer 208.

Situation: On the River Fit in central Bedfordshire. 9 miles south east of Bedford.

About the Base: Chicksands, a village with easy access to the trails.

Parking: Sandy Lane Car Park in Rowney Warren Woods, north of the village. **Grid Ref:** TL124404. **Post Code:** SG17 5QG.

Route Idea

From Sandy Lane car park, E to take trail along Chicksands Wood. Roads to Houghton Conquest and then Millbrook. Trails to Lidlington. Cross A421 then onto Wootton via Marston Thrift, Roxhill Manor Farm, & Wooton Wood. SE to Kempston Hardwick, N on B530 then E to Elstow. S - on John Bunyan Trail to Haynes. Road back to car park. Distance 58km.

Also see Chicksands Bike Park (p337).

Other trails possibility: See Chicksands Bike Park for trails around the woods.

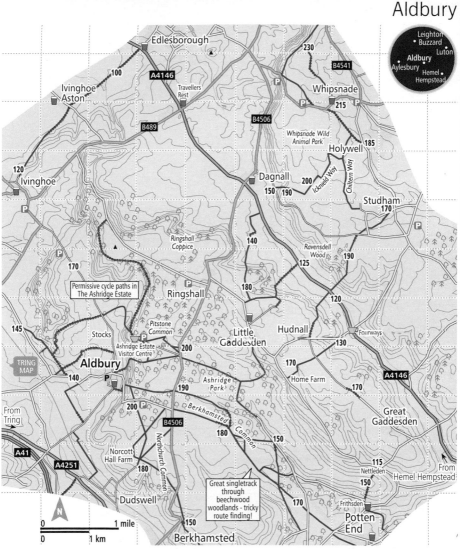

Situation: At the north eastern end of the Ridgeway National Trail in the Chiltern Hills. 3 miles east of Tring and 8 miles south west of Dunstable.

About the Base: Aldbury, a village with two pubs.

Parking: Roadside in the centre of Aldbury. Car parks at Pitstone Common Visitor Centre. Other car parks marked on the map. *Grid Ref: Aldbury SP964124, Pitstone Common SP970130. Post Code: Aldbury HP23 5RR, Pitstone Common Visitor Centre HP4 1LX*

Drive Times: Oxford 1hr, Northampton 1hr, London 1hr10, Birmingham 1hr50, Bristol 2hr20.

Trains: Tring & Berkhamsted Stations are on the London-Watford-Milton Keynes line.

Refreshments: At Aldbury, The Valiant Trooper 01442 851 203 and The Greyhound Inn 01442 851228. Brownlow Cafe 01442 851670 at Pitstone Common National Trust Visitor Centre. The Rose & Crown 01296 668 472 at Ivinghoe, The Village Swan 01525 220 544 at Ivinghoe Aston, The Bell 01525 222 957 at Eddlesborough, The Travellers Rest 01525 221 841 and The Old Hunters Lodge 01582 872228 at Whipsnade. The Bridgewater Arms 01442 842408 at Little Gaddesden. Fourways Cafe 01442 842764, The Alford Arms 01442 864 480 at Frithsden

Bike Shops: Dyson Cycles 01582 665 533 in Dunstable.

Maps: OS Explorer 181.

Routes on Web: www.goodmtb.co.uk/a133

Route Idea

From Aldbury, SE across Berkhamsted Common and onto Nettleden, Great Gaddesden and then N to Hudnall. Trails and roads to Studham, Whipsnade and Edlesborough. SW on trails to Ivinghoe. Roads back to the start. Distance 32km.

Extend the area: Tring Map to the W.

Tring

Leighton Buzzard • Luton
Tring
Aylesbury • Hemel Hempstead

140
150
160 140
200
Ashridge Estate Visitor Centre
Aldbury
Aldbury Common
ALDBURY MAP
Grand Union Canal
Towpath
Tring Station
Tring
B4635
From Aylesbury A41
A4251
140
200
B4506
Berkhamsted Common
180
180
160
Wigginton
150
240
Hastoe
Hamberlins Farm
Norcott Hall Farm
170
Northchurch Common
160
170
Longcroft
High Scrubs
Champneys
Northchurch
Northchurch Farm
240
Leylands Farm
180
190
Tring Grange Farm
A41
Berkhamsted
A416
St Leonards
Cholesbury
160
Hawridge Common
170
Buckland Common

N
0   1 mile
0   1 km

Situation: In the Tring Gap, a low point in the Chiltern Hills, in Hertfordshire. Close to the border with Buckinghamshire, 8 miles south east of Aylesbury.

About the Base: Tring, a small market town with pubs, cafés and accommodation. **Parking:** Car park in the centre of Tring, Pitstone Common Visitor Centre & Berkhamsted Common. *Grid Ref: Tring SP925114, Pitstone Common SP970130, Berkhamsted Common SP972118. **Post Code:** Tring HP23 5AG, Pitstone Common Visitor Centre HP4 1LX.*

Drive Times: London 1hr, Oxford 1hr, Northampton 1hr10, Birmingham 1hr50, Bristol 2hr20.

Trains: Tring & Berkhamsted Stations are on the London-Watford-Milton Keynes line.

Refreshments: Plenty of pubs and cafés at Tring. The Valiant Trooper 01442 851 203 at Aldbury and Brownlow Cafe 01442 851670 at Pitstone Common National Trust Visitor Centre. The George & Dragon 01442 864 533 at Northchurch or pubs and cafés at Berkhamsted. The Rose & Crown 01494 758944 at Hawridge, The Full Moon 01494 758 959 at Hawridge Common and The White Lion 01494 758 387 at St Leonards. The Greyhound 01442 824 631 at Wigginton.

Bike Shops: Mountain Manie Cycles 01442 822 458.

Books: MTB Rides to the SE (M.Darkins).

Maps: OS Explorer 181.

Route Idea

From Tring, NE over the canal. Trails around Aldbury Common, Berkhamsted Common then Northchurch Common to Berkhamsted. Road and trails W to Tring. Grange Farm, through High Scrubs to Hastoe. N on trails and roadback to Tring.
Distance 32km.

Extend the area: Aldbury Map to the W.

Also see the purpose-built trails at Aston Hill (p339), which are just to the west of this area.

Riders: MTB Berkhamsted. © Steve Lloyd

Princes Risborough

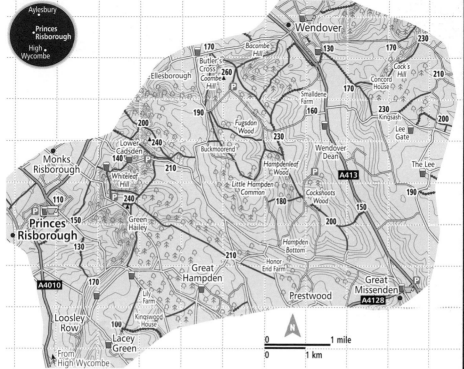

Situation: Between the Vale of Aylesbury and the Chiltern Hills Escarpment on The Ridgeway National Trail. 8 miles south of Aylesbury and 9 miles north west of High Wycombe.

About the Base: Princes Risborough, a small town with a choice of pubs and cafés.
Further Info: www.princesrisborough.com.
Parking: Car park in the centre of Princes Risborough. Also at Whiteleaf Hill, Lower Cadsden, Coombe Hill, Wendover Dean & Great Missenden. *Grid Ref: Princes Risborough SP807034, Whiteleaf Hill SP823036, Lower Cadsden SP833045, Coombe Hill SP851062, Wendover Dean SP871043, Great Missenden SP894014. Post Code: Princes Risborough HP27 9AX, Great Missenden HP16 9AL.*

Drive Times: Oxford 40 mins, London 1hr10, Northampton 1hr20, Birmingham 1hr40.

Trains: Princes Risborough & Monks Risborough Stations are on the London-Birmingham West Coast Main Line. Great Missendon & Wendover Stations are on the London-Aylesbury line.

Refreshments: Choice of pubs or Le Cafe de la Gare 01844 274 555 at Princes Risborough. The Red Lion 01844 344 980 at Whiteleaf or The Plough at Cadsden 01844 343 302. The Russell Arms 01296 622 618 at Butlers Cross, pubs and cafés at Wendover, The Fire Crest 01296 628 041 at Wendover Dean, The Gate Inn 01494 837 368 at Lee Gate and The Cock & Rabbit 01494 837512 at

The Lea. Pubs, The Village Café 01494 866 393 or Café-Toria 01494 863 367 at Great Missenden. The Hampden Arms 01494 488255 at Great Hampden, The Black Horse, The Pink & Lily 01494 488308 and The Whip 01844 344060 at Lacey Green.

Bike Shops: Risborough Cycles 01844 345 949 for bikes, parts, repairs & hire.

Books: South East MTB – Ridgeway & Chilterns (N.Cotton). MTB Rides to the SE (M.Darkins).

Maps: OS Explorer 181.

Routes on Web: www.goodmtb.co.uk/a134

Route Idea

From Whiteleaf Hill car park, first N then E to take trails towards Little Hampden Common then through Hampdenleaf Wood, past Cockshoots Wood to join the A413 S. Roads to Kingsash then on to Wendover via trails across Cock's Hill. Trails across Bacombe Hill and Fugsden Wood. Return to Princess Risborough as reverse of outbound start. Distance 31km. Various road and trail links to shorten as required.

Watlington (east)

Thame
Watlington
High Wycombe

Crowel
Kingston Blount 145
CHINNOR MAP
B4009
Aston Rowant
Crowell Hill 240
Crowellhill Wood
200
A480
130
From Oxford
140
Lewknor
6
Grove Wood
200
Crowell Wood
230
240
160
Little London Wood
Stokenchurch
150
250
Hailey Wood
210
5
B4009
Ridgeway
Cowleaze Wood
Lydall's Wood
Wellground Farm
High Wycombe
Watlington
Shirburn Wood
Portobello Farm
140
Commonhill Wood
100
130 140
240
Shotridge Wood
Christmas Common
Hungryhill Wood
Ibstone Common
130
Watlington Hill
WATLINGTON (South) MAP
230
Launder's Farm 210
Queen Wood
210 Northend
N
170

0 _____ 1 mile
0 _____ 1 km

Situation: Close to The Ridgeway National Trail in Oxfordshire, on the fringes of the Chiltern Hills. 10 miles north of Henley on Thames and 3 miles from M40 junction 6.

About the Base: Watlington, a market town with pubs and a café. **Parking:** Car parks in the centre of Watlington & at Watlington Hill, south east of the town. Also at Cowleaze Wood & Little London Wood. **Grid Ref:** *Watlington SU690944, Watlington Hill SU709935, Cowleaze Wood SU726958, Little London Wood SU731966.* **Post Code:** *Watlington OX49 5BD.*

Drive Times: Oxford 30 mins, London 1hr, Birmingham 1hr30, Southampton 1hr40, Bristol 1hr50.

Refreshments: At Watlington, The Carriers Arms 01491 613470, The Chequers 0149161 2874, The Fox & Hounds 01491 613040 or The Pantry Café 01491 614820. The Leathern Bottle 01844 351 482 at Lewknor, The Lambert Arms 01844 351 496 at Aston Rowant and The Cherry Tree 01844 352 273 at Kingston Blount. Pubs at Stokenchurch and The Fox Country Inn 01491 639 333 at Ibstone Common or The Fox & Hounds 01491 612599 at Christmas Common.

Bike Shops: Rides on Air, 8 miles away in Wallingford. Henley Cycles 01491 578 984 in Henley on Thames also do hire.

Books: South East MTB – Ridgeway & Chilterns (N.Cotton).

Maps: OS Explorer 171.

Route Idea

From Watlington, NE on Ridgeway. S to Crowell Hill, Crowell Wood, Hailey Wood to Northend. W to Christmas Common on trails through Queen Wood. Trail to the Ridgeway and back to Watlington. Distance 27km.

Extend the area: Chinnor Map to the NE. Watlington South Map to the S.

Christmas Common. © Alex Leigh

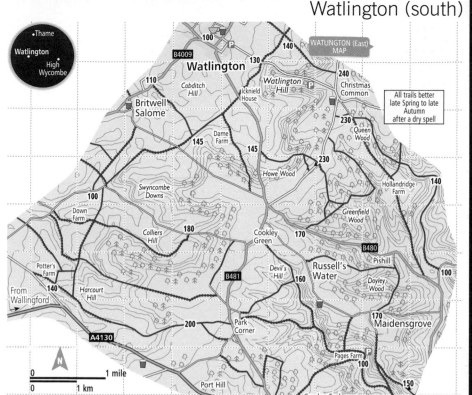

Situation: At the foot of the Chiltern Hills, close to The Ridgeway National Trail in Oxfordshire. 10 miles north of Henley on Thames and 3 miles from M40 junction 6.

About the Base: Watlington, a market town with pubs and a café. **Parking:** Car parks in the centre of Watlington & at Watlington Hill, south east of the town. *Grid Ref: Watlington SU690944, Watlington Hill SU709935. Post Code: Watlington OX49 5BD.*

Drive Times: Oxford 30 mins, London 1hr, Birmingham 1hr30, Southampton 1hr40, Bristol 1hr50.

© Alex Leigh

Refreshments: At Watlington, The Carriers Arms 01491 613470, The Chequers 0149161 2874, The Fox & Hounds 01491 613040 or The Pantry Café 01491 614820. The Fox & Hounds 01491 612599 at Christmas Common, The Crown Inn 01491 638 364 at Pishill and The Five Horseshoes 01491 641 282 at Russell's Water. The White Hart 01491 641 245 at Nettlebed, The Crown 01491 641 335 at Nuffield and The Goose 01491 612 304 at Britwell Salome.

Bike Shops: Rides on Air, 8 miles away in Wallingford. Henley Cycles 01491 578 984 in Henley on Thames also do hire.

Books: South East MTB – Ridgeway & Chilterns (N.Cotton). MTB Rides to the SE (M.Darkins).

Maps: OS Explorer 171.

Routes on Web: www.goodmtb.co.uk/a135

Route Idea

E from Watlington on roads and trails to Christmas Common. Trails SE through Queen Wood to the B480. S from Pishill to Maidensgrove. Trails S then N to pass Pages Farm and W on to Park Corner. Trails W to Harcourt Hill then N to the base of Watlington Hill. Road back to the finish. Distance 28km.

Extend the area: Watlington East Map.

Chinnor

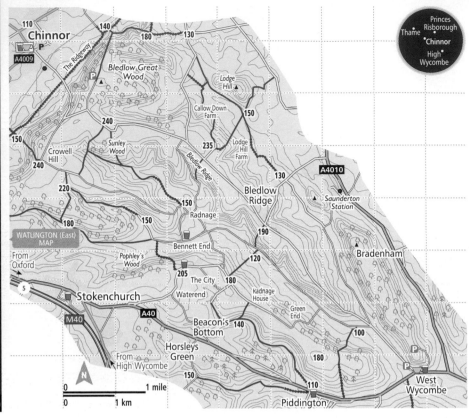

Situation: On the Ridgeway National Trail below the Chiltern Hills Escarpment in South Oxfordshire. 4 miles south east of Thame and 10 miles north west of High Wycombe.

About the Base: Chinnor, a large village with several pubs and a café. **Parking:** Roadside parking by the church in Chinnor & car park outside the village at Bledlow Great Wood. Car parks at West Wycombe. **Grid Ref:** *Chinnor SP756009, Bledlow Great Wood SP766002, West Wycombe SU827951 or SU825947.* **Post Code:** *Chinnor OX39 4PH, West Wycombe HP14 3AP.*

Drive Times: Oxford 30mins, London 1hr, Northampton 1hr20, Birmingham 1hr40, Bristol 2hrs.

Trains: Saunderton Station is on the London-Birmingham West Coast Main Line.

Refreshments: At Chinnor, several pubs and The Daisy Chain Tea Room 01844 355 912 at Chinnor Nurseries. The Swan Inn 01494 527 031 and Tea Rooms at Hellfire Caves 01494 533 739 at West Wycombe. The Dashwood Arms 01494 882 935 at Piddington, The Crown Inn 01494 482 301 and The Three Horseshoes 01494 483 273 at Bennett End.

Bike Shops: 2 Wheels 01844 212 455 in Thame, Cycle Care 01494 447908 & Freewheelin 01494 258189 in High Wycombe.

Books: South East MTB – Ridgeway & Chilterns (N.Cotton). MTB Rides to the SE (M.Darkins).

Maps: OS Explorer 171 & 172.

Route Idea

From Chinnor, on to then NE on The Ridgeway then trails & roads S&W past Lodge Hill to Bledlow Ridge. S to Piddington mostly on trails then W to Horsleys Green & Beacon's Bottom. Road and trails NW to Crowell Hill. Trail down to The Ridgeway and back to Chinnor. Distance 25km.

Extend the area: Watlington East Map to the E.

© Mark James

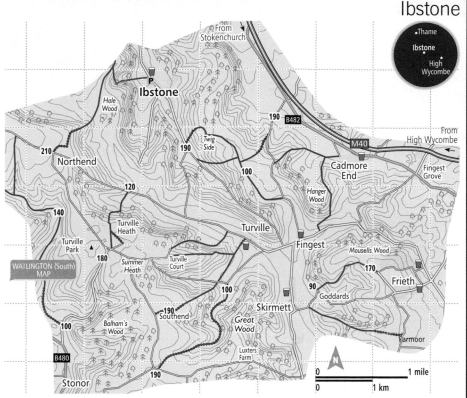

Ibstone

Situation: In the Chiltern Hills, on the Buckinghamshire/Oxfordshire border. 8 miles north west of Marlow and 10 miles west of High Wycombe.

About the Base: Ibstone, a village with a pub and easy access to the trails.

Parking: Layby in Ibstone opposite the pub. *Grid Ref: SU750939. Post Code: HP14 3XT.*

Drive Times: Oxford 1hr, London 1hr, Birmingham 1hr30, Southampton 1hr40, Bristol 2hrs.

Refreshments: The Fox & Country Inn 01491 639333 at Ibstone. The Old Ship 01494 883 496 at Cadmore End, The Prince Albert 01494 881 683 or The Yew Tree 01494 882 330 at Frieth, The Frog at Skirmett 01491 638996, The Chequers Inn 01491 638335 at Fingest and The Bull & Butcher 0149163 8283 at Turville.

Bike Shops: Saddle Safari 01628 477 020 in Marlow.

Books: MTB Rides to the SE (M.Darkins).

Maps: OS Explorer 171.

Route Idea

From Ibstone to Frieth via Twig Side & Hanger Wood. W to Skirmett. Road S then W past Luxters Farm. Trail N through Great Wood and on to Turville. Trails and roads W to Turville Heath & Northend. Trails back to Ibstone. Distance 28km.

Extend the area: Watlington South Map to the SW.

Stoke Row

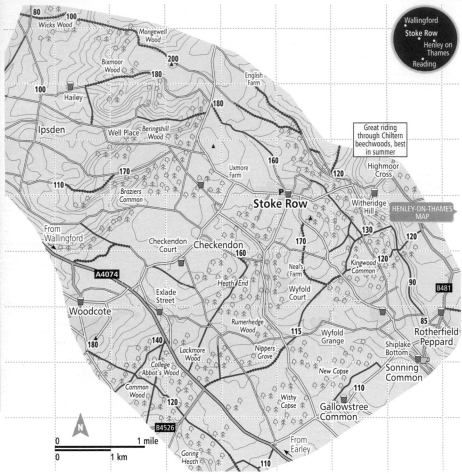

Situation: In the Chiltern Hills in South Oxfordshire. 6 miles west of Henley on Thames.

About the Base: Stoke Row, a village with a pub and village store. Further Info: www.stokerow.net.

Parking: Roadside parking in Stoke Row.
Grid Ref: SU680840. Post Code: RG9 5QL.

Drive Times: Oxford 40 mins, London 1hr10, Southampton 1hr30, Bristol 1hr40, Birmingham 1hr50.

Trains: Henley on Thames Station has services to London.

Refreshments: At Stoke Row, The Cherry Tree Inn 01491 680 430 and refreshments at Stoke Village Stores 01491 681430. The Rising Sun 01491 640 856 at Witheridge Hill, The Unicorn 01491 628 452 and The Red Lion 01491 628 329 at Rotherfield Peppard, Fresh as a Daisy Cafe 0118 972 4061 or The Greyhound 0118 972 2227 at Sonning Common and The Reformation 0118 972 3126 at Gallowstree Common. The Highwayman 01491 682 020 at Exlade Street, The Red Lion 01491 680 483 at Woodcote and King William IV at Hailey. The Four Horse Shoes 01491 680 325 at Checkendon.

Bike Shops: Rides on Air, 5 miles away in Wallingford, Trailjunkies Mountain Bike Centre 01491 871 721 at Streatley or Mountain High 0118 984 1851 in Pangbourne, both 7 miles away. Henley Cycles 01491 578 984 in Henley on Thames also do hire.

Books: South East MTB – Ridgeway & Chilterns (N.Cotton). MTB Rides to the SE (M.Darkins).

Maps: OS Explorer 171.

Route Idea

From Stoke Row, SE on trails across Kingwood Common. Trails W past Nippers Grove. Road S to cross the A4074 then trails N through Goring Heath and Common Wood to Woodcote. N on trail then road to pass Ipsden & up to Wicks Wood. SE on trails and roads back to finish. Distance 24km.

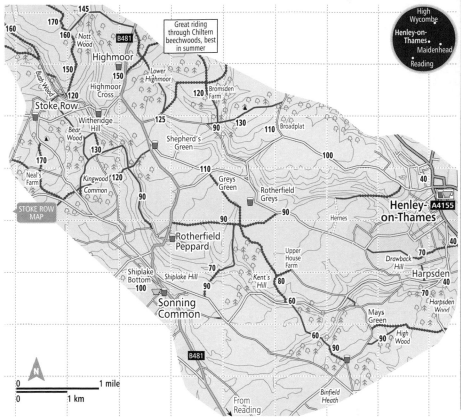

High
Wycombe
Henley-on-Thames.
Maidenhead
Reading

Situation: At the foot of the Chiltern Hills on the River Thames in South Oxfordshire. Close to the borders of Berkshire and Buckinghamshire, 8 miles north east of Reading.

About the Base: Henley on Thames, a town with pubs, cafés and accommodation.
Further Info: www.henley-on-thames.org.
Parking: Car Park at Henley Railway Station.
Grid Ref: SU766821. Post Code: RG9 1BF.

Drive Times: Oxford 50mins, London 1hr, Southampton 1hr30, Birmingham 1hr50, Bristol 1hr50.

Trains: Henley on Thames Station has services to London. Reading Station is on the Oxford-Southampton & London-Exeter-Plymouth lines.

Refreshments: Good choice of pubs and cafés at Henley on Thames. The Bottle & Glass 01491 575755 at Binfield Heath, The Red Lion 01491 628 329 and The Dog Inn 01491 628 343 at Rotherfield Peppard or Fresh as a Daisy Cafe 0118 972 4061 and The Greyhound 0118 972 2227 at Sonning Common. The Cherry Tree Inn 01491 680 430 and refreshments at Stoke Village Stores 01491 681430 at Stoke Row, The Rising Sun 01491 640 856 at Witheridge Hill, The Dog & Duck 01491 641261 at Highmoor, The Lamb Inn 01491 628 482 at Shepherd's Green and The Maltsters Arms 01491 628 400 at Rotherfield Greys.

Bike Shops: Henley Cycles 01491 578 984 for bikes, parts, repairs & hire.

Books: South East MTB – Ridgeway & Chilterns (N.Cotton).
Maps: OS Explorer 171.

Route Idea

Roads S through Harpsden Wood. Trails W through High Wood. Trails W to Rotherfield Peppard. Trails NW to Stoke Row, then on to Nott Wood and B481. Trails and roads back to Henley via Lower Highmoor, Bromsden Farm & Broadplat. Distance 28km.

Extend the area: Stoke Row Map to the W.

©Jeremy Stevens

Great Offley

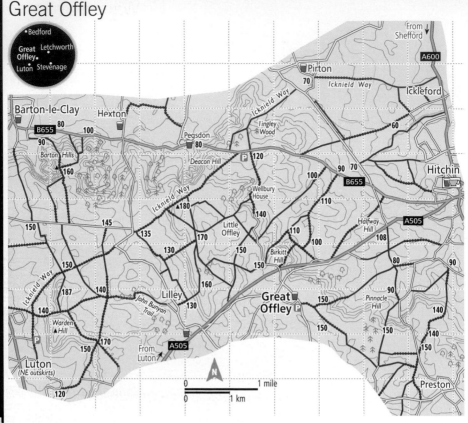

334

Situation: On the most north eastern ridge of the Chiltern Hills in Hertfordshire, close to the Bedfordshire. 3 miles south west of Hitchin and 7 miles north east of Luton.

About the Base: Great Offley, a village with two pubs.

Parking: Car park in Great Offley. Also on B655 for the Icknield Way & north east of Luton at Warden Hill. *Grid Ref: Great Offley TL143267, Icknield Way TL132300, Warden Hill TL086259. **Post Code:** Great Offley SG5 3EN, Warden Hill LU2 7AJ,*

Drive Times: Northampton 1hr, Cambridge 1hr, Reading 1hr 10, London 1hr10, Peterborough 1hr15, Birmingham 1hr50, Bristol 2hr30.

Trains: Hitchin Station is on the Peterborough-London line. Luton Station is on the Bedford-St Albans-London line.

Refreshments: At Great Offley, The Green Man 01462 768256 and The Gloucester Arms 0146276 8046. The Silver Lion 0146276 8386 at Lilley and The Motte & Bailey 01462 712 641 at Pirton. Detour to pubs at Barton-le-Clay, The Raven 01582 881 209 at Hexton, The Live & Let Live 01582 881739 at Pegsdon or pubs & cafes at Hitchin.

Bike Shops: Cycledealia 01462 631 555 in Hitchin.

Books: MTB Rides to the SE (M.Darkins).

Maps: OS Explorer 207.

Route Idea

From Great Offley, road N to Birkett Hill then W on trails to Lilley. John Bunyan Trail W past Warden Hill then NE on Icknield Way to Deacon Hill. S past Wellbury House back to Great Offley.
Distance 19km.

Watton at Stone

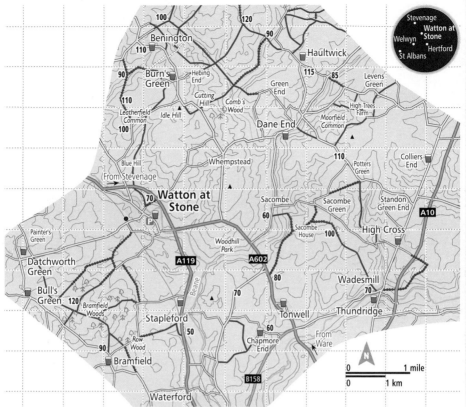

Situation: In the valley of the River Beane in Hertfordshire. 5 miles south east of Stevenage and north west of Hertford.

About the Base: Watton at Stone, a village with two pubs. **Parking:** Car park in Watton at Stone opposite The Bull pub. *Grid Ref: TL302192. Post Code: SG14 3SB.*

Drive Times: Cambridge 1hr, London 1hr10, Northampton 1hr20, Birmingham 2hr10, Bristol 2hr30.

Trains: Watton at Stone Station is on the London-Peterborough line.

Refreshments: At Watton at Stone, The George & Dragon 01920 830 285 and The Bull Inn 01920 831 032. The Tilbury 01438 815 550 at Datchworth or The Horns Pub 01438 798 052 at Bulls Green. The Grandison 01992 554 077 at Bramfield, Papillon Woodhall Arms 01992 535123 at Stapleford, The Woodman 01920 463 143 at Chapmore End, The Robin Hood & Little John 01920 463 352 at Tonwell, The Anchor 01920 462 861 at Wadesmill and The White Horse 01920 462 996 at High Cross. The Lamb & Flag 01920 823222 at Colliers End or The Boot 01920438770 at Dane End. The Rest & Welcome 01920 438 323 at Haultwick, The Bell Inn 01438 869 270 at Benington and The Lordship Arms 01438 869 665 at Burns Green.

Bike Shops: Marshalls Cycles in Hertford 01992 503 868 or Stevenage 01438 748 104.

Books: MTB Rides to the SE (M.Darkins).

Maps: OS Explorer 194 & 182.

Route Idea

From Watton at Stone, trails SW to & through Bramfield Woods to Bramfield. Roads to Waterford then NE to A602. Trails past Sacombe House and on to Wadesmill and High Cross. Trail N towards Potters Green then NE over Moorfield Common to Levens Gereen. NW to Haultwick then trail to Cutting Hill. W to Leatherfield Common and trail S back to Watton at Stone. Distance 36km.

Letty Green

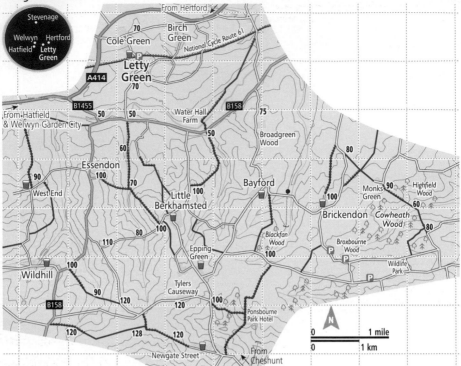

Situation: Just north of the River Lea in Hertfordshire. 4 miles south east of Welwyn Garden City and south west of Hertford.

About the Base: Letty Green, a small village with a pub and easy access to the trails. **Parking:** Green Way car park next to the Cowper Arms as you approach the village from the north. Car parks at Broxbourne Wood, south of Brickendon. **Grid Ref:** *Letty Green TL284111, Broxbourne Wood TL324070.* **Post Code:** *Letty Green SG14 2NS.*

Drive Times: Cambridge 1hr, London 1hr, Northampton 1hr10, Birmingham 2hr, Bristol 2hr20.

Trains: Bayford Station is on the London-Hertford line. Hertford & Welwyn Garden City Stations have services to London & Peterborough.

Refreshments: At Letty Green, The Cowper Arms 01707 330202. The Five Horseshoes 01707 875 055 at Little Berkhamstead, The Beehive 01707 875 959 at Epping Green and The Bakers Arms 01992 511235 at Bayford. The Farmers Boy 01992 511 610 at Brickendon, The Crown 01707 872 107 at Newgate Street, The Woodman 01707 642 618 at Wildhill or The Candlestick 01707 261 322 at West End.

Bike Shops: Marshalls Cycles in Hertford 01992 503 868 or Welwyn Garden City 01707 393 322.

Books: MTB Rides to the SE (M.Darkins).

Maps: OS Explorer 174 & 182.

Route Idea

From Letty Green, E on National Cycle Route 61 then trails SW to Little Berkhamsted. Roads to Blackfan Wood then trail N and road E to Brickendon. Trail N then SE to Monks Green. Trails and roads to pass Ponsbourne Park Hotel & onto Newgate Street. Trail W then roads to Little Berkhamsted. Trails N to B158. Roads back to start. Distance 33km.

Greensands Bike Park

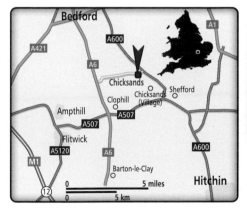

Opened in 2010, a 41 acre site in Bedfordshire, continually being developed with more tracks planned and under construction. Offering a 4X track, Dual Slalom, Pump Track, Jump Track, XC trail and massive dirt jumps to challenge even the most experienced rider. Families are also welcome as younger riders will find tracks to suit them too.

Facilities:
Refreshments on site. Pay to ride
Parking:
Grid Ref: TL210486. Post Code: SG19 2NQ
Web: www.goodmtb.co.uk/b68

The Trails
❶ 4X
❷ Dual Track
❸ Pump Track
❹ Jump Track
❺ XC

Chicksands Bike Park

A small area of Forestry Commission land in Bedfordshire. Waymarked XC trails and a popular Freeride Area, with dirt jumps, drops and northshore, are constantly improved and maintained by Chicksands Bike Park. A National standard 4X course and Dual slalom cater for evryone from novices wanting to improve their off road bike handling skills to expert, experienced riders.

Facilities:
Truly Thai 'take away' on site weekends and bank holidays. Pay to Ride.
Parking:
Grid Ref: TL115416.
Web: www.goodmtb.co.uk/b66

337

The Trails
❶ XC, Blue, 4km.
❷ XC, Red, 5.5km.
❸ The Bull Run, DH.
❹ The Snake Run, DH.
❺ Old Faithful, Dual Slalom.
❻ 4X.
❼ Freeride.

Riders: Neil Webster
Rider: Mark James
Rider: Scott Hogan
3 photos © Mark James

Woburn Trails & Aspley Woods

On the Greensands Ridge close to Milton Keynes, riding for all abilities. Plenty of dirt jumps, drops and northshore built, maintained and constantly updated by local riders. Short downhill runs 20-30 seconds in length. All year round riding on umarked XC loops with fast technical singletrack and long wide bridleways.

Facilities:
None on site. Refreshments in nearby Woburn. Pay to ride.

Parking:
Grid Ref: SP925336.

Web: www.goodmtb.co.uk/b70a & /b70b

The Trails
❶ Freeride
❷ XC
❹ 5 DH runs

Moto X. Rider:Jim Holgate. ©Jason Curtis

Epping Forest

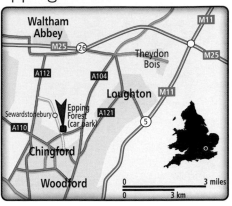

The largest public open space in the London area. Deciduous forest with plenty of unmarked singletrack and forest roads to explore.

Facilities:
Epping Forest Visitor Centre. Refreshments in nearby Chingford.

Parking:
Grid Ref: TQ394949

Web: www.goodmtb.co.uk/b67

The Trails

No waymarked trails. Explore or meet up with local riders.

Hainault Forest Park

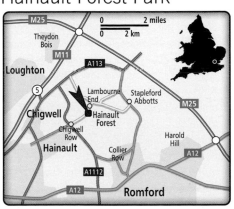

Built by the London Development Agency in 2008, Redbridge Cycling Centre has a purpose built, all weather MTB track in Hainault Forest Park north east of London. With a large descent section as well as berms, jumps and a 'pump track' suitable for BMXs.

Facilities:
Café at Hainault Forest Country Park Visitor Centre. Redbridge Cycling Centre 020 8500 9359.

Parking:
Grid Ref: TQ478943. Post Code: RM4 1NB

Web: www.goodmtb.co.uk/b69

The Trails
XC, 3.25km

Aston Hill

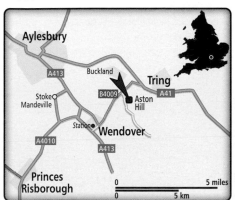

In the Chiltern Hills Area of Outstanding Natural Beauty. Several purpose built trails including a cross country loop, five graded downhill runs and a 4X course.

Facilities:
None on site. Café in the Woods at nearby Wendover Woods. Pay to Ride.

Parking:
Grid Ref: SP891101. Post Code: HP22 5NQ

Web: www.goodmtb.co.uk/b65a & /b65b

The Trails
❶ XC, 8km.
❷ DH: Red, Black, DH3, DH4 and DH5(423).
❸ 4X

The Ridgeway & Hampshire Downs

D ating back 5000 years, the Ridgeway is claimed to be the oldest road in Europe. The broad chalk and flint track starts at Overton Hill, near Marlborough (and the stone circle at *Avebury*) and passes many ancient hill forts and burial mounds such as Barbury Castle, Uffington Castle and Waylands Smithy on its way to the Thames at Goring. It passes through a rolling landscape of vast arable fields, hillside sheep pastures and gallops. Don't be surprised to see large numbers of fine racehorses training on the springy grass gallops that run parallel with many of the tracks in the area, especially around *Lambourn*. The area has a denser concentration of bridleways and byways than anywhere else in the country, meaning that many circular rides are possible using sections of the Ridgeway. In places the bridleway and byway network dwarfs the road network. There are good bases at *Avebury*, *Ogbourne St George*, *Aldbourne*, *Lambourn*, *East Ilsley* and *Streatley*.

Riding times vary enormously from summer to winter as the chalk and clay gets sticky when wet. In the summer, after a hot, dry spell, it wouldn't be out of the question to contemplate 100km rides as you can blast along the fast, wide chalk tracks at a good lick. In the depths of winter, a ride half this length might use up the same amount of energy.

South of the Ridgeway and the valley formed by the River Kennet lies another fine mountain biking area known as the North Hampshire Downs. Walbury Hill to the southwest of Newbury is the highest chalk upland in all of Southern England, rising to a dizzying 297m (975ft). There is some excellent riding to the south of the ridge that is not unlike the South Downs, and in the area to the east as far as *Kingsclere* (location of *Watership Down*) and south towards Andover. The area is more wooded than the Ridgeway but is still predominantly open with fine wide-ranging views. One of the more extraordinary sights is the gibbet that was used for hanging criminals high up on the ridge at Combe Gibbet, above Inkpen (see *Hurstbourne Tarrant*). Further good bases are at *Collingbourne Kingston* and *Kingsclere*.

Martinsell Hill, Pewsey Downs. © Dave Robinson SPAM

Avebury

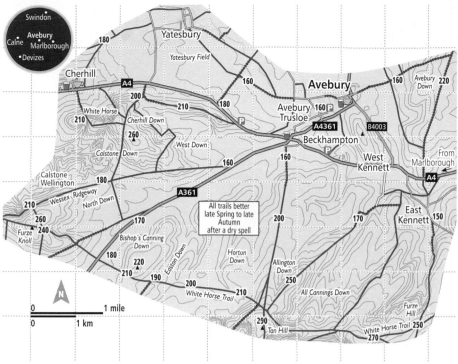

Situation: In an area of chalkland in the Upper Kennett Valley. At the western end of the Ridgeway and the Berkshire Downs in Wiltshire. 6 miles west of Marlborough and 11 miles south of Swindon.

About the Base: Avebury, a village with a pub and a café. **Parking:** National Trust car park south of the village on A4361, also east & west of Beckhampton on A4. *Grid Ref: Avebury SU099695, Beckhampton East SU096686, Beckhampton West SU077691. Post Code: Avebury SN8 1RD.*

Drive Times: Bristol 1hr, Reading 1hr, Oxford 1hr10, Southampton 1hr30, London 1hr50, Birmingham 2hrs.

Refreshments: At Avebury, The Red Lion 01672 539 266 and Circles National Trust Café 01672 539250. The Wagon and Horses 01672 539 418 at Beckhampton and Divine Café 01249 815 979 or The Black Horse 01249 813 365 at Cherhill.

Bike Shops: Bertie Maffoon's Bicycle Company 01672 519 119 in Marlborough.

Books: South East MTB – Ridgeway & Chilterns (N.Cotton). MTB Guide Wiltshire (I.White). MTB Rides to the SW (M.Darkins).

Maps: OS Explorer 157.

Route Idea

❶ From Avebury, E around Avebury Down to East Kennett. So to Furze Hill then along the White Horse Trail to Furze Knoll. E on Wessex Ridgeway then N over Calstone Down to Cherhill, then Yatesbury and back to Avebury. Distance 34km.

❷ Use the N-S trail from Beckhampton to Tan Hill to split the above route.
E loop distance 19km.
W loop distance 26km.

Pewsey Downs. © Dave Robinson SPAM

Ogbourne St George

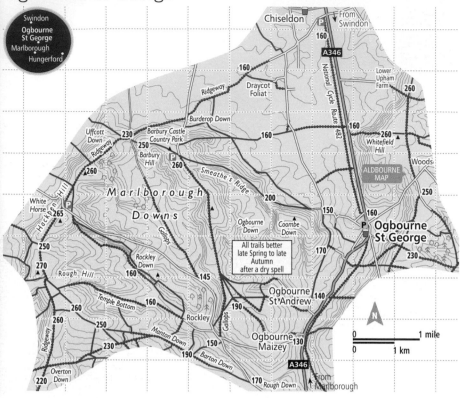

Swindon
Ogbourne St George
Marlborough
Hungerford

Situation: In the Og Valley between the Marlborough Downs and the Aldbourne Downs in Wiltshire. On the Ridgeway National Trail, 4 miles north of Marlborough and 10 miles south of Swindon.

About the Base: Ogbourne St George, a village with a pub and easy access to the trails. Further info: www.ogbournestgeorge.org.uk. **Parking:** Roadside parking next to the Parklands Hotel in Ogbourne St George. Car parks at Barbury Castle Country Park & Hackpen Hill.
Grid Ref: Ogbourne St George SU202743, Barbury Castle SU157760, Hackpen Hill SU129747.
Post Code: Ogbourne St George SN8 1SJ.

Drive Times: Bristol 50mins, Reading 50mins, London 1hr40, Birmingham 1hr50, Manchester 3hr10, Leeds 3hr40.

Refreshments: The Inn with the Well 01672 841 445 at Ogbourne St George. The Patriots Arms 01793 740 331 at Chiseldon and Silks on the Downs 01672 841 229 at Ogbourne St Andrew.

Bike Shops: Bertie Maffoon's Bicycle Company 01672 519 119 in Marlborough.

Books: South East MTB – Ridgeway & Chilterns (N.Cotton). MTB Guide Wiltshire (I.White). MTB Rides to the SW (M.Darkins). MBR Ride Guide 2010

Maps: OS Explorer 157.

Route Ideas

❶ From Ogbourne St George, N along National Cycle Route 482 towards Chiseldon. SW along The Ridgeway. At Barbury Hill SE along the Gallops to road & onto Ogbourne St Andrew. Cycle Route 482 back to start. Distance 23km.

❷ Extend the above by continuing along The Ridgeway to Hackpen Hill then Overton Down. E along Manton Down to Road at Rockley. E to Ogbourne Maizey and Cycle Route 482 back to start. Distance 27km.

Extend the area Aldbourne Map to the E.

Aldbourne p343. Riders: MB Swindon. © Tom Stickland

Aldbourne

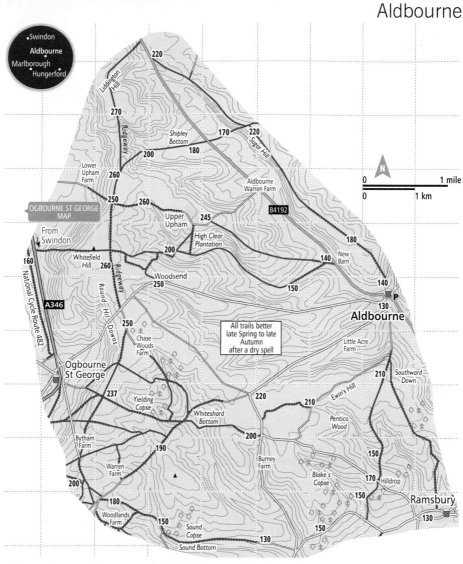

Situation: Set in a valley on the south slope of the Lambourne Downs, east of the Ridgeway National Trail in Wiltshire. 8 miles north east of Marlborough and north west of Hungerford.

About the Base: Aldbourne, a village with three pubs Further info: www.aldbourne.net.
Parking: Roadside in the centre of Aldbourne.
Grid Ref: SU264756. Post Code: SN8 2DU.

Drive Times: Oxford 50mins, Reading 50mins, Bristol 1hr, Southampton 1hr10, London 1hr30, Birmingham 1hr50.

Refreshments: At Aldbourne, The Pub on the Green 01672 540 237, The Crown at Aldbourne 01672 540 214 and The Masons Arms 01672 540 124. The Bell 01672 520 230 at Ramsbury or The Inn with the Well 01672 841 445 at Ogbourne St George.

Bike Shops: Bertie Maffoon's Bicycle Company 01672 519 119 in Marlborough or Supernova Cycles 01488 644 667 in Hungerford.

Books: South East MTB – Ridgeway & Chilterns (N.Cotton). MTB Guide Wiltshire (I.White).

Maps: OS Explorer 157.

Route Ideas

❶ From Aldbourne, S past Hilldrop. W along Sound Bottom. Trails NE from Bytham Farm. N along Round Hill Downs. E to Upper Upham, New Barn and road back to start. Distance 22km.

❷ Roads S from Aldbourne along Ewin's Hill. Trails and roads to Whiteshard Bottom. SE to pass Warren Farm then N to Bytham Farm. NE to Round Hill Downs. Ridgeway N to Liddington Hill and B4192. Back to start via trails E of the B4192. 25km.

Extend the area: Ogbourne St George Map to the W.

Lambourn

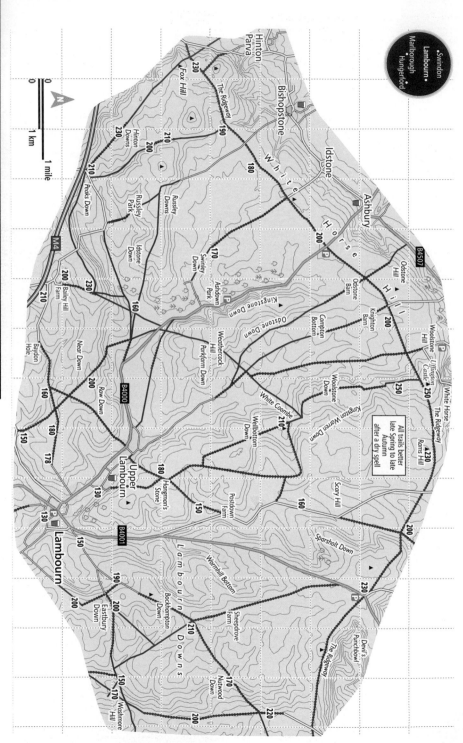

All trails better late spring to late Autumn after a dry spell

- Swindon
- Lambourn
- Marlborough
- Hungerford

Situation: In the Lambourn Downs, south of the Ridgeway in Berkshire. 7 miles north of Hungerford and 7 miles south west of Wantage.

About the Base: Lambourn, a village with three pubs. Further Info: www.lambourn.info.

Parking: Car parks in the centre of Lambourn, at National Trust Ashdown Park & Woolstone Hill. Also on The Ridgeway south west of Ashbury & at Devils Punchbowl. *Grid Ref: Lambourn SU325788, Ashdown Park SU292825, Woolstone Hill SU292866, Ashbury SU274843, Devils Punchbowl SU344849.*
Post Code: Lambourn RG17 8XL.

Drive Times: Reading 45mins, Oxford 50mins, Bristol 1hr, Southampton 1hr10, London 1hr30, Birmingham 2hrs.

Refreshments: At Lambourn, The George Hotel 01488 71889, The Wheelwright Arms 01488 71643 and The Lamb Inn 01488 71552. The Malt Shovel 01488 72916 at Upper Lambourn. The Rose & Crown 01793 710222 at Ashbury, The Bacon Wizard Breakfast Shop, The Royal Oak 01793 790 481 or The True Heart Inn 01793 790 080 at Bishopstone.

Bike Shops: Ridgeway Cycles 01235 764 445 in Wantage or Supernova Cycles 01488 644 667 in Hungerford.

Books: South East MTB – Ridgeway & Chilterns (N.Cotton). MTB Guide Wiltshire (I.White). MTB Rides to the SE (M.Darkins).

Maps: OS Explorer 158 & 170.

Route Ideas

❶ From Lambourn, N to Hangman's Stone, Postdown Farm and road up to the Ridgeway. W along the Ridgeway to Fox Hill. SE to Peaks Down. Road E to Blaydon Hole. Trails and road E to Lambourn. Distance 30km.

❷ From Lambourn, NE over Bockhampton Down & Nutwood Down to link to the Ridgeway. W along the Ridgeway to Uffington Castle. S over Woolstone Down & Wellbottom Down to Hangman's Stone & back to Lambourn. Distance 23km.

MTB Berkhamsted. © Steve Lloyd

East Ilsley

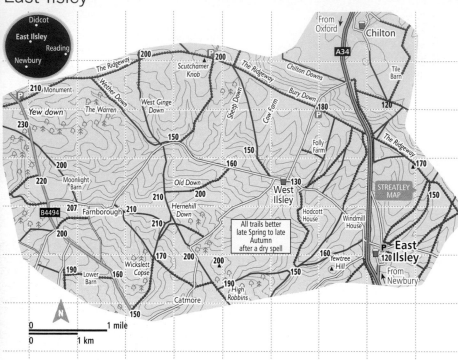

Situation: Just south of the Ridgeway National Trail in West Berkshire. 9 miles south east of Wantage and 10 miles north of Newbury.

About the Base: East Ilsley, a village with two pubs.

Parking: Roadside parking in East Ilsley. Car parks along The Ridgeway at Bury Down, Scutchamer Knob & Yew Down. *Grid Ref: East Ilsley SU493811, Bury Down SU479840, Scutchamer Knob SU457850, Yew Down SU418841.* **Post Code:** *East Ilsley RG20 7LH, Bury Down SU479840, Scutchamer Knob SU457850, Yew Down SU418841.*

Drive Times: Oxford 30mins, Reading 35mins, Southampton 1hr, Bristol 1hr10, London 1hr20, Birmingham 1hr40.

Refreshments: At East Ilsley, The Star Inn 0163528 1215 and The Crown & Horns 01635 281 545. The Harrow Inn 01635 281260 at West Ilsley or The Rose & Crown 01235 862 992 and The Ridgeway Café 01235 821 444 at Chilton.

Bike Shops: Trailjunkies Mountain Bike Centre 01491 871 721, 8 miles away at Streatley, Ridgeway Cycles 01235 764 445 in Wantage or Banjo Cycles 01635 43186 in Newbury.

Books: South East MTB – Ridgeway & Chilterns (N.Cotton).

Maps: OS Explorer 158 & 170.

Route Idea

From East Ilsley, trails NW to the Ridgeway. W along the Ridgeway. S across West Ginge Down & Hernehill Down to High Robbins. E back to East Ilsley. Distance 19km.

Extend the area: Streatley Map to the E.

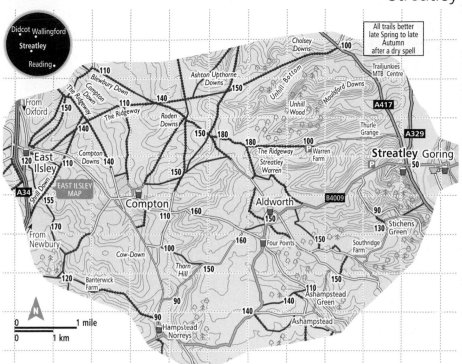

Situation: In the Goring Gap on the River Thames in Berkshire. On the Ridgeway National Trail, close to the Oxfordshire border, 10 miles north west of Reading.

About the Base: Streatley, a village with a pub and easy access to the trails.
Further Info: www.streatley.org. **Parking:** Car park west of Streatley on B4009 or car park on The Ridgeway at Warren Farm. **Grid Ref:** Streatley SU583806, Warren Farm SU566811. **Post Code:** Streatley RG8 9RB.

Drive Times: Reading 30mins, Oxford 40mins, Southampton 1hr20, Bristol 1hr20, London 1hr30, Birmingham 1hr50.

Trains: Goring & Streatley Station is on the Reading-Oxford line.

Refreshments: The Bull at Streatley 01491 872 392 at Streatley and a choice of pubs or Pierreponts Cafe 01491 874 464 across the river at Goring. The Star Inn 0163528 1215 and The Crown & Horns 01635 281 545 at East Ilsley, The White Hart 01635 202 248 at Hampstead Norreys, The Four Points 01635 578 367 and The Bell Inn 01635 578 272 at Aldworth. The Compton Swan 01635 579 400 at Compton.

Bike Shops: Trailjunkies Mountain Bike Centre 01491 871 721, north of Streatley off the A417 or Mountain High 0118 984 1851, 4 miles away in Pangbourne.

Books: South East MTB – Ridgeway & Chilterns (N.Cotton). MTB Rides to the SE (M.Darkins).

Maps: OS Explorer 171, 170 & 158.

Route Idea

From Warren Farm car park, W along the Ridgeway almost to East Ilsley. S to Hampstead Norreys via Shrill Down and Banterwick Farm. Road to Aldworth. N to the Ridgeway and back to the start. Distance 22km.

Extend the area: East Ilsley Map to the W.

Collingbourne Kingston

Situation: On the River Bourne in Wiltshire. 10 miles south of Marlborough. **About the Base:** Collingbourne Kingston, a village with a pub and easy access to the trails. Further Info: www.collingbournekingston. org.uk. **Parking:** Roadside in Collingbourne Kingston. Layby north of the village on A338. **Grid Ref:** *Collingbourne Kingston*

SU238557, A338 Layby SU237574. **Post Code:** *Collingbourne Kingston SN8 3SZ, A338 Layby SN8 3RY.*

Drive Times: Oxford 1hr, Reading 1hr, Southampton 1hr, Bristol 1hr10, London 1hr50, Birmingham 2hr10.

Refreshments: The Barleycorn Inn 01264

850 368 at Collingbourne Kingston. The Blue Lion 07973 915951 at Collingbourne Ducis, The Shears Inn 01264 850 304 ay Cadley, The Cross Keys 01264 730 295 at Upper Chute and The Hatchet Inn 01264 730 229 at Lower Chute.

Bike Shops: The Bike Shop 07795 574

492, 4 miles away in Luggershall, Bertie Maffoon's Bicycle Company 01672 519 119 in Marlborough or Behind the Bikeshed 01264 338 794 in Andover.

Books: MTB Rides to the SW (M.Darkins).

Maps: OS Explorer 131 & 130.

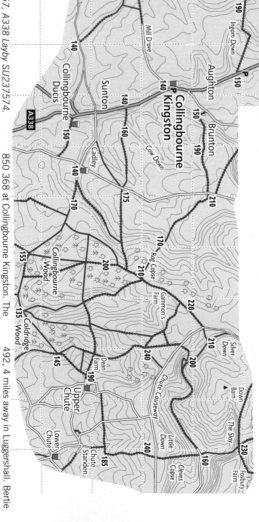

Route Idea

W along Mill Drove and on to Lower Everleigh. N past Down Farm and Milton Hill Farm. SE to Aughton Down and E across Ingham Down to A338. Road to Brunton. Trails to Rag Copse. NE to Silver Down & on to Down Barn, The Slay, Little Down. Trails to Upper Chute. W to Cadley via Coldridge & Collingbourne Woods. Road back to start. Distance 42km. W to Cadley via loops, both of which can be started at Collingbourne Kingston. The W loop is 19km. The E loop is 23km.

Extend the area: Hurstbourne Tarrant Map to the NE.

Hurstbourne Tarrant

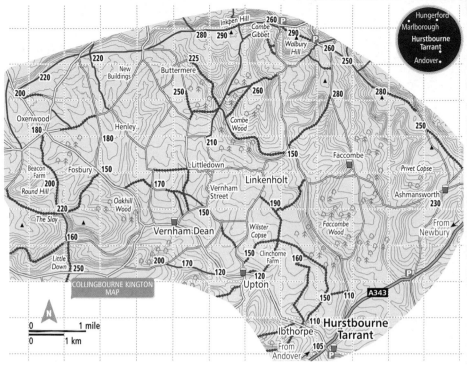

Situation: South of Walbury Hill in the Test Valley in Hampshire. Close to the Wiltshire and Berkshire borders, 5 miles north west of Andover and 11 miles south west of Newbury.

About the Base: Hurstbourne Tarrant, a village with a pub. Further Info: www.hbt.org.uk. **Parking:** Car park at parish hall, south east of Hurstbourne Tarrant on B3048. Parking on A343 to Newbury. Car parks at Walbury Hill. **Grid Ref:** *Hurstbourne Tarrant SU382530, A343 SU406550, Walbury Hill SU378616 or SU365622.* **Post Code:** *Hurstbourne Tarrant SP11 0AD.*

Drive Times: Reading 45mins, Oxford 50mins, Southampton 50mins, Bristol 1hr20, London 1hr30, Birmingham 2hrs.

Trains: Andover Station is on the Salisbury-Reading & Salisbury-London lines.

Refreshments: The George & Dragon 01264 736 277 at Hurstbourne Tarrant. The Plough 01635 253 047 at Ashmansworth, The Jack Russell Inn 01264 737 315 at Faccombe, The George Inn 01264 737 279 at Vernham Dean and The Crown Inn 01264 736265 at Upton.

Bike Shops: Behind the Bikeshed 01264 338 794 in Andover. North Hants Bikes 01256 893 501, 7 miles away in Whitchurch, for parts & hire.

Books: South East MTB – Ridgeway & Chilterns (N.Cotton). MTB Guide Wiltshire (I.White). MTB Rides to the SW (M.Darkins).

Maps: OS Explorer 131.

Route Ideas

❶ Hurstbourne Tarrant, NW to Ibthorpe. Trails N then roads to Faccombe & Ashmansworth. Trails NW to Inkpen Hill then W to road N of Oxenwood. Trails and roads S to The Slay and Little Down. Road and trails to Upton. N to pass Clinchorne Farm then S to Ibthorpe & back to start. Distance 42km.

❷ Hurstbourne Tarrant, road & trails N to Linkenholt. Trails through Combe Wood to Buttermere to join above route after Inkpen Hill. Distance 35km.

Extend the area:
Collingbourne Kington Map to the S.

Kingsclere

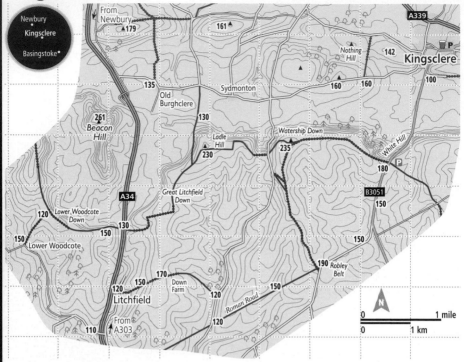

Situation: Near to Watership Down in Hampshire, close to the Berkshire border. 8 miles south west of Newbury and 9 miles north west of Basingstoke.

About the Base: Kingsclere, a large village with three pubs and accommodation.
Further Info: www.kingsclere.gov.uk. **Parking:** Car park in the centre of Kingsclere or White Hill Car Park south of the village on the B3051. **Grid Ref:** *Kingsclere SU516564, White Hill SU516565.*
Post Code: *Kingsclere RG25 3EJ.*

Drive Times: Reading 40mins, Oxford 50mins, Southampton 50mins, London 1hr20, Bristol 1hr30, Birmingham 2hrs.

Trains: Overton Railway Station, 5 miles away, is on the Salisbury-Reading & Salisbury-London lines.

Refreshments: At Kingsclere, The Crown 01635 299 558, The George & Horn 01635 299 130 and The Swan Hotel 01635 298 314.

Bike Shops: Pedal On 0118 982 1021, 5 miles away near Tadley,.

Books: South East MTB – Ridgeway & Chilterns (N.Cotton). MTB Rides to the SE (M.Darkins).

Maps: OS Explorer 144.

Route Idea

Set out from from White Hill car park, to the S of Kingsclere. W past Watership Down, Ladle Hill, Great Litchfield Down, Lower Woodcote Down. Roads to Litchfield. Trails and road to join the Roman Road. At Robley Belt follow roads back to start.
Distance 23km.

Cherhill White Horse. © Dave Robinson SPAM

Marlborough Downs. © Dave Robinson SPAM

North Downs & Surrey Hills

Unlike the South Downs Way, the North Downs Way, running east from Farnham to Canterbury and on to Dover, is a mixture of footpaths (where you are NOT allowed to ride), bridleways and byways (where you may ride). It is also known as the Pilgrims Way as it was the course of the pilgrimage made by people on their way to Canterbury. Routes tend to consist of lots of short sections of trails linked by tarmac and they are definitely better second and third time around when you know in advance where to go at each junction without looking at the map. One unusual feature of the North Downs is the underlying sandy soils on parts of the trails: there are times in a dry spell when riding on the North Downs, say around Leith Hill, is like riding along a soft beach. This is one of the few places where wet weather is sometimes a bonus as the sand is harder packed.

© Nick Cotton

© Richard Kelly www.allbikedup.com

There are several areas with dense concentrations of rideable tracks: around Guildford there are good bases at **Puttenham**, with access to what feels like a mountain bike playground on Puttenham Common; east from **Shalford** the North Downs Way climbs up through sand to the cathedral on the hill; from **Godalming** bridleways radiate south-east over the wooded slopes of Hyde Heath and Hascombe Hill; whilst **Shere** makes a good centre for exploring tracks north into the densely wooded chalk hills stretching from Newlands Corner to Westhumble and south into the sandy soils leading towards Pitch Hill, Holmbury Hill and Leith Hill. The latter, at 294m, represents the highest point in the South East.

Further east, **Reigate Hill** and **Godstone** both give access to bridleways running through broadleaf woodland either side of the M25. The views from **Reigate Hill** are particularly fine.

In the Sevenoaks-Maidstone area you will notice the transition from sandy heathland to Kentish orchards. There are good bases at **Ide Hill** and **Ightham** - trails go right past the extraordinary house at Ightham Mote and also into the very spooky Mereworth Woods. North of here the Pilgrims Way from **Trottiscliffe** goes past the ancient long barrow at Coldrum.

Deep into Kent, north of Ashford, one of the longest rideable sections of the North Downs Way runs east from Hollingbourne (east of Maidstone) for almost 20km, passing north of **Charing** to reach Westwell (north of Ashford). The attractive village of **Chilham** is an excellent place to be based for a weekend with a good network of bridleways stretching from King's Wood southeast to the Roman Road of Stone Street. Towards the coast and the famous white cliffs there are several rides starting from **Hythe** and

Lyminge running east above Folkestone towards Dover, the endpoint of the North Downs Way.

Although there are no Trail Centres in this area, there are singletrack trails to explore around Holmbury Hill near Reigate (**The Hurtwood Estate**) and cross country trails at **Fowlmead Country Park**.

© Richard Kelly www.allbikedup.com

353

© Richard Kelly www.allbikedup.com

Yateley Common

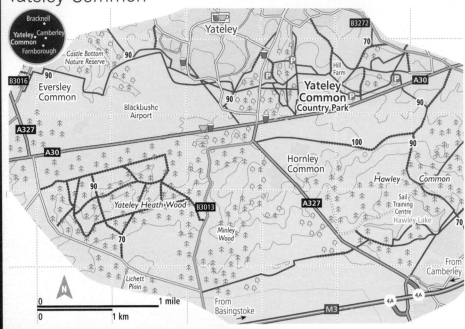

Bracknell
Yateley Common • Camberley • Farnborough
Yateley
Castle Bottom Nature Reserve
B3016
Eversley Common
A327
A30
Blackbushe Airport
90
90
B3272
70
Hill Farm
Yateley Common Country Park
A30
90
100
Hornley Common
Hawley   Common
A327
Sail Training Centre
Hawley Lake
70
Yateley Heath Wood
B3013
Minley Wood
Lichett Plain
From Basingstoke
From Camberley
M3
4A 4A

N

0   1 mile
0   1 km

Situation: South of Yateley in Hampshire, close to the Berkshire and Surrey borders. 5 miles north of Fleet and 6 miles north west of Farnborough.

About the Base: Yateley Common, a country park with easy access to the trails. Further info: www3.hants.gov.uk/countryside/yateley-country-park.htm

Parking: Car parks at Yateley Common Country Park.

Grid Ref: Wyndham's Pool SU821596, Cricket Hill SU824597, A30 SU833592, Hayward's Cottage SU837595,

Drive Times: Southampton 45mins, London 1hr, Oxford 1hr10, Bristol 1hr40, Birmingham 2hr20.

Trains: Blackwater Railway Station, 3 miles away, is on the Guildford-Reading line. Fleet Station is on the London-Salisbury & London-Southampton lines.

Refreshments: Choice of pubs and cafés at Yateley. The Cricketers 01252 872 105 in the start of the ride. The Bushe Café 07949 574 524 at Blackbushe Airport and The Ely 01252 860444 at Yateley Common.

Bike Shops: Cycle Kingdom 01252 624 136 in Fleet.

Books: MTB Rides to the SE (M.Darkins).

Maps: OS Explorer 145.

Route Idea

From The Country Park, trails W to Eversley Common. S through Yateley Heath Wood. Trails E to and around Hawley Lake, over Hawley Common and back to start. Distance 19km.

© Dirt Divas / Graeme Warren

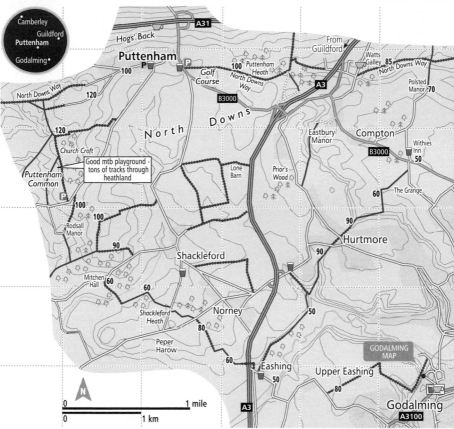

Situation: Just south the chalk ridge of the North Downs, The Hog's Back. 5 miles west of Guildford and 7 miles east of Farnham.

About the Base: Puttenham, a village with two pubs and easy access to the trails. **Parking:** Roadside parking in Puttenham. Car parks at Puttenham Golf Course & Puttenham Common. *Grid Ref: Puttenham SU931478, Puttenham Golf Course SU935477,Puttenham Common SU919462, A31 SU927482. Post Code: Puttenham GU3 1AR, Puttenham Golf Course GU3 1AJ.*

Drive Times: London 1hr, Southampton 1hr10, Brighton 1hr20, Bristol 2hrs, Birmingham 2hr20.

Trains: Godalming Railway Station, in the south east of the map, is on the London-Portsmouth line.

Refreshments: At Puttenham, The Good Intent 01483 810387 and The Jolly Farmer 01483 810374. The Hog's Back café 01483 813724 on A31. Tea Shop at Watt's Gallery, The Withies Inn 01483 421158 or The Harrow Inn 01483 810379 at Compton. The Squirrel 01483 860223 at Hurtmore and The Stag on the River 01483 421568 at Eashing. Pubs & cafés at Guildford or The Cyder House Inn 01483 810360 at Shackleford.

Bike Shops: Godalming Cycles 01483 420036 in Godalming, Cycleworks 01483 302210, Pedal Pushers 01483 502327 & Raleigh Cycle Centre 01483 504932 in Guildford.

Books: South East MTB – N & S Downs (N.Cotton).

Maps: OS Explorer 145.

Route Idea

From Puttenham Common, trails N to the North Downs Way. E on North Downs Way past Puttenham, Puttenham Heath & the A3. S past Polsted Manor to Hurtmore & on to Eashing. NW to Mitchen Hall. Road & trails to Rodsall Manor & back to start. Distance 19km.

Extend the area: Godalming Map to the SE.

Puttenham Common. Riders: VCGH © Mark Reynolds

Godalming

Map labels: Farncombe, Catteshall, PUTTENHAM MAP, A3100, Godalming, Munstead Heath 120, Busbridge, Busbridge Lakes, Tuesley, Milford Sta, Enton Green, Hydestile, Hydon Heath, Hydon's Ball 150, 140, Vann Hill 150, Juniper Valley, B2130, Winkworth Arboretum, The Hurtwood 130, 160, Bramley, 80 50, SHERE/SHALFORD MAP, Birtley Green, National Cycle Route 22, Thorncombe Street, A281, Rushett Common, Grafham, Selhurst Common, Hascombe, 110, 170, 150, Nore, Hascombe Hill

Tricky route-finding around Hascombe: loads of tracks on ground

Woking, Guildford, Godalming, Cranleigh

0 1 mile
0 1 km

N

Situation: On the River Wey, surrounded by the Surrey Hills Area of Outstanding Natural Beauty. 4 miles south west of Guildford.

About the Base: Godalming, a market town with pubs, cafés and accommodation.
Further Info: www.godalming-tc.gov.uk.

Parking: Car parks in Godalming, at Winkworth Arboretum & Hydon Heath. **Grid Ref:** *Godalming SU971440, Winkworth Arboretum SU989411, Hydon Heath SU978401.* **Post Code:** *Godalming GU7 1HW, Winkworth Arboretum GU8 4AD.*

Drive Times: London 1hr10, Brighton 1hr20, Southampton 1hr20, Bristol 2hr10, Birmingham 2hr30.

Trains: Godalming, Farncombe & Milford Stations are on the London -Portsmouth line.

Refreshments: Plenty of pubs & cafés at Godalming. Hectors Café 01483 418769 at Catteshall, The Jolly Farmer 01483 893355 or The Bramley Café 01483 894037 at Bramley. The White Horse 01483 208 at Hascombe or National Trust café at Winkworth Arboretum.

Bike Shops: Godalming Cycles 01483 420036 in Godalming, Beyond Mountain Bikes 01483 267676, south of Bramley on the A281, or bike shops in Guildford.

Books: MTB Rides to the SE (M.Darkins).

Maps: OS Explorer 145.

Route Idea

From Godalming, Roads E to Catteshall. Trails to Bramley. S on National Cycle Route 22 to Birtley Green. Trails & roads S to Selhurst Common, S to Nore. W to Hascombe across The Hurtwood to Vann Hill. N across Hydon Heath to Busbridge Lakes and back to Godalming. Distance 22km.

Extend the area: Puttenham Map to the NW. Shalford/ Shere Map to the NE

Rider: VCGH ©Mark Reynolds

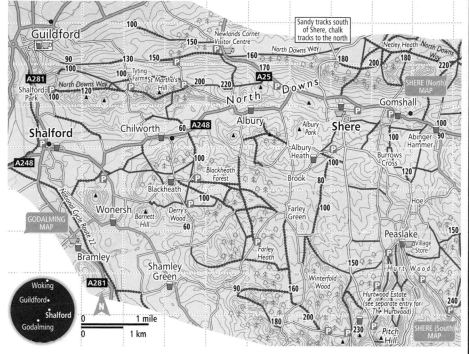

Situation: At the confluence of the River Tillingbourne and the River Wey, Shalford lies at the edge of the Surrey Hills, 2 miles south fo Guildford. Shere, 5 miles to the east, is in the Tillingbourne Valley at the foot of the North Downs.

About the Base: Shalford, a village with two pubs and a railway station. **Parking:** Car park in Shalford Park or next to the railway station in Shalford. Car parks in the centre of Shere near to The Manor House, at Albury Heath south of the village or Gomshall to the east. Several car parks on the Hurtwood Estate & throughout the map area. *Grid Ref: Shalford Park TQ003483, Shalford Station TQ001470, Shere TQ072479, Albury Heath TQ071469, Gomshall TQ085478. Post Code: Shalford GU4 8AW, Shalford Station GU4 8JZ, Shere GU5 9HF, Gomshall GU5 9LB.*

Drive Times: London 1hr, Brighton 1hr10, Southampton 1hr30, Bristol 2hr10, Birmingham 2hr30.

Trains: Shalford, Chilworth & Gomshall Stations are on the Guildford-Dorking North Downs line.

Refreshments: At Shalford, The Queen Victoria 01483 561733, The Seahorse 01483 514351 and The Parrot Inn 01483 561400. New Barn Café at Newlands Corner Visitor Centre 01483 222820, The Drummond 01483 202039 at Albury and The William IV 01483 202685 at Albury Heath. Pubs & cafés at Shere, Compasses Inn 01483 202685 at Gomshall and The Abinger Arms 01306 730145 at Abinger Hammer. The Hurtwood Inn 01306 730851 or refreshments at Peaslake Village Stores 01306 730474 at Peaslake. The Windmill 01483 277566 at Pitch Hill. The Jolly Farmer 01483 893355 or The Bramley Café 01483 894037 at Bramley, The Grantley Arms 01483 893351 at Womersh, The Villagers Inn 01483

893152 at Blackheath and The Percy Arms 01483 561765 at Chilworth.

Bike Shops: Pedal & Spoke 01306 731639 in Peaslake, Beyond Mountain Bikes 01483 267676, south of Bramley on the A281, Cycleworks 01483 302210, Pedal Pushers 01483 502327 & Raleigh Cycle Centre 01483 504932 in Guildford.

Books: South East MTB – N & S Downs (N.Cotton).

Maps: Surrey Hills Map Pack, Surrey Hills Maps 2 & 3 (Trailmaps). OS Explorer 145.

Route Ideas

❶ From Shalford Park, trails E to Albury, S to Blackheath via Blackheath Forest. N on the Downs Link towards St Martha's Hill. W on The North Downs Way back to start. Distance 15km.

❷ From Shalford Park, trails E to Albury, Albury Heath, Shere & Abinger Hammer. N to the North Downs Way.W on North Down From Shalford Park, trails E to Albury, S to Blackheath via Blackheath Forest. N on s Way back to start. Distance 27km.

❸ Explore the unmapped trails on the Hurtwood Estate, see the Surrey Hills entry for further info.

Extend the area: Godalming Map to the SW, Shere (south) Map to the E. Shere (north) Map to the NE.

Also see trail info for The Hurtwood Estate, SE corner of the map on (p375) and Leith Hill (p376) which is just to the east of the map.

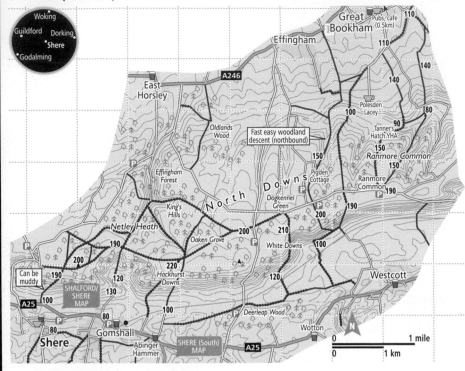

Shere (north)

Woking
Guildford Dorking
Shere
Godalming

Great Bookham — Pubs, cafe (0.5km) 110
Effingham
110
140
A246
East Horsley
140
Polesden Lacey
100
90
80
Tanner's Hatch YHA
Oldlands Wood
Fast easy woodland descent (northbound)
150
150
Ranmore Common
150
Effingham Forest
Pigden Cottage
Ranmore Common 190
King's Hills
North Downs
Dogkennel Green
190
200
Netley Heath
Oaken Grove
200
210
White Downs 100
190
200
220
Hackhurst Downs
120
Westcott
Can be muddy
190
120
130
120
SHALFORD/ SHERE MAP
A25 100
100
Deerleap Wood
80
80
Gomshall
Wotton
Shere
Abinger Hammer
SHERE (South) MAP
A25

0 — 1 mile
0 — 1 km

Situation: In the Tillingbourne Valley, between the North Downs and the Surrey Hills. 6 miles south east of Guildford and 6 miles west of Dorking.

About the Base: Shere, a village with two pubs and tearooms. **Parking:** Car parks in the centre of Shere near to The Manor House, in Gomshall & throughout the map area. *Grid Ref: Shere TQ072479, Gomshall TQ085478.* **Post Code:** *Shere GU5 9HF, Gomshall GU5 9LB.*

Drive Times: London 1hr, Brighton 1hr10, Southampton 1hr30, Bristol 2hr20, Birmingham 2hr30.

Trains: Gomshall Station is on the Guildford-Dorking North Downs line.

Refreshments: At Shere, The Prince of Wales 01483 202313, The White Horse 01483 202518, The Lucky Duck Tea Room 01483 202445 and Nell's Country Kitchen 01483 202445. The Duke of Wellington 01483 282164 at East Horsley. Courtyard Coffee Shop 01372 458203 at National Trust Polesdon Lacey, The Crown Inn 01306 885414 at Westcott, The Wotton Hatch 01306 887694 at Wotton, The Abinger Arms 01306 730145 at Abinger Hammer or Compasses Inn 01483 202685 at Gomshall.

Bike Shops: Nirvana Cycles 01306 740300 in Westcott for hire, parts & repairs. Head for the Hills 01306 885007 in Dorking or bike shops in Guildford.

Books: South East MTB – N & S Downs (N.Cotton).

Maps: Surrey Hills Map Pack, Surrey Hills Map 4 (Trailmaps). OS Explorer 145 & 146.

Route Idea

From Shere, trails N to Netley Heath. E across King's Hills towards Dogkennel Green. Trails N past Pigden Cottage and on to outskirts of Great Bookham. Trails S across Ranmore Common & on to Westcott. W past Deerleap Wood to Abinger Hammer. Trails & roads back to Shere. Distance 28km.

Extend the area: Shalford/ Shere Map to the SW. Shere (south) Map to the south.

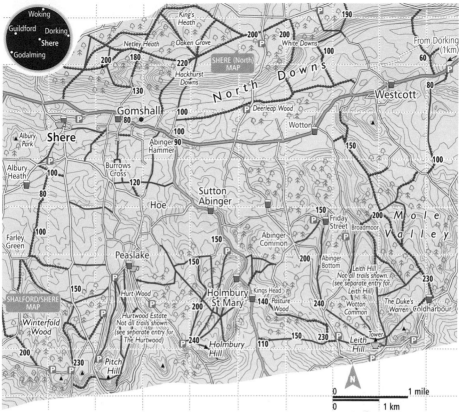

Situation: Between the North Downs and the Surrey Hills in the Tillingbourne Valley. 6 miles south east of Guildford and 6 miles west of Dorking.

About the Base: Shere, a village with two pubs and tearooms. **Parking:** Car parks in the centre of Shere near to The Manor House, at Albury Heath south of the village or Gomshall to the east. Several car parks on the Hurtwood Estate & throughout the map area. *Grid Ref: Shere TQ072479, Albury Heath TQ071469, Gomshall TQ085478. Post Code: Shere GU5 9HF, Gomshall GU5 9LB.*

Drive Times: London 1hr, Brighton 1hr10, Southampton 1hr30, Bristol 2hr20, Birmingham 2hr30.

Trains: Gomshall Station is on the Guildford-Dorking North Downs line.

Refreshments: At Shere, The Prince of Wales 01483 202313, The White Horse 01483 202518, The Lucky Duck Tea Room 01483 202445 and Nell's Country Kitchen 01483 202445. Compasses Inn 01483 202685 at Gomshall, The Abinger Arms 01306 730145 at Abinger Hammer, and The Crown Inn 01306 885414 at Westcott. The Plough Inn 01306 711793 at Coldharbour or refreshments at National Trust Leith Hill Tower 01306 712711. The Stephan Langton 01306 730775 at Friday Street, The Abinger Hatch 01306 730737 at Abinger Common, The Volunteer 01306 730798 at Sutton Abinger, The Royal Oak 01306 730120 or The Kings Head 01306 730282 at Holmbury St Mary. The

Hurtwood Inn 01306 730851 or refreshments at Peaslake Village Stores 01306 730474 at Peaslake.

Bike Shops: Pedal & Spoke 01306 731639 in Peaslake, Nirvana Cycles 01306 740300 in Westcott for hire, parts & repairs. Head for the Hills 01306 885007 in Dorking or bike shops in Guildford.

Books: South East MTB – N & S Downs (N.Cotton). MTB Rides to the SE (M.Darkins).

Maps: Surrey Hills Map Pack, Surrey Hills Map 1 (Trailmaps). OS Explorer 145 & 146.

Route Ideas

❶ From Shere, trails & road S through Winterfold Wood & on to Pitch Hill. Trail N on E side of Pitch Hill to Peaslake. Road SE towards Holmbury Hill. Trails towards The Kings Head then across Pasture Wood. N to Friday Street, E past Broadmoor and trails to Westcott. Back to Shere via Deerleap Wood & Abinger Hammer. Distance 28km.

❷ Large choice of alternative trails and roads to lengthen or shorten as required.

❸ Many unmarked trails to explore in the Hurtwood Estate & around Leith Hill (see Surrey Hills entry for further info).

Extend the area: Shere (north map). Shalford/Shere Map to the W.

Also see trail info for The Hurtwood Estate (p375) and Leith Hill (p376), both in the south area of the map.

Reigate Hill

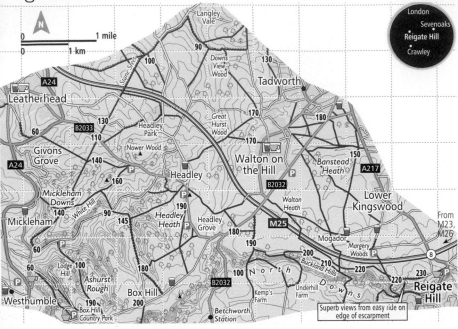

Situation: East of the Mole Valley, on the edge of the North Downs in Surrey. 2 miles north of Reigate and close to M25 Junction 8.

About the Base: Reigate Hill a rural location with a car park and refreshments. **Parking:** National Trust car park at Reigate Hill. Car parks north of the M25 at Margery Wood & Walton on the Hill. Parking at several points west of the M25. Car park next to the River Mole at Westhumble & at Boxhill Country Park. *Grid Ref: Reigate Hill TQ262523, Margery Wood TQ245527, Walton on the Hill TQ227544, Westhumble TQ171520, Boxhill TQ178513. Post Code: Reigate Hill RH2 9RP, Walton on the Hill KT20 7QS, Westhumble RH5 6BX.*

Drive Times: London 50mins, Brighton 50mins, Southampton 1hr20, Bristol 2hr10, Birmingham 2hr20.

Trains: Reigate & Betchworth Stations are on the London Bridge-Reading line. Westhumble Station is on the London Victoria-Littlehampton line. Tadworth Station has services to London Bridge.

Refreshments: At Reigate Hill, The Yew Tree 01737 244944 and Café at Reigate Hill Car Park. The Mint Arms 01737 242957 at Lower Kingswood, The Sportsman 01737 246655 at Mogador, pubs &cafés at Walton on the Hill. The Cock Inn 01372 377258 at Headley. The Running Horses 01372 372279 at Mickleham, Rykas Café 01306 884454 next to the river at Westhumble, National Trust Cafe 01306 885502 at Boxhill Country Park or The Hand at Hand 01737 843352 at Boxhill.

Bike Shops: Finch Cycles 01737 242 163 in Reigate for parts & repairs & hire at National Trust Visitor Centre 01306 885502 in Boxhill. Cycle Hire 01306 886944 at Westhumble Station.

Books: South East MTB – N & S Downs (N.Cotton).

Maps: OS Explorer 146.

© Nick Cotton

Route Idea

From Reigate Hill, mostly trails towards Lower Kingswood then NW across Banstead Heath, through Walton on the Hill, past Downs View Wood towards Langley Vale. SW along Stane Street (Roman Road). Across Mickleham Downs. Across Ashurst Rough to Box Hill. Trails over Headley Heath towards Headley. Trails SE, along the Buckland Hills and back to the start. Distance 30km.

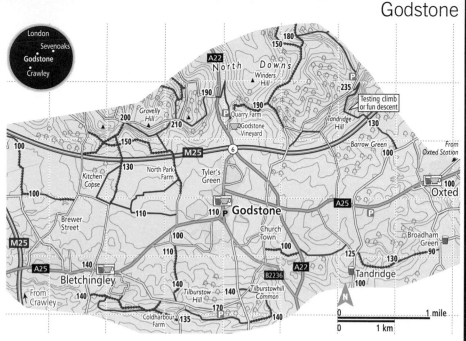

Situation: On the southern edge of the North Downs in Surrey. 5 miles east of Redhill and close to M25 Junction 6.

About the Base: Godstone, a village with pubs & café. Further Info: www.godstone.net.

Parking: Roadside, around The Green in the centre of Godstone. Layby on the A25 west of Oxted. Car park nr Quarry Farm on A22 & at Tilburstow Hill. *Grid Ref: Godstone TQ350516, A25 TQ375518, Quarry Farm TQ350533, Tilburstow Hill TQ349500. Post Code: Godstone RH9 8LU.*

Drive Times: Maidstone 40mins, Brighton 50mins, London 50mins, Bristol 2hr20, Birmingham 2hr30.

Trains: South Godstone Station, a mile south of the map, is on the London-Ashford line.

Refreshments: At Godstone, The Whitehart 01883 742521, The Bell Inn 01883 741877, The Hare and Hounds 01883 742296 and The Old Forge Café 01883 743230. The Barley Mow 01883 713770 at Tandridge, The Haycutter Inn 01883 712550 at Broadham Green. Pubs & cafés at Oxted. Cafe at Godstone Vineyard 01883 744590. Pubs & cafés at Bletchingley.

Bike Shops: Petra Cycles 01883 715114 in Oxted.

Books: South East MTB – N & S Downs (N.Cotton). MTB Rides to the SE (M.Darkins).

Maps: OS Explorer 146.

Route Idea

From the car park at Tilburstow Hill, trail W then N to outskirts of Godstone. Trails W towards Kitchen Copse then E along Gravelly Hill. On to Oxted via Quarry Farm, Tandridge Hill then Barrow Green. S to Broadham Green. W towards Tandridge and Church Town. N over Tilburstowhill and back to start. Distance 23km.

© Nick Cotton

Ide Hill

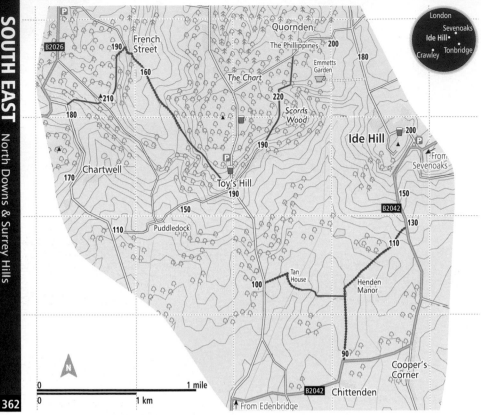

London
Sevenoaks
Ide Hill •
Crawley • • Tonbridge

B2026 French Street 190 160 210 180

Quornden 200 The Phillippines 180 Emmetts Garden The Chart 220 Scords Wood 190

Ide Hill 200 From Sevenoaks

190 Toy's Hill 150 B2042 150 130

Chartwell 170 150 110 Puddledock 110

100 Tan House Henden Manor

90 Cooper's Corner

B2042 Chittenden

From Edenbridge

0 ——— 1 mile
0 ——— 1 km

Situation: One of the highest points on a sandstone ridge of the North Downs in Kent. 4 miles south west of Sevenoaks and 9 miles north west of Tonbridge.

About the Base: Ide Hill, a small village with two pubs and easy access to the trails.
Further Info: www.ide-hill.co.uk. **Parking:** Car parks in Ide Hill, Toy's Hill & at National Trust Emmetts Garden. *Grid Ref: Ide Hill TQ488517, Toy's Hill TQ469516, Emmetts Garden TQ477524. Post Code: Ide Hill TN14 6JG, Toy's Hill TN16 1QG, Emmetts Garden TN14 6BA.*

Drive Times: Maidstone 40mins, London 1hr, Brighton 1hr10, Bristol 2hr30, Birmingham 2hr40.

Trains: Edenbridge Railway Station, 3 miles south east of the map is on the London-Ashford line. Edenbridge Town Station is on the London-Uckfield line. Sevenoaks Station is on the London-Hastings line.

Refreshments: At Ide Hill, The Cock Inn 01732 750310 and The Woodman 01732 750296. The Fox and Hounds 01732 750328 at Toy's Hill and Tearooms 01732 868381 at National Trust Emmetts Garden.

Bike Shops: The Bike Warehouse 01732 464997 in Sevenoaks or Cycles UK 01732 365718 in Tonbridge.

Books: MTB Guide Kent (G.Tompsett).

Maps: OS Explorer 147.

Route Idea

From Ide Hill, S past Henden Manor to Chittenden. Roads N to Toy's Hillthen Chartwell. Trails to French Street and on to Toy's Hill. Back to Ide Hill via Scords Wood and Quorndon. Distance 17km.

© Dirt Divas / Graeme Warren

Ightham

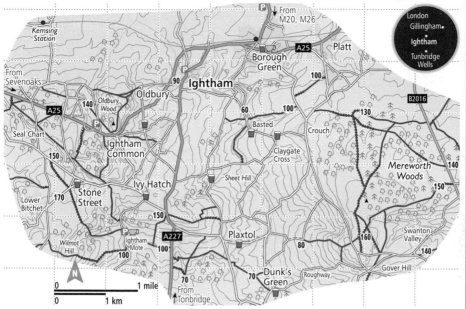

Situation: At the source of the River Bourne in the Kent Downs Area of Outstanding Natural Beauty. 5 miles north east of Sevenoaks and 7 miles north of Tonbridge.

About the Base: Ightham, a village with two pubs. Further Info: www.ightham.org. **Parking:** Car parks at Ightham Village Hall, Oldbury Wood & National Trust Ightham Mote. **Grid Ref:** *Ightham TQ594566, Oldbury Wood TQ578558, Ightham Mote TQ584535.* **Post Code:** *Ightham TN15 9HA, Ightham Mote TN15 0NT.*

Drive Times: Maidstone 30mins, London 1hr, Brighton 1hr10, Bristol 2hr40, Birmingham 2hr40.

Trains: Borough Green & Kemsing Stations are on the London Victoria-Ashford line.

Refreshments: At Ightham, The Chequers Inn 01732 882396 and The George & Dragon 01732 882440. The Harrow Inn 01732 885912 at Ightham Common, The Padwell Arms 01732 761532 at Stone Street, The Plough at Ivy Hatch and Café at National Trust Ightham Mote 01732 810378. The Papermakers Arms 01732 810407 and The Golding Hop 01732 882150 at Plaxtol or The Kentish Rifleman 01732 810727 at Dunk's Green. Chequers Inn 01732 884829 at Claygate Cross and The Plough 01732 885689 at Basted. If arriving by train, Cafe King 01732 886207 and The Black Horse 01732 885332 at Borough Green.

Bike Shops: The Bike Warehouse 01732 464997 in Sevenoaks or Cycles UK 01732 365718 in Tonbridge.

Books: South East MTB – N & S Downs (N.Cotton). MTB Rides to the SE (M.Darkins).

Maps: OS Explorer 147 & 148.

Route Idea

From Ightham, W through Oldbury Wood , then road and trails W. Cross over the A25 then SE to Ivy Hatch. Trail and roads E to climb up and into Mereworth Woods to the B2016 and head N. Back into Mereworth Woods towards Crouch then roads and trails to Ightham. Distance 23km.

© Nick Cotton

Trottiscliffe

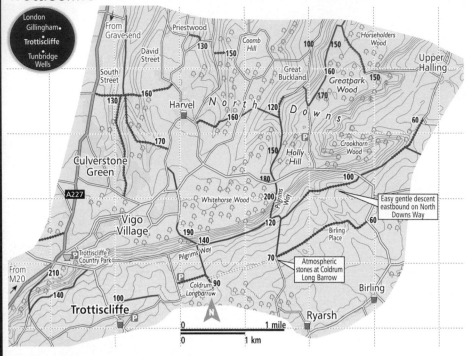

Situation: Above the Medway Valley, at the edge of the Kent Downs Area of Outstanding Natural Beauty, on the North Downs. 9 miles north west of Maidstone and 10 miles north east of Sevenoaks.

About the Base: Trottiscliffe, a village with two pubs. Further Info: www.trottiscliffevillage.co.uk.

Parking: Car parks at Trottiscliffe Village Hall, Trottiscliffe Country Park, Coldrum Longbarrow & Holly Hill. *Grid Ref: Trottiscliffe TQ643602, Country Park TQ632610, Coldrum Longbarrow TQ650607, Holly Hill TQ669629. Post Code: Trottiscliffe ME19 5EH, Country Park DA13 0SG, Coldrum Longbarrow ME19 5EL.*

Drive Times: Maidstone 20mins, London 1hr, Brighton 1hr10, Bristol 2hr40, Birmingham 2hr40.

Trains: Halling Railway Station, 1 mile east of the map, is on the Snood-Maidstone line. Borough Green Railway Station, 3 miles south west of the map, is on the London Victoria-Ashford line.

Refreshments: At Trottiscliffe, The Plough 01732 822233 and The George Inn 01732 822462. The Amazon & Tiger 01474 814705 at Harvel and Tealeaves Café 01732 823833 at Trottiscliffe Country Park.The Duke of Wellington 01732 842318 at Ryarsh or The Nevill Bull 01732 843193 at Birling.

Bike Shops: Larkfield Cycles 01732 847438, 4 miles away in Larkfield, The Bike Warehouse 01732 464911 in Sevenoaks or Cycles UK 01622 688162 in Maidstone.

Books: South East MTB – N & S Downs (N.Cotton). MTB Rides to the SE (M.Darkins). MTB Guide Kent (G.Tompsett).

Maps: OS Explorer 148.

Route Idea

From Trottiscliffe, E past Coldrum Longbarrow to join Pilgrims Way for short distance then other trails and road to Upper Halling. W through Greatpark Wood. S on trails past Holly Hill. Pilgrims way W and back to Trottiscliffe. Distance 21km.

Aylesford

Situation: In the Medway Valley at the edge of the Kent Downs Area of Outstanding Natural Beauty. 4 miles north west of Maidstone and close to M20 Junction 5.

About the Base: Aylesford, a village with three pubs and easy access to the trails. **Parking:** Car park next to the river in Aylesford. Layby as you turn off A229 towards Aylesford opposite The Lower Bell Inn. *Grid Ref: Aylesford TQ731588, Lower Bell Inn TQ747606. Post Code: Aylesford ME20 7AU, Lower Bell Inn TQ747606.*

Drive Times: Canterbury 40mins, London 1hr, Brighton 1hr20, Bristol 2hr40, Birmingham 2hr50.

Trains: Aylesford Station is on the London-Maidstone-Gatwick line.

Refreshments: The Bush Inn 01622 717446 at Aylesford. The Red Bull 01622 718135 at Eccles, The Medway Inn 01634 666619 at Wouldham, The Robin Hood or The Windmill Inn 01634 861919 at Burham. The Lower Bell 01634 861127 or Café 01622 662012 at Tyland Barn Visitor Centre.

Bike Shops: Larkfield Cycles 01732 847438, 2 miles away in Larkfield, or Cycles UK 01622 688162 in Maidstone.

Books: MTB Guide Kent (G.Tompsett).

Maps: OS Explorer 148.

Route Idea

From Aylesford, road and trails NW to Burnham Court then Wouldham. NW to Nashenden Farm. Trails through Bridge Woods and on to Burham. Trail NE towards Burham Common. Road to Blue Bell Hill. Trail and roads S to Pratling Street then Aylesford. Distance 25km.

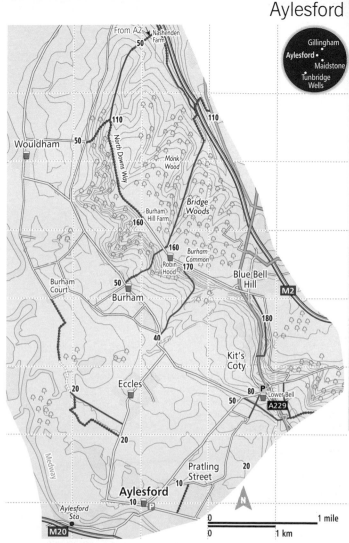

© www.kent-trails.co.uk

Charing (west)

150
190
Ringlestone
110 Wichling
Ashdown Hill
Wichling Wood
Filmer Wood
120
190
100 120
130
Dean's Hill
North Downs Way
Stedehill Wood
Oakenpole Wood
CHARING (North) MAP
100
West Street
Woodside Green
160
Warren Street
110
From Maidstone
120 150 140
80 100
150
130
160
Stalisfield Green
M20
Harrietsham
Dickley Wood
150
160
160
180
Lenham
North Downs Way
150
N
0   1 mile
0   1 km
Long flat section of North Downs Way: Hollingbourne to Charing Hill
A20
130
140
Charing Hill
150
A252
Charing
P
110
A252

Maidstone • Canterbury •
Charing •
Ashford

Situation: On the North Downs Way National Trail at the foot of the North Downs in Kent. 6 miles north west of Ashford.

About the Base: Charing, a small village with pubs and cafés. Further Info: www.charingkent.co.uk.
Parking: Roadside in the centre of Charing.
Grid Ref: TQ954495. Post Code: TN27 0LB.

Drive Times: Maidstone 30mins, London 1hr20, Brighton 1hr20, Bristol 3hrs, Birmingham 3hrs.

Trains: Charing, Lenham & Harrietsham Stations are on the Maidstone-Ashford line.

Refreshments: At Charing, The Oak 01233 712612, The Queens Head 01233 712253, The Pilgrim's Tea Rooms 01233 712170 and Oliver's Coffee Shop 01233 713838. The Bowl Inn 01233 712256 at Charing Hill, The Plough 01795 890256 at Stalisfield and The Harrow Inn 01622 858727 at Warren Street. The Red Lion 01622 858531 or Pippa's Tea Room 01622 851360 at Lenham. The Ringlestone Inn 01622 859900 to the north west of the map area.

Bike Shops: Cranbrook Cycle Centre 01233 639558 in Ashford.

Books: MTB Guide Kent (G.Tompsett). MTB Rides to the SE (M.Darkins).

Maps: OS Explorer 137.

Route Idea

NW along the North Downs Way, past Dean's Hill. N past Ringlestone to Wichling. S through Filmer Wood and   Okenpole Wood to Warren Street. North Downs Way SE back to the start. Distance 26km.

Extend the area: Charing North Map.

Charing (north) p367 ©www.kent-trails.co.uk

Maidstone
Canterbury
Charing
Ashford

Eastling

Barn Wood

45

Wilgate Green

70

South Wilderton

80

Yewhedges

95

Throwley

Hockley

100

Divan Wood

Throwley Forstal

110

Tong Green

100

130

Bell's Forstal

120

Hall's Place

Woodsell

90

Heel Farm

140

130

150

Riggshill Farm

Stalisfield Green

100

90

190

North

Downs

120

Bowl Inn

130

170

Waggon & Horses

Longbeech Wood

Landews Meadow Farm

Dormestone Farm

170

150

Hart Hill

140

North Downs Way

Stoker's Head

Paddock

A252

A20

Charing Hill

150

Charing

P 100

From Ashford

190

N

0 —————————————— 1 mile
0 —————————————— 1 km

Situation: On the southern edge of the Kent Downs Area of Outstanding Natural Beauty at the foot of the North Downs. 6 miles north west of Ashford.

About the Base: Charing, a small village with pubs and cafés. Further Info: www.charingkent.co.uk.

Parking: Roadside in the centre of Charing.
Grid Ref: TQ954495. Post Code: TN27 0LB.

Drive Times: Maidstone 30mins, London 1hr20, Brighton 1hr20, Bristol 3hrs, Birmingham 3hrs.

Trains: Charing Station is on the Maidstone-Ashford line.

Refreshments: At Charing, The Oak 01233 712612, The Queens Head 01233 712253, The Pilgrim's Tea Rooms 01233 712170 and Oliver's Coffee Shop 01233 713838. The Bowl Inn 01233 712256, The Plough 01795 890256 at Stalisfield. The Carpenters Lodge 01795 890234 at Eastling or The Waggon & Horses 01233 712249.

Bike Shops: Cranbrook Cycle Centre 01233 639558 in Ashford.

Books: MTB Guide Kent (G.Tompsett).

Maps: OS Explorer 137.

Route Idea

From Charing, W on North Downs Way. N past HartHill. Trails and roads N past Hall's Place, through Divan Woods to Yewhedges. N through Barn Wood. Roads S past Hockley. Trails SW past Woodsell to road near The Bowl Inn. Roads back to start. Distance 24km.

Extend the area: Charing East Map

Chilham

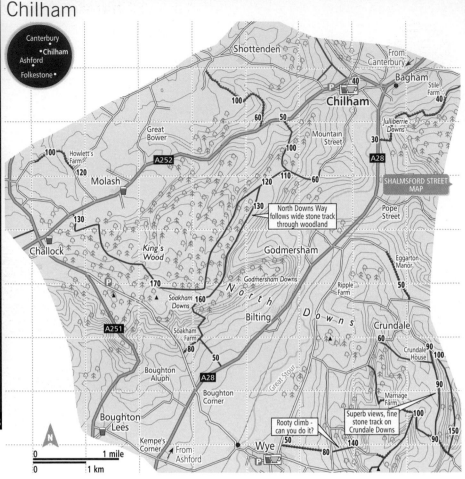

Situation: High above the Stour Valley in the North Downs. 6 miles south west of Canterbury and 9 miles north east of Ashford.

About the Base: Chilham, a village with two pubs and easy access to the trails. **Parking:** Car parks in the centre of Chilham, Wye & SE of Challock. *Grid Ref: Chilham TR066536, Challock TR023500, Wye TR052467. Post Code: Chilham CT4 8BZ, Wye TN25 5DP.*

Drive Times: Maidstone 40mins, London 1hr30, Brighton 1hr50, Bristol 3hr10, Birmingham 3hr10

Trains: Bagham Station, Ashford-Canterbury line.

Refreshments: At Chilham, The Woolpack 01227 730351 and The White Horses Inn 01227 730355. The Halfway House 01233 740258 at Challock. The Tickled Trout 01233 812227 & Crown Coffee Shop 01233 812798 at Wye.

Bike Shops: Downland Cycles 01227 479643 & Cycles UK 01227 457956 in Canterbury. Downland Cycles also do seasonal hire.

Books: South East MTB – N & S Downs (N.Cotton). MTB Rides to the SE (M.Darkins). MTB Guide Kent (G.Tompsett).

Maps: OS Explorer 137.

Route Idea

From Chilham. S through Mountain Street, then trails NW towards Shottenden. Roads SW. Trail NE from Howlett's Farm then road to link to trails through King's Wood. Back to Mountain Street and Chilham. Distance 23km.

Extend the area: Shalmsford Street Map to the E.

Near Crundale © www.kent-trails.co.uk

Shalmsford Street

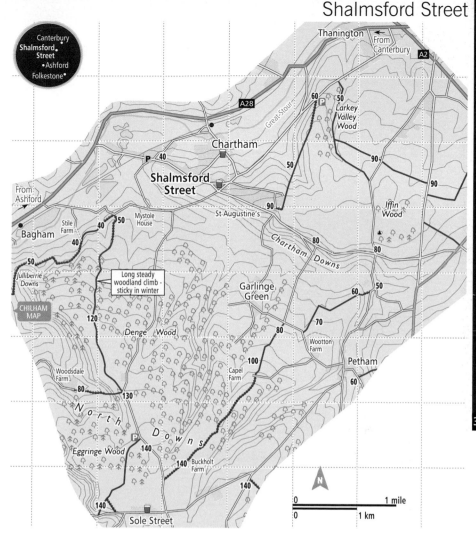

Situation: At the foot of the North Downs in the valley of the Great Stour River in Kent. 4 miles south west of Canterbury.

About the Base: Shalmsford Street, a village with a pub and easy access to the trails. **Parking:** Roadside verge at the east end of Shalmsford Street. Car parks at Larkeyvalley Wood & Eggringe Wood. *Grid Ref: Shalmsford Street TR107543, Larkeyvalley Wood TR123556, Eggringe Wood TR097503. Post Code: Shalmsford Street CT4 7PY.*

Drive Times: Maidstone 40mins, London 1hr30, Brighton 1hr50, Bristol 3hr10, Birmingham 3hr10.

Trains: Bagham & Chartham Stations are on the Ashford-Canterbury line.

Refreshments: The George Inn 01227 732527 at Shalmsford Street, The Artichoke Inn 01227 738316 or The Local 01227 738080 at Chartham and The Compasses Inn 01227 700300 at Sole Street.

Bike Shops: Downland Cycles 01227 479643 & Cycles UK 01227 457956 in Canterbury. Downland Cycles also do seasonal hire.

Books: South East MTB – N & S Downs (N.Cotton).

Maps: OS Explorer 150, 137 & 138.

Route Idea

From Shalmsford Street head towards Mystole House then S on trails through Denge Wood and Eggringe Wood to Sole Street. NE past Buckholt Farm, on to Wootton Farm. N past Iffin Wood. Around Larkey Valley Wood and back to Shalmsford Street. Distance 21km.

Extend the area: Chilham Map to the W.

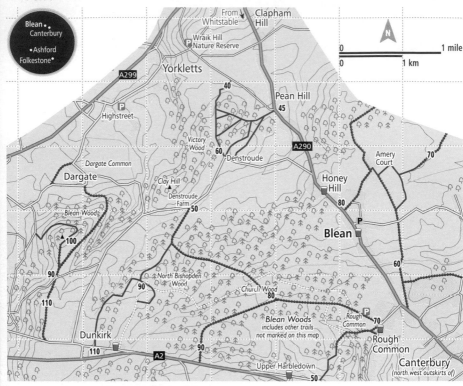

Yorkletts

Pean Hill
45

40

A299

Highstreet

Victory
Wood
60
Denstroude

A290

Amery
Court

70°

Dargate Common

Dargate

Clay Hill

Honey
Hill

80

Denstroude
Farm
50

Blean Wood

100

Blean

P

60°

90

North Bishopden
Wood

90

110

Church Wood
80

Blean Woods
includes other trails
not marked on this map

Rough
Common

70

Dunkirk

110

A2

90

Rough
Common

Upper Harbledown

50

Canterbury
(north west outskirts of)

Situation: In the heart of The Forest of Blean in Kent. 4 miles north west of Canterbury and south of Whistable.

About the Base: Blean, a small village with a pub and easy access to the trails. Further Info: www.theblean.co.uk. **Parking:** Roadside in the centre of Blean. Car parks at Rough Common Nature Reserve south of Blean & Wraik Hill Nature Reserve near Yorkletts. *Grid Ref: Blean TR122608, Rough Common TR121594, Wraik Hill TR096635, Victory Wood TR085626. **Post Code:** Blean CT2 9HP, Rough Common CT2 9DB, Wraik Hill CT5 3AW.*

Church Wood ©www.kent-trails.co.uk

Drive Times: Maidstone 40mins, London 1hr30, Brighton 1hr50, Bristol 3hr10, Birmingham 3hr10.

Trains: Canterbury Station, London-Dover line. Whitstable Station, London-Margate line.

Refreshments: The Dog & Bear 01227 464825 at Rough Common, The Hare & Hounds 01227 471594 at Blean, The Royal Oak 01227 760149 at Honey Hill, The Dove Inn 01227 760149 at Dargate, The Red Lion 01227 750224 at Dunkirk or The Plough Inn 01227 763882 at Upper Harbledown.

Bike Shops: Herberts Cycles 01227 272072 in Whitstable, Downland Cycles 01227 479643 & Cycles UK 01227 457956 in Canterbury. Downland Cycles also do seasonal hire.

Books: MTB Guide Kent (G.Tompsett). MTB Rides to the SE (M.Darkins).

Maps: OS Explorer 150 & 149.

Route Ideas

❶ From Blean, NW to Denstroude , trails N through Victory Wood. Road through Yorkletts, High Street to Dargate. Trails S through the Blean Wood. On to Dunkirk then trails N to Denstroude Farm. Road to Denstoude then back to the start. Distance 19km.

❷ From Rough Common Car Park, trails W then NW then NE to Denstroude Farm. On to Dargate and trails S through the woods. Trails N from Dunkirk then back through Church Wood to the start. Distance 16km.

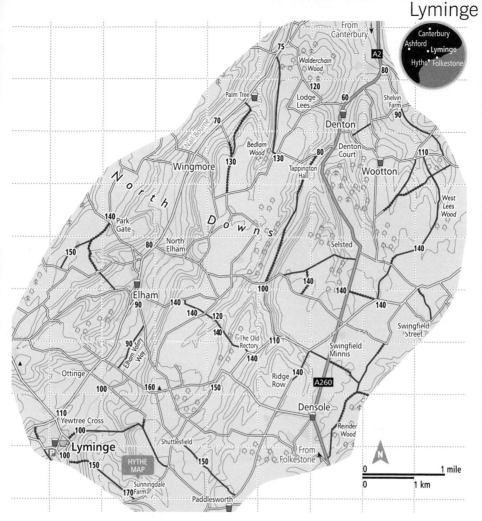

Situation: In the Elham Valley, close to the North Downs Way National Trail and the south Kent coast. 7 miles north west of Folkestone and 12 miles south of Canterbury.

About the Base: Lyminge, a village with a pub and a coffee shop. Further Info: www.lyminge.org.uk.

Parking: Car park at Lyminge village hall on the south edge of the village. *Grid Ref: TR158409. Post Code: CT18 8EN.*

Drive Times: Maidstone 40mins, London 1hr30, Brighton 1hr50, Bristol 3hr10, Birmingham 3hr20.

Trains: Shepherdswell Railway Station, 2 miles east of the map, is on the Dover-Canterbury line. Sandling Railway Station, 3 miles away, & Folkestone Station are on the Ashford-Dover line.

Refreshments: At Lyminge, The Coach & Horses 01303 862694 and Lyminge Coffee Shop 01303 864222. The Kings Arms 01303 840242, The Rose & Crown 01303 840226 and The Cosy Tea Rooms 01303 840344 at Elham. The Palm Tree 01227 831463 at Wingmore, The Jackdaw 01303 844663 at Denton, The Endeavour Inn 01303 844268 at

Wootton and The Black Horse Inn 01303 892263 at Densole.

Bike Shops: Biketart 01227 832582 at Wingmore. The Hub 01303 210311 at Sandgate & Activ 01303 240110 or Renhams Cycle Centre 01303 241884 in Folkestone.

Books: MTB Rides to the SE (M.Darkins).

Maps: OS Explorer 138.

Route Idea

From Lyminge, NE to Elham on roadsand section of Elham Valley Way. E to The Old Rectory. N to Tappington Hall. W towards Bedlam Wood then trail N. Roads SE to Denton. E to Shelvin Farm. Trails S past West Lees Wood. Road link then trails along Reinden Wood. Roads towards Paddlesworth. Trail to Shuttlesfield. S towards Sunningdale Farm then trail back to Lyminge. Distance 35km. Possibility of using various roads to shorten as required.

Extend the area: Hythe Map to the S.

Hythe

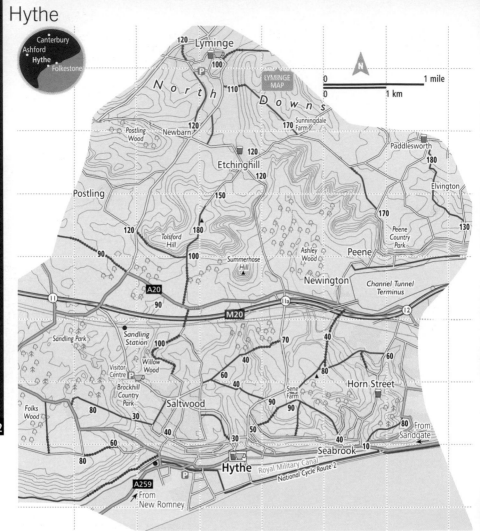

Situation: At the foot of the North Downs on the south coast of Kent. 4 miles west of Folkestone.

About the Base: Hythe, a small coastal market town with pubs, cafés and accommodation. Further Info: www.hythe-tourism.com. **Parking:** Several car parks in Hythe, try Portland Road. Car park at Brockhill Country park. Car park at Lyminge village hall on the south edge of the village. *Grid Ref: Hythe TR157345, Brockhill Country Park TR149360, Lyminge TR158409,.* **Post Code:** Hythe CT21 6JD, Brockhill Country Park CT21 4HL, Lyminge CT18 8EN.

Drive Times: Maidstone 40mins, London 1hr30, Brighton 1hr50, Bristol 3hr10, Birmingham 3hr20.

Trains: Sandling Railway Station, 2 miles away, & Folkestone Station are on the Ashford-Dover line.

Refreshments: Good choice of pubs & cafés at Hythe. The New Inn 01303 862026 at Etchinghill, The Coach & Horses 01303 862694 and Lyminge Coffee Shop 01303 864222 at Lyminge. The Cat and Custard Pot 01303 892205 at Paddlesworth or The Britannia 01303 238502 at Horn Street.

Bike Shops: The Hub 01303 210311, 2 miles away at Sandgate. Activ 01303 240110 or Renhams Cycle Centre 01303 241884 in Folkestone.

Books: MTB Guide Kent (G.Tompsett).

Maps: OS Explorer 138.

Route Idea

From Hythe, NW to Saltwood. Trail N past Willow Wood. N to Etchinghall. On to Newbarn and trail to Lyminge. SE to Sunningdale Farm, then Peene and Newington. SW to Sene Farm then SE to Seabrook and National Cycle Route 2 back to Hythe. Distance 21km.

Extend the area: Lyminge Map to the N.

Hamstreet

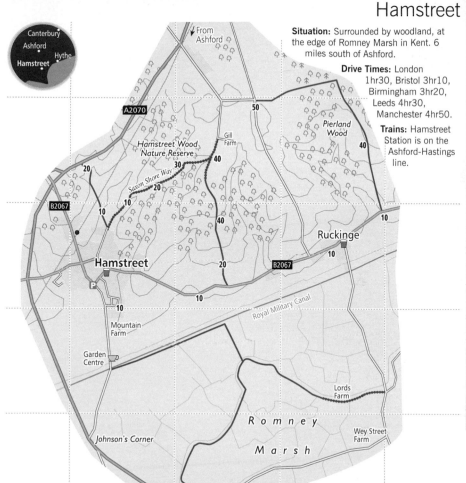

Situation: Surrounded by woodland, at the edge of Romney Marsh in Kent. 6 miles south of Ashford.

Drive Times: London 1hr30, Bristol 3hr10, Birmingham 3hr20, Leeds 4hr30, Manchester 4hr50.

Trains: Hamstreet Station is on the Ashford-Hastings line.

Hythe p372. ©www.kent-trails.co.uk

About the Base: Hamstreet, a village with a pub and café. Further Info: www.hamstreet.info. **Parking:** Car park next to the recreation ground in the south of the village. *Grid Ref: TR001331. Post Code: TN26 2JF.*

Refreshments: The Dukes Head 01233 733701 and Coffee Shop 01233 732988 at Hamstreet Garden Centre at Hamstreet. The Blue Anchor 01233 732387 at Ruckinge.

Bike Shops: Cranbrook Cycle Centre 01233 639558 in Ashford or Romney Cycles, 8 miles away in New Romney. Romney Cycles also do hire.

Books: MTB Guide Kent (G.Tompsett).

Maps: OS Explorer 125 & 137.

Route Idea

From Hamstreet, S past the garden centre , Trails across Romney Marsh past Lords Farm. Roads to Ruckinge. Trails through Pierland Wood. Back to Hamstreet on the Saxon Shore Way. Distance 12km.

Swinley Forest

An area of Windsor Forest, owned and managed by The Crown Estate, comprising 2600 acres of coniferous woodland. Cycling is permitted on hard tracks and within a specific expert mountain bike area.

Facilities:
Café and Wellington Trek Bike Hire
01344 874 611 at The Look Out
Discovery Centre.

Parking:
Grid Ref: SU876661.
Post Code: RG12 7QW

Web: www.goodmtb.co.uk/b55

The Trails

A network of forest roads and a wide variety of purpose built, umarked trails, including plenty of singletrack within a dedicated Expert MTB area.

Suitable for everyone from families to XC riders, freeriders and downhillers.

It is a condition of cycling within Swinley Forest that you must hold a cycle permit if over 16 years of age.

374

©Dirt Divas/ Graeme Warren

Esher X

Opening in 2011. Set in 3 acres of woodland in Surrey, a brand new bike park being built on the site of the old 'esher shore' freeride park.

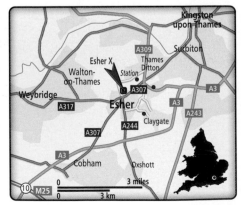

Facilities:
Refreshments on site to be confirmed.

Parking:
Grid Ref: TQ138649. Post Code: KT10 8AN

Web: www.goodmtb.co.uk/b52

The Trails

Due to open in 2011.

Competition standard Dual Slalom Track with gated racing, Play Track with big tabletops, berms and jumps, Pump Track and singletrack Bike Test Track.

The Hurtwood Estate

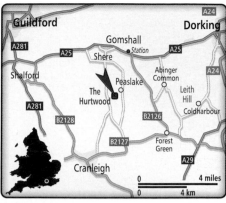

© Richard Kelly www.allbikedup.com

© Richard Kelly www.allbikedup.com

In the Surrey Hills Area of Outstanding Natural Beauty around Holmbury Hill and Pitch Hill, two magnificent greensand peaks which, with the Winterfold Ridge, are criss crossed by a network of trails to explore. Private land, with open access to the public, maintained by Friends of the Hurtwood.

Facilities:
Refreshments at Peaslake Village Stores in Peaslake.

Parking:
Near Peaslake - Grid Ref: TQ083441. Post Code: GU5 9RP. Also other car parks situated around the area.

Web: www.goodmtb.co.uk/b54

The Trails

There are several recognised unwaymarked trails:

Telegraph Road, Yoghurt Pots, Doc, BKB, Reservoir Dogs, I should Coco. The T Trails (1-5) on Pitch Hill.

Orange Clawhammer, Christmas Pud on Winterfold Ridge.

Also many other trails to explore.

To make sure you ride all the best bits several companies offer guided rides, such as All Biked Up and Singletrack School.

Please follow the Code of Conduct for riding at The Hurtwood

- Only cycle at speeds safe for the trail ahead. You don't know what is around the next corner. Please be aware that dogs are allowed to exercise freely, without leads, on The Hurtwood.

- Make sure your presence is known, by calling out a greeting if approaching walkers from the rear.

- Always give way to horse riders and walkers.

- Do not cycle in groups of more than 6.

- Be respectful and courteous to other users.

- Choose your route carefully, especially when the ground is wet, to minimise erosion.

- Avoid harsh braking and skidding, thus reducing trail damage.

- Riders must not create new trails, please use the existing network.

- Make sure your bike is safe to ride and be prepared for emergencies.

- Wear a helmet and use protective clothing.

Leith Hill

In the Surrey Hills Area of Outstanding Natural Beauty, Leith Hill is the highest point in the south east. Recognised XC and Downhill trails, including Summer Lightning a fun, fast stretch of downhill singletrack, are built and maintained by local mountain bikers The Redlands Project in partnership with local landowners.

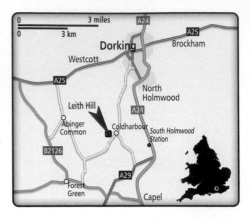

Facilities:
The Plough Inn at Coldharbour.

Parking:
Grid Ref: TQ150440. Post Code: RH5 6HE

Web: www.goodmtb.co.uk/b72

The Trails

These tend to involve a good amount of forest singletrack.

Some waymarking for the Summer Lightning trail. For other trails maybe best to pay for a guided ride or hook up with local riders.

Other trails include:

Waggle Dance

Crooked Furrow

Regurgitator

Wind in the Willows

Will-o'-the-Wisp

Caspers

Fowlmead Country Park

A 200 acre regenerated green space and leisure park on the site of the former Betteshanger Colliery in Kent.

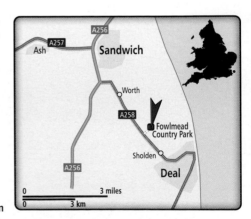

Facilities:
Café and MTB Hire 01304 615390 at Fowlmead Country Park Visitor Centre.

Parking:
Grid Ref: TR352539. Post Code: CT14 0BF

Web: www.goodmtb.co.uk/b53

The Trails

Plenty of off road trails with undulating all weather singletrack, BMX Track and a 3.5km tarmac race/time trial cycle circuit open to all.

South Downs, South Hampshire & Isle of Wight

378

© Nick Cotton

The biggest, toughest and most spectacular rides in the South east are to be found along the South Downs, a great whaleback of chalk that runs for almost 100 miles from Winchester to Eastbourne. The South Downs Way is a long distance National Trail that has bridleway or byway status along its entire length offering a tough weekend challenge or an extremely strenuous summer's day ride. Either side of the trail there are hundreds of miles of well waymarked tracks enabling riders to devise routes to suit all abilities. The area is a mixture of beech woodland and huge open grassy areas with panoramic views out over the Sussex Weald to the north and the English Channel to the south.

As is the case for most of Southern England, chalk and flint tracks dominate in Hampshire. There are several rides in the Winchester area running west from **Broughton** along the Monarch's Way or east from **King's Somborne** towards Winchester itself. North and west of Petersfield rides use the extensive network of wide tracks, formerly ox droves. These run south from

Dummer though the handsome town of **New Alresford** and down towards the Meon Valley and **East Meon**. South of Petersfield, the **Queen Elizabeth Country Park** lies on the course of the South Downs Way and also has waymarked mountain bike rides.

There are many excellent bases all the way along the South Downs, from **Cocking** to **Alfriston,** with places such as **Ditchling Beacon** offering shorter ridge rides with all the benefits of the views yet without the 200m of ascent up out of valleys. Attractive towns to stay for a weekend include **Midhurst**, **Haslemere** and **Lewes**.

The Isle of Wight is a separate world, linked to the mainland by ferry or hovercraft. Once again, chalk dominates and the rides in the west of the island are some of the finest along the whole of the South Coast with stunning views north over the Solent and south over the English Channel. Good bases on the Isle of Wight are **Yarmouth**, **Godshill** and **Shanklin**.

There is plenty of easy cycling on the broad gravel tracks that cover the **New Forest**. This is not one unbroken area of woodland - there is plenty of open heathland as well. Look out for the wild New Forest ponies and vast numbers of deer whist you ride. It is essential to pick up (or download) a forest map showing the waymarked posts as this will enable you to plan your route and to orientate yourself while out riding.

Trail Centres in the area include **Bedgebury**, **Friston** and **Queen Elizabeth Country Park**. There are also smaller Bike Parks at **Deers Leap** (East Grinstead) and **Penshurst**.

Riders: VCGH © Mark Reynolds

Broughton

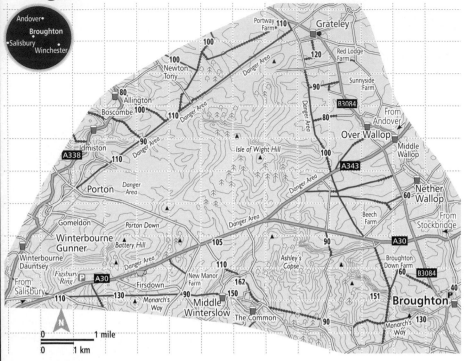

Situation: On the western side of the Test Valley in Hampshire. 12 miles east of Salisbury and 13 miles west of Winchester.

About the Base: Broughton, a village with a pub and easy access to the trails.
Further Info: www.broughton-hants.net. **Parking:** Roadside in Broughton. National Trust Car Park at Figsbury Ring. **Grid Ref:** Broughton SU309328, Figsbury Ring SU192338. **Post Code:** Broughton SO20 8AA.

Drive Times: Southampton 40mins, London 1hr40, Bristol 1hr50, Birmingham 2hr30.

Trains: Grately Railway Station, in the north of the map, is on the London-Salisbury & Reading-Salisbury lines.

Refreshments: The Tally Ho 01794 301280 at Broughton. The Five Bells 01264 782621 at Nether Wallop, The George Inn at Middle Wallop 01264 782772 or The White Hart 01264 781331 at Over Wallop. The Shire Horse 01264 889373 at Grateley, The Old Inn 01980 619045 at Allington, The Earl of Normanton 01980 610251 at Idmiston, The Winterbourne Arms 01980 611306 at Winterbourne Dauntsey. The Hilltop Diner 01980 863086 at Firsdown, The Lord Nelson 01980 862218 at Middle Winterslow and The Lions Head 01980 862234 at The Common.

Bike Shops: Cycleworld 01794 513344, 10 miles away in Romsey. Hargroves Cycles 01962 860005 & Peter Hansford Cycles 01962 877555 in Winchester, Stonehenge Cycles 01722 334915 & Cycle World 01722 440372 in Salisbury.

Books: MTB Rides to the SW (M.Darkins).

Maps: OS Explorer 131.

Route Idea

From Broughton, N to Grateley on trails running parallel to the B3084. Trails SW to Porton. S through Winterbourne Dauntsey then W on trails to Middle Winterslow and on to Broughton.
Distance 34km.

King's Somborne p381 © Jonathan Russell

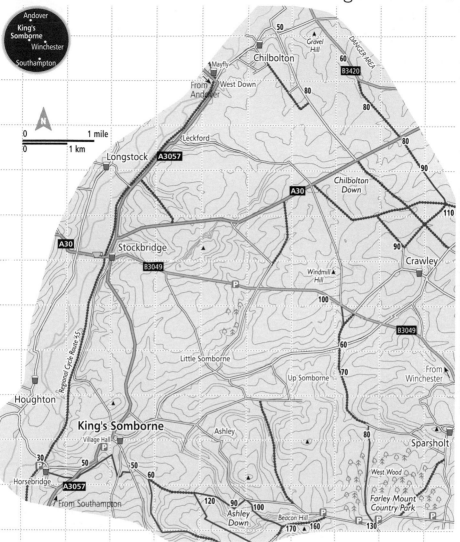

Situation: At the edge of the Test Valley in Hampshire. 9 miles west of Winchester.

About the Base: King's Somborne, a village with a pub and easy access to the trails. Further Info: www.thesombornes.org.uk. **Parking:** Car parks at King's Somborne Village Hall & next to the river in Horsebridge. Several car parks at Farley Mount Country Park. **Grid Ref:** *King's Somborne SU358308, Horsebridge SU344304, Farley Mount Country Park SU432293.* **Post Code:** *King's Somborne SO20 6PR, Horsebridge SO20 6PU.*

Drive Times: Southampton 40mins, London 1hr40, Bristol 1hr50, Birmingham 2hr20.

Refreshments: The Crown 01794388360 at Kings Somborne. The John of Gaunt 01794 388394 at Horsebridge, The White Hart 01264 810663 or Lillies Café 01264 810754 at Stockbridge. Cross the river to the Boot Inn 01794 388310 at Houghton,

The Peat and Spade 01264 810612 at Longstock or The Mayfly at Testcombe. The Abbots Mitre 01264 860 348 at Chilbolton The Fox and Hounds 01962 776006 at Crawley and The Plough 01962 776353 at Sparsholt.

Bike Shops: Cycleworld 01794 513344, 6 miles away in Romsey. Hargroves Cycles 01962 860005 & Peter Hansford Cycles 01962 877555 in Winchester.

Books: MTB Rides to the SE (M.Darkins).

Maps: OS Explorer 131 & 132.

Route Idea

From King's Somborne, S on a short stretch of main road or use bridleway across the fields. At Horsebridge, N on Cycle Route 65 to West Down. Roads & trails past Chilbolton & Gravel Hill to Crawley. S to Farley Mount Country Park. W across Ashley Down and back to King's Somborne. Distance 36km.

Dummer

Situation: In the heart of Hampshire, 6 miles south west of Basingstoke and 12 miles north west of Alton, close to the M3 motorway.

About the Base: Dummer, a small village with a pub and easy access to the trails. **Parking:** Roadside in the centre of Dummer. *Grid Ref: SU588460. Post Code: RG25 2AY.*

Drive Times: Southampton 40mins, London 1hr10, Bristol 1hr40, Birmingham 2hr20.

Refreshments: The Queen Inn 01256 397367 at Dummer. The Purefoy Arms 01256 389777 at Preston Candover or The Crown at Axford 01256 389492.

Bike Shops: Action Bikes 01256 465266 in Basingstoke & First Gear Cycles 01420 543922 in Alton.

Books: MTB Rides to the SE (M.Darkins).

Maps: OS Explorer 144 & 132.

Route Idea

S past Tidley Hill, The Holt, Furzedown, Lone Barn House and Brown Candover. Trails NE past Preston Down. Trails N past Moundsmere Manor, Windmill Hill, Nutley Wood and back to Dummer. Distance 26km.

Extend the area: Alton Map to the E.

© Nick Cotton

New Alresford

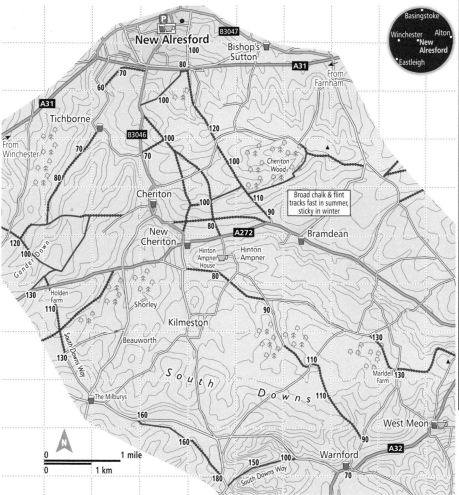

Broad chalk & flint tracks fast in summer, sticky in winter

Situation: At the foot of the South Downs and the northern edge of the South Downs National Park in Hampshire. 8 miles north east of Winchester.

About the Base: New Alresford, a small town with a choice of pubs and cafés.
Further Info: www.alresford.org. **Parking:** Car park next to the station in New Alresford. *Grid Ref: SU588324. Post Code: SO24 9JQ.*

Drive Times: Southampton 40mins, London 1hr30, Bristol 1hr50, Birmingham 2hr30.

Refreshments: At New Alresford, plenty of pubs, Tiffin Tearooms 01962 734394 or The Courtyard Tearooms 01962 733303.The Tichborne Arms 01962 733760 at Tichborne, The Milburys 01962 771248 and The George & Falcon 01730 829623 at Warnford. The Thomas Lord 01730 829244 and Tazzina Cafe 01730 829882 at West Meon. Tea Rooms 01962 771305 at National Trust Hinton Ampner, The Hinton Arms 01962 771252 at New Cheriton and The Flower Pots 01962 771534 at Cheriton.

Bike Shops: Alresford Cycles 01962 733145 in New Alresford. Hargroves Cycles 01962 860005 & Peter Hansford Cycles 01962 877555 in Winchester.

Books: South East MTB – N & S Downs (N.Cotton). MTB Rides to the SE (M.Darkins). MTB on S Downs (P.Edwards)
Maps: OS Explorer 132.

Route Idea

S to Tichborne, South Downs Way to Warnford. Road NE to Mardell Farm. Trails and roads NW to Hinton Ampner then continue N to New Alresford.
Distance 32km

Fawley Down ©www.trailbreak.co.uk

Alton

Situation: On the northern edge of the South Downs National Park in Hampshire. 10 miles south west of Farnham and 11 miles south of Basingstoke.

About the Base: Alton, a market town with pubs, cafés and accommodation. **Parking:** Car parks in the centre of Alton & at Chawton Park Woods at Four Marks. *Grid Ref: Alton SU71639, Chawton Park Woods SU672361. Post Code: Alton GU34 2BF, Chawton Park Woods GU34 5ED.*

Drive Times: Southampton 50mins, London 1hr20, Bristol 2hrs, Birmingham 2hr40.

Trains: Alton Station has services to London Waterloo.

Refreshments: Plenty of pubs and cafés at Alton. The Star Inn 01420 561224 and The Sun Inn 01420 562338 at Bentworth. The Golden Pot 01420 80655 at Shalden. The Royal Oak 01256 381213 at Lasham. The Yew Tree Inn 01256 389224 at Lower Wield and The Castle of Comfort 01420 562112 at Medstead.

Bike Shops: First Gear Cycles 01420 543922 in Alton, Owens Cycles 01420 768 227 at Four Marks & Farnham Cycles 01420 520661, north east of the town on A31.

Books: MTB Rides to the SE (M.Darkins).

Maps: OS Explorer 144 & 132.

Routes on Web: www.goodmtb.co.uk/a130

Route Ideas

❶ SW from Alton on National Cycle Route 24. Through Chawton Park Wood. N to Holt End and Bentworth. Trails & roads S to Beech. Trail through Bushy Leaze Wood. Roads back into Alton. Distance 18km.

❸ From Chawton Park Wood, NE towards Alton, main road and trail to Beech. Roads & trails to Bentworth and then Shalden. Roads N to Shalden Green then E to the A339. Trails to Bradley. Back to start via Ashley Farm and Jennie Green Lane. Distance 36km.

Extend the area: Dummer Map to the W.

Selborne

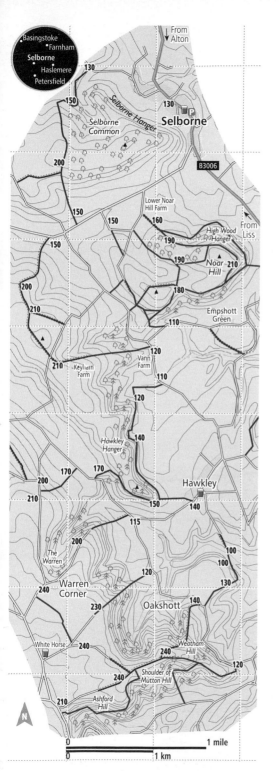

Situation: Just within the northern boundary of the South Downs National Park in East Hampshire. 4 miles south of Alton.

About the Base: Selborne, a village with a pub and easy access to the trails.

Parking: Car park in the centre of Selbourne. *Grid Ref: SU742335. Post Code: GU34 3JR.*

Drive Times: Southampton 50mins, London 1hr20, Brighton 1hr30, Bristol 2hrs, Birmingham 2hr40.

Trains: Liss Railway Station, 2 miles south east of the map, is on the London-Portsmouth line. Alton Station has services to London Waterloo.

Refreshments: The Selborne Arms 01420 511247 at Selborne. The Hawkley Inn 01730 827205 at Hawkley and The White Horse Inn 01420 588387 at Warren Corner.

Bike Shops: Gleaming Bikes 01420 488899, 3 miles away at Oakhanger, Owens Cycles 01730 260446, just south of the map at Steep, & First Gear Cycles 01420 543922 in Alton.

Books: MTB Rides to the SE (M.Darkins). MTB Rides to the SE (M.Darkins).

Maps: OS Explorer 133.

Route Idea

From Selborne, roads S past Lower Noar Hill Farm. S through High Wood Hanger and around Noar Hill. S past Vann Farm and through Hawkley Hanger. On to Warren Corner, Ashford Hill, Shoulder of Mutton Hill, Weatham Hill and Oakshott & Hawkley. Rejoin trial though Hawkley Hanger. After Vann Farm, trails W past Keyham Farm then N to link to trails on W of Selborne Common. Roads back to start. Distance 27km.

The above consists of two loops so easy shortcut options available.

Haslemere

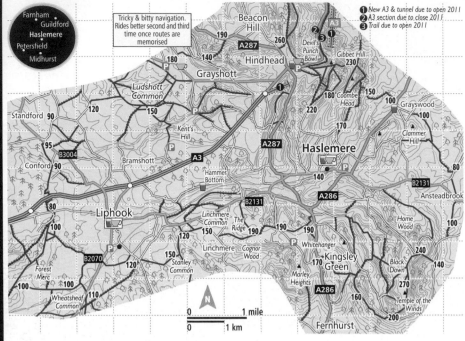

Tricky & bitty navigation. Rides better second and third time once routes are memorised

1 New A3 & tunnel due to open 2011
2 A3 section due to close 2011
3 Trail due to open 2011

Situation: Surrounded by hills and heathland in the south west corner of Surrey, close to the borders with Hampshire and West Sussex. 14 miles south west of Guildford.

About the Base: Haslemere, a market town with a choice of pubs, cafés and accommodation. Further Info: www.haslemere.com. **Parking:** Car parks at Devils Punchbowl near Hindhead, in the centre of Haslemere & next to the station at Liphook. Alternative parking marked on map. **Grid Ref:** Devils Punchbowl SU890357, Haslemere SU904330, Liphook. **Post Code:** Devils Punchbowl GU26 6AE, Haslemere GU27 2AN, Liphook GU30 7DN.

Drive Times: Southampton 1hr10, London 1hr20, Brighton 1hr20, Bristol 2hr20, Birmingham 2hr40.

Trains: Haslemere Station is on the London-Portsmouth line.

Refreshments: Plenty of pubs &d cafés at Haslemere. National Trust Café 01428 608771 and Devils Punchbowl Inn 01428 606565 at Hindhead. Applegarth Farm Café 01428 712777 at Grayshott, pubs & cafés at Liphook, The Prince of Wales 01428 652600 at Hammer Bottom and The Wheatsheaf Inn 01428 644440 at Grayswood.

Bike Shops: Cycleworks 01428 648424 in Haslemere & Liphook Cycles 01428 727858 at Liphook.

Books: MTB Rides to the SE (M.Darkins).

Maps: OS Explorer 133.

Route Idea

Anticlockwise loop around Haslemere. Start to N of Haslemere at the Devil's Punchbowl, W past Hindhead and Grayshott, across Ludshott Common. S past Conford to Forest Mere and Wheatsheaf Common. E past Stanley Common and Linchmere to Kingsley Green. Trails around Temple of the Winds. N to Ansteadbrook, Grayswood, Gibbet Hill & back to start. Distance 43km.

Riders: VCGH © Mark Reynolds

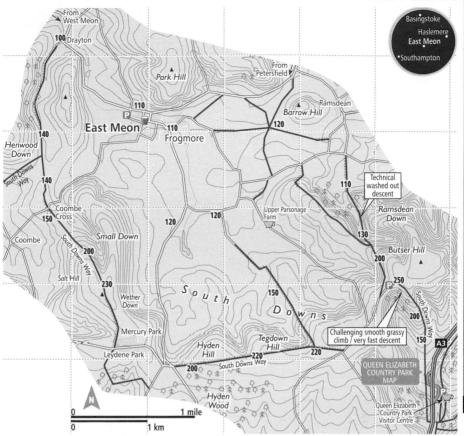

Situation: In the Meon Valley at the heart of the South Downs National Park. 5 miles west of Petersfield and 18 miles north of Portsmouth.

About the Base: East Meon, a village with two pubs and easy access to the trails. Further Info: www.eastmeon.net. **Parking:** Car park in East Meon on Workhouse Lane. Car parks at Butser Hill & Queen Elizabeth Country Park Visitor Centre. *Grid Ref: East Meon SU677222, Butser Hill SU711200, Queen Elizabeth Country Park SU718185. Post Code: East Meon GU32 1PF, Queen Elizabeth Country Park PO8 0QE.*

Drive Times: Southampton 50 mins, London 1hr30, Bristol 2hrs, Birmingham 2hr40.

Trains: Petersfield Station is on the London-Portsmouth line.

Refreshments: At East Meon, Ye Olde George Inn 01730 823481 and The Izaak Walton 01730 823252. Café 023 9259 6345 at Queen Elizabeth Country Park Visitor Centre. Harvesting Cream Teas 01730 823490 (April-Sept only) at Upper Parsonage Farm.

Bike Shops: Cycleworks 01730 266007 & Cyclelife Petersfield 01730 266644.

Books: South East MTB – N & S Downs (N.Cotton).

Maps: OS Explorer 1119 & 120.

Route Idea

From East Meon, road NW to Drayton. Trails S to Coombe Cross and Leydene Park. E across Hyden Hill and Tegdown Hill. Road NE then trails N passing Ramsdean Down. Trails S of Barrow Hill (or use roads when ground is wet) & back to start. Distance 16km.

Extend the area: Queen Elizabeth Country Park Map to the E.

Queen Elizabeth Country Park

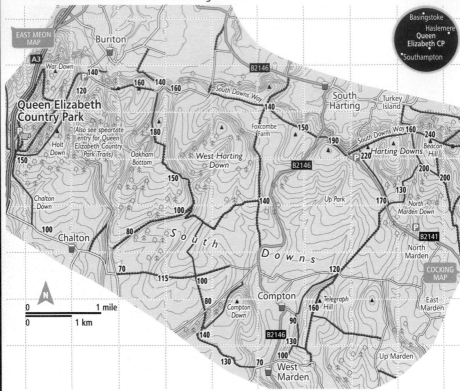

Situation: On the South Downs Way in the heart of the South Downs National Park in Hampshire, close to it's border with West Sussex. 4 miles south of Petersfield and 14 miles north of Portsmouth on the A3.

About the Base: Queen Elizabeth Country Park, a rural location with a café and a visitor centre. Further info: www3.hants.gov.uk/countryside/qecp.

Parking: Car parks at Queen Elizabeth Country Park Visitor Centre, Harting Downs & North Marden Down. **Grid Ref:** *Queen Elizabeth Country Park SU718185, Harting Downs SU794172, North Marden Down, SU803163.* **Post Code:** *Queen Elizabeth Country Park PO8 0QE.*

Drive Times: Southampton 40moins, Brighton 1hr20, London 1hr30, Bristol 2hrs, Birmingham 2hr40.

Trains: Petersfield Station is on the London -Portsmouth line.

Refreshments: Café 023 9259 6345 at Queen Elizabeth Country Park Visitor Centre. The Red Lion Inn 023 9259 2246 at Chalton, The Coach & Horses 023 9263 1228 at Compton or The Victoria Inn 023 92631330 at West Marden. The Ship Inn 01730 825302 at South Harting and The Five Bells 01730 263584 at Buriton.

Bike Shops: Cycleworks 01730 266007 & Cyclelife Petersfield 01730 266644.

Books: South East MTB – N & S Downs (N.Cotton). MTB Rides to the SE (M.Darkins). MBR Ride Guide 2010

Maps: OS Explorer 120.

Route Idea

From the Visitor Centre, S across Chalton Down to Chalton. Road & trails to West Marden. N over Telegraph Hill to the B2141. Trails NE across North Marden Down to South Downs Way. South Downs Way back to car park.
Distance 24km.

Extend the area: East Meon Map to the NW. Cocking Map to the E.

Also see Queen Elizabeth Country Park Trails on page 410.

© Nick Cotton

Midhurst

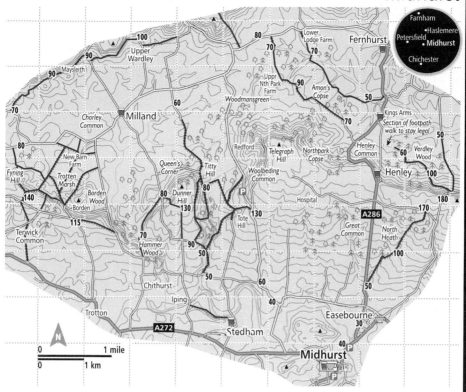

Situation: On the River Rother in West Sussex, within the South Downs National Park. 9 miles south of Haslemere and 10 miles east of Petersfield.

About the Base: Midhurst, a market town with plenty of pubs, cafés and accommodation. Further Info: www.midhurst.org. **Parking:** Car park next to the information point in Midhurst. Also at Woolbedding Common. *Grid Ref: Midhurst SU885213, Woolbedding Common SU864253.* **Post Code:** *Midhurst GU29 9LT.*

Drive Times: Southampton 1hr, Brighton 1hr10, London 1hr30, Bristol 2hr20, Birmingham 2hr50.

Trains: Liphook Railway Station, 3 miles north of the map, is on the London-Portsmouth line.

Refreshments: Good choice of pubs & cafés at Midhurst. Cowdray Farm Café 01730 812799 at Easebourne and The Hamilton Arms at Steadham. The Rising Sun 01428 741347 at Milland or The Red Lion 01428 643112 at Fernhurst. The Kings Arms 01428 652005 at Henley Common and The Duke of Cumberland 01428 652280 at Henley.

Bike Shops: Liphook Cycles 01428 727858, 3 miles north of the map at Liphook, Cycleworks in Haslemere 01428 648424 & Petersfield 01730 266007.

Books: MTB Rides to the SE (M.Darkins).

Maps: OS Explorer 133.

Route Idea

From Midhurst, N to Easebourne. Roads W. Trails N to Dunner Hill and S through Hammer Wood. Road & trail W past Fyning Hill then on to Maysleith, Upper Wardley and Lower Lodge Farm. Trail SE to the A286. Through Verdley Wood then S across North Heath. Roads back to start. Distance 34km.

Rider: VCGH © Mark Reynolds

Cocking

(Map of Cocking area showing South Downs Way, Cocking, Singleton, Charlton, East Dean, West Dean, Chilgrove, Goodwood Race Course, Queen Elizabeth Country Park and surrounding hills with spot heights. Annotations include: "Fast ridge cruising", "Tough 120m climb east or west from main road". Scale 0–1 mile / 0–1 km. Inset locator map showing Farnham, Haslemere, Cocking, Chichester.)

Situation: At the foot of the South Downs and the edge pf the Rother Valley Area of Outstanding Natural Beauty in West Sussex. 10 miles north of Chichester.

About the Base: Cocking, a village with tea rooms and a village store.
Further Info: www.gravelroots.net/cocking
Parking: Cocking Hill car park on A286 south of the village. Layby on A286 north of Singleton. Car parks at Goodwood Country Park & Stoughton Down or layby on B2141 south of Chilgrove. *Grid Ref: Cocking Hill SU875166, Singleton SU875139, Goodwood Country Park SU888111, Stoughton Down SU815125, Chilgrove SU832137,*

Drive Times: Brighton 1hr10, Southampton 1hr, London 1hr30, Bristol 2hr30, Birmingham 3hrs.

Refreshments: At Cocking, Moonlight Cottage Tea Rooms 01730 813336 and Cocking Post Office and Stores 01730 815081. The Star and Garter 01243 811318 at East Dean, The Fox Goes Free 01243 811461 at Charlton and The Royal Oak 01243 535257 at Hooksway. The Gallery Tea Rooms 01243 811899 and The Partridge Inn 01243 811251 at Singleton.

Bike Shops: Shed End Bikes 01243 811766 at West Dean for hire, delivery & collection. Geared Bikes 01243 784479 & Hargroves Cycles 01243 537337 in Chichester.

Books: South East MTB – N & S Downs (N.Cotton). MTB Rides to the SE (M.Darkins). MTB on S Downs (P.Edwards).

Maps: OS Explorer 120 & 121.

Route Ideas

❶ From Cocking Hill car park, E on South Downs Way. S past Court Hill to East Dean. Roads & trails past Goodwood Race Course. Trails W to the A286 and on to the B2141. Trails around Kingley Vale then N past Bow Hill and Lambdown Hill and on to Chilgrove. Back to Cocking via Westdean Woods and Bepton Down. Distance 28km.

❷ As above to Lambdown Hill then N to Hooksway via Chilgrove Hill. NE to South Downs Way. South Downs Way back to start. Distance 34km.

Extend the area: Queen Elizabeth Country Park Map to the W.

© Nick Cotton

Whiteways Lodge

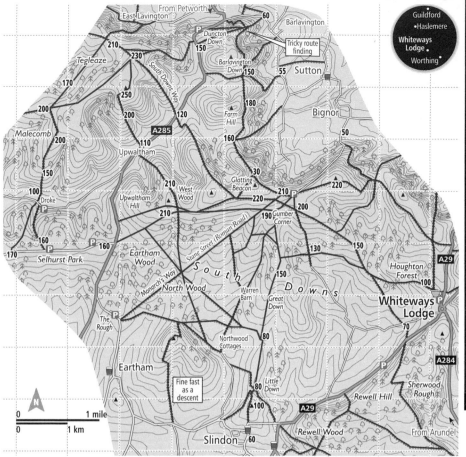

Guildford
•Haslemere
Whiteways Lodge •
Worthing•

Situation: At the edge of the Arundel Estate in the South Downs, 6 miles south west of Storrington and 7 miles north of Littlehampton.

About the Base: Whiteways Lodge, a rural location with a car park. **Parking:** Car parks at Whiteways Lodge & throughout the map area. *Grid Ref: Whiteways Lodge TQ000101, Rewell Hill SU991096, Glatting Beacon SU973129, Duncton Down SU955160, Eartham Wood SU938106, Selhurst Park SU927119,*

Drive Times: Brighton 45mins, Southampton 1hr, London 1hr50, Bristol 2hr40, Birmingham 3hr10.

Trains: Amberley Railway Station, 2 miles away, is on the London-Littlehampton line.

Refreshments: Cafe at Whiteways Lodge car park.

Bike Shops: South Downs Bikes 01903 745534 in Storrington. The Bike Shed 01903 715111 & Blazing Saddles 01903 850418 in Littlehampton.

Books: South East MTB – N & S Downs (N.Cotton). MTB Rides to the SE (M.Darkins). MTB on S Downs (P.Edwards).

Maps: OS Explorer 121.

Route Ideas

❶ From Whiteways Lodge, trails W then S, over A29 and across Sherwood Rough. W through Rewell Wood. N to Little Down & NW onto North Wood. W to Selhurst Park. N past past Malecomb & Tegleaze to South Downs Way. Trails E to Duncton Down then S across Barlavington Down, passed Farm Hill and Glatting Beacon. SE through Houghton Forest and back to start. Distance 33km.

❷ From Whiteways Lodge, NW to Gumber Corner. S past Northwood Cottages. W to The Rough. Trail N to Upwaltham. Trails N then E to Duncton Down. Then back to start as above route. Distance 27km.

© Nick Cotton

South Downs Way near Storrington p393. © www.southdownsmountainbiking.co.uk

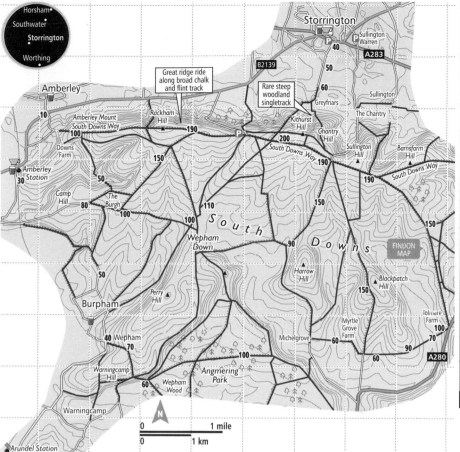

Situation: At the foot of the South Downs in West Sussex, on the northern edge of the South Downs National Park. 10 miles north west of Worthing.

About the Base: Storrington, a large village with pubs, a café and accommodation.
Further Info: www.storrington.org.uk. **Parking:** Large car park in the centre of Storrington. Car parks at National Trust Sullington Warren in the village & on the South Downs Way. *Grid Ref: Storrington TQ087143, Sullington Warren TQ098141, South Downs Way TQ069124. Post Code: Storrington RH20 4DH, Sullington Warren RH20 3LY.*

Drive Times: Brighton 40mins, London 1hr40, Bristol 2hr50, Birmingham 3hr10.

Trains: Amberley & Arundel Stations are on the London-Littlehampton line.

Refreshments: At Storrington, The New Moon 01903 744773, The Anchor Inn 01903 742665 and Vintage Rose Café 01903 744100. The Black Horse 01798 831552, The Bridge Inn 01798 831619 and Riverside Café 01798 831558 at Amberley or The George & Dragon 01903 883131 at Burpham.

Bike Shops: South Downs Bikes 01903 745534 in Storrington. M's Cycle Hire 07852 986163 in Worthing for hire, delivery & collection.

Books: South East MTB – N & S Downs (N.Cotton). MTB Rides to the SE (M.Darkins). MTB on S Downs (P.Edwards).

Maps: OS Explorer 121.

Route Idea

From Storrington, S to to join the South Downs Way on E side of Kithurst Hill. W towards Amberley Mount. S past The Burgh to Burpham & Wepham. E through Angmering Park and on to Michelgrove and Tolmare Farm. N to Chantry Hill joining South Downs Way. N back to Storrington. Distance 26km.

Extend the area: Findon Map to the E.

Findon

Situation: In the heart of the South Downs, 4 miles north of Worthing.

About the Base: Findon, a village with several pubs and easy access to the trails. **Further Info:** www.findon.info. **Parking:** Roadside around the crossroads in the centre of Findon parking north of Findon on A24, south at Findon Valley or east at Cissbury Ring. **Grid Ref:** Findon TQ122088, A24 TQ120118, Findon Valley TQ129076, Cissbury Ring TQ139085.

Post Code: Findon BN14 0TE, Findon Valley BN14 0HT.

Drive Times: Brighton 30mins, Southampton 1hr20, London 1hr40, Bristol 2hr50, Birmingham 3hr10.

Trains: Worthing Station (3 miles south), on Brighton-Southampton line. Plus services to Gatwick & London Victoria.

Refreshments: At Findon, The Gun Inn 01903 873206, The Black Horse 01903 872301 and John Henrys 01903 877277. Pubs & cafés at Steyning.

Bike Shops: Splash Mountain Bikes 01903 872300, one mile south of Findon, & Quest Adventure 01903 573700 in Worthing. M's Cycle Hire 07852 986163 in Worthing for hire, delivery & collection.

Books: N & S Downs (N.Cotton). Rides SE (M.Darkins). S Downs (P.Edwards).

Maps: OS Explorer 121 & 122.

Route Ideas

❶ From Findon, road E towards Cissbury Ring. Trails SW to Findon Valley. Trails past West Hill then N towards Sullington Hill to join The South Downs Way. E on The South Downs Way past Chantonbury Ring to Chalkpit Wood. S towards Cissbury Ring. Road back to Findon. Dist 26km.

❷ From Findon, road E towards Cissbury Ring. Trails SE to Beggars rush via Lychpole Hill. N to the South Downs Way. E to Annington and Steyning. W on Monarch's Way past Steyning Bowl. NW on South Downs Way. Pass Chantonbury Ring. Trail SW towards but not as far as North End. Trails towards Cissbury Ring. W back to Findon. Distance 24km.
Extend: Storrington Map to the W.

STORRINGTON MAP

Chantonbury Ring - superb descents in every direction

N

0   1 km
0   1 mile

South Downs

A280   A24   A283   A2037

Sullington Hill, Barnsfarm Hill, South Downs Way, Highden Hill, From Horsham, Blackpatch Hill, Church Hill, West Hill, Tolmare Farm, Windlesham House School, North Farm, North End, Gallops Farm, Findon, Findon Valley (North outskirts of Worthing), From Worthing, Cissbury Ring, Chalkpit Wood, Monarch's Way, Park Brow, Lychpole Hill, Beggars Bush, Steyning Bowl, Steyning Round Hill, Steyning, Monarch's Way, Annington Hill, Annington, Winding Bottom, Botolphs, South Downs Way, Bramber, Upper Beeding

Southwater, Storrington, Findon, Worthing, Steyning

Alfriston West, p400. Riders: Brighton MTB © Mike Gill

Stanmer Park, Ditchling Beacon, p400. Riders: Brighton MTB © Mike Gill

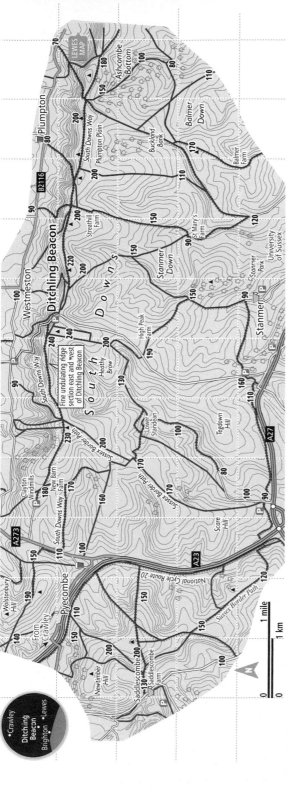

Situation: High on the South Downs ridge in East Sussex. 6 miles north of Brighton.

About the Base: Ditchling Beacon, a rural location with a car park and easy access to the trails. **Parking:** Car parks at Ditchling Beacon & at the foot of the hill on Underhill Lane. Also at Clayton Windmills, Saddlescombe, north of the A27 & at Stanmer Park. **Grid Ref:** Ditchling Beacon TQ333129, Underhill Lane TQ325137, Clayton Windmills TQ302134, Saddlescombe TQ26911, Stanmer Park TQ336096. **Post Code:** Ditchling Beacon BN6 8RJ, Stanmer BN1 9PZ.

Drive Times: Brighton 20mins, London 1hr30, Southampton 1hr40, Bristol 2hr50, Birmingham 3hrs.

Trains: Hassocks Railway Station, 3 miles away, is on the London Victoria-Brighton line.

Refreshments: No refreshments at Ditchling Beacon. The Plough Inn 01273 842796 at Pyecombe, Hikers Café at National Trust Saddlescombe Farm 01273 857712 at Saddlescombe. Stanmer Park Tea Rooms 01273 604041 at Stanmer.

Bike Shops: Freedom Bikes 01273

681698, Evans Cycles 01273 772357 or Action Bikes 01273 605160 in Brighton. Go Cycle 01273 697104 in Brighton for hire.

Books: South East MTB – N & S Downs (N.Cotton). MTB Rides to the SE (M.Darkins). MBR Ride Guide 2010

Maps: OS Explorer 122.

Route Ideas

❶ From Ditchling Beacon, W on the South Downs Way. Trail S of Wolstonbury Hill then S to Pyecombe. SW to Saddlescombe. Sussex Border Path S then N to link back to South Downs Way. E back to start. Distance 20km.

❷ Start as above. Leave the Sussex Border Path to head E to Lower Standean. Trails to High Peak Farm, Stanmer Down, St Marys's Farm, Balmer Down, across Ashcombe Bottom to South Downs Way. W back to start.

Extend the area: Lewes Map to the E.

397

Lewes

DITCHLING BEACON MAP

Crawley
Hayward s
Heath
Lewes
Brighton

South Downs Way
Plumpton Plain
Blackcap
Courthouse Farm
B2116
A2029
Offham
200
150
180
190
Mount Harry
Ashcombe Bottom
150
Offham Hill
40
170
100
130
Buckland Bank
80
10
Balmer Down
South Downs Way
100
Houndean Bottom
100
Lewes
50
110
170
150
150
Balmer Farm
70
Bunkershill Plantation
110
100
120
Housedean Farm
60
Long Hill
"Pavement Path"
A27
50
From Brighton
60
Falmer
50
70
Kingston near Lewes
50
P
30
From Eastbourne
Loose Bottom
South Downs Way
100
140
140
South Downs Way
190
170
170
South Downs
30
Iford
190
180
Castle Hill
Swanborough Hill
50
B2123
Newmarket Hill
100
180
20
160
P
190
Bullock Hill
150
Iford Hill
Front Hill
150
Woodingdean
80
180
South Downs Way
Rodmell
Standean Bottom
100
150
100
Pickers Hill
Whiteway Bottom
80
70
120
Harvey's Cross Monument
120
Highdole Hill
Fore Hill
30
120
110
110
High Hill
Pickers Hill Farm
50
80
120
Telscombe
60
30
100
Saltdean
90

N
0   1 mile
0   1 km

Situation: On the banks of the River Ouse in the South Downs National Park in East Sussex. 7 miles north of Newhaven and 10 miles north east of Brighton.

About the Base: Lewes, a county town with pubs, cafés and accommodation. Further Info: www.lewes.co.uk. **Parking:** Car parks in the centre of Lewes & just north of Woodingdean. Roadside parking in Kingston near Lewes. **Grid Ref:** *Lewes TQ418103, Woodingdean TQ356063, Kingston near Lewes TQ393082.* **Post Code:** *Lewes BN7 2LP, Woodingdean BN2 6NT, Kingston near Lewes BN7 3NT.*

Drive Times: Brighton 30mins, London 1hr30, Bristol 2hr50, Birmingham 3hrs.

Trains: Lewes Station is on the London-Newhaven & Brighton-Eastbourne lines.

Refreshments: Good choice of refreshments at Lewes. The Swan Inn 01903 232923 at Falmer and The Juggs 01273 472523 at Kingston near Lewes. The Blacksmiths Arms 01273 472971 at Offham or The Abergavenny Arms 01273 472416 at Rodmell.

Bike Shops: Lewes Cycle Shack 01273 479688.

Books: South East MTB – N & S Downs (N.Cotton). MTB on S Downs (P.Edwards). MBR Ride Guide 2010

Maps: OS Explorer 122.

Route Idea

From Kingston near Lewes, trail links to skirt the W of Lewes. Climb NW towards and past Mount Harry. S on South Downs Way, crossing the A27 then to outskirts of Woodingdean. E around Bullock Hill, Standean Bottom to Harvey's Cross Monument. SE to Telescombe. NE past Fore Hill. NW on South Downs Way then NE descent to Kingston near Lewes. Distance 35km.

Extend the area: Ditchling Beacon Map to the W.

© Nick Cotton

Alfriston (west)

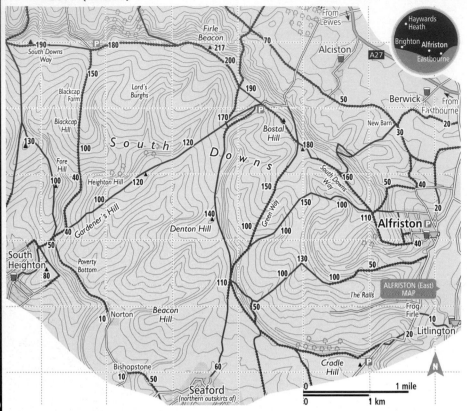

Situation: At the foot of Firle Beacon on the South Downs. In the Cuckmere Valley and the South Downs National Park in East Sussex. 7 miles east of Newhaven and 9 miles north west of Eastbourne.

About the Base: Alfriston, a village with several pubs, cafés and tea rooms.
Further Info: www.alfriston-village.co.uk. **Parking:** Car park near to the river in Alfriston & south of the village at Cradle Hill. Also either side of Firle Beacon. *Grid Ref: Alfriston TQ521032, Cradle Hill TQ509010, Firle Beacon TQ494050 or TQ468058.* **Post Code:** *Alfriston BN26 5UQ.*

Drive Times: Brighton 40mins, London 1hr40, Bristol 3hrs, Birmingham 3hr10.

Trains: Berwick Railway Station, 2 miles north of Alfriston, is on the London-Eastbourne line.

Refreshments: A choice of pubs and cafés at Alfriston. The Cricketers Arms 01323 870469 at Berwick and The Rose Cottage Inn 01323 870377 at Alciston. The Flying Fish 01273 515440 at South Heighton, Litlington Tea Gardens and The Plough and Harrow at Litlington.

Bike Shops: Cuckmere Cycle Centre 01323 870310, 2 miles south of the map at Seven Sisters Country Park for bikes, parts, repairs, hire & guided rides.

Books: South East MTB – N & S Downs (N.Cotton). MTB on S Downs (P.Edwards). MBR Ride Guide 2010.

Maps: OS Explorer 123.

Route Idea

From Alfriston, NW on South Downs Way past Firle Beacon to Junction.S past Blackcap Hill and on to Bishopstone thenSeaford. Trails NE on Green Way. South Downs Way back to Alfriston. Distance 21km.

Extend the area: Alfriston E Map.

Near Firle Beacon. ©www.trailbreak.co.uk

Alfriston West. Riders: Brighton MTB © Mike Gill

Alfriston East. Riders: Brighton MTB © Mike Gill

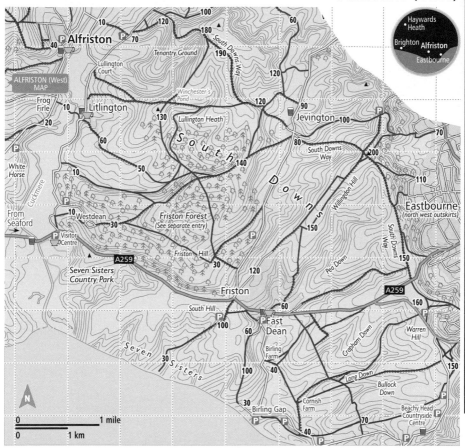

Situation: On the South Downs Way, in the Cuckmere Valley and the South Downs National Park in East Sussex. 7 miles east of Newhaven and 9 miles north west of Eastbourne.

About the Base: Alfriston, a village with several pubs, cafés and tea rooms. Further Info: www.alfriston-village.co.uk. **Parking:** Car parks near to the river in Alfriston, east of the village across Long Bridge & south at The White Horse. Also at Westdean, Seven Sisters Country Park, Friston Forest, South Hill & Eastdean. Several car parks along the coast, at Beachy Head Countryside Centre & west of Eastbourne. *Grid Ref: Alfriston TQ521032, East Alfriston TQ531032, White Horse TQ509010, Westdean TQ517001, Seven Sisters TV518994, Friston Forest TV555993, South Hill TV549978, Eastdean TV557977.* **Post Code:** *Alfriston BN26 5UQ, Westdean BN25 4AJ, Seven Sisters BN25 4AD, Eastdean BN20 0DL.*

Drive Times: Brighton 40mins, London 1hr40, Bristol 3hrs, Birmingham 3hr10.

Trains: Berwick Station, 2 miles north of Alfriston, is on the London-Eastbourne line.

Refreshments: A choice of pubs and cafés at Alfriston. Litlington Tea Gardens and The Plough and Harrow at Litlington. Café 01323-871095 at Seven Sisters Country Park and The Golden Galleon 01323 892247 at Westdean. The Hikers Rest Coffeee Shop 01323 423 733 and The Tiger Inn 01323 423209 at East Dean. The Beachy Head 01323 728060 near Beachy Head Countryside Centre. The Eight Bells 01323 484442 at Jevington.

Bike Shops: Cuckmere Cycle Centre 01323 870310 at Seven Sisters Country Park in Westdean for bikes, parts, repairs, hire & guided rides.

Books: South East MTB – N & S Downs (N.Cotton). MTB Rides to the SE (M.Darkins). MTB on S Downs (P.Edwards).

Maps: OS Explorer 123.

Route Ideas

❶ From car park east of Alfriston, S to Lullington Court. E to Winchester Pond. S through Friston Forest to Friston. NE along Willingdon Hill. South Downs way back to the start. Distance 21km.

❷ Start as above to Friston then trail S tof East Dean and trails over to Birling Gap. Trails past Cornish Farm to Warren Hill. South Downs Way back to the start. Distance 31km.

Extend the area: Alfriston West Map.

Netherfield

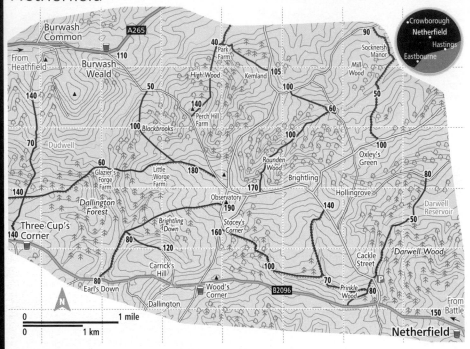

Situation: On a high point, overlooking the surrounding forest in East Sussex. 8 miles north west of Hastings.

About the Base: Netherfield, a village with two pubs and easy access to the trails.

Further Info: www.villagenet.co.uk/esussex-iron/villages/netherfield. **Parking:** Opposite the Netherfield Arms in Netherfield. Car parks at Darwell Wood, west of the village, & National Trust Batemans at Burwash. *Grid Ref: Netherfield TQ711186, Darwell Wood TQ695195, Batemans TQ670237. Post Code: Netherfield TN33 9QD, Batemans TN19 7DS.*

Drive Times: Brighton 1hr, London 1hr40, Bristol 3hr10, Birmingham 3hr20.

Trains: Battle Railway Station, 3 miles away, is on the London-Hastings line.

Refreshments: At Netherfield, The White Hart 01424 838382 and The Netherfield Arms 01424 838282. The Swan Inn 01424 838242 at Woods Corner, The Three Cup's Inn 01435 830252 at Three Cup's Corner and The Wheel Inn 01435 882758 at Burwash Weald. Tea Rooms at National Trust Batemans.

Bike Shops: Cycle Revival 01435 866118, 4 miles west of the map in Heathfield.

Books: MTB Rides to the SE (M.Darkins).

Maps: OS Explorer 124.

Route Idea

From Darwell Wood Car Park. Trails through Prinkle Wood and on to Stacey's Corner. Trails across Brightling Down. Road to Three Cup's Corner. Trails E through Dallington Forest then N past Blackbrooks. Trails N through High Wood then SE to Kemland. Road S then trail NE through Rounden Wood. Roads to Hollingrove then E to take trail through Darwell Wood and back to the start.
Distance 27km.

Findon p394, Chanctonbury Ring. ©www.trailbreak.co.uk

Shanklin (Isle of Wight)

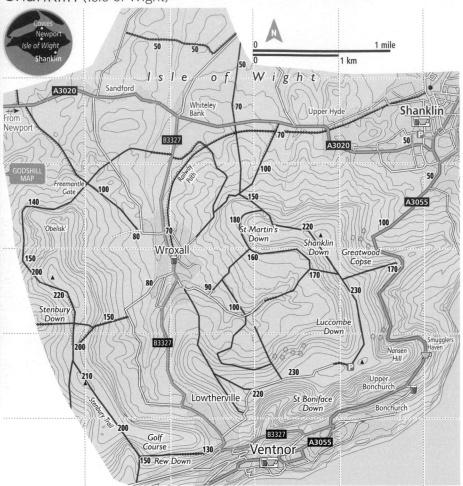

Situation: At the foot of Luccombe Down in the south east corner of the Isle of Wight, at the southernmost tip of Sandown Bay. 10 miles south east of Newport.

About the Base: Shanklin, a seaside resort with pubs, cafés and accommodation. Further Info: www.isleofwight.com/shanklin. **Parking:** Car park in the centre of Shanklin. Also at Luccombe Down. *Grid Ref: Shanklin SZ580813, Luccombe Down SZ573786. Post Code: Shanklin PO37 7NP.*

Trains: Shanklin Station has services to the high speed ferry terminal at Ryde Pier for connections to Portsmouth Harbour & onward trains to London, Brighton, Southampton, Bristol & Cardiff.

Refreshments: Plenty of pubs & cafés at Shanklin, Smugglers Haven Café 01983 852992, The Bonchurch Inn 01983 852611 at Bonchurch, pubs & cafés at Ventnor. The Four Seasons Inn 01983 854701 at Wroxhall.

Bike Shops: Extreme Cycles 01983 852232 in Ventnor, Wight Mountain 01983 533445 in Newport. The Wight Cycle 0800 112 3751 in Ventor for hire.

Maps: OS Explorer OL29.

Routes on Web: www.goodmtb.co.uk/a131

Route Idea

From Shanklin, S on A3055 past Greatwood Copse. Trail W then S across Luccombe Down. W to Lowtherville and along Rew Down. N past Stenbury Down to Freemantle Gate. SE to Wroxall. Railway path N then W back to Shanklin. Distance 18km.

Extend the area: Godshill Map to the W.

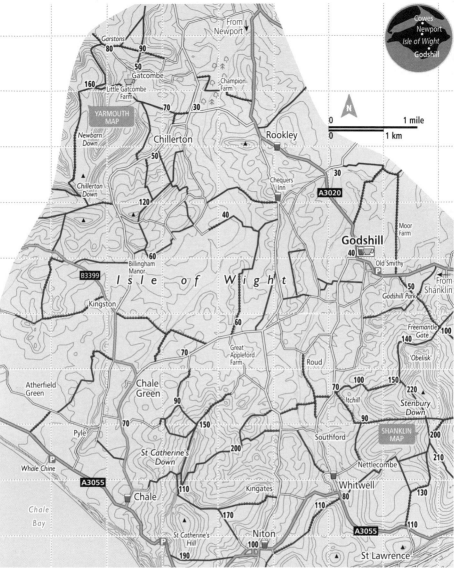

Situation: In the south of the Isle of Wight.

About the Base: Godshill, a small village with pubs and cafés. Further Info: www.godshilliow.info.

Parking: Car parks in Godshill. *Grid Ref: SZ530816 Post Code: Godshill PO38 3JD*

Ferry: High speed ferry terminal at Ryde Pier, connections to Portsmouth Harbour for onward trains to London, Brighton, Southampton, Bristol & Cardiff.

Refreshments: At Godshill, The Taverners 01983 840707, The Griffin 01983 840039, Old Smithy Tea Rooms 01983 840426 and Hollies Tea Gardens 01983 840011. Tea Rooms at Little Gatcombe Farm 01983 721580. The Buddle Inn 01983 730243 at Niton and The White Horse 01983 730375 at Whitwell.

Bike Shops: Extreme Cycles 01983 852232 in

Ventnor, Wight Mountain 01983 533445 in Newport. Wight Cycle 0800 112 375 in Ventor for hire.

Books: MTB Rides to the SE (M.Darkins).

Maps: OS Explorer OL29.

Route Idea

From Godshill, along the A3020 then trail N past Moor Farm. On to Rookley. Trail past Champion Farm to join roads and trails to Garstons. S across Newbarn Down and Chillerton Down to the B3399. E to Billingham Manor. Road & trails past Great Appleford Farm, across St Catherine's Down to Niton. NE to pass Whitwell. N across Stenbury Down to Freemantle Gate and back to start. Distance 34km. Use of other roads & trails to shorten if required.

Extend the area: Yarmouth Map to the NW. Shanklin Map to the E.

Yarmouth (Isle of Wight)

Situation: On the Yar Estuary, western side of the Isle of Wight.

About the Base: Yarmouth, a small harbour town with a choice of pubs and cafés. Further Info: www.isleofwight. com/yarmouth. **Parking:** Car parks in Yarmouth, Freshwater Bay, at Carisbrooke Castle & throughout the area (see map). **Grid Ref:** Yarmouth SZ353895, Freshwater Bay SZ346857, Carisbrooke Castle SZ489875. **Post Code:** Yarmouth PO41 0NU, Freshwater Bay PO40 9US, Carisbrooke Castle PO30 1YS.

Ferry: Ferry Services from Yarmouth to Lymington, 18 miles south west of Southampton. The high speed ferry terminal at Ryde Pier has connections to Portsmouth Harbour for onward trains to London,

Brighton, Southampton, Bristol & Cardiff.

Refreshments: Several pubs & cafés at Yarmouth. The Red Lion 01983 754925 at Freshwater, Apple Tree Café 07979 386 584 at Afton and Tea Rooms at Freshwater Bay. Tea Rooms at Little Gatcombe Farm 01983 721580 or Carisbrooke Castle 01983 522107. Eight Bells Inn 01983 825501 at Carisbrooke.

Bike Shops: Wight Mountain 01983 533445 in Newport. Wight Cycle Hire 01983 761800 in Yarmouth.

Books: MTB Rides to the SE (M.Darkins).

Maps: OS Explorer OL29.

Routes on Web: www.goodmtb.co.uk/ a132a &/a132b

Route Idea

From Yarmouth, S to Afton along the inlet to join Tennyson Trail. Follow E & NE all the way to Newport. S to Gatcombe & on to Chillerton Down. W past Lorden Copse and then Fore Down. Rejoin Tennyson Trail and reverse outward section back to start. Distance 43km. Possible to use various road and trails to shorten as required.

Possibly the best chalk trail in the UK

Brightstone Down ©Patrick Eden. Isle of Wight Cycling Festival

Alice Holt

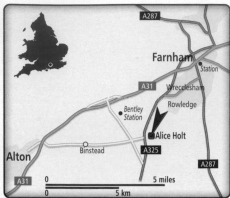

Within the South Downs National Park in Surrey. A circular trail in ancient oak forest suitable for novice and family riders.

Facilities:
Café on the Green at Alice Holt Visitor Centre. Quench Cycles 01420 520355 for MTB hire, parts and repairs.

Parking:
Grid Ref: SU811417. Post Code: GU10 4LS

Web: www.goodmtb.co.uk/b56

The Trails

Family Trail, XC, 4.8km

The family trail makes a launch point to build skills and confidence before heading out into the wider woodland.

Queen Elizabeth Country Park Trails

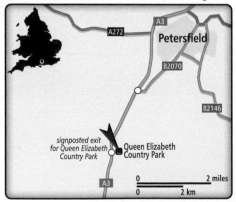

In the Butser Hill National Nature Reserve at the highest point on the South Downs, 1,400 acres of open access woodland and downland within the East Hampshire Area of Outstanding Natural Beauty. Two shorter waymarked cross country trails as well as longer, more challenging trails to explore.

Facilities: The Coach House Café at the Visitor Centre.

Parking:
Grid Ref: SU716182. Post Code: PO8 0QE

Web: www.goodmtb.co.uk/b62

The Trails

❶ Novice Trail, XC, 6km.
❷ Advanced Trail, XC, 5km.
❸ Queen Elizabeth, XC, 16km.
❹ Meon Valley, XC, 16km.

Tilgate Forest

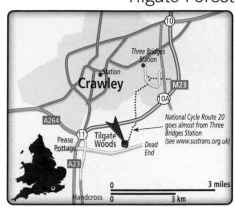

Tilgate Forest near Crawley, West Sussex has been a favourite spot for mountain bikers in the South East of England for more than a decade. Recently a dedicated few have brought together individual groups of riders and trail builders to work with the Forestry commission and CTC to form Ride Tilgate, the official extreme mountain biking park in the forest.

Facilities:
Refreshments in nearby Horsham or Crawley.

Parking:
Grid Ref: TQ274345. Post Code: RH10 5LY

Web: www.goodmtb.co.uk/b71

The Trails

Various trails to suit variety of abilities. If you want to ride here you must be a member, a member's guest or a day ticket holder. See above web link for further information.

Deers Leap Park

In the High Weald Area of Outstanding Natural Beauty in Mid Sussex, just south of East Grinstead. Waymarked, dedicated MTB trails include singletrack, northshore and family trails.

Facilities:
Deers Leep Bikes 01342 325 858 for MTB hire, parts and repairs on site.

Parking:
Grid Ref: TQ384357. Post Code: RH19 4NG

Web: www.goodmtb.co.uk/b59

The Trails

240 acres of dedicated mountain bike tracks of every grade from family-friendly trails to singletrack and northshore in the woods. Generally easy trails with not much to test experienced riders.

Viceroy's Wood (PORC)

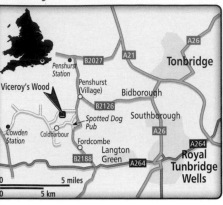

In the Kent countryside and the High Weald Area of Outstanding Natural Beauty, purpose-built, waymarked trails for all abilities from very technical to family leisure.

Facilities:
Refreshments and MTB Hire at the Shimla Clubhouse.

Parking:
Grid Ref: TQ512426. Post Code: TN11 8DX

Web: www.goodmtb.co.uk/b64

The Trails

XC. DH. Dirt Jump

4x Competition Track

Bedgebury

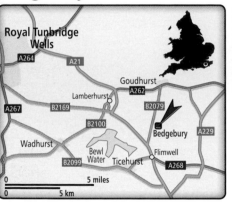

In Kent, a 2000 acre Forestry Commission managed forest. Developed and maintained by Boars on Bikes Bedgebury Forest Cycle Club, a 15km single-track XC trail with added technical features, Freeride Area with dirt jumps and Family Trails to explore.

Facilities:
Café at Bedgebury Forest Visitor Centre. Quench Cycles 01580 879694 for MTB hire, parts and repairs.

Parking:
Grid Ref: TQ718339. Post Code: TN17 2SL

Web: www.goodmtb.co.uk/b57a & /b57b

The Trails

Green, XC, 9km.

Wanda's Trail, Red, XC, 15km.

Freeride

Bewl Water

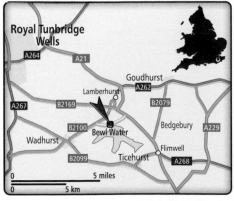

Within the High Weald Area of Outstanding Natural Beauty, a circular route, on a variety of surfaces, around the largest reservoir in the South East.

Facilities:
Food Court Restaurant & Bar at Bewl Water Visitor Centre.

Parking:
Grid Ref: TQ677340. Post Code: TN3 8JH

Web: www.goodmtb.co.uk/b58

The Trails

Family friendly riding around the reservoir, 19km. The route is open to cyclists from May to October.

Friston Forest

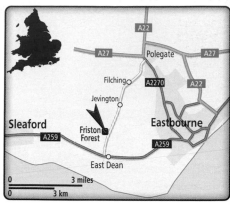

In the Cuckmere Valley and the South Downs National Park in East Sussex, umarked and waymarked trails on smooth flowing woodland singletrack with short downhill, northshore, jumps & drops.

Facilities:
Refreshments at nearby East Dean. Cuckmere Cycle Centre 01323 870310 for MTB hire at Seven Sisters Country Park Visitor Centre.

Parking:
Grid Ref: TV555995.

Web: www.goodmtb.co.uk/b60

The Trails

One waymarked XC, 11.3km.

New Forest

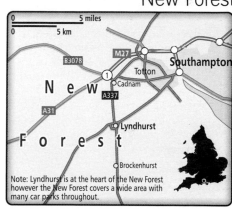

A National Park stretching from east of the Avon Valley to Southampton Water and from the Solent coast to the edge of the Wiltshire chalk downs. Over one hundred miles of waymarked trails for beginners and families.

Facilities:
New Forest Visitor Centre. AA Bike Hire 02380 283349. Cyclexperience 01590 624204. Country Lanes Cycle Hire 01590 622627. Forest Leisure Cycling 01425 403584 .

Parking:
Many car parks all around the New Forest. For Lyndhurst. Post Code: SO43 7NY.

Web: www.goodmtb.co.uk/b61

The Trails

Cycling only allowed on marked cycle routes; maps of which can be downloaded from the web (link above). General easy family riding on forest tracks.

SOUTH WEST

The South West offers the greatest variety of mountain biking in all of England, from the granite tors of Dartmoor rising to 621m, to rides along the chalk cliffs of Dorset; from the bewildering network of bridleways criss-crossing Exmoor and the Quantocks with views out over the Bristol Channel to the tracks through the Cotswolds linking the famous honey coloured stone villages. Throw in the limestone ridge of the Mendips, Salisbury Plain, the start of the Ridgeway National Trail and various Trail Centres and clearly there is a massive choice in the region. Whilst the rides in the Cotswolds and on the chalk of Wiltshire and Dorset suffer the heavy mud in winter that is prevalent throughout Southern England, Dartmoor, Exmoor and the Quantocks offer year round riding as these areas consist of older, harder rocks giving easier winter riding conditions.

The Cotswolds & The Mendips

The area covered by an arc 20 miles around Cheltenham and to the east of the M5 contains the best of Cotswolds mountain biking. Woodland tracks suddenly pop you out in fine little villages of honey coloured stone with pubs and tea shops. The Cotswolds are like a slice of cake on its side: the steep edge represents the escarpment dropping down sharply into the Severn Vale with some of the toughest climbs and best descents. The more gentle slope represents the gradual tilt of the Cotswolds from their highpoint 326m, on Cleeve Common south west of **Winchcombe** down to the Thames at **South Cerney**.

Set to the northeast of Tewkesbury and separated from the main bulk of the Cotswolds, Bredon Hill rises to 294m and offers plenty of options, best explored from **Kemerton**.

Broadway, **Chipping Campden** and **Winchcombe** are stunningly attractive towns at the northern end of the Cotswolds, connecting via woodland tracks to similarly beautiful smaller villages such as **Blockley**, **Snowshill** and **Naunton**. The views from the top of the escarpment near to **Snowshill** are vast, looking west towards the Malverns and across the Severn Valley into Wales. For easier riding try the bridleways that cross the gentle slope of the Cotswolds starting from picturesque **Bibury** and exploring the Coln

© Peter Joyner

Valley or weaving in and out of the lakes in the Cotswold Water Park at **South Cerney.**

The topography of the Cotswolds becomes more fractured around the Stroud Valleys with rides starting north of here at **Bisley** or to the south from **Nailsworth**. Similarly the area around **Wotton under Edge** and Dursley is surrounded by extraordinary shaped hills like Cam Long Down or Uley Bury and lots of hidden valleys like the wonderfully named Ozleworth Bottom. There are also rides further south: the Cotswold escarpment extends right down to **Bath**, one of Britain's most famous and beautiful cities, with the Kennet & Avon Canal and the Bristol & Bath Railway Path offering links out into the countryside to join trails climbing steeply up to **Lansdown** and the race course.

East of **Cheddar**, the Cheddar Gorge is the most famous feature of the Mendips, a

carboniferous limestone ridge just to the south of Bristol. This area of drystone walls and high sheep pastures at times has the feel of the Peak District. Ride up to the highest point of the Mendips, Beacon Batch / Black Down (325m). There are some fine descents from here to the south, west and north. Be warned that this is winter mud territory and best enjoyed after a few dry days from late spring to late autumn.

Trail Centres for the area include **Ashton Court** & **Leigh Woods** (new trails opening 2011) and **Forest of Dean** on the other side of the Severn Bridge. There are also trails at **Spirt Hill** near Swindon.

© Sheldon Attwood

© Sheldon Attwood

Kemerton

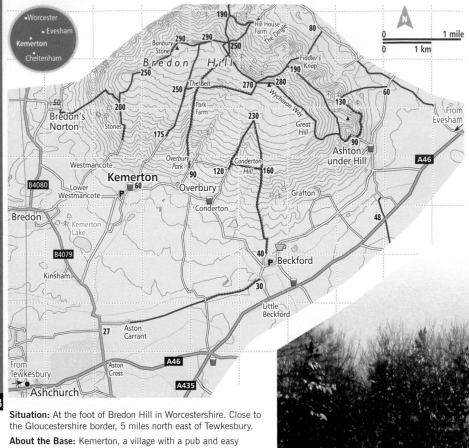

Situation: At the foot of Bredon Hill in Worcestershire. Close to the Gloucestershire border, 5 miles north east of Tewkesbury.

About the Base: Kemerton, a village with a pub and easy access to the trails. **Parking:** Roadside in the centre of Kemerton or Beckford. *Grid Ref: Kemerton SO945371, Beckford SO976357, **Post Code:** Kemerton GL20 7HP, Beckford GL20 7AD.*

Drive Times: Birmingham 1hr, Bristol 1hr, Oxford 1hr30, Southampton 2hr10, London 2hr30.

Trains: Ashchurch for Tewkesbury Railway Station, in the south west of the map, is on the Birmingham-Cheltenham & Worcester-Cheltenham lines.

Refreshments: The Crown Inn 01386 725 293 at Kemerton. The Yew Tree 01386 725 364 at Conderton, The Beckford Inn 01386 881 532 or Two Jays Café 07796 034 799 at Beckford, The Gardeners Arms 01242 620 257 at Alderton and The Star 01386 881 325 at Ashton under Hill.

Bike Shops: Halfords 01684 854990 in Tewkesbury.

Books: MTB Guide W Midlands (D.Taylor). Cotswolds MTB (T.Fenton).

Maps: OS Explorer 190.

Route Idea

From Kemerton, N to the Belt. E along the Belt & onto Fiddler's Knap then road. S to Ashton under Hill. NW along Wychavon Way. Up to Banbury Stone. Down to Lower Westmancote and back to start. Distance 20km.

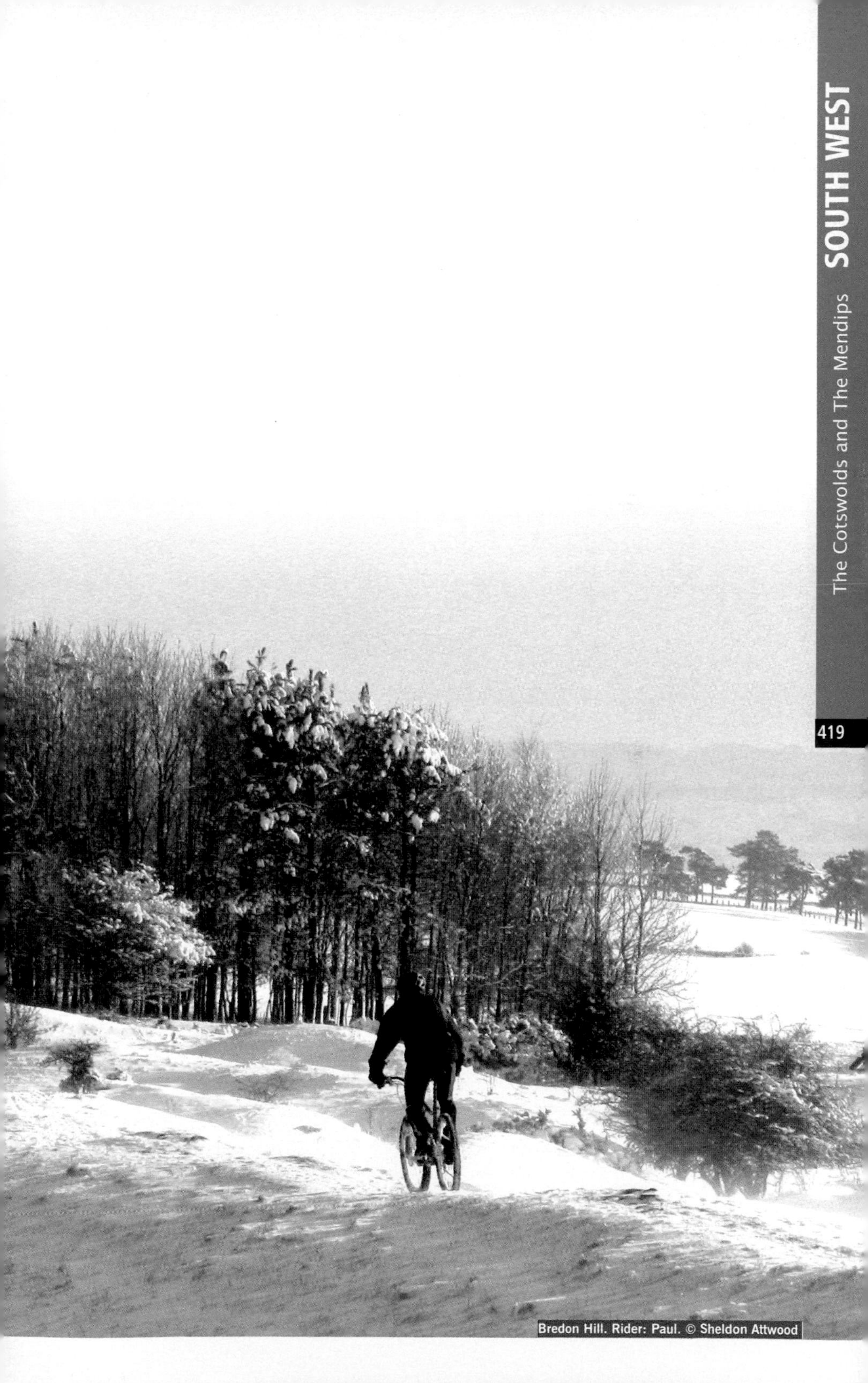

Bredon Hill. Rider: Paul. © Sheldon Attwood

Broadway

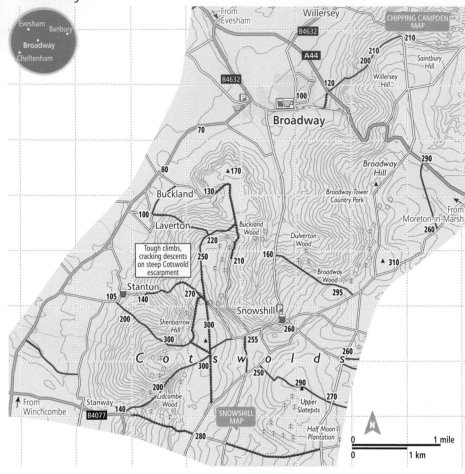

Situation: Beneath the Worcestershire Hills on the western Cotswold escarpment. 7 miles south east of Evesham.

About the Base: Broadway, a village with pubs, cafés and accommodation.
Further Info: www.beautifulbroadway.com.

Parking: Car parks west of Broadway village & at Snowshill Manor. *Grid Ref:* Broadway SP090376, Snowshill SP095340, **Post Code:** Broadway WR12 7HA, Snowshill WR12 7JR.

Drive Times: Birmingham 1hr, Bristol 1hr10, Oxford 1hr10, Manchester 2hr30, London 2hr20.

Trains: Honeybourne Railway Station, 5 miles away, is on the Worcester-Oxford line.

Refreshments: At Broadway, a choice of pubs, Foxy Browns Café 01386 852155 or Tisanes Tea Rooms 01386 853296. Corners Café 01386 852 142 on the edge of the village. The Snowshill Arms 01386 852 653 or Tea Rooms at National Trust Snowshill Manor.

Bike Shops: Vale Cycles 01386 41204 in Evesham.

Books: MTB Guide W Midlands (D.Taylor).

Maps: OS Explorer OL45.

Route Idea

From Broadway, NE past Willersey Hill. Road S. Trail S from A44 then roads S to Half Moon Plantation. Trail W towards Stanway, NE through Lidcombe Wood & onto Buckland Wood and Buckland. Roads back to start. Distance 27km.

© Sheldon Attwood

Chipping Campden

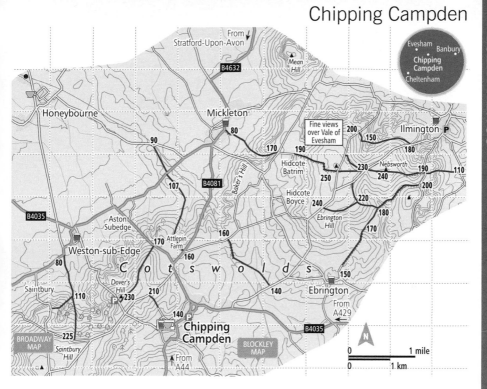

Situation: In the Ilmington Downs on the northern edge of the Cotswolds. 10 miles south east of Evesham and 12 miles south of Stratford-upon-Avon.

About the Base: Chipping Campden, a small market town with pubs, cafés and accommodation. Further Info: www.chippingcampden.co.uk. **Parking:** In the centre of Chipping Campden. Car park west of the town at Dover's Hill. Parking in Ilmington village. *Grid Ref: Chipping Campden SP150391, Dover's Hill SP137395, Ilmington SP213434,* **Post Code:** *Chipping Campden GL55 6AP, Ilmington CV36 4LZ.*

Drive Times: Birmingham 1hr10, Oxford 1hr10, Bristol 1hr30, London 2hr20, Southampton 2hr40.

Trains: Honeybourne Railway Station, in the west of the map, is on the Worcester-Oxford line.

Refreshments: Plenty of pubs and cafés at Chipping Campden. The Seagrave Arms 01386 840192 at Weston-sub-Edge, The Kings Arms 01386 438 257 at Mickleton, The Howard Arms 01608 682 226 at Ilmington and The Ebrington Arms 01386 593 223 at Ebrington. If arriving by train, The Thatched Tavern 01386 830 454 or Speckled Hen Tea Room 01386 833083 at Honeybourne.

Bike Shops: Cycle Cotswolds 01789 720 193 for hire, delivery & collection. Cotswold Country Cycles 01386 438 706 for hire & guided tours.

Books: MTB Guide W Midlands (D.Taylor).

Maps: OS Explorer 205.

Route Idea

From Chipping Campden, N to Mickleton via Dover's Hill & Attlepin Farm. E past Hidcote Batrim & Nebsworth. Trails SW to Ebrington and roads back to the start. Distance 24km

Blockley

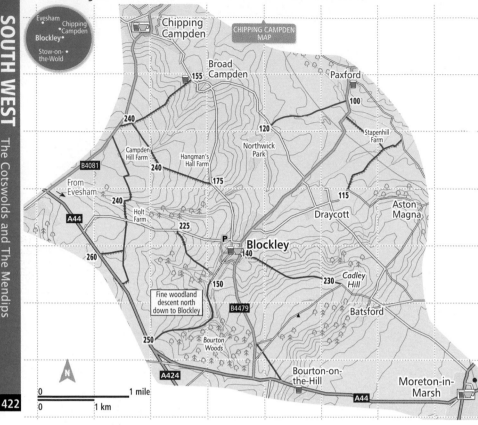

Situation: In the north east corner of the Cotswolds in Gloucestershire. 3 miles south of Chipping Campden and 4 miles north west of Moreton-in-Marsh.

About the Base: Blockley, a village with a pub, shop and café. **Parking:** Roadside parking in Blockley.

Grid Ref: SP165348, Post Code: GL56 9DS.

Drive Times: Birmingham 1hr10, Oxford 1hr, Bristol 1hr20, Southampton 1hr50, London 2hr.

Trains: Moreton-in-Marsh Station is on the Oxford-Worcester line.

Refreshments: At Blockley, The Great Western Arms 01386 700 362 or Blockley Village Shop and Café 01386 701411. The Bakers Arms 01386 840 515 at Broad Campden and The Churchill Arms 01386 593046 at Paxford. The Horse & Groom 01386 700 413 at Bourton-on-the-Hill or pubs and cafés at Chipping Campden and Moreton-in-Marsh.

Bike Shops: Country Lanes Cycle Centre in Moreton-in-Marsh or Cycle Cotswolds 01789 720 193 & Cotswold Country Cycles 01386 438 706 in Chipping Campden for hire & guided tours.

Books: Cotswolds MTB (T.Fenton).

Maps: OS Explorer OL45.

Route Idea

From Blockley, SW past Bourton Woods to the A44. Road & trails N to Broad Campden via Holt Farm. W to Paxford on road & trail. Road S then trail towards Draycott, road to Aston Magna and Batsford. Trail at Cadley Hill back to Blockley. Distance 21km.

Extend the area Chipping Campden map to the N.

Riders: Old Blokes on Bikes. © Peter Joyner

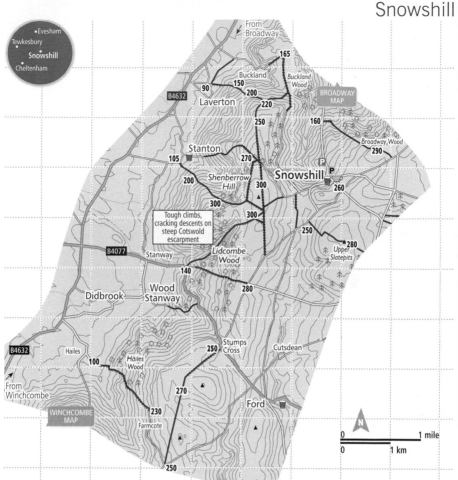

Situation: On an escarpment above Broadway in the Gloucestershire Cotswolds. 6 miles south west of Chipping Campden and 9 miles south east of Evesham.

About the Base: Snowshill, a small village with a pub.

Parking: Roadside Parking in Snowshill or car park at National Trust Snowshill Manor. *Grid Ref: Snowshill SP096337, Snowshill Manor SP096340, Post Code: Snowshill WR12 7JU, Snowshill Manor WR12 7JR.*

Drive Times: Bristol 1hr10, Birmingham 1hr10, Oxford 1hr10, Southampton 2hr10, London 2hr10.

Trains: Moreton-in-Marsh Railway Station, 7 miles away, is on the Oxford-Worcester line.

Refreshments: At Snowshill, The Snowshill Arms 01386 852 653 or Tea Rooms at National Trust Snowshill Manor. The Plough Inn 01386 584215 at Ford and The Mount Inn 01386 584 316 at Stanton.

Bike Shops: Vale Cycles 01386 41204 in Fvesham. Cycle Cotswolds 01789 720 193 or Cotswold Country Cycles 01386 438 706 in Chipping Campden for hire & guided tours.

Books: Cotswolds MTB (T.Fenton).

Maps: OS Explorer OL45.

Route Idea

From Snowshill, S to Stumps Cross, on to Farmcote and NW to the B4632. NE to Didbrook, Stanway, through Lidcombe Wood, over Shenberrow Hill then W to Stanton. Roads To Laverton then trails back towards Shenberrow Hill. Roads back to Snowshill. Distance 27km.

Extend the area: Broadway Map to the N. Winchcombe Map to the S.

Around Snowshill p423 ©Sheldon Attwood

Winchcombe

Evesham
Tewkesbury
Winchcombe
Cheltenham

From A44

SNOWSHILL MAP

70 B4632 Hailes 100 Hailes Wood

Greet

B4078

230

Farmcote

100 Winchcombe Stancombe Wood

170

Lynes Barn Farm 220

B4632

Round Hill

260 220 Postlip 140 Parks Farm 270

220 Cleeve Hill 180

250 150 Corndean Hall 135 Newmeadow Farm

From Cheltenham 290

Cleeve Common

Highest point on Cotswolds: 330m (1083ft)

290 210

From Stow-on-the-Wold

300 Charlton Abbots Roel Hill Farm

310 225

West Down 290 West Wood 210 Roel Gate 240

300 270

Puckham Woods 210 270

Brockhampton 275

Sevenhampton 200

250

Great descent, challenging climb

Syreford 180

N

0 ———————— 1 mile
0 ———————— 1 km

Situation: At the foot of Cleeve Hill in the Cotswolds. 7 miles north east of Cheltenham and 8 miles south west of Broadway.

About the Base: Winchcombe, a town with pubs, cafés and accommodation. Further Info: www.winchcombe.co.uk. **Parking:** Car park in the centre of Winchcombe. Also at Cleeve Hill, south of Cleeve Common & at West Down. *Grid Ref: Winchcombe SP025284, Cleeve Hill SO989271, Cleeve Common SO994248, West Down SP010236 Post Code: Winchcombe GL54 5HY.*

Drive Times: Bristol 1hr10, Oxford 1hr10, Birmingham 1hr10, Southampton 2hr10, London 2hr10.

Trains: Cheltenham Spa Station is on the Birmingham-Bristol line.

Refreshments: Choice of pubs or Juri's Café 01242602469 at Winchcombe. The Craven Arms 01242 820 410 at Brockhampton.

Bike Shops: Cheltenham Cycles 01242 255414, Roylan Cycles 01242 235948, Leisure Lakes Bikes & Halfords in Cheltenham.

Books: Cotswolds MTB (T.Fenton). MBR Ride Guide 2010

Maps: OS Explorer OL45 & 179.

Route Ideas

❶ From Winchcombe, S to Newmeadow Farm. On to Corndean Hall & S to West Down. N over Cleeve Common, around Cleeve Hill to Postlip. Roads back to Winchcombe. Distance 20km.

❷ From Winchcombe, N on B4632. S on roads & trails to Roel Gate via Hailes Wood, Farmcote & Roel Hill Farm. SW to Syreford. Road & trails through Puckham Woods, over Cleeve Common, around Cleeve Hill to Postlip. Roads back. Distance 34km.

Extend the area: Snowshill Map to the N.

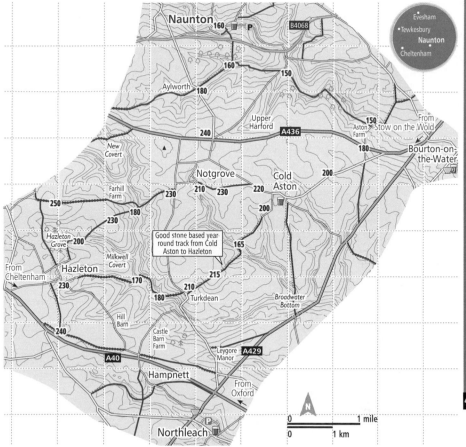

Evesham
• Tewkesbury
Naunton
• Cheltenham

Situation: In the heart of the Cotswolds in Gloucestershire. 5 miles north west of Bourton on the Water and 12 miles east of Cheltenham.

About the Base: Naunton, a village with a pub and easy access to the trails. **Parking:** Roadside parking in Naunton. Car park in Northleach. *Grid Ref: Naunton SP119234, Northleach SP113145,* **Post Code:** *Naunton GL54 3AD, Northleach GL54 3EE.*

Drive Times: Oxford 1hr, Bristol 1hr10, Birmingham 1hr30, Southampton 2hrs. London 2hr10.

Refreshments: At Naunton, The Black Horse Inn 01451 850 565. The Red Lion Inn 01451 860 251 or Blades Coffee Shop 01451 860 715 at Northleach and The Plough nn 01451 821 459 at Cold Aston.

Bike Shops: Bourton Cycles 01451 822323 & Bourton Bikes 01451 824488, In Bourton on the Water, for bikes, parts, repirs & hire.

Books: Cotswolds MTB (T.Fenton).

Maps: OS Explorer OL45.

Route Idea

From Naunton, W then S on road to Aylworth. Roads S to Notgrove then Cold Aston. Trails to Turkdean and Hazleton. S to cross the A40. Roads then trails E to Hampnett. Trails E to junction with the A40 & A429. N to Leygore Manor, Broadwater Bottom & Cold Aston. NE to Aston Farm. Trails back to Naunton. Distance 34km.

© Sheldon Attwood

Cleeve Hill (Winchcombe p426). Rider: Kiren Bennett. © Sheldon Attwood

Charlbury (west)

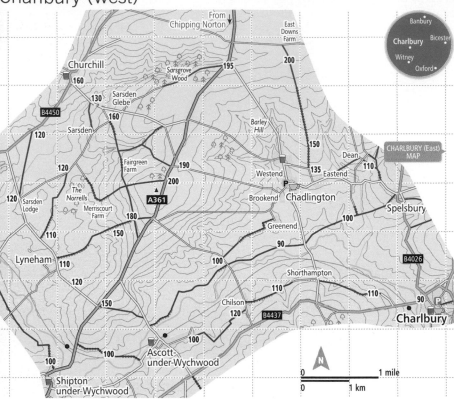

Situation: In the Evenlode Valley, on the edge of Wychwood Forest and the Cotswold Hills in west Oxfordshire. 7 miles south east of Chipping Norton and 8 miles north of Witney.

About the Base: Charlbury, a small market town with pubs, cafés and accommodation. Further Info: www.charlbury.info. **Parking:** Car park in Charlbury. Roadside Parking in Chadlington. *Grid Ref: Charlbury SP358196, Chadlington SP327219, Post Code: Charlbury OX7 3PQ, Chadlington OX7 3BL.*

Drive Times: Oxford 40mins, Bristol 1hr30, Birmingham 1hr30, Southampton 1hr40, London 1hr40.

Trains: Charlbury, Ascott-under-Wychwood & Shipton Stations are on the Oxford-Worcester line.

Refreshments: At Charlbury, The Bull Inn 01608 810 689, Ye Olde Three Horseshoes 01608 810780 and The Bell Hotel 01608 810278. Cafés at The Good Food Shop 01608811157 and News and Things 01608 810228. The Tite Inn 01608 676 475 or Cafe De la Poste at Chadlington. The Chequers Village Inn 01608 659 393 at Churchill, The Red Horse 01993 830 391 at Shipton-under-Wychwood and The Swan Inn 01993 830 345 at Ashton-under-Wychwood.

Bike Shops: Velo Specialist Cycles 01993 771847 in Witney.

Books: Cotswolds MTB (T.Fenton).

Maps: OS Explorer 180, 191 & OL45.

Route Idea

From Charlbury, N to Spelsbury. Trails to Eastend then N towards East Downs Farm. W through Sarsgrove Wood then S past Fairgreen Farm and on to Lyneham. Roads & trails to Shipton under Wychwood, Ascott-under-Wychwood, Chilson, Shorthampton & back to Charlbury. Distance 28km.

Extend the area: Charlbury East Map.

Rider:Andrew Querelle. © Simon Clayson

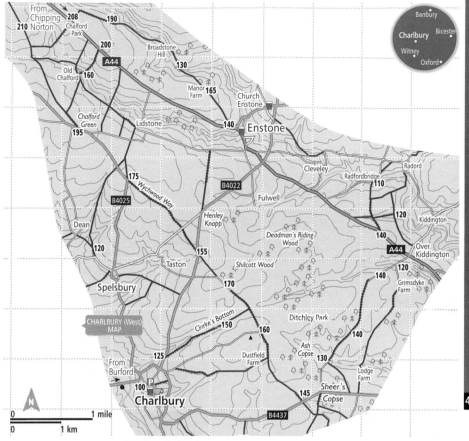

Banbury
Charlbury • Bicester
Witney •
Oxford •

From Chipping Norton 208 210
190
Chalford Park
200
Broadstone Hill
130
A44
Old Chalford 160
Manor Farm 165
Church Enstone
Chalford Green 195
Lidstone
140
Enstone
175
Cleveley
Radfordbridge 110
Radord
B4022
Fulwell
B4025
Wychwood Way
120
Kiddington
Dean
Henley Knapp
140
Deadman's Riding Wood
A44
Over Kiddington
120
155
Taston
Shilcott Wood
120
140
Spelsbury
170
Grimsdyke Farm
CHARLBURY (West) MAP
Clarke's Bottom
150
Ditchley Park
140
160
Ash Copse
140
125
Dustfield Farm
130
From Burford
Lodge Farm
P 100
145
Sheer's Copse
Charlbury
B4437

0 ————— 1 mile
0 ————— 1 km
N

Riders: Old Blokes on Bikes © Chris Green

Situation: On the edge of the Cotswolds and Wychwood Forest in west Oxfordshire. In the Evenlode Valley, 7 miles south east of Chipping Norton and 8 miles north of Witney.

About the Base: Charlbury, a small market town with pubs, cafés and accommodation. Further Info: www.charlbury.info. **Parking:** Car park in Charlbury. *Grid Ref: SP358196, Post Code: OX7 3PQ.*

Drive Times: Oxford 40mins, Bristol 1hr30, Birmingham 1hr30, Southampton 1hr40, London 1hr40.

Trains: Charlbury, Ascott-under-Wychwood & Shipton Stations are on the Oxford-Worcester line.

Refreshments: At Charlbury, The Bull Inn 01608 810 689, Ye Olde Three Horseshoes 01608 810780 and The Bell Hotel 01608 810278. Cafés at The Good Food Shop 01608811157 and News and Things 01608 810228. The Harrow Inn 01608 677 366 at Enstone or The Crown Inn 01608 677 262 at Church Enstone.

Bike Shops: Velo Specialist Cycles 01993 771847 in Witney.

Books: Cotswolds MTB (T.Fenton).

Maps: OS Explorer 191.

Route Idea

From Charlbury, NE along Clarke's Bottom. Trails & roads NW to Chalford Green & on to Chalford Park. S to Enstone via Broadstone Hill. S to Over Kiddington via Cleveley & Radfordbridge. SW to Lodge Farm. Back to Charlbury via Dustfield Farm. Distance 29km.

Extend the area: Charlbury West Map

Birdlip

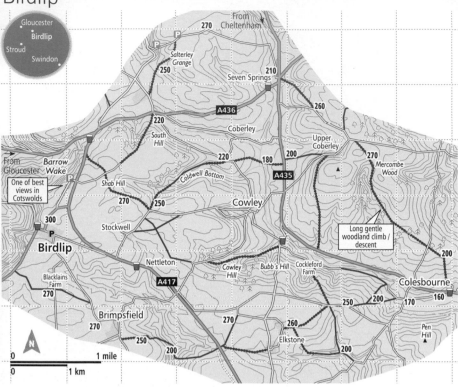

432

Situation: In the heart of Gloucestershire and the Cotswolds Area of Outstanding Natural Beauty. 6 miles south of Cheltenham, 9 miles south east of Gloucester and 9 miles north east of Stroud.

About the Base: Birdlip, a small village with a hotel and easy access to the trails. **Parking:** Roadside in the centre of Birdlip. Car park at Barrow Wake viewpoint, north of Birdlip on the A417. Also at Salterley Grange in the north of the map. *Grid Ref: Birdlip SO927142, Barrow Wake SO931153, Salterley Grange SO946176 or SO950178, Post Code: Birdlip GL4 8JH.*

Drive Times: Bristol 50mins, Oxford 1hr10, Birmingham 1hr10, Southampton 1hr40, London 2hrs.

Trains: Cheltenham Spa Station is on the Birmingham-Bristol line.

Refreshments: The Royal George Hotel 01452 862506 at Birdlip. The Golden Heart 01242 870261 at Nettleton or The Green Dragon Inn at Cockleford. The Colesbourne Inn 01242 870376 at Colesbourne, The Hungry Horse 01242 870219 at Seven Springs and the Air Balloon 01242 870219 at Crickley Hill.

Bike Shops: Several in Cheltenham.

Books: Cotswolds MTB (T.Fenton).

Maps: OS Explorer 179.

Route Idea

From Barrow Wake, S in to Birdlip then on to Blacklains Farm, Brimpsfield, Elkstone, Cockleford Farm & Colesbourne. NW to Seven Springs and back to start via Salterley Grange then Shab Hill. Distance 29km.

Rider: Simon. © Sheldon Attwood

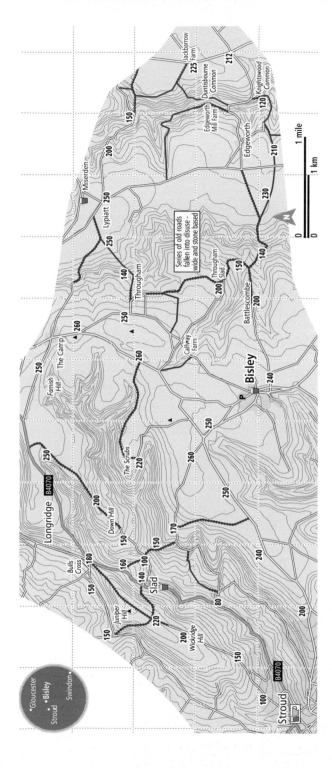

Situation: On top of the Cotswold Hills in Gloucestershire. 4 miles east of Stroud and 9 miles north west to Cirencester.

About the Base: Bisley, a village with two pubs. Further Info: www.bisleyonline.net. **Parking:** Roadside in Bisley opposite The Bear Inn. *Grid Ref: SO903060, Post Code: GL6 7BD.*

Drive Times: Bristol 50mins, Oxford, 1hr20, Birmingham 1hr20, Southampton 1hr50, London 2hr10.

Trains: Stroud Station is on the Gloucester-London line.

Refreshments: At Bisley, The Bear Inn 01452 770265 and

The Stirrup Cup 01452 770280. The Woolpack Inn 01452 813429 at Slad and The Carpenters Arms 01285 821283 at Miserden.

Bike Shops: Noahs Ark 01453 884738, 4 miles away on A419 at Brinscombe or Cytek 01453 753330 in Stroud.

Books: Cotswolds MTB (T.Fenton).

Maps: OS Explorer 168 & 179.

Route Idea

From Bisley, NW to Slad then clockwise on the roads and trails around Juniper Hill then NE over downhill. Roads to Througham. Anticlockwsie loop back to Througham via Througham Slad, Knightswood Common, Jackbarrow Farm & Lypiatt. Back to Bisley via Calfway Farm, or repeat to Througham Slad then on to Battlescombe then Bisley. Distance, 30km.

Series of old roads fallen into disuse - wide and stone based

Nailsworth

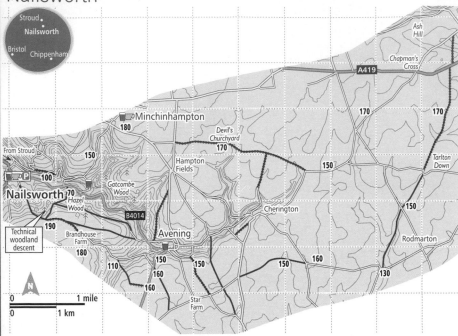

Stroud
Nailsworth
Bristol
Chippenham

Ash Hill
Chapman's Cross
A419
170   170
Minchinhampton
180
Devil's Churchyard
170
Hampton Fields
150
Tarlton Down
From Stroud
150
Gatcombe Wood
100
Nailsworth 70
Hazel Wood
150
Cherington
150
B4014
190
Technical woodland descent
Brandhouse Farm
Avening
Rodmarton
180
110   150   150   150   160   130
160
160
Star Farm

0   1 mile
0   1 km

Situation: In one of the Stroud Valleys, 5 miles south of Stroud, in the Gloucestershire Cotswolds Area of Outstanding Natural Beauty.

About the Base: Nailsworth, a market town with pubs and cafés. Further Info: www.nailsworth.com. **Parking:** Several car parks in Nailsworth. *Grid Ref: ST849995, Post Code: GL6 0DD.*

Drive Times: Bristol 40mins, Cardiff 1hr20, Oxford 1hr30, Birmingham 1hr30, Southampton 2hrs, London 2hr20.

Trains: Stroud Station is on the Gloucester-London line.

Refreshments: Good choice of refreshments at Nailsworth. The Weighbridge Inn 01453 832520 at Gatcombe Wood. The Crown Inn 01453 882357 or The Kitchen Café 01453 882655 at Minchin-hampton, The Bell Inn 01453 836422 and The Cross Inn 0844 412 3100 at Avening.

Bike Shops: The Bike Works 01453 872824, 2 miles north of Nailsworth on the A46, Noahs Ark 01453 884738, 4 miles away on A419 at Brinscombe or Cytek 01453 753330 in Stroud.

Books: Cotswolds MTB (T.Fenton).

Maps: OS Explorer 168.

Route Idea

From Nailsworth to Minchinhampton, E past Devil's Churchyard and N past Chapman's Cross. S past Tarlton Down. W to Avening. S on B4014 then trails and roads back to Nailsworth via Brandhouse Farm. Distance 30km.

Wotton-under-Edge

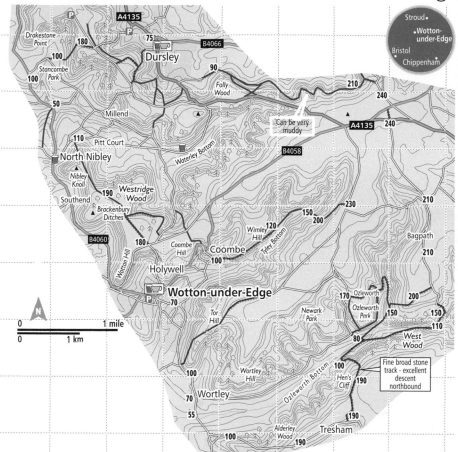

Situation: At the foot of the Cotswold Edge and the southern end of the Cotswold Hills in Gloucestershire. 6 miles south of Dursley, 13 miles south west of Stroud and 13 miles north east of Bristol.

About the Base: Wotton-under-Edge, a small market town with pubs, cafés and accommodation. Further Info: www.cotswolds.info/places/wotton-under-edge.

Parking: Car park in the centre of Wotton-under-Edge & at Dursley Leisure Centre. Also west of Dursley at Drakestone Point. *Grid Ref: Wotton-under-Edge ST756931, Dursley ST754982, Drakestone Point ST751982, Post Code: Wotton-under-Edge GL12 7AF, Dursley GL11 4BW.*

Drive Times: Bristol 30mins, Cardiff 1hr, Birmingham 1hr30, Oxford 1hr40, Southampton 2hrs, London 2hr20.

Trains: Cam & Dursley Railway Station, 7 miles away is on the Bristol-Gloucester & Bristol-Birmingham lines.

Refreshments: At Wotton-under-Edge, The Royal Oak 01453 842316, The Full Moon 01453 843792, The Swan Hotel and The Ark Café 01453 521838. The Black Horse Inn 01453 546841 at North Nibley. The New Inn 01453 543659 at Waterley Bottom.

Bike Shops: The Cycle Shop 01453 842259 in Wotton-Under-Edge or Severn Cycles 01453 544866 in Dursley.

Books: MTB Rides to the SW (M.Darkins).

Maps: OS Explorer 167 & 168.

Route Idea

From Wotton-under-Edge, S to Wortley then Tresham. Trails thorough West Wood then N past Bagpath and over the A4135. Trails W to Dursley. W to to Stancombe Park. S to North Nibley. Trails through Westridge Wood and roads back to the start. Distance 32km.

Bibury

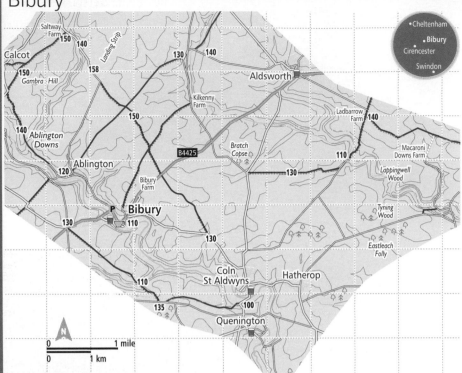

Rider: Rich. © Sheldon Attwood

Situation: On the River Coin in the Gloucestershire Cotswolds. 7 miles north east of Cirencester.

About the Base: Bibury, a village with two pubs, a café and accommodation. Further Info: www.bibury. com. **Parking:** Roadside parking in Bibury. *Grid Ref: SP114068, Post Code: GL7 5NW.*

Drive Times: Oxford 50mins, Bristol 1hr10, Southampton 1hr40, Birmingham 1hr30, London 2hrs.

Refreshments: At Bibury, The Catherine Wheel 01285 74 0250, The Swan Hotel 01285 740 695 and Café at Bibury Trout Farm 01285 740215. The New Inn at Coln 01285 750 651 at Coln St Aldwyns. The Keepers Arms 01285 750 349 at Quenington and The Sherborne Arms 01451 844 346 at Aldsworth.

Bike Shops: Ride 24-7 01285 642 247 in Cirencester. Pedal Power 01285 640 505 in Cirencester also do repairs & hire.

Books: Cotswolds MTB (T.Fenton).

Maps: OS Explorer OL45.

Route Ideas

❶ Roads from Bibury to Coln St Aldwyns, Hatherop & past Tyning Wood. N towards Macaroni Downs Farm. On to Ladbarrow Farm, Bratch Copse & Kilkenny Farm. Trail SW then NW to Saltway Farm. Around Gambra Hill to Ablington Downs and on to Ablington and Bibury. Distance 30km.

❷ To shorten the above and avoiding a lot of roads, head N from Bibury to pick up route to Salway Farm, around Gambra Hill & back to Bibury. Distance 11km.

South Cerney

Situation: In the Cotswold Water Park, south east of the Cotswold Hills on the Gloucestershire/Wiltshire border. 4 miles south of Cirencester and 15 miles north west of Swindon.

About the Base: South Cerney, a village with three pubs. Further Info: www.southcerney.com.

Parking: Roadside parking in the centre of South Cerney. Parking in the water park, south east of the village & at North End. Car parks at Waterhay Bridge & at The Gateway Centre. *Grid Ref: South Cerney SU048971, Water Park SU061967 or SU063962, North End SU051951, Waterhay Bridge SU060933, Gateway Centre SU072970, Post Code: South Cerney GL7 5UA, Gateway Centre GL7 5TL.*

Drive Times: Bristol 1hr, Oxford 1hr, Birmingham 1hr30, Southampton 1hr30, London 1hr50.

Trains: Kemble Railway Station, 4 miles away is on the Swindon-Gloucester line.

Refreshments: At South Cerney, The Royal Oak 01285 860 298, The Eliot Arms 01285 860 215 and The Old George Inn 01285 869 989. Coots' Café at The Gateway Visitor Centre 01793 752413 and The Lakeside Brasserie 01285 862 894 in the Water Park. The Crown Inn 01793 750 369 at Cerney Wick and The Horse and Jockey 01285 861 270 at Ashton Keynes.

Bike Shops: Ride 24-7 01285 642 247 in Cirencester. Pedal Power 01285 640 505 in Cirencester also do repairs & hire.

Books: MTB Guide Wiltshire (I.White).

Maps: OS Explorer 169.

Route Idea

A flat loop ridden in either direction using National Cycle Route 45, the Thames Path plus trails & roads, and linking the lakes with Ashton Keynes and South Cerney.
Distance 14km.

Castle Combe

Situation: At the southernmost edge of the Cotswolds in north west Wiltshire. 6 miles north west of Chippenham.

About the Base: Castle Combe, a village with two pubs and easy access to the trails. Further Info: www.castle-combe.com. **Parking:** Car park on north side of Castle Combe next to B4039. **Grid Ref:** ST845776, **Post Code:** SN14 7HH.

Drive Times: Bristol 30mins, Oxford 1hr20, Southampton 1hr40, Birmingham 2hrs, London 2hrs.

Trains: Chippenham Station is on the Bath Spa-London & Swindon-Exeter lines.

Refreshments: At Castle Combe, The Castle Inn Hotel 01249 783030 and The White Hart 01249 782295. The Jolly Huntsman 01249 750305 at Kington St Michael or The Plough at Kington Langley. The Neeld Arms 01249 782 470 at Grittleton. The Salutation Inn 01249 782460 at The Gibb. The Old House at Home 01454 218227 at Burton.

Bike Shops: Cycology Bikes 01249 461997 in Chippenham.

Books: MTB Guide Wiltshire (I.White).

Maps: OS Explorer 156.

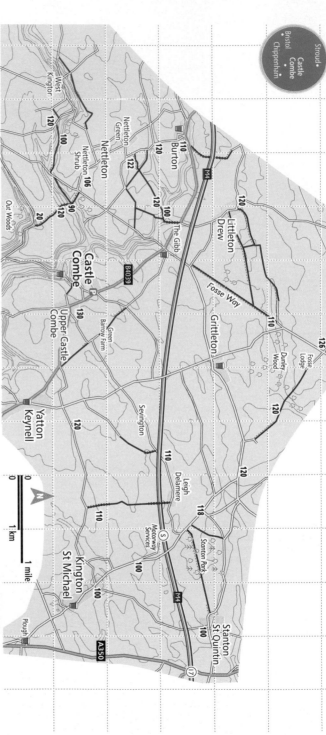

Route Idea

From Castle Combe, Road NE then trail S past Green Barrow Farm. Road NE past Sevington then trail S at Leigh Delamere. Road to Kington St Michael then Stanton St Quinton. W through Stanton Park, roads and trails NW to pass Fosse Lodge. Fosse Way SW, trails to Nettleton and onto West Kington. Trails towards Out Woods and roads back to Castle Combe. Dist 33km.

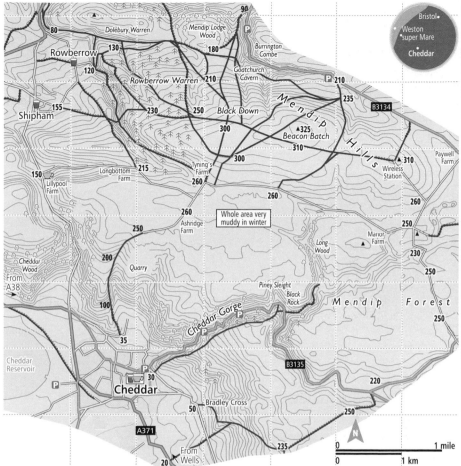

Bristol•
Weston
super Mare
•
Cheddar

B3134

B3135

A371

N
0   1 mile
0   1 km

Situation: At the foot of the Cheddar Gorge on the southern edge of the Mendip Hills in Somerset, 13 miles south east of Weston Super Mare.

About the Base: Cheddar a large vilage with pubs, cafés and accommodation.
Further Info: www.cheddarvillage.co.uk.

Parking: Large car park in the centre of Cheddar. Car parks at Cheddar Reservoir & Burrington Combe. Parking in Cheddar Gorge. *Grid Ref: Cheddar ST461536, Cheddar Reservoir ST446534, Burrington Combe ST476588 or ST489581, Cheddar Gorge ST469542 or ST474544, Post Code: Cheddar BS27 3PX, Cheddar Reservoir BS27 3DR.*

Drive Times: Bristol 40mins, Exeter 1hr20, Southampton 2hr10, Birmingham 2hr10, London 2hr50.

Refreshments: Good choice of pubs and cafés at Cheddar. The Burrington Inn 01761 462227 at Burrington Combe, The Swan Inn 01934 852371 at Rowberrow, The Miners Arms 01934 842146 at Shipham or Lillypool Café & Farm Shop 01934 743994.

Bike Shops: Cheddar Cycle Store 01934 741300 for bikes, parts, repairs & hire.

Books: South West MTB (N.Cotton). MTB Rides to the SW (M.Darkins). MBR Ride Guide 2010.

Maps: OS Explorer 141.

Route Ideas

❶ From Cheddar, SE to Bradley Cross. Trails NE to the B3135. Roads N to the Wireless Station. W across Beacon Batch, W down Rowberrow Warren to Rowberrow. SE to Tyning's Farm. Road past Ashridge Farm then to Cheddar. Distance 29km.

❷ There is a maze of trails worth exploring around Black Down, Beacon Batch & Rowberrow Warren. Park at Burrington Combe and ride until you've had your fill!

Riders: Dorset Rough Riders. © Steve J Gordon

Bath (north)

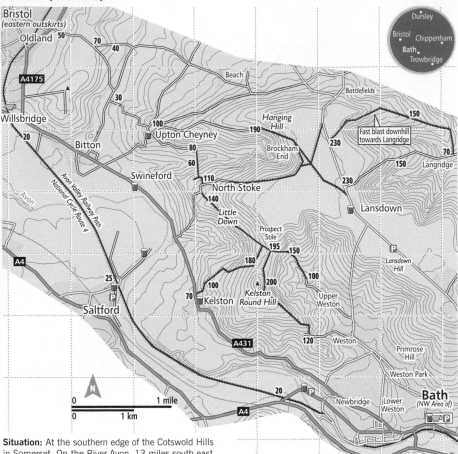

Bristol (eastern outskirts)
Oldland 50
70
40
A4175
30
Willsbridge
20
Bitton
25
P
Saltford
Beach
100
Upton Cheyney
80
60
Swineford
110
140
Little Down
100
70
Kelston
A431
A4
Battlefields
Hanging Hill
190
Brockham End
North Stoke
Prospect Stile
195
150
180
200
Kelston Round Hill
100
120
20
P
Newbridge
150
230
230
Lansdown
150
100
Upper Weston
Weston
Lower Weston
Fast blast downhill towards Langridge
150
70
Langridge
P
Lansdown Hill
Primrose Hill
Weston Park
Bath (NW Area of)
P

N

0 _____ 1 mile
0 _____ 1 km

Dursley
Bristol   Chippenham
Bath
Trowbridge

Situation: At the southern edge of the Cotswold Hills in Somerset. On the River Avon, 13 miles south east of Bristol.

About the Base: Bath, a small city with a great choice of pubs, cafés and accommodation. Further info: www.visitbath.co.uk. **Parking:** Plenty of car parks in Bath city centre. Lansdown Park & Ride or Newbridge Park & Ride NW of Bath are best. Also car park next to the river in Saltford. *Grid Ref: Lansdown Park & Ride ST731680, Newbridge Park & Ride ST717658, Saltford ST686672, Post Code: Lansdown Park & Ride BA1 9BJ, Newbridge Park & Ride BA1 3NB, Saltford BS31 3EU.*

Drive Times: Bristol 30mins, Cardiff 1hr10, Southampton 1hr50, Birmingham 2hrs, London 2hr20.

Trains: Bath Spa Station is on the Bristol-London, Bath-Exeter & Bristol- Portsmouth lines.

Refreshments: Plenty of refreshments at Bath. The Blathwayt 01225 421995 at Lansdown, The Old Crown 01225 423032 at Kelston and The Boat House 01225 482584 at Newbridge. The Riverside Inn 01225 873862 or The Jolly Sailor 01225 873002 at Saltford. The Swan Inn 0117 932 3101 at Swineford, The Buffet Cafe at Avon Valley Railway at Willsbridge and The Upton Inn 0117 932 4489 at Upton Cheyney.

Bike Shops: Several in Bath including Cadence 01225 446887, Total Fitness 01225 444164 & Hares Cycleworks 01225 422674.

Books: MTB Rides to the SW (M.Darkins).

Maps: OS Explorer 155.

Route Idea

From Lansdown Park & Ride, trails to North Stoke, Little Down, Kelston Round Hill, Weston. Roads to join National Cycle Route 4 & follow to Oldland. Roads to Hanging Hill and trails back to Lansdown. Distance 28km.

©Andy Stewart, Bath MTB

Situation: At the south edge of the Cotswold Hills in Somerset. 13 miles SE of Bristol.

About the Base: Bath, a small city with a great choice of pubs, cafés and accommodation.
Further info: www.visitbath.co.uk.

Parking: Plenty of car parks in Bath city centre. Odd Down Park & Ride (closed Sunday) on A367 SW of Bath. Also car park at Canal Visitor Centre in Monkton Combe. *Grid Ref: Odd Down Park and Ride ST733616, Monkton Combe ST781621, **Post Code:** Odd Down Park & Ride BA2 2SL, Monkton Combe BA2 7JD.*

Drive Times: Bristol 30mins, Cardiff 1hr10, Southampton 1hr50, Birmingham 2hrs.

Trains: Bath Spa Station is on the Bristol-London & Bristol- Portsmouth lines with services to Taunton & Weymouth. Freshford Station is on the Bath-Taunton & Bath-Weymouth lines.

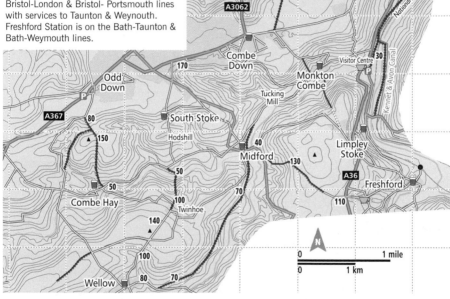

©Andy Stewart. Bath MTB

Refreshments: Plenty of refreshments at Bath. The Packhorse Inn 01225 832060 at South Stoke and The Horseshoe Inn 01225 837114 at Combe Down. The Wheelwrights Arms 01225 722287 or Angelfish Cafe 0845 2021125 in the Canal Visitor Centre at Monkton Combe. The Hop Pole Inn 01225 723134 at Limpley Stoke, The Inn at Freshford 01225 722250 at Freshford, The Hope and Anchor 01225 832296 at Midford and The Wheatsheaf 01225 833504 at Combe Hay.

Bike Shops: Cadence 01225 446887, Total Fitness 01225 444164, Avon Valley Cyclery 01225 461880 & Hares Cycleworks 01225 422674. Bath & Dundas Canal Company 01225 722292 at the visitor centre in Monkton Combe for hire, parts & repairs.

Books: MTB Rides to the SW (M.Darkins).

Maps: OS Explorer 155, 156 & 142.

Route Idea

From Odd Down Park & Ride, roads to Combe Down then trails and roads N to Bathampton. National Cycle Route 4 to Limpley Stoke. Trails to Midford and SW to Wellow. Trail N from Twinhoe then road to Combe Hay. Trail N and back to start. Distance 30km.

Forest of Dean

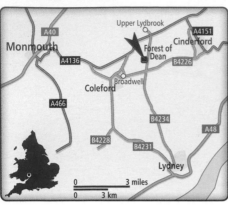

On the Wales/England border in West Gloucestershire, Forestry Commission land with miles of unmarked trails to explore. Waymarked trails include a Family Cycle Trail on surfaced tracks as well as a challenging and varied 100 % singletrack with tricky switchback climbs, rooty drops and hairpin bends. A dedicated downhill area offers several downhill trails for experienced off road riders.

Facilities:
Café, MTB Hire, parts, repairs and Bike Wash at Pedalabikeaway Cycle Centre 01594 860065. Flyup Uplift Service 01453 873533

Parking:
Grid Ref: SO606125. Post Code: GL16 7EH

Web: www.goodmtb.co.uk/b89a & /b89b

The Trails

❶ Family Cycle Trail, Green, XC, 17.7km.

❷ FODCA/Freeminer Trail, Red, 4.5km.

❸ DH

Rider: Mandi. © Sheldon Attwood

Leigh Woods

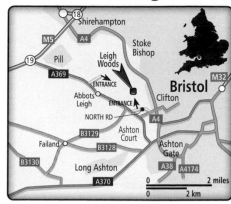

On the edge of the Avon Gorge at the out-skirts of Bristol, a National Nature Reserve managed jointly by the Forestry Commission and the National Trust. Several well-used unofficial trails as well as an all ability waymarked trail. New official mtb trail opening in Summer 2011.

Facilities:
No facilities on site. Coach House Café at nearby Ashton Court Visitor Centre.

Parking:
Grid Ref: ST553739.

Web: www.goodmtb.co.uk/b90a & /b90b

The Trails

Mountain bikers are welcome to use the established unofficial trails, providing they avoid any specific "no cycling" areas and refrain from creating any new trails. An official trail is opening Summer 2011.

Ashton Court - Timberland Trail

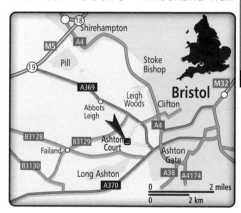

In the Forest of Avon, west of Bristol, a waymarked trail built and maintained in conjunction with the Bristol Trails Group. In two parts, a figure of eight family trail suitable for riders of all abilities links to a more challenging trail with berms, jumps, drop-offs, rock gardens and an 8 metre log ride. 11km of new and reconstructed trails, designed by Phil Saxena, will be built and should be ready to be ridden by Summer 2011. Riders of all abilities will be able to use the trails, most of which will be on or close to the line of existing routes but will be able to be enjoyed throughout the year.

Facilities:
Coach House Café at Ashton Court Visitor Centre. A new trail centre opening Summer 2011 will include a cafe and cycle hire.

Parking:
Grid Ref: SJO37547. Post Code: BS41 9JJ

Web: www.goodmtb.co.uk/b88a & /b88b

The Trails

Avon Timberland Trail, 10km, XC.

Croft Trails

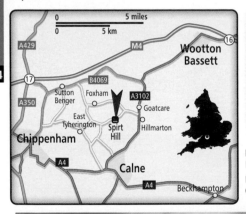

At Croft Country Park in Swindon, two waymarked trails built and maintained entirely by volunteers from MB Swindon and funded by donations. A wide, relatively flat, surfaced trail with small technical features for families and beginners. Steeper, tougher, singletrack trail with variable surfaces and lots of features including boardwalks, berms, rocks, roots and drop-offs for the more experienced. Ride both together for a longer ride.

Facilities:
Picnic Area. Refreshments in nearby Swindon.
Parking:
Grid Ref: SU155821. Post Code: SN3 1TA
Web: www.goodmtb.co.uk/b87

The Trails
Blue, XC, 1.2km.
Red, XC, 5km.

Spirt Hill Trail

Situated on a working farm in Wiltshire, waymarked trails suitable for all abilities through grassland, woodland and arable land with added bridges, jumps and technical features. Areas for speed, raised banks and tough climbs with alternative routes for the less experienced mean that there is something for everyone.

Pay to Ride.

Facilities:
Picnic Area
Parking:
Grid Ref: ST996756. Post Code: SN11 9HW
Web: www.goodmtb.co.uk/b63

444

The Trails
XC, 4km. XC, 7km. Blue with Red & Black sections

Riders: Andy Phillips & Billy Dyer / SPAM. © Duncan Snow

445

North Cotswolds. Riders: Old Blokes on Bikes. © Peter Joyner

Salisbury Plain & Dorset

446

The great slab of chalk that covers southern England starts on the Dorset coast then spreads northeast through Wiltshire and Hampshire to the Ridgeway and the Chiltern Hills and along the English Channel to the famous white cliffs of Dover.

Wiltshire has a higher proportion of bridleways and byways to road network than any other county in England. These broad chalk and flint trails are best explored from late spring to late autumn after a few dry days, offering big days out where rides of up to 100km are quite possible. Set right in the heart of the county, Salisbury Plain may be better known as a military training area but it is also crossed over and over with great lengths of broad chalk and flint trails. South of **Urchfont** the Wessex Ridgeway links the Ridgeway at **Avebury** with the Coastal Path at **Lyme Regis** and has many long stretches of rideable tracks, including the Imber Range Perimeter Path that runs through Chitterne and forms a circuit around the military training ground centred on the ghost village of Imber. Other trails from **Urchfont** cross

the Plain towards **Enford** and the valley of the River Avon which flows south to **Salisbury**. Southwest of **Salisbury** and its satellite village of **Wilton** there are a series of excellent lengths of byway running along the ridges that are a real blast on crisp autumn days. **Bishopstone** in the Ebble valley is a good link between the ridges. A little further west **Mere** gives access to trails over the extraordinarily shaped White Sheet Hill and Rodmead Hill to the north of the A303.

Like Wiltshire, Dorset also has a vast network of byways and bridleways although the riding tends to be harder as the hills are steeper and the chalk is more frequently cut through by streams and rivers. Some of the best mountain biking in Dorset runs along the grass covered coastal hills with stunning views out over the English Channel. A tough route can be followed east from **Charmouth** to **West Bay**, with links to **Bridport**. Try also the ridge between **West Lulworth** past **Osmington** to the Hardy Monument and **Abbotsbury** to the southwest of Dorchester or the inland route known as the Wessex Ridgeway between **Beaminster** and Iwerne

Courtney, close to **Stourpaine**. The triangle formed by **Melbury Osmond**, **Milton Abbas** and **Dorchester**, taking in bases at **Cerne Abbas**, **Puddletown** and **Charminster** contains much of the best mountain biking in Dorset's heartland: hidden valleys, woodland tracks, chalk and flint ridges, the great chalk giant at **Cerne Abbas** and clusters of pretty villages, often with good pubs. To the east of **Blandford Forum** the gradients are more gentle and the riding easier: have a look at the trails from **Tarrant Keyneston** or **Cranborne**. Finally, the Isle of Purbeck, explored from the dramatic setting of **Corfe** **Castle** does almost have the feeling of an island, a great lump of higher land by the coast, surrounded by the sea to the south and low-lying woodland and heath to the north.

Although there are no major Trail Centres, there are purpose-built trails at **Puddletown Woods** east of **Dorchester**, and **Watchmoor Wood** north of Bournemouth, or try the **UK Bike Park** west of Blandford Forum

Park Bottom, Wylye Map p449. ©Dave Robinson SPAM

Enford

Map labels:
Chirton Maggot, Danger Area, 210, 200, 190, 190, Danger Area, URCHFONT MAP, 200, 170, Wilsford Down, Rushall Down, Casterley Camp, West Chisenbury, East Chisenbury, 180, Danger Area, Water Dean Bottom, Danger Area, 140, Avon, Urchfont Down, Chariton Down, Thornham Down, Compton, 90, Enford P, 120, 170, Black Heath, Danger Area, 130, Salisbury, Plain, A345, Coombe, 160, Larkhill Artillery Range, Danger Area, Fittleton, Honeydown Bottom, Enford Down, 130, Lavington Folly, 100, 150, 120, Netheravon, Danger Area, 110, 100, 90, Wexland Hanging, From Amesbury, 120, 100

Marlborough, Devizes, Enford, Andover

0 — 1 mile
0 — 1 km

Situation: On the Salisbury Plain and the banks of the River Avon in Wiltshire. 12 miles south east of Devizes and 15 miles north of Salisbury.

About the Base: Enford, a small village with a pub and easy access to the trails. **Parking:** Roadside near the church in Enford. Car park at Chirton Maggot. *Grid Ref: Enford SU140515, Chirton Maggot SU059553. Post Code: Enford SN9 6DJ.*

Drive Times: Southampton 1hr, Bristol 1hr20, London 1hr50, Exeter 2hr10, Birmingham 2hr20.

Refreshments: The Swan 01980 670338 at Enford. The Red Lion 01980 671124 at East Chisenbury and The Dog and Gunn 01980 671287 at Netheravon.

Bike Shops: Hills Cycles 01980 622705, 6 miles away in Amesbury, Bikes & Boards 01380 729621 in Devizes, Stonehenge Cycles 01722 334915 & Cycle World 01722 440372 in Salisbury.

Books: MTB Rides to the SW (M.Darkins). MTB Guide Wiltshire (I.White).

Maps: OS Explorer 130.

Route Idea

From Enford, minor roads S to Netheravon. Trails W past Wexland Hanging then N across Salisbury Plain. Trails E at Chirton Maggott back to Enford. Distance 28km.

Extend the area: Urchfont Map to the NW.

© Dave Robinson SPAM

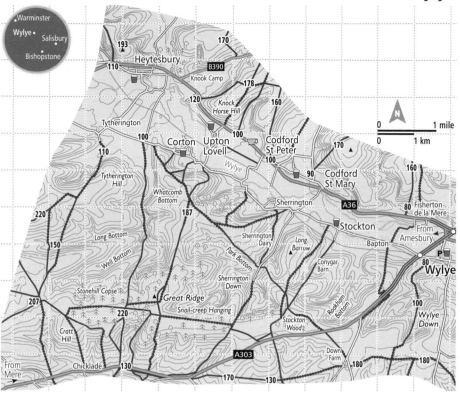

Situation: In the Wylye Valley at the foot of the Great Ridge in Wiltshire. 11 miles north west of Salisbury and south east of Warminster.

About the Base: Wylye, a village with a pub and easy access to the trails. **Parking:** Car park in Wylye next to the playground. *Grid Ref: SU007378.* **Post Code:** *BA12 0QP.*

Drive Times: Southampton 1hr, Bristol 1hr10, Exeter 1hr50, London 1hr50, Birmingham 2hr40.

Trains: Tisbury Railway Station, 4 miles south of the map, is on the Salisbury-Exeter line.

Refreshments: The Bell Inn 01985 248338 at Wylye. The Carriers 01985 850653 at Stockton and The Dove Inn 01985 850109 at Corton. The George 01985 850270 at Codford, The Prince Leopold 01985 850460 at Upton Lovell or The Angel Inn 01985 213225 at Heytesbury.

Bike Shops: Stonehenge Cycles 01722 334915 & Cycle World 01722 440372 in Salisbury, Batchelors Bikz 01985 213221 in Warminster.

Books: MTB Rides to the SW (M.Darkins). MTB Guide Wiltshire (I.White).

Maps: OS Explorer 130 & 143.

Route Idea

From Wylye, W to Stockton. Trail SW past Long Barrow. Trail NW along Park Bottom. Road to Tytherington. Trails S then E through woods and over A303 to Down Farm and back to Wylye via trail over Wylye Down. Distance 33km.

South of Stockton Woods © Phil Miles SPAM

Wilton

Situation: At the confluence of the Rivers Wylye and Nadder in Wiltshire. 3 miles west of Salisbury.

About the Base: Wilton, a small town with several pubs and tea rooms. **Parking:** Car park Wilton centre on Minster Road. *Grid Ref: SU100311. Post Code: SP2 0BH.*

Drive Times: Southampton 50mins, Bristol 1hr30, Exeter 2hrs, London 2hrs, Birmingham 2hr40.

Trains: Salisbury Station is on the London-Exeter & the Bristol-Southampton lines.

Refreshments: A choice of pubs and tea rooms at Wilton. The Bell Inn 01722 743336 at South Newton, Royal Oak 01722 790079 at Great Wishford and The Barford Inn 01722 742242 at Barford St Martin.

Bike Shops: Stonehenge Cycles 01722 334915 & Cycle World 01722 440372 in Salisbury.

Books: MTB Guide Wiltshire (I.White).

Maps: OS Explorer 130.

Route Idea

From Wilton, NW to Heath Wood then W along the Roman road to Dinton Beeches. Section of road then Monarch Way E then over Crouch's Down, Barford Down, Groveley Hill and back to Wilton. Distance 21km.

© Phil Miles SPAM

Urchfont

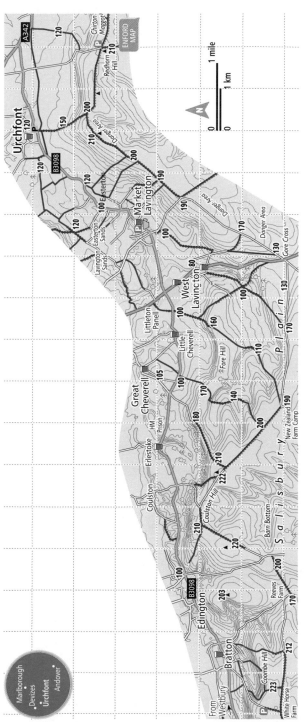

Situation: At the northern edge of Salisbury Plain in Wiltshire. 6 miles south east of Devizes.

About the Base: Urchfont, a rural village with a pub.

Parking: Roadside in Urchfont. Car park south east of Urchfont at Redhorn Hill, at Market Lavington & west of Bratton at Westbury White Horse. **Grid Ref:** *Urchfont SU039568, Redhorn Hill SU059553, Market Lavington SU015542, Westbury White Horse ST898513. **Post Code:** Urchfont SN10 4RW, Market Lavington SN10 4AF.*

Drive Times: Bristol 1hr10, Southampton 1hr20, London 2hrs, Exeter 2hr20, Birmingham 2hr30.

Trains: Westbury Station, 3 miles west of the map, is on the Salisbury-Exeter line.

Refreshments: The Lamb 01380 848848 at Urchfont. The Green Dragon 01380 813235 at Market Lavington, The Well 01380 828287 and The Bridge Inn 01380 813213 at West Lavington. The Duke at Bratton 01380 830242 and The Lamb 01380 830263 at Edington. The George & Dragon 01380 830167 at Erlestoke, The Bell In 01380 813277 at Great Cheverell or The Owl 01380 812263 at Little Cheverell.

Bike Shops: Bikes & Boards 01380 729621 in Devizes.

Books: MTB Guide Wiltshire (I.White).

Maps: OS Explorer 130 & 143.

Route Idea

From car park at Redhorn Hill. Trails W then road to Gore Cross. Road W to New Zealand Farm Camp then trails & roads NW over Coulston Hill to Edington then Bratton. SW to White Horse Farm then Reeves Farm and NE to Coulston Hill. Repeat outward section back to the start. Distance 42km.

Extend the area: Enford Map to the SE.

Salisbury Plain and Dorset **SOUTH WEST**

451

Salisbury

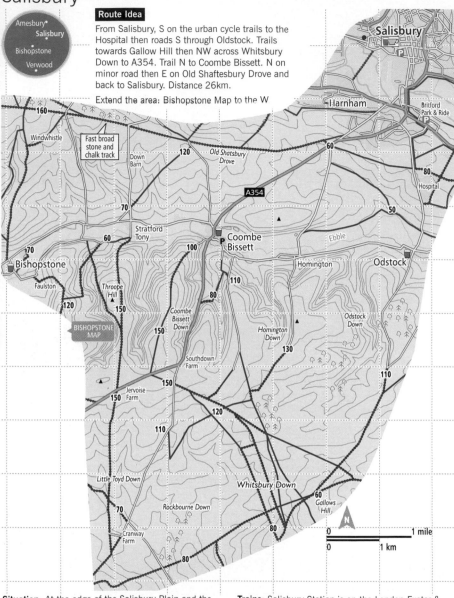

Route Idea

From Salisbury, S on the urban cycle trails to the Hospital then roads S through Oldstock. Trails towards Gallow Hill then NW across Whitsbury Down to A354. Trail N to Coombe Bissett. N on minor road then E on Old Shaftesbury Drove and back to Salisbury. Distance 26km.

Extend the area: Bishopstone Map to the W

Amesbury
Salisbury
Bishopstone
Verwood

Situation: At the edge of the Salisbury Plain and the confluence of the River Avon with four of its tributaries in South East Wiltshire. 24 miles north west of Southampton.

About the Base: Salisbury, a cathedral city with plenty of pubs, cafés and accommodation. Further Info: www.visitwiltshire.co.uk/salisbury. **Parking:** Several car parks in Salisbury. Park & Ride at Britford is best for the ride. Roadside in Coombe Bissett, near to the village store. *Grid Ref: Salisbury SU145297, Britford Park & Ride SU148278, Coombe Bissett SU109263.* **Post Code:** *Salisbury SP1 2PJ, Britford Park & Ride SP2 8BH, Coombe Bissett SP5 4LS.*

Drive Times: Southampton 45mins, Bristol 1hr30, London 2hrs, Exeter 2hr10, Birmingham 2hr40.

Trains: Salisbury Station is on the London-Exeter & the Bristol-Southampton lines.

Refreshments: Good choice of refreshments at Salisbury. The Yew Tree Inn 01722 329786 at Odstock, The Fox & Goose 01722 718437 or refreshments at Coombe Bissett Stores 01722 718852 at Coombe Bissett. The Horseshoe Inn 01722 780474 and The White Hart 01722 780244 at Bishopstone.

Bike Shops: Stonehenge Cycles 01722 334915 & Cycle World 01722 440372 in Salisbury.

Books: MTB Rides to the SW (M.Darkins).

Maps: OS Explorer 130.

Bishopstone

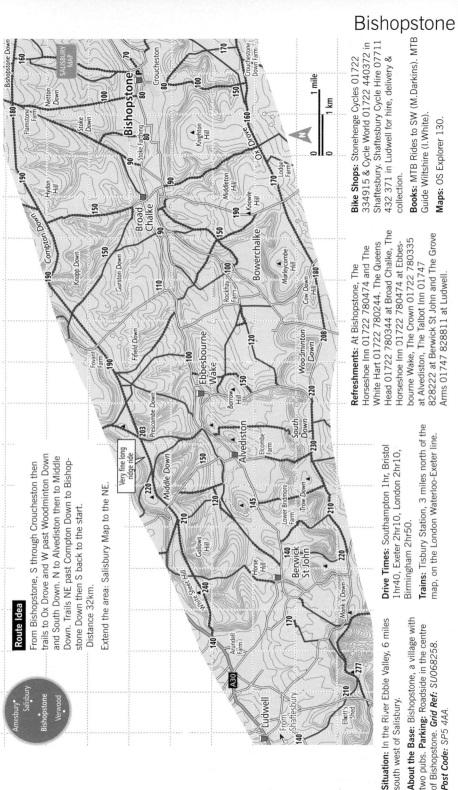

Route Idea

From Bishopstone, S through Croucheston then trails to Ox Drove and W past Woodminton Down and South Down. N to Alvediston then to Middle Down. Trails NE past Compton Down to Bishopstone then S back to the start. Distance 32km.

Extend the area: Salisbury Map to the NE.

Situation: In the River Ebble Valley, 6 miles south west of Salisbury.

About the Base: Bishopstone, a village with two pubs. **Parking:** Roadside in the centre of Bishopstone. *Grid Ref:* SU068258. *Post Code:* SP5 4AA.

Drive Times: Southampton 1hr, Bristol 1hr40, Exeter 2hr10, London 2hr10, Birmingham 2hr50.

Trains: Tisbury Station, 3 miles north of the map, on the London Waterloo-Exeter line.

Refreshments: At Bishopstone, The Horseshoe Inn 01722 780474 and The White Hart 01722 780244. The Queens Head 01722 780344 at Broad Chalke, The Horseshoe Inn 01722 780474 at Ebbesbourne Wake, The Crown 01722 780335 at Alvediston, The Talbot Inn 01747 828222 at Berwick St John and The Grove Arms 01747 828811 at Ludwell.

Bike Shops: Stonehenge Cycles 01722 334915 & Cycle World 01722 440372 in Shaftesbury. Shaftesbury Cycle Hire 07711 432 371 in Ludwell for hire, delivery & collection.

Books: MTB Rides to SW (M.Darkins). MTB Guide Wiltshire (I.White).

Maps: OS Explorer 130.

Salisbury Plain (p451). Riders: SPAM. © Duncan Snow

Cranborne

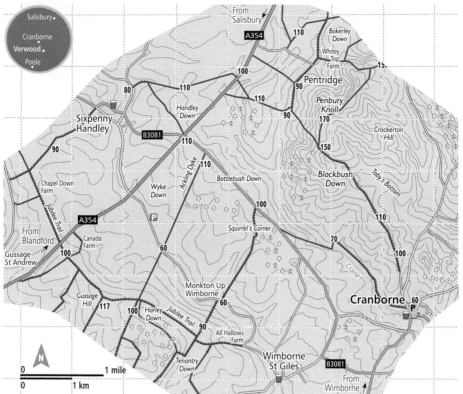

Situation: In the Cranborne Chase Area of Outstanding Natural Beauty in East Dorset. 15 miles south west of Salisbury and 18 miles north of Bournemouth.

About the Base: Cranborne, a village with a pub and a cafe. **Parking:** Roadside in the centre of Cranborne. Car park at Wycke Down. **Grid Ref:** *Cranborne SU055133, Wycke Down SU005150. **Post Code:** Cranborne BH21 5PR.*

Drive Times: Southampton 50mins, Bristol 1hr50, Exeter 2hr10, London 2hr10, Birmingham 3hrs.

Refreshments: At Cranborne, The Fleur de Lys 01725 551249, The Sheaf of Arrows 01725 517456 and Café at Cranborne Manor Garden Centre 01725 517248. The Bull Inn 01725 517300 at Wimborne St Giles and The Roebuck Inn 01725 552002 at Sixpenny Handley.

Bike Shops: Common Assault 01425 482797 & Bicycle World 01425 470835, 9 miles away in Ringwood.

Books: MTB Guide Dorset (C.Dennis).

Maps: OS Explorer 118

Route Idea

From Cranborne, N on trails over Blackbush Down then Penbury Knoll and on to Pentridge. S on A354 then trails W to Sixpenny Handley. Trail W out of the village then Jubilee Trail to Monkton Up Wimborne. N to Squirrel's Corner then back to Cranborne by the trail running alongside the River Crane. Distance 28km.

Verwood

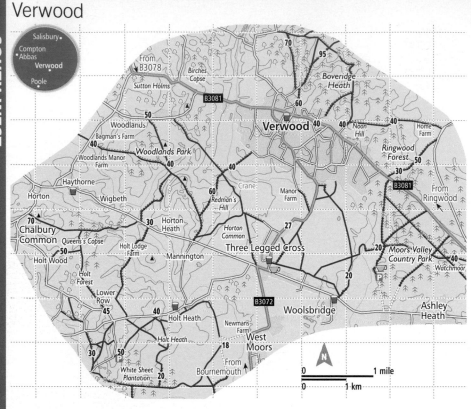

Situation: West of the New Forest National Park in Dorset, close to the Hampshire border. 14 miles north of Bournemouth and 18 miles south of Salisbury.

About the Base: Verwood, a small town with several pubs. **Parking:** Car park in the centre of Verwood opposite the recreation ground. Also at Moors Valley Country Park & at White Sheet Plantation.
Grid Ref: Verwood SU087090, Moors Valley SU107056, White Sheet Plantation SU048036.
Post Code: Verwood BH31 7AQ, Moors Valley BH24 2ET.

Drive Times: Southampton 40mins, Bristol 2hrs, London 2hrs, Exeter 2hr10, Birmingham 2hr50.

Refreshments: Choice of pubs at Verwood. Drusillas Inn 01258 840297 at Haythorne, The Cross Keys 01202 822555 at Holt Heath, The Woodcutters Arms 01202 828866 and Cottage Coffee Shop 01202 820480 at Three Legged Cross. The Old Barn Farm 01202 826052 at Woolsbridge and Café at Moors Valley Country Park 01425 470537.

Bike Shops: Common Assault 01425 482797 & Bicycle World 01425 470835, 5 miles away in Ringwood.

Books: MTB Rides to the SW (M.Darkins).

Maps: OS Explorer OL22 & 118.

Route Idea

From Verwood, SW across the River Crane, past Redman's Hill then NW through Woodlands Park to road near Bagman's Farm. S past Haythorne then Horton. Trail through Queen's Copse and Holt Forest to Lower Row. Roads & trails S to White Sheet Plantation. E to the B3072 near Newman Farm. On to Three Legged Cross then trails E in to Moors Country Park. Cross the B3081 then NE through Ringwood Forest. Trail E past Home Farm to Noon Hill. Trails N over Boveridge Heath then S back to Verwood. Distance 37km.

Also see purpose-built trails at Moors Valley (p477) and northshore trails at Watchmoor Bike Park (p477).

Mere

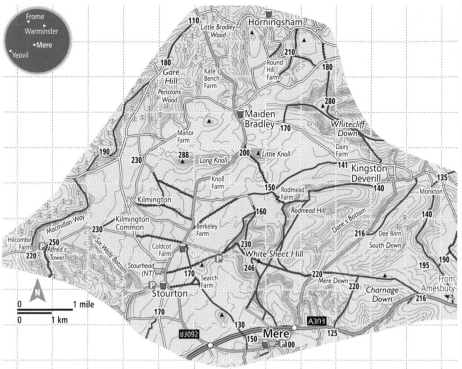

Situation: On the south western edge of the Salisbury Plain in Wiltshire, close to the borders of Dorset and Somerset. 9 miles south west of Warminster and 12 miles south of Frome.

About the Base: Mere, a small town with two pubs and a tea room. **Parking:** Car park in the centre of Mere. Also at White Sheet Hill & National Trust Visitor Centre in Stourton. National Trust car park at Alfred's Tower. Layby on A303 at Willoughby Hedge.
Grid Ref: Mere ST815324, White Sheet Hill ST797350, Stourton ST777340, Alfred's Tower ST748353, Willoughby Hedge ST863335.
Post Code: Mere BA12 6ET, Stourton BA12 6SH.

Drive Times: Bristol 1hr10, Southampton 1hr20, Exeter 1hr30, London 2hr10, Birmingham 2hr40.

Trains: Gillingham Railway Station, 5 miles south of the map, is on the Salisbury-Exeter line. Bruton, 5 miles west, & Frome, 6 miles north of the map, are on the Reading-Exeter line. Warminster Railway Station, 6 miles north east of the map is on the Salisbury-Bristol line.

Refreshments: At Mere, The Walnut Tree 01747 861220, The George Inn 01747 860427 and Angel Corner Tea Rooms 01747 860187. The Spread Eagle Inn 01747 840587 at Stourton, refreshments at National Trust Stourhead and The Red Lion 01985 844263 near White Sheet Hill. The Bath Arms 0844 815 0099 at Horningsham adn The Somerset Arms 01985 844207 at Maiden Bradley.

Bike Shops: Batchelors Bikz 01985 213221 in Warminster, Live 2 Ride 01373 469590 in Frome. Shaftesbury Cycle Hire 07711 432 371, 8 miles away in Ludwell for hire, delivery & collection.

Books: MTB Rides to the SW (M.Darkins).

Maps: OS Explorer 143 & 142.

Route Idea

From Mere, N to White Sheet Hill, W on trails and roads past Kilmington Common towards Hilcombe Farm. N on Macmillan Way then on to Gare Hill then Horningsham. SE across Whitecliff Down to Kingston Deverill. Trails S of Monkton to the A303. Trail W across Charnage Down to White Sheet Hill, S back to Mere. Distance 44km.

Winter at Shearwater. ©Dave Robinson.SPAM

Compton Abbas

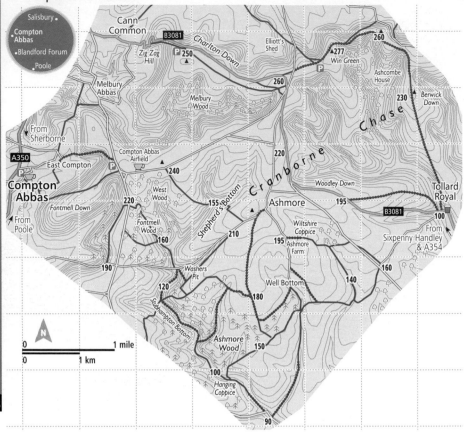

Situation: In Blackmore Vale, at the foot of Cranbourne Chase in North Dorset. 3 miles south of Shaftesbury and 9 miles north of Blandford Forum.

About the Base: Compton Abbas, a village with tea rooms and easy access to the trails. **Parking:** Car parks at Milestone Tea Rooms in Compton Abbas & at Compton Abbas Airfield. Parking at Win Green & Charlton Down. *Grid Ref: Compton Abbas ST868184, Compton Abbas Airfield ST886187, Charlton Down ST897207, Win Green ST923204. Post Code: Compton Abbas SP7 0NL, Compton Abbas Airfield SP5 5AP.*

Drive Times: Southampton 1hr20, Bristol 1hr30, Exeter 1hr50, London 2hr20, Birmingham 2hr50.

Refreshments: Milestones Tea Rooms 01747 812197 at Compton Abbas. Café at Compton Abbas Airfield 01747 811767 and The King John Inn 01725 516207 at Tollard Royal.

Bike Shops: Shaftesbury Cycle Hire 07711 432 371 in Shaftesbury for hire, delivery & collection. Offcamber 01258 458677 in Blandford Forum.

Books: MTB Rides to the SW (M.Darkins). MTB Guide Dorset (C.Dennis).

Maps: OS Explorer 118.

Route Idea

From the car park at Charlton Down, W then SW on road & trails to East Compton. E on trails and roads past the airfield. Trails SE to Shepherd's Bottom, to road then SW past Washers Pit, SE along Stubhampton Bottom to Hanging Coppice. NE to Well Bottom then to Ashmore. Roads & trails E to Tollard Royal. Trails N across Berwick Down then W past Win Hill. Trail S of B3081 back to the start. Distance 28km.

Stourpaine

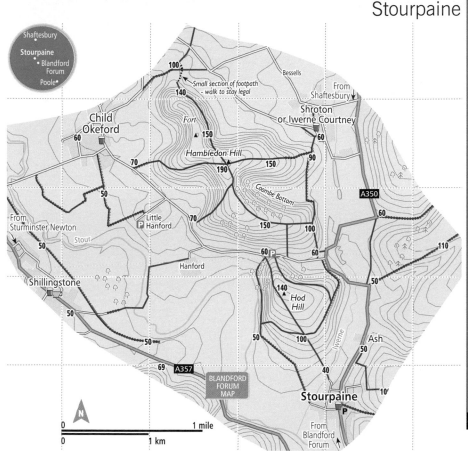

Shaftesbury
Stourpaine
• Blandford
Forum
Poole•

Bessells

Small section of footpath
- walk to stay legal

From
Shaftesbury

Child
Okeford

Fort

Shroton
or Iwerne Courtney

Hambledon Hill

Coombe Bottom

From
Sturminster Newton

Little
Hanford

Stour

A350

Hanford

Shillingstone

Hod
Hill

Iwerne

Ash

Stour

BLANDFORD
FORUM
MAP

A357

Stourpaine

From
Blandford
Forum

0 ——————— 1 mile
0 ——————— 1 km

N

Situation: On the River Stour in north Dorset. In the south east corner of Blackmore Vale at the foot of Cranborne Chase. 3 miles north west of Blandford Forum and 10 miles south of Shaftesbury.

About the Base: Stourpaine, a village with a pub and easy access to the trails. **Parking:** Layby opposite the post office in Stourpaine. National Trust car park at Hod Hill. **Grid Ref:** *Stourpaine ST861094, Hod Hill ST853112.* **Post Code:** *Stourpaine DT11 8SS.*

Drive Times: Southampton 1hr10, Bristol 1hr40, Exeter 2hrs, London 2hr30, Birmingham 3hr.

Refreshments: The White Horse 01258 453535 at Stourpaine. The Old Ox Inn 01258 860211 or The Willows Tea Rooms 01258 861167 at Shillingstone. The Baker Arms 01258 860260 or the Post Office and Tea Rooms 01258 860281 at Child Okeford and The Cricketers 01258 860421 at Iwerne Courtney.

Bike Shops: Offcamber 01258 458677 in Blandford Forum for bikes, parts, repairs & hire.

Books: MTB Guide Dorset (C.Dennis).

Maps: OS Explorer 118.

Route Idea

From Stourpaine, trails NW over Hod Hill. Road W. Just before reaching Child Okeford trail E to Hambledon Hill. NW past the site of old fort then road SE to Shroton. Trails W, back Hambledon Hill, then SE descent to road. Trails around the back of Hod Hill then back to the start. Distance 14km.

Extend the area: Blandford Forum Map to the SW.

Hod Hill. Dorset Rough Riders. © Steve J Gordon

Blandford Forum

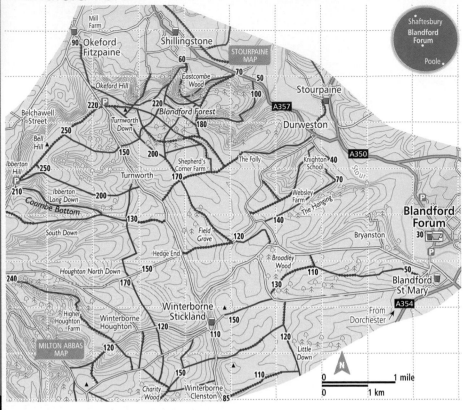

Situation: On the River in Stour between the Dorset Downs and Cranborne Chase in North Dorset. 15 miles north west of Poole and 18 miles north east of Dorchester.

About the Base: Blandford Forum, a market town with a choice of pubs and cafés. **Parking:** Car parks in Blandford Forum at Blandford Bridge & near to the river north of the town. Parking at Ibberton Hill & next to the picnic area at Okeford Hill. **Grid Ref:** *Blandford Bridge ST883061, Blandford North ST882073, Ibberton Hill ST791071, Okeford Fitzpaine ST812092.* **Post Code:** *Blandford Bridge DT11 7AW, Blandford North DT11 7SH.*

Drive Times: Southampton 1hr10, Bristol 1hr40, Exeter 1hr50, London 2hr30, Birmingham 3hr10.

Refreshments: Plenty of pubs & cafés at Blandford Forum. The Milton Arms 01258 880306 at Blandford St Mary, The Crown 01258 880838 at Winterbourne Strickland, The Royal Oak 01258 861561 at Okeford Fitzpaine and The Old Ox Inn 01258 860211 or The Willows Tea Rooms 01258 861167 at Shillingstone.

Bike Shops: Offcamber 01258 458677 in Blandford Forum for bikes, parts, repairs & hire.

Books: MTB Rides to the SW (M.Darkins). MTB Guide Dorset (C.Dennis).

Maps: OS Explorer 117.

Route Idea

From Blanford Forum, road SW then trails to Winterborne Clenston via Little Down. Road N past Winterborne Stickland and Hedge End. Trail W along Combe Bottom to road. Trail NE past Bell Hill. Cross the road then trails towards Eastcombe Wood then S through Blandford Forest. On to Durweston via The Folly. Pass Knighton School then trail close to The Hanging. Road S followed by trail to Blandford St Mary and road N back to start. Distance 37km.

Extend the area: Milton Abbas Map to the SW.

Tarrant Keyneston

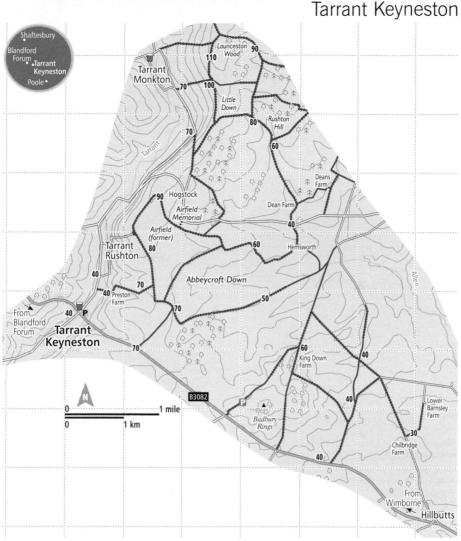

Situation: In the Tarrant Valley in North Dorset. 4 miles south east of Blandford Forum and 13 miles north west of Poole.

About the Base: Tarrant Keyneston, a village with a pub and easy access to the trails. **Parking:** Layby on B3082 in Tarrant Keyneston, or ask at the pub. Car park at Badbury Rings. *Grid Ref: Tarrant Keyneston ST930041, Badbury Rings ST961031.* **Post Code:** *Tarrant Keyneston DT11 9JE.*

Drive Times: Southampton 1hr, Exeter 1hr50, Bristol 1hr50, London 2hr20, Birmingham 3hr10.

Refreshments: The True Lovers Knot 01258 452209 at Tarrant Keyneston or The Langton Arms 01258 830225 at Tarrant Monkton.

Bike Shops: Offcamber 01258 458677 in Blandford Forum for bikes, parts, repairs & hire.

Books: MTB Guide Dorset (C.Dennis).

Maps: OS Explorer 118

Route Idea

From Tarrant Keyneston, road NE to Tarrant Rushton, trails around north edge of the old airfield to the memorial. Road N past Hogstock then trails N to Launceston Wood then S past Rushton Hill to Dean Farm. S past Hemsworth, over Abbeycroft Down, past Preston Farm and back to start. Distance 16km.

Milton Abbas

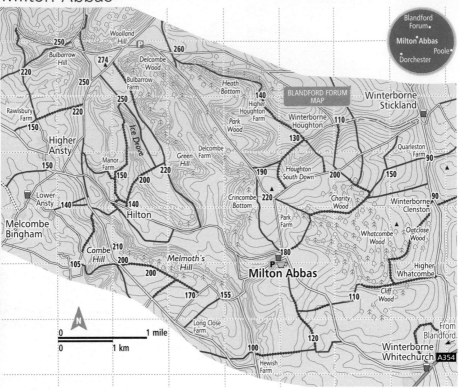

Situation: On the southern edge of the Dorset Downs. 7 miles south west of Blandford Forum and 12 miles north east of Dorchester.

About the Base: Milton Abbas, a village with a pub and a café. Further Info: www.miltonabbas.org.uk.

Parking: Roadside in the centre of Milton Abbas. Car park at Delcombe Wood.

Grid Ref: Milton Abbas ST806017. Post Code: Milton Abbas DT11 0BN.

Drive Times: Southampton 1hr10, Exeter 1hr40, Bristol 1hr50, London 2hr30, Birmingham 3hr20.

Refreshments: At Milton Abbas The Hambro Arms 01258 880233 and Tea Clipper Café 01258 880223. The Fox Inn 01258 880328 at Lower Ansty, The Crown 01258 880838 at Winterbourne Strickland or The Milton Arms 01258 880306 at Winterbourne Whitechurch.

Bike Shops: Offcamber 01258 458677 in Blandford Forum, Mud Sweat & Gears 01305 260202 or Dorchester Cycles 01305 268787 in Dorchester. Offcamber also do hire.

Books: MTB Rides to the SW (M.Darkins). MTB Guide Dorset (C.Dennis).

Maps: OS Explorer 117.

Route Idea

From Milton Abbas, SW on road past the lake. Trails across Melmoth's Hill to Combe Hill. Road & trials N to Hilton. Trail NE then N along Ice Drove. Road N then E to take trail SE across Heath Bottom, then SW past Houghton South Down. On to Winterborne Clenston via trails through Charity Wood. Back to Milton Abbas via Oatclose Wood & Cliff Wood. Distance 23km.

Extend the area: Blandford Forum Map to the NE.

Cerne Abbas

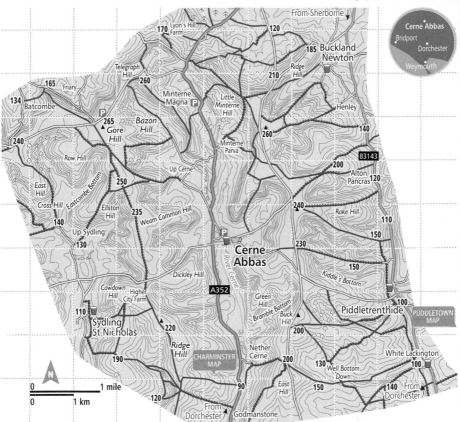

Situation: At the heart of Dorset in the valley of the River Cerne and the Dorset Downs. 8 miles north of Dorchester.

About the Base: Cerne Abbas, a village with three pubs and a café.

Further Info: www.cerneabbas.org.uk. **Parking:** Car park in Cerne Abbas at the north end of the village. Car parks at Minterne Magna & next to the picnic area at Gore Hill. *Grid Ref: Cerne Abbas ST662015, Minterne Magna ST657042, Gore Hill ST636039. Post Code: Cerne Abbas DT2 7AL, Minterne Magna DT2 7AR.*

Drive Times: Southampton 1hr30, Exeter 1hr30, Bristol 1hr40, London 2hr50, Birmingham 3hr10.

Trains: Maiden Newton Railway Station, 4 miles west of the map, is on the Weymouth-Castle Cary line.

Refreshments: The New Inn 01300 341274, The Royal Oak 01300 341797, The Fox & Hounds 01300 320444 and The Singing Kettle Tea Rooms 01300 341349 at Cerne Abbas. The Greyhound Inn 01300 341303 at Sydling St Nicholas, The European Inn 01300 348308 at White Lackington, The Piddle Inn 01300 348468 or The Poachers 01300 348358 at Piddletrenthide and The Gaggle of Geese 01300 345249 at Buckland Newton.

Bike Shops: Mud Sweat & Gears 01305 260202 or Dorchester Cycles 01305 268787. Cycloan 01305 251521 for hire.

Books: MTB Rides to the SW (M.Darkins). MTB Guide Dorset (C.Dennis).

Maps: OS Explorer 117.

Route Idea

From Cerne Abbas, roads then trails N past Up Cerne and Blazon Hill towards Telegraph Hill. Road SW to Gore Hill then trails S past Ridge Hill to Godmanstone. NE to Nether Cerne then trails E to White Lackington. N on trail past Piddletrenthide then W back to Cerne Abbas. Distance 29km.

Extend the area: Puddletwon Map to the SE. Charminster Map to the S.

Melbury Osmond

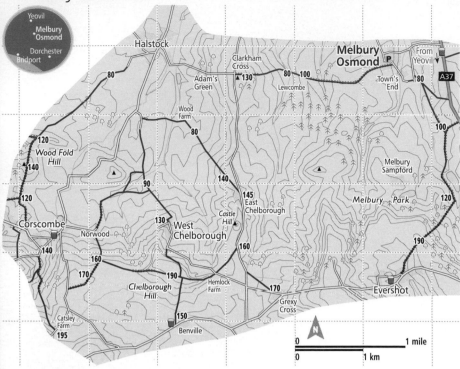

Situation: At the foot of the Dorset Downs in North West Dorset. 7 miles south of Yeovil and 15 miles north west of Dorchester.

464

About the Base: Melbury Osmond, a small village with a pub and easy access to the trails.
Parking: Roadside near the church in Melbury Osmond. *Grid Ref: Melbury Osmond ST574078.*
Post Code: Melbury Osmond DT2 0LU.

Drive Times: Exeter 1hr20, Bristol 1hr30, Southampton 1hr40, London 2hr50, Birmingham 3hrs.

Trains: Chetnole Railway Station, 2 miles away, is on the Bristol-Weymouth line.

Refreshments: The Rest & Welcome 01935 83248 at Melbury Osmond. The Acorn Inn 01935 83228 at Evershot, The Talbot Arms 01935 83381 at Benville and The Fox Inn 01935 891330 at Corscombe.

Bike Shops: Rock & Road 01935 313250, Yeovil Cycle Centre 01935 422000 & Tri UK 01935 414142 in Yeovil.

Books: MTB Guide Dorset (C.Dennis).

Maps: OS Explorer 117.

Route Idea

From Melbury Osmond, S to Evershot. W to Grexy Cross then Hemlock Farm. Trails W over Cherlborough Hill to Norwood. To Corscombe then N to Halstock via Wood Fold Hill. Roads & trails E back to Melbury Osmond. Distance 23km.

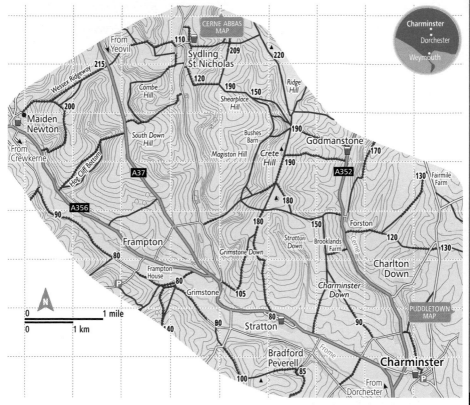

Situation: On the River Cerne, close to its confluence with the River Frome in the foothills of the Dorset Downs. 2 miles north of Dorchester.

About the Base: Charminster, a village with a pub. **Parking:** Car park near to the pub in Charminster. Car park south of the river at Frampton. *Grid Ref: Charminster SY676926, Frampton SY619944.*
Post Code: Charminster DT2 9QT, Frampton DT2 9NQ.

Drive Times: Exeter 1hr20, Southampton 1hr30, London 2hr10, Bristol 2hr20, Birmingham 3hrs.

Trains: Maiden Newton Station & Dorchester West Stations are on the Weymouth-Swindon & Weymouth-Gloucester lines. Dorchester South Station is on the Southampton-Weymouth line.

Refreshments: The Three Compasses 01305 263618 at Charminster, The Saxon Arms 01305 260020 at Stratton, The Chalk & Cheese 01300 320600 at Maiden Newton, The Greyhound Inn 01300 341303 at Sydling St Nicholas and The Smiths Arms at Godmanstone.

Bike Shops: Mud Sweat & Gears 01305 260202 or Dorchester Cycles 01305 268787. Cycloan 01305 251521 for hire.

Books: MTB Guide Dorset (C.Dennis).

Maps: OS Explorer OL15 & 117.

Route Idea

From Charminster, W to Bradford Peverell then mainly trails heading NW on S of the River Frome to Maiden Newton. NE to Stydling St Nicholas. Trails SE over Shearplace Hill and to Crete Hill. S back to Charminster via trails across Charminster Down. Distance 28km.

Dorchester

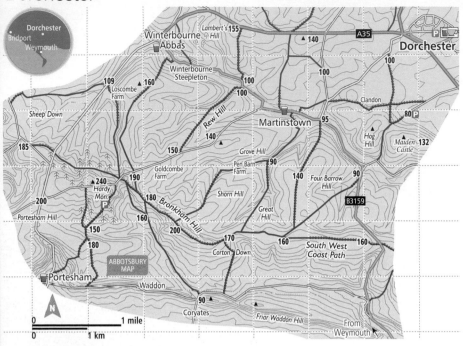

Situation: On the River Frome at the foot of the Dorset Downs. 8 miles north of Weymouth and 24 miles west of Poole.

About the Base: Dorchester, a historic market town with plenty of pubs, cafés and accommodation.
Further Info: www.visit-dorchester.co.uk. **Parking:** Several car parks in the centre of Dorchester. Car park south of Dorchester at Maiden Castle. National Trust car park at the Hardy Monument.
Grid Ref: Dorchester SY693904, Maiden Castle SY668889, Hardy Monument SY613875.
Post Code: Dorchester DT1 1DZ.

Drive Times: Southampton 1hr20, Exeter 1hr30, Bristol 1hr50, London 2hr40, Birmingham 3hr20.

Trains: Dorchester South Station is on the Southampton-Weymouth line. Dorchester West Station is on the Weymouth-Swindon & Weymouth-Gloucester lines.

Refreshments: Good choice of refreshments at Dorchester. The Kings Arms 01305 871342 at Portesham, The Coach & Horses 01305 889340 at Winterbourne Abbas and The Brewers Arms 01305 889361 at Martinstown.

Bike Shops: Mud Sweat & Gears 01305 260202 or Dorchester Cycles 01305 268787. Cycloan 01305 251521 for hire.

Books: MTB Rides to the SW (M.Darkins).

Maps: OS Explorer OL15.

Route Idea

From car park near Maiden Castle, SW on trail past the castle then S on the B3159. W along the South West Coast path and along Bronkham Hill. NE on road past Goldcombe Farm then trail NE across Rew Hill. Road through Martinstown then road N followed by trail E past Clandon and back to start. Distance 16km.

Extend the area: Abbotsbury Map to the SW.

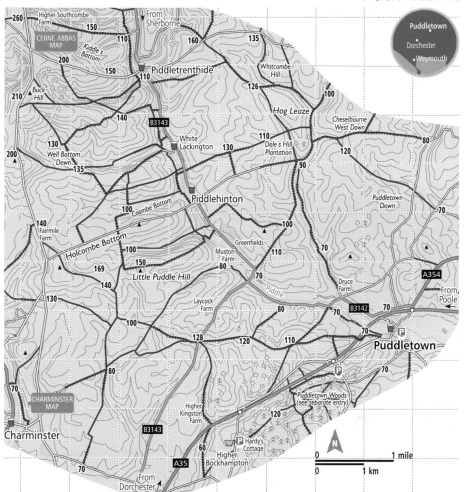

Situation: At the edge of Puddletown Woods in the heart of Dorset. 5 miles from Dorchester.

About the Base: Puddletown, a small village with a pub. Info: www.dorsets.co.uk/puddletown-village.htm.
Parking: Cycle friendly car park at The Blue Vinny pub in Puddletown. Beacon Corner car park SW of the village at Puddletown Woods. *Grid Ref:* Puddletown SY756947, Beacon Corner SY742936, Higher Bockhampton SY725921. *Post Code:* Puddletown DT2 8TE, Higher Bockhampton DT2 8QH.

Drive Times: Southampton 1hr10, Exeter 1hr30, Bristol 1hr50, London 2hr30, Birmingham 3hr20.

Trains: Dorchester South Station, on the Southampton-Weymouth line. Dorchester West Station, on the Weymouth-London & Weymouth-Gloucester lines.

Refreshments: The Blue Vinny Inn 01305 848228 at Puddletown. Tea Rooms at Greenwood Grange Farm 01305 268874 near to Hardy's Cottage. Piddle Inn 01300 348468 or Poachers 01300 348358 at Piddletrenthide, The European Inn 01300 348308 at White Lackington and The Thimble Inn 01300 348270 at Piddlehinton.

Bike Shops: Mud Sweat & Gears 01305 260202 or Dorchester Cycles 01305 268787. Cycloan 01305 251521 for hire.

Books: MTB Rides to the SW (M.Darkins). MTB Guide Dorset (C.Dennis).

Maps: OS Explorer OL15 & 117.

Route Ideas

❶ From car park at Puddletown Woods, trails W through the wood to and past Higher Bockhampton. Trails N past Higher Kingston Farm to B3143 Trail W then N past Little Puddle Hill to Holcombe Bottom. Trails N past Well Bottom Down to Buck Hill. Road N then trail E past Higher Southcombe Farm to Piddletrenthide. Trails E towards Hog Leaze then S past Dole's Hill Plantation to Druce Farm. Back to start using the trails W of Puddletown. Dist 33km.

❷ Shorten the above, when at the road in Holcombe Bottom head E straight to Dole's Hill Plantation, then see above. Distance 22km.

Extend the area: Charminster Map to the W.

Bere Regis

Situation: On the River Bere and the edge of Wareham Forest in South Dorset. 11 miles north east of Dorchester and 12 miles west of Poole.

About the Base: Bere Regis, a large village with two pubs and a café nearby. Further Info: www.bereregis.org. **Parking:** Car parks in Bere Regis & Wareham Forest. *Grid Ref: Bere Regis SY846947, Wareham Forest SY888917 or SY880926.* **Post Code:** Bere Regis BH20 7LY.

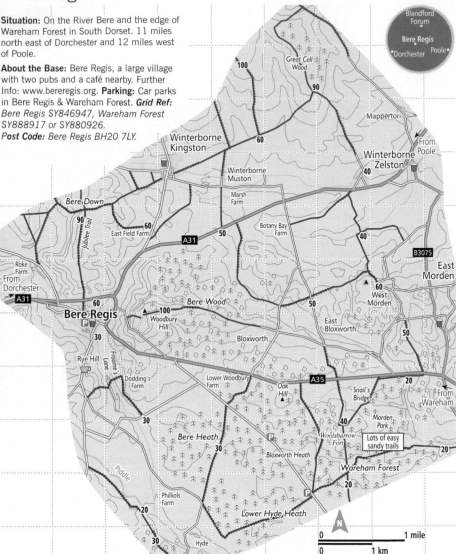

Drive Times: Southampton 1hr10, Exeter 1hr40, Bristol 1hr50, London 2hr30, Birmingham 3hr20.

Trains: Wareham Station, 6 miles away, is on the Southampton-Weymouth line.

Refreshments: At Bere Regis, The Drax Arms 01929 471386, The Royal Oak 01929 471203 and The Pampered Pigs Pantry 01929 472327 at Rye Hill, south of the village. The Cock & Bottle 01929 459238 at East Morden, Botany Bay Inn 01929 459227 at Winterbourne Zelston. The Greyhound 01929 471332 at Winterbourne Kingston.

Bike Shops: Purbeck Cycle Hire & Cycle Experience 01929 556601, 6 miles away at Wareham Station. Offcamber 01258 458677, 9 miles away in Blandford Forum.

Books: MTB Guide Dorset (C.Dennis).

Maps: OS Explorer 117.

Route Ideas

❶ From Bere Regis, S past Rye Hill, trail SE along the River Piddle. Road N then trail E past Lower Hyde Heath and into Wareham Forest. N past Woolsbarrow Fort and Snail's Bridge to the A35. Minor road to Bloxworth. SW to cross the A35 then trails over Bere Heath. Road NW past Philliols Farm. Trail past Dodding's Farm then Froome's Lane back to Bere Regis. Distance 26km.

❷ From Bere Regis, E to trails through Bere Wood. Road N from Bloxworth then trails & roads E to the B3075 via West Morden. N to Winterborne Zelston. N through Mapperton and onwards, trails S around Great Coll Wood then trails SW to Winterborne Kingston then Bere Down. Section of the Jubilee Trail S to Bere Regis. Distance 23km.

Osmington

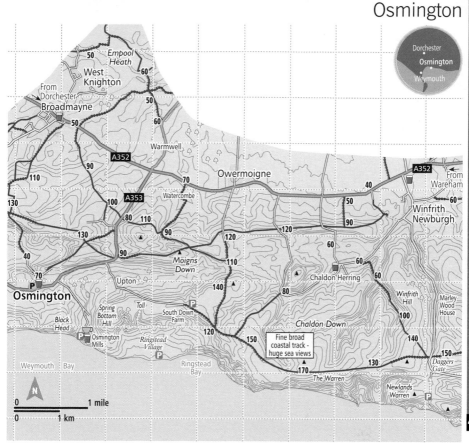

Situation: 4 miles north east of Weymouth and 7 miles south east of Dorchester.

About the Base: Osmington, a village with a pub and easy access to the trails. Further Info: www.osmington.info. **Parking:** Roadside near to the church in Osmington. National Trust car park at Ringstead & South Down Farm. Also at Newlands Warren. **Grid Ref:** *Osmington SY724829, Ringstead SY752817, South Down Farm SY759823, Newlands Warren SY810804.* **Post Code:** *Osmington DT3 6EJ, Ringstead DT2 8NG.*

Drive Times: Southampton 1hr10, Exeter 1hr30, Bristol 2hrs, London 2hr40, Birmingham 3hr30.

Swyre Head. Rider: Nigel Parker. © Alex Leigh

Trains: Weymouth Station has services to London Waterloo & Gloucester. Dorchester South Station is on the Southampton-Weymouth line. Dorchester West Station is on the Weymouth-London & Weymouth-Gloucester lines.

Refreshments: The Sunray 01305 832148 at Osmington. The Smugglers Inn 01305 833125 and The Cottage Café 01305 833237 at Osmington Mills. The Sailors Return 01305 854571 at Chaldon Herring. The Red Lion 01305 852814 at Winfrith Newburgh and The Black Dog 01305 852360 at Broadmayne.

Bike Shops: Mud Sweat & Gears 01305 260202 or Dorchester Cycles 01305 268787 in Dorchester. Mud Sweat & Gears 01305 784849 or Westham Cycles 01305 776977 in Weymouth. Westham Cycles also do hire

Books: MTB Rides to the SW (M.Darkins). MTB Guide Dorset (C.Dennis).

Maps: OS Explorer OL15.

Route Idea

From Car Park next to South Down Farm, E on trails to Daggers Gate. Trails N past Winfrith Hill. Road NE to outskirts of Winfrith Newburgh then trails W, to and past Moigns Down to the A353. S past Upton and back to the car park. Distance 23km.

Corfe Castle (west)

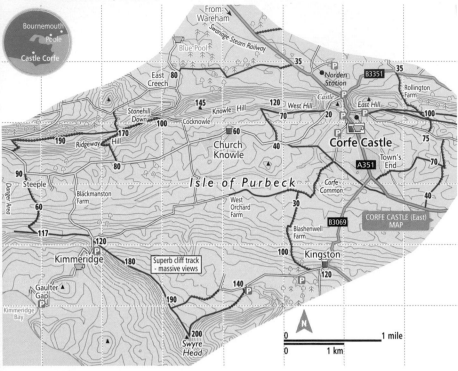

Situation: South of Poole Harbour in Dorset. Lying in a gap in the Purbeck Hills on the Isle of Purbeck. 14 miles south west of Poole.

About the Base: Corfe Castle, a large village with several pubs, cafés and accommodation. Further info: www.corfe-castle.co.uk. **Parking:** Car parks in Corfe Castle, at Corfe Castle Visitor Centre, east of the village at Challow Hill & north at Norden Station. Also at Kimmeridge, Gaulter Gap & west of Kingston. *Grid Ref: Corfe Castle SY958817, Corfe Castle Visitor Centre SY959824, Challow Hill SY963821, Norden Station SY958829, Blue Pool SY934835, Kimmeridge SY918800, Gaulter Gap SY909790, Kingston SY943792 or SY952794. Post Code: Corfe Castle BH20 5EB, Corfe Castle Visitor Centre BH20 5DR, Norden Station BH20 5DW, Blue Pool BH20 5AR, Kimmeridge BH20 5PH, Kingston BH20 5LL.*

Drive Times: Southampton 1hr20, Exeter 2hrs, Bristol 2hr20, London 2hr40, Birmingham 3hr30.

Trains: Poole Station is on the Southampton-Weymouth line. There is a frequent ferry service with a 4 minute crossing to the ferry terminal at Studalnd.

Refreshments: At Corfe Castle, The Castle Inn 01929 480208, The Fox Inn 01929 480449, The Greyhound Inn 01929 480205, Model Village Courtyard Café 01929 481234 and National Trust Tea Rooms 01929 481332. Blue Pool Tea Rooms at Furzebrook. The New Inn 01929 480 357 at Church Knowle, Clavell's Café & Farm Shop 01929 480701 at Kimmeridge and The Scott Arms 01929 480270 at Kingston.

Bike Shops: Primera Sports 01202 749674, Ridebike 01202 741744, Bikelab 01202 330011 & Cycle Paths 01202 680123 in Poole. Ridebike also do guided rides in the Purbeck Hills. Cycle Safaris in 07785 317 410 Swanage for hire & guided rides.

Books: MTB Rides to the SW (M.Darkins). MTB Guide Dorset (C.Dennis).

Maps: OS Explorer OL15.

Route Idea

Out of Corfe Castle NW on the A351. Trails W towards East Creech. Road towards Stonehill Down then trails W along Ridgeway Hill. Road and trails SE to Swyre Head then to Kingston. Trails N past Blashenwell Farm across Corfe Common and back to the start. Distance 19km.

Extend the Area: Corfe Castle East Map.

Rider: Davey Sprocket, Dorset Rough Riders.

© Steve J Gordon

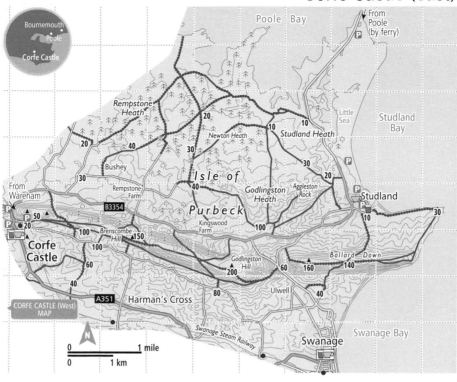

Bournemouth
Poole
Corfe Castle

Poole Bay

From Poole (by ferry)

Rempstone Heath

20

Newton Heath

10

Little Sea

Studland Bay

Studland Heath

20

40

Bushey

30

30

20

Isle of

40

Godlington Heath

Aggleston Rock

Studland

From Wareham

50

20

Rempstone Farm

B3354

Purbeck

Kingswood Farm

100

10

30

100

Brenscombe Hill

150

100

Corfe Castle

60

Godlingston Hill

200

60

160

Ballard Down

140

40

Ulwell

80

40

A351

CORFE CASTLE (West) MAP

Harman's Cross

N

Swanage Steam Railway

Swanage

Swanage Bay

0 ——— 1 mile
0 ——— 1 km

Situation: In the heart of the Isle of Purbeck, south of Poole Harbour in Dorset. Lying in a gap in the Purbeck Hills, 14 miles south west of Poole.

About the Base: Corfe Castle, a large village with several pubs, cafés and accommodation. Further info: www.corfe-castle.co.uk. **Parking:** Car parks in Corfe Castle, at National Trust Visitor Centre & east of the village at Challow Hill. Also at Studland Ferry Terminal, Studland Bay Visitor Centre, National Trust car park at Studland Beach & Studland village. *Grid Ref: Corfe Castle SY958817, National Trust Visitor Centre SY959824, Challow Hill SY963821, Studland Ferry Terminal SZ035863, Studland Bay Visitor Centre SZ033834, Studland Beach SZ035828, Studland Village SZ033824. Post Code: Corfe Castle BH20 5EB, National Trust Visitor Centre BH20 5DR, Studland Ferry Terminal BH19 3BA, Studland Bay Visitor Centre BH19 3AH, Studland Beach BH19 3AX, Studland Village BH19 3BT.*

Drive Times: Southampton 1hr20, Exeter 2hrs, Bristol 2hr20, London 2hr40, Birmingham 3hr30.

Trains: Poole Station is on the Southampton-Weymouth line. There is a frequent ferry service with a 4 minute crossing to the ferry terminal at Studalnd.

Refreshments: At Corfe Castle, The Castle Inn 01929 480208, The Fox Inn 01929 480449, The Greyhound Inn 01929 480205, Model Village Courtyard Café 01929 481234 and National Trust Tea Rooms 01929 481332. The Bankes Arms 01929 450225 or Middle Beach Café 01929 450411 at Studland or choice of pubs & cafés at Swanage.

Bike Shops: Primera Sports 01202 749674, Ridebike 01202 741744, Bikelab 01202 330011 & Cycle Paths 01202 680123 in Poole. Ridebike also do guided rides in the Purbeck Hills. Cycle Safaris in 07785 317 410 Swanage for hire & guided rides.

Books: MTB Rides to the SW (M.Darkins). MTB Guide Dorset (C.Dennis).

Maps: OS Explorer OL15.

Route Idea

Out of Corfe Castle on the B3354 then minor road and trails N across Rempstone Heath to Studland Heath. Roads to Studland. Trails E along the coast then SW along Ballard Down. Continue on trails past Godlington Hill, Brenscombe Hill and back to Corfe Castle. Distance 30km.

Extend the Area: Corfe Castle West Map.

Rider: Jason Nash. © Alex Leigh

Charmouth

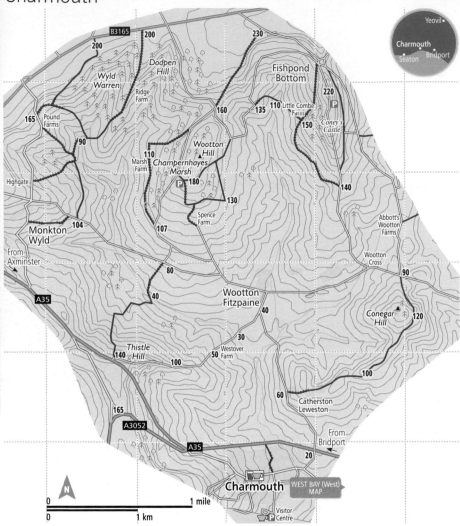

Situation: At the mouth of the River Char on the Jurassic Coast in West Dorset. 3 miles east of Lyme Regis and 7 miles west of Bridport.

About the Base: Charmouth, a coastal village with two pubs, cafés and accommodation. Further Info: www.charmouth.org. **Parking:** Car park at Charmouth Heritage Coast Centre. Also at Champernhayes Marsh & National Trust car park at Coneys Castle. *Grid Ref: Charmouth SY364930, Champernhayes Marsh SY354968, Coneys Castle SY371976. Post Code: Charmouth DT6 6QX.*

Drive Times: Exeter 50mins, Bristol 1hr40, Southampton 1hr50, London 3hr10, Birmingham 3hrs.

Trains: Axminster Railway Station, 4 miles west of the map, is on the Salisbury-Exeter line.

Refreshments: At Charmouth, The Royal Oak 01297 560277, The George 01297 560280, The Old Bank Café 01297 561600 and Beach Café 01297 560265 at Charmouth Heritage Coast Centre.

Bike Shops: Revolutions 01308 420586 in Bridport & Bikenutz 01297 631202 6 miles away in Axminster.

Books: MTB Guide Dorset (C.Dennis).

Maps: OS Explorer 116.

Route Idea

From Charmouth, roads N to Wootton Fitzpaine then SW to Thistle Hill. Trail N then roads W to Highgate. Trails NE past Wyle Warren to B3165. Trails & roads to Marsh Farm then NE over Wootton Hill to Little Combe Farm. Trails & roads S to Wootton Cross. Trails S past Conegar Hill to Catherston Leweston. Roads back to the start. Distance 24km.

Extend the Area: West Bay West Map.

Bridport

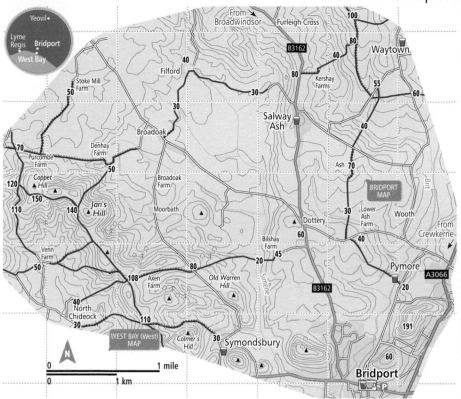

Situation: On the River Brit in West Dorset. Close to the Jurassic Coast at the western end of Chesil Beach. 15 miles west of Dorchester

About the Base: Bridport, a historic market town with a choice of pubs, cafés and accommmodation. Further Info: www.bridportandwestbay.co.uk. **Parking:** Long stay car park in the centre of Bridport. **Grid Ref:** *Bridport SY463928. Post Code: Bridport DT6 3RB.*

Drive Times: Exeter 1hr, Southampton 1hr40, Bristol 1hr50, London 3hrs, Birmingham 3hr10.

Refreshments: Plenty of pubs and cafés at Bridport. The Ilcheseter Arms 01308 422600 at Symondsbury, The Anchor Inn 01308 488398 at Salway Ash, The Hare & Hounds 01308 488203 at Waytown and The Pymore Inn 01308 422625 at Pymore.

Bike Shops: Revolutions 01308 420586 in Bridport.

Books: MTB Guide Dorset (C.Dennis).

Maps: OS Explorer 116.

Route Idea

From Bridport, W to Symondsbury then North Chideock. N to Venn Farm then trails to Jan's Hill, Coppett Hill, Purscombe Farm and Stoke Mill Farm. Roads to Broadoak. Trails to Filford then Salway Ash. N past Kershay Farms then S mainly on trails to Pymore. Road back to Bridport. Distance 26km.

Extend the Area: Bridport Map to the NW. West Bay West Map to the SW.

West Bay (west)

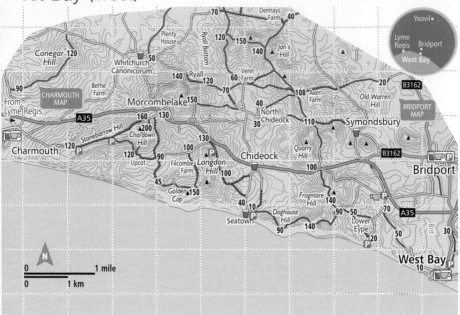

Situation: On the Jurassic Coast and the South West Coastal Path, at the mouth of the River Brit in West Dorset. 2 miles south of Bridport and 17 miles west of Dorchester.

About the Base: West Bay, a coastal resort with a choice of refreshments and accommodation.

Parking: Long stay car park in West Bay. Long stay car park in the centre of Bridport. Also next to picnic area on A35 at Eype, Langdon Hill west of Chideock & Stonebarrow Hill east of Charmouth.

Grid Ref: *West Bay SY465906, Bridport SY463928, Langdon Hill SY412930, Eype SY451922, Chardownhill SY390935, Stonebarrow Hill SY381932.* **Post Code:** *West Bay DT6 4EH, Bridport DT6 3RB.*

Drive Times: Exeter 30mins, Plymouth 1hr, Bristol 1hr50, London 3hrs, Birmingham 3hr20.

Refreshments: A choice of pubs and cafés at West Bay. The Ilcheseter Arms 01308 422600 at Symondsbury and The Five Bells 01297 489262 at Whitchurch Canonicorum. Pubs and cafés at Charmouth, The George Inn 01297 489419 at Chideock, Anchor Inn 01297 489215 at Seatown, New Inn 01308 423254 and Corner Café 01308 421256 at Eype.

Bike Shops: Revolutions 01308 420586 in Bridport.

Books: MTB Guide Dorset (C.Dennis).

Maps: OS Explorer 116.

Route Idea

From West Bay, NW to Symondsbury on trail and road. W to North Chideock then Ryall. Roads through Whitchurch Canonicorum. Trails S over Conegar Hill Then roads to Charmouth.E to Upcot, Golden Cap, skirting Langdon Hill to reach Seatown. Trails E to Lower Eype then back to West Bay. Distance 32km.

Extend the Area: Charmouth Map to the NW.

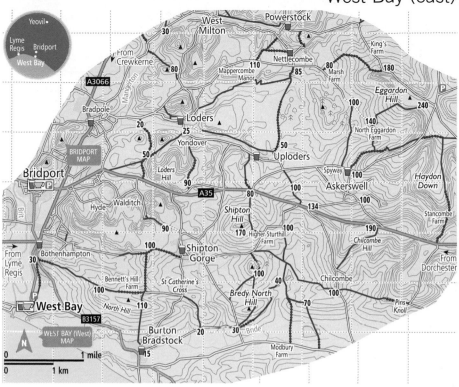

Situation: On the Jurassic Coast at the mouth of the River Brit and the western end of Chesil Beach in West Dorset. 2 miles south of Bridport and 17 miles west of Dorchester.

About the Base: West Bay, a coastal resort with plenty of refreshments and accommodation.
Further Info: www.westbay.co.uk. **Parking:** Long stay car park in West Bay. Long stay car park in the centre of Bridport. *Grid Ref: West Bay SY465906, Bridport SY463928. Post Code: West Bay DT6 4EH, Bridport DT6 3RB.*

Drive Times: Exeter 30mins, Plymouth 1hr, Bristol 1hr50, London 3hrs, Birmingham 3hr20.

Refreshments: A choice of pubs and cafés at West Bay. The Crown Inn 01308 422037 at Bothenhampton. Pubs and cafés at Bridport or The Kings Head 01308 422520 at Bradpole. The New Inn 01308 897302 at Shipton Gorge, The Crown Inn 01308 485356 at Uploders and The Loders Arms 01308 422431 at Loders. The Marquis of Lorne 01308 485236 at Nettlecombe, The Three Horses 01308 485328 at Powerstock, The Spyway Inn 01308 485250 at Askerswell and The Anchor 01308 897228 at Burton Bradstock.

Bike Shops: Revolutions 01308 420586 in Bridport.

Books: MTB Guide Dorset (C.Dennis).

Maps: OS Explorer OL15.

Route Idea

From West Bay , N to Bothenhampton. E to Shipton Gorge and Higher Sturthill Farm. Trails N past Shipton Hill, to Uploaders. N to Nettlecombe. SE to North Eggardon Farm then N up Eggardon Hill to Road. S on roads & trails to Stancombe Farm and A35. S to Pins Knoll then trail W to Chilcombe. Trails & roads W to skirt S of Bredy North Hill. St Catherine's Cross, trails to Bothenhampton and back to West Bay. Distance 33km.

Extend the Area: West Bay West Map. Bridport Map to the NW.

Abbotsbury

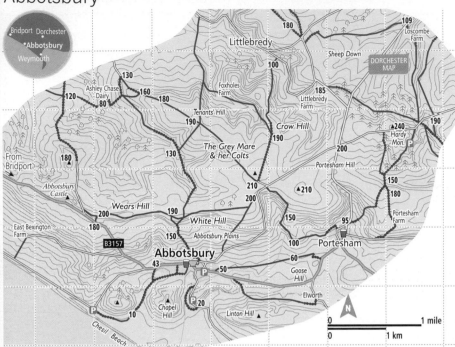

Situation: On the Jurassic Coast in West Dorset. 10 miles south west of Dorchester and north west of Weymouth.

About the Base: Abbotsbury, a large village with two pubs and several tea rooooms. Further Info www.abbotsbury.co.uk. **Parking:** Car park in the centre of Abbotsbury. Car parks at Chapel Hill & Chesil Beach, south of the village. National Trust car park at the Hardy Monument. *Grid Ref: Abbotsbury SY578852, Chesil Beach SY560846, Hardy Monument SY613875. Post Code: Abbotsbury DT3 4JL.*

Drive Times: Exeter 1hr20, Southampton 1hr40, Bristol 1hr50, London 2hr50, Birmingham 3hr30.

Refreshments: At Abbotsbury, The Swan Inn 01305 871249, The Ilchester Arms 01305 871243 and a choice of tea rooms. The Kings Arms 01305 871342 at Portesham.

Bike Shops: Mud Sweat & Gears 01305 260202 or Dorchester Cycles 01305 268787 in Dorchester. Mud Sweat & Gears 01305 784849 or Westham Cycles 01305 776977 in Weymouth. Westham Cycles also do hire

Books: MTB Rides to the SW (M.Darkins).

Maps: OS Explorer OL15.

Route Idea

From Abbotsbury, trail N then W along Wears Hill. Road N then trail N then E past Ashley Chase Dairy. SE on trail past The Grey Mare & her Colts then N past Crow Hill to road. Road SE past Littlebredy Farm then trails E past Hardy Monument then S to Portesham. Road & trails back to Abbotsbury. Distance 21km.

Hardy's Monument. © Dave Robinson SPAM

Moors Valley Country Park

West of the New Forest in Dorset, a single-track trail designed by Dafydd Davis, aimed at novice mountain bikers who want to progress their riding. A central waymarked family circuit on wide gravel tracks plus three additional loops to extend your ride, trailquest course and network of paths and tracks through Moors Valley Country Park and Forest provide something for everyone.

Facilities:
Moors Valley Visitor Centre and Seasons Restaurant. MTB hire, service & repair at Cycle Hire Centre 01425 470721.

Parking:
Grid Ref: BH24 2ET. Post Code: SU106056

Web: www.goodmtb.co.uk/b84

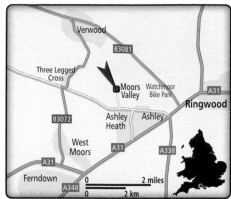

The Trails

❶ Corsican, Family, XC, 3.2km.

❷ Crane, Family, XC, 4.8km. Somerley Loop, XC, 1.6km.

❸ Watchmoor Loop, XC, 2.3km.

❹ Family Trailquest.

❺ Singletrack, Blue, XC, 7km

© Forestry Commission

Watchmoor Bike Park

North of Poole in East Dorset, a one-hectare site, developed in conjunction with the Forestry Commission, containing a northshore mountain bike network designed for beginner to advanced riders.

© Forestry Commission

Facilities:
Nearby Moors Valley Visitor Centre and Seasons Restaurant. MTB hire, service & repair at Cycle Hire Centre 01425 470721 in nearby Moors Valley Country Park.

Parking:
Grid Ref: SU128058.

Web: www.goodmtb.co.uk/b86

The Trails

Network of northshore, to suit various abilities

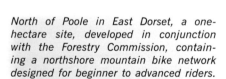

Puddletown Woods

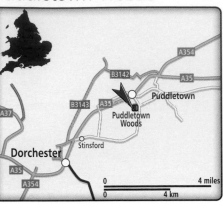

In the heart of Dorset. Constantly chang-ing with new trails emerging all the time as the forest is managed.

Facilities:
Tea Rooms at Greenwood Grange Farm 01305 268874 near to Hardy's Cottage.

Parking:
Grid Ref: SY745934. Post Code: DT2 8QS

Web: www.goodmtb.co.uk/b85

The Trails

Short singletrack trails; tight, technical downhills; freeride jumps & drops on twisty forest tracks

UK Bike Park

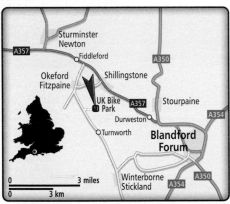

A In North Devon, a free ride park designed by riders for riders. A great downhill race course, jump area, skills area, northshore and dedicated 4X course. All the existing trails have been redeveloped and a wide range of new trails added from super wide, safe & easy trails suitable for beginners, to fast fun trails with tons of jumps, drops and berms. The bottom bowl will go ex-treme with massive step ups, wall rides, drops, dirt jumps, road gaps and more all culminating with a proper finish line & arena. Ukbikepark will now be open 5 days a week and FREE to ride.

Facilities:
Now with uplift service, refreshments at The Cabin, Mini Bike Shop with spares & MTB hire.

Parking:
Grid Ref: ST814093.

Web: www.goodmtb.co.uk/b81

The Trails

❶ Seven downhill courses

❷ A National Competition standard 4X Track

❸ Northshore trail.

❹ The Dakine Ladder Ally Freeride trail as well as dirt jumps and freeride features. 'Chicken Runs' enable anyone still to have a run down a trail.

❺ Beginners Trails

478

© Paul Howell www.ukbikepark.com

Wareham Forest. Rider: Steve J Gordon, Dorset Rough Riders. © Rob Koppenhol

Exmoor & The Quantocks

Located on the north coast of Devon and spreading eastwards into Somerset, Exmoor boasts a fine mixture of woodland, moorland and coast. Although smaller than Dartmoor, Exmoor is criss-crossed by many more miles of bridleways and byways, rideable year round. Unlike Dartmoor there are no large inaccessible moorland plateaus at the heart of the National Park and the waymarking throughout the area is probably the best of any National Park in England and Wales. Many of the rides on Exmoor offer fine views out over Bridgwater Bay and the Bristol Channel.

Lynton makes a fine base for rides at the western edge of the National Park; to the west lie the unusual rock formations of The Valley of the Rocks and excellent woodland tracks zig-zagging up from the stunning coastline; to the east is the beautiful wooded valley of the East Lyn River (and beyond that, a testing trail down the famous Doone Valley); to the south the bleakest part of Exmoor, known as The Chains, offering some tough moorland crossings.

Porlock Weir is perhaps the best centrally located base on the coast with access to the steep tracks through the ancient oaks of Horner Wood, singletrack descents from **Pittcombe Head** and perhaps most stunning of all, the sandstone tracks up and over heather-clad Selworthy Beacon east to **Minehead**.

Dunkery Beacon (519m) is the highest point on Exmoor and is easily reached from **Horner**. **Withypool** and **Winsford**, together with **Dulverton**, enclose a triangle with a great variety of stone based trails exploring the wooded valleys and rounded moorland slopes that characterise Exmoor.

Moving further east there are circuits around **Wimbleball Lake**, Exmoor's only reservoir, a one-off ride from **Monksilver** finishing with one of the best descents on Exmoor and plenty to choose from to the west of **Carhampton**.

Nr Porlock Weir p486 ©Tom Ivory

For waymarked trails, the private estates at *Dunster Forest* and **Combe Sydenham Country Park** offer both cross country trails and competition level downhills.

Located just to the west of Bridgwater The Quantocks are a perfect gem of a mountain biking area offering year-round riding. Measuring only 16km x 7km, this whaleback has an incredible quantity of top grade trails. The backbone of the area is the southeast-northwest ridge trail that runs for 11km from Triscombe Stone to Beacon Hill above *West Quantoxhead*, a wide stone-based track offering fine views out into the surrounding countryside. Dropping off this to north and south are myriad trails of varying width and degrees of difficulty. *Holford* is the preferred base for most mountain bikers to the Quantocks but it would be just as easy to start from *West Quantoxhead*, at the north end of the hills, or *Hawkridge Reservoir* and *Enmore* to the south.

West Quantoxhead p496. Bicknoller Post © Matt Cope

Lynton

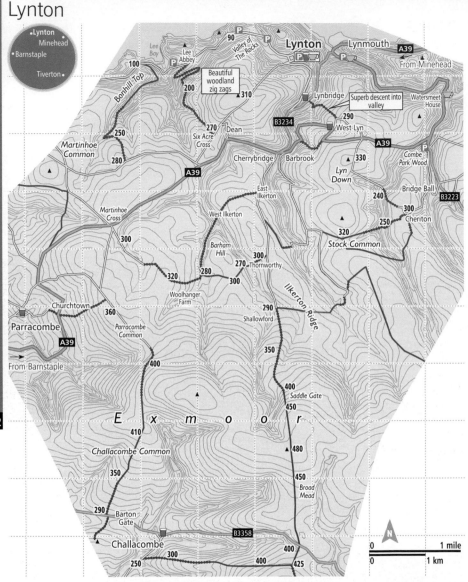

Situation: Just west of the East Lyn River, on the coast of Exmoor National Park in North Devon. 18 miles east of Ilfracombe and west of Minehead.

About the Base: Lynmouth, a small holiday town with pubs, cafés and accommodation.
Further Info: www.lynton-lynmouth-tourism.co.uk.
Parking: Car parks in Lynton & Lynmouth. Parking west of Lynton at The Valley of the Rocks & Lee Bay or east at Watersmeet House & Combe Park Wood.
Grid Ref: Lynton SS721492, Lynmouth SS723494, Valley of the Rocks SS711496, Lee Bay SS694491, Watersmeet House SS743487, Combe Park Wood SS739477. **Post Code:** Lynton EX35 6JD, Lynmouth EX35 6ES, Watersmeet House EX35 6NT.

Drive Times: Exeter 1hr30, Plymouth 2hr10, Bristol 2hr10, Birmingham 3hr30, London 4hrs.

Refreshments: Good choice of pubs and cafés at Lynton and Lynmouth. The Bridge Inn 01598 753425 at Lynbridge, The Beggars Roost 01598 752404 at West Lyn and Tea Rooms at National Trust Watersmeet House 01598 753348. The Fox & Goose 01598 763239 at Challacombe or The Black Venus Inn 01598 763251 at Parracombe.

Bike Shops: Exmoor Cycle Hire 01643 705307 for hire & Pompy's Cycles 01643 704077 for bikes, parts, repairs & hire, both in Minehead. Porlock Cycle Hire 01643 862535, 12 miles away in Porlock.

Books: South West MTB (N.Cotton). MTB Rides to the SW (M.Darkins).

Maps: OS Explorer OL9.

Routes on Web: www.goodmtb.co.uk/a122

Route Ideas

❶ From Lynton, road W to Lee Abbey. Trail S to Six Acre Cross. Road W towards Martinhoe Common then S to Martinhoe Cross. Road SE then trails past Woolhanger then N to East Ilkerton. Road S then trails and roads E over Stock Common to Cheriton. N across Lyn Down, over the A39 then roads & trails to Lynbridge. Roads back to Lynton. Distance 22km.

❷ Start as above to Six Acre Cross, then on to Dean. E along the A39 to Cherrybridge. Roads S past East Ilkerton. Keep S on trail past Shallowford then all the way to and over the B3358. Trails to Challacombe. W on the B3358 then trails N across Challacombe Common followed by road to Martinhoe Cross then Martinhoe Common. Road E then trails N past Bonhill Top. Road back to Lynton. Distance 31km.

© Matt Cope

Pittcombe Head

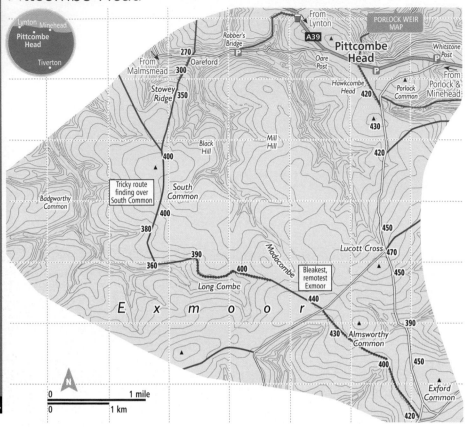

Situation: On the A39, above the Oare valley on the northern edge of Exmoor National Park in Somerset. 3 miles west of Porlock and 9 miles west of Minehead.

About the Base: Pittcombe Head, a rural location with a car park and easy access to the trails. **Parking:** Car parks at Whitcombe Head, east at Whitstone Post or west at Robbers Bridge. *Grid Ref: Pittcombe Head SS845461, Whitstone Post SS855462, Robber's Bridge SS821464.* **Post Code:** Robber's Bridge TA24 8JP.

Drive Times: Exeter 1hr30, Plymouth 2hrs, Bristol 2hrs, Birmingham 3hr10, London 3hr50.

Refreshments: The Culbone Stables Inn 07791 878 527 or The Buttery Café 01598 741106 and Cloud Farm Tearooms 01598 741278 just north west of the map at Malmshead.

Bike Shops: Porlock Cycle Hire 01643 862535 in Porlock. Pompy's Cycles 01643 704077, in Minehead, for bikes, parts, repairs & hire.

Books: South West MTB (N.Cotton).

Maps: OS Explorer OL9.

Routes on Web: www.goodmtb.co.uk/a125

Route Idea

From Pittcombe Head, S on trails across Hawkcombe Head then roads S to Lucott Cross to Exford Common. Trails NW across Almsworthy Common to Long Combe, South Common, Stowey Ridge to Oareford. Roads back to the start. Distance 18km.

Extend the area: Porlock Weir map to the N.

© Tom Ivory

Carhampton

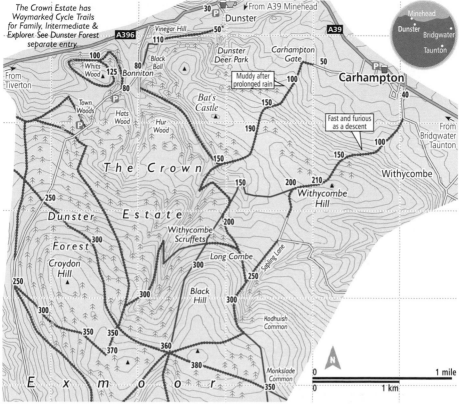

The Crown Estate has Waymarked Cycle Trails for Family, Intermediate & Explorer. See Dunster Forest separate entry.

Situation: On the north east edge of Exmoor National Park, close to the Bristol Channel coast. 4 miles south east of Minehead.

About the Base: Carhampton, a small village with a pub and easy access to the trails. Further Info: www.carhampton.org. **Parking:** Car parks at Carhampton, next to the river in Dunster and in Dunster Forest. *Grid Ref: Dunster SS989432, Dunster Forest SS973420 or SS977423, Carhampton ST008426. Post Code: Dunster TA24 6SP, Carhampton TA24 6LX.*

Drive Times: Taunton 40mins, Exeter 1hr20, Bristol 1hr40, Plymouth 1hr50, Birmingham 3hrs, London 3hr30.

Trains: Dunster Railway Station, on the West Somerset Railway line, has services to Minehead & Taunton. Groups should book ahead 01643 704996. Taunton Station is on the Bristol-Exeter & Swindon-Exeter lines.

Refreshments: At Dunster, a good choice of pubs and cafes or Riverside Tearooms 01643 821759 at Dunster Water Mill. The Butchers Arms 01643 821333 at Carhampton.

Bike Shops: Exmoor Cycle Hire 01643 705307 for hire & Pompy's Cycles 01643 704077 for bikes, parts, repairs & hire, both in Minehead.

Books: South West MTB (N.Cotton). MTB Rides to the SW (M.Darkins).

Maps: OS Explorer OL9.

Route(s) on Web: www.goodmtb.co.uk/a120

Route Idea

From Carhampton, W to Carhampton Gate. Trails SW then NW through the woods around Bat's Castle to Bonniton. Road SW then trails to the west side of the road through Town Woods then S followed by SE to cross the road, in to Dunster Forest ,to north side of Croydon Hill, and on to Monkslade Common. Trails N along Sapling Lane then trails NE over Withycombe Hill.

Also see the trail info for Dunster Forest (p502).

© Phil Miles SPAM

Porlock Weir

Situation: On the South West Coastal Path and the north coast of Exmoor, overlooking the Bristol Channel in Somerset. 7 miles west of Minehead.

About the Base: Porlock Weir, a small harbour with a pub and easy access to the trails. Further Info: www.porlock.co.uk. **Parking:** Car parks at Porlock Weir, Porlock & County Gate Visitor Centre. Several parking points on A39 & at Robber's Bridge. **Grid Ref:** Porlock Weir SS864478, Porlock SS885468, County Gate Visitor Centre SS792486, Robber's Bridge SS821464. **Post Code:** Porlock Weir TA24 8PB, Porlock TA24 8PX, County Gate Visitor Centre EX35 6NQ, Robber's Bridge TA24 8JP.

Drive Times: Exeter 1hr30, Bristol 1hr50, Plymouth 2hr10, Birmingham 3hr10, London 3hr50.

Refreshments: The Bottom Ship 01643 863288 at Porlock Weir, The Ship Inn 01643 862507, The Royal Oak 01643 862798, Whortleberry Tearooms 01643 862337 or The Home Cook Café 01643 862015 at Porlock. Culbone Stables Inn 07791 878 527 at Culbone Hill, Cafe 01598 741321 at County Gate Visitor Centre, The Buttery Café 01598 741106 or Cloud Farm Tearooms 01598 741278 at Malmshead.

Bike Shops: Porlock Cycle Hire 01643 862535 in Porlock. Pompy's Cycles 01643 704077, in Minehead, for bikes, parts, repairs & hire.

Books: South West MTB (N.Cotton). MTB Rides to the SW (M.Darkins).

Maps: OS Explorer OL9.

Routes on Web: www.goodmtb.co.uk/a126

Route Idea

From Porlock Weir, SE to Porlockford Bridge, trails W through Worthy Wood. Roads S then N (before Pitt Farm) past Ash Farm and on to trails on the north side of Culbone Hill and follow to the A39 at County Gate Visitor Centre. Trails SE to Oare. Roads E to Robber's Bridge. Trails NE. Cross the A39 then road E to Pitt Farm followed by S to Pittcombe Head. S over Hawkcombe Head then E on trails through Shillett Wood to Porlock. Back to Porlock Weir on the B3225. Distance 28km.

Extend the area: Pittcombe Head map to the S. Horner map to the SE.

Minehead

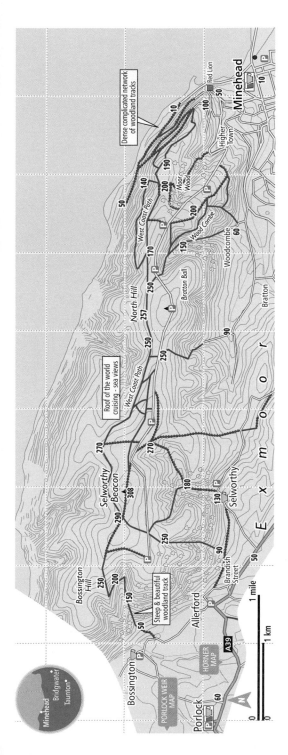

Situation: On the Bristol Channel Coast and the South West Coastal Path, at the edge of Exmoor national Park in Somerset. 21 miles north west of Taunton.

About the Base: Minehead, a coastal town with pubs, cafés and accommodation. Further Info:www.mineheadsomerset. co.uk. **Parking:** Car park near to the railway station in Minehead. Also north west of the town at Moor Wood & at several points en route to the "End of the Road" car park at Selworthy Beacon. Car parks in Bossington, Porlock, Allerford & Selworthy. **Grid Ref:** Minehead SS977460, Moor Wood SS954474, Selworthy Beacon SS910476, Bossington SS897480, Porlock SS885468, Allerford SS904469, Selworthy SS919467. **Post Code:** Minehead TA24 6DG, Bossington TA24 8HF, Porlock TA24 8PX, Allerford TA24 8HN, Selworthy TA24 8TR.

Drive Times: Exeter 1hr20, Bristol 1hr40, Plymouth 2hrs, Birmingham 3hrs, London 3hr40.

Trains: Minehead Railway Station, on the West Somerset Railway line, has services to Taunton. Groups should book ahead 01643 704996. Taunton Station is on the Bristol-Exeter & Swindon-Exeter lines.

Refreshments: Good choice of refreshments at Minehead. The Red Lion 01643706507, opposite the harbour, is best for the ride. Kitnors Tea Rooms 01643 862643 at Bossington, pubs and cafés at Porlock or Periwinkle Cottage Tea Rooms 01643 862769 at Selworthy.

Bike Shops: Exmoor Cycle Hire 01643 705307 for hire & Pompy's Cycles 01643 704077.

Books: South West MTB (N.Cotton). MTB Rides to the SW (M.Darkins).

Maps: OS Explorer OL9.

Routes on Web: www.goodmtb.co.uk/a123

Route Idea

From Minehead, roads through Higher Town then trails NW along Wood Combe. Continue to the West Coast Path just south of North Hill. Out & back section to Selworthy Beacon. When back at North Hill follow trails E back Minehead. Distance 15km.

Exmoor and The Quantocks **SOUTH WEST**

487

Horner

Map labels:
- Lynton
- Minehead
- Horner
- Tiverton
- From Minehead
- Porlock
- From Lynton
- A39
- MINEHEAD MAP
- PORLOCK WEIR MAP
- Hawkcombe
- Crawter Hill
- West Luccombe
- Horner
- 70
- 100
- 150
- 200
- 250
- 280
- 290
- Doverhay Down
- Ley Hill
- E x m o o r
- All very steep - all very beautiful
- 110
- 150
- Horner Wood
- Horner Hill 200
- Luccombe
- 230
- Pool Farm
- 250
- 230
- 200
- 200 180 210
- 310
- Stoke Pero
- 300
- Horner Wood
- 150
- 200
- Cloutsham Ball
- 250
- Cloutsham
- 70
- N
- 0   1 mile
- 0   1 km

Situation: On Horner Water, at the edge of Horner Wood in West Somerset. At the foot of Dunkery Beacon within Exmoor National Park, 1 mile south east of Porlock and 6 miles west of Minehead.

About the Base: Horner, a National Trust village with tea rooms and easy access to the trails.

© Singletrack Safari

Parking: Car park in Horner or north of the rout in Porlock. *Grid Ref: Horner SS897454, Porlock SS885468. Post Code: Horner TA24 8HY, Porlock TA24 8PX.*

Drive Times: Exeter 1hr20, Bristol 1hr50, Plymouth 2hrs, Birmingham 3hr10, London 3hr50.

Refreshments: At Horner, Horner Vale Tea Rooms 01643 862506 and Horner Tea Gardens 01643 862380. Pubs and cafés at Porlock.

Bike Shops: Porlock Cycle Hire 01643 862535 in Porlock. Pompy's Cycles 01643 704077, in Minehead, for bikes, parts, repairs & hire.

Books: South West MTB (N.Cotton).

Maps: Exmoor Mountain Bike Routes (Goldeneye). OS Explorer OL9.

Routes on Web: www.goodmtb.co.uk/a121

Route Idea

From Horner, trails N past Crawter Hill. Roads S then trails S past Ley Hill and in to Horner Wood. Follow the trails through the wood then on to Cloutsham Ball and to the road E of Horner Hill. Roads N back to Horner. Distance 10km.

Extend the area: Porlock Weir map to the NW.

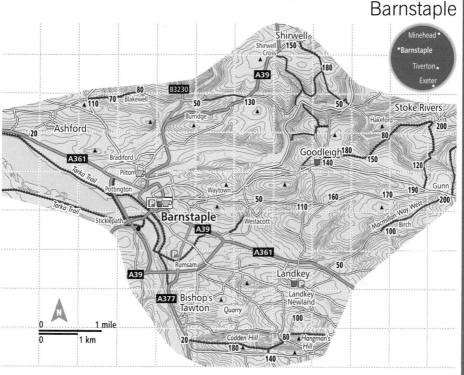

Situation: On the River Taw at the head of the Taw Estuary in North Devon. 30 miles north west of Tiverton and 40 miles north west of Exeter.

About the Base: Barnstaple, a coastal town with a choice of pubs, cafés and accommodation.
Further Info: www.barnstapletowncentre.co.uk.

Parking: Car parks in the centre of Barnstaple or Park & Ride on south edge of town. Car park in the centre of Landkey. *Grid Ref: Barnstaple SS560328, Park & Ride SS562318, Landkey SS598311. **Post Code:** Barnstaple EX32 8GP, Park & Ride EX32 9AX, Landkey EX32 0NF.*

Drive Times: Exeter 1hr10, Plymouth 1hr50, Bristol 2hrs, Birmingham 3hr20, London 4hrs.

Trains: Barnstaple Station has services to Exeter.

Refreshments: Plenty of pubs and cafés at Barnstaple, The New Inn 01271 342488 at Goodleigh and The Castle Inn 01271 830438 at Landkey.

Bike Shops: Bike-It 01271 323873. The Bike Shed 01271 328628. Tarka Trail Cycle Hire 01271 324202.

Books: MTB Rides to the SW (M.Darkins).

Maps: OS Explorer OL9.

Route Idea

From Barnstaple, NW on Tarka Trail then roads through Ashford. Trail and roads E past Blakewell, overt he B3230 and on to A39. NE to Shirwell Cross. Trails and roads to Goodleigh then trails NE to Stoke Rivers. S to Gunn then trails and roads SW to A361. Roads through Landkley Newland then trails W over Codden Hill. N back to Barnstaple on A377 then urban cycle trails. Distance 36km.

Withypool

Simonsbath
B3224
Two Moors Way
380
340
320
Barle
390
Horsen Farm
280
390
350
Great Ferny Ball
300
Two Moors Way
350
Two Moors Way
Horsen Hill
430
Mudbath after rain
350
E x m o o r
Withypool
250
290
350
Withypool Common
400
300
350
Fine stone track through heather
Withypool Hill
400
Withypool Cross
360
Worth Hill
388
Sandyway Cross
Sportsman's
400
Humber's Ball
Twitchen Ridge
310
390
360
White Post
N

Minehead
Withypool Taunton
Tiverton

0 — 1 mile
0 — 1 km

Situation: In the Barle Valley, at the foot of Withypool Common in the centre of Exmoor National Park. 17 miles south west of Minehead and 20 miles east of Barnstaple.

About the Base: Withypool, a small village with a pub and tea rooms.
Further Info: www.withypoolexmoor.co.uk. **Parking:** Car parks in Withypool & Simonsbath, next to the information points or north west of the village at Withypool Common. *Grid Ref: Withypool SS844354, Simonsbath SS773394, Withypool Common SS815360. Post Code: Withypool TA24 7RA, Simonsbath TA24 7SH.*

Drive Times: Exeter 1hr10, Plymouth 1hr50, Bristol 1hr50, Birmingham 3hr10, London 3hr50.

Refreshments: The Royal Oak Inn 01643 831506 at Withypool, The Exmoor Forest Inn 01643 831341 at Simonsbath and The Sportsmans Inn 01643 831109.

Bike Shops: Kustom Bikes 01643 841818, 7 miles away at Wheddon Cross. Pompy's Cycles 01643 704077, in Minehead, for bikes, parts, repairs & hire.

Books: South West MTB (N.Cotton). MTB Rides to the SW (M.Darkins).

Maps: OS Explorer OL9.

Routes on Web: www.goodmtb.co.uk/a129

Route Ideas

❶ From Withypool, NW on road (Two Moors Way) then follow on to the Two Moors Way path to the River Barle. Leave the Two Moors Way and follow trails W past Horsen Farm then S over Horsen Hill and on to Withypool Cross. Roads SW then SE along Twitchen Ridge to White Post. Trails NE back to Withpool, Distance 22km.

❷ Extend the route by 7km and add in a refreshment stop with an out & back section along the Two Moors Way to Simonsbath.

© Phil Miles SPAM

© Phil Miles SPAM

© Julie Young

Winsford (east)

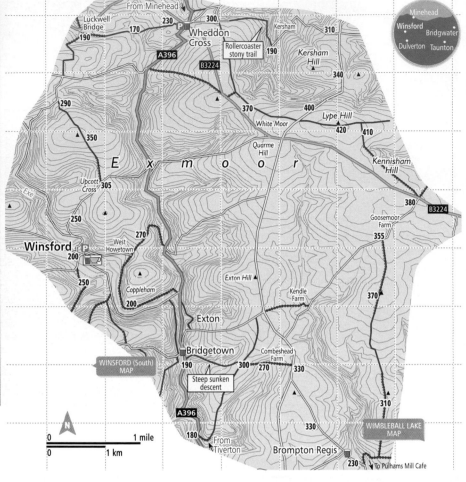

Situation: On the banks of the River Exe at the foot of the Bendon Hills in the heart of Exmoor National Park. 14 miles south west of Minehead, 19 miles north of Tiverton and 19 miles north west of Taunton.

About the Base: Winsford, a village with a pub and tearooms. **Parking:** Car parks in Winsford & at Wheddon Cross. **Grid Ref:** *Winsford SS906349, Wheddon Cross SS923387.* **Post Code:** *Winsford TA24 7JQ, Wheddon Cross TA24 7DU.*

Drive Times: Exeter 1hr10, Plymouth 1hr40, Bristol 1hr50, Birmingham 3hr10, London 3hr50.

Refreshments: At Winsford, The Royal Oak Inn 01643 851455, Bridge Cottage Tea Rooms 01643 851362 and Tea Rooms at Karslake House 01643 851242. The Rest & Be Thankful 01643 841222 at Wheddon Cross. The George Inn 01398 371273 or Pulhams Mill Cafe 01398 371366 at Brompton Regis or The Badgers Holt 01643 851204 at Bridgetown.

Bike Shops: Kustom Bikes 01643 841818 at Wheddon Cross. Exmoor Cycle Hire 01643 705307 for hire & Pompy's Cycles 01643 704077 for bikes, parts, repairs & hire, both in Minehead.

Books: South West MTB (N.Cotton). MTB Rides to the SW (M.Darkins).

Maps: OS Explorer OL9.

Routes on Web: www.goodmtb.co.uk/a128

Route Idea

From Winsford, roads N to Upcott Cross. Trails and roads N to Luckwell Bridge. Trails E to Wheddon Cross. Roads & trails E past Kersham and around Kersham Hill. Roads SW past Goosemoor Farm then trails S to Brompton Regis. Roads N then trails W to Bridgetown. Trail N along west side of river then roads back to Winsford. Distance 28km.

Extend the area: Winsford South map. Wimbleball Lake map to the SE.

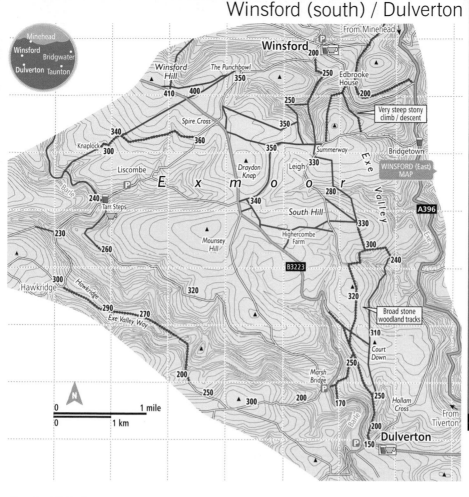

Situation: Within Exmoor National Park in West Somerset, Winsford is on the banks of the River Exe, 14 miles south west of Minehead. Dulverton is 6 miles south on the edge of the park. At the foot of the Barle Valley, close to it's confluence with the River Exe, it is close to the Devon border.

About the Base: Dulverton, a small town with plenty of refreshments or Winsford, a village with a pub and tearooms. Further Info: www.dulverton.net. **Parking:** Car parks next to the river in Dulverton & north of the village at Marsh Bridge. Car parks in Winsford & at Tarr Steps. **Grid Ref:** *Dulverton SS912279, Marsh Bridge SS907289, Winsford SS906349, Tarr Steps, SS872323. **Post Code:** Dulverton TA22 9AA, Winsford TA24 7JQ, Tarr Steps TA22 9PY.*

Drive Times: Exeter 1hr, Bristol 1hr40, Plymouth 1hr40, Birmingham 3hrs, London 3hr40.

Refreshments: Good choice of pubs and cafés at Dulverton. The Tarr Farm Inn and Tea Rooms 01643 851 507 at Tarr Steps. The Royal Oak Inn 01643 851455, Bridge Cottage Tea Rooms 01643 851362 and Tea Rooms at Karslake House 01643 851242 at Winsford or The Badgers Holt 01643 851204 at Bridgetown.

Bike Shops: Kustom Bikes 01643 841818, 4 miles away at Wheddon Cross. Exmoor Cycle Hire 01643 705307 for hire & Pompy's Cycles 01643 704077 for bikes, parts, repairs & hire, both in Minehead.

Books: South West MTB (N.Cotton). MTB Rides to the SW (M.Darkins).

Maps: OS Explorer OL9 & 114.

Routes on Web: www.goodmtb.co.uk/a119

Route Idea

From Winsford, roads W to The Punchbowl. Trails SW past Knaplock to the River Barle. SE to Tarr Farm. Roads SW then E along the Exe Valley Way followed by roads to Dulverton. N on the B3223. Trails N (just before Marsh Bridge) then on to road N past South Hill, then Leigh to Summerway. Trail N to Edbrooke House. Road back to Winsford. Distance 25km.

Extend the area: Winsford East map.

Wimbleball Lake

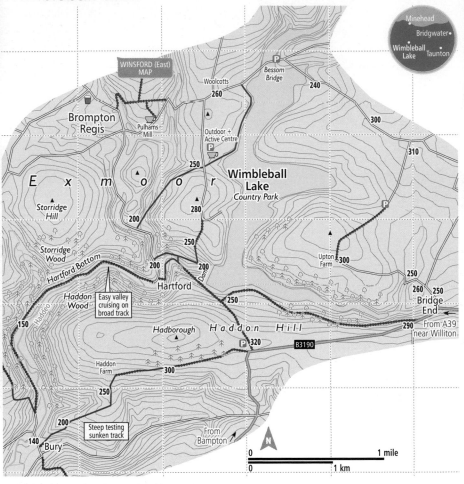

Situation: In the south east corner of Exmoor. 15 miles south of Minehead. 16 miles north of Tiverton.

About the Base: Wimbleball Lake, a reservoir and country park with a café and outdoor centre. Further Info: www.swlakestrust.org.uk.

Parking: Car parks at Wimbleball Lake Outdoor & Active Centre, north of the lake at Bessom Bridge & south at Haddon Hill.

Grid Ref: *Wimbleball Lake SS965308, Bessom Bridge SS974317, Haddon Hill SS969284.*

Post Code: *Wimbleball Lake TA22 9NU.*

Drive Times: Exeter 1hr, Plymouth 1hr40, Bristol 1hr40, Birmingham 3hrs, London 3hr40.

Refreshments: Wimbleball Lake Cafe 01398 371257. The George Inn 01398 371273 or Pulhams Mill Café 01398 371366 at Brompton Regis.

Bike Shops: Kustom Bikes 01643 841818, 6 miles away at Wheddon Cross. Exmoor Cycle Hire 01643 705307 for hire & Pompy's Cycles 01643 704077 for bikes, parts, repairs & hire, both in Minehead. Ralphies 01823 275822 & The Bicycle Chain 01823 252499 in Taunton or Rons Cycle Centre 01884 255750 in Tiverton.

Books: South West MTB (N.Cotton).

Maps: OS Explorer OL9 & 114.

Routes on Web: www.goodmtb.co.uk/a127

Route Idea

From the car park at the Activity Centre, a figure of 8 ride. Roads & trails S to Haddon Hill and the B3190. Trails W past Haddon Farm to Bury. N along Hartford Bottom to Hartford. Anticlockwise around the lake: Bridge End, Upton Farm, Bessom Bridge and back to the Activity Centre. Distance 22km.

Extend the area: Winsford East map.

Monksilver

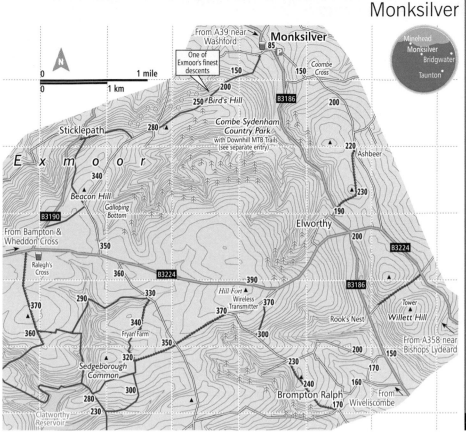

Situation: On the eastern slopes of the Brendon Hills and the edge of Exmoor National Park in Somerset. 10 miles south east of Minehead and 14 miles north west of Taunton.

About the Base: Monksilver, a small village with a pub and easy access to the trails. **Parking:** Car park next to the village hall on the south east edge of Monksilver. *Grid Ref: ST075374. Post Code: TA4 4JE.*

Drive Times: Exeter 1hr, Bristol 1hr30, Plymouth 1hr40, Birmingham 2hr50, London 3hr30.

Trains: Williton Railway Station, 3 miles away on the West Somerset Railway line, has services to Minehead & Taunton. Groups should book ahead 01643 704996. Taunton Station is on the Bristol-Exeter & Swindon-Exeter lines.

Refreshments: The Notley Arms at Monksilver 01984 656217 or The Ralegh's Cross Inn 01984 640343.

Bike Shops: Exmoor Cycle Hire 01643 705307 for hire & Pompy's Cycles 01643 704077 for bikes, parts, repairs & hire, both in Minehead. Ralphies 01823 275822 or The Bicycle Chain 01823 252499 in Taunton.

Books: South West MTB (N.Cotton).

Maps: OS Explorer OL9.

Routes on Web: www.goodmtb.co.uk/a124

Route Idea

From Monksliver, roads SE to Coombe Cross then Ashbeer. Trails to Elworthy. B3186 and minor roads S to Brompton Ralph. Trails then road NW towards the wireless transmitter, then trails SW. Cross the road then trails N past Fryan Farm. Roads NW to Beacon Hill then trails to Sticklepath. NE back to Monksilver via trail past Bird's Hill. Distance 19km.

West Quantoxhead

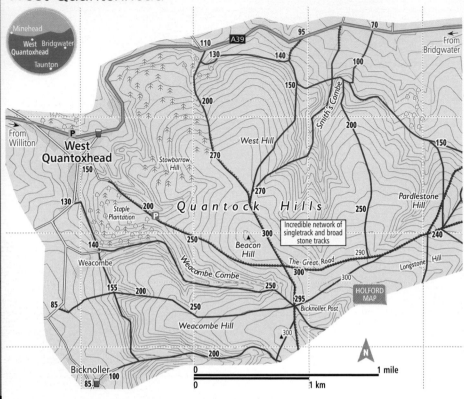

Situation: At the foot of the Quantock Hills in West Somerset, close to the Bristol Channel. 10 miles east of Minehead, 15 miles west of Bridgewtaer and north of Taunton.

About the Base: West Quantoxhead, a small village with a pub and easy access to the trails.
Further Info: www.quantockonline.co.uk/quantocks/villages/westquantoxhead.

Parking: Layby opposite the post office on A39 in West Quantoxhead. National Trust car park at Staple Plantation just south of the village. **Grid Ref:** *West Quantoxhead ST108418, Staple Plantation ST116410.*
Post Code: *West Quantoxhead TA4 4DF.*

Drive Times: Exeter 1hr10, Bristol 1hr20,Plymouth 1hr50, Birmingham 2hr40, London 3hr20.

Trains: Williton Railway Station, 2 miles away on the West Somerset Railway line, has services to Minehead & Taunton. Groups should book ahead 01643 704996. Taunton Station is on the Bristol-Exeter & Swindon-Exeter lines.

Refreshments: The Windmill Inn 01984 633004 at West Quantoxhead. The Bicknoller Inn 01984 656234 at Bicknoller.

Bike Shops: Exmoor Cycle Hire 01643 705307 for hire & Pompy's Cycles 01643 704077 for bikes, parts, repairs & hire, both in Minehead. The Bicycle Chain 01278 431269 in Bridgwater, Ralphies 01823 275822 or The Bicycle Chain 01823 252499 in Taunton.

Books: MBR Ride Guide 2010

Maps: OS Explorer 140.

Route Idea

From Staple Plantation, SE past Beacon Hill. N to Smith's Combe then trail SE past Pardlestone Hill. Back towards Beacon Hill then S to Bicknoller Post. W along Weacombe Combe. Road towards West Quantoxhead Head then SE back to start. Distance 11km.

Extend the area: Holford Map to the SE.

West Quantoxhead, Bicknoller © Matt Cope

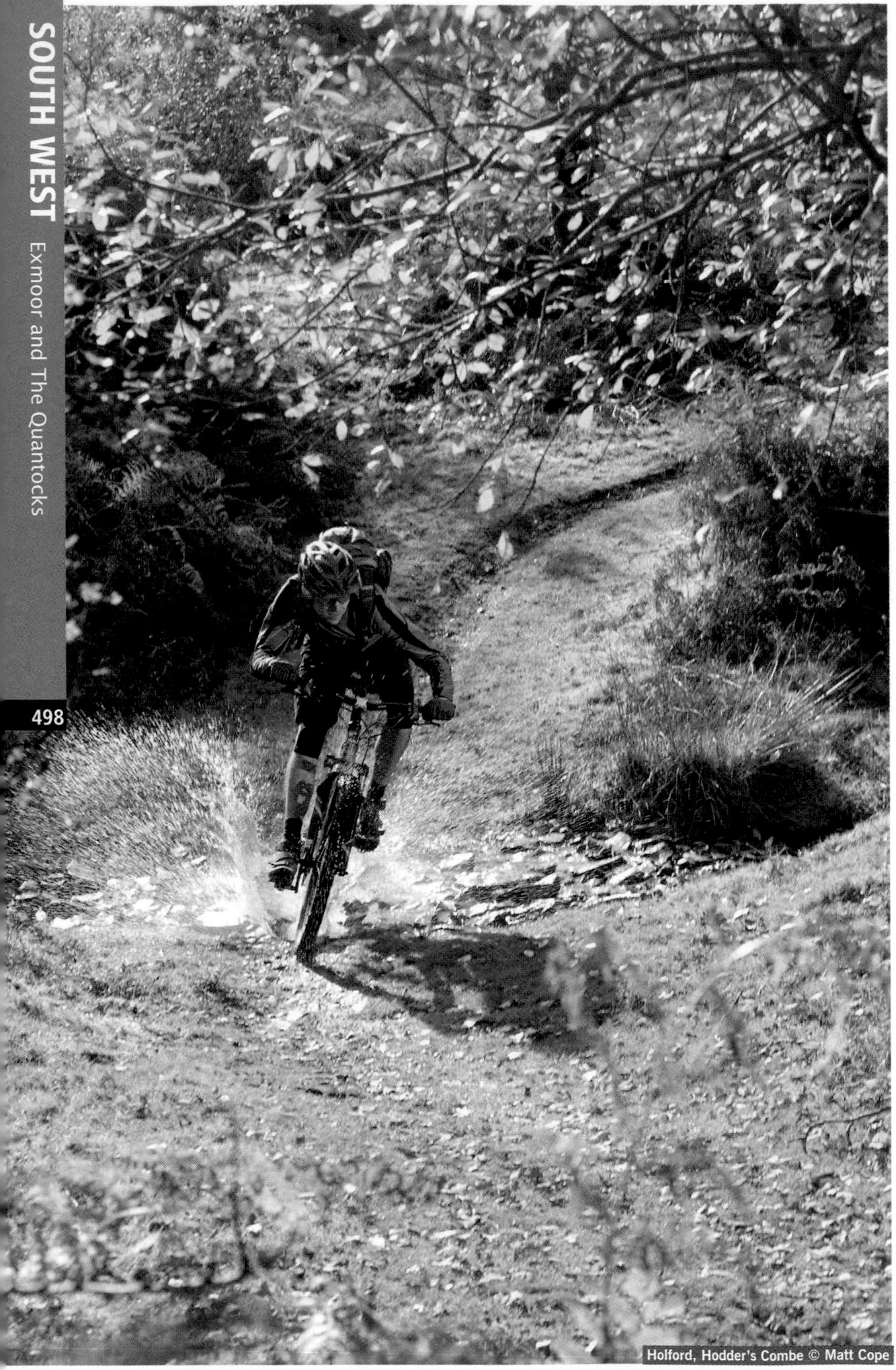

Holford, Hodder's Combe © Matt Cope

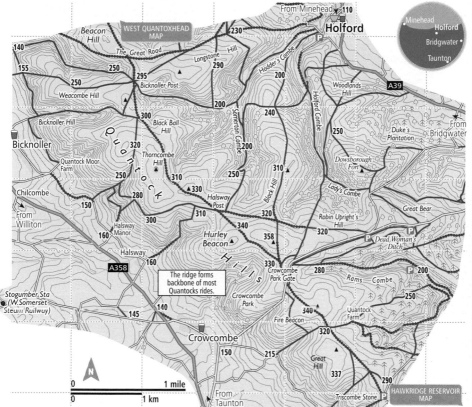

Situation: On the River Holford and the edge of The Quantock Hills in West Somerset. 10 miles west of Bridgewater and 14 miles north of Taunton.

About the Base: Holford, a small village with a pub, tea rooms and easy access to the trails.
Further Info: www.quantockonline.co.uk/quantocks/villages/holford. **Parking:** Car park in Holford just south of the village. Also at Dead Woman's Ditch, Great Bear & Rams Combe. Car park at Triscombe Stone **Grid Ref:** *Holford ST154410, Dead Woman's Ditch ST161381, Great Bear ST168382, Rams Combe ST167376, Triscombe Stone ST163359. **Post Code:** Holford TA5 1SA, Triscombe Stone TA4 3HE.*

Drive Times: BExeter 1hr10, Bristol 1hr10, Plymouth 1hr50, Birmingham 2hr30, London 3hr10.

Refreshments: The Plough Inn 01278 741232 and Stella's Tea Garden 01278 741529 at Holford, The Carew Arms 01984 618631 at Crowcombe and The Bicknoller Inn 01984 656234 at Bicknoller.

Bike Shops: The Bicycle Chain 01278 431269 in Bridgwater, Ralphies 01823 275822 or The Bicycle Chain 01823 252499 in Taunton. Sedgemoor Cycles 01278 453357, 8 miles away in Chilton Trinity, for hire.

Books: South West MTB (N.Cotton). MTB Rides to the SW (M.Darkins). MBR Ride Guide 2010

Maps: OS Explorer 140.

Route Ideas

❶ From Holford, S along Holford Combe and Lady's Combe. S on road. W along trail to Halswell Post. NW past Bicknoller Post. E on The Great Road back to Holford. Distance 14km.

❷ From Holford, W on the Great Road then S to Bicknoller Post. W along Weacombe Hill then S then E along Bicknoller Hill towards Black Ball Hill. SE past Halsway Post to Crowcombe Park Gate. N along Black Hill then W to drop in to Somerton Combe. NE along Hodder's Combe back to Holford. Distance 15km.

Extend the area: West Quantoxhead Map to the NW. Hawkridge Reservoir map to the SE.

Hawkridge Reservoir

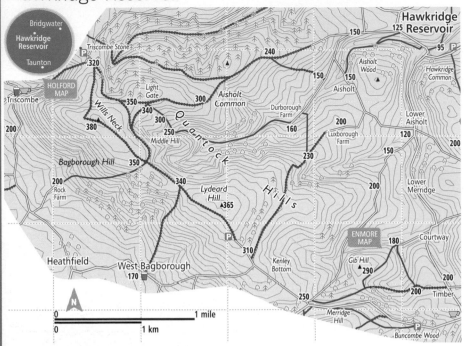

Rider: Martin Buckley. © Alex Leigh

Situation: In a small valley on the Quantock Hills, in an Area of Outstanding Natural Beauty. 6 miles west of Bridgwater and 8 miles north of Taunton.

About the Base: Hawkridge Reservoir, a rural location with a car park and easy access to the trails. **Parking:** Car parks at Hawkridge Reservoir, Triscombe Stone, Lydeard Hill & Buncombe Wood. *Grid Ref: Hawkridge Reservoir ST207360, Triscombe Stone ST163359, Lydeard Hill ST180338, Buncombe Wood ST200328. Post Code: Hawkridge Reservoir TA5 1AL.*

Drive Times: Exeter 1hr, Bristol 1hr10, Plymouth 1hr40, Birmingham 2hr30, London 3hr.

Trains: Bridgwater Station is on the Bristol-Taunton-Exeter line. Taunton Station is on the Bristol-Exeter & Swindon-Exeter lines.

Refreshments: No refreshments at the reservoir. The Rising Sun Inn 01823 432 575 at West Bagborough, The Pines café 01823 451245 at Buncombe Wood or The Blue Ball Inn 01984 618242 and Stable Cottage Tea Rooms 01984 618239 at Triscombe.

Bike Shops: The Bicycle Chain 01278 431269 in Bridgwater, Ralphies 01823 275822 or The Bicycle Chain 01823 252499 in Taunton. Sedgemoor Cycles 01278 453357, 6 miles away in Chilton Trinity, for hire.

Books: South West MTB (N.Cotton). MTB Rides to the SW (M.Darkins).

Maps: OS Explorer 140.

Route Idea

From Hawkridge Reservoir, road and trails W to Aisholt and Luxborough Farm then trails SW. NW to Skirt the top of Lydeard Hill then S to West Bagborough. Roads to Rock Farm. Climb Bagborough Hill then along to Light Gate. Trails & roads W back to the start. Distance 16km. Shorten the above, when skirting Lydeard Hill continue straight to Light Gate. Distance 12km.

Enmore

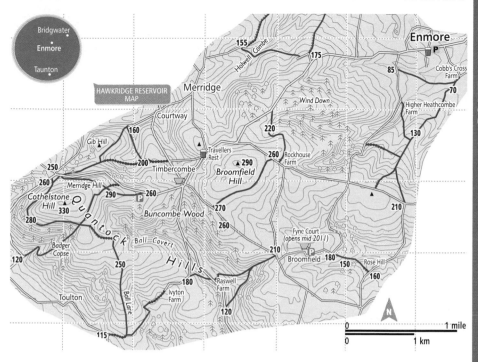

Situation: On the Eastern Edge of the Quantock Hills in Somerset. 4 miles west of Bridgwater and 8 miles north of Taunton.

About the Base: Enmore, a small village with a pub and easy access to the trails. Further Info: www.quantockonline.co.uk/quantocks/villages/enmore.

Parking: Roadside in the centre of Enmore. Car parks at Buncombe Wood & Fyne Court. *Grid Ref: Enmore ST240349, Buncombe Wood ST200328, Fyne Court ST221321. Post Code: Enmore TA5 2DT, Fyne Court TA5 2EQ.*

Drive Times: Exeter 1hr, Bristol 1hr, Plymouth 1hr40, Birmingham 2hr20, London 3hrs.

Trains: Bridgwater Station is on the Bristol-Taunton-Exeter line. Taunton Station is on the Bristol-Exeter & Swindon-Exeter lines.

Refreshments: The Tynte Arms 01278 671351 at Enmore. The Traveller's Rest 01278 671367, The Pines café 01823 451245 at Buncombe Wood and Café at National Trust Fyne Court 01823 451587.

Bike Shops: The Bicycle Chain 01278 431269 in Bridgwater, Ralphies 01823 275822 or The Bicycle Chain 01823 252499 in Taunton. Sedgemoor Cycles 01278 453357, 6 miles away in Chilton Trinity, for hire.

Books: South West MTB (N.Cotton).

Maps: OS Explorer 140.

Route Idea

From Enmore, W to Merridge via Holwell Combe. SW past Courtway past and around Cothelstone Hill then S down Ball Lane. NE past Ivyton Farm to Broomfield then E to Rose Hill. Roads & trails NE to Cobb's Cross Farm & back to Enmore. Distance 19km.

Rider: Pedro. © Sheldon Attwood

Dunster Forest

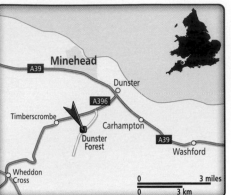

In West Somerset at the north eastern corner of Exmoor National Park, overlooking the Bristol Channel. A private estate with waymarked trails including a short family trail, intermediate and explorer trails with steady climbs, minor technical sections and stunning views.

Facilities:
None on site. Plenty of refreshments at Dunster village.

Parking:
Grid Ref: SS980426. Post Code: TA24 6TB

Web: www.goodmtb.co.uk/b83

The Trails

❶ **Green Family Trail, XC, 1.6km.**
❷ **Intermediate Orange Trail, XC, 9.7km.**
❸ **Brown Explorer Trail, XC, 14.5km.**

© Phil Miles SPAM

Combe Sydenham Country Park

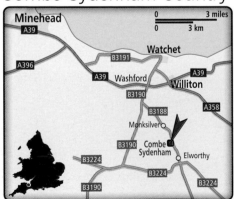

At the edge of Exmoor National Park in Somerset. Competition standard downhill courses, some suitable for all abilities, in privately owned Combe Sydenham Country Park.

Facilities:
Refreshments available for group tours.

Parking:
Grid Ref: ST076366. Post Code: TA4 4JG

Web: www.goodmtb.co.uk/b82

The Trails

DH courses, various abilities, pay per bike to ride.

near Minehead, p487. © Phil Miles SPAM

North of Challacombe, Lynton p482. ©Matt Cope

Dartmoor & Cornwall

D artmoor is the larger of two National Parks in Devon (the other is Exmoor) and its granite tors create quite an extraordinary landscape. Dartmoor offers year-round riding with a good variety of testing singletrack mixed in with broad stone or grass tracks. Dartmoor is like a clockface: the best rides lie around the edge of the clock or right in the centre. The bleak expanse of the high central plateau is crossed by just two roads, which meet in **Princetown**, location of the famous Dartmoor Prison.

Princetown is a good base and some purpose built trails radiate out from the town: follow the old tramway west around the distinctive outcrops of rocks at King's Tor or head south on a much improved track towards Nun's Cross with the option of a teeth rattling descent down to Burrator Reservoir. Alternatively go east on a much rougher and rugged track past the improbably located ruins at Swincombe.

Postbridge is the other base in the centre of Dartmoor and has one of the most unforgettable rides you will ever do, useing a series of stepping stones (huge boulders) to cross a succession of rivers.

Around the edge of the moor there are rides north from **South Brent** up towards the remote Avon Dam. *Lustleigh* gives access to the steep wooded cleaves on the east side of the moor and, hopping over the hills to the ancient delights of Grimspound, fast grassy blasts and testing

Near Princetown © Singletrack Safari

singletrack through rock gardens down in the valleys.

To the north of the National Park, **Okehampton** is connected via a disused railway path called the Granite Way to **Lydford** with trails returning along the flanks of the moor past Meldon Reservoir and some open tracks through fern-covered moorland.

Elsewhere in South Devon there are trails to the east of Exeter around **Woodbury**, between the Exe Estuary and the valley of the River Otter and to the north of **Sidmouth** either side of the woodland ridge along the top of East Hill.

For such a large county Cornwall offers very little good mountain biking - there are plenty of easy family trails such as the Camel Trail, the Clay Trails around St Austell or the Coast to Coast Trail from **Portreath** to Devoran.

There is the start of a new network of trails in the Poldice Valley but in much of the rest of the county it is a case of making the most of the the the odd bridleway or small Forestry Commission holding.

With regard to Trail Centres, the main one is at **Haldon Forest Park**, south west of Exeter with much smaller centres/bike parks in Devon at **Stoke Woods** (north of Exeter), **Abbeyford Woods** (north of Okehampton), **South West Extreme** (Bideford) and **Maddacleave Woods** (Plymouth). In Cornwall (near Redruth) there is a bike park at **The Track** and freeride trails at **Poldice Valley**.

Around Lustleigh © Singletrack Safari

Okehampton (west)

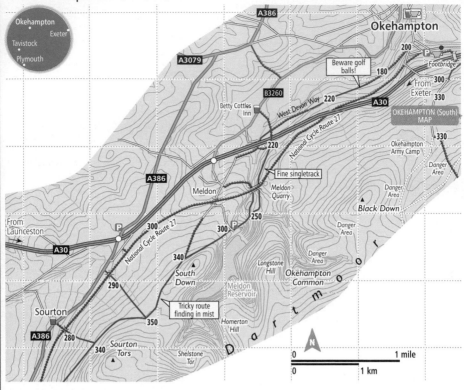

Situation: In West Devon, on the northern edge of Dartmoor National Park. Close to the A30, 23 miles west of Exeter.

About the Base: Okehampton, a town with pubs, cafés and an adventure centre.
Further Info: www.okehamptondevon.co.uk.
Parking: Car park at YHA Okehampton. Also at Meldon Reservoir & next to the picnic area on A30.
Grid Ref: YHA Okehampton SX591944, Car park at Meldon Reservoir SX561918, A30 Picnic Area SX543913.
Post Code: YHA Okehampton EX20 1EW.

Drive Times: Bristol 1hr50, Birmingham 3hr10, London 3hr50, Manchester 4hr30, Leeds 5hrs.

Trains: Okehampton Station has services to Exeter.

Refreshments: Plenty of pubs and cafés at Oke-hampton. Refreshments at YHA Okehampton 01837 53916 south of the town. Betty Cottles Inn 01837 55339 and The Highwaymans Inn 01837 861243 at Sourton.

Bike Shops: Okehampton Cycles 01837 53248 & Moor Cycles 01837 659677 in Okehampton. hire at Adventure Okehampton 01837 53916.

Books: South West MTB (N.Cotton). MTB Rides to the SW (M.Darkins).

Maps: Dartmoor Mountain Bike Routes (Goldeneye). Dartmoor British Mountain Map (Harvey). OS Explorer OL28.

Route Idea

From Okehampton, National Cycle Route 27 SW to Sourton. Trail SE towards Sourton Tors then NE across South Down. Follow past Meldon Quarry, over the A30 then E along the West Devon Way back to Okehampton. Distance 16km.

© Nick Cotton

Okehampton (south)

Situation: On the northern edge of Dartmoor National Park in West Devon. Close to the A30, 23 miles west of Exeter.

About the Base: Okehampton, a town with pubs, cafés and an adventure centre. Further Info: www.okehamptondevon.co.uk.
Parking: Car park at YHA Okehampton.
Grid Ref: YHA Okehampton SX591944.
Post Code: YHA Okehampton EX20 1EW.

Drive Times: Bristol 1hr50, Birmingham 3hr10, London 3hr50, Manchester 4hr30, Leeds 5hrs.

Trains: Okehampton Station has services to Exeter.

Refreshments: Plenty of pubs and cafés at Okehampton. Refreshments at YHA Okehampton 01837 53916 south of the town. The Tors Inn 01837 840689 at Belstone.

Bike Shops: Okehampton Cycles 01837 53248 & Moor Cycles 01837 659677 in Okehampton. hire at Adventure Okehampton 01837 53916.

Books: MTB Rides to the SW (M.Darkins).

Maps: Dartmoor Mountain Bike Routes (Goldeneye). Dartmoor British Mountain Map (Harvey). OS Explorer OL28.

Route Idea

From Okehampton, trails E close to the A30 then roads SE to Belstone. Trails SW then S towards Okement Hill. Trails N to join road near the Army Camp and back to Okehampton. Distance 24km.

507

Map

Okehampton

Exeter
Tavistock
Plymouth

From Exeter

160
200
Footbridge
A30
270
300
East Hill
330
OKEHAMPTON (West) MAP
150

Belstone
320
350
380

330
Okehampton Army Camp
Danger Area
Wide, stone track
Scarey Tor 360
Belstone Common
420
Cullever Steps 350
Danger Area 400
Rowtor
430
West Mill Tor
Danger Area
Danger Area
Okehampton Common
Danger Area 450
New Bridge
East Mill Tor
400
Military Loop Road - almost all tarmac
Danger Area
Danger Area
Danger Area
500
Danger Area
450
D a r t m o o r
Danger Area
Danger Area 500
Okehampton Army Range
Phone 0800 4584868 for firing notices
Danger Area
560
Okement Hill

N

0   1 mile
0   1 km

Fine fast grassy descent

© Nick Cotton

Drewsteignton

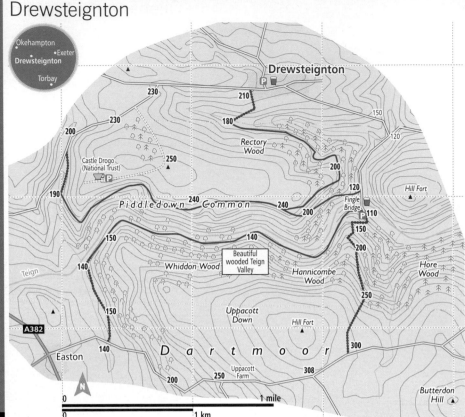

Situation: In the Teign Valley and the north of Dartmoor National Park in west Devon. 10 miles south east of Oakhampton and 14 miles west of Exeter.

About the Base: Drewsteignton, a village with a pub and easy access to the trails.
Further Info: www.drewsteigntonparish.co.uk.

Parking: Parking in Drewsteignton Square. Car park at Fingle Bridge & National Trust Castle Drago. *Grid Ref: Drewsteignton Square SX735908, Fingle Bridge SX743898, Castle Drago SX723901. Post Code: Drewsteignton Square EX6 6QN, Castle Drago EX6 6PB.*

Drive Times: Bristol 1hr50, Birmingham 3hr10, London 3hr50, Manchester 4hr30, Leeds 5hrs.

Refreshments: The Drewe Arms 01647 281224 at Drewsteignton. Café 01647 433306 at National Trust Castle Drago and The Fingle Bridge Inn 01647 281287.

Bike Shops: Okehampton Cycles 01837 53248 & Moor Cycles 01837 659677 in Okehampton.

Maps: Dartmoor Mountain Bike Routes (Goldeneye). Dartmoor British Mountain Map (Harvey). OS Explorer OL28.

© Phil Miles SPAM

Route Idea

From Drewsteigton, S on trails through Rectory Wood then E to Fingle Bridge. SW then W along the south side of the river and then follow S to road. Road E then trails S back to Fingle Bridge. Cross the river then W on trails across Piddledown Common. Roads back to Drewsteignton.
Distance 13km.

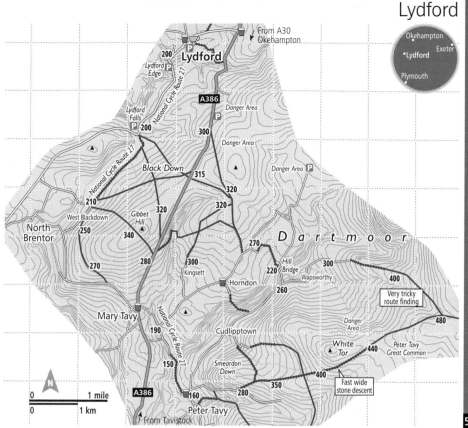

Situation: On the western edge of Dartmoor National Park in West Devon. 9 miles north east of Tavistock and south west of Okehampton.

About the Base: Lydford, a village with two pubs and tea rooms nearby. Further Info: www.lydford.co.uk.

Parking: Car park in Lydford near to the Castle Inn. National Trust car parks at Lydford Gorge & Lydford Falls. Parking on A386 south of Lydford.

Grid Ref: Lydford SX510847, Lydford Gorge SX508843, Lydford Falls SX500831, A386 SX516832. **Post Code:** Lydford EX20 4BH.

Drive Times: Bristol 2hr10, Birmingham 3hr20, London 4hrs, Manchester 4hr40, Leeds 5hr10.

Refreshments: The Castle Inn 01822 820241 at Lydford, The Dartmoor Inn 01822 820221 east of the village and National Trust Tea Rooms 01822 820320 at Lydford Gorge. The Elephant's Nest Inn 01822 810273 at Horndon and The Peter Tavy Inn 01822 810348 at Peter Tavy. The Mary Tavy Inn 01822 810326 and Royal Standard Inn 01822 810011 at Mary Tavy.

Bike Shops: Dartmoor Cycles 01822 618 178 & Tavistock Cycles 01822 617630 in Tavistock, Okehampton Cycles 01837 53248 & Moor Cycles 01837 659677 in Okehampton. Devon Cycle Hire 01837 861141, 5 miles away in Sourton Down, for hire.

Books: South West MTB (N.Cotton). MTB Rides to the SW (M.Darkins).

Maps: Dartmoor Mountain Bike Routes (Goldeneye). Dartmoor British Mountain Map (Harvey). OS Explorer OL28 & 112.

Route Ideas

❶ From Lydford Falls car park, SE on trails over Black Down. Cross the A386 then trails and roads SE to Hill Bridge. Roads to Peter Tavy. National Cycle Route 27 through Mary Tavy and back to the start. Distance 17km.

❷ As above to Hill Bridge then E on road and clockwise on trails around White Tor to Cudlipptown. S to Peter Tavy then National Cycle Route 27 N through Mary Tavy and back to the start. Distance 24km.

© Nick Cotton

Postbridge (east)

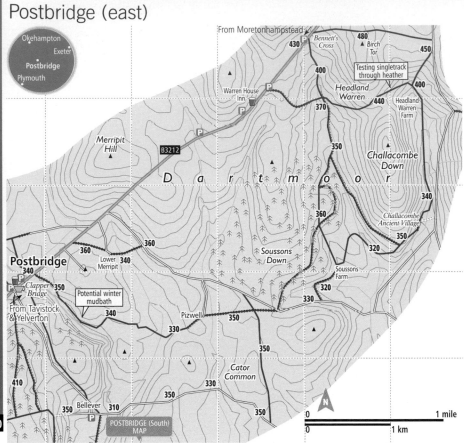

Okehampton
Exeter
● Postbridge
Plymouth

From Moretonhampstead

Bennett's Cross
430
480 ▲ Birch Tor
450
400
Testing singletrack through heather
400
Warren House Inn
Headland Warren
440
Headland Warren Farm
370
350
Merripit Hill ▲
B3212
Challacombe Down ▲

D a r t m o o r

340
360
Challacombe Ancient Village
350

360
360
Soussons Down
320

Postbridge
340
Lower 340 Merripit
Soussons Farm
350

Clapper Bridge 350
Potential winter mudbath
320

From Tavistock & Yelverton
340
Pizwell
350
330

330
350

350

Cator Common

410
330
350

Bellever 310
350
350
POSTBRIDGE (South) MAP

N

0 — 1 mile
0 — 1 km

510

Situation: On the East Dart River below Challacombe Down, at the centre of Dartmoor National Park in Devon. 6 miles north east of Postbridge and 13 miles north east of Tavistock.

About the Base: Postbridge, a small village with a pub, post office store and information centre. Further Info: www.postbridge.net. **Parking:** Car park next to the information centre in Postbridge. Parking at Bellever, Bennett's Cross & on B3212 close to The Warren House Inn. *Grid Ref: Postbridge SX646788, Bellever SX655771, Bennett's Cross SX680817, Warren House Inn SX673808.* **Post Code:** *Postbridge PL20 6TH.*

Drive Times: Bristol 2hr10, Birmingham 3hr30, London 4hrs, Manchester 4hr50, Leeds 5hr20.

Refreshments: At Postbridge, The East Dart Hotel 01822 880213 and refreshments at Postbridge Post Office Stores 01822 880201. The Warren House Inn 01822 880208.

Bike Shops: Big Peaks, 11 miles away in Ashburton, Dartmoor Cycles 01822 618 178 & Tavistock Cycles 01822 617630 in Tavistock. Tavistock Cycles also do hire.

Books: South West MTB (N.Cotton). MTB Rides to the SW (M.Darkins).

Maps: Dartmoor British Mountain Map (Harvey). OS Explorer OL28.

Route Idea

From Postbridge, trails E to Pizwell. Trails and roads E to Soussons Farm. Anticlockwise on trails around Challacombe Down. SW through the woods on Soussons Down. NW on road then trails past Lower Merripit and back to Postbridge. Distance 16km.

© Nick Cotton

Postbridge (south)

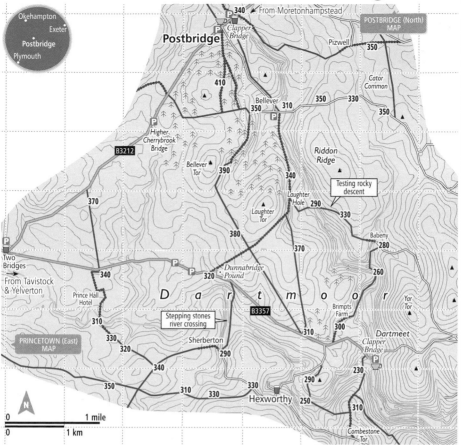

Situation: At the centre of Dartmoor National Park in Devon. 6 miles north east of Postbridge and 13 miles north east of Tavistock.

About the Base: Postbridge, a small village with a pub, post office store and information centre. Further Info: www.postbridge.net. **Parking:** Car parks next to the information centre in Postbridge & south of the village. Also at Bellever, Higher Cherrybrook Bridge, Two Bridges, Dunnabridge Pound & Dartmeet.
Grid Ref: *Postbridge SX646788, Postbridge South SX646786, Bellever SX655771, Higher Cherrybrook Bridge SX638768, Two Bridges SX609750, Dunnabridge Pound SX639747 or SX641746, Dartmeet SX672733.* **Post Code:** *Postbridge PL20 6TH, Dartmeet PL20 6SG.*

Drive Times: Bristol 2hr10, Birmingham 3hr30, London 4hrs, Manchester 4hr50, Leeds 5hr20.

Refreshments: At Postbridge, The East Dart Hotel 01822 880213 and refreshments at Postbridge Post Office Stores 01822 880201. Brimpts Farm Tea Rooms 01364 631450 at Dartmeet and The Forest Inn 01364 631211 at Hexworthy.

Bike Shops: Big Peaks, 8 miles south east of the map in Ashburton, Dartmoor Cycles 01822 618 178 & Tavistock Cycles 01822 617630 in Tavistock. Tavistock Cycles also do hire.

Books: South West MTB (N.Cotton). MTB Rides to the SW (M.Darkins).

Maps: Dartmoor Mountain Bike Routes (Goldeneye). Dartmoor British Mountain Map (Harvey). OS Explorer OL28.

Route Idea

From Postbridge, S on trails through the woods then on to Bellever. Trails S to Laughter Hole then SW to Dunnabridge Pound. W on the B3357 then trail S followed by roads to Hexworthy. Road NE then before reaching the B3357 trails S then N to Clapper Bridge. Road W then trails N past Brimpts Farm. On to Babeny and back to Laughter Hole. N to Bellever and back to Postbridge. Distance 21km.

© Nick Cotton

Princetown (south)

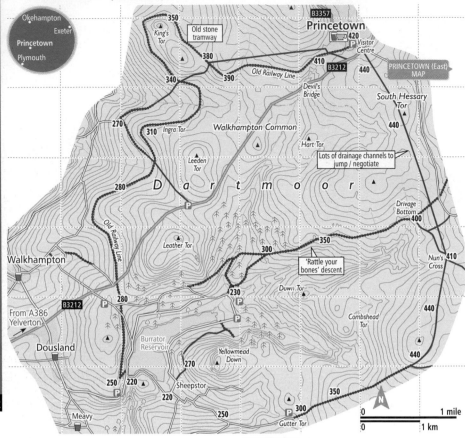

Okehampton
Exeter
Princetown
Plymouth

King's Tor
350
Old stone tramway
B3357
Princetown
420
Visitor Centre
380
410
B3212
440
PRINCETOWN (East) MAP
340
390
Old Railway Line
Devil's Bridge
South Hessary Tor
270
310 Ingra Tor
Walkhampton Common
Hart Tor
440
Leeden Tor
Lots of drainage channels to jump / negotiate
280
D a r t m o o r
Drivage Bottom
400
Leather Tor
300
350
Nun's Cross
410
Walkhampton
'Rattle your bones' descent
B3212
280
230
Down Tor
440
From A386 Yelverton
Combshead Tor
Dousland
Burrator Reservoir
Yellowmead Down
440
270
250 220
Sheepstor
220
350
Meavy
250
300
Gutter Tor
0 .... 1 mile
0 .... 1 km

512

Situation: On high moorland, in the heart of Dartmoor National Park in Devon. 8 miles east of Tavistock.

About the Base: Princetown, a small town with pubs, cafes and a visitor centre. Further Info: www.devonlink.co.uk/smtowns/princetown.

Parking: Car park next to Highland Moor Visitor Centre in Princetown. Parking on B3212 at Leeden Tor, around Burrator Reservoir & at Gutter Tor in the south of the map. *Grid Ref: Princetown SX589735, Leedon Tor SX560709, Burrator West SX547692, Burrator South SX549677, Burrator East SX569693 or SX568689. Post Code: Princetown PL20 6QF.*

Drive Times: Plymouth 30mins, Exeter 50mins, Bristol 2hr10, Bournemouth 2hr20, B'ham 3hr30.

Refreshments: At Princetown, The Prince of Wales 01822 890219, Plume of Feathers Inn 01822 890240, Fox Tor Café 01822 890238, Badgers Holt Tea Rooms, The Old Police Station 01822 890407.

Bike Shops: Dartmoor Cycles 01822 618 178 & Tavistock Cycles 01822 617630 in Tavistock. Tavistock Cycles also do hire.

Books: South West MTB (N.Cotton). MTB Rides to the SW (M.Darkins).

Maps: Dartmoor Mountain Bike Routes (Goldeneye). Dartmoor British Mountain Map (Harvey). OS Explorer OL28.

Route Ideas

❶ From Princetown, S on trails past South Hessary Tor then W across Drivage Bottom to Burrator Reservoir. Roads along the south of the reservoir to Sheepstor. Road then trails E to Nun's Cross and trail back over South Hessary Tor to Princetown. Distance 21km.

❷ As above to Burrator Reservoir. Along roads on the south side of the reservoir, followed by trails N on the old railway line back to Princetown. Distance 23km.

© Singletrack Safari

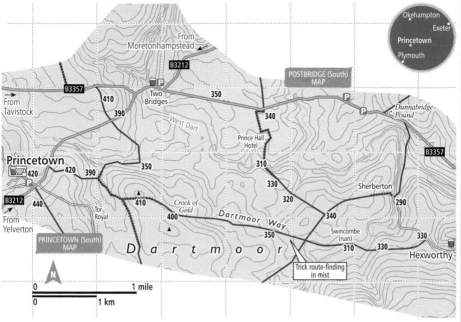

Situation: In the heart of Dartmoor National Park in Devon. On high moorland, 8 miles east of Tavistock.

About the Base: Princetown, a small town with pubs, cafes and a visitor centre. Further Info: www.devonlink.co.uk/smtowns/princetown.
Parking: Car park next to Highland Moor Visitor Centre in Princetown. Also at Two Bridges & Dunnabridge Pound. *Grid Ref: Princetown SX589735, Two Bridges SX609750, Dunnabridge Pound SX639747 or SX641746. Post Code: Princetown PL20 6QF.*

Drive Times: Bristol 2hr10, Birmingham 3hr30, London 4hr10, Manchester 4hr50, Leeds 5hr20.

Refreshments: At Princetown, The Prince of Wales 01822 890219, Plume of Feathers Inn 01822 890240, Fox Tor Café 01822 890238, Badgers Holt Tea Rooms and The Old Police Station 01822 890407. The Two Bridges Hotel 01822 892300 and The Forest Inn 01364 631211 at Hexworthy.

Bike Shops: Dartmoor Cycles 01822 618 178 & Tavistock Cycles 01822 617630 in Tavistock. Tavistock Cycles also do hire.

Books: South West MTB (N.Cotton).

Maps: Dartmoor British Mountain Map (Harvey). OS Explorer OL28.

Route Idea

From Princetown, E along the Dartmoor Way to road near Hexworthy. N to Sherberton. W then NW on trails past Prince Hall Hotel to the B3357 and follow back to Princetown. Distance 16km.

Rider: Simon Leigh. © Alex Leigh

South Brent

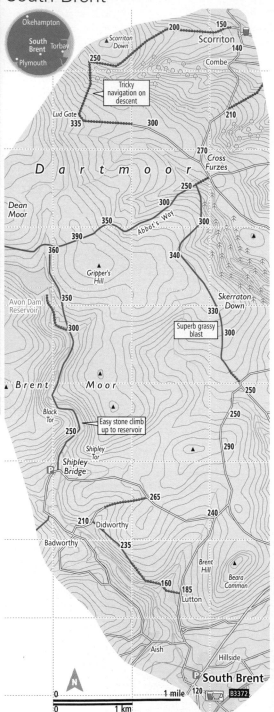

Situation: In the Avon Valley at the foot of Brent Moor, on the southern edge of Dartmoor National Park. 6 miles north east of Ivybridge and 7 miles west of Totnes.

About the Base: South Brent, a large village with two pubs and a café. **Parking:** Car Park at the north end of South Brent next to the railway line. Also at Shipley Bridge. *Grid Ref: South Brent SX698602, Shipley Bridge SX679628. Post Code: South Brent TQ10 9AL.*

Drive Times: Bristol 1hr50, Birmingham 3hr10, London 3hr50, Manchester 4hr30, Leeds 5hrs.

Trains: Ivybridge & Totnes Stations are on the Newton Abbot-Plymouth line.

Refreshments: At South Brent, The Royal Oak 01364 72133, The Packhorse Inn 01364 72283 and Crumbs & Cuppa Café 01364 73004. The Tradesmans Arms 01364 631206 at Scorriton.

Bike Shops: Ivybridge Cycle Centre 01752 893435 in Ivybridge, Hot Pursuit Cycles 01803 865174 in Totnes. Hot Pursuit also do hire.

Books: South West MTB (N.Cotton). MTB Rides to the SW (M.Darkins). MBR Ride Guide 2010

Maps: Dartmoor British Mountain Map (Harvey). OS Explorer OL28.

Route Ideas

❶ From South Brent, roads N to Lutton, trails NW to Didworthy then on to Shipley Bridge. N on trails across Brent Moor then along Abbot's Way to Cross Furzes. Clockwise loop via Lud Gate and Scorriton back to Cross Furzes. Trail S over Skerraton Down. Roads back to South Brent. Distance 24km.

❷ Shorten the above by missing out the loop at Cross Furzes. Distance 17km

© Singletrack Safari

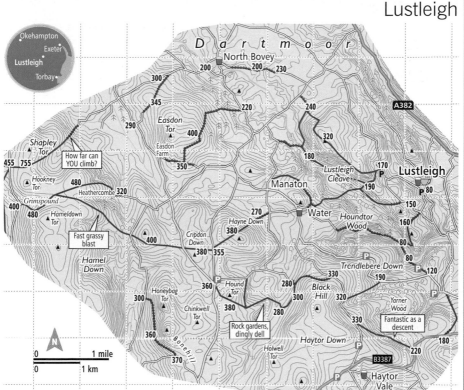

Situation: In the Wrey Valley, close to the eastern edge of Dartmoor National park in Devon. 9 miles north west of Newton Abbott.

About the Base: Lustleigh, a small village with a pub and tea rooms. **Parking:** Roadside parking by the church in Lustleigh & west of the village at Lustleigh Cleave. Car parks at Trendlebere Down, Hound Tor, next to the information point in Haytor Vale, Haytor Down & Yarner Wood. *Grid Ref: Lustleigh SX785812, Lustleigh Cleave SX774815, Trendlebere Down SX771796, Hound Tor SX739792, Haytor Vale SX765771, Haytor Down SX770778, Yarner Wood SX785788.* **Post Code:** Lustleigh TQ13 9TJ, Haytor Vale TQ13 9XS.

Drive Times: Bristol 1hr50, Birmingham 3hr10, London 3hr50, Manchester 4hr30, Leeds 5hrs.

Refreshments: At Lustleigh, The Cleave Inn 01647 277223 and Primrose Cottage Tea Room 01647 277365. The Keator Inn 01647 221626 at Manaton, The Ring of Bells 01647 440375 at North Bovey or The Rock Inn 01364 661305 at Haytor Vale.

Bike Shops: Hot Pursuit 01626 354082 & Rydon Cycles 01626 337228, 9 miles away in Kingsteignton. Hot Pursuit also do hire.

Books: South West MTB (N.Cotton). MTB Rides to the SW (M.Darkins).

Maps: Dartmoor Mountain Bike Routes (Goldeneye). Dartmoor British Mountain Map (Harvey). OS Explorer OL28.

Route Idea

From the roadside parking to the west of Lustleigh, trails NW along Lustleigh Cleave, across river then S on road to Manaton. Roads then trial W to Easdon Farm. Road NW then SW on to trails past Shapley Tor. S to Grimspound then trails E to Cripdon Down. Road S. Trails E over Hound Tor and follow to road north of Black Hill. Road S then SE on trails to the B3387. E on the road then trails and roads N then NW through Houndtor Wood to Water. Trails NE back to the start. Distance 31km.

© Phil Miles SPAM

Shaldon

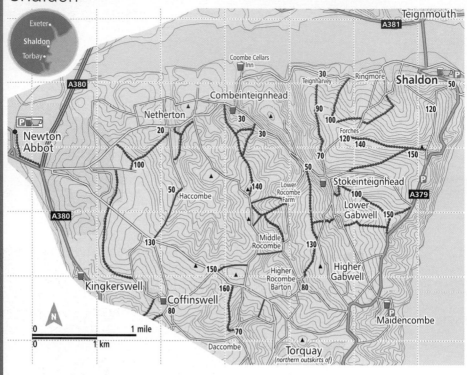

Exeter•
Shaldon•
Torbay•

Teignmouth
A381
Coombe Cellars Inn
Combeinteignhead
Netherton
Newton Abbot
A380
A380
30
Teignharvey
30
Ringmore
Shaldon
50
90
100
Forches
120
140
70
150
120
20
30
30
50
100
Haccombe
50
140
Lower Rocombe Farm
Stokeinteignhead
100
Lower Gabwell
150
A379
130
Middle Rocombe
130
150
Higher Rocombe Barton
80
Higher Gabwell
Kingkerswell
160
Coffinswell
80
70
Daccombe
Maidencombe
Torquay
(northern outskirts of)

N
0   1 mile
0   1 km

Situation: At the mouth of the River Teign, on Babbacombe Bay in South Devon. One mile across the river from Teignmouth, 6 miles east of Newton Abbot and north of Torquay.

About the Base: Shaldon, a coastal village with pubs, cafés and accommodation.
Further Info: www.shaldon-devon.co.uk. **Parking:** Car park near to the information point in Shaldon. Also on A379 south of the village & at Maidencombe Beach. **Grid Ref:** Shaldon SX937718, A379 SX929701, Maidencombe SX926684. **Post Code:** Shaldon TQ14 0HP, Maidencombe TQ1 4TS.

Drive Times: Bristol 1hr50, Birmingham 3hr10, London 3hr50, Manchester 4hr30, Leeds 5hrs.

Trains: Teignmouth Station is on the Exeter-Newton Abbot line.

Refreshments: Good choice of pubs and cafés at Shaldon. The Church House Inn 01626 872475 at Stokeinteignhead. The Thatched Tavern 01803 329155 or Beach Café at Maidencombe. The Linny 01803 873192 at Coffinswell, The Barn Owl 01803 872130 at Kingkerkwell, The Wild Goose 01626 872241 at Combeteignhead and The Coombe Cellars Inn 01626 872423.

Butterfly Lane © Jonathan Neale

Bike Shops: Hot Pursuit 01626 354082 & Rydon Cycles 01626 337228, 5 miles away in Kingsteignton, Bike-in Motion 01803 214145 in Torquay. Hot Pursuit also do hire.

Books: MTB Rides to the SW (M.Darkins).

Maps: OS Explorer 110.

Route Idea

From the car park on the A379 south of Shaldon, S on the A379 then trails SW then NW to Stokeinteighnhead. Roads and trails SW to Higher Rocombe Barton then on to Daccombe and Coffinswell. Road N then trails NE to Haccombe. To Combeinteighnhead then E to Teighnharvey. Trail S towards Stokeinteighnhead. Road NE to Forches then trail E. Join the A379 back to the start. Distance 19km.

Woodbury

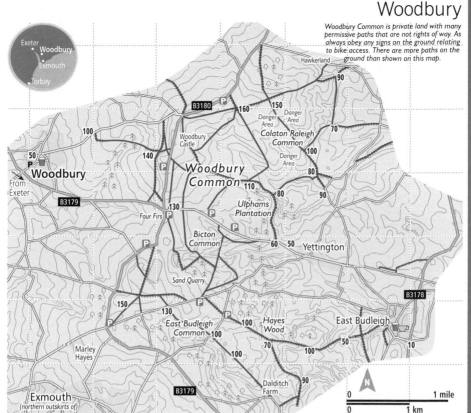

Woodbury Common is private land with many permissive paths that are not rights of way. As always obey any signs on the ground relating to bike access. There are more paths on the ground than shown on this map.

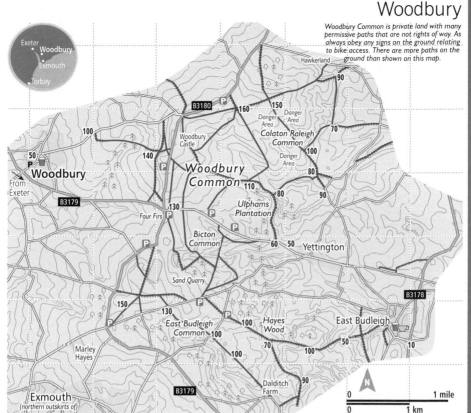

© Jonathan Neale

Situation: West of Woodbury Common in East Devon. 5 miles north of Exmouth and 8 miles south east of Exeter.

About the Base: Woodbury, a village with two pubs. **Parking:** Roadside parking in the centre of Woodbury. Four Firs car park at Woodbury Common. Several others if this is full. *Grid Ref: Woodbury SY008870, Four Firs SY032863.* ***Post Code:*** *Woodbury EX5 1LL.*

Drive Times: Bristol 1hr40, Birmingham 2hr50, London 3hr30, Manchester 4hr10, Leeds 4hr40.

Trains: Lympstone Railway Station, 2 miles west of the map, is on the Exeter-Exmouth line.

Refreshments: At Woodbury, The Malsters Arms 01395 232218 and The White Hart Inn. The Sir Walter Raleigh, The Rolle Arms and Old Granary Tea Rooms 01395 445919 at East Budleigh.

Bike Shops: Knobblies 01395 270182 in Exmouth. Exmouth Cycle Hire 01395 225656 for hire.

Books: MTB Rides to the SW (M.Darkins).

Maps: OS Explorer 115.

Route Idea

From Four Firs car park, trails S past the quarry then trails across East Budleigh Common to Dalditch Farm. N to Hayes Wood then NW back towards the quarry. Trails N to skirt the east of Ulpahams Plantation then around Colaton Raleigh Common first heading towards Hawkerland then W to Woodbury Castle. Trails S back to the start. Distance 18km.

Sidmouth

Situation: At the mouth of the River Sid on the Jurassic Coast, in the East Devon Area of Outstanding Natural Beauty. 10 miles north east of Exmouth and 15 miles south east of Exeter.

About the Base: Sidmouth, a small coastal town with pubs, cafés and accommodation. Further Info: www.visitsidmouth.co.uk. **Parking:** Long stay car park in Sidmouth. Car parks at Peak Hill & Salcombe Hill outside the town. Parking at Big Wood, East Hill & in Ottery St Mary. **Grid Ref:** *Sidmouth SY121873, Peak Hill SY109872, Salcombe Hill SY139881, Big Wood SY118932, East Hill SY119932, Ottery St Mary SY097954.* **Post Code:** *Sidmouth EX10 8RW, Ottery St Mary EX11 1ET.*

Drive Times: Bristol 1hr50, Birmingham 3hr, London 3hr30, Manchester 4hr30, Leeds 4hr50.

Trains: Honiton Railway Station, 3 miles north of the map, is on the London Waterloo-Exeter line.

Refreshments: Plenty of refreshments at Sidmouth. The Rising Sun 01395 513722 and The Blue Ball Inn 01395 514062 at Sidford, The Red Lion 01395 597313 at Sidbury and Hare & Hounds 01404 41760 at Putts Corner. Pubs and cafés at Ottery St Mary or The Bowd Inn 01395 513328 at Bowd.

Bike Shops: Sidmouth Cycles 01395 579786, Knobblies in Exmouth 01395 270182, Cycle 01404 47211, 3 miles north of the map in Honiton.

Books: MTB Guide Dorset (C.Dennis).

Maps: OS Explorer 115.

Route Ideas

❶ From Sidmouth, road and trails NE to Salcombe Regis. N on trails past Orleigh's Hill, then N past Harcombe Hill to Rakeway Head bridge. Trails to Lower Mincombe Farm then on to Knapp Copse, Putts Corner and Chineway Head. Road S then trail E through Core Copse. Roads to Sidbury then back to Sidmouth mainly on minor roads. Distance 33 km.

❷ Use the trails around Bulverton Hill and Mutter's Moor as a short blast, about 7km, or combine with the first option.

© Jonathan Neale

Portreath

Portreath
Redruth
Falmouth
Penzance

50 20
Chapel Combe
90 80
Towan Cross
90 100
Beach 100 100
20 Trevissick Farm 70 90
Porthtowan 60
80 20 Mount Hawke
60 50
90
Menagissey 100
Nancekuke Common 80
Airfield (disused) 11
Laity Moor Mawla
50 Cycle Lane
Portreath Cambrose Forge Mineral Tramway 110
Mineral Tramway 10 70
B3300 30 Wheal Rose
Bridge B3300
The Track
From A30 & Redruth

0 ——— 1 mile
0 ——— 1 km

Situation: On the north coast of Cornwall. 5 miles north west of Redruth.

About the Base: Portreath, a coastal village with pubs and cafés. **Parking:** Car parks in Portreath, east of the village & at Portreath Beach. **Grid Ref:** *Portreath Beach SW654453, Porthreath East SW659456. Post Code: Portreath Beach TR16 4NN.*

Drive Times: Bristol 3hr10, Birmingham 4hr30, London 5hr10, Manchester 5hr50, Leeds 6hr20.

Trains: Redruth Station is on the Plymouth-Penzance line.

Refreshments: At Portreath, The Bassett Arms 01209 842077, The Waterfront Inn 01209 842777 and The Harbour Café 01209 844888. The Bridge Inn 01209 842532 at Bridge, The Old School 01209 891158 at Mount Hawke and The Victory Inn 01209 890359 at Towan Cross. The Unicorn 01209 890244 and The Beach Cafe 01209 899016 at Porthtowan.

Bike Shops: The Bike Barn 01209 891498 at Cambrose for bikes, parts, repairs, hire & tuition.

Books: MTB Rides to the SW (M.Darkins).

Maps: OS Explorer 104.

Route Idea

From Portreath, E on the Mineral Tramway to Cambrose then roads N towards Porthtowan. Trails towards the coast then dropping down to Porthtowan Beach. Trails NE along coast then SE to Towan Cross. Trails past Trevissick Farm then SW to road. Roads S to Mawla then roads and the Mineral Tramway back to Portreath. Distance 21km.

Also see the freeride bike park The Track (p524) in the south of the area, and Poldice Valley (p524) south of Redruth.

© Roger Knight The Bike Barn

South West Extreme Freeride Park

In North Devon, a free ride park designed by riders for riders. A great downhill race course, a jump area, skills area, north-shore and a dedicated 4X course with challenging jumps and turns. Designed by riders for riders, the park is being constantly changed and updated by TT Freeriders in conjunction with the SW Extreme team.

Pay to Ride.

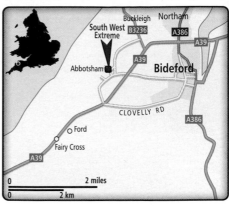

Facilities:
None on site. Refreshments in nearby Bideford.

Parking:
Grid Ref: SS423265. Post Code: EX39 5AP

Web: www.goodmtb.co.uk/b77

The Trails
DH

4X

Skills Area

Abbeyford Woods

At the northern edge of Dartmoor National Park in Devon, Forestry Commission land, developed and maintained by local MTB group Okefreeriders.

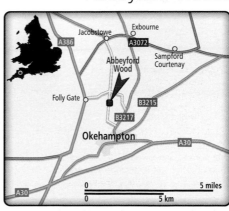

Facilities:
None on site. Train station and refreshments in nearby Okehampton.

Parking:
Grid Ref: SX589975. Post Code: EX20 1RN

Web: www.goodmtb.co.uk/b73a & /b73b

The Trails
DH, various grades.

Tavistock Woods

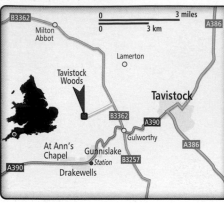

A downhill venue on private land in the Tamar Valley Area of Outstanding Natural Beauty west of Dartmoor. There's something for everyone with more than a dozen tracks varied from fast and flowing to slower and more technical. Managed and maintained by the Woodland Riders, you must be a member to ride (day passes available).

Facilities:
None on site. Refreshments in nearby Gunnislake. Regular uplifts organised by Gawton Uplift (Dartmoor Cycles) 01822 618178. Book at Advance.

Parking:
Grid Ref: SX425735.

Web: www.goodmtb.co.uk/b79

The Trails

DH, blue, red & black.

Maddacleave Woods (Gawton Downhill)

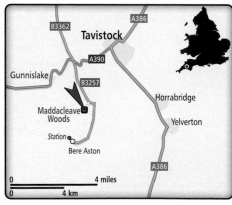

In the Tamar Valley Area of Outstanding Natural Beauty west of Dartmoor. A downhill venue on private land managed and maintained by the Woodland Riders. Competition standard, technically challenging downhills and an easier trail for less experienced riders. You must be a member to ride (day passes available).

Facilities:
None on site. Refreshments in nearby Calstock. Regular uplifts organised by Gawton Uplift (Dartmoor Cycles) 01822 618178. Book in Advance.

Parking:
Grid Ref: SX458696.

Web: www.goodmtb.co.uk/b75

The Trails

DH:
❶ **HSD, blue.**
❷ **Super Tavi, black.**
❸ **Egypt, black.**

Stoke Woods

Just north of Exeter. Fast, technical downhill and freeride trails, a dirt jump area with a total of six jumps and unmarked singletrack to explore.

Facilities:
None on site. Refreshments in nearby Cowley.

Parking:
Grid Ref: SX919959.

Web: www.goodmtb.co.uk/b78

The Trails
XC. DH.

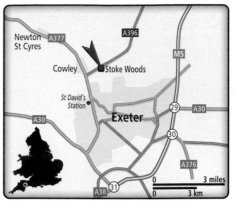

Haldon Forest Park

3,500 acres of woodland just fifteen minutes from Exeter with something to suit everyone. Great forest singletrack for families or beginners and technical, fast flowing, challenging trails for the experienced rider. Purpose built skills area with numerous features for all abilities.

Facilities:
The Ridge Café and Forest Cycle Hire 01392 833768 on site.

Parking:
Grid Ref: SX881848. Post Code: EX6 7XR

Web: www.goodmtb.co.uk/b74a & /b74b

The Trails
❶ Discovery Trail, Green, XC, 2.4km.

❷ Challenge Trail, Blue, XC, 9.6km or extend to 12km.

❸ Ridge Ride Trail, Red, XC, 9.6km.

❹ Ridge Ride Extreme, Black, XC, 1km.

❺ Pump Tail, Blue.

❻ Skills Area.

© Jonathan Neale

The Track

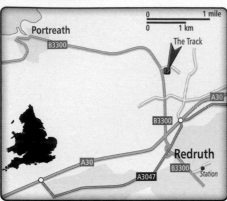

Close to Redruth in North Cornwall, a purpose built freeride park with something for everyone. Dirt Jumps offer beginners sections suitable for all abilities, intermediate with small doubles and pump bumps or advanced to test the most experienced riders. A Foam Pit and a Resi Ramp are great for practising tricks. A Slopestyle course with start ramp, KONA wall ride, VANS platform and 3 wooden kickers as well as a national standard, all weather BMX Race Track, suitable for all ages and abilities. Pay to Ride.

Facilities:
Refreshments at The Track Snax Shax. MTB Hire
enquiries@the-track.co.uk

Parking:
Grid Ref: SW690444. Post Code: TR16 4HZ

Web: www.goodmtb.co.uk/b80

The Trails
❶ Freeride
❷ 4X.

Poldice Valley Trails

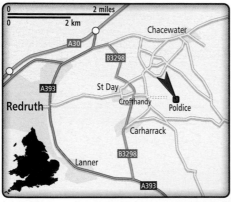

In central Cornwall, a steep valley with a "lunar landscape" in this disused mining area.

Facilities:
The Bike Barn 01209 891498 at Cambrose for refreshments, bikes, parts, repairs, MTB hire and tuition.

Parking:
Grid Ref: SW750424. Post Code: TR4 8SH

Web: www.goodmtb.co.uk/b76

The Trails
The focus is on downhill tracks, dirtjumps and freeride features but with some short XC runs.

524

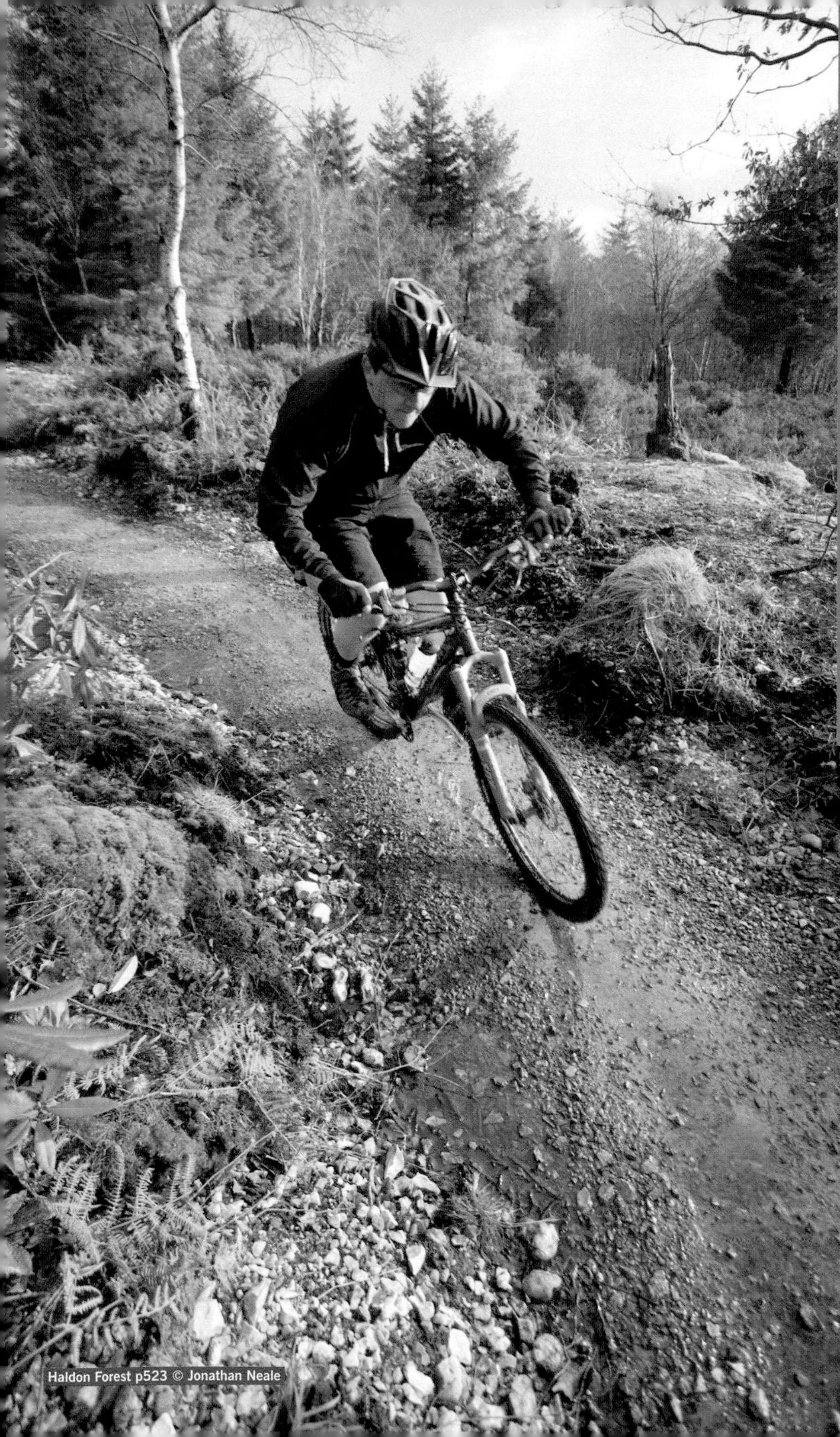

Haldon Forest p523 © Jonathan Neale

WALES

In many ways Wales is the perfect destination for mountain biking: it is almost all mountainous, there is a far greater proportion of forestry than in England and, with the exception of the far south, the country is sparsely populated. There are brilliant Trail Centres across the country and a great variety of scenery. The only oddity seems to be the rather haphazard provision of bridleways and byways ie legal trails on the Rights of Way network: the vast county of Powys in the centre of the country is blessed with a huge network of such trails whereas West Wales, Northwest Wales and Anglesey have very few. By good chance there are excellent Trail Centres in Snowdonia and at Brechfa in Ceredigion. For many mountain bikers living in the winter mudbaths of Southern England, Wales represents a real destination for year-round riding.

526

Dothie Valley, Llyn Brianne p574. Rider: Mandi. ©Sheldon Attwood

Snowdonia, Clwyds and North Wales

The largest National Park in Wales is home to the highest mountain in all of England and Wales (Snowdon at 1085m), some of the most famous and long established mountain bike trails at **Coed y Brenin**, The **Marin Trail**, north of **Betws-y-Coed** and some excellent cross-country routes. Right up on the north coast a tough linear route links **Llanfairfechan** to the attractive walled town of **Conwy** with its dramatically located castle. Lying at the base of Snowdon on its northern side, **Llanberis** is the start point for two bridleways that climb right to the top of the mountain, either via the Snowdon Ranger Path or the Llanberis Path, the highest bridleways in the whole of the UK. Also at the base of the Snowdon range, this time on its eastern side, **Capel Curig** and **Dolwyddelan** each have BOATs (byways open to all traffic), UCRs (unclassified roads), RUPPs (roads used as public paths) and bridleways leading to the four points of the compass, often through Forestry Commission holdings and crossing from one valley to the next in this most mountainous of regions.

Pont Scethin p548 © Singletrack Safari

Cilcain and *Ruthin* are the two bases used to explore the compact gem of The Clwyds.

To the south and west, the Berwyn Mountains, rising to 827m on Moel Sych, offer a far more gentle profile than the rocky crags of Snowdonia. *Llandrillo* on the western side is an ideal base to explore The Berwyns (pronounced 'Berra-wins'). Beware the legal trails that suddenly turn to footpaths at the county boundaries or just run out halfway up the hillside. Over on the eastern side of the Berwyns *Llanarmon Dyffryn Ceiriog* & *Llanrhaeadr-ym-Mochnant* lie at one end of the mighty crossing of the range, climbing to almost 600m on its way to *Llandrillo*. *Llangollen* in the Dee Valley (also known as the Vale of Llangollen at this point) is linked to *Glyn Ceiriog* in the Ceiriog valley by a series of steep tracks and impossibly steep narrow lanes. Elsewhere in this region, trails radiate out north, east and south from Llanwddyn at the eastern end of *Lake Vyrnwy*. On the coast, inland from *Tal-y-bont* and *Barmouth*, there are many challenges up into the hills that rise to over 600m, climbing steeply north from the spectacular wooded Mawddach Estuary.

This region has popular Trail Centres at *Coed y Brenin*, the *Marin Trail* & *Penmachno* both close to Betws y Coed, and *Llandegla*. Other smaller centres have also joined the party, there are some shorter trails at *Beddgelert Forest*, **Alwen Reservoir** and *Foel Gasnach.*

North of Barmouth p548 ©Singletrack Safari

Conwy / Llanfairfechan

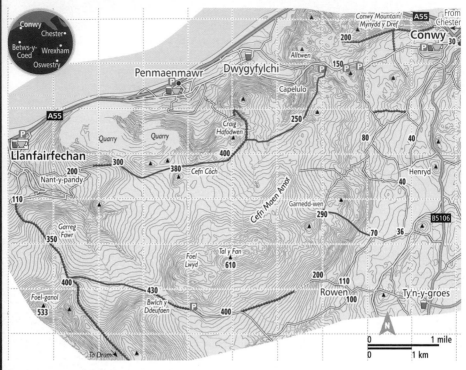

Situation: On the Conwy estuary and the North Wales coast. Conway is 45 miles west of Chester. Llanfairfechan, 7 miles to the south west is 12 miles north east of Bangor.

About the Base: Conwy, a walled market town with pubs, cafés and accomommodation or Llanfairfechan, a village with a pub and beach side café.
Further Info: www.conwy-wales.com
& www.llanfairfechan.org.uk.

Parking: Car parks west of Conwy are best for the ride. Parking on sea front at Llanfairfechan & Penmaenmawr. **Grid Ref:** *Conwy SH781773, Conwy West SH759768 or SH754768, Llanfairfechan SH678752, Penmaenmawr SH717766. Post Code: Conwy LL32 8LS, Llanfairfechan LL33 0BL, Penmaenmawr LL34 6AT.*

Drive Times: Manchester 1hr40, Leeds 2hr10, Birmingham 2hr20, Bristol 3hr40, London 4hr25.

Trains: Conwy & Llanfairfechan Railway Stations are on the Chester-Holyhead line.

Refreshments: Plenty of pubs and cafés at Conwy. The Groes Inn 01492 650545 or The Red Lion 01492 650 245 at Tyn-y-groes. The Llanfair Arms 01248 680 521 or Beach Pavillion Café 01248 680 035 at Llanfairfechan. The Bron Eryri 01492 623 978 or Oasis Café 01492 622 322 at Penmaenmawr and The Gladstone 01492 623 231 at Dwygyfylchi.

Books: MTB Trails Snowdonia (Savege, Barbier, Davis).

Maps: OS Explorer OL17.

Routes on Web: www.goodmtb.co.uk/a114

Bike Shops: West End Cycles 01492 530269, 5 miles away in Colwyn Bay, for parts & repairs. Halfords 01492 868110, 4 miles away in Llandudno.

530

© Andrew Hill

Route Idea

A clockwise loop. From one of the car parks W of Conwy, S to Garnedd-wen then Rowen. W to Llanfairfechan then back to Conwy via Cefn Côch. Distance 26km.

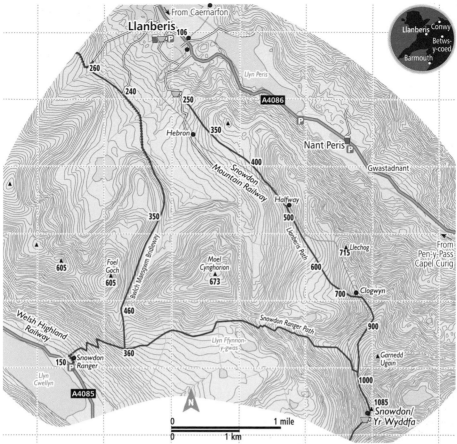

Situation: At the foot of Snowdon and on the north west edge of Snowdonia National Park, 6 miles east of Caernarfon.

About the Base: Llanberis, a village with pubs, cafés and accommodation. Further Info: www.llanberis.com. **Parking:** Lakeside car parks in Llanberis & south of Llyn Peris. Car park in Nant Peris. Also at Llyn Cwellyn. **Grid Ref:** *Llanberis SH577605, Llyn Peris SH598587, Nant Peris SH606583, Llyn Cwellyn SH563550. Post Code: Llanberis LL55 4ER, Nant Peris LL55 4UG.*

Drive Times: Manchester 2hr10, Birmingham 2hr40, Leeds 2hr40, Bristol 4hr, London 4hr40.

Trains: Snowdon Mountain Railway runs between Llanberis & the summit of Snowdon. Bikes not allowed.

Refreshments: At Llanberis, several pubs, Pete's Eats 01286 870 117 and Pen y Ceunant Tea Rooms 01286 872 606. Cafés at Snowdon Mountain Railway Station and Hafod Eryri, the new summit visitor centre. The Vaynol Arms 01286 872 672 at Nant Peris. Pennceunant Isaf Café 01286 872606 on the Snowdon Path.

Books: Wales MTB (T.Hutton). MTB Guide North Wales (P.Bursnall). MTB Trails Snowdonia (Savege, Barbier, Davis). MBR Ride Guide 2010

Maps: Snowdonia British Mountain Map (Harvey). OS Explorer OL17.

Bike Shops: Beddgelert Bikes 01766 890434, 14 miles away in Beddgelert for bikes, parts, repairs & hire.

Route Ideas

❶ An out and back to Snowdon along the Llanberis path. Distance 16km.

❷ Leave a car at Llanberis & Llyn Cwellyn. From Llanberis to Snowdon along the Llanberis path. Descend to Llyn Cwellyn along the Ranger Path. Distance 14km.

❸ As above but don't desend all the way to Llyn Cwellyn. Instead follow the Bwlch Maesgwm bridleway back to Llanberis. Distance 21km.

Note: between 10.00am & 5pm from 1st May to 30th September cyclists should not cycle on the Snowdon bridleways. This is a voluntary agreement to help avoid accidents when the paths to the summit of Snowdon are extremely busy. If not adhered to is likley to invoke a total ban on riding in the area. Keep up to date: www.eryri-npa.gov.uk

Capel Curig

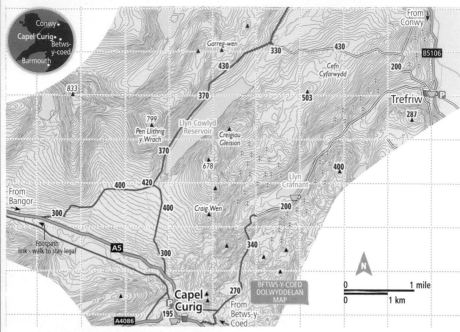

© Andrew Hill

Situation: In the Carneddau and the north of Snowdonia National Park on the River Llugwy. 5 miles west of Betwys y Coed and 16 miles south west of Bangor.

About the Base: Capel Curig, a small village with a pub and a café. **Parking:** Car parks in Capel Curig or Trefriw. **Grid Ref:** *Capel Curig SH719582, Trefriw SH781630.* **Post Code:** *Capel Curig LL24 0EW, Trefriw LL27 0RY.*

Drive Times: Manchester 2hr, Birmingham 2hr20, Leeds 2hr40, Bristol 3hr40, London 4hr20.

Trains: Betwys y Coed Railway Station is on the Conwy Valley line.

Refreshments: At Capel Curig, The Bryn Tyrch Hotel 01690 720 223 or The Pinnacle 01690 720201. Glanrafon Stores and 01492 642177 or The Princes Arms 01492 640 592 at Trefriw. Lakeside at Llyn Crafnant.

Books: Wales MTB (T.Hutton).

Maps: Snowdonia British Mountain Map (Harvey). OS Explorer OL17.

Routes on Web: www.goodmtb.co.uk/a112

Bike Shops: Beics Betwys 01690 710766 or Ultimate Outdoors 01690 710888 in Betwys y Coed for parts & hire.

Route Idea

Clockwise loop from Capel Curig. W along trail parallel with A5. Up and over to Trefriw via Llyn Cowlyd. Back to Capel Curig via Llyn Crafnant. Distance 27km.

Extend the area: Betwys-y-Coed/Dolwyddelan Map to the SE.

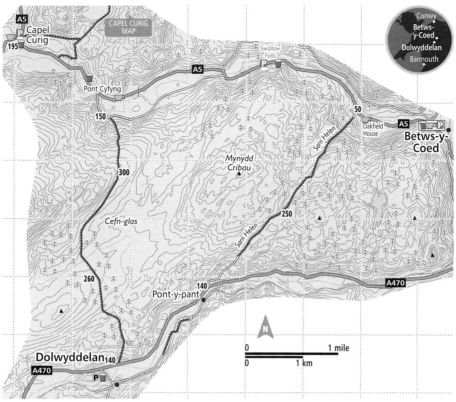

Situation: In the north east of Snowdonia National Park. Betwys-y-Coed is in the Gwydyr Forest, at the confluence of the Rivers Conway, Llugy and Lledr in the Conway valley. Dolwyddelan is 5 miles to the south west in the Lledr valley.

About the Base: Betwys-y-Coed, a village with pubs, cafés and accommodation or Dolwyddelan, a small village with a pub and easy access to the trails. Further Info: www.betws-y-coed.co.uk & www.dolwyddelan.org. **Parking:** Car Parks at Betws-y-Coed, Capel Curig & Swallow Falls. Roadside parking in Dolwyddelan. **Grid Ref:** *Betws-y-Coed SH794566, Capel Curig SH719582, Swallow Falls SH763576, Dolwyddelan SH734523.* **Post Code:** *Betws-y-Coed LL24 0AH, Capel Curig LL24 0EW, Dolwyddelan LL25 0NZ.*

Drive Times: Manchester 1hr50, Birmingham 2hr10, Leeds 2hr30, Bristol 3hr30, London 4hr15.

Trains: Betws-y-Coed & Dolwyddelan Railway Stations on are on the Conwy Valley line.

Refreshments: Good choice of pubs and Cafés at Betws-y-Coed. The Gwydyr Hotel 01690 750 209 at Dolwyddelan. Bryn Glo 01690 720215 at Pont Cyfyng. The Bryn Tyrch Hotel 01690 720 223 or The Pinnacle 01690 720201 at Capel Curig. The Swallow Falls Inn 01690 710796 at Swallow Falls.

Books: MTB Guide North Wales (P.Bursnall).

Maps: Snowdonia British Mountain Map (Harvey). OS Explorer OL17 & OL18.

Bike Shops: Beics Betwys 01690 710766 or Lightspeed Bikes @ Ultimate Outdoors 01690 710888 in Betwys y Coed for parts & hire.

Route Idea

From Betwys-y-Coed, W on A5 past Swallow Falls then minor road leading SW towards trail to Dolwyddelan. Minor roads and trails S of A470 towards Pont-y-pant. Sarn Helen NE to the A5 & back to the start. Distance 21km.

© Singletrack Safari

Llyn Brenig

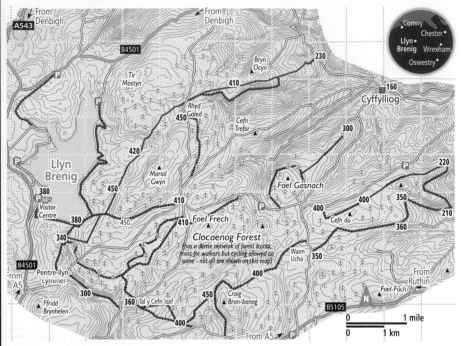

Situation: On the edge of the Clocaenog Forest in the heart of the Denbigh Moors of North Wales. 9 miles south west of Denbigh and 11 miles east of Betwys y Coed.

About the Base: Llyn Brenig, a rural location with a visitor centre and cafés. **Parking:** Car parks at Llyn Brenig Visitor Centre, lakeside or north on B4501. Parking in Clocaenog Forest & south east on B5105 Ruthin-Cerrigy-drudion road. **Grid Ref:** *Visitor Centre SH967547, Lakeside SH962559 or SH983573, B4501 SH970580, Clocaenog Forest SJ024546 or SJ065556, B5105 SJ036512. Post Code: Visitor Centre LL21 9TT.*

Drive Times: Manchester 1hr40, Birminham 2hr10, Leeds 2hr20, Bristol 3hr30, London 4hr10.

Refreshments: at Llyn Brenig Visitor Centre 01490 420463 or Red Lion Hotel 01824 710 664 at Cyffylliog.

Bike Shops: Beics Betwys 01690 710766 or Lightspeed Bikes @ Ultimate Outdoors 01690 710888 in Betwys y Coed for parts & hire.

Books: MTB Trails NE Wales (S.Savege & T.Griffiths).

Maps: OS Explorer 264.

Route Ideas

❶ From the Visitor Centre, E across Dam & towards Foel Frech, Trail SW to Tal y Cefn Isaf. Return NW back to Llyn Brenig. Distance 15km.

❷ Extend the above when at Tal y Cefn Isaf by a loop to Craig Bron-banog and back. Distance 22km.

❸ From the Visitor Centre, E across the dam towards Foel Frech then N to Rhyd Galed. E on trails and road To Cyffylliog. SW to Foel Gasnach then passing close to Foel Frech its mainly forest tracks back to the start. Distance 30km.

❹ Extend the above, after Foel Gasnach head SE to Cefn du then trails to loop E then W to Waen Ucha. SW to Tal y Cefn Isaf and back to start. Distance 37km.
5. A 15km loop around Llyn Brenig which can also be used to extend any of the above.

Ruthin

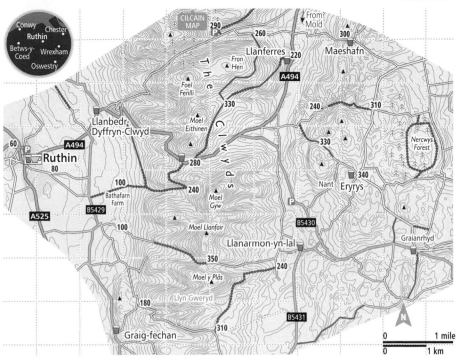

Situation: On the banks of the River Clwyd at the foot of the Clwydian Hills of North East Wales. 18 miles north west of Wrexham.

About the Base: Ruthin, a market town with plenty of pubs, cafés and accommodation. Further Info: www.visitruthin.com. **Parking:** Car park next to the information centre in Ruthin. Also west of Llanferres & north of Llanarmon-yn-Ial. **Grid Ref:** *Ruthin SJ124586, Llanferres SJ161605, Llanarmon-yn-Ial SJ188573.* **Post Code:** *Ruthin LL15 1BB.*

Drive Times: Manchester 1hr20, Birmingham 2hr, Leeds 2hr, Bristol 3hr20, London 4hr.

Refreshments: Good choice of refreshments at Ruthin. The Three Pigeons Inn 01824 703 178 at Graig-fechan, The Raven Inn 01824 780 833 at Llanarmon-yn-Ial, Rose & Crown 01824 780 727 at Graianrhyd, The Sun Inn 01824 780 402 at Eryrys.

The Miners Arms 01352 810 464 at Maeshafn, The Druid Inn 01352 810 225 at Llanferres.

Bike Shops: Cellar Cycles 01824 707 133 in Ruthin.

Books: MTB Trails NE Wales (S.Savege & T.Griffiths).

Maps: OS Explorer 265 & 256.

Routes on Web: www.goodmtb.co.uk/a118

535

Route Idea

From Ruthin, SE on roads and trails to Llanarmon-yn-Ial. Roads SE then trail N to Graianrhyd. N through Nercwys Forest & on to Maeshafn. Road W then trails skirting Fron Hen and Moel Eithinen. Back to Ruthin via trails past Bathafarn Farm and final road section. Distance 33km.

Extend the area: Cilcain Map to the N.

© Angus Muir

Cilcain

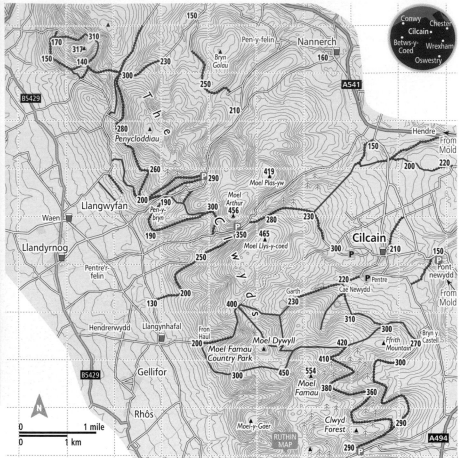

Situation: North of the Clwyd Forest in the foothills of the Clwydian Hills in north east Wales. 4 miles west of Mold and 14 miles west of Chester.

About the Base: Cilcain, a village with a pub and easy access to the trails. **Parking:** Roadside west of Cilcain or south of the village at Pentre. Car parks at Pont-newydd, Clwyd Forest & Moel Arthur. **Grid Ref:** *Cilcain SJ171652, Pentre SJ171647, Pont-newydd SJ187651, Clwyd Forest SJ172611, Moel Arthur SJ146657 or SJ138668.*

Drive Times: Manchester 1hr10, Leeds 1hr50, Birmingham 2hr, Bristol 3hr20, London 4hr.

Refreshments: White Horse Inn 01352 740 142 at Cilcain. Golden Lion 01824 790 451 at Llangynhafal, White Horse Inn 01824 790 582 and Kinmel Arms 01824 790 291 at Llandyrnog or The Cross Foxes 01352 741 293 at Nannerch.

Books: Wales MTB (T.Hutton). MTB Trails NE Wales (S.Savege & T.Griffiths). MBR Ride Guide 2010

Bike Shops: Cellar Cycles 01824 707 133, 7 miles away in Ruthin. RPM Cycles 01244 541 135, 9 miles away in Buckley.

Maps: OS Explorer 265.

Routes on Web: www.goodmtb.co.uk/a113

Route Ideas

❶ Road S towards Bryn y Castell. Trails W to N of Ffrith Mountain and S of Moel Dywyll to Fron Haul. Return NE to Cilcain via Garth. Distance 14km.

❷ From Cilcain towards Ffrith Mountain via Cae Newydd. W to Llangynhafal via Moel Farnau Country Park. NE on the trail running around the N of Moel Llys-y-coed and almost back to Cilcain. SW up the track towards Moel Dywyll then trails past Garth & back to Cilcain. Distance 20km.

❸ As option 2 but when at car park S of Moel Arthur head on a clockwise loop on the trails and minor roads around Penycloddiau to return to the same car park. Continue down to Cilcain. Distance 34km.

Extend the area: Ruthin Map to the S.

Cilcain p536. © Angus Muir

Cilcain p536 © Angus Muir

Llangollen

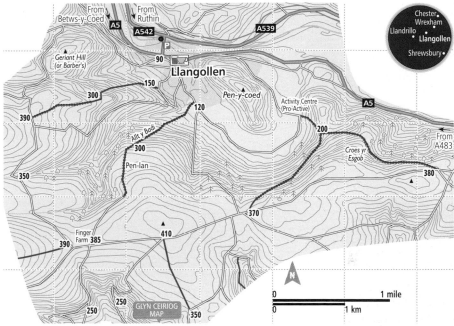

Situation: At the edge of the Berwyn Mountains on the River Dee in north east Wales. 12 miles north west of Oswestry and 12 miles south east of Wrexham.

About the Base: Llangollen, a small town with a good choice of refreshments and accommodation. Further Info: www.llangollen.org.uk. **Parking:** Car park in the town centre. **Grid Ref:** *SJ214419*. *Post Code: LL20 8PS.*

Drive Times: Manchester 1hr30, Birmingham 1hr30, Leeds 2hr, Bristol 2hr50, London 3hr40.

Trains: Ruabon Railway Station, 6 miles away, is on the Chester-Wrexham-Shrewsbury line.

Refreshments: Several pubs and Cafés at Llangollen.

Bike Shops: Llangollen Bike Hire 01978 860605, ProAdventure in Llangollen also sell parts. Stuart Barkley Cycles 01691 658705 & Halfords 01691 677920 in Oswestry. Alf Jones 01978 261580 & Halfords 01978 264550 in Wrexham.

Books: MTB Trails NE Wales (S.Savege & T.Griffiths).

Maps: OS Explorer 256.

Route Idea

SE from Llangollen past the activity centre and Croes yr Esgob. Road W to Finger Farm then NE along Allt y Badi & back to start. Distance 14km.

Extend the area: Glyn Ceiriog Map to the S.

© Andrew Hill

Glyn Ceiriog

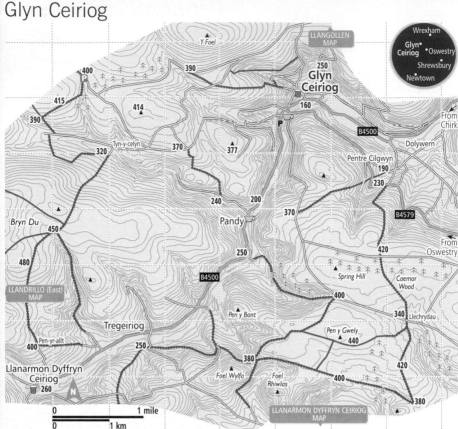

Bridleway from Pandy to Spring Hill. ©Margaret Wilson

Situation: On the River Ceiriog in the Ceiriog Valley. 3 miles south of Llangollen and 9 miles north west of Oswestry.

About the Base: Glyn Ceiriog, a village with a pub, and hotel. Further Info: www.ceiriog.co.uk/glynceiriog. **Parking:** Roadside in the centre of Glyn Ceiriog or car park at the waterfalls west of the village. **Grid Ref:** *Glyn Ceiriog SJ201377, Waterfalls SJ165382. Post Code: Glyn Ceiriog LL20 7ET.*

Drive Times: Manchester 1hr30, Birmingham 1hr30, Leeds 2hr10, Bristol 2hr50, London 3hr30.

Trains: Chirk Railway Station, 6 miles away, is on the Chester-Wrexham-Shrewsbury line.

Refreshments: At Glyn Ceiriog, The Oak 01691 718 810, The Glyn Valley Hotel 01691 718896 or at The Christian Centre 01691 718753. The Woolpack Tea Rooms 01691 718 382 at Pandy. The West Arms Hotel 01691 600 665 or The Hand Hotel 01691 600 666 at Llanarmon Dyffryn Ceiriog.

Bike Shops: Stuart Barkley Cycles 01691 658705 & Halfords 01691 677920 in Oswestry.

Books: MTB Trails NE Wales (S.Savege & T.Griffiths).

Maps: OS Explorer 255.

Routes on Web: www.goodmtb.co.uk/a115

Route Idea

W from Glyn Ceiriog on trails then road to Tyn-y-celyn. Trails S past Bryn Du to Pen-yr-allt then E to Tregeiriog. Trails E skirting Foel Rhiwlas & Craig-yr-hwch then N to Llechrydau. Trail N through Caemor Wood & road back to start. Distance 26km.

Extend the area: Llangollen Map to the N, Llanarmon Dyffryn Ceiriog Map to the S, Llandrillo East Map to the W.

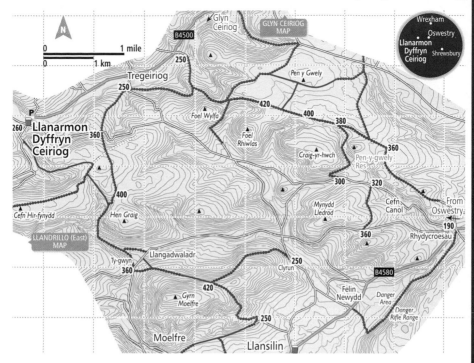

Situation: In the Upper Ceiriog Valley on the banks of the River Ceiriog. 8 miles south of Llangollen and 10 miles north west of Oswestry.

About the Base: Llanarmon Dyffryn Ceiriog, a village with two pubs and easy access to the trails. **Parking:** Roadside in the centre of the Llanarmon Dyffryn Ceiriog. **Grid Ref:** *SJ156328. Post Code: LL20 7LD.*

Drive Times: Manchester 1hr40, Birmingham 1hr40, Leeds 2hr20, Bristol 3hr, London 3hr40.

Refreshments: The West Arms Hotel 01691 600 665 or The Hand Hotel 01691 600 666 at Llanarmon Dyffryn Ceiriog. The Wynnstay Inn at Llansilin.

Bike Shops: Stuart Barkley Cycles 01691 658705 & Halfords 01691 677920 in Oswestry.

Books: MTB Trails NE Wales (S.Savege & T.Griffiths).

Maps: OS Explorer 255.

Route Idea

From Llanarmon Dyffryn Ceiriog, E on minor road then trail N almost down to Tregeiriog. Trails SE to Rhydycroesau then SW past the rifle range to Felin Newydd. Road to Clyrun then trails W to Llangadwaladr. Trails N to meet road (before the descent to Tregeiriog), head W here back to the start. Distance 26km.

Extend the area: Llandrillo East Map to the W. Glyn Cieiriog Map to the N.

© Turnip Towers

Llandrillo (north)

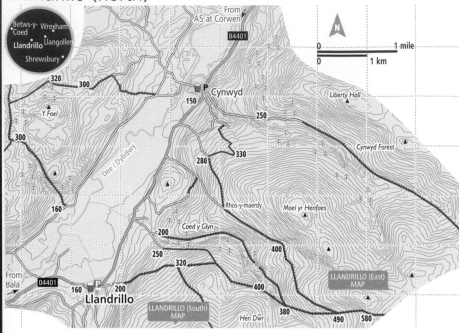

Situation: South of the River Dee in the Berwyn Mountains. 8 miles east of Bala and 25 miles south west of Wrexham.

About the Base: Llandrillo, a small village with a pub and easy access to the trails. **Parking:** Car parks in Llandrillo. Roadside parking in Cynwyd.
Grid Ref: Llandrillo SJO35371, Cynwyd SJO56411.
Post Code: Llandrillo LL21 0TG, Cynwyd LL21 0LD.

Drive Times: Manchester 1hr40, Birmingham 2hr, Leeds 2hr20, Bristol 3hr10, London 4hr.

Refreshments: The Dudley Arms Hotel 01490 440 223 at Llandrillo. The Blue Lion Hotel 01490 412106 at Cynwyd.

Bike Shops: RH Roberts 01678 520 252 in Bala for parts, repairs & hire.

Books: MTB Guide Mid Wales & The Marches (J.Dixon). MTB Trails NE Wales (S.Savege & T.Griffiths).

Maps: OS Explorer 255.

Route Idea

From Llandrillo, road then trails E skirting Hen Dwr then NW along the flanks of Moel yr Henfaes to Rhos-y-maerdy. N to Cynwyd then W around Y Foel back to Llandrillo. Distance 23km.

542

© www.flattyres-mtb.co.uk

Llandrillo (east) / Llanrhaeadr-ym-Mochnant

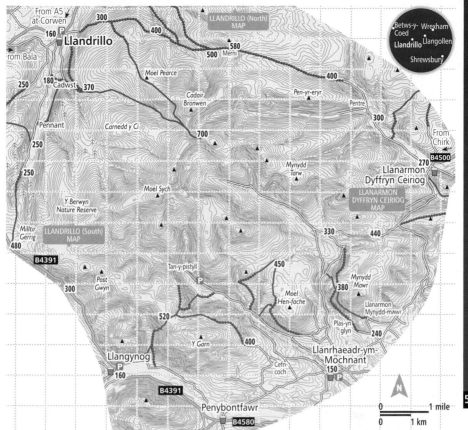

Situation: In the Berwyn Mountains east of Snowdonia National Park. Llandrillo is at the foot of Craig Berwyn, 8 miles east of Bala. Llanrhaeadr-ym-Mochnant, 14 miles to the south east, is on the River Rhaeadr 12 miles west of Oswestry.

About the Base: Llandrillo or Llanrhaeadr-ym-Mochnant, both small villages with pubs and accommodation. **Parking:** Car parks in Llandrillo, Llangynog, at Tan-y pistyll or Llanrhaeadr-ym-Mochnant. **Grid Ref:** *Llandrillo SJ035371, Llangynog SJ053261, Tan-y pistyll SJ076293, Llanrhaeadr-ym-Mochnant SJ124260.* **Post Code:** *Llandrillo LL21 0TG, Llangynog SY10 0EX, Llanrhaeadr-ym-Mochnant SY10 0JL.*

Drive Times: Manchester 1hr40, Birmingham 2hr, Leeds 2hr20, Bristol 3hr10, London 4hr.

Refreshments: The Dudley Arms Hotel 01490 440 223 at Llandrillo. The West Arms Hotel 01691 600 665 or The Hand Hotel 01691 600 666 at Llanarmon Dyffryn Ceiriog. The Plough Inn 01691 780 654 at Llanrhaeadr-ym-Mochnant or The Railway Inn 01691 860 447 at Penybontfawr. The Tanat Valley Inn 01691 860 227 or The New Inn 01691 860 229 at Llangynog.

Bike Shops: RH Roberts 01678 520 252 in Bala for parts, repairs & hire.

Books: Wales MTB (T.Hutton). MTB Guide Mid Wales & The Marches (J.Dixon).

Maps: OS Explorer 255.

Route Idea

E from Llandrillo to Llanarmon Dyffryn Ceiriog. SW on road then trail to W of Mynydd Mawr and onto Llanrhaeadr-ym-Mochnant. Roads NW then trail N of Y Garn to Llangynog. Road to Milltir Gerrig. Trails and road N back to start. Distance 50km.

Extend the area: Llandrillo North Map, Llandrillo South Map, Llanarmon Dyffryn Ceiriog Map to the E.

© www.flattyres-mtb.co.uk

Llandrillo (south)

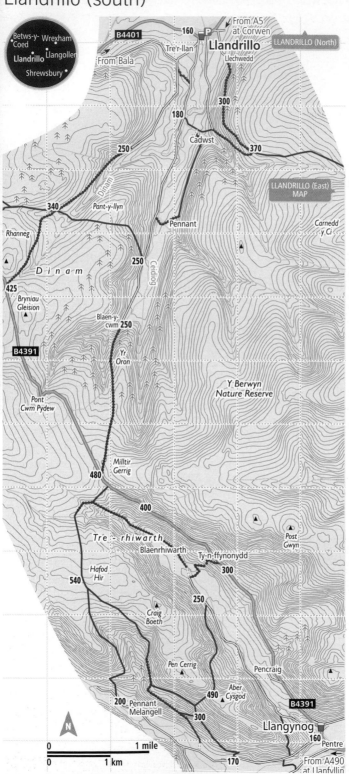

Situation: South of the River Dee in the Berwyn Mountains. 8 miles east of Bala and 25 miles south west of Wrexham.

About the Base: Llandrillo, a small village with a pub and easy access to the trails.

Parking: Car parks in Llandrillo & Llangynog.

Grid Ref: *Llandrillo SJ035371, Llangynog SJ053261.*

Post Code: *Llandrillo LL21 0TG, Llangynog SY10 0EX.*

Drive Times: Manchester 1hr40, Birmingham 2hr, Leeds 2hr20, Bristol 3hr10, London 4hr.

Refreshments: The Dudley Arms Hotel 01490 440 223 at Llandrillo. The Tanat Valley Inn 01691 860 227 or The New Inn 01691 860 229 at Llangynog.

Books: MBR Ride Guide 2010.

Maps: OS Explorer 255.

Bike Shops: RH Roberts 01678 520 252 in Bala for parts, repairs & hire.

Routes on the web: www.goodmtb.co.uk/a117

Route Idea

From Llandrillo, SW on roads & trails past Dinam to B4391. S on B4391 to Milltir Gerrig. Trails to Llangynog via Hafod Hir. N on B4391 to Milltir Gerrig. N on trails to Blaen-y-cwm. Road back to Llandrillo. Distance 36km. Shorten above by heading back to Llandrillo when first at Milltir Gerrig. Distance 16km.

Llandrillo (south) p544 © www.flattyres-mtb.co.uk

Conwy p530. The Tribe MBC. © Vic Cheetham

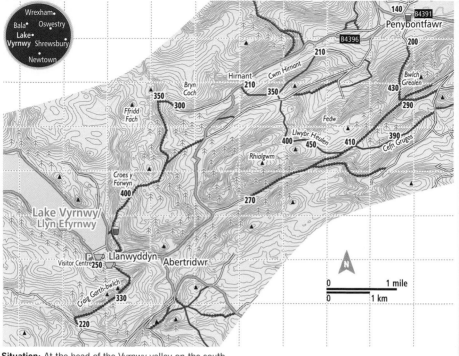

Situation: At the head of the Vyrnwy valley on the south east edge of Snowdonia National Park. 12 miles south of Bala and 25 miles south west of Oswestry.

About the Base: Lake Vyrnwy, a rural location with a visitor centre and a hotel. Further Info: www.lake-vyrnwy.com. **Parking:** Car Park at Lake Vyrnwy Visitor Centre. **Grid Ref:** *SJO16191.* **Post Code:** *SY10 ONA.*

Drive Times: Birmingham 1hr45, Manchester 2hr, Leeds 2hr40, Bristol 3hr10, London 3hr50.

Refreshments: At Lake Vyrnwy, at Visitor Centre 01691 870278 or The Tavern Bar 01691 870 692 at Lake Vyrnwy Hotel. The Old Barn Café 01691 870377 or Artisans Coffee Shop 01691 870317 at Llanwyddyn. The Railway Inn 01691 860 447 at Penybontfawr.

Bike Shops: Cycle hire at The Old Barn Café 01691 870377 or Artisans 01691 870317 in Llanwyddyn.

Books: MTB Trails NE Wales (S.Savege & T.Griffiths). MTB Guide Mid Wales & The Marches (J.Dixon).

Maps: OS Explorer 239.

Routes on Web: www.goodmtb.co.uk/a116

Route Ideas

❶ From the Visitor Centre, S along Craig Garth-bwlch. NE to Abertridwr & on towards Hirnant. Just before Hirnant head W to take trails back to Lake Vyrnwy. Distance 18km.

❷ Start as above to Abertridwr then head NE on road and trails to and along Cefn Grugos then E to and along Llwybr Heulen to Hirnant. Head W to take trails back to Lake Vyrnwy. Distance 28km.

Tal-y-bont / Barmouth (north)

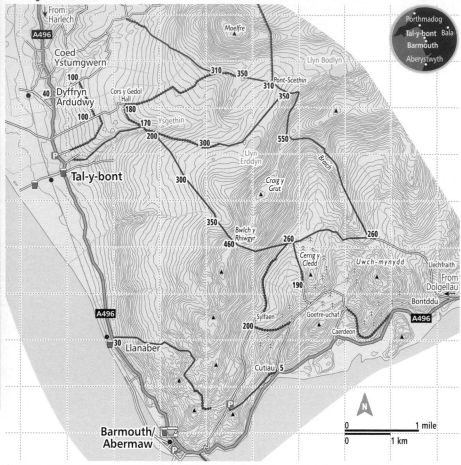

Situation: On the Mawddach estuary and Cardigan Bay on the west coast of North Wales. In the south west corner of Snowdonia National Park, 50 miles south of Conwy.

About the Base: Barmouth, a small town with pubs, cafés and accommodation or Tal-y-Bont, a village with a pub and easy access to the trails. Further Info: www.barmouth.org.uk. **Parking:** Car park on sea front in Barmouth or north east of the town. Car park at Tal-y-Bont. **Grid Ref:** *Barmouth SH613155 or SH625166, Tal-y-Bont SH590218. Post Code: Barmouth LL42 1EF, Tal-y-Bont LL43 2AW.*

Drive Times: Manchester 2hr30, Birmingham 2hr30, Leeds 3hr, Bristol 3hr40, London 4hr30.

Trains: Barmouth & Tal-y-Bont Railway Stations are on the Shrewsbury-Pwllheli line.

Refreshments: Good choice of pubs and cafés at Barmouth. The Wayside 01341 280 200 at Llanaber, The Black Rock 01341 247 578 or The Sands 01341 247 771 at Tal-y-Bont.

Bike Shops: Birmingham Garage 01341 280644 in Barmouth for parts & hire.

Books: Wales MTB (T.Hutton). MTB Guide Mid Wales & The Marches (J.Dixon).
Maps: Rhinogs Map (Harvey). OS Explorer OL18.

Routes on Web: www.goodmtb.co.uk/a111

Route Ideas

❶ From Talybont, NE to Pont Scethin via Cors y Gedol Hall. S along Braich then back to start via Bwlch y Rhiwgyr and trail just north of Yagethin river. Distance 19km.

❷ From Barmouth, NE to Cutiau then N past Cerrig y Cledd. Anticlockwise loop, Brach, Pont Scethin, Cors y Gedol Hall, Bwlch y Rhiwgyr. Back to start via Sylfaen. Distance 28km.

© Singletrack Safari

Tal-y-bont p548. © Singletrack Safari

Tal-y-bont p548. © Singletrack Safari

Llandegla

With views of the Clwydian Hills in North East Wales, a purpose built trail centre with something for everyone. Waymarked forest trails for beginners and families, more challenging routes for experienced bikers with fast, flowing, swooping singletrack and technical, downhill sections including the new black Parallel Universe. Freeride Area, Skills Area, Pump Track and Duel Slalom.

Facilities:
One Planet Café, MTB Hire and Repairs 01978 751656 at Coed Llandegla Visitor Centre.

Parking:
Grid Ref: SJ236522. Post Code: LL11 5UL

Web: www.goodmtb.co.uk/b31a & /b31b

The Trails

❶ Green, XC, 5km.

❷ Blue, XC, 12 km.

❸ Red, XC, 18 km.

❹ Black, XC, 21km combines red with several black options.

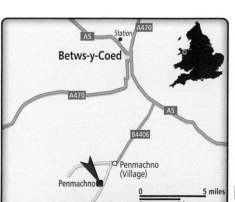

Rider: George Allgood © Darren Allgood

Marin Trail (Gwydyr)

In the heart of Snowdonia, a waymarked trail combining big climbs with amazing views, and big descents on singletrack which varies from tight and technical to open and flowing; from deep forest to exposed ridgeline.

Facilities:
None on site. Refreshments and train station at Betws y Coed.

Parking:
Grid Ref: SH790609. Post Code: LL27 0HX

Web: www.goodmtb.co.uk/b25

The Trails
Red, XC, 25km.

Penmachno

Built and maintained as part of a community project in the heart of Snowdonia, a waymarked cross country trail with stunning scenery and plenty of flowing singletrack. Put some money in the honesty box at the trail head and help to maintain the trails.

Facilities:
None on site. Refreshments at The Eagles in Penmachno.

Parking:
Grid Ref: SH786497. Post Code: LL24 0YP

Web: www.goodmtb.co.uk/b35

The Trails
Red, XC, 22km.

Coed y Brenin

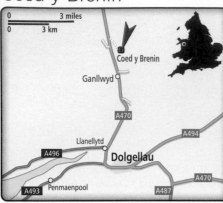

In the heart of Snowdonia, an ever increasing network of varied all weather singletrack on several technical cross country trails. Additional family trail and fantastic views of Snowdonia.

Facilities: Café at Coed y Brenin Visitor Centre. Beics Brenin 01341 440728 on site for MTB hire, parts & repairs.

Parking:
Grid Ref: SI1723269. Post Code: LL40 2HZ

Web: www.goodmtb.co.uk/b29a & /b29b

The Trails

❶ Yr Afon, Green, XC, 7 or 11 km.

❹ Temtiwr, Red, XC, 8.7 km.

❸ Cyflym Coch, Red, 10.8 km.

❻ Dragons Back, Red, 31 km.

❺ MBR Black, XC, 18.4 km.

❻ Tarw, Black, XC, 20.2 km.

❼ Beast of Brenin, Black, X C, 38 km.

Rider: Caroline Chauvin, The Tribe MBC. © Alistair Websdell

Foel Gasnach

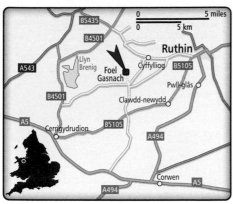

In the Clocaenog Forest and the Clwydian Hills of North Wales, a relatively new downhill race track managed and developed by FoelDHRiders. Seriously technical trails with big drops and gaps.

Facilities: None on site. The Red Lion, 2 miles away at Cyffiliog.

Parking:
Grid Ref: SJ037547. Post Code: LL15 2DR

Web: www.goodmtb.co.uk/b30

The Trails

DH. 4 Trails.

Riders are required to join the FDHR club.

Alwen Reservoir

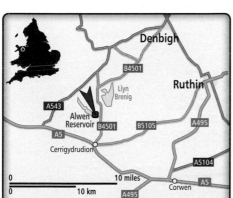

In the Hiraethog Moors of North Wales. An off-road family friendly trail around Alwen Reservoir with superb views.

Facilities: None on site. Refreshments 3 miles away at Llyn Brenig Visitor Centre.

Parking:
Grid Ref: SH956529. Post Code: LL21 9TT

Web: www.goodmtb.co.uk/b26a & /b26b

The Trails

Blue, XC, 11.3km.

Beddgelert Forest

In Snowdonia National Park, circular waymarked trails including a trailquest facility with easy, predominantly flat riding on forest roads.

Facilities: None on Site. Refreshments one mile away at Beddgelert. Beddgelert Bikes 01766 890 434 for MTB hire, parts & repairs.

Parking:
Grid Ref: SH573501. Post Code: LL55 4UU

Web: www.goodmtb.co.uk/b27

The Trails

**Family Trailquest
(mountain bike orienteering).**

Coed Llyn y Garnedd

In the Ffestiniog Valley at the heart of Snowdonia National Park. A natural combination of tough climbs and great downhill for a short technical ride with fantastic scenery.

Facilities: Tan-Y-Bwlch Café at Tan-y-Bwlch Ffestiniog Railway Station 1/2 mile away.

Parking:
Grid Ref: SH652413. Post Code: LL41 3AQ

Web: www.goodmtb.co.uk/b28

The Trails

Red, XC.

Moelfre

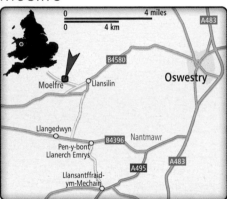

In North Wales. A super fast, rolling, downhill track with many high speed corners, off camber sections and fast straights. With regular uplift days the track should not be ridden outside organised events.

Facilities: Uplift days arranged by Borderline Events 01524 388 388.

Parking:
Grid Ref: SJ189284

Web: www.goodmtb.co.uk/b33

The Trails

DH.

Moelfre. © Turnip Towers

Revolution Bike Park

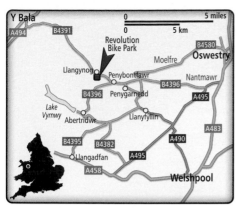

In the picturesque Tanat Valley, near Oswestry, North Wales, a 106 acre woodland and quarry with an elevation of 300m. Building will start in early 2011 to create an exciting new freeride and downhill mountain biking facility. Family run, owned and built; plans include Red and Black grade Freeride and Downhill tracks, an uplift service, Downhill Pump Track, Skills Area and family Fun Run.

Facilities: Refreshments on site to be confirmed.

Parking:
Grid Ref: SJ055259

Web: www.goodmtb.co.uk/b32

The Trails

Trails due to open in 2011.

Nant Gwrtheyrn. © Turnip Towers

Nant Gwrtheyrn

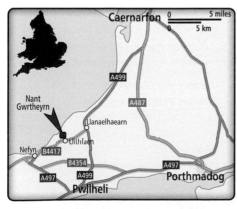

On the Llyn Peninsula. The run is on private land and should not be ridden outside organised races and uplift days. Alternative lines means the course can be ridden by a range of abilities (always walk & study the track before riding).

Facilities: Bar & Café at Welsh Language Centre open on event days. Uplift Days arranged by Simply Downhill. To book ahead email simplydownhill@hotmail.co.uk.

Parking:
Grid Ref: SH359432. Post Code: LL53 6NL

Web: www.goodmtb.co.uk/b34a & /b34b

The Trails

DH

Mid Wales

This part of Wales offers tough, remote, big country rides where you should always be prepared for a sudden change in weather. It is not a place to go unprepared as the nearest bike shop or hospital may be a long way away. Mid Wales is blessed with the best network of byways and bridleways of the three Welsh regions described in this guide. By some anomaly, the huge county of Powys, stretching from the Brecon Beacons in the south to beyond **Caersws** in the north, has probably more miles of bridleways and byways than the rest of Wales put together.

Trails cross the moorland south of **Barmouth**, with scenic views towards the coast, beneath the slopes of brooding Cadair Idris. Base yourself at **Abergynollwyn** to explore the summit. Located about halfway between **Machynlleth** and **Llanidloes**, the small settlement of **Dylife** (it rhymes with 'Gulliver' and not 'High Life') offers trails exploring the rugged landscape in all directions, including some expedition-style challenges through high passes and past isolated lakes southwest to **Nant-y-Moch Reservoir** or north to the Dovey Valley. **Llangurig**, a small village close to the junction of two A roads, offers options heading in almost all directions, some of which might be accessed via Lôn Las Cymru (National Cycle Network Route 8), the long distance trail that runs across Wales from Holyhead to Cardiff.

Rhayader, the **Elan Valley** and further south, **Llanwrtyd Wells** have been at the heart of mountain biking from its very early days back in the 1980s. A combination of motivated people, excellent trails, **Rhayader**'s position at a crossroads in the heart of Mid Wales and of course the stunning scenery of the Elan Valley reservoirs (**Elan**) have

556

Riders: Amanda & Stu. ©Sheldon Attwood

all conspired to make this something of a mecca for mountain biking.

Llanwrtyd Wells has gained its reputation as scene of the famous Man v Horse v Mountain Bike event. There are several trails west from here which link to those around the remote setting of **Llyn Brianne** Reservoir.

In the south east of the Mid Wales region, close to the border with England, is another area densely packed with stunning trails, with potential bases at **Aberedw**, **Hundred House**, **Gladestry** and **New Radnor**.

The main Trail Centre in Mid Wales is at **Nant yr Arian**, east of Aberystwyth. There are also various waymarked trails around **Machynlleth** as well as smaller centres at **Crychan**, **Cwm Rhaeadr** and **Coed Trallwm** in the south.

© Sheldon Attwood

Barmouth (south)

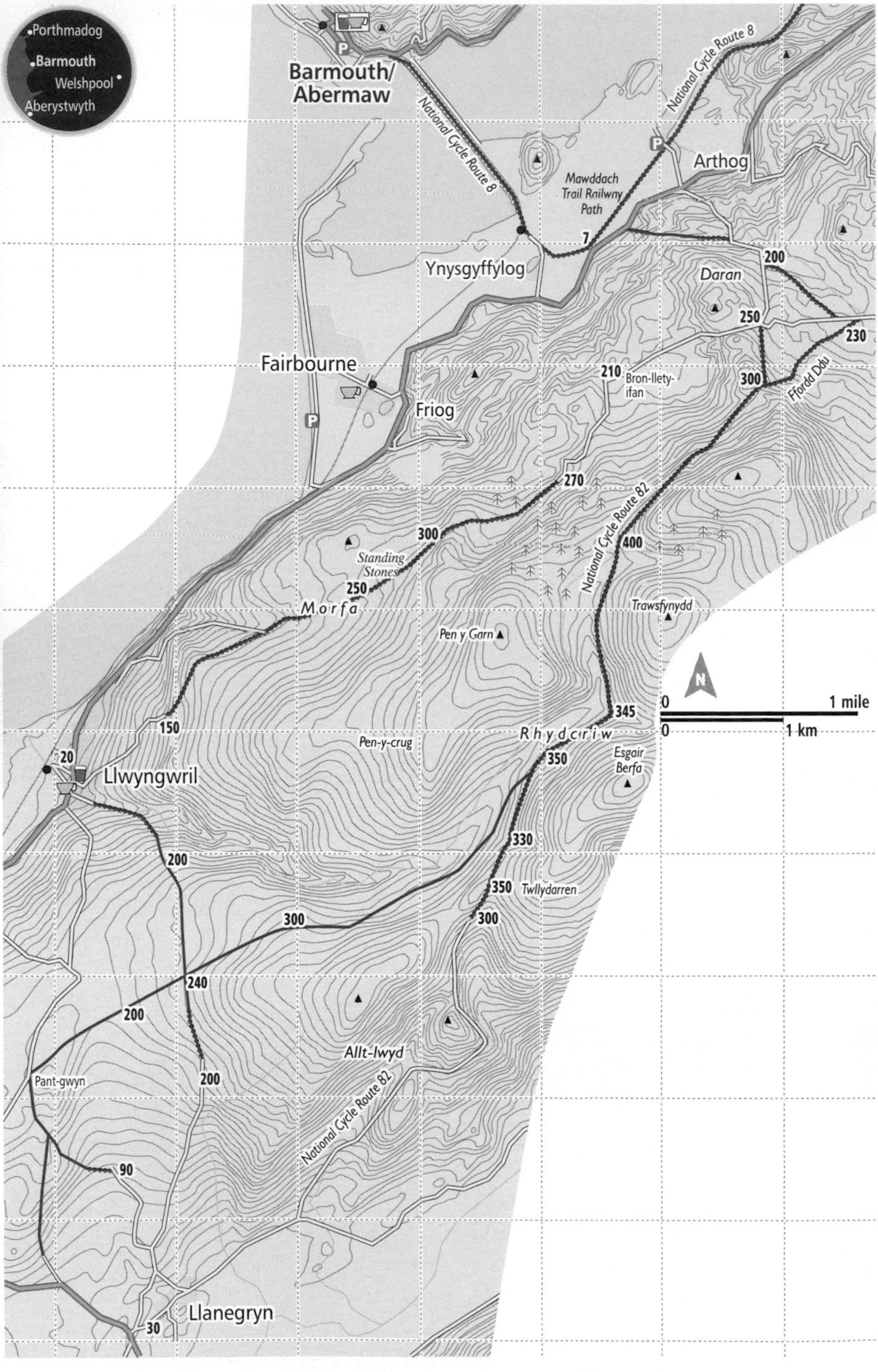

- Porthmadog
- Barmouth
- Welshpool
- Aberystwyth

Barmouth/
Abermaw

Arthog

National Cycle Route 8

Mawddach
Trail Railway
Path

7

Ynysgyffylog

Daran

200

250

230

Bron-llety-
ifan

210

300

Fairbourne

Ffordd Ddu

Friog

270

Standing
Stones

300

400

250

Morfa

Trawsfynydd

Pen y Garn

National Cycle Route 82

150

345

Rhydcriw

Pen-y-crug

350

Esgair
Berfa

20

Llwyngwril

330

200

350

Twllydarren

300

300

240

200

Allt-lwyd

Pant-gwyn

200

90

National Cycle Route 82

30

Llanegryn

0   1 mile
0   1 km

N

Situation: On the Mawddach estuary and Cardigan Bay on the west coast of Wales. In the south west corner of Snowdonia National Park, 50 miles south of Conwy.

About the Base: Barmouth, a small town with pubs, cafés and accommodation.
Further Info: www.barmouth.org.uk.

Parking: Car parks on sea front in Barmouth, at Fairbourne & at Arthog. *Grid Ref: Barmouth SH613155, Fairbourne SH611125, Arthog SH640147. Post Code: Barmouth LL42 1EF, Fairbourne LL38 2DZ, Arthog LL39 1YY.*

Drive Times: Manchester 2hr30, Birmingham 2hr30, Leeds 3hr, Cardiff 3hr30, Bristol 3hr40, London 4hr30.

Trains: Barmouth, Morfa Mawddach, Fairbourne & Llwyngwril Stations are on the Shrewsbury-Pwllheli line.

Refreshments: Good choice of pubs and cafés at Barmouth. The Garthangharad Inn 01341 250 484 or Café Gwril 01341 250327 at Llwyngwril or Harlequin Café 01341 250 007 at Fairbourne.

Bike Shops: Birmingham Garage 01341 280644 in Barmouth for parts & hire.

Books: Wales MTB (T.Hutton). MTB Guide Mid Wales & The Marches (J.Dixon).

Maps: OS Explorer OL23.

Route Ideas

❶ SE from Barmouth. Around E of Daran then SW along National Cycle Route 82 to Llanegryn. N to Pant-gwyn. Road to Llwyngwril. NE across Morfa to Arthog and Cycle Route 8 back to Barmouth. Distance 39km.

❷ Shorten the above, when W of Esgair Berfa head on trails to Pant-gwyn to avoid the Llanegryn section. Distance 31km.

© Singletrack Safari

Abergynolwyn

Barmouth
• Abergynolwyn
  Newtown •
• Aberystwyth

Map labels:
560
Pony Path
700
560
893 Cadair Idris
700
600
700
600
490
500
400
Craig Cau
350 Hafotty Gwastadfryn
300
200
Craig Cwm Amarch
766
150
Craig Ysgiog
60
Foel Ddu
Mynydd Tyn-y-fach
409
From A487
Llanfihangel-y-pennant
20
Foel Cae'rberllan
B4405
60
From Tywyn
40 Abergynolwyn
Talyllyn Steam Railway

N
0 | 1 mile
0 | 1 km

Situation: Below Cadair Idris in the south of Snowdonia National Park. 12 miles north west of Machynlleth and south west of Dolgellau.

About the Base: Abergynolwyn, a village with a pub and a café. Further Info: www.abergynolwyn.com.

Parking: Parking in the centre of Abergynolwyn or car parks at Llanfihangel-y-pennant. *Grid Ref: Abergynolwyn SH677069, Llanfihangel-y-pennant SH672088 or SH669085. Post Code: Abergynolwyn LL36 9UU.*

Drive Times: Birmingham 2hr20, Manchester 2hr30, Cardiff 3hr10, Bristol 3hr20, London 4hr20.

Trains: Tywyn Railway Station, 7 miles away, is on the Shrewsbury-Pwllheli line.

Refreshments: At Abergynolwyn, The Railway Inn 01654 782 279 or Café in the Community Centre.

Bike Shops: Holey Trail Bike Shop 01654 700 411 in Machynlleth. Dolgellau Cycles 01341 423 332 in Dolgellau, also do hire.

Maps: OS Explorer OL23.

Routes on Web: www.goodmtb.co.uk/a108

Route Idea

An out and back to the top of Cadair Idris. This involves carrying your bike a huge and steep ascent and a gnarly decent. For experienced riders and fine weather only. Distance 19km from Llanfihangel-y-pennant.

© www.chasingtrails.com

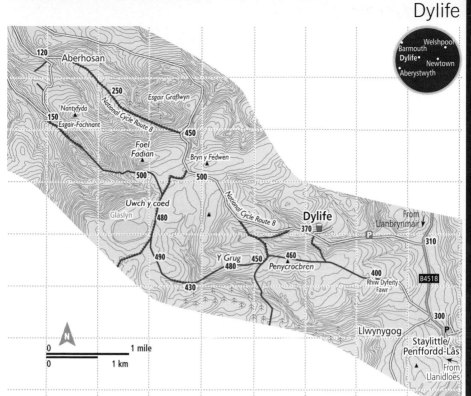

Situation: At the head of Afon Twymyn, south east of Foel Fadian in the Cambrian Mountains. 10 miles south east of Machynlleth and 20 miles west of Newtown.

About the Base: Dylife, a hamlet with a pub and easy access to the trails.

Parking: Car park next to the waterfalls east of Dylife. Roadside parking on B4518 at Staylittle.

Grid Ref: Dylife SN873939, Staylittle SN884924.

Drive Times: Birmingham 2hr10, Cardiff 2hr30, Manchester 2hr40, Bristol 2hr50, Leeds 3hr20, London 4hr20.

Refreshments: The Star Inn 01650 521 345 at Dylife.

Bike Shops: Holey Trail Bike Shop 01654 700 411 in Machynlleth.

Books: Wales MTB (T.Hutton). MTB Guide Mid Wales & The Marches (J.Dixon).

Maps: OS Explorer 215.

Route Ideas

❶ From car park by the waterfalls, head W to Dylife then trail S to join trails W past Penycrocbren, Y Grug, Uwch y coed to Esgair-Fochnant. Road to Aberhosan then National Cycle Route 8 back to Dylife. Distance 20km.

❷ For a 4km extension head to Penycrobren (before the final return to Dylife, above), then E to Rhiw Dyfeity Fawr and roads back to the start.

Nant-y-Moch Reservoir

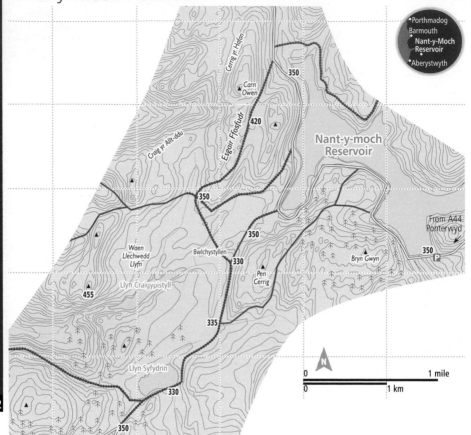

Rider: Amanda. © Sheldon Attwood

Situation: At the source of the River Rheidol in the west of the Cambrian Mountains of Mid Wales. 17 miles north east of Aberystwth.

About the Base: Nant-y-Moch Reservoir, a rural location with easy access to the trails. **Parking:** Car park next to the dam on the south shore of the reservoir. *Grid Ref: SN756861,*

Drive Times: Cardiff 2hr40, Birmingham 2hr40, Bristol 2hr50, Manchetser 3hr10, Leeds 3hr40, London 4hr40.

Refreshments: No refreshments.

Books: MTB Guide Mid Wales & The Marches (J.Dixon).

Maps: OS Explorer 213.

Route Idea

From the car park, W along road to reach N end of Nant-y-moch Reservoir. S along Esgair Ffosfudr to Llyn Syfydrin. Road around Llyn Blaenmelindwr then retrace route back to start. Distance 28km.

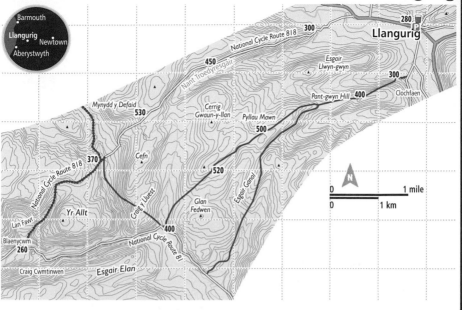

Rider: Mark. © Sheldon Attwood

Situation: On the River Wye, high in the Cambrian Mountains of Mid Wales. 5 miles south west of Llanidloes and 9 miles north west of Rhayader.

About the Base: Llangurig, a small village with a pub. **Parking:** Car park in Llangurig. *Grid Ref: SN908798. Post Code: SY18 6SG.*

Drive Times: Cardiff 2hr10, Birmingham 2hr10, Bristol 2hr20, Manchester 2hr40, Leeds 3hr20, London 4hr10.

Refreshments: The Bluebell Inn 01686 440 254 at Llangurig.

Bike Shops: Hafren Cycle Hire 01686 413565 at Llanidloes. Clive Powell Mountain Bikes 01597 811343 in Rhayader for bikes, parts, repairs & hire.

Books: MTB Guide Mid Wales & The Marches (J.Dixon).

Maps: OS Explorer 214.

Route Idea

Anticlockwise loop from Llangurig, SW along National Cycle Route 818 to Blaenycwm. Road E then trail to N of Glan Fedwen passing Pyllau Mawn and Pant-gwyn Hill. Road to finish. Distance 23km.

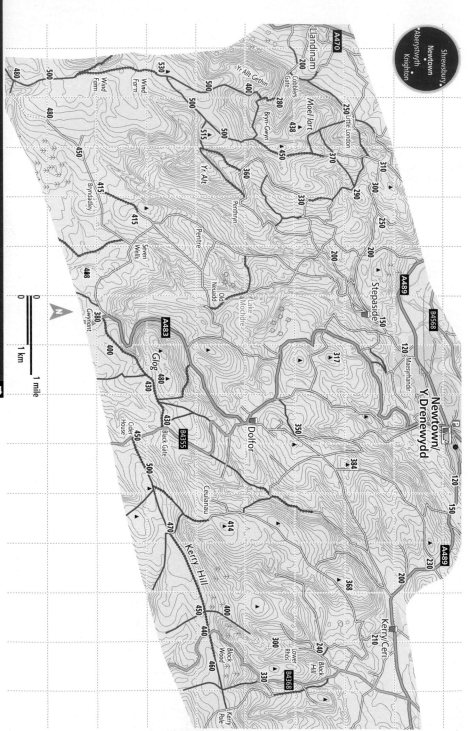

Situation: In a narrow valley on the River Severn in Mid Wales, 10 miles west of the Wales-England border. 30 miles south west of Shrewsbury and north west of Ludlow.

About the Base: Newtown, a large town with pubs, cafés and accommodation.

Further Info: www.newtown.org.uk.

Parking: Car park in the centre of Newtown next to the information centre. *Grid Ref: Newtown SO106916. Post Code: Newtown SY16 2NH.*

Drive Times: Birmingham 1hr40, Manchester 2hr10, Bristol 2hr40, Leeds 2hr50, London 3hr40.

Trains: Newtown Station is on the Shrewsbury-Aberystwyth line.

Refreshments: Choice of refreshments at Newtown. The Dolau Inn 01686 629 538 at Stepaside, The Dolfor Inn 01686 626 531 at Dolfor, The Kerry Lamb 01686 670 226 and The Herbert Arms 01686 670 638 at Kerry.

Bike Shops: Brooks Cycles 01686 610 021.

Books: MTB Guide Mid Wales & The Marches (J.Dixon).

Maps: OS Explorer 214.

Route Idea

W from Newtown to Stepaside, Little London, Cobblers Gate. Trails S past Yr Allt Gethin and the Wind Farms. NE to Bryndadley & Seven Wells. Road SE towards Gwynant. Trails to Black Gate, along Kerry Hill & down to Lower Rhôs. Roads back to Newtown. Distance 43km.

© Drover Holidays

Rhayader

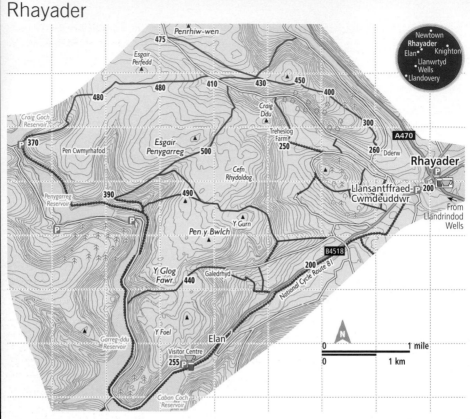

Situation: On the River Wye, close to its source in the Cambrian Mountains. 10 miles north west of Llandrindod Wells and 14 miles north of Builth Wells.

About the Base: Rhayader, a market town with pubs, cafés and accommodation.

Further Info: www.rhayader.co.uk. **Parking:** Car parks in the centre of Rhayader at the start of the Elan Valley Trail, west of Rhayader on B4518. Car parks next to Elan Valley Visitor Centre & at Caban Coch Dam in Elan village. Also north of Elan at Garreg-ddu & Penygarreg Reservoirs. *Grid Ref: Rhayader SN970682, Elan Valley Trail SN965678, Elan Valley Visitor Centre SN928646, Caban Coch Dam SN924645, Garreg-ddu SN914673, Penygarreg SN901671 or SN894686. Post Code: Rhayader LD6 5DD, Elan Village LD6 5HR.*

Drive Times: Cardiff 2hr, Bristol 2hr10, Birmingham 2hr20, Manchester 2hr50, Leeds 3hr30, London 4hr.

Refreshments: Plenty of pubs and cafés at Rhayader. Elan Valley Hotel 01597 810448 and Café at Elan Valley Visitor Centre 01597 810899 at Elan village.

Bike Shops: Clive Powell Mountain Bikes 01597 811343 for bikes, parts, repairs & hire.

Books: Wales MTB (T.Hutton). MBR Ride Guide 2010

Maps: OS Explorer 200.

Route Ideas

❶ Road NW from Llansantffraed-Cwmdeuddwr then trail SW past Esgair Penygarreg. Trail N along Penygarreg Reservoir and then E at junction with Craig Goch reservoir to road. N towards Penrhiw-wen. Trail SE to Dderw and roads back to start. Distance 24km.

❷ Extend the above, instead of descending to Penygarreg Reservoir follow trails around Pen y Bwlch to Galedrhyd and descend to Garrg-ddu Reservor. Continue N along the reservoirs then E to road. N towards Penrhiw-wen. Trail SE to Dderw and roads back to start. Distance 33km.

Rider: Alex. © Sheldon Attwood

Elan

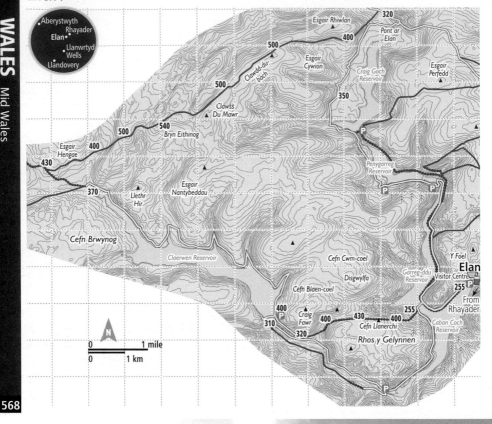

Situation: In the Elan Valley at the head of Caban Coch Reservoir in the heart of Mid Wales. 3 miles south west of Rhayader and 15 miles north of Builth Wells.

About the Base: Elan, a small village with a visitor centre. Further Info: www.elanvalley.org.uk.

Parking: Car parks next to Elan Valley Visitor Centre & at Caban Coch Dam in Elan village. At the southern end of Caban Coch & at Caerwen Reservoir. Also north of Elan at Garreg-ddu & Penygarreg Reservoirs. *Grid Ref: Elan Valley Visitor Centre SN928646, Caban Coch Dam SN924645, Caban Coch South SN901616, Caerwen Reservoir SN870633, Garreg-ddu SN914673, Penygarreg SN901671 or SN894686.* **Post Code:** *Elan Village LD6 5HR.*

Drive Times: Cardiff 2hr, Bristol 2hr10, Birmingham 2hr20, Manchester 2hr50, Leeds 3hr30, London 4hr10.

Refreshments: At Elan Village, Elan Valley Hotel 01597 810448 and Café at Elan Valley Visitor Centre 01597 810899.

Bike Shops: Clive Powell Mountain Bikes 01597 811343, in Rhayader for bikes, parts, repairs & hire.

Books: Wales MTB (T.Hutton). MTB Guide Mid Wales & The Marches (J.Dixon).

Maps: OS Explorer 200.

Route Ideas

❶ SW from Elan. Road along Caban Coch Reservoir then trail towards Caerwen Reservoir. Head back to Elan via Cefn Llanerchi. Distance 16km.

❷ N from Elan. At N end of Penygarreg Reservoir/S end of Craig Coch Reservoir follow road N to join trail near Pont ar Elan. Trail SW, road along Caerwen Reservoir. Trail back to Elan via Cefn Llanerchi. Distance 43km.

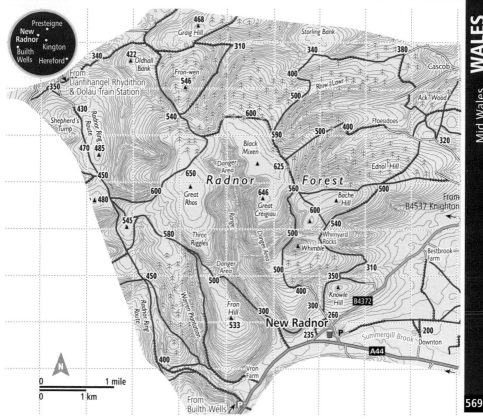

Situation: At the foot of Radnor Forest in Mid Wales. 6 miles north west of Kington and 14 miles north east of Builth Wells.

About the Base: New Radnor, a village with two pubs and a café. **Parking:** Roadside in New Radnor or car park south west of the village on A44. **Grid Ref:** New Radnor SO214607, A44 SO19359.
Post Code: New Radnor LD8 2SS.

Drive Times: Bristol 2hr, Birmingham 2hr, Manchester 2hr50, Leeds 3hr30, London 3hr40.

Trains: Dolau Railway Station, in the north west of the map, is on the Shrewsbury-Carmarthen line.

Refreshments: At New Radnor, The Radnor Arms 01544 350 232, The Royal Oak 01544 260 842 and Lornas Sandwich Shop/Café.

Bike Shops: Builth Wells Cycles 01982 552 923 for parts & repairs, MTB Hire & guided rides.

Books: Wales MTB (T.Hutton). MTB Guide Mid Wales & The Marches (J.Dixon). MBR Ride Guide 2010

Maps: OS Explorer 200 & 201.

Routes on Web: www.goodmtb.co.uk/a110

Route Ideas

❶ An anti-clockwise loop from New Radnor around Great Creigiau, Black Mixen, Great Rhos & Three Riggles. Distance 17km.

❷ From the car park on A44 SW of New Radnor. N on Radnor Ring Route. Pass Shepherd's Tump then E to Oldhall Bank. S to pass Great Rhos and rejoin Radnor Ring Route back to car park. Distance 26km.

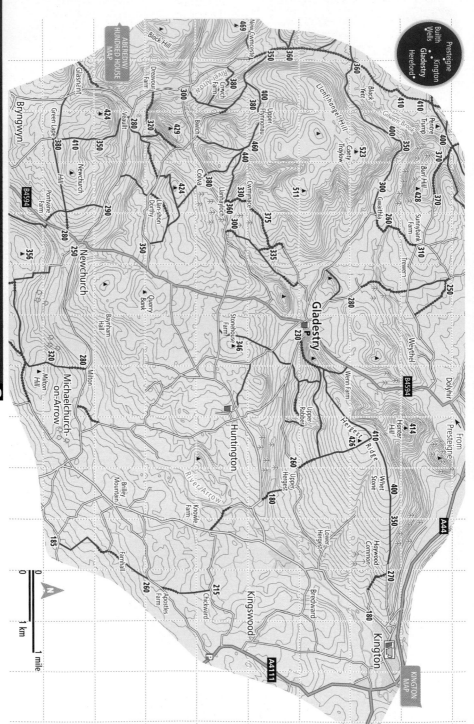

Situation: In Mid Wales, close to the border with England at the end of Hergest Ridge. 5 miles west of Kington and 10 miles north of Hay-on-Wye.

About the Base: Gladestry, a village with a pub. Further Info: www.gladestry.org.uk.

Parking: Roadside in the centre of Gladestry. Car park on A4111 at Kingswood. *Grid Ref: Gladestry SO232551, Kingwood SO297533. Post Code: Gladestry HR5 3NR.*

Drive Times: Bristol 1hr50, Birmingham 2hr, Manchester 3hr, Leeds 3hr30, London 3hr40.

Refreshments: At Gladestry, The Royal Oak Inn 01544 370 669. The Swan 01544 370 656 at Huntington or plenty of refreshments at Kington.

Bike Shops: no

Books: MTB Guide Mid Wales & The Marches (J.Dixon).

Maps: OS Explorer 200 & 201.

Routes on Web: www.goodmtb.co.uk/a109

Route Ideas

❶ An out and back along the Hergest Ridge to Kington. Distance 14km, or vary by returning from Kington on roads to Upper Hergest then trail N (but not to top of ridge) & trails W to Gladestry. Distance 15km.

❷ From Gladestry, Road NW to Gwaithla. Trail NE to Sunnybank Farm then W past Burl Hill to Black Yett. Back to Gladestry via Upper Ffynnonau & Cwmynace. Distance 18km.

❸ Extend the above route, from Black Yett continue S to Veaullt. Trails to Newchurch then to Michaelchurch-on-Arrow via trails over Milton Hill. Road N past Knowle Farm then NW to Upper Hergest. Trail N (but not to top of ridge) & trails W to Gladestry. Distance 35km.

© Drover Holidays

Aberedw / Hundred House

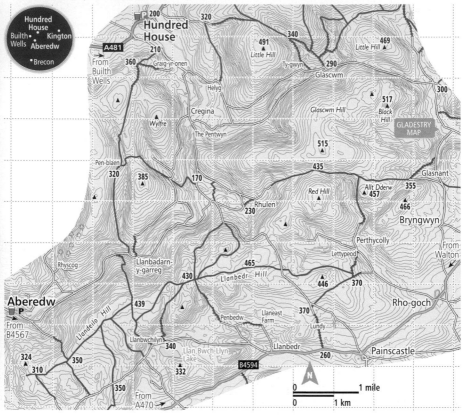

Situation: At the confluence of the River Edw and the River Wye, Aberedw is 5 miles south east of Builth Wells. Hundred House, at the source of the Edw, is 5 miles to the north east.

About the Base: Aberedw or Hundred House, both small villages with a pub. **Parking:** Roadside in the centre of Aberedw. Car park in Hundred House. **Grid Ref:** *Aberedw SO080473, Hundred House SO112544.* **Post Code:** *Aberedw LD2 3UW, Hundred House LD1 5RY.*

Drive Times: Bristol 1hr50, Birmingham 2hr20, Manchester 3hr10, Leeds 3hr40, London 3hr40.

Trains: Builth Road Station in Builth Wells is on the Shrewsbury-Carmarthen line.

Refreshments: The Seven Stars Inn 01982 560 494 at Aberedw or The Hundred House Inn 01982 570 231 at Hundred House.

Bike Shops: Builth Wells Cycles 01982 552 923 for parts & repairs, MTB Hire & guided rides.

Books: Wales MTB (T.Hutton). MTB Guide Mid Wales & The Marches (J.Dixon).

Maps: OS Explorer 188 & 200.

Routes on Web: www.goodmtb.co.uk/a107

Route Idea

From Hundred House, S past Pen-blaen. Road SW towards Aberedw. Trails across Llandeilo Hill & Llanbedr Hill. N past Perthycolly to Allt Dderw then E to road. N to Glascwm then trails to N of Little Hill and back to start. Distance 37km.

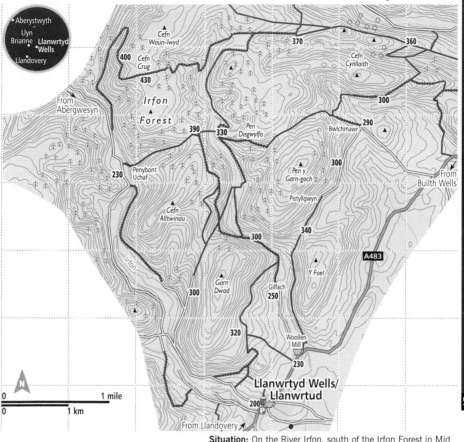

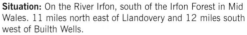

N

| 0 | | 1 mile |
| 0 | 1 km | |

Irfon Forest. © Job Hutchings

Situation: On the River Irfon, south of the Irfon Forest in Mid Wales. 11 miles north east of Llandovery and 12 miles south west of Builth Wells.

About the Base: Llanwrtyd Wells, a small town with two pubs and tea rooms. Further Info: www.llanwrtyd.com.
Parking: Car park in Llanwrtyd Wells next to the river.
Grid Ref: SN877466. Post Code: LD5 4SS.

Drive Times: Cardiff 1hr40, Bristol 2hr, Birmingham 2hr40, Manchester 3hr10, Leeds 3hr50, London 4hr.

Trains: Llanwrtyd Wells Station is on the Shrewsbury-Carmarthen line.

Refreshments: At Llanwrtyd Wells, The Stonecroft Inn 01591 610 327, The Neuadd Arms 01591 610 236 and Drovers Rest Tea Rooms 01591 610264. Café at Cambrian Woollen Mill 01591 610 363.

Bike Shops: Cycles Irfon 01591 610710 for hire & repairs. Cool Biking Mid Wales 01591 610508 for hire & guided rides.

Books: Wales MTB (T.Hutton).

Maps: OS Explorer 187.

Route Idea

From Llanwrtyd Wells, N to Gilfach via the Wollen Mill. Trails NW through Irfon Forest to Penybont Uchaf. N then SE past Cefn Crug then E in clockwise direction around Cefn Cynllaith to Bwlchmawr. S to Pistyllgwyn. Trail back to the Woollen Mill and road to Llanwrtyd Wells. Distance 23km.

Llyn Brianne

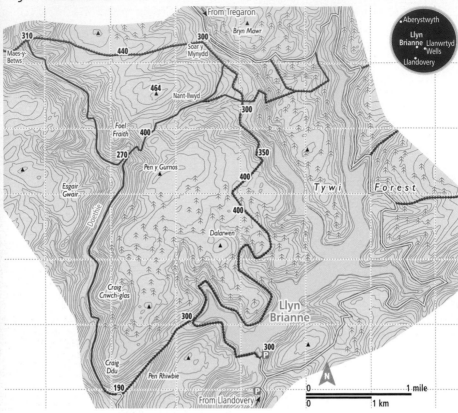

Situation: In the Tywi Forest at the head of the River Tywi in the Cambrian Mountains. 5 miles north west of Llanwrtyd Wells and 10 miles north of Llandovery.

About the Base: Llyn Brianne, a rural location with easy access to the trails.

Parking: Car parks at the southern end of the Reservoir. *Grid Ref: SN793484 or SN792479.*

Drive Times: Cardiff 1hr50, Bristol 2hr20, Birmingham 3hr, Manchester 3hr30, Leeds 4hr10, London 4hr10.

Trains: Llanwrtyd Wells Station is on the Shrewsbury-Carmarthen line.

Refreshments: No refreshments. Try The Royal Oak Inn 01550 760201 or Post Office Tea Rooms 01550 760293, 4 miles south of the map at Rhandirmwyn.

Bike Shops: Cycles Irfon 01591 610710 in Llanwrtyd Wells for hire & repairs.

Books: Wales MTB (T.Hutton). MBR Ride Guide 2010

Maps: OS Explorer 187.

Route Idea

Head W from car park at S end of Llyn Brianne then N to Soar y Mynydd. W almost to Maes-y-Betws. Along the Doethie river towards Craig Ddu then NE to the reservoir and back to the start. Distance 23km.

Dothie Valley, Llyn Brianne p574. Riders: Paul & Jess. © Sheldon Attwood

Cli-machx

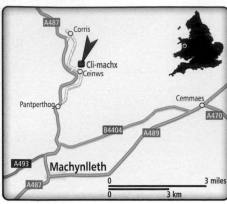

In the Dyfi Forest and the Cambrian Mountains of Mid West Wales. A purpose built singletrack trail with rocky jumps and technical climbs. Managed and maintained by volunteers, please show your appreciation in the donations box at the trail head.

Facilities:
None on site. Tafarn Dwynant Inn at Ceinws. Refreshments, Railway Station and Holey Trail bike shop 01654 700 411 at Machynlleth.

Parking:
Grid Ref: SH759062. Post Code: SY20 9HB

Web: www.goodmtb.co.uk/b19a & /b19b

The Trails
Red, XC, 15 km.

Machynlleth

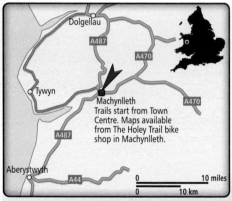

Natural challenging trails in the south of Snowdonia National Park, improved and maintained by community groups Dyfi Mountain Biking and Ecodyfi. Waymarked, cross country trails exploring the local countryside with some fast finishes and fabulous views.

Facilities:
Refreshments, Railway Station and Holey Trail bike shop 01654 700 411 at Machynlleth.

Parking:
Grid Ref: SH745008. Post Code: SY20 8AG

Web: www.goodmtb.co.uk/b23a & /b23b

The Trails
❶ Mach 1, Blue , XC, 16km.
❷ Mach 2, Red, XC, 24km.
❸ Mach 3, Black, XC, 30km.

Mach 3. Rider: Tom Stickland MB Swindon. © Job Hutchings

Coed Trallwm

At the edge of the Irfon Forest in Mid Wales. Three waymarked cross country trails with plenty of great singletrack.

Facilities:
Forest Café at Coed Trallwm MTB Centre.

Parking:
Grid Ref: SN882543. Post Code: LD5 4TS

Web: www.goodmtb.co.uk/b20

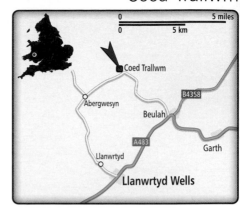

The Trails

❶ Blue, XC, 4km.

❷ Red, XC, 5km.

❸ Black, XC, 5km

Nant yr Arian

In the Cambrian Mountains high above Aberystwyth in West Wales, miles of way-marked trails on natural singletrack with mountain climbs, river crossings and technical rocky descents.

Facilities:
Café at Nant yr Arian Forest Visitor Centre.

Parking:
Grid Ref: SN718813. Post Code: SY23 3AD

Web: www.goodmtb.co.uk/b24

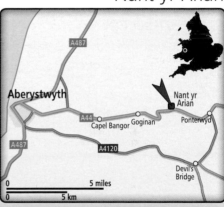

The Trails

❶ Pendam Trail, Red, XC, 9km.

❷ Summit Trail, Red, XC, 16km.

❸ Syfydrin Trail, Black, XC, 35km.

Riders: Mandi and Amanda. © Sheldon Attwood

Cwm Rhaeadr

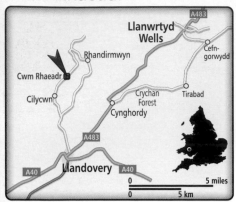

In the upper Tywi valley at the southern edge of the Cambrian Mountains. A short cross country trail on Forestry Commission land, designed by Rowan Sorrell. Mostly all weather singletrack with variable surfaces and plenty of technical trail features.

Facilities:
None on site. The Royal Oak Inn at Rhandirmwyn or Neuadd Fawr Arms at Cilycwm nearby.

Parking:
Grid Ref: SN765422. Post Code: SA20 0TL

Web: www.goodmtb.co.uk/b22a & /b22b

The Trails

Red, XC, 6.7km

Crychan Forest

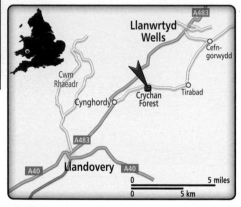

Between the Cambrian Mountains and the Brecon Beacons National Park. Miles of waymarked family trails with scenic views.

Facilities:
None on site. Refreshments 4 miles away at Llandovery.

Parking:
Routes can be joined from any one of four car parks, where information on the trails is provided. Grid Refs: SN837412, SN848411, SN813387, SN834327.

Web: www.goodmtb.co.uk/b21

The Trails

Family graded waymarked trails:
1. Golygfa Epynt 13.5km.
2. Cwm Coed Oeron 12.8km.
3. Brynffo-Esgair Fwyog, 7.1km.
4. Allt Troedrhiw-fer, 4km.
5. Allt Troedrhiw-fer-Golygfa Epynt link, 4.9km.

Caersws

On the River Severn, just west of the Wales/England border. A downhill race venue with regular organised uplift days throughout the year. A choice of fast, technical tracks on private land which should not be riden outside organised events.

Facilities:
None on site. Refreshments at The Red Lion at Caerws village.
Uplift days arranged by Borderline Events 01524 388 388.

Parking:
Grid Ref: SO010938. Post Code: SY17 5JE

Web: www.goodmtb.co.uk/b18a & /b18b

The Trails

DH

© Turnip Towers

Brecon Beacons & South Wales

Along with Exmoor and Dartmoor, the tracks and trails of the Brecon Beacons National Park offer the closest, top quality, winter riding for mountain bikers in Southern England wishing to escape the sticky mud and clay that can make riding anywhere, from the Cotswolds to the White Cliffs of Dover, very hard work through the wet, dark months. The valleys of South Wales are also a surprisingly good area for off road riding, bearing in mind their past history as one of the world's greatest coal mining regions. Many of the ridges above the valleys offer some excellent trails with views down to the terraced houses so typical of the old mining areas.

In West Wales, in the area to the west of the Valleys, namely Carmarthenshire and Pembrokeshire, there are very few off road riding opportunities with the exception of a magnificent ride around the dramatic Gower Peninsula from **Rhossili**, with panoramic sea views and some rough tracks from **Rosebush** over the Preseli Hills. To the east of the old mining valleys there are some rides from **Wyesham** in the stunning broadleaf woodland of the Wye Valley.

The Brecon Beacons National Park covers three areas which often cause confusion: to the west is the Black Mountain (no 's'); in the centre are the Brecon Beacons and to the northeast, the Black Mountains (with an 's'). The land rises to 886m on Pen y Fan and there are several trails which climb to over 500m. Wooded valleys lead up to open moorland past ancient trees battered by the prevailing westerly winds. There are good bases for the Black Mountains from **Talgarth**

Talybont-on-Usk (west) p586. Rider: Conor. © Sheldon Attwood

and for the Brecon Beacons at *Sennybridge*, *Talybont-on-Usk*, *Llangors*, *Crickhowell* and *Govilon* (Abergavenny).

Up in the hills above the old coal mining valleys of South Wales lie the forests with the mountain bike trails. These stretch from *Aberdulais* in the Neath Valley to the west, through *Aberdare* and *Cwm Darran* to *Abersychan* in the east. The valleys can also be approached from the south from *Blackmill*, *Tongwynlais* and *Cross Keys*, the latter located on the Monmouthhire &

Brecon Canal, offering a good escape route from Newport.

There are four well known Trail Centres in South Wales at *Brechfa*, north east of Carmarthen, *Afan Forest* and *Glyncorrwg* inland from Port Talbot and *Cwmcarn* to the north west of Newport. A smaller centre can be found at *Coed Taf Fawr*, plus downhill enthusiasts are catered for at *Rheola*, *Gethin* and *Wentwood*.

Torpantau, Talybont-on-Usk (west) p586. © www.bikesandhikes.co.uk

Sennybridge

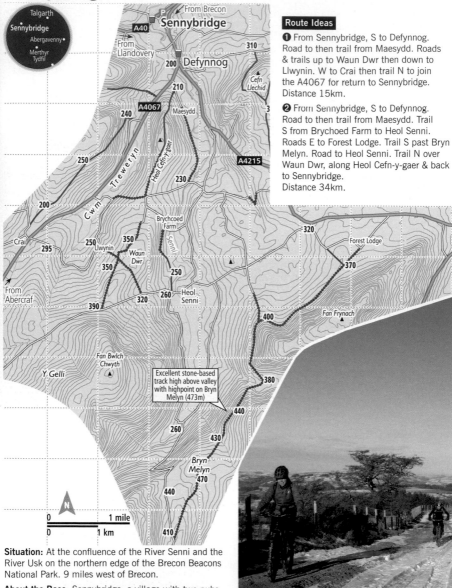

Route Ideas

❶ From Sennybridge, S to Defynnog. Road to then trail from Maesydd. Roads & trails up to Waun Dwr then down to Llwynin. W to Crai then trail N to join the A4067 for return to Sennybridge. Distance 15km.

❷ From Sennybridge, S to Defynnog. Road to then trail from Maesydd. Trail S from Brychoed Farm to Heol Senni. Roads E to Forest Lodge. Trail S past Bryn Melyn. Road to Heol Senni. Trail N over Waun Dwr, along Heol Cefn-y-gaer & back to Sennybridge. Distance 34km.

Excellent stone-based track high above valley with highpoint on Bryn Melyn (473m)

Situation: At the confluence of the River Senni and the River Usk on the northern edge of the Brecon Beacons National Park. 9 miles west of Brecon.

About the Base: Sennybridge, a village with two pubs. Further Info: www.visit-brecon-beacons.co.uk/places/sennybridge. **Parking:** Car park in Sennybridge. *Grid Ref: SN923288, Post Code: LD3 8RR.*

Drive Times: Cardiff 1hr10, Bristol 1hr40, Birmingham 2hr30, London 3hr40, Manchester 3hr40, Leeds 4hr20.

Refreshments: The Red Lion 01874 636958 and Abercamlais Arms 01874636461 at Sennybridge or The Tanners Arms 01874 638032 at Defynnog.

Bike Shops: Bi Ped Cycles 01874 622296 or Dirt Sky 01874 625734 in Brecon. Bi Ped also do hire.

Maps: OS Explorer OL12.

Routes on Web: www.goodmtb.co.uk/a100

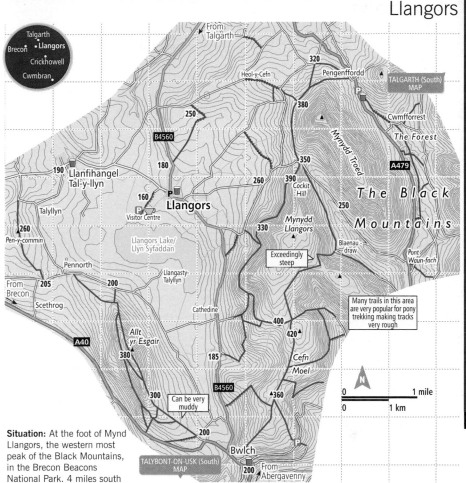

Talgarth
Brecon • Llangors
Crickhowell
Cwmbran

From Talgarth

320

Heol-y-Cefn

Pengenffordd

TALGARTH (South) MAP

380

Cwmfforrest

The Forest

250

B4560

A479

180

350

Mynydd Troed

190 Llanfihangel Tal-y-llyn

260

390 Cockit Hill

The Black

Talyllyn

160

Llangors

Visitor Centre

330

250 Mynydd Llangors

Mountains

260
Pen-y-commin

Llangors Lake/ Llyn Syfaddan

Exceedingly steep

Blaenau-draw

Pont Waun-fach

Pennorth

200

Llangasty-Talyllyn

From Brecon

205

Scethrog

Cathedine

400

420

Many trails in this area are very popular for pony trekking making tracks very rough

A40

Allt yr Esgair

380

185

Cefn Moel

300

B4560

360

Can be very muddy

200

0 ——— 1 mile
0 ——— 1 km

N

583

Bwlch

TALYBONT-ON-USK (South) MAP

200 From Abergavenny

Situation: At the foot of Mynd Llangors, the western most peak of the Black Mountains, in the Brecon Beacons National Park. 4 miles south west of Talgarth and 6 miles east of Brecon.

About the Base: Llangors, a small village with two pubs and accommodation. Further Info: www.wiz.to/llangors. **Parking:** Roadside in the centre of Llangors. Car park at Llangors Lake. *Grid Ref: Llangorse SO134275, Llangors Lake SO128272, Post Code: Lllangors LD3 7UB.*

Drive Times: Cardiff 1hr20, Bristol 1hr20, Birmingham 2hr20, London 3hr20, Manchester 3hr30, Leeds 4hrs.

Refreshments: At Llangors, The Castle Inn 01874 658225 and The Red Lion 01874 658238. Café next to National Park Information Centre at Llangors Lake. The Castle inn 01874 711353 at Pengenf-ffordd, The New Inn 01874 730215 at Bwlch and The Black Cock Inn 01874 658697 at Llanfihangel Tal-y-Llyn.

Bike Shops: Bi Ped Cycles 01874 622296 or Dirt Sky 01874 625734 in Brecon. Bi Ped also do hire.

Books: Wales MTB (T.Hutton).

Maps: OS Explorer OL13.

Routes on Web: www.goodmtb.co.uk/a97

Route Ideas

❶ From Llangors, roads E to join the trail just North of Cockit Hill then anti-clockwise around Mynydd LLangors to Blaenau-draw. E across the A479. Roads and trails N to Pengenffordd Trail to road at base of Cockit Hill. Roads back to Llangors. Distance 23km.

❷ From Llangors, roads NE. Trail to Heol-y-Cefn. Road and trails to Pengenffordd. Trail on W side of Mynydd Troed and Mynydd Llangors then across to Cefn Moel and down to Bwlch. NW over Allt yr Esgair then Pen-y-commin. Roads back to Llangors. Distance 31km.

Extend the area: Talgarth (South) Map to the NE. Talybont-on-Usk (South) Map to the S.

Talgarth (north)

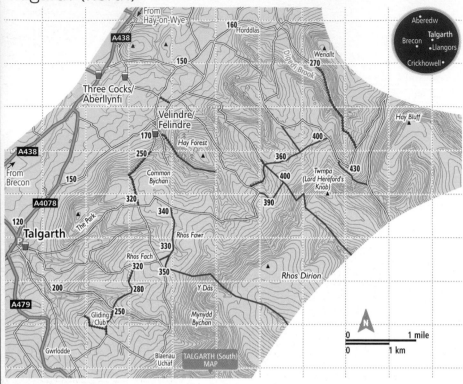

Situation: In the foothills of the Black Mountains and the north east corner of the Brecon Beacons National Park. 7 miles south west of Hay-on-Wye and 9 miles north east of Brecon.

About the Base: Talgarth, a small market town with pubs, a café and accommodation.
Further Info: www.visittalgarth.co.uk. **Parking:** Car parks in Talgarth. **Grid Ref:** Talgarth SO152336, Pengenffordd SO173297, **Post Code:** Talgarth LD3 0PQ.

Drive Times: Cardiff 1hr20, Bristol 1hr30, Birmingham 2hr10, London 3hr20, Manchester 3hr20, Leeds 4hrs.

Refreshments: At Talgarth, The New Inn 01874 711581, The Tower Hotel 01874 711253, The Bridge End Inn 01874 711936 and The Strand Café 01874 711195. The Three Horseshoes 01497 847304 at Velindre. The Three Cocks Coaching Inn 01497 847215 and The Old Barn Inn 01497 847861 at Three Cocks.

Bike Shops: MTB hire at The Activity Centre 01497 847897 in Three Cocks & Drover Holidays 01497 821134 in Hay on Wye. Bi Ped Cycles 01874 622296 or Dirt Sky 01874 625734 in Brecon. Bi Ped also do hire.

Maps: OS Explorer OL13.

Routes on Web: www.goodmtb.co.uk/a101

Route Idea

From Talgarth, roads SE past Gwrlodde then on to and past Blaenau Uchaf. Trails N across Rhos Fawr. Road E then trails across the base of Twmpa. Trails N along Digedi Brook. Roads to Felindre. Trail S up Common Bychan. Road to Rhos Fach. Trail S then road back to Talgarth. Distance 33km.

Extend the area: Talgarth South Map

Talgarth (south)

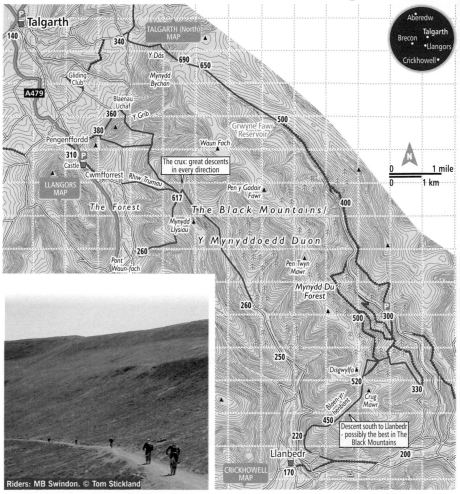

Aberedw

Brecon • Talgarth •Llangors

Crickhowell •

Riders: MB Swindon. © Tom Stickland

Situation: Beneath the Black Mountains, east of the Brecon Beacons in the north east of the National Park. 7 miles south west of Hay-on-Wye and 9 miles north east of Brecon.

About the Base: Talgarth, a small market town with pubs, a café and accommodation.
Further Info: www.visittalgarth.co.uk.
Parking: Car parks in Talgarth,next to the information point in Myndd Du Forest & just south of Pengenffordd. *Grid Ref:* Talgarth SO152336, Myndd Du Forest SO252284, Pengenffordd SO173297, *Post Code:* Talgarth LD3 0PQ.

Drive Times: Cardiff 1hr20, Bristol 1hr30, Birmingham 2hr10, London 3hr20, Manchester 3hr20, Leeds 4hrs.

Refreshments: At Talgarth, The New Inn 01874 711581, The Tower Hotel 01874 711253, The Bridge End Inn 01874 711936 and The Strand Café 01874 711195. The Red Lion 01873 810754 at Llanbedr or The Castle inn 01874 711353 at Pengenffordd.

Bike Shops: MTB hire at The Activity Centre 01497 847897 in Three Cocks & Drover Holidays 01497 821134 in Hay on Wye. Bi Ped Cycles 01874 622296 or Dirt Sky 01874 625734 in Brecon. Bi Ped also do hire.

Maps: OS Explorer OL13.

Routes on Web: www.goodmtb.co.uk/a102

Route Ideas

❶ From the car park just S of Pengenffordd. Road & trails NE to and past Blaenau Uchaf. Trail S past Gwyne Fawr Reservoir and through Mynydd Du Forest. Over Blaen-yr-henbant. Roads then trails N past Mynydd Llysiau, along Rhiw Trumau and back to start. Distance 40km. If starting the above from Talgarth add about 12km to the distance.

❷ From the car park in Mynydd Du Forest. An anticlockwise loop, through the forest, over Blaen-yr-henbant then continue on road & trails back to the start. Distance 21km.

Extend the area: Talgarth North Map, Crickhowell Map to the S. Llangors Map to the SE.

Talybont-on-Usk (west)

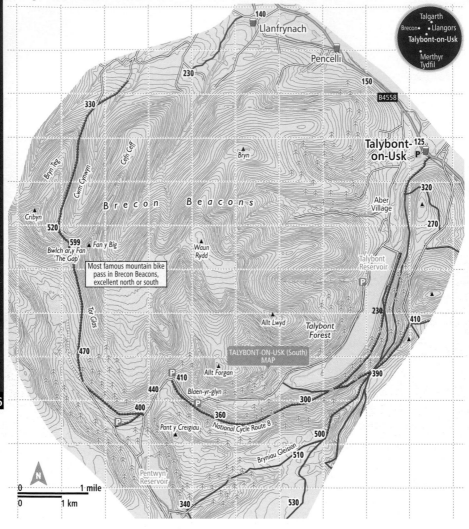

Situation: On the River Usk, north east of Talybont Forest and Reservoir. In the heart of the Brecon Beacons National Park, 6 miles south east of Brecon.

About the Base: Talybont-on-Usk, a village with pubs, a café and village store.

Further Info: www.wiz.to/talybont. **Parking:** Roadside in Talybont-on-Usk. Car Parks at Talybont Reservoir, Blaen-y-Glyn Waterfalls & Pentwyn Reservoir.

Grid Ref: Talybont SO115225, Talybont Reservoir SO099196, SO062170, Blaen-y-Glyn Waterfalls SO062170 or SO056175, Pentwyn Reservoir SO042163, Post Code: Talybont LD3 7JD.

Drive Times: Cardiff 1hr10, Bristol 1hr20, Birmingham 2hr10, London 3hr20, Manchester 3hr30, Leeds 4hrs.

Refreshments: At Talybont-on-Usk, The Usk Inn 01874 676251, The Star Inn 01874 676635, The White Hart Inn and Bunkhouse 01874 676227, The Traveller's Rest 01874 676233 or Café at Talybont Stores 01874 676663. The Royal Oak 01874

665396 at Pencelli and The White Swan 01874 665276 at Llanfrynach.

Bike Shops: Cyclebasket 01874 730368, 4 miles away in Llangynidr, Bi Ped Cycles 01874 622296 or Dirt Sky 01874 625734 in Brecon. Bi Ped also do hire.

Maps: OS Explorer OL12. Brecon Beacons East Map (Harvey).

Routes on Web: www.goodmtb.co.uk/a104

Route Idea

An anticlockwise loop. From Talybont-on-Usk, trails S (stay on National Cycle Route 8 or the more adventurous trail over Bryniau Gleision). N to Bwlch ar y Fan. Roads & trails to Llanfrynach then Pencelli. Road back to start. Distance 34km.

Extend the area: Talybont-on-Usk (South) map.

The Gap, Talybont-on-Usk (west) p586. Riders: SPAM. © Dave Robinson

Talybont-on-Usk (south)

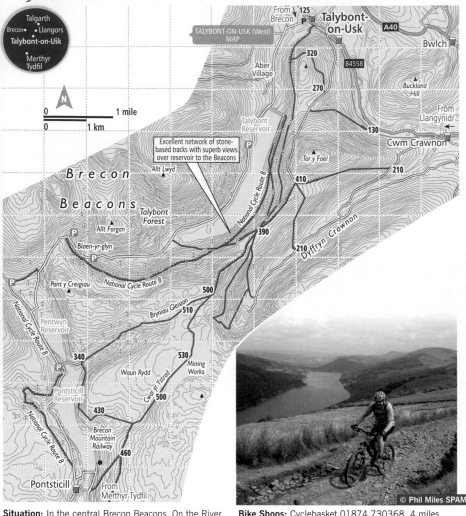

© Phil Miles SPAM

Situation: In the central Brecon Beacons. On the River Usk, north east of Talybont Forest and Reservoir, 6 miles south east of Brecon.

About the Base: Talybont-on-Usk, a village with pubs, a café and village store. Further Info: www.visit-brecon-beacons.co.uk. **Parking:** Roadside in Talybont-on-Usk. Car Parks at Talybont Reservoir, Blaen-y-Glyn Waterfalls & Pentwyn Reservoir. **Grid Ref:** *Talybont SO115225, Talybont Reservoir SO099196, SO062170, Blaen-y-Glyn Waterfalls SO062170 or SO056175, Pentwyn Reservoir SO042170,*

Drive Times: Cardiff 1hr10, Bristol 1hr20, Birmingham 2hr10, London 3hr20, Manchester 3hr30.

Refreshments: At Talybont-on-Usk, The Usk Inn 01874 676251, The Star Inn 01874 676635, The White Hart Inn and Bunkhouse 01874 676227, The Traveller's Rest 01874 676233 or Café at Talybont Stores 01874 676663. The Coach and Horses 01874 730245 at Cwm Crawnon and The Butchers Arms 01685 723544 at Pontsticill.

Bike Shops: Cyclebasket 01874 730368, 4 miles away in Llangynidr, Bi Ped Cycles 01874 622296 or Dirt Sky 01874 625734 in Brecon. Bi Ped also do hire.

Maps: OS Explorer OL13. Brecon Beacons East Map (Harvey).

Routes on Web: www.goodmtb.co.uk/a103

Route Ideas

❶ A figure of eight loop. S from Talybont-on-Usk on trails to E of the reservoir. Climb over Cwar yr Ystrad then down to Pontsticill Reservoir. National Cycle Route 8 to the north of the reservoir then climb NE past Bryniau Gleision. Just S of Tor y Foel head down to Cwm Crawnon. Road back to start. Distance 34km.

❷ Options to start at various car parks by the reservoirs & use National Cycle Route 8 to link with part of the route above.

Extend the area: Talybont-on-Usk (West) Map.

Crickhowell

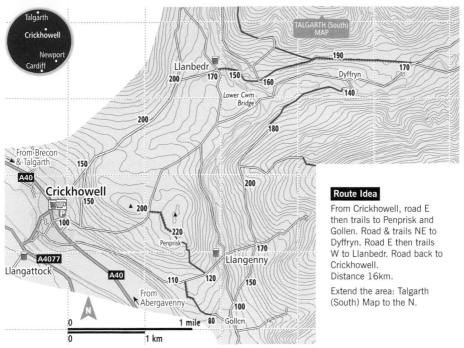

Route Idea

From Crickhowell, road E then trails to Penprisk and Gollen. Road & trails NE to Dyffryn. Road E then trails W to Llanbedr. Road back to Crickhowell.
Distance 16km.

Extend the area: Talgarth (South) Map to the N.

Talybont-on-Usk (south) p588

Rider: K. ©Sheldon Atwood

Situation: On the River Usk between the Black Mountains and the Brecon Beacons. In the east of the Brecon Beacons National Park, 6 miles north west of Abergavenny.

About the Base: Crickhowell, a small market town with pubs, cafes and accommodation. Further Info: www.crickhowellinfo.org.uk. **Parking:** Car park in the centre of Crickhowell. **Grid Ref: SO219183, Post Code: NP8 1AE.**

Drive Times: Cardiff 40mins, Bristol 1hr10, Birmingham 2hrs, London 3hrs, Manchester 3hr20, Leeds 3hr50.

Trains: Abergavenny Station is on the Hereford-Newport-Cardiff line.

Refreshments: At Crickhowell, choice of pubs, The Courtroom Café 01873 812497or Askews Family Bakery 01873 810345. The Vine Tree Inn 01873 810514 or The Horseshoe Inn 01873 810393 at Llangattock. The Red Lion 01873 810754 at Llanbedr and The Dragons Head Inn 01873 810350 at Llangenny.

Bike Shops: Cyclebasket 01874 730368, 4 miles away in Llangynidr. Bike Base 01873 855999, Gateway Cycles 01873 858519 or M&D Cycles 01873 854980 in Abergavenny for bikes parts & repairs.

Books: Wales MTB (T.Hutton).

Maps: OS Explorer OL13.

Routes on Web: www.goodmtb.co.uk/a95a & /a95b

Ystradfellte

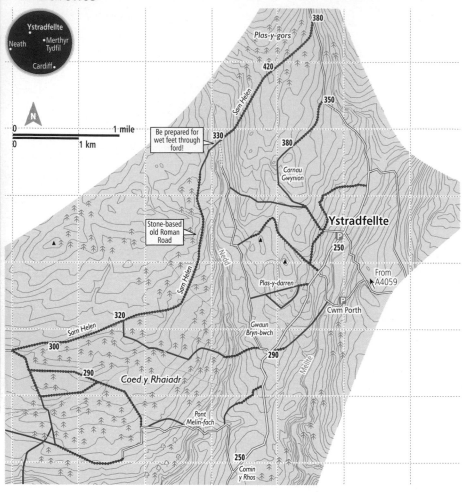

Be prepared for wet feet through ford!

Stone-based old Roman Road

Plas-y-gors

Carnau Gwynion

Ystradfellte

From A4059

Plas-y-darren

Cwm Porth

Gwaun Bryn-bwch

Sarn Helen

Nedd

Mellte

Coed y Rhaiadr

Pont Melin-fach

Comin y Rhos

Ystradfellte • Merthyr Tydfil
Neath
Cardiff

0 — 1 mile
0 — 1 km

Situation: On the Afon Mellte in the Fforest Fawr area of the Brecon Beacons National Park. 10 miles north west of Aberdare.

About the Base: Ystradfellte, a small village with a pub. **Parking:** Car parks in Ystradfellte & south of the village at Cwm Porth. *Grid Ref: Ystradfellte SN929134, Cwm Porth SN928124, Post Code: Ystradfellte CF44 9JE.*

Drive Times: Cardiff 1hr, Bristol 1hr40, Birmingham 2hr40, London 3hr30, Manchester 3hr50, Leeds 4hr30.

Refreshments: The New Inn 01639 720211 at Ystradfellte.

Bike Shops: Dare Valley Cycles 01685 886797 in Aberdare. Halfords 01685 388466 in Merthyr Tydfil.

Books: MTB Guide Valleys S Wales (N.Cotton).

Maps: OS Explorer OL12. Brecon Beacons West Map (Harvey).

Routes on Web: www.goodmtb.co.uk/a106

Route Idea

Roads S from Ystradfellte to Comin y Rhos. W to cross Pont Melin-fach. Trails into Coed y Rhaiadr then Sarn Helen NE to road near Plas-y-gors. Road S then trails past Carnau Gwynion & back to Ystradfellte. Distance 21km.

Rider: The Tribe MBC. © Vic Cheetham

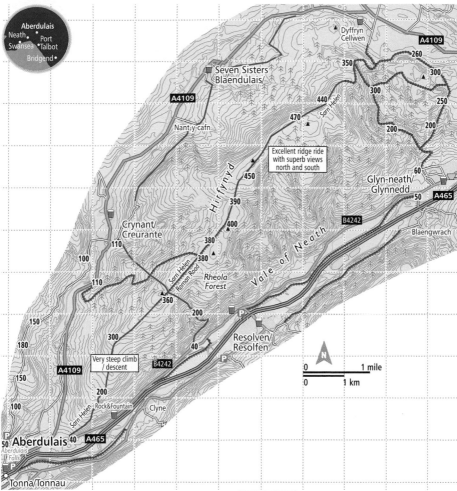

Situation: On the River Neath, 11 miles north east of Neath.

About the Base: Aberdulais, a village with a pub and tea rooms. **Parking:** National Trust Car Park at Aberdulais Falls or car park next to the picnic area. Also car park next to the river at Resolven.
Grid Ref: National Trust Car Park SS771993, Picnic Area SN769000, Resolven SN826030, Post Code: National Trust Car Park SA10 8EU, Picnic Area SA10 8DB, Resolven SA11 4LG.

Drive Times: Cardiff 50mins, Bristol 1hr20, Birmingham 2hr40, London 3hr20, Leeds 4hr30.

Refreshments: At Aberdulais, The Dulais Rock Inn 01639 644611 and National Trust Tea Rooms 01639 636674 at Aberdulais Falls. Pubs and Java Bean Cafe 01639 729904 at Glyn-neath, The Farmers Arms 01639 710264 & Vaughan Arms 01639 710212 at Resolven.

Bike Shops: Lodge Cycles 01639 821100 & Halfords 01639 635731 in Neath.

Books: MTB Guide Valleys S Wales (N.Cotton).

Maps: OS Explorer 165.

Route Ideas

❶ Minor road N to Crynant. Trails up to the Sarn Helen. Sarn Helen back to Aberdulais. Distance 20km

❷ NE on the Sarn Helen then forest trails down to Glyn-neath. Back to Aberdulais along the B4242. Distance 32km.

© Sheldon Attwood

Aberdare

Merthyr
Tydfil
• Aberdare
• Neath
Cardiff •

Heolgerrig
(SW Outskirts of
Merthyr Tydfil)
300

416

350

350

Descent of 300m on
stone then tarmac into
Dare valley

Blaencanaid

Garn Las ▲

400
Pen-y-lan
Hill

Abernant

360

130
Aberdare
Aberdâr

Cefn
Pennar

Cycle Path

Mynydd

Cynon

150

200

Merthyr

420

A4059

Ffynnon-
y-gôg
300

N

Cwmbach

460

0   1 mile
0   1 km

Situation: In the Cynon Valley, just south of the Brecon Beacons National Park and at the foot of Mynydd Merthyr. 4 miles south west of Merthyr Tydfil.

About the Base: Aberdare, a large town with plenty of refreshments.

Parking: Car park at Sports Centre in Aberdare. *Grid Ref: SO006026, Post Code: CF44 0JE.*

Drive Times: Cardiff 40mins, Bristol 1hr20, Birmingham 2hr30, London 3hr10, Manchester 3hr50, Leeds 4hr20.

Trains: Aberdare & Cwmbach Stations have services to Cardiff.

Refreshments: Plenty of pubs and cafes at Aberdare. The Royal Oak 01685 877106 at Cwmbach or The Ynyscynon inn 01685 883846 near Cwmbach Railway Station. The Rhoswenallt Inn 01685 875851 at Abernant.

Bike Shops: Dare Valley Cycles 01685 886797 in Aberdare. Halfords 01685 388466 in Merthyr Tydfil.

Books: MTB Guide Valleys S Wales (N.Cotton).

Maps: OS Explorer 166.

Route Idea

An anticlockwise loop from Aberdare, around Mynydd Merthyr, N to outskirts of Helogerrig and S back to Aberdare.
Distance 24km.

Cwm Darran

Situation: In the smaller Darran Valley between the Rymney and Taff Welsh Valleys. 4 miles north west of Bargoed and 7 miles south east of Merthyr Tydfill.

About the Base: Cwm Darran, a country park with a café and a visitor centre.

Parking: Car parks at Cwm Darran Country Park next to the visitor centre & at the south end of the lake. *Grid Ref: Visitor Centre SO113034, Lakeside SO118030, Post Code: Visitor Centre CF81 9NR.*

Drive Times: Cardiff 45mins, Bristol 1hr20, Birmingham 2hr20, London 3hr10, Manchester 3hr40, Leeds 4hr10.

Trains: New Tredegar & Bargoed Stations are on the Rhymney-Cardiff line.

Refreshments: Lakeside Café at Cwm Darran Visitor Centre 01443 875557. The Darran Hotel 01443 830257 at Deri, pubs and cafes at Bargoed, The Village Café 01443 879518 or Ruperra Arms 01443 834782 at New Tredegar, The Rising Sun 01685 841435 at Fochriw or The White Horse Inn at Pentwyn.

Bike Shops: Taff Vale Cycles 01685 382700 in Merthyr Tydfil. Halfords 01685 388466 at Merthyr Tydfil.

Books: MTB Guide Valleys S Wales (N.Cotton).

Maps: OS Explorer 166.

Route Idea

S along National Cycle Route 469 then road link to Cycle Route 468. NE of New Tredegar follow roads S to Brithdir then NW over Cefn Brithdir. Trail S back to start.
Distance 22km.

Govilon

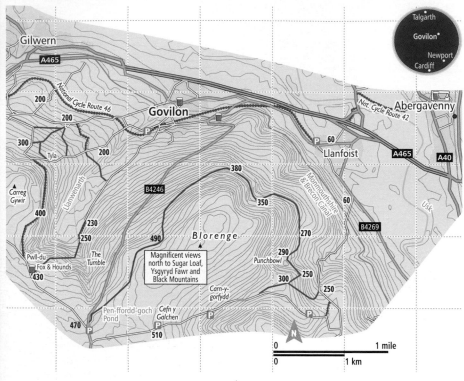

Situation: In the Usk Valley at the foot of the Black Mountains. On the south east edge of the Brecon Beacons National Park in South Wales, 3 miles south west of Abergavenny.

About the Base: Govilon, a village with pubs and a village shop. Further Info: www.govilon.com.

Parking: Car parks just west of Govilon or at Llanfoist Crossing on the edge of Llanfoist. Parking south of The Blorenge & at Pen-fford-goch Pond. **Grid Ref:** *Govilon SO262134, Llanfoist SO285133, Blorenge SO284109, SO270109 or SO263107, Pen-ffordgoch Pond SO254107,* **Post Code:** *Govilon NP7 9RS, Llanfoist NP7 9LP.*

Drive Times: Cardiff 1hr, Bristol 1hr, Birmingham 1hr50, London 3hrs, Manchester 3hr10, Leeds 3hr40.

Trains: Abergavenny Station is on the Hereford-Newport-Cardiff Railway line.

Refreshments: At Govilon, The Bridgend Inn 01873 831812, The Lion Inn 01873 830404 and The Cordell Country Inn 01873 830436. The Lamb and Fox 01495 790196 at Pwlldu. Pubs and cafes at Abergavenny.

Bike Shops: Bike Base 01873 855999, Gateway Cycles 01873 858519 or M&D Cycles 01873 854980 in Abergavenny for bikes parts & repairs.

Books: Wales MTB (T.Hutton).

Maps: OS Explorer OL13.

Routes on Web: www.goodmtb.co.uk/a96

Route Idea

Out of Govilon W on National Cycle Route 46. Roads N to then take trail past Carreg Gwyir. Trail around the Blorenge from Pen-fford-goch Pond. On to Llanfoist, Cycle Route 46 back to Govilon. Distance 23km.

Blorenge from Monmouthshire & Brecon Canal

© www.treadsandtrails.co.uk

Wyesham

Situation: West of the Forest of Dean, on the River Wye in south east Wales, close to the border with England. 2 miles south east of Monmouth.

About the Base: Wyesham, a village with a pub and a shop. **Parking:** Roadside in the centre of Wyesham near the school. Parking at Broadstones and at Marian's Inclosure. **Grid Ref:** *Wyesham SO519122, Broadstones SO537123, Marian's Inclosure SO537123.* **Post Code:** *Wyesham NP25 3LF.*

Drive Times: Cardiff 50mins, Bristol 50mins, Birmingham 1hr30, London 2hr40, Manchester 2hr50, Leeds 3hr20.

Refreshments: The Mayhill Hotel 01600 712280 at Wyesham. Good choice of pubs and cafes at Monmouth or The White Horse Inn 01594 834001 at Staunton.

Bike Shops: The Pedalabikeaway Cycle Centre 01600 772821 for hire. Bridge Cycles 01600 719941 in Monmouth.

Books: MTB Guide Valleys S Wales (N.Cotton).

Maps: OS Explorer OL14.

Route Idea

SE from Wyesham on Offa's Dyke Path. Road to Staunton. N through the Woods past Suck Stone to join the Peregrine Path. S through Highmeadow Woods, around Marion's Inclosure. S through Blake's Wood. Return as outward start. Distance 24km.

Wye Valley. © Sheldon Attwood

Abersychan

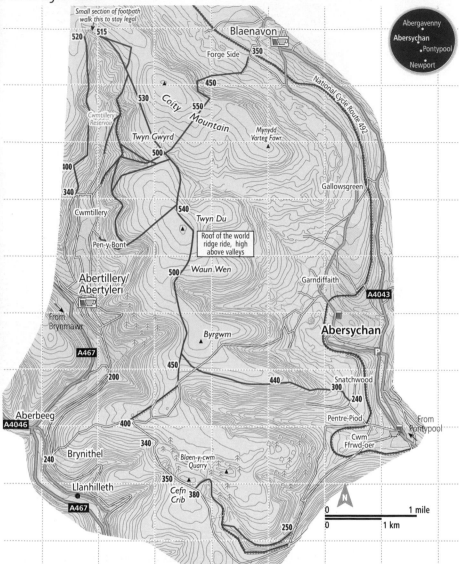

Situation: In the Afon Llwyd valley, below Coity Mountain, just outside the south east corner of the Brecon Beacons National Park. 2 miles north west of Pontypool.

About the Base: Abersychan, a town with a choice of refreshments. **Parking:** Car park in Abersychan. *Grid Ref: SO269033, Post Code: NP4 7EW.*

Drive Times: Cardiff 45mins, Bristol 1hr, Birmingham 2hrs, London 2hr50, Manchester 3hr20, Leeds 3hr50.

Trains: Pontypool & New Inn Stations are on the Hereford-Newport-Cardiff line.

Refreshments: Choice of pubs at Abersychan. Pubs and cafes at Blaenavon, Abertillery and Pontypool.

Bike Shops: XTrail Cycles 01495 755240 in New Inn, Pontypool.

Books: MTB Guide Valleys S Wales (N.Cotton).

Maps: OS Explorer 152 & OL13.

Route Idea

S on National Cycle Route 492. Roads & trails to Cefn Crib. N to follow trails past Waun Wen and the flanks of Coity Mountain, walk small section to stay legal then S on trail to the W of Cwmtillery Reservoir. From Cwmtillery NE towards Twyn Gwwryd then S along outward trail to road by Byrgwm. E on trail to Snatchwood and back to start.
Distance 32km.

Situation: On the River Usk in south east Wales 7 miles east of Pontypool and 13 miles north east of Newport.

About the Base: Usk, a small market town with a good choice of pubs, cafes and accommodation. Further Info: www.usktown.co.uk. **Parking:** Car park in the centre of Usk & at Wentwood in the south of the map. **Grid Ref:** Usk SO377008, Wentwood ST424943, **Post Code:** Usk NP15 1BJ.

Drive Times: Cardiff 35mins, Bristol 40mins, Birmingham 1hr40, London 2hr40, Manchester 3hrs, Leeds 3hr30.

Trains: Pontypool & New Inn Station is on the Hereford-Newport-Cardiff line.

Refreshments: Several pubs and cafes at Usk. The Greyhound Inn 07979 963 005.

Bike Shops: XTrail Cycles 01495 755240 in New Inn, Pontypool. Halfords 01633 875151 in Cwmbran.

Books: MTB Guide Valleys S Wales (N.Cotton).

Maps: OS Explorer 152.

Route Idea

S from Usk on National Cycle Route 42. Trails through Darren Wood to Bertholau Graig. E towards Nine Wells & The Five Paths. N to road. Return to Usk via White Horse Farm, Yew Tree Farm & Cwmbir. Distance 27km.

Cross Keys

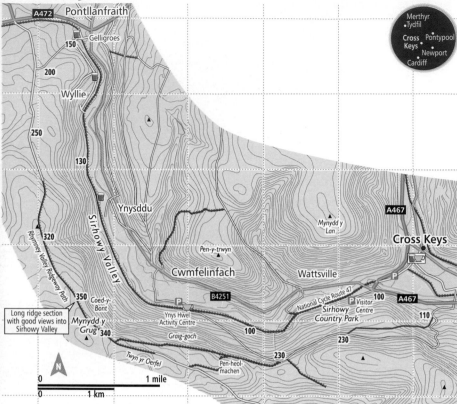

Situation: At the junction of the Sirhowy Valley and the River Ebbw in South Wales. 8 miles north west of Newport.

About the Base: Cross Keys, a small village with pubs and a café. Further Info: www.crosskeys.me.uk. **Parking:** Car park next to the river in Crosskeys. Also at Sirhowy Valley Country Park & Ynys Hywel Activity Centre. *Grid Ref:* Crosskeys ST218917, Sirhowy Valley Visitor Centre ST212913, Ynys Hywel ST185914, **Post Code:** Crosskeys NP11 7PL, Sirhowy Valley Visitor Centre NP11 7PX, Ynys Hywel NP11 7GZ.

Drive Times: Cardiff 40mins, Bristol 50mins, Birmingham 2hr10, London 2hr50, Manchester 3hr30, Leeds 4hrs.

Trains: Crosskeys Station is on the Ebbw Vale-Cardiff line.

Refreshments: At Crosskeys, The Eagle Inn 01495 272964, The Crosskeys Hotel 01495 270317 and Tonys Café 01495 272800. Café at Ynys Hywel Activity Centre 01495 272800, The Black Prince 01495 200193 at Ynysddu, The Islwyn Inn 01495 200659 at Wylie and The Halfway House 01495 220255 at Pontllanfraith.

Bike Shops: PS Cycles 01495 246555, 2 miles away in Abercam near Cwmcarn Trail Centre. Halfords 01633 875151 in Cwmbran.

Books: MTB Guide Valleys S Wales (N.Cotton).

Maps: OS Explorer 152 & 166.

Route Idea

From Sirhowy Country Park, National Cycle Route 47 and roads towards Cross Keys then S followed by W towards Mynydd y Grug and along Ryhmney Ridgeway Path. N to Gelligores and National Cycle Route 47 back to the start. Distance 20km.

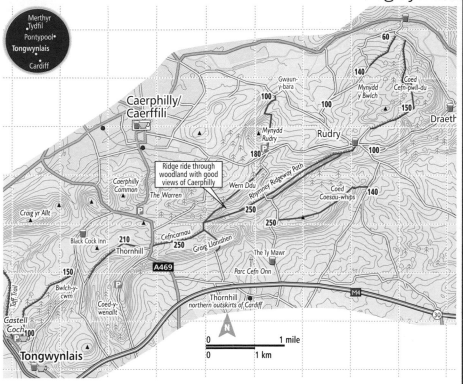

Merthyr Tydfil •
Pontypool •
Tongwynlais •
Cardiff •

60

140

Gwaun-y-bara

100

100

Mynydd y Bwlch

Coed Cefn-pwll-du

150

Draeth

Caerphilly/ Caerffili

Mynydd Rudry

Rudry

100

180

Ridge ride through woodland with good views of Caerphilly

Wern Ddu

Rhymney Ridgeway Path

Caerphilly Common

The Warren

Coed Coesau-whips

140

Craig yr Allt

250

250

Black Cock Inn 210

Cefncarnau 250

Graig Llanishen

Thornhill

The Ty Mawr

A469

Parc Cefn Onn

150

Bwlch-y-cwm

Coed-y-wenallt

Thornhill
northern outskirts of Cardiff

M4

30

Castell Coch 100

Tongwynlais

N

0 ——————— 1 mile

0 ——————— 1 km

Situation: Surrounded by Forest Fawr in the Taff Valley, south of the Welsh Valleys. 5 miles south west of Caerphilly, 5 miles north west of Cardiff and 8 miles south east of Pontypridd.

About the Base: Tongwynlais, a village with pubs and a café. **Parking:** Roadside in the centre of Tongwynlais. Car Parks at Castell Coch, Caerphilly Common, Coed-y-Wenallt & Mynnyd Rudry. *Grid Ref: Tongwynlais ST133821, Castell Coch ST130826, Caerphilly Common ST155850, Coed-y-Wenallt ST152836, Mynnyd Rudry ST182864, Post Code: Tongwynlais CF15 7LF, Castell Coch CF15 7JS.*

Drive Times: Cardiff 15mins, Bristol 50mins, Birmingham 2hrs, London 2hr40, Manchester 3hr30.

Trains: Caerphilly Station is on the Cardiff-Rhymney line. Taffs Well Railway Station, 1 mile away, is on the Cardiff-Pontypridd-Merthyr Tydfil line.

Refreshments: At Tongwynlais, The Lewis Arms 029 2081 0330, The Old Ton 029 2081 1865 and Julies Snack Attack Café 029 2081 4370. The Bakestone Café 029 2081 0101 at Castell Coch. The Maen Llwyd 029 2088 2372 at Rudry. The Ty Mawr 029 2075 4456 or The Hollybush 01633 441326 at Draethen. Pubs and cafes at Caerphilly. The Black Cock Inn 029 2088 0534 near the A469

Bike Shops: Castle Bikes 029 2132 8131 in Caerphilly. Halfords 0292 0621222 in Gabalfa.

Books: MTB Guide Valleys S Wales (N.Cotton).

Maps: OS Explorer 151 & 166.

Routes on Web: www.goodmtb.co.uk/a105

© Matt Cope

Route Idea

From Castell Coch, trail NE through the forest then on to Thornhill, Cefncarnau, Wern Ddu, Gwaun-y-bara. Roads towards Mynydd y Bwlch then through Coed Cefn-pwll-du and along Rhymney Ridgeway Path. Return as outward start. Distance 24km.

Blackmill

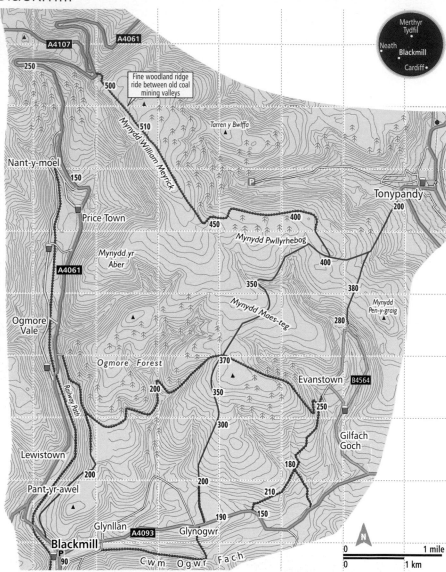

Fine woodland ridge ride between old coal mining valleys

Situation: At the confluence of the River Ogmore and Cwm Ogwr Fach in the Welsh Valleys. 6 miles north east of Bridgend.

About the Base: Blackmill, a small village with a pub and easy access to the trails. **Parking:** Roadside in the centre of Blackmill near to the pub. *Grid Ref: SS933866, Post Code: CF35 6DR.*

Drive Times: Cardiff 30mins, Bristol 1hr10, Birmingham 2hr20, London 3hrs, Manchester 3hr40, Leeds 4hr10.

Trains: Bridgend Station is on the Cardiff-Swansea line.

Refreshments: The Fox and Hounds 01656 841652 at Blackmill. Lite Bite Café 01656 840207, The Corbett Arms 01656 840386 or The Wyndham Arms 01656 842050 at Ogmore Vale. The Blaenogwr

01656 840437 at Price Town, pubs and cafes at Tonypandy or Molly O'D's Irish at Gilfach Coch.

Bike Shops: Rush Cycles 01656 728568, 3 miles away at Brynmenyn on the road to Bridgend. Halfords 01656 648846 in Bridgend.

Books: MTB Guide Valleys S Wales (N.Cotton).

Maps: OS Explorer 166.

Route Idea

From Blackmill, trails N, then continue N on minor & main roads past Nant-y-moel. Trail SE over Mynydd William Meyrick, across Mynydd Maes-teg, through Ogmore Forest and back to Blackmill. Distance 24km.

© Matt Cope

Rhossili

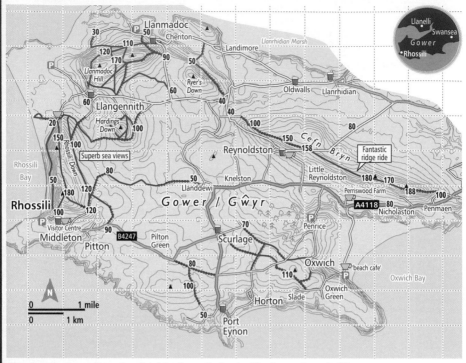

Situation: On the south western tip of the Gower Peninsula, 18 miles south west of Swansea.

About the Base: Rhossili, a small village with cafes and accommodation.
Further Info: www.the-gower.com/villages/Rhossili.

Parking: Car parks in Rhossili, Llangenith, Llanmadoc, Oxwich Bay & Penrice.

Grid Ref: Rhossili SS414880, Llangenith SS416925, Llanmadoc SS439934, Oxwich Bay SS502865, Penrice SS493882, Post Code: Rhossili SA3 1PR, Llangenith SA3 1JP, Llanmadoc SA3 1DE, Oxwich Bay SA3 1LS, Penrice SA3 1LN.

Drive Times: Cardiff 1hr30, Bristol 2hrs, Birmingham 3hr20, London 4hrs, Leeds 5hr10.

Refreshments: At Rhossili, The Worms Head Hotel 01792 390512, The Bay Coffee House 01792 390519 and Jolly Joe's Café. The Ship Inn 01792 390204 at Port Eynon, The Countryman 01792 390597 at Scurlage, Beach Café at Oxwich Bay and Café at Perriswood Farm 01792 371661 at Nicholaston. The King Arthur Hotel 01792 390775 or Compass Coffee Shop 01792 391145 at Reynoldston, Greyhound Inn 01792 391027 at Old Walls and Dolphin Inn 01792 391069 at Llanrhidian. The Britannia Inn 01792 386624 at Llanmadoc, Kings Head 01792 386212 or Eddy's Cafe at Llangenith.

Bike Shops: Tredz 01792 702555, Wheelies 01792 472612 & Action Bikes 01792 464640 in Swansea. Halfords 01554 785980 in Llanelli.

Books: MTB Guide Valleys S Wales (N.Cotton).

Maps: OS Explorer 164.

Routes on Web: www.goodmtb.co.uk/a98

Route Ideas

❶ North from Rhossili, across Rhossili Down, anticlockwise around Hardings Down to Llangennith. Over Llanmadoc Hill to Llanmadoc. SE past Ryer's Down, along section of Cefn Bryn to Reynoldston. Roads to Llanddewi then trails back to Rhossili. Distance 32km.

❷ As above but continue along Cefn Bryn to Penmaen, roads to Oxwich then trails to Scurlage. N to Llanddewi then trails back to start. Distance 39km.

Cefn Bryn. © Phil Reynolds

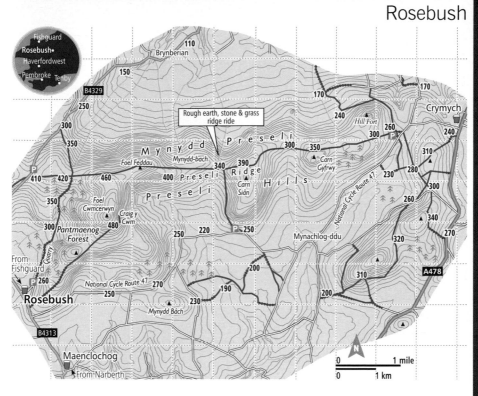

Situation: South of the Preseli Hills on the edge of the Pembrokeshire Coast National Park in West Wales. 9 miles south east of Fishguard.

About the Base: Preseli, a small village with a pub and easy access to the trails.

Parking: In the centre of Rosebush. Car parks north of the village on the B4329, in the Preseli Hills & west of Crymych. Grid Ref: *Rosebish SN075294, B4329 SN075322, Preseli Hills SN126309, Crymych SN164331,* Post Code: *Rosebush SA66 7QU.*

Drive Times: Cardiff 2hrs, Bristol 2hr30, Birmingham 3hr50, London 4hr30, Leeds 5hrs.

Refreshments: At Rosebush, Tafarn Sinc Preseli 01437 532214 and The Old Post Office Restaurant and Tea Rooms 01437 532205. The Globe Inn 01437 532269 at Maenclochog and The Crymych Arms 01239 831435 at Crymych.

Bike Shops: Pembrokeshire Bikes 01348 874170 in Fishguard.

Maps: OS Explorer OL35.

Routes on Web: www.goodmtb.co.uk/a99

Route Idea

From Rosebush, N past the quarry and through Pantmaenog Forest. E along the Preseli Ridge. National Cycle Route 47 back to Rosebush. Distance 25km.

Brechfa

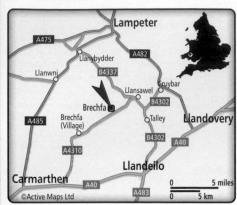

West of the Brecon Beacons four purpose built, waymarked cross country trails designed by downhill rider Rowan Sorrell. All weather trails of every grade suit all abilities and include some fantastic downhills as well as big berms and jumps. The green trail is a an ideal introduction to mountain biking.

Facilities:
Drop Off Double Decker Diner open on site at weekends. The Black Lion at Abergorlech near the start of the Gorlech trail.

Parking:
Grid Ref: SN585340. Post Code: SA32 7SL

Web: www.goodmtb.co.uk/b38a & /b38b

The Trails

❶ Derwen, Green, XC, 9km
❷ Derwen, Blue, XC, 5km.
❸ Gorlech, Red, XC, 19km.
❹ Raven, Black, XC, 18.5km.

Coed Taf Fawr

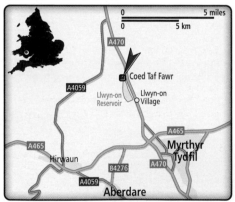

In the south of the Brecon Beacons National Park. A waymarked cross country trail through mature forest and open land with some steep climbs on the extended route. Two mini trails to improve riding skills.

Facilities:
Refreshments at Garwnant Visitor Centre.

Parking:
Grid Ref: SO002130. Post Code: CF48 2HU

Web: www.goodmtb.co.uk/b39

The Trails

❶ Rowan, Green, 0.5km.
❷ Mini Trails Spruce, Blue, 0.5km.
❸ Garwnant, Blue, 8km to 17.7 km.

Glyncorrwg Mountain Bike Centre

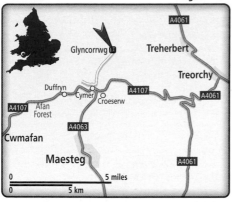

Glyncorrwg is in Afan Forest (also see below) but has its own base. The Centre has good facilities and is the trailhead for Whites level and Skyline mountain biking trails. There is a bike shop, café, lounge area, open air deck, changing/shower rooms and a bike park.

Facilities:
Drop off café at Glyncorrwg Mountain Bike Centre. Skyline Cycles 01639 850011 for MTB hire, parts and repairs.

Parking:
Grid Ref: SS874991. Post Code: SA13 3BA

Web: www.goodmtb.co.uk/b37a & /b37b

The Trails

❹ Rheilffordd Low Level Family Cycleway 16/22.5km links Afan and Glyncorrwg.

❶ Whites Level, Red, XC, 17km.

❷ Skyline, Red, XC, 46km.

❸ W2, Black, 44km combines Whites Level with The Wall at Afan Forest.

Afan Forest Park Centre

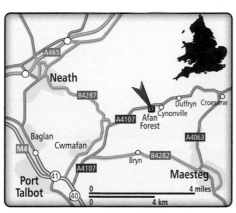

Afan Forest Park Visitor Centre is the main point of contact to find out about everything to see and do in Afan Forest Park, (which also includes Glyncorrwyg, see above). This Centre is the starting point for the Penyhydd and Y Wall mountain bike trails.

Facilities:
Café at Afan Forest Park Visitors Centre. Skyline Cycles 01639 850011 at Glyncorrwg for MTB hire, parts and repairs.

Parking:
Grid Ref: SS821950. Post Code: SA13 3HG

Web: www.goodmtb.co.uk/b36a & /b36b

The Trails

❶ Rheilffordd Low Level Family Cycleway 16/22.5km links Afan and Glyncorrwg.

❶ Y Wall, Red, XC, 23km.

❷ Penhydd, Red, XC, 17km.

❸ W2, Black, 44km combines The Wall with Whites Level at Glyncorrwg

Y Wall, Afan Forest. © Singletrack Safari

Gethin Woods

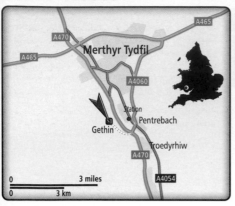

Just south of the Brecon Beacons National Park in the valleys of South Wales, a long, technically challenging downhill course. The future looks bright for Gethin with plans to turn it into an International Mountain Bike Centre.

Facilities:
None on site. Refreshments and Pentre-Bach Railway Station at nearby Abercanaid. Welsh Downhill Mountain Bike Association run regular uplift days. Register online: www.wdmba.co.uk

Parking:
Grid Ref: SO050035.

Web: www.goodmtb.co.uk/b41

The Trails
DH.

Wentwood Downhill

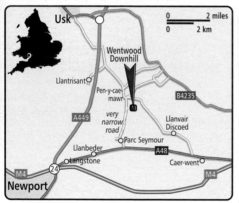

Over 1000 acres of woodland close to Newport in South Wales. A fast, fun, purpose built downhill track maintained by local riders Wentwood Downhill in conjunction with the Forestry Commission. Plenty of unmarked cross country trails to explore.

Facilities:
None on site. Refreshments at nearby Parc Seymour.

Parking:
Grid Ref: ST417945.

Web: www.goodmtb.co.uk/b43

The Trails
Dragons Track, DH, 759m.

Rheola

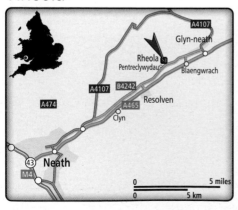

Just south of the Brecon Beacons National Park in the valleys of South Wales, a fast, steep and rocky natural downhill trail. A technically challenging race venue with regular uplift days arranged by the Welsh Downhill Mountain Bike Association.

Facilities:
None on site. Welsh Downhill Mountain Bike Association run regular uplift days. Register online via the wdmba website www.wdmba.co.uk

Parking:
Grid Ref: SN852051. Post Code: SA11 4DU

Web: www.goodmtb.co.uk/b42

The Trails
DH.

Cwmcarn

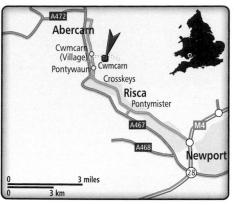

In the Nantcarn Valley in South Wales. Purpose built, all weather singletrack combining flowing descents, demanding technical sections and scenic views. Also extreme downhill run and a freeride area.

Facilities:
Café at Cwm Carn Forest Visitor Centre. Cwm Down Uplift. Book ahead online www.cwmdown.co.uk

Parking:
Grid Ref: ST228936. Post Code: NP11 7EX

Web: www.goodmtb.co.uk/b40

Polly Summerhayes on the Twrch Trail © Cat Williams

The Trails

❶ Twrch Trail, Red, XC, 15.5 km.

❷ Y Mynydd Downhill, Black, 1.9km (year round uplift, book a pass with www.cwm-down.co.uk)

❸ Freeride, full of jump packs, berms, wall rides and a complete corkscrew.

© Matt Cope

608

Anne & Douglas Ross, Top of Cumberland Brook, Wildboarclough. Langley map p243

Abbreviations

N, S, E, W - North, South, East, West
DH - Downhill
XC - Cross Country
4X - Four Cross
DJ - Dirt Jumping
MTB - Mountain Biking

Index

609

John at Afan Forest. ©Sheldon Attwood

611

Brecon Beacons ©Matt Cope

613

614

Hayden at Forest of Dean. © Sheldon Attwood

Near Kentmere, Steve Wroe, Nick Matthews and Neil Fleetwood © Nick Matthews

Reservoir Chicks. © Mark James

631

© Dirt Divas / Graeme Warren

635

Jim Holgate at Woburn. © Neil Tydeman

637

The Wild Boar Maps
Mountain Bike
Map & Routes

with sealed Waterproof Covers

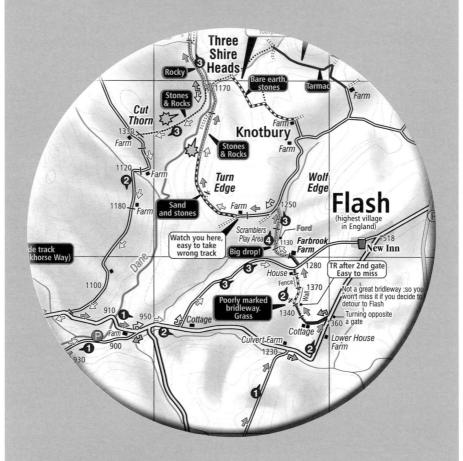

See the detailed picture

available from
www.BikeMaps.co.uk

South Downs Way, Lewes, p398. Brighton MTB © Mike Gill

Help us make the next edition of The Good Mountain Biking Guide even better...

This is the first edition of the book and we hope that it will become essential to every mountain biker who wants to get the best out of their bike. We would be delighted to feel, in part, responsible for people discovering new areas and riding in a greater variety of terrain. We have spent thousands of hours collecting and sifting relevant information, drawing maps, sorting photographs and presenting the information in a simple and clear fashion. Even as the book goes to print we know that some things will change by the time it reaches the shelves. New trails will be added as access arrangements improve, Trail Centres will be built and sadly some may also end up closing. Pubs, cafés and bike shops will also come into existence or stop trading.

We would like your help on keeping **The Good Mountain Biking Guide** as up to date as possible. There are some areas where you can specifically help:

- If you have a photograph that illustrates an area that where we don't currently have a photograph then please send it to us (or if you think you can improve on a photograph we have used in the book). We will provide a free copy of the next edition to the photographer and credit both photographer and rider if appropriate (please see www.goodmtb.co.uk for more details)

- If we have made any errors of fact in the text or the maps then we would like to correct them next time around.

- If you have better or alternative route ideas for particular bases then please send us details and, most importantly, if you are aware of new trails or areas that we have simply missed then let us know. We would also like to hear from you if you think any of our existing choice of bases do not provide attractive riding but do please recognise that this is fairly subjective and some riders may get enjoyment from a trail which others consider mundane.

Please send any suggestions to: editor@goodmtb.co.uk